Oracle Distributed Systems

Oracle Distributed Systems

Charles Dye

O'REILLY®

Beijing · Cambridge · Köln · Paris · Sebastopol · Taipei · Tokyo

Oracle Distributed Systems

by Charles Dye

Copyright © 1999 O'Reilly & Associates, Inc. All rights reserved.
Printed in the United States of America.

Published by O'Reilly & Associates, Inc., 101 Morris Street, Sebastopol, CA 95472.

Editor: Deborah Russell

Production Editor: Melanie Wang

Printing History:

April 1999: First Edition.

ISBN: 1-56592-432-0

Table of Contents

Preface

In my nearly 10 years of Oracle database administration experience, I've witnessed the emergence of a distributed database technology whose sophistication level has risen while the average user's understanding of that technology has not. With the advent of Oracle's advanced replication facilities, relatively few DBAs are well versed in all aspects of Oracle's distributed systems offerings, and few engineers fully recognize the implications that distributed systems have for their code. As a result, many hours are spent struggling to implement doomed solutions, and still more hours are spent supporting hobbled architectures.

Oracle's exploding feature set is not to blame these lost hours. There is a vast gap between the theoretical, or academic, knowledge base surrounding distributed systems and the practical, or applied, knowledge base. In general, the people who understand the principles and nuances of a distributed environment are not the same people who are out there building systems. The publications on distributed systems reflect this divide; most books are either very theoretical and contain little specific advice or are rather simplistic cookbooks for those on the front lines (or in the kitchen, as the case may be). Needless to say, it can be rather frustrating to find the information you need when one book discusses set theory and another says "point here, click there."

This book strives to close the gap between the theoretical and the applied by explaining the objectives of the ideal distributed system in the context of Oracle's technology. I examine the reasons why distributed systems should have certain properties and discuss how Oracle is designed to deliver these properties. I also provide design recommendations for various common requirements. And, finally, I deliver programming examples and scripts and tricks for the DBA. I wish I had had this book 10 years ago.

Audience for This Book

This book is intended primarily for Oracle database administrators, developers, system administrators, network administrators, and others who need to build or maintain distributed database systems.

About Replication

This book contains a substantial amount of detail about Oracle's advanced replication facilities. Most of this information has been obtained through several real-world implementations, and my advice is based on experiences and situations that are, for the most part, not addressed in Oracle's documentation.

In addition to sharing the benefit of my experience, this book tries to convey a fundamental understanding of how the advanced replication facilities actually work. I describe its underpinnings, its limitations, and how to use it successfully to solve a variety of problems.

One thing this book does *not* attempt to describe is Oracle's GUI tool—Replication Manager. Although this tool may be useful for the administration of a pre-existing, stable environment, using it does not give you any insight into how replication works or into the viability of your environment. In addition, the tool is not very useful for solving the inevitable problems that arise in a replicated environment. If you are interested in using Oracle's Replication Manager, we refer you to the *Oracle8 Server Replication Guide*.

About Oracle Versions and Platforms

At this point, I work with Oracle8 almost exclusively in both production and development environments. Therefore, most of the specific examples and recommendations in this book are proven on Oracle8. In cases in which I refer to Oracle7, I mean Version 7.3.0 and later. When I am aware of how a feature will work under the upcoming release, Oracle8*i*, I have noted that as well.

As a general observation, my experience with Oracle8 has been quite positive, especially where replication is concerned. If you have not yet migrated to Oracle8, my advice is to do so as soon as possible.

Most of the examples described in this book were developed on a Unix operating system; however, SQL scripts are very portable, and most of them will run as is on Windows NT and other operating systems.

Structure of This Book

This book is divided into three parts:

Part I, The Distributed System

Chapter 1, *Introduction to Distributed Systems*, is an overview of distributed systems—terminology, basic concepts, benefits and perils, and the various options provided by Oracle.

Chapter 2, *SQL*Net and Net8*, describes the underlying protocols Oracle supplies to support communication with distributed Oracle databases over a network.

Chapter 3, *Configuration and Administration*, explains how to set up a distributed database environment; it discusses initialization parameters, database links, how distributed transactions work, and the basics of distributed backup and recovery.

Chapter 4, *Distributed Database Security*, describes special security concerns for distributed systems; it looks at privilege management, various authentication methods, the encryption of network traffic, and the use of the Oracle Security Server (OSS) and the Advanced Networking Option (ANO).

Chapter 5, *Designing a Distributed System*, examines the design of a distributed system; it introduces C. J. Date's fundamental principles of distributed databases, discusses the global data dictionary, and recommends a particular approach to data partitioning.

Chapter 6, *Oracle's Distributed System Implementation*, examines how Oracle's RDBMS and networking products meet Date's objectives for distributed database systems.

Chapter 7, *Sample Configurations*, focuses on the most common distributed architectures: the high-availability system, systems illustrating geographic data distribution, workflow partitioning, and data collection and consolidation, and the loosely coupled federation.

Chapter 8, *Engineering Considerations*, examines the special requirements of distributed systems that must be taken into account during the engineering process: schema design and integration, application tiering, and the design of a replicated application.

Part II, Replication

Chapter 9, *Oracle Replication Architecture*, takes a deeper look at Oracle's replication architecture; it examines the various types of replication available through Oracle, specific architectural components, installation tips, and enhancements for Oracle8 and Oracle8*i*.

Chapter 10, *Advanced Replication Installation*, describes how to set up an advanced replication environment, including the setting of initialization parameters, the selection of redo logs and rollback segments, the size and placement of data dictionary objects, and the use of administrative accounts, privileges, and database links.

Chapter 11, *Basic Replication*, is a detailed analysis of Oracle's basic replication (snapshot) facility.

Chapter 12, *Multi-Master Replication*, is a detailed analysis of Oracle's multi-master replication facility.

Chapter 13, *Updateable Snapshots*, is a detailed analysis of Oracle's updateable snapshot facility.

Chapter 14, *Procedural Replication*, is a detailed analysis of Oracle's procedural replication facility.

Chapter 15, *Conflict Avoidance and Resolution Techniques*, describes a variety of techniques for avoiding conflicts among the various distributed sites where data is replicated.

Part III, Appendixes

Appendix A, *Built-in Packages for Distributed Systems*, is the Application Programming Interface (API) reference; it contains summaries of all specifications, parameters, exceptions, and restrictions for the procedures and functions available through the Oracle built-in packages used with distributed systems.

Appendix B, *Scripts and Utilities*, contains the code for a variety of scripts mentioned in this book.

Conventions Used in This Book

Indicates a tip, suggestion, or general note. For example, we'll tell you if you need to use a particular Oracle version or if an operation requires certain privileges.

Indicates a warning or caution. For example, we'll tell you if Oracle does not behave as you'd expect or if a particular operation has a negative impact on performance.

Italic

> Used for script names, filenames, directory names, and operating system commands. Also used for replaceables in text, for emphasis, and to introduce new terms.

`Constant width`

> Used for code examples.

`Constant width italic`

> Used in code examples to indicate elements (e.g., filenames) that you supply.

`Constant width bold`

> Used occasionally to highlight particular items in code being discussed.

UPPERCASE

> In code examples, generally indicates Oracle keywords.

`lowercase`

> In code examples, generally indicates user-defined items such as variables, parameters, and so forth.

`punctuation`

> In code examples, enter exactly as shown.

`*` *and* `*/`

> In code examples, these characters delimit a comment, which can extend from one line to another.

`--/` *or* `#`

> In code examples, these characters indicate the start of a comment line.

`[ ]`

> In syntax descriptions, square brackets enclose optional items.

`{}`

> In syntax descriptions, curly brackets enclose a set of items; you must choose only one of them.

`|`

> In syntax descriptions, a vertical bar separates the items enclosed in curly brackets, as in {VARCHAR | DATE | NUMBER}.

About the Scripts

All of the scripts described or mentioned in this book are also included on the accompanying diskette. In addition, these scripts are available at the O'Reilly web site (see "Comments and Questions").

Comments and Questions

Please address comments and questions concerning this book to the publisher:

O'Reilly & Associates, Inc.
101 Morris Street
Sebastopol, CA 95472
800-998-9938 (in the U.S. or Canada)
707-829-0515 (international or local)
707-829-0104 (fax)

You can also send us messages electronically. To be put on our mailing list or request a catalog, send email to:

nuts@oreilly.com

To ask technical questions or comment on the book, send email to:

bookquestions@oreilly.com

For corrections and amplifications for the book, as well as for copies of the scripts found in this book, check out *http://www.oreilly.com/catalog/oradistsys*. See the ads at the end of the book for information about all of O'Reilly & Associates' online services.

Acknowledgments

Fortunately many people have supported me in the writing of this book; trite as it may sound, I definitely could not have done it by myself. While my name may appear on the byline, there are numerous people whose contributions, technical and otherwise, have been invaluable.

This is the second book I have written for O'Reilly & Associates, and my first solo effort. Debby Russell, my editor, has provided guidance and encouragement, as well as a measure of admonishment, all of which have led to a successful project. Debby has two abilities which result in great books for O'Reilly: motivating writers and envisioning a high-quality product. Many thanks as well to Steve Abrams, who converted files, did lots of preproduction work on the text, and otherwise helped move things along efficiently. And finally, thanks to the entire production staff; you did a great job.

My first line of support for solving intractable replication issues and one of the primary reviewers of this book was Jenny Tsai of Oracle Corporation. Jenny has been able to help me research issues with the utmost thoroughness and has devoted a significant amount of time to validating the accuracy of the material presented here. And most importantly, Jenny introduced me to Oracle's advanced replication several years ago when she taught the symmetric replication class for Oracle Education.

Other folks at Oracle have been most generous with their time and have provided significant assistance with various portions of this book. Harvey Eneman, the architect of multi-threaded server (MTS), provided extensive consultation. Sue Jang, who probably has more experience with implementing replication than anybody, has provided valuable input into the replication chapters. Virtually all members of the replication team have been very helpful, not only with the contents of this book but also with the resolution of real-world issues. They include Al Demers, Alan Downing, Pat McElroy, Maria Pratt, Benny Souder, Jim Stamos, Harry Sun, and Lik Wong.

Other reviewers who have provided insight from the consumer point of view include Jeremy Brinkley, Peter Grendler, and Teresa Shaw. All of these people have been working with Oracle for a number of years, and were able to provide commentary from the point of view of DBAs and engineers.

Wittingly or not, my managers at Excite also have contributed to the quality of this book. Dan Nater and Jon Prall have asked me to push Oracle's replication technology to its limits, which I have. Their insatiable thirst for solutions has enhanced my ability to optimize a replicated environment, and the knowledge I have gained meeting their requests is all available here. Chances are, you will not ever need to push Oracle replication as far as Dan and Jon have.

Finally, I thank my wife, Kathy, who has been incredibly patient and understanding throughout the course of my writing this book. Nobody is looking forward to its completion more than she is.

I

The Distributed System

Part I introduces distributed database systems and provides information on the networking, configuration, security, and design of these systems. It contains the following chapters:

- Chapter 1, *Introduction to Distributed Systems*, is an overview of distributed systems—terminology, basic concepts, benefits and perils, and the various options provided by Oracle.

- Chapter 2, *SQL*Net and Net8*, describes the underlying protocols Oracle supplies to support communication with distributed Oracle databases over a network.

- Chapter 3, *Configuration and Administration*, explains how to set up a distributed database environment; it discusses initialization parameters, database links, how distributed transactions work, and the basics of distributed backup and recovery.

- Chapter 4, *Distributed Database Security*, describes special security concerns for distributed systems; it looks at privilege management, various authentication methods, the encryption of network traffic, and the use of the Oracle Security Server (OSS) and the Advanced Networking Option (ANO).

- Chapter 5, *Designing a Distributed System*, examines the design of a distributed system; it introduces C. J. Date's fundamental principles of distributed databases, discusses the global data dictionary, and recommends a particular approach to data partitioning.

- Chapter 6, *Oracle's Distributed System Implementation*, examines how Oracle's RDBMS and networking products meet Date's objectives for distributed database systems.

- Chapter 7, *Sample Configurations*, focuses on the most common distributed architectures: the high-availability system, systems illustrating geographic data distribution, workflow partitioning, and data collection and consolidation, and the loosely coupled federation.

- Chapter 8, *Engineering Considerations*, examines the special requirements of distributed systems that must be taken into account during the engineering process: schema design and integration, application tiering, and the design of a replicated application.

1

Introduction to Distributed Systems

Any organization that uses the Oracle relational database management system (RDBMS) probably has multiple databases. There are a variety of reasons why you might use more than a single database in a distributed database system:

- Different databases may be associated with particular business functions, such as manufacturing or human resources.

- Databases may be aligned with geographic boundaries, such as a behemoth database at a headquarters site and smaller databases at regional offices.

- Two different databases may be required to access the same data in different ways, such as an order entry database whose transactions are aggregated and analyzed in a data warehouse.

- A busy Internet commerce site may create multiple copies of the same database to attain horizontal scalability.

- A copy of a production database may be created to serve as a development test bed.

Sometimes the relationship between multiple databases is part of a well-planned architecture, in which distributed databases are designed and implemented as such from the beginning. In other cases, though, the relationship is unforeseen; it is quite common for distributed databases to evolve as businesses expand, requirements grow, and applications spawn. But common to all cases is the need to copy or reference data in one or more remote databases.

A distributed database system will meet one or more of the following objectives:

Availability
> Data must be available at the local site even when a remote site is unreachable.

Survivability
> The failure of any single database instance must not impact the ongoing business.

Data collection
> Regional data such as sales receipts is consolidated and aggregated at a single site.

Data extraction
> A data warehouse extracts transaction records from an online transaction processing (OLTP) system.

Decentralized data
> Data may be updated in several databases.

Maintenance
> There must be support for activities such as load testing with data from production in a benchmarking database.

Oracle Corporation introduced interdatabase connectivity with SQL*Net in Oracle Version 5 and simplified its usage considerably with the database links feature in Oracle Version 6, opening up a world of distributed possibilities. Oracle now supplies a variety of techniques that you can use to establish interdatabase connectivity and data sharing. Each technique has its advantages and disadvantages, but in many cases the best solution is not immediately obvious.

Before delving into Oracle's offerings in the distributed database systems area, I'll clarify some terminology and concepts.

Terminology and Concepts

I have found that there is a great deal of confusion surrounding the various products and terminology from Oracle. I think it's worthwhile to clarify some of these terms up front so you'll get the most benefit from this book.

Database/database instance
> These terms are often used interchangeably, but they are not the same thing. In Oracle parlance, a *database* is the set of physical files containing data. These files comprise tablespaces, redo logs, and control files. A *database instance* (or simply *instance*) is the set of processes and memory structures that manipulate a database.

A database may be accessed by one or more database instances, and a database instance may access exactly one database.

Oracle parallel server

Oracle parallel server (OPS) is a technology that allows two or more database instances, generally on different machines, to open and manipulate one database, as shown in Figure 1-1. In other words, the physical data files (and therefore data) in a database can be seen, inserted, updated, and deleted by users logging on to two or more different instances; the instances run on different machines but access the same physical database.

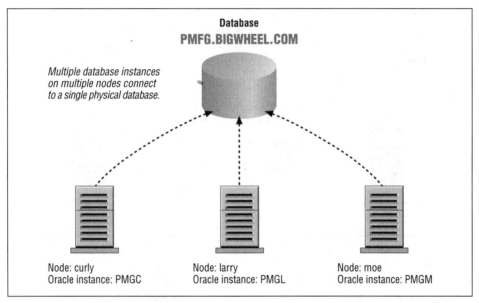

Database
PMFG.BIGWHEEL.COM

Multiple database instances on multiple nodes connect to a single physical database.

Node: curly
Oracle instance: PMGC

Node: larry
Oracle instance: PMGL

Node: moe
Oracle instance: PMGM

Figure 1-1. Parallel server architecture

Oracle parallel server requires an operating system that supports clustering and a distributed lock manager because the multiple database instances must share information about the data that is updated, the lock resources, and so on. For example, if a user on instance A updates a row, and a user on instance B performs a query that would return that row, instance B must instruct instance A to write the updated data to the physical database so that the query will deliver the updated information.

Oracle parallel server is intended to provide *failover capabilities*—capabilities that allow a second machine to take over the processing being performed by the first in the event of machine failure (e.g., CPU or motherboard failure). It does not provide any protection from disk failure. Occasionally, parallel server technology is used to achieve horizontal scalability, a concept I'll discuss later in this chapter.

Standby database

Oracle introduced the standby database in Version 7.2, although some sites had created their own homegrown varieties earlier. A standby database is one that shadows a normal database and is always in recovery mode. Whenever a redo log is archived in the primary database, the archived redo log is applied to the standby database, as shown in Figure 1-2. Generally, the standby database resides on a separate machine and uses separate storage.

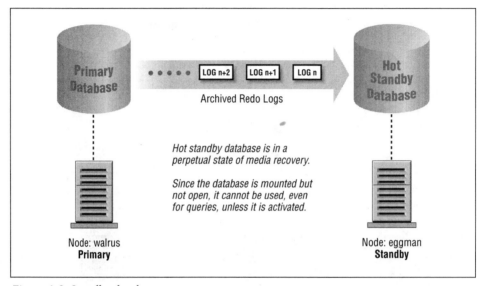

Figure 1-2. Standby database

If the primary database fails, the DBA can open the standby database and point users to it instead of to the primary database. Once this occurs, what had been the standby database becomes the primary database, and it cannot be put back into standby mode again.

Advanced replication

Advanced replication, also known as *symmetric replication* or *multi-master replication*, refers to maintaining a table or tables in multiple databases such that DML (Data Manipulation Language) can be issued in any of the databases and applied to the others automatically. The DML may be propagated *synchronously* (i.e., DML is committed locally and remotely as a single transaction) or *asynchronously* (i.e., DML committed locally is placed in a queue from which it is applied at the remote site later). Advanced replication can be used to deliver high availability, in the sense that the unavailability of any one site does not affect the others, or it may be used as part of a *survivability policy* in which *every* database has a replicated copy that can be used in the event of failure. Unlike parallel server, advanced replication involves numerous databases and numerous database instances.

Parallel query

The parallel query option (PQO) is a technology that can divide complicated or long-running queries into several independent queries and allocate separate processes to execute the smaller queries. A coordinator process collects the results of the smaller queries and constructs the final result set. Parallel queries are effective only on machines that have multiple CPUs.

Parallel DML

Oracle introduced the parallel DML feature in Oracle8. Parallel DML is similar to parallel query, except that the independent processes perform DML. For example, an update of several hundred thousand rows can be doled out to several processes that execute the update on separate ranges of the table.

What Is a Distributed Database System?

A distributed database system, illustrated in Figure 1-3, is an environment in which data in two or more database instances is accessible as though this data were in a single instance. This access may be read-only, or it may permit updates to one or many instances. The referenced data may be real time, or it may be seconds, hours, or days old. Generally, the different database instances are housed on different server nodes, and communication between them is via SQL*Net (for Oracle7) or Net8 (for Oracle8). Chapter 2, *SQL*Net and Net8*, describes this communication.

In addition to database servers, a distributed database system usually includes application servers and clients. The focus of this book is on the interaction among database servers, but a brief review of the entire distributed environment will clarify their raison d'être.

Application servers, like database servers, typically are high-capacity machines that run intensive utilities such as web applications, Oracle's application cartridges, report generators, and so forth.

The *clients* in this environment are typically PCs or Macintoshes or other lightweight computers running web browsers. The client's role is to provide an interface to the user, such as Forms (in Oracle Developer 2000) and web browsers. Client machines are characterized by low cost and the absence of a local database.

Implicit in this distributed system architecture is the *network*. It links database servers, application servers, and clients. SQL*Net and Net8 are network interfaces that are protocol-independent and that provide communication to networked databases.

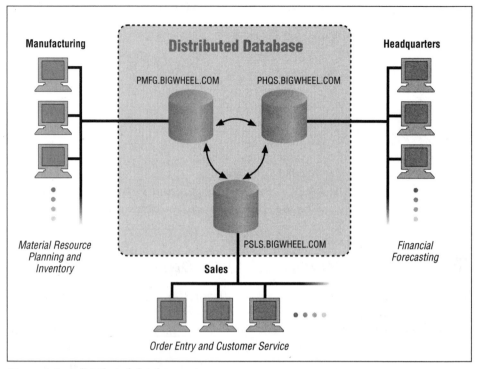

Figure 1-3. A distributed database system

Benefits of Distributed Databases

The separation of the various system components, especially the separation of application servers from database servers, yields tremendous benefits in terms of cost, management, and performance.

Tunability

A machine's optimal configuration is a function of its workload. Machines that house web servers, for example, need to service a high volume of small transactions, whereas a database server with a data warehouse has to service a relatively low volume of large transactions (i.e., complex queries). Separating the web server from the database server in this example allows the system administrators to optimize these machines without compromise. A machine configured as a web server will differ from a machine configured as a data warehouse database server. If performance problems arise in a distributed architecture, it is much easier not only to identify problems but also to solve them without the risk of compromising other components.

Platform Autonomy

Since applications and databases do not reside on the same machines, there is no particular reason why they even need to reside on the same *type* of machine. SQL*Net and Net8 provide a protocol-independent network interface allowing connectivity among disparate platforms and even disparate database engines. This openness allows DBAs, developers, and desktop users to choose their platforms without being restricted by anybody else's preferences or requirements. Whether you perform a major platform change such as moving from VMS to Unix or a minor upgrade such as from Solaris 2.5 to Solaris 2.6, you can make these changes without risking functionality changes in the Oracle database engine.

Fault Tolerance

The failure of a single component in a distributed architecture is much less drastic than in an environment in which databases and applications are housed on the same machine. Administrators can design failover methodologies that are appropriate to each component's functionality. For example, database machines might implement parallel server or synchronous replication to protect against failure of a database machine, whereas application servers may have backup hardware available so that the application can run on a new machine if an application server fails. Protecting against failure of machines that house data is generally much more complicated than protecting against failure of machines that simply run applications.

Scalability

A server that houses nothing other than an Oracle database scales very predictably; sites taking advantage of the parallel query option (and/or parallel DML in Oracle8) can expect performance to be a nearly linear function of the number of processors (up to the point of at least 30 processors on Solaris). Other applications may or not scale this way, but if the applications have their own host, system administrators can understand their requirements and allocate hardware resources appropriately.

Location Transparency

Location transparency means that neither applications nor users need to be concerned with the logistics of where data actually resides or how it is distributed. Needless to say, being shielded from these specifics enhances the usability of a database because developers and users do not need to consider such details as connect strings. Moreover, data can be relocated from one database instance to another with minimal impact on users and applications.

Site Autonomy

Distributed databases allow various locations to share their data without conceding administrative control. If a database instance at headquarters contains particularly sensitive information or has high availability requirements, it can still share data without compromising its security or availability. In addition, any given site in a distributed database environment can follow its own administrative procedures and upgrade paths, within reason. Of course, we hope that administrators from various sites are in communication with one another and that they coordinate their activities, but they are in no way handcuffed to one another.

Enhanced Security

The components of the distributed architecture are completely independent of one another, which means that every site can be maintained independently. You can share data without sharing accounts and passwords. Each site can have its own administrators and its own sets of accounts, and private data can be kept private.

As an example, you can implement a replicated environment with updateable snapshots that would allow users at a branch office to update something as sensitive as the salary table without having any access to the salary data for headquarters (*horizontal partitioning*). As another example, you can use *workflow partitioning* (discussed in Chapter 15, *Conflict Avoidance and Resolution Techniques*) in a multi-master replicated environment to limit the set of rows that can be updated at any given site.

You also can configure a distributed environment to provide security in the sense of survivability—that is, you can maintain two or more versions of entire schema by replicating them to different machines at different locations.

There is no reason for developers or end users to have accounts on a database server, because all database access is through network APIs (Application Programming Interfaces). The database server's exposure to malicious intruders and careless users is minimal. In fact, it is not uncommon for users to have no idea whatsoever where the database resides!

Multiple Schema Versus Multiple Databases

Most designers and database administrators associate one schema with one application. (By *schema*, I mean an Oracle database account that owns the database objects that an application uses.) Whenever a new schema is introduced, the designers and DBAs must choose between giving the schema its own database or placing it with other schema in an existing database. A number of factors affect this decision

The Single Database with Multiple Schema

Quite often, it makes sense to let schema and applications share a database instance. The two primary advantages of this approach are lower administrative overhead and lower hardware costs. Every Oracle database instance carries a certain amount of overhead: disk space must be allocated to system, temporary, and rollback tablespaces; and memory must be allocated to the SGA (System Global Area). In addition, a DBA must manage users, SQL*Net configuration, database links, and so on. If you can minimize this overhead, by all means do so.

If the schemas share data, then you may realize additional benefits. For example, an inventory application that shares a VENDORS table with an accounts payable application can access the table without depending on the availability of two databases. The administrative work is simplified because no database links are required, and application code is simplified because no error trapping need exist to handle the unavailability of the VENDORS table.

Even if applications do not share data, you should consider placing different schema in the same database if you can answer "Yes" to all questions in Table 1-1.

Table 1-1. Conditions for Locating Application Schema in the Same Database Instance

Requirement	Yes	No
Are most users in the same location or using the same access path?		
Do the applications have the same administrative support staff?		
Do the applications have compatible availability requirements?		
Do the applications have compatible database and OS version requirements and upgrade paths?		
Are the applications reasonably similar in functionality and load characteristics?		
Do the applications have the same usage level (e.g., QA, development, production, maintenance, etc.)?		

As a general rule, it is more economical to house schemas in a single database instance than to devote an instance to every application that comes down the pike. Don't create additional instances without good reason.

Database Instances Devoted to a Single Application

If you answered "No" to any of the conditions in Table 1-1, then your schemas probably belong in separate database instances, even if they share data.

Options for Distributed Data

Oracle provides several methods for accessing data that is distributed among two or more database instances. All of these methods provide *location transparency*, which means that users and applications can manipulate data as though it were all in one single database instance. These various methods are summarized here and are described in detail throughout this book.

Export/Import

The Oracle export and import utilities (illustrated in Figure 1-4) are the most primitive method of sharing data among databases and are also used as part of a backup and recovery strategy. Export (*exp*) creates a file that is essentially a set of SQL statements that invoke the DDL (Data Description Language) and DML (Data Manipulation Language) required to create objects and insert data. Import (*imp*) is the utility that reads this file and executes the SQL statements to re-create the objects and populate tables. A full database export creates a file that you can use to re-create the entire database.

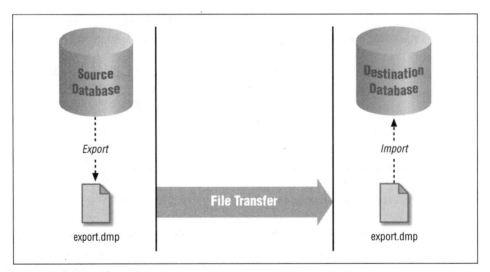

Figure 1-4. Export/import

Unlike any of the other options, export and import are static. An export file contains the data from the time of the export and cannot be updated. In fact, an export file could easily be out of date before the export job is finished. In addition, you must specify the export option CONSISTENT=Y in order for all of the data in the export file to be consistent as of a single point in time. Exports are only one part of a comprehensive backup strategy.

Database Links

Database links are the invisible glue that makes location transparency possible. In more technical terms, a database link defines a connection from one database instance to another, and this definition is stored in the Oracle data dictionary. Since database link connections log in to a normal account in the remote database instance, you have complete control over its privileges and quotas.

Used in conjunction with synonyms, database links (shown in Figure 1-5) can make remote objects appear to be local as far as applications and users are concerned.

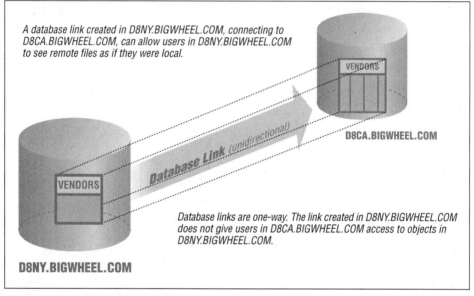

Figure 1-5. Database links

If your inventory application at a manufacturing site needs to reference the VENDORS table at headquarters, you could provide location transparency with the following three SQL statements:

```
CREATE PUBLIC DATABASE LINK D8CA.BIGWHEEL.COM
    USING 'hqaccounting.bigwheel.com'

CREATE PUBLIC SYNONYM vendors FOR vendors@D8CA.BIGWHEEL.COM

GRANT SELECT ON vendors TO inventory_reader
```

Since the CREATE DATABASE LINK statement in this example creates a PUBLIC link without specifying an account to connect to in the D8CA.BIGWHEEL.COM database, this particular implementation assumes that every application user in the inventory database has an account in the remote database with the same password and with privileges to see the VENDORS table. If the remote database is unavailable, the VENDORS table also will be unavailable.

Of course, there are several ways to provide location transparency; these are described in greater detail later in this book.

Read-Only Snapshots

If you have an application that cannot risk a dependency on the availability of a remote database, you could use a read-only snapshot (shown in Figure 1-6). A read-only snapshot is essentially a local table whose data is refreshed at specified intervals by performing a query against one or more remote tables. The inventory application could create the same functionality as the database link described in the previous section by following these steps:

```
CREATE PUBLIC DATABASE LINK D8CA.BIGWHEEL.COM
    USING 'hqaccounting.bigwheel.com'

CREATE SNAPSHOT vendors
    REFRESH COMPLETE
    START WITH SYSDATE
    NEXT TRUNC(sysdate + 1) + 10/1440
AS
SELECT vendor_id, company_name
FROM vendors@D8CA.BIGWHEEL.COM

CREATE PUBLIC SYNONYM vendors FOR vendors

GRANT SELECT ON vendors TO inventory_reader
```

This snapshot is populated when the CREATE SNAPSHOT statement executes, and is then refreshed every day from that point on at 10 minutes after midnight. Again, this is just one example of how the technique could be implemented; the details come later. Snapshots use the Oracle built-in package DBMS_JOB to schedule refreshes and require the *INIT.ORA* parameter JOB_QUEUE_PROCESSES to be greater than zero.

The benefit of read-only snapshots over database links and public synonyms is that the snapshot is available even when the remote site is not. The disadvantages are that the data is neither real time nor updateable.

 Oracle introduced read-only snapshots with Oracle Version 7.0. The infrastructure this feature required has been expanded with each subsequent release, with additional functionality such as updateable snapshots and advanced replication. The base components include the job queue and triggers. The feature set is continuing to expand.

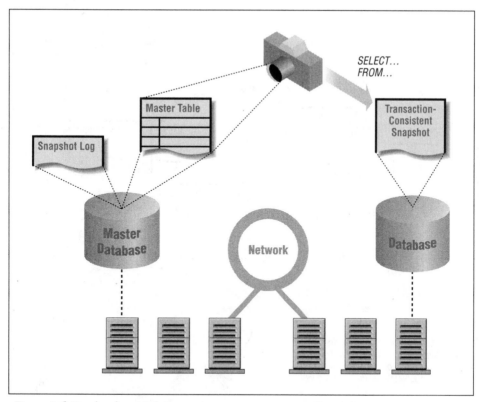

Figure 1-6. Read-only snapshot

Updateable Snapshots

If your application needs to change data in a snapshot and send the changes back to the master site, you can use updateable snapshots, shown in Figure 1-7. A trigger on the snapshot table logs updates that are applied at the master site when the snapshot refreshes. Updateable snapshots require the advanced replication facilities. A common use of updateable snapshots is an application that consolidates data from various sites into a single master site. For example, a bicycle company might collect sales transactions from its distributors every night, or travelling salespeople might enter customer leads on their laptops and upload this information to the headquarters database when they return to the office.

Two important characteristics of updateable snapshots, which distinguish them from multi-master replicated tables, are:

- They update only the master site.

- They can be disconnected from the master site for extended periods.

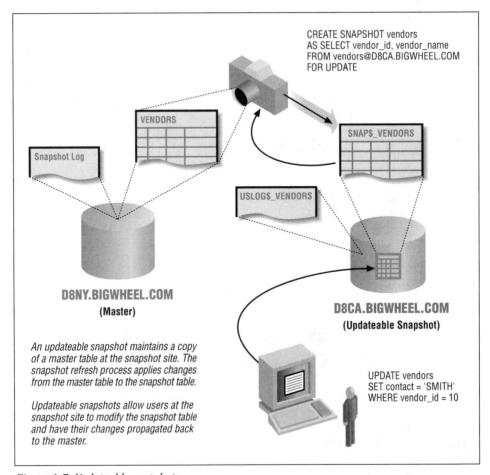

CREATE SNAPSHOT vendors
AS SELECT vendor_id, vendor_name
FROM vendors@D8CA.BIGWHEEL.COM
FOR UPDATE

VENDORS

Snapshot Log

SNAP$_VENDORS

USLOG$_VENDORS

D8NY.BIGWHEEL.COM
(Master)

D8CA.BIGWHEEL.COM
(Updateable Snapshot)

An updateable snapshot maintains a copy of a master table at the snapshot site. The snapshot refresh process applies changes from the master table to the snapshot table.

Updateable snapshots allow users at the snapshot site to modify the snapshot table and have their changes propagated back to the master.

UPDATE vendors
SET contact = 'SMITH'
WHERE vendor_id = 10

Figure 1-7. Updateable snapshots

You also can configure an updateable snapshot such that the updates are *not* sent back to the master. You can use this configuration to perform "What if" analyses against the local data without fear of overwriting the definitive values at the master site.

Advanced Replication

Advanced (or multi-master) replication (shown in Figure 1-8) is the most powerful of the replication options. You can use it to maintain a table at numerous sites, with updates at any one location being applied at all the other locations. There is no single "master" table, although there is a *master definition site*, from which schema maintenance must be performed. Unlike the situation with snapshots, you can configure a multi-master environment to provide real-time data; this technique is known as *synchronous replication*. If you use *asynchronous replication* (by far the more common implementation), updates to a table are placed in the *deferred queue* and pushed to other participating sites at user-defined intervals.

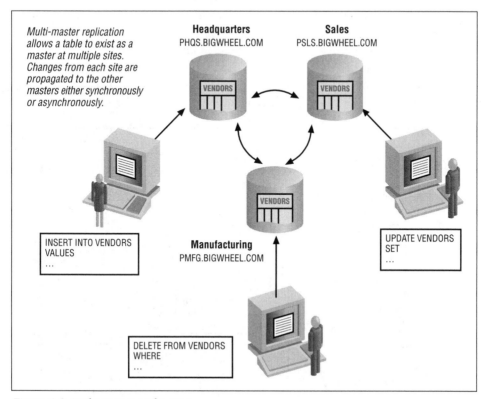

Figure 1-8. Multi-master replication

Since updates can occur at several locations, these updates can conflict with one another. Oracle provides a number of built-in methods to assist in resolving these conflicts, such as Latest Timestamp and Site Priority, but these techniques must be selected carefully to guarantee that data always converges. Conflict resolution, described in detail in Chapter 15, *Conflict Avoidance and Resolution Techniques*, is usually the biggest challenge to creating and maintaining a successful implementation.

Advanced replication also has some significant limitations:

- No support for sequences

- No support for LONG or LONG RAW or HHCODE data, although Oracle8 supports replication of binary large objects (BLOBs) and character large objects (CLOBs)

- Not recommended for applications performing massive updates (i.e., updates to tens of thousands of rows per hour)

Procedural Replication

Procedural replication (shown in Figure 1-9) is the preferred way to perform the massive updates that are not recommended with advanced replication. Instead of queuing up row-level changes and sending them to the other database instances, procedural replication queues calls to procedures and sends them to the other participants. If, for example, you wanted to mark up the prices of all your products by five percent, you could replicate the procedure call UPDATE_PRICES(pct_increase => 5). The procedure will execute at every site with the same parameters.

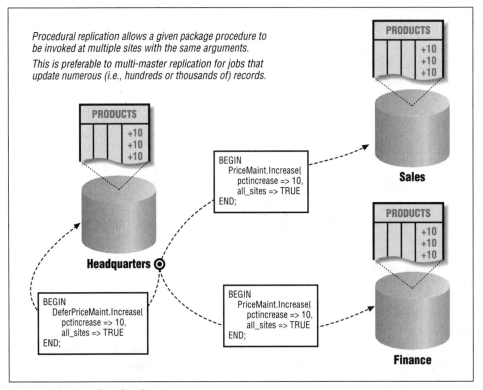

Figure 1-9. Procedural replication

Oracle does not provide any conflict handlers that work in conjunction with procedural replication, so any routines that you want to use in this way must account for conflicts. In the price increase example, suppose that a price for one item had been changed at a remote site, and the change had not yet propagated to the site initiating the UPDATE_PRICES call. The data would not converge to the same values at both sites. Table 1-2 summarizes the kinds of conflicts that may occur with procedural replication.

It is safest to perform procedural replication during periods of low or no activity.

Table 1-2. Potential Conflicts with Procedural Replication

Time	Activity	CA Price	NY Price
12:00	Sites agree	$100	$100
12:05	CA calls UPDATE_PRICES(pct_increase => 5)	$105	$100
12:10	NY site updates price to $120 before procedure replicates	$105	$120
12:15	Procedure call replicates to NY site	$105	$126
12:20	Update from NY at 12:10 arrives at CA site	$120	$126

Perils of Distributed Databases

Nobody ever said that the administration of distributed databases is easy; it's not. For one thing, it can be difficult to keep track of who needs what sort of access to a given database instance, and what access needs to be available from it to other instances. If users are experiencing difficulties or applications are unable to perform, how do you know which database is causing the problem? When you create a new user, what database instances should have the account? What is USER_A really seeing when he references the VENDORS table? None of these difficulties exist in a standalone system. Some of the more significant perils are summarized here and are discussed in detail in the chapters that follow.

Security

Didn't this topic appear under the "Benefits" section, too? Yes, because there are two sides to the security story. Because it can be difficult to know and to control who is coming into a database via a database link, the accounts to which database links connect should be given no more access rights than absolutely necessary. Similarly, the CREATE PUBLIC DATABASE LINK system privilege should be granted sparingly because whoever has it can effectively create a public doorway into any system to which she has access. If you use operating system validated (OPS$) accounts, be extremely careful of using them in the CONNECT clause of database links. Be aware that holes to exploit do exist.

In an advanced replication environment, security issues can become complicated because the user community can be the sum of all users in all databases participating in replication. The maintenance of accounts in and of itself can become a full-time job. Oracle8 alleviates this chore somewhat, but you will need to decide if replicated transactions should be performed at remote sites by the original user or by a generic replication account.

It is possible to configure an extremely well controlled and robust distributed environment, but it takes care and planning as I'll describe in Part II of this book.

Data Consistency

If you are using multi-master replication or procedural replication or if you have written your own code to perform DML on remote tables, one of your most formidable tasks will be to guarantee that data converges. This responsibility is shared among designers, developers, and DBAs (who should be coordinating their efforts). Designers must consider potential conflicts in their architecture; developers must code so that conflicts are addressed; and DBAs must resolve the unresolved conflicts. In general, the design and realization of a replicated system necessitates the solution of far more problems than does a standalone system, and the bulk of these problems concern data convergence.

Transaction Management

Do you want to update 15,000 records in the VENDORS table to reflect an area code change? Well, if that transaction needs to be replicated to five other sites, you'd better think twice about it because it's going to queue up 15,000 × 5 = 75,000 transactions across your replicated environment. Do you want to use procedural replication to do it tonight at midnight California time? What about your site in Hong Kong where users are at work and updating the table? The point is that any batch updates in a replicated environment must be carefully coordinated with all sites in order to avoid massive conflicts and logjams.

The initial load and distribution of data among sites also requires coordination. For example, you might want to lock users out of all instances until you can guarantee that the data is identical everywhere.

Monitoring

The additional workload a distributed environment demands of the DBA can be considerable. In addition to the normal DBA responsibilities such as monitoring space utilization and extent allocation, the DBA must monitor objects such as snapshot logs, job queues, transaction queues, and error queues. If left unresolved, problems in a distributed environment can become so difficult to solve that it is easier to reload data from scratch than try to resolve specific errors.

For that reason, most people consider alert mechanisms to be essential in a replicated environment. For example, if unresolved conflicts put entries into the error queue (*deferror*), the DBA should be notified as soon as possible. You will find utilities for this sort of automated notification in Appendix B, *Scripts and Utilities*, of this book, and on the accompanying diskette.

Recovery

If a database that is part of a distributed environment fails, the recovery process must ensure not only the complete restoration of the local data but also the restoration of distributed data, such as snapshots and deferred transactions. It may be necessary to refresh snapshots at remote sites, to requeue deferred transactions, and so on. The point is that the recovery of the local system does not necessarily mean that the overall distributed database is recovered.

Performance

Several factors can affect performance in a distributed database. If the application references data over a database link, the performance of the network will have a direct bearing on performance. Replication components that utilize store-and-forward techniques, such as snapshots and multi-master replication, also exact their toll on overall system performance. If, for example, a snapshot master has a snapshot log, all DML on that table will cause a row-level trigger to fire that inserts records into the snapshot log. Similarly, DML against a replicated table will either put entries into the deftran queue (in the case of asynchronous replication) or require the successful delivery of every transaction to remote sites before completing (in the case of synchronous replication).

The storing and forwarding of transactions will impact overall system performance, and you should take this impact into consideration when specifying hardware requirements. In addition, activities such as snapshot refreshes and application of pushed transactions at destination sites impact performance. Oracle has taken great steps to minimize the impact of data distribution, but it still is a factor to consider.

Differences Between Oracle7 and Oracle8

Oracle has added a wide variety of capabilities into the Oracle8 server. Some of the more significant enhancements relevant to distributed databases are highlighted here.

Global users and global roles

Oracle8 provides a user management scheme that supports maintenance of users and roles across multiple database instances. Instead of having to visit every instance to grant privileges, create users, and so on, you can define users and roles in such a way that changes from a central location take effect everywhere.

System security model

The management of users in an advanced replication environment is simplified tremendously in Oracle8, with the introduction of *propagator* and *receiver* accounts. Instead of having to create a user in all instances participating in the replication *and* having to create and verify private database links for each user, you can designate one account to queue DML and one account to apply DML.

Parallel propagation

Oracle8 is able to push replicated transactions either in parallel or serially. The replication option can determine which transactions are independent of one another so that transactional consistency is preserved. The net result is a significant improvement in throughput.

Reduced data propagation

With Oracle8 you can omit columns in a table from replication. What this means is that the replication facility does not check the before and after values of the columns that you so designate. Since these columns are not replicated, less data is transmitted, and less time is spent checking for conflicts.

Snapshot registration at master sites

When you create a snapshot in Oracle8, it is automatically registered at the master site, with relevant information stored in the DBA_REGISTERED_SNAPSHOTS data dictionary view. This registration occurs regardless of whether the master table has a snapshot log on it, but if there is a snapshot log, you can query DBA_REGISTERED_SNAPSHOTS and DBA_SNAPSHOTS to obtain information about the latest refreshes, and so on, as shown in the following:

```
SELECT r.owner,
       r.name,
       r.snapshot_site,
       l.current_snapshots
  FROM dba_registered_snapshots r,
       dba_snapshot_logs l
 WHERE r.snapshot_id = l.snapshot_id(+)
```

Deferred constraint validation

Oracle8 supports deferred constraint checking, which means that you can now create uniqueness and integrity constraints on snapshot tables. Oracle enforces deferred constraints only after refreshes are complete, not during the actual snapshot refresh, during which constraints are not necessarily respected. You also can use deferred constraints during imports so that records in parent tables can be imported after child tables without violating foreign key constraints.

Fine-grained quiesce

Although Oracle7 provides an API to *quiesce* replication (i.e., suspend DML activity against replicated objects) at the group level, it doesn't actually work, even in the latest Version 7.3 releases. Oracle8 corrects this problem, making it possible to administer multiple replication groups completely independently.

Internalized triggers

The triggers required to support replication are internalized in Oracle8, which means that they are compiled C code as opposed to PL/SQL. The enhancement results in improved performance and easier maintenance.

2

SQL*Net and Net8

SQL*Net and Net8 are the network protocols Oracle supplies to support communication with an Oracle database over a network. Net8 is the new moniker for SQL*Net which Oracle has introduced with Oracle8.

Protocol Overview

Even if a process is running on the same machine as the database instance, it requires SQL*Net or Net8 to establish its database connection and to perform operations such as record fetching. SQL*Net or Net8 is required for communication between servers and clients and between servers and other servers. This software makes the entire networked database environment appear as a single machine even though multiple machines and network protocols may be involved. Before delving into the architecture and management of SQL*Net/Net8, I'll provide an introduction to this software's role in a distributed database environment.

Distributed Processing

Although database transactions are performed on the database server, they are usually not *initiated* there. A transaction may originate from a mouseclick on a web page or a bar code scan at a grocery store or a button pushed on a Touch-Tone phone—to name a few examples. SQL*Net/Net8 coordinates the communications associated with distributed transactions by establishing connections between clients and servers (or servers and servers), transmitting data back and forth, and disconnecting cleanly. SQL*Net/Net8 is also responsible for translating any differences in character sets or data representations that may exist at the operating system level. SQL*Net/Net8 does not, however, perform tasks such as converting a bar code or key tone into its respective ASCII representation; that is the application's responsibility.

SQL*Net/Net8 establishes a connection from a client to a server or a server to a server by passing the connection request to the Transparent Network Substrate (TNS). TNS, in turn, determines which server should handle the request and sends the request using the corresponding network protocol.

Network Transparency and Network Independence

The details of the SQL*Net/Net8 configuration and network protocols are completely invisible to database applications. Oracle provides network drivers (called *protocol adapters*) that allow SQL*Net/Net8 to function with all network protocols. These drivers function on any media or topology that supports the protocol. For example, the TCP/IP SQL*Net/Net8 protocol adapter works on Ethernet, token ring, or any other media and topology on which TCP/IP runs.

Multiple Network Protocol Interoperability

Besides facilitating communication between machines that are connected with the same network protocol, SQL*Net/Net8 also supports communication between machines running *different* network protocols. Oracle accomplishes this with the MultiProtocol Interchange in Oracle7 and connection manager (CMAN) in Oracle8. A computer that runs both network protocols provides the link between network communities, and the MultiProtocol Interchange software runs on this machine to translate TNS communications from one protocol to the other, as illustrated in Figure 2-1.

Oracle Names

Oracle Names is a product that stores connection information about all databases in a distributed environment in a single location. Any time an application issues a connection request, it consults the Oracle Names repository to determine the location of the database server. Oracle Names is primarily an administrative aid that makes the maintenance of this information easier. Its use is not required; the alternative is to provide local *tnsnames.ora* files on every client machine.

Architecture

Oracle supplies three key components that interact to locate services, establish connections, transport data, and handle exceptions. They are:

- SQL*Net/Net8
- Transparent Network Substrate (TNS)
- Oracle Listener

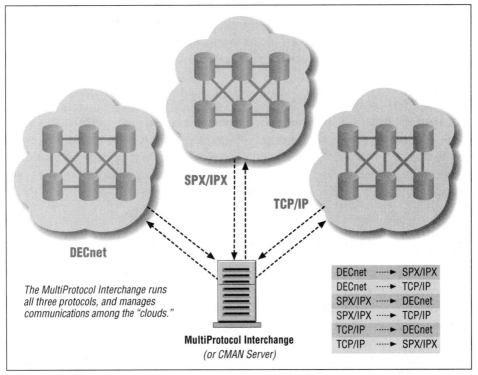

Figure 2-1. Disparate network communities linked with the MultiProtocol Interchange

While the interaction among these products does not generally require intervention beyond the initial installation, some customizations are often beneficial in an environment that is making heavy use of snapshots, symmetric replication, or other distributed functionality.

SQL*Net/Net8, TNS, and the OSI Reference Model

Both TNS and the Oracle protocol adapters may be described by the seven-layer Open Systems Interconnection (OSI) model, as seen in Table 2-1.

The OSI model uses the concept of a stack to describe the interaction of networked machines. Each layer of the stack communicates with its peer on a remote machine and with adjacent layers on the local machine, where data is passed down from the application through the various layers and finally passed to the remote machine at the physical layer.

There are different Oracle networking components associated with layers 4, 5, 6, and 7. The lower layers of the stack are related to routing and physical characteristics of the network; they are not specifically relevant to the data being transmitted.

Table 2-1. TNS and Oracle Protocol Adapters in the OSI Model

Client-Side Stack	Layer	Server-Side Stack
Client application	7 (application)	Oracle server
SQL*Net/Net8	6 (presentation)	SQL*Net/Net8
TNS	5 (session)	TNS
Oracle protocol adapter	4 (transport)	Oracle protocol adapter
	3 (network)	
	2 (data link)	
	1 (physical)	

Application layer

The application layer is what the user sees and interacts with. It is a user interface, such as a web browser or a Forms application or even a bar code scanner. The application initiates requests on behalf of the user, such as connection requests, queries, and updates. All applications that interact with an Oracle database do so through the OCI (Oracle Call Interface). This code contains API calls to do the following:

- Connect and disconnect from the database server

- Parse SQL statements

- Open cursors

- Bind variables from the application to server memory

- Describe fields in tables and views

- Execute SQL statements

- Fetch rows of data

- Close cursors

- Handle exceptions

Within the application layer, OCI calls are made at a layer known as the User Programmatic Interface (UPI) on the client side and the Oracle Programmatic Interface (OPI) on the server side.

Applications that use stored PL/SQL procedures and packages can significantly reduce the volume of data that is sent over the network because there are fewer network round trips between the client and the server (i.e., the client does not need to ship SQL statements to the server if the SQL statements reside in a stored procedure).

Presentation layer

Two-Task Common is the SQL*Net/Net8 code that resides on the presentation layer and is used by the OCI. If and when necessary, this code translates between character sets and data representations on the client and the server.

Session layer

The session layer establishes and terminates database connections and carries data and data requests. It also determines whether data can be transported asynchronously or synchronously. The session layer is the realm of TNS, which is layered within the session layer. TNS translates OCI messages from the application layer (the messages have been translated if necessary at the presentation layer) into SEND messages. Similarly, it passes RECEIVE messages up the stack in OCI format. TNS exchanges data with the Oracle protocol adapter, which formats for the transport layer using standards that are specific to the protocol in use. TNS also provides error and interrupt handling.

Transport, network, data link, and physical layers

The activity that takes place at these lower levels of the OSI stack are specific to the protocols and media in use. The Oracle software residing at the session layer shields us from any involvement at this level.

SQL*Net/Net8 Elements

SQL*Net/Net8 consists of three components:

The client
> The client is the application or software that initiates the connection. It may be an end user application, such as a web page, or it may be another Oracle server.

The server
> This is the software to which the client connects; it may be an Oracle server or an external procedure.

The listener
> The listener (also known as the TNS listener or the SQL*Net listener) creates listen end points on the machine housing the Oracle server or external procedure. The addresses of these end points are established in advance and published in the *tnsnames.ora* file, stored in an Oracle Names server (the location of which is published in the *names.ora* file) or stored in some other name server.

SQL*Net and WANs

As you can imagine, the translations that occur between and within various levels of the OSI stack have an impact on performance, and when a wide area network (WAN) is involved, the impact can be significant. SQL*Net and TNS are essentially layered protocols, which in turn are layered on a network protocol. Every frame of every protocol layer has a header portion and a data portion. The more layers, the more headers, and the more headers, the less data.

Consider the overhead encountered translating a single 1514-byte Ethernet frame from Ethernet to IP to TCP to TNS:

- Ethernet frame: 14 bytes header, 1500 bytes data. (This is an IP frame.)

- IP frame: 20 bytes header, 1480 bytes data. (This is an IP frame.)

- TCP frame: 20 bytes header, 1460 bytes data. (This is an IP frame.)

- TNS frame: 10 bytes header, 1450 bytes data. Note that the TNS frame size is configurable with the SDU parameter in the configuration files *listener.ora, tnsnames.ora*, and, in the case of the multi-threaded server (MTS) in Oracle8, *INIT.ORA*.

Here we see that 64 bytes (approximately four percent) of the Ethernet frame was lost to overhead. In tests we ran with a Forms application on a PC connected to a Unix database server, we saw an average of only 60 bytes of actual data per frame. And for each SQL*Net packet sent to a destination, an acknowledgment SQL*Net packet must come back. The acknowledgment messages can cause a severe performance degradation on a WAN because of message latency and a potentially high number of raindrop messages.

Connection Scenarios

There are two scenarios for which SQL*Net establishes a connection to a database:

- When a user or program specifically initiates a connection (e.g., a Forms login screen).

- When one server needs to communicate with another, as the result of either an explicit or implicit request. An example of this type of connection is an application that accesses a table over a database link in a distributed database environment.

In both cases, the initiator sends a connection request to a predefined address on which a listener is accepting requests. The listener passes the request to the appropriate server.

Bequeathed and Redirected Connections

The TNS listener establishes all connections by performing either a bequeath or a redirect. A bequeathed connection is one that the listener passes to the Oracle server directly. In the case of a redirect, the listener redirects the client to establish a connection to a different address in order to connect to the targeted server. You have control over whether the TNS listener performs bequeathed or redirected connections. Table 2-2 compares the two types of connections.

Table 2-2. Bequeathed Versus Redirected Connections

Connection Type	Operating System and Protocol Requirements	Examples
Bequeathed	Operating system can pass a connection end point to another process during creation of connection process. Protocol must allow connection to be given to another process.	Most Oracle server dedicated processes are bequeathed.
Redirected	No operating system requirements. Protocol must allow process to perform a wildcard listen or else use configuration files.	All Oracle multi-threaded server (MTS) processes are redirected.

If an operating system and network protocol are capable of handing a listener end point from the listener to the server during the creation of an operating system process, then a bequeathed connection may be used.

How a bequeathed connection is established on Unix

If the TNS listener and the Oracle server have a parent-child relationship, then the listener can establish bequeathed connections. The series of events is as follows:

1. The TNS listener is started, and it listens on an address it obtained from the *listener.ora* file or an appropriate default.

2. The client sends a connection request to the TNS listener's address. The client determines this address from the *tnsnames.ora* file, the Oracle Names server, or another name server.

3. The client and TNS listener perform a handshake, during which the client supplies the connect string. The TNS listener accepts or rejects the connection request based on the information supplied. If the connection is rejected, it sends a REFUSE to the client and continues waiting for more connection requests.

4. If the TNS listener accepts the connection request, it spawns a new operating system process which inherits the TNS listener's open connections.

5. The TNS listener closes its open connection, and continues waiting for more connection requests.

6. The new operating system process created in Step 4 uses the connection it inherited to communicate with the client.

How a redirected connection is established

If the TNS listener and the Oracle server do not have a parent-child relationship, then the TNS listener will use redirected connections. This is the method used by the multi-threaded server and from any configuration in which the TNS listener is on a different machine from the Oracle server. The TNS listener also uses redirected connections when the protocol and/or operating system in use cannot pass connection end points between processes.

The first three steps of establishing a redirected connection are the same as for establishing a bequeathed connection. If the TNS listener accepts the connection request, the following events complete the request:

1. The TNS listener either creates a new operating system process or (in the case of a multi-threaded server configuration) communicates with an existing operating system process (the MTS dispatcher). This operating system process establishes a listening end point of its own, and the TNS listener is informed of the end point's address. This end point is usually a wildcard listen, which means that the operating system process tells the underlying protocol stack that it does not care what address is used. Most operating systems then choose a listening address that is not in use and assign it to the process.

2. The TNS listener communicates the new listening address to the client. This step is known as the REDIRECT.

3. The client disconnects from the TNS listener, issues a new connection request to the address provided in the redirect message, and establishes a connection.

Because redirected connections generally do not have the overhead of starting a new process, these connections are generally faster to establish, and the methodology is portable across more operating systems and protocols.

Because the TNS listener's role is only to process new connection requests, you can stop and start it at any time without affecting connections that are *already* established.

Example: Connecting to a Multi-Threaded Server

The multi-threaded server allows you to service many client connections with a relatively small number of server processes, thereby reducing memory and processing requirements. This technique is well suited for applications that must support a high number of connections that do not transmit a high volume of data. A Forms-based application would be a good candidate for MTS connections. Oracle export/import utilities, on the other hand, are examples of applications that should use dedicated server processes.

In order to use the multi-threaded server option with a database instance, you must set parameters in the instance's *INIT.ORA* file, as outlined in Table 2-3.

Table 2-3. Multi-Threaded Server INIT.ORA Parameters

Parameter Name	Description
MTS_DISPATCHERS	Used to configure a group of dispatchers. This is the only required parameter in Oracle8*i*.
MTS_LISTENER_ADDRESS	The address on which the listener is to listen; specify at least one address per protocol. Obsolete in Oracle8.
MTS_MAX_DISPATCHERS	The maximum number of dispatcher processes that can run simultaneously. Optional.
MTS_MAX_SERVERS	The maximum number of shared server processes that can run simultaneously. Optional.
MTS_MULTIPLE_LISTENERS	If TRUE, syntax of MTS_LISTENER_ADDRESS can support multiple protocols. Obsolete in Oracle8.
MTS_RATE_LOG_SIZE	The sample size used to calculate dispatcher statistics. Oracle8 only. Deprecated in Oracle8*i*.
MTS_RATE_SCALE	The scale, in hundredths of a second, with which dispatcher statistics are calculated. Oracle8 only. Deprecated in Oracle8*i*.
MTS_SERVERS	The initial number of server processes. Optional in Oracle8*i*.
MTS_SERVICE	The name of the service to which the dispatcher connects. Typically the ORACLE_SID defaults to DB_NAME. Deprecated in Oracle8*i*.

When a multi-threaded server Oracle instance and listener start up, the following events typically take place:

1. The TNS listener begins listening on the addresses configured in the *listener.ora* file.

2. The Oracle multi-threaded server background processes (dispatchers and servers) start with the database instance, using the configuration specified in the *INIT.ORA* file. Each dispatcher listens on its protocol on the specified (or dynamically generated) address.

3. Each dispatcher informs the TNS listener of the wildcard address it is listening on. In Oracle7, each dispatcher connects to each listener. In Oracle8, the PMON background process connects to each listener.

Although you can start the database before you start the TNS listener, Oracle Corporation recommends that you start the listener first. The reason is that if you start the Oracle instance first, the dispatchers (Oracle7) or PMON (Oracle8) will not contact the listener as described in Step 3. In this case, the dispatcher or PMON processes loop and attempt to reconnect to the listener every 60 seconds.

At this point, the multi-threaded server processes and TNS listener are ready to accept connections. The command:

```
lsnrctl services listener_name
```

reports what dispatchers are registered with the TNS listener, as shown in the following example:

```
oracle@socrates% lsnrctl services LISTENER

LSNRCTL for Solaris: Version 8.0.4.0.0 - Production on 23-NOV-98 23:26:08

(c) Copyright 1997 Oracle Corporation.  All rights reserved.

Connecting to (ADDRESS=(PROTOCOL=IPC)(KEY=prodsales.bigwheel.com))
Services Summary...
  PSLS            has 9 service handler(s)
    DEDICATED SERVER established:1401 refused:0
      LOCAL SERVER
    DISPATCHER established:174381 refused:0 current:28 max:254 state:ready
      D000 <machine: socrates, pid: 3198>
      (ADDRESS=(PROTOCOL=tcp)(DEV=21)(HOST=199.172.152.166)(PORT=63409))
    DISPATCHER established:211990 refused:0 current:28 max:254 state:ready
      D001 <machine: socrates, pid: 3222>
      (ADDRESS=(PROTOCOL=tcp)(DEV=21)(HOST=199.172.152.166)(PORT=63415))
    DISPATCHER established:220539 refused:0 current:28 max:254 state:ready
      D004 <machine: socrates, pid: 3272>
      (ADDRESS=(PROTOCOL=tcp)(DEV=21)(HOST=199.172.152.166)(PORT=63439))
    DISPATCHER established:179663 refused:0 current:28 max:254 state:ready
      D003 <machine: socrates, pid: 3256>
      (ADDRESS=(PROTOCOL=tcp)(DEV=21)(HOST=199.172.152.166)(PORT=63436))
    DISPATCHER established:175661 refused:0 current:28 max:254 state:ready
      D002 <machine: socrates, pid: 3232>
      (ADDRESS=(PROTOCOL=tcp)(DEV=21)(HOST=199.172.152.166)(PORT=63428))
    DISPATCHER established:184766 refused:0 current:28 max:254 state:ready
      D005 <machine: socrates, pid: 3279>
      (ADDRESS=(PROTOCOL=tcp)(DEV=21)(HOST=199.172.152.166)(PORT=63446))
    DISPATCHER established:218292 refused:0 current:27 max:254 state:ready
      D006 <machine: socrates, pid: 3291>
      (ADDRESS=(PROTOCOL=tcp)(DEV=21)(HOST=199.172.152.166)(PORT=63455))
    DISPATCHER established:204115 refused:0 current:27 max:254 state:ready
      D007 <machine: socrates, pid: 3307>
      (ADDRESS=(PROTOCOL=tcp)(DEV=21)(HOST=199.172.152.166)(PORT=63458))
The command completed successfully
```

The steps for handling connection requests with the multi-threaded server are as follows:

1. The client sends a connection request to the TNS listener's address. The client determines this address from the *tnsnames.ora* file, the Oracle Names server, or another name server.

2. The TNS listener receives the request and performs the handshake to determine whether the client can connect. If the connection is denied, the TNS listener sends a REFUSE to the client and continues listening for other requests.

3. If the client request is accepted, the TNS listener sends a REDIRECT to the client, informing it of the address of the dispatcher that is listening on the client's protocol.

4. The client terminates its connection with the TNS listener and establishes a new connection with the dispatcher using the address the TNS listener provided.

5. The TNS listener continues listening for connection requests.

A client can override the multi-threaded server and use a dedicated server by specifying SERVER=DEDICATED in the connect string. In addition, if all multi-threaded server connections are exhausted, subsequent connection requests will use dedicated servers.

Example: Connecting to a Prespawned Server Process

As the name suggests, *prespawned server processes* are processes that the TNS listener starts at startup time. These processes can be handed off to clients that are requesting dedicated processes. Prespawned processes are typically not used in conjunction with the multi-threaded server.

The *listener.ora* file contains configuration information required to use prespawned servers. The relevant parameters are described in Table 2-4.

Table 2-4. listener.ora Parameters Governing Prespawned Servers

Parameter Name	Description
POOL_SIZE	Number of unused prespawned processes to maintain for each protocol. This number should be between 1 and PRESPAWN_MAX, inclusive.
PRESPAWN_MAX	Number of prespawned processes to create for each protocol.
TIMEOUT	Number of seconds an inactive server should wait for a new connection before shutting down. Affects only processes that have carried a client connection.

These parameters can be set individually for each ORACLE_SID the TNS listener services.

The sequence of events for using prespawned server processes is as follows:

1. The TNS listener starts and listens on the addresses specified in *listener.ora.*

2. The TNS listener spawns POOL_SIZE server processes for each ORACLE_SID defined in *listener.ora.*

3. Each prespawned server process performs a wildcard listen and informs the TNS listener of the address it is using.

4. The client sends a connection request to the TNS listener's address. The client determines this address from the *tnsnames.ora* file or from the Oracle Names server.

5. The TNS listener receives the request, and performs the handshake to determine whether the client can connect. If the connection is denied, the TNS listener sends a REFUSE to the client and continues listening for other requests.

6. If the client's request is accepted, the TNS listener sends the client a REDIRECT message informing it of the address of one of the prespawned processes. Then the TNS listener marks the prespawned process as ACTIVE.

7. The client terminates its connection with the TNS listener and establishes a new connection with the prespawned process using the address the TNS listener provided.

8. If PRESPAWN_MAX is less than the number of active and idle prespawned processes, the TNS listener spawns a new process to replace the one that the client took.

9. The TNS listener continues listening for new connections.

When PRESPAWN_MAX processes exist for the ORACLE_SID, the TNS listener stops prespawning server processes. When a client disconnects from one of the prespawned processes, it is marked as IDLE (i.e., available) and, if more than POOL_SIZE servers are not ACTIVE, it remains alive for TIMEOUT seconds. If no connection has been established in that time, the idle prespawned process terminates.

Prespawned connections are an aging technology that was primarily intended for use with operating systems on which process startup costs are high (most notably VMS). In this day and age, the multi-threaded server technology is a preferable choice.

SQL*Net/Net8 Tuning

The most effective network tuning you can do for SQL*Net/Net8 is to reduce the
number of round-trip messages between the client machines and database server.
You can control this behavior in various ways, such as setting your application's
ARRAY_SIZE (the number of records that are processed with each fetch), the size
of the session data unit (SDU), and the use of stored procedures. In addition, scalability issues can be improved by tuning your MTS configuration. Net8 introduces
additional multiplexing and connection pooling capabilities which scale to support tens of thousands of users.

Do You Have a Problem?

The first step in addressing SQL*Net/Net8 scalability is to recognize whether your
system is experiencing a performance degradation and act accordingly. If you are
using multi-threaded server, your primary concerns are whether the dispatchers
are keeping up with the rate of requests and whether the server processes are able
to handle the volume of activity. If you are using prespawned servers, your concerns are whether you have enough servers and whether the machine has the
resources to accommodate their memory and CPU usage. Methods of diagnosing
all of these situation are included here.

Tuning the multi-threaded server

Tuning the multi-threaded server amounts to configuring more dispatchers and
adding or reducing server processes. The book *Oracle Performance Tuning*, 2nd
edition, by Mark Gurry and Peter Corrigan (O'Reilly & Associates, 1996) includes
SQL scripts that help to diagnose multi-threaded usage. Slightly modified versions
of these scripts, which are useful primarily for Oracle7, follow. You'll find copies
on the diskette accompanying this book.

To determine whether you have enough dispatcher processes to service the rate of
connection requests, you can query the V$DISPATCHER dynamic data dictionary
view:

```
----------------------------------------------------------------------
-- Filename:    busydisp.sql
-- Purpose:     Provides stats indicating whether the dispatcher processes
--              are overly taxed.
-- Author:      Chas. Dye (cdye@excitecorp.com)
-- Date:        6-Aug-1998
----------------------------------------------------------------------
column network    heading "Protocol"                           format a40
column rate       heading "Total Busy Rate|>50%=>Add Dispatchers" format 99.99
```

```
SELECT  network,
        100*(sum(busy)/(sum(busy)+sum(idle))) rate
FROM    v$dispatcher
GROUP BY network
/
column protocol heading "Protocol"                              format a40
column Wait     heading "Average Wait|(hundredths of seconds)"  format a30

SELECT  network Protocol,
        decode( sum(totalq), 0, 'No Responses',
        to_char(sum(wait)/sum(totalq), 'FM9999.90')) Wait
FROM    v$queue q, v$dispatcher d
WHERE   q.type = 'DISPATCHER'
AND     q.paddr = d.paddr
GROUP BY network
/
```

Here is sample output from this script:

```
                        Total Busy Rate
Protocol                >50%=>Add Dispatchers
-------------------------  ---------------------
ipc                                       .00
tcp                                       .48

2 rows selected.



                  Average Wait
Protocol          (hundredths of seconds)
----------------  ------------------------------
ipc                            No Responses
tcp                                     .00

2 rows selected.
```

The metrics from the V$DISPATCHER are cumulative since the time that the database instance was started. If the workload on your database varies over time, you should examine the delta in values from V$DISPATCHER over a set interval. In Oracle8, the data dictionary view V$DISPATCHER_RATE provides metrics that reflect current utilization rates.

In this case, we see that the dispatchers are not overly taxed. Had we seen a Busy Rate above approximately 50% or an appreciable value for Average Wait, we would be advised to add more dispatchers dynamically (as follows) or by modifying the *INIT.ORA* file.

Oracle7 syntax:

```
ALTER SYSTEM SET mts_dispatchers = 'tcp, 5';
```

Oracle8 syntax:

```
SQL> ALTER SYSTEM SET mts_dispatchers = '(PROTOCOL=TCP)(DISPATCHERS=5)';
```

Note that adding dispatcher processes can lead to excessive context switching, which may degrade performance.

 Changes in Oracle8 make this tuning advice somewhat less relevant. In Oracle8, the BUSY and IDLE fields in V$DISPATCHER are cumulative and therefore do not reflect the current statistics. You must query V$DISPATCHER at set intervals and observe the change in BUSY/IDLE over time.

Tuning multi-threaded server dispatchers in Oracle8

In Oracle8, the dynamic data dictionary view V$DISPATCHER_RATE provides statistics that can help to determine whether you have an appropriate number of dispatchers.

The following script reports on dispatchers in an Oracle8 database:

```
---------------------------------------------------------------------------
-- Filename:     disprate.sql
-- Purpose:      Queries v$dispatcher_rate.
-- Author:       Chas. Dye (cdye@excitecorp.com)
-- Date:         24-Nov-1998
---------------------------------------------------------------------------

col name format a8

col CUR_MSG_RATE   format 999999
col MAX_MSG_RATE   format 999999
col AVG_MSG_RATE   format 999999

SELECT name,
       CUR_MSG_RATE,
       MAX_MSG_RATE,
       AVG_MSG_RATE
FROM   v$dispatcher_rate
/

col CUR_SVR_BYTE_PER_BUF   format 999999 heading "CUR|SVR|BYTE|PER|BUF"
col CUR_CLT_BYTE_PER_BUF   format 999999 heading "CUR|CLT|BYTE|PER|BUF"
col MAX_SVR_BYTE_PER_BUF   format 999999 heading "MAX|SVR|BYTE|PER|BUF"
col MAX_CLT_BYTE_PER_BUF   format 999999 heading "MAX|CLT|BYTE|PER|BUF"
col AVG_SVR_BYTE_PER_BUF   format 999999 heading "AVG|SVR|BYTE|PER|BUF"
col AVG_CLT_BYTE_PER_BUF   format 999999 heading "AVG|CLT|BYTE|PER|BUF"

SELECT name,
       CUR_SVR_BYTE_PER_BUF,
       CUR_CLT_BYTE_PER_BUF,
       MAX_SVR_BYTE_PER_BUF,
       MAX_CLT_BYTE_PER_BUF,
       AVG_SVR_BYTE_PER_BUF,
       MAX_CLT_BYTE_PER_BUF
```

```
FROM    v$dispatcher_rate
/
```

Here is sample output:

```
SQL> @disprate

NAME     CUR_MSG_RATE MAX_MSG_RATE AVG_MSG_RATE
-------- ------------ ------------ ------------
D000               62         8000         1937
D001              233         8500         2099
D002               26         7300         1770
D003              269         7900         2836
D004              333         8100         2158
D005              274         9400         2968
D006              339         8600         2171
D007              212         8300         2372

8 rows selected.
```

	CUR SVR BYTE PER	CUR CLT BYTE PER	MAX SVR BYTE PER	MAX CLT BYTE PER	AVG SVR BYTE PER	MAX CLT BYTE PER
NAME	BUF	BUF	BUF	BUF	BUF	BUF
D000	155	973	7446	40465	14	40465
D001	263	593	6169	49080	37	49080
D002	161	1380	7709	45152	83	45152
D003	319	980	9508	50433	9	50433
D004	254	337	19246	37949	41	37949
D005	228	753	5837	43968	8	43968
D006	374	1347	44276	36661	43	36661
D007	103	119	21710	56071	21	56071

```
8 rows selected.
```

Tuning multi-threaded server server processes

The other concern with multi-threaded servers is whether the server processes are overly busy. If you see many requests on the COMMON queue (visible in the dynamic data dictionary via V$QUEUE), you should consider adding more servers. The following script provides useful statistics:

```
-------------------------------------------------------------------------
-- Filename:    busyq.sql
-- Purpose:     Provides stats indicating whether a given queue is overly
--              taxed in a Multi-Threaded Server environment.
--              If the COMMON queue is overly taxed, consider adding more
--              servers.
-- Author:      Chas. Dye (cdye@excitecorp.com)
-- Date:        6-Aug-1998
-------------------------------------------------------------------------
```

```
column type        heading "Queue|Type"              format a10
column circuit     heading "Name"                    format a8
column queued      heading "Items|Queued"            format 999,999
column wait        heading "Total|Time|Waited"       format 999,999,999
column totalq      heading "Total|Items|Processed"   format 999,999,999,999
column avgwait     heading "Average|Wait"            format 9,999.90

set head off
set feedback off

SELECT  sysdate
FROM    dual
/
set head on
set feedback on

SELECT paddr,
       type,
       queued,
       wait,
       totalq,
       decode(totalq, 0, 0, wait)/decode(totalq, 0, 1, totalq) avgwait
FROM    v$queue
/
```

Here is sample output:

```
system@live SQL> @busyq

24-Nov-1998 00:36:30


                      Total    Total
             Queue    Items    Time                Items    Average
PADDR        Type     Queued   Waited          Processed       Wait
--------  ----------  -------  -------  ----------------  ---------
00           COMMON         0        0       484,422,948        .20
8C612E88 DISPATCHER         0        0        74,413,276        .04
8C60C1D8 DISPATCHER         0        0        81,077,489        .04
8C614BE8 DISPATCHER         0        0        68,060,821        .05
8C614028 DISPATCHER         0        0        98,532,257        .04
8C6151C8 DISPATCHER         0        0        83,142,628        .04
8C608A08 DISPATCHER         0        0       102,410,058        .04
8C60D958 DISPATCHER         0        0        83,688,178        .05
8C610B48 DISPATCHER         0        0        86,438,327        .06

9 rows selected.
```

Because the COMMON queue does not show any items queued and an average wait time of zero, we can conclude that the server allocation for this system is adequate. If you see a high number of items on the COMMON queue, and there are no significant wait events occurring (such as latch waits) you should consider adding more multi-threaded server processes (controlled with the *INIT.ORA* parameters MTS_SERVERS and MTS_MAX_SERVERS).

Measuring multi-threaded server server activity

Finally, we also can check the volume of activity of the individual connections that are associated with a given server. The query is as follows:

```
-------------------------------------------------------------------------
-- Filename:    busycirc.sql
-- Purpose:     Provides stats indicating whether a given circuit is
--              overly taxed in a Multi-Threaded Server environment.
-- Author:      Chas. Dye (cdye@excitecorp.com)
-- Date:        6-Aug-1998
-------------------------------------------------------------------------
column server   heading "Server"                             format a8
column circuit  heading "Name"                               format a8
column status   heading "Status"                             format a8
column message0 heading "Bytes|in|First|Msg|Buf"             format 9,999
column message1 heading "Bytes|in|Second|Msg|Buf"            format 9,999
column messages heading "Messages|Processed"                 format 999,999
column queue    heading "Queue"                              format a10
column bytes    heading "Bytes"                              format 9,999,999
column breaks   heading "Brks"                               format 999

SELECT   server,
         circuit,
         status,
         queue,
         message0,
         message1,
         messages,
         bytes,
         breaks
FROM     v$circuit
ORDER BY server
/
```

Here is sample output:

Server	Name	Status	Queue	Bytes in First Msg Buf	Bytes in Second Msg Buf	Messages Processed	Bytes	Brks
00	D7009B30	NORMAL	NONE	0	0	4,687	428,048	5
00	D7009F54	NORMAL	NONE	0	0	4,217	469,556	0
00	D700A378	NORMAL	NONE	0	0	8	273	0
00	D700A79C	NORMAL	NONE	0	0	4,405	500,308	0
00	D700ABC0	NORMAL	NONE	0	0	2,328	246,359	0
00	D700AFE4	NORMAL	NONE	0	0	2,328	246,352	0
00	D700B408	NORMAL	NONE	0	0	4,432	471,695	0
00	D700B82C	NORMAL	NONE	0	0	4,013	449,682	0
00	D700BC50	NORMAL	NONE	0	0	2,328	246,355	0
00	D700C074	NORMAL	NONE	0	0	2,328	246,361	0
00	D700C498	NORMAL	NONE	0	0	2,328	246,365	0
00	D700C8BC	NORMAL	NONE	0	0	5,357	559,594	11

```
00          D700CCE0 NORMAL    NONE          0     0      5,260    537,766   11
00          D700D104 NORMAL    NONE          0     0      5,499    582,824   12
00          D700D528 NORMAL    NONE          0     0      5,195    535,113    9
00          D700D94C NORMAL    NONE          0     0      5,546    584,801   14
00          D7011B8C NORMAL    NONE          0     0      2,328    246,352    0
00          D7011768 NORMAL    NONE          0     0      4,439    421,834    3
00          D7011344 NORMAL    NONE          0     0      2,328    246,355    0
00          D7010F20 NORMAL    NONE          0     0      2,340    248,940    0
00          D7010AFC NORMAL    NONE          0     0      4,761    435,934    5
00          D70102B4 NORMAL    NONE          0     0     40,402  8,519,935    0
00          D700FE90 NORMAL    NONE          0     0     42,936  9,030,261    0
00          D700DD70 NORMAL    NONE          0     0      2,328    246,352    0
00          D7012C1C NORMAL    NONE          0     0      2,328    246,352    0
00          D70123D4 NORMAL    NONE          0     0          8        283    0
00          D7011FB0 NORMAL    NONE          0     0      2,328    246,352    0
00          D700E194 NORMAL    NONE          0     0     45,406  9,534,634    0
00          D700E5B8 NORMAL    NONE          0     0      4,569    425,801    4
00          D700E9DC NORMAL    NONE          0     0          8        283    0
00          D700EE00 NORMAL    NONE          0     0      4,337    409,904    0
00          D700F224 NORMAL    NONE          0     0     41,002  8,628,613    0
00          D700F648 NORMAL    NONE          0     0      3,926    439,282    0
D805482C    D700FA6C NORMAL    SERVER        0   235        521     68,737    1

34 rows selected.
```

Here we see that all but one of the circuits are idle and that there are no clogged message buffers, indicating that the network is able to keep up with the traffic volume. If you do see messages accumulating in the buffer, you can consider adding more multi-threaded server processes over which to spread the load.

The possible values of the STATUS and QUEUE fields of V$CIRCUIT are listed in Table 2-5.

Table 2-5. V$CIRCUIT STATUS and QUEUE Fields

Field	Values
STATUS	BREAK (circuit has been interrupted); EOF (circuit is about to exit); NORMAL (normal circuit for the local database); OUTBOUND (waiting to establish an outbound connection)
QUEUE	COMMON (circuit is on the common queue, available to be picked up by a server process); DISPATCHER (waiting for a dispatcher); SERVER (currently in user); OUTBOUND (waiting to establish an outbound connection); NONE (circuit is idle)

Tuning Dedicated Processes and Prespawned Processes

Unlike with a multi-threaded server configuration, a DBA using dedicated or prespawned processes does not have an arsenal of V$ tables to assist in diagnosing connection-specific performance problems. Since dedicated processes (whether prespawned or not) require an operating system process for each user connection, one of the problems you are likely to encounter is a memory shortage. Memory problems manifest themselves in different ways on different operating systems, and it is not our intention to provide a primer on system administration. However, suffice it to say that if you plan to support a large number of users with dedicated processes, you should be prepared to configure your machine with a large amount of memory.

Apart from memory problems, you and your user community may find that it takes them a long time to connect with a dedicated process configuration. If this is the case, and you are not currently using prespawned processes, you should consider doing so, particularly if your operating system is one that does not create processes quickly (e.g., VMS).

Break Out the Sniffer

If you have exhausted the remedies indicated by the V$ tables and operating system statistics, but performance is still slow, you may have to perform an analysis of your network traffic with a sniffer in order to analyze the efficiency of your network traffic.

SQL*Net sends data in packets of session data unit (SDU) bytes. The default value for SDU is 2048 bytes. That means that if you want to send 4097 bytes of data, SQL*Net will actually send 2048 + 2048 + 2048 = 3 packets. You can experiment with changing the value of SDU to see how it affects your performance, but there is no magic formula to help you. However, you will benefit significantly by tuning the SDU if your application does at least one of the following:

- Sends multiple packets of data

- Sends consistently sized packets

- Sends large amounts of data

- Runs over a WAN

If you elect to change SDU, bear in mind that it is negotiated to the lower of the values configured for the client and the server. The server configuration file is *listener.ora* (for dedicated connections) or *INIT.ORA* (for MTS). The client configuration file is *tnsnames.ora*.

Here is a sample portion of *tnsnames.ora*:

```
D7CA.BIGWHEEL.COM =
    (DESCRIPTION =
        (SDU=8192)
        (ADDRESS = .........
```

Here is a sample portion of *listener.ora*:

```
SID_LIST_LISTENER =
    (SID_LIST =
        (SID_DESC =
            (SDU = 8192)
            (SID_NAME = V7323)
.............................
```

You also have other tuning options that are not really specific to SQL*Net and whose benefits can be confirmed only by analyzing your network traffic. Among these other options are:

- Increase ARRAYSIZE. Most Oracle applications allow you to set the number of records that are sent at one time. In SQL*Plus, the parameter is ARRAYSIZE. Forms has an analogous setting. By increasing the value of this setting, you often can improve the efficiency of your network transmissions dramatically by reducing the number of round-trip messages.

- Set MTU (maximum transmission unit) on the WAN.

Load Balancing

If your application is one that must process a high volume of connection requests in a short amount of time (e.g., a popular web site), you might consider TNS listener load balancing. You can configure multiple TNS listeners to process your connection requests to a single database. Or, if you have a symmetric replication environment that allows clients to connect to any of several masters, you can configure TNS listeners that send connection requests to the masters with the least busy dispatchers (assuming that you are also using a multi-threaded server).

Multiple TNS Listeners and Multi-Threaded Server with a Single Database Instance

If you are using a multi-threaded server, you can run TNS listeners on multiple nodes for your database instance. The TNS listener does not need to run on the same node as the database because dispatchers are able to register with listeners on whatever node(s) you specify with the *INIT.ORA* parameter MTS_LISTENER_ADDRESS (Oracle7). In Oracle8, use the LISTENER attribute of the MTS_DISPATCHERS parameter. Figure 2-2 depicts a configuration with multiple listeners on multiple machines for a single database.

The relevant multi-threaded server *INIT.ORA* parameters for this configuration are as follows:

```
mts_multiple_listeners = TRUE
mts_listener_address = "(ADDRESS=(PROTOCOL=TCP)(host=eggman)(port=1521))"
mts_listener_address = "(ADDRESS=(PROTOCOL=TCP)(host=walrus)(port=1521))"
```

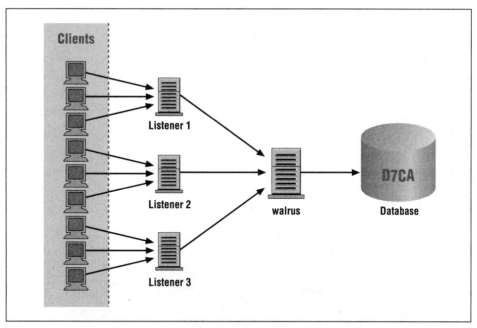

Figure 2-2. Multiple listeners on multiple nodes for a single database instance

On the client side, the *tnsnames.ora* file must also reflect that the database instance has two listeners by having two DESCRIPTION sections for the same CONNECT_DATA section. The client will pick one of the two listeners at random. However, if the connection fails, the client will reattempt the connection with the second listener.

```
penguin = (DESCRIPTION_LIST =
   (DESCRIPTION =
        (ADDRESS =
           (PROTOCOL = TCP)
           (Host = eggman)
           (Port = 1521)
         )
   )
   (DESCRIPTION =
        (ADDRESS =
           (PROTOCOL = TCP)
           (Host = walrus)
           (Port = 1521)
         )
   )
     (CONNECT_DATA =
        (SID = D7CA)
      )
 )
```

Note that the listeners do not have to be listening on the same protocol.

Multiple TNS Listeners and Multi-Threaded Server with Multiple Database Instances

If you are configuring a symmetric replication or Oracle parallel server environment that allows clients to connect to any of several masters, you can configure your listeners such that they hand off connections to the least busy dispatchers among all your masters. You will recall that the dispatcher processes update the TNS listener with information relevant to load balancing. Figure 2-3 depicts such a configuration.

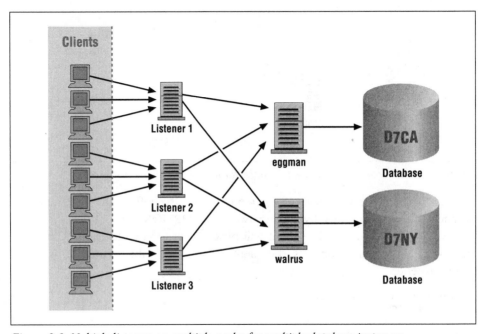

Figure 2-3. Multiple listeners on multiple nodes for multiple database instances

In this case, you must update the *tnsnames.ora* client configuration files to reflect the fact that there are two separate database instances available for the alias *penguin*:

```
penguin = (DESCRIPTION_LIST =
   (DESCRIPTION =
        (ADDRESS =
          (PROTOCOL = TCP)
          (Host = eggman)
          (Port = 1521)
        )
     (CONNECT_DATA =
        (SID=D7NY)
     )
   )
```

```
     (DESCRIPTION =
         (ADDRESS =
            (PROTOCOL = TCP)
            (Host = walrus)
            (Port = 1521)
         )
      (CONNECT_DATA =
         (SID = D7CA)
      )
    )
  )
```

In this case, there are two CONNECT_DATA sections, one for each DESCRIPTION_LIST. As with the multiple TNS listeners for a single database configuration, clients will randomly select a listener to process their connection requests but will fail over to the other listener if the connection fails.

If you are using dedicated processes, all listeners must reside on the same machine as the database instance. For a multi-threaded server configuration, you can run multiple listeners on multiple machines because dispatchers are able to register with listeners on different nodes.

Multiple TNS Listeners and Dedicated Processes

To configure multiple TNS listeners for dedicated process connections, either you can create individual *listener.ora* files for each one and store them in different locations or you can use one *listener.ora* file with multiple named listeners in it. The processes that start the listeners must each have the appropriate environment variable set to the location of *listener.ora*. In Unix, this environment variable is TNS_ADMIN.

If you are finding that your listener is not able to handle all of the connection requests, you should consider setting the QUEUESIZE in your *listener.ora* file (boldfaced in the following example). This parameter sets the number of connection requests the listener can queue—that is, the number of requests that it will allow to wait while it processes earlier requests. If your clients are experiencing timeouts when trying to connect, setting this parameter can alleviate the problem, but only by making the connection requests wait for the listener to process them. If you are still experiencing timeouts, you should run additional listeners.

```
###############
# Filename......: listener.ora
# Name.........: walrus
# Date.........: 08-SEP-98 11:44:31
###############
LISTENER =
  (ADDRESS_LIST =
      (ADDRESS =
         (PROTOCOL = TCP)
```

```
                    (Host = walrus)
                    (Port = 1521)
                    (Queuesize = 20)
                )
        )
    STARTUP_WAIT_TIME_LISTENER = 0
    CONNECT_TIMEOUT_LISTENER = 10
    TRACE_LEVEL_LISTENER = OFF
    SID_LIST_LISTENER =
      (SID_LIST =
        (SID_DESC =
          (SID_NAME = D7CA)
          (ORACLE_HOME = /usr/home/oracle/product/7.3.3)
        )
      )
```

Oracle8 Scalability Options

Oracle has introduced connection pooling and multiplexing with Net8, the network component of Oracle8. Both of these features build on the functionality that
exists with the multi-threaded server that first shipped with Oracle7. With the
added benefits of connection pooling and multiplexing, Oracle has racked up
some very impressive benchmark results with tens of thousands of users. Your
mileage may vary.

Connection Pooling

Connection pooling maximizes the utilization of a dispatcher's existing network
connections by detecting clients that are connected but idle for a predetermined
time and reallocating their transport connection to an incoming client connection.
The default timeout value is determined by Net8 and may vary by platform. If the
idle client resumes activity, the connection is reestablished.

You enable connection pooling by specifying the POOL attribute of the MTS_DIS-
PATCHERS *INIT.ORA* parameter—for example:

```
mts_dispatchers="(PROTOCOL=TCP)(POOL=ON)"
```

This enables connection pooling for the dispatcher, using the default values.

Connection pooling applies to both incoming and outgoing connections, and you
can specify the timeout (in network ticks) for both types of connections:

```
mts_dispatchers="(PROTOCOL=TCP)(POOL=(IN=20)(OUT=100))"
```

You can also enable connection pooling for inbound (or outbound) connections
only:

```
mts_dispatchers="(PROTOCOL=TCP)(POOL=(IN=20))"
```

Obviously, connection pooling works better with some types of applications than others. In order to profit from it, your application should be characterized by a relatively low ratio of active data requests to concurrent sessions. Examples include decision support systems (DSS), online transaction processing (OLTP), and messaging applications.

Session Multiplexing

Multiplexing is a solution for applications that must support a high number of active users, for those that use connection manager already, or for those that have a high reconnect cost (WAN or satellite). It uses the Oracle connection manager to service multiple network sessions through a single transport connection. The connection manager is essentially a concentrator for client sessions.

The connection manager has three components, each with a corresponding executable, described in Table 2-6.

Table 2-6. Connection Manager Components

Executable Name (Unix and VMS/Desktop)	Description
cmgw/cmgw80	The gateway process. This process registers with the connection manager administrative process, listens for incoming SQL*Net/Net8 connection requests, initiates connection request to Net8 listeners for clients, and answers requests initiated by *cmctl*.
cmadm/cmadm80	The connection manager administrative process. Primarily responsible for maintaining address information in the Oracle Names server (if any). It also processes *cmgw* and listener registration, locates the local name server (if any), identifies all listeners that are serving one or more database instances, updates the Oracle Names server (if any) with network updates, and answers requests initiated by *cmctl*. Note that all communication between *cmgw* and *cmadm* is via IPC.
cmctl/cmctl80	The connection manager utility program, analogous to *lsnrctl*. This utility includes four basic commands: START [cman | cm | adm] starts either or both the gateway process and administrative process. STOP [cm] stops the connection manager. Stopping the gateway process also stops the administrative process. STATUS [cman | cm | admin] provides status information about the three components. VERSION provides version information.

If you are using TCP/IP, you can enable the default behavior of the connection manager simply by modifying the following *INIT.ORA* parameter:

```
mts_dispatchers="(PROTOCOL=TCP)(MULTIPLEX=ON)"
```

You can also enable multiplexing for incoming or outgoing connections individually:

```
mts_dispatchers="(PROTOCOL=TCP)(MULTIPLEX=IN)"
mts_dispatchers="(PROTOCOL=TCP)(MULTIPLEX=OUT)"
```

By default, the connection manager listens on port 1600, and you can start it by issuing the command *cmctl start*.

In order to customize the behavior of multiplexing and the connection manager, you must create a configuration file, called *cman.ora*.

```
# Connection Manager config file
# cman.ora - The file is used by cman and cman_admin.
#
# These are cman's listening addresses (one or more) for the purpose of
# relaying TNS sessions.
#
CMAN=(ADDRESS=(PROTOCOL=TCP)(Host=walrus.bigwheel.com)(Port=1600)))

CMAN=
    (ADDRESS_LIST=
        (ADDRESS=
            (PROTOCOL=TCP)
            (HOST=walrus.bigwheel.com)
            (PORT=1600)
        )
    )
#
#
# These parameters control the connection managers logging and capacity.
CMAN_PROFILE = (PARAMETER_LIST=
                    (MAXIMUM_RELAYS=10240)
                    (LOG_LEVEL=ADMIN)
                    (TRACING=no)
                    (RELAY_STATISTICS=no)
                    (SHOW_TNS_INFO=no)
                    (USE_ASYNC_CALL=yes)
                    (AUTHENTICATION_LEVEL=0)
                    (ANSWER_TIMEOUT=0)
                )

# CMAN_RULES defines where connections are accepted or rejected.
CMAN_RULES=(RULE=(SRC=x.x.x.x)(DST=189.221.84.120)(SRV=D8CA)(ACT=accept))
```

The usage of the parameters CMAN, CMAN_PROFILE, and CMAN_RULES is summarized in Tables 2-7 through 2-9.

Table 2-7. cman.ora: CMAN Section

Parameter Name	Description
CMAN	CMAN contains one or more addresses for the ports on which the connection manager is processing connection requests. You must specify the address parameters PROTOCOL, HOST, and PORT.

Table 2-8. cman.ora: CMAN_PROFILE Section

Parameter Name	Default	Value Range	Description
ANSWER_TIMEOUT	0	0–unlimited	Number of seconds the connection manager uses to instruct NS (Network Services) to time out a connection request. A value of 0 indicates that no timeouts should occur.
AUTHENTICATION_LEVEL	0	0, 1	0 implies no authentication. 1 causes the connection manager to reject connection attempts that are not using SNS (Secure Network Services) to perform client authentication.
LOG_LEVEL	0	0–4	Level of logging performed.
MAXIMUM_RELAYS	8	1–10,240	The maximum number of hops that the connection manager will support.
RELAY_STATISTICS	no	no, yes	If "yes," connection manager maintains statistics about relay I/O.
SHOW_TNS_INFO	no	no, yes	If "yes," connection manager maintains TNS information in its logging.
TRACING	no	no, yes	If "yes," connection manager will create trace files.
USE_ASYNC_CALL	no	no, yes	If "yes," connection manager uses asynchronous NS functions nsanwer, nsaccept, and nscall.

The optional CMAN_RULES parameter provides a method of restricting access to the database based on the origination of the connection request, its target host, and its target ORACLE_SID. The parameter is included in the *cman.ora* file using this syntax:

```
CMAN_RULES = (RULE_LIST=<rule1><rule2>...<rulen>)
```

Table 2-9. cman.ora: CMAN_RULES Section

Parameter	Description
ACT	The action to perform: "accept" to accept the connection request or "reject" to reject it.
DST	The target (destination) hostname or IP address. The character "x" may be used as a wildcard in IP addresses.
SRC	Name or IP address of the source of the connection request. The character "x" may be used as a wildcard in IP addresses.
SRV	The ORACLE_SID of the target database.

If the CMAN_RULES parameter is present, then the only connection requests that are accepted are those that meet the rules defined. Note that CMAN_RULES is applicable only in a TCP/IP network.

You must also modify the *tnsnames.ora* on the client side to "teach" it to use the correct addressing to the connection manager. If you are running a single protocol, you would modify the *tnsnames.ora* to look something like this:

```
d8ca.bigwheel.com =
  (DESCRIPTION =
    (ADDRESS_LIST =
        (ADDRESS=
          (PROTOCOL=TCP)
          (HOST=walrus.bigwheel.com)
          (PORT=1600)
         )
        (ADDRESS =
          (PROTOCOL = TCP)
          (Host = eggman.bigwheel.com)
          (Port = 1521)
         )
     )
    (CONNECT_DATA =
       (SID = D8CA)
     )
    (SOURCE_ROUTE=YES)
   )
```

The ADDRESS section instructs the client to connect to WALRUS.BIGWHEEL.COM on port 1600 (where it will find the connection manager waiting). Then, it tells the connection manager to connect to the listener that is listening on port 1521. Essentially, the ADDRESS section is the route that the client will use to connect to the database.

The really nice thing about the connection manager is that you can specify a route that has multiple protocols in it. In fact, Oracle's stated direction is to replace the MultiProtocol Interchange with the connection manager. In the preceding example, the protocol between the client and the connection manager could have been, for example, SPX, and the *tnsnames.ora* entry would then look like this:

```
d8ca.bigwheel.com =
  (DESCRIPTION =
    (ADDRESS_LIST =
        (ADDRESS=
          (PROTOCOL=SPX)
          (HOST=walrus.bigwheel.com)
          (PORT=1600)
         )
        (ADDRESS =
          (PROTOCOL = TCP)
```

```
            (Host = eggman.bigwheel.com)
            (Port = 1521)
        )
   )
   (CONNECT_DATA =
       (SID = D8CA)
   )
   (SOURCE_ROUTE=YES)
)
```

You can even have a route to a connection manager that maps to another connection manager on another node.

Scalability: Summary

Net8 provides additional network scalability capacity by offering connection pooling and multiplexing. Connection pooling is well suited for applications that may service a high number of connections with a high proportion of idle connections. Multiplexing is intended for applications that must support a high volume of connections, all of which are active. The dynamic performance tables V$DISPATCHER and V$DISPATCHER_RATE provide statistics about the efficiency of both connection pooling and multiplexing.

SQL*Net/Net8 Client Configuration

The *sqlnet.ora* file on a client machine contains parameters that govern the client's behavior. The attributes that can be modified fall into five categories:

* Dead connection detection
* Tracing and logging
* Default domains
* Oracle Names parameters
* Other optional parameters

These attributes are described in the sections that follow.

Dead Connection Detection

SQL*Net/Net8 can automatically detect and terminate connections that are no longer valid. This feature is particularly useful for environments in which the clients are PCs, because users may reboot their PCs or otherwise terminate their sessions without logging out of the database. Rebooting a PC does not in and of itself cause the corresponding database session to terminate, because the underlying transport, such as TCP/IP, does not recognize it as such. The worst-case scenario is that the user reboots his PC while he has a lock on a table! Although you can assign a profile to your users that limits connect time and idle time, you usually have to set these limits high enough to accommodate users who want to go out to lunch without logging out of the application (e.g., several hours).

You can use dead connection detection to search and destroy invalid connections every 10 minutes or so. To do so, you must specify the optional parameter SQL-NET.EXPIRE_TIME in the *sqlnet.ora* file. The number you specify is the frequency in minutes with which SQL*Net/Net8 probes connections to confirm their validity. Sessions that are dead or invalid are terminated.

If dead connection detection is enabled, SQL*Net sends a probe periodically to determine whether there is an invalid connection that should be terminated. If it finds a dead connection, or a connection that returns an error, it causes the server to terminate the connection.

Of course, there is a certain amount of overhead associated with using dead connection detection:

- Additional network traffic for the dead connection probes every SQL-NET.EXPIRE_TIME minutes.

- Potential performance degradation on the Oracle server which must distinguish between connection probing events and other events. You should perform your own analysis to determine whether your platform is adversely affected.

Some protocols have their own dead connection detection algorithms, which may obviate the need to use SQL*Net/Net8's version.

Tracing and Logging

The *sqlnet.ora* file contains several optional parameters for logging and tracing that you can use to collect statistics on client/server activity. You can use the parameters described in Table 2-10 to analyze network activity.

Table 2-10. sqlnet.ora: Tracing and Logging Parameters

Parameter Name	Description
LOG_DIRECTORY_CLIENT	Directory in which to place output log file. Default location is the current working directory.
LOG_FILE_CLIENT	Name of the output file for logging information. Default filename is *sqlnet.log*.
TNSPING.TRACE_DIRECTORY	Directory in which to place TNSPING log files. Default location is platform-specific.

Table 2-10. sqlnet.ora: Tracing and Logging Parameters (continued)

Parameter Name	Description
TNSPING.TRACE_LEVEL	Determines level of tracing for TNSPING activity. Possible values are OFF, USER, and ADMIN. OFF indicates no tracing. USER indicates end-user tracing (information includes such diagnostics as invalid address). ADMIN indicates full tracing is enabled, including protocol and configuration errors.
TRACE_DIRECTORY_CLIENT	Location of trace file. Default value is current directory.
TRACE_FILE_CLIENT	Name of trace file. Default value is *sqlnet.trc*.
TRACE_LEVEL_CLIENT	Determines level of trace file details for client activities. Possible values are OFF, USER, and ADMIN. OFF indicates not tracing. USER indicates tracing of errors such as addressing errors and missing protocol stack errors. ADMIN provides full tracing capabilities, including third-party software inconsistencies.

Default Domains

The *sqlnet.ora* parameter DEFAULT_DOMAIN specifies the domain to use when the client's connect string does not specify a fully qualified path. For example, if the *sqlnet.ora* file contains the entry:

```
NAMES.DEFAULT_DOMAIN = BIGWHEEL.COM
```

then the connect string:

```
SCOTT@SALES
```

will resolve to:

```
SCOTT@SALES.BIGWHEEL.COM
```

This parameter may be present in *sqlnet.ora* regardless of whether you are using Oracle Names.

Oracle Names Parameters

The parameter NAMES.DIRECTORY_PATH determines the order in which name resolution services are attempted. The default value is TNSNAMES, ONAMES. The default setting

```
NAMES.DIRECTORY_PATH = (TNSNAMES, ONAMES)
```

indicates that the *tnsnames.ora* file is probed first to resolve the SQL*Net alias, followed by the Oracle Names server.

If you are using Oracle Names, you must specify the parameter NAMES.PRE-FERRED_SERVERS, which includes one or more addresses of the name servers the client should use.

Additional Parameters

Table 2-11 describes additional, optional parameters you can include in the client *sqlnet.ora* file.

Table 2-11. sqlnet.ora: Optional Parameters

Parameter Name	Default	Value Range	Description
AUTOMATIC_IPC	ON	ON, OFF	If OFF, client connections will not attempt to use an IPC address to establish connections.
DISABLE_OOB	OF	ON, OFF	Disables use of Out-of-Band Breaks. Note that this may boost performance for applications that return many rows of data at a time because the server does not check for breaks after each SEND.
USE_DEDICATED_SERVER	OFF	ON, OFF	Forces use of dedicated processes for client connection.

SNMP Support

Beginning with Oracle Version 7.2 and SQL*Net Version 2.2, Oracle has included SNMP (Simple Network Management Protocol) support in its products. This functionality provides administrators with "hooks" they can use to gather performance and diagnostic information from Oracle for analysis in a third-party tool (such as Hewlett-Packard's OpenView). The SNMP hooks are integrated into the Oracle product line; however, you must run an SNMP master agent in order to run Oracle's subagent. Oracle does not provide the SNMP master agent; they provide SNMP subagents that communicate with the master agent. Oracle's subagent is a separate executable (*dbsnmp* on the Unix port).

The primary use of Oracle SNMP is that DBAs or data center operators can use a tool such as OpenView to monitor the status of all Oracle databases and listeners on the network. The range of information includes:

- Database instance status
- Performance problems
- Discovery of new databases

- Ability to set alerts for various events and configure automatic notification of the appropriate personnel

- Ability to store and report on historical data

Configuring SNMP Support

Essentially, the only way to configure the Oracle SNMP subagents is with the Oracle Network Manager product, which (as of this writing) exists only on the Windows NT platform. The Network Manager provides an interface for setting parameters and generating the *SNMP.ORA* configuration file, which is required for each managed node. The *SNMP.ORA* file resides in the same directory as the other network configuration files (*tnsnames.ora*, etc.). The parameters you can set are:

- SNMP VISIBLE

- SNMP INDEX

- SNMP CONTACT

- USERNAME (if subagent monitors an Oracle database server)

- PASSWORD (if subagent monitors an Oracle database server)

After creating the *SNMP.ORA* files, you must also run the *CATSNMP.SQL* script to create the SNMPAGEN role and DBSNMP user, which are both required in databases that are visible to SNMP.

Using SNMP

In addition to starting the master agent, encapsulator, and native SNMP agent for your platform, you also must start the Oracle SNMP subagents for the Oracle database and for the Oracle network services.

Use the *lsnrctl* utility to control the Oracle database subagent:

```
LSNRCTL> dbsnmp_start    starts the database subagent
LSNRCTL> dbsnmp_stop     stops the database subagent
LSNRCTL> dbsnmp_status   reports status information for the database subagent
```

The subagents for the TNS listener, MultiProtocol Interchange, and Oracle Names server are started automatically with the respective service.

Security

Oracle has been bundling security products with SQL*Net and the RDBMS since Version 7.1.4 of the database. They have moved the security software from Secure Network Services into the Advanced Networking Option, which includes additional naming services as well. But whatever the name, the product provides encryption and authentication services for SQL*Net/Net8.

Table 2-12 depicts the matrix of RDBMS releases, bundled security software, and functionality. The installation and configuration of these services is platform-specific.

Table 2-12. Security Products Provided with the RDBMS

RDBMS Version	Security Product	Encryption Services	Authentication Services
7.1.4	Secure Network Services 1.0.1	RSA RC4 40	NA
7.1.5	Secure Network Services 1.0.2	RSA RC4 40	NA
7.1.6	Secure Network Services 1.0.3	RSA RC4 40	NA
7.2.2	Secure Network Services 1.1.x	RSA RC4 40, 56 DES 40, 56	NA
7.2.x	Secure Network Services 2.0.x	RSA RC4 40, 56 DES 40, 56	Kerberos, CyberSAFE, SecurID
7.3.x	Advanced Networking Option 2.3.x	RSA RC4 40, 56 DES 40, 56	Kerberos, CyberSAFE, SecurID
8.0.x	Advanced Networking Option 8.0.x	RSA RC4 40, 56, 128 DES 40, 56 Diffie-Hellman Key Fold-In MD5	Kerberos, CyberSAFE, SecurID, Identix TouchNet II, DCE GSSAPI

In this chapter:
- *Initialization Parameters*
- *Database Links*
- *Distributed Queries and Transactions*
- *Distributed Backup and Recovery*
- *Multiversion Interoperability*

3

Configuration and Administration

The ease with which you can administer a distributed database environment is, to a large degree, a function of how well it is configured. With proper planning and implementation, your distributed database environment can attain a very high degree of location transparency, expandability, and security regardless of how many individual database instances comprise it. These objectives are not the only goals; systems must also be:

Maintainable

> The DBA has the flexibility to move databases to different machines, change ORACLE_SIDs, apply patches, relocate tables, and so on, without requiring changes to application code or changes to client configurations. The interoperability and interdependencies of the various databases must be readily understood.

Robust

> The failure of one database instance does not render others inoperable.

Concurrent

> Distributed transactions meet the ACID criteria (autonomous, consistent, isolated, durable).

In this chapter, we examine the DBA's responsibilities and concerns for providing such an environment. In Chapter 5, *Designing a Distributed System*, we consider the application designer's point of view.

Initialization Parameters

Oracle provides a number of initialization parameters (summarized in Table 3-1) that govern various aspects of your distributed environment. These parameters are specified in the *INIT.ORA* file, the location of which is platform-specific. This section describes how and when you should use these parameters.

Table 3-1. Initialization Parameters Relevant to Distributed Databases

Parameter Name	Description
COMMIT_POINT_STRENGTH	Determines the commit point site in distributed transactions
DB_DOMAIN	String identifying the domain in which the database instance resides
DBLINK_ENCRYPT_LOGIN (Oracle8)	Determines whether connections over database links should send encrypted passwords
DISTRIBUTED_LOCK_TIMEOUT	Number of seconds a distributed transaction will wait to acquire a lock
DISTRIBUTED_RECOVERY_ CONNECTION_HOLD_TIME	Number of seconds to hold a connection open in the event that a distributed transaction fails
DISTRIBUTED_TRANSACTIONS	Maximum number of concurrent distributed transactions
GLOBAL_NAMES	Enforces the use of global naming
JOB_QUEUE_INTERVAL	Period (in seconds) of dormancy for job queue background processes
JOB_QUEUE_PROCESSES	Number of job queue background processes
MAX_TRANSACTION_BRANCHES	Maximum number of database instances that can participate in a distributed transaction
OPEN_LINKS	Maximum number of open database links per session
OPEN_LINKS_PER_INSTANCE (Oracle8)	Maximum number of open database links for the database instance
REMOTE_DEPENDENCIES_MODE	Specifies algorithm for determining validity of stored procedures (TIMESTAMP or SIGNA- TURE)
REMOTE_LOGIN_PASSWORD_FILE	Determines method of validating privileged accounts
REMOTE_OS_AUTHENT	Determines whether operating system validated accounts are allowed from remote machines
REMOTE_OS_ROLES	Determines whether to use operating system roles or database roles for remote clients
REPLICATION_DEPENDENCY_ TRACKING (Oracle8)	Enables or disables dependency tracking
SNAPSHOT_REFRESH_INTERVAL	Period (in seconds) of dormancy for snapshot background processes
SNAPSHOT_REFRESH_PROCESSES	Number of snapshot background processes

COMMIT_POINT_STRENGTH

Datatype: Integer
Default: 10
Range: 0 through 255

The database instance with the highest COMMIT_POINT_STRENGTH is the commit point site in a distributed transaction. The commit point site retains information required for transactions that use a two-phase commit. In general, the higher a database's availability, the higher its COMMIT_POINT_STRENGTH should be.

DB_DOMAIN

Datatype: Character string
Default: WORLD
Range: Any string starting with an alphanumeric character and consisting only of alphanumeric characters and periods (.), underscores (_), and pound signs (#).

The global name of every Oracle database is of the form *DB_NAME.DB_DOMAIN* so the name you select for DB_DOMAIN should match the domain name of your site, for example, US.ORACLE.COM. The setting of the NAMES.DEFAULT_DOMAIN parameter in your *sqlnet.ora* file should also have the same value. Following these conventions simplifies the administration of your distributed environment.

DBLINK_ENCRYPT_LOGIN (Oracle8)

Datatype: Boolean
Default: FALSE
Range: TRUE or FALSE

By default, Oracle sends encrypted passwords over the network to establish connections over database links. If the connection attempt fails, Oracle tries again with an unencrypted password. Setting DBLINK_ENCRYPT_LOGIN to TRUE prevents Oracle from reattempting the connection with the unencrypted password.

DISTRIBUTED_LOCK_TIMEOUT

Datatype: Integer
Default: 60 (seconds)
Range: Minimum value 1; no maximum limit

Although you can set DISTRIBUTED_LOCK_TIMEOUT to an arbitrarily high value, the highest value Oracle uses is 2,808,348,671 (seconds). Since this value equates to more than 88 years, it is not likely to be a limitation. If you are using the advanced replication facilities, the default value of 60 seconds may not be adequate; a setting of 300 is a reasonable starting point.

DISTRIBUTED_RECOVERY_CONNECTION_HOLD_TIME

Datatype: Integer
Default: 200 (seconds)
Range: Minimum value 0; no maximum limit

The DISTRIBUTED_RECOVERY_CONNECTION_HOLD_TIME parameter dictates how long Oracle will keep a failed transaction's connection open. If the transaction is reattempted, it will not have to spend time reestablishing the connection. Although you can specify an arbitrarily high value for this parameter in the *INIT.ORA* file, the highest value Oracle uses is 4,294,967,295. However, since the recoverer (RECO) background process wakes up every 30 minutes to resolve failed distributed transactions, any value above the following:

30 minutes × 60 seconds/minute = 1800 seconds

effectively specifies an infinite hold time. Maintaining a failed transaction's open connection consumes system resources; this could be an issue if you have a large number of distributed transactions.

DISTRIBUTED_TRANSACTIONS

Datatype: Integer
Default: Operating-system specific; derived from TRANSACTIONS
Range: 0 through TRANSACTIONS

The DISTRIBUTED_TRANSACTIONS parameter sets the maximum number of distributed transactions in which the database can simultaneously participate. This value must be less than or equal to the value of TRANACTIONS. By default, Oracle sets DISTRIBUTED_TRANSACTIONS to TRANSACTIONS/4. (Unless otherwise specified, TRANSACTIONS = 1.1 × PROCESSES.) Oracle does not start the recoverer (RECO) background process if DISTRIBUTED_TRANSACTIONS is zero, which means that no distributed transactions are permitted. The derived value for DISTRIBUTED_TRANSACTIONS is suitably high for most applications; in fact, it may be too high. If you experience a high number of failed distributed transactions, you should consider reducing DISTRIBUTED_TRANSACTIONS to decrease the number of concurrent distributed transactions and therefore the number of in-doubt transactions.

GLOBAL_NAMES

Datatype: Boolean
Default: FALSE
Range: TRUE or FALSE

Setting GLOBAL_NAMES to TRUE enforces the global naming of database links. That is, the name of a database link must be the same as the global name of the database to which it connects. By default, a database's global name is *DB_ NAME.DB_DOMAIN* (e.g., D7NY.BIGWHEEL.COM). You must set GLOBAL_NAMES to TRUE in order to use any components of advanced replication. Even if you are not using replication, it is a good idea to enforce global naming because the resulting consistency eases database administration.

JOB_QUEUE_INTERVAL

Datatype: Integer
Default: 60 (seconds)
Range: 1 through 3600 (seconds)

The JOB_QUEUE_INTERVAL parameter specifies how often the snapshot background processes (SNPn) wake up to check for snapshots to fire or jobs to execute. (The values for n range from 0–9 and A–Z.) Although use of the job queue is not restricted to distributed environments, it plays a critical role in advanced replication, so we include it here. In an environment using snapshots and/or multimaster replication, JOB_QUEUE_INTERVAL should be less than the time it takes to perform all of the snapshot refreshes and queue pushes and less than the interval at which your jobs are scheduled. Jobs in the DBMS_JOB queue cannot run more often than every JOB_QUEUE_INTERVAL seconds. This parameter replaces SNAPSHOT_REFRESH_INTERVAL, which still exists in Oracle8 as an undocumented parameter.

JOB_QUEUE_PROCESSES

Datatype: Integer
Default: 0
Range: 0 through 36

The JOB_QUEUE_PROCESSES parameter specifies how many snapshot background processes (SNPn) the database instance should use. (The values for n range from 0–9 and A–Z.) Since the default is zero, you must specify this parameter if you wish to run these background processes. If you have numerous snapshots or scheduled jobs that run simultaneously, you must have multiple SNPn background processes. A single SNPn process performs snapshot refreshes and job executions serially. Oracle recommends setting JOB_QUEUE_PROCESSES to at least two at sites using multi-master replications. This parameter replaces SNAPSHOT_REFRESH_PROCESSES, which still exists in Oracle8 as an undocumented parameter.

MAX_TRANSACTION_BRANCHES

Datatype: Integer
Default: 8
Range: 1 through 32

The MAX_TRANSACTION_BRANCHES parameter specifies the maximum number of branches the session tree of a distributed transaction can have. Oracle introduced this parameter with Version 7.1.6, presumably to alleviate restrictions that the kernel had been imposing on certain transaction process monitoring software: Here is a note from the 7.1.6 *README.doc*:

> This parameter controls the number of branches in a distributed transaction. For example, the TopEnd TP Monitor uses one branch per process involved in a distributed transaction. The Tuxedo TP monitor uses one branch per process group involved in a distributed transaction. The previously fixed maximum number of branches limited the number of TopEnd servers involved in a distributed transaction to 8 per Oracle instance. With the MAX_TRANSACTION_BRANCHES parameter, the maximum number of branches can be increased to 32, allowing for 32 TopEnd processes per Oracle instance to work on one distributed transaction. Setting MAX_TRANSACTION_BRANCHES to a lower value will reduce shared pool memory usage slightly ($n \times$ distributed_transactions $\times$ 72 bytes).

OPEN_LINKS

Datatype: Integer
Default: 4
Range: 0 through 255

The OPEN_LINKS parameter specifies the maximum number of open database links a single session can have; it should be at least as large as the maximum number of databases referenced in a single transaction.

OPEN_LINKS_PER_INSTANCE (Oracle8)

Datatype: Integer
Default: 4
Range: 0 through 255

The OPEN_LINKS_PER_INSTANCE parameter sets the maximum number of open database links that can exist simultaneously in the entire database instance.

REMOTE_DEPENDENCIES_MODE

Datatype: Character string
Default: TIMESTAMP
Range: TIMESTAMP or SIGNATURE

The REMOTE_DEPENDENCIES_MODE parameter designates the method of validating PL/SQL objects (packages, procedures, and triggers) that have remote dependencies. If you specify the TIMESTAMP dependencies mode, objects require recompilation if the remote object has a modification time that is later than the local object. In SIGNATURE mode, no recompilation is required as long as the remote objects exist.

REMOTE_LOGIN_PASSWORD_FILE

Datatype: Character string
Default: None
Range: NONE, SHARED, or EXCLUSIVE

The REMOTE_LOGIN_PASSWORD_FILE parameter specifies whether users are to be validated through a password file. A setting of NONE indicates that there is no password file. SHARED indicates that the same password file is used by user SYS (or INTERNAL) for multiple databases. EXCLUSIVE indicates that the password file is for a single database, with all named users represented in the file.

REMOTE_OS_AUTHENT

Datatype: Boolean
Default: FALSE
Range: TRUE or FALSE

The REMOTE_OS_AUTHENT parameter enables or disables operating system validated (OPS$) accounts from remote machines. If you specify TRUE, then these accounts can log in regardless of the machine from which the process originates. If you specify FALSE, then operating system validated accounts work only for processes that are running on the same machine as the database instance. If you set this parameter to TRUE, you should be very careful not to create privileged OPS$ accounts (such as OPS$ORACLE) because it is quite easy to masquerade as a different user from, for example, a computer running Windows.

REMOTE_OS_ROLES

Datatype: Boolean
Default: FALSE
Range: TRUE or FALSE

The REMOTE_OS_ROLES parameter determines how Oracle enforces role privileges. If you specify FALSE, Oracle uses the role definitions from the database, as seen in DBA_ROLE_PRIVS. If you specify TRUE, Oracle uses operating system roles for remote clients. This method is relevant only for roles using operating system validation, that is, those that have been created with the following syntax:

```
CREATE ROLE {rolename} IDENTIFIED EXTERNALLY
```

which implies that the parameter REMOTE_OS_ROLES is also set to TRUE. Oracle validates users of operating system validated roles differently for each operating system. For example, under Unix, members of group ora_*sid_role* are members of the OS validated group role in the database instance with ORACLE_SID *sid*.

REPLICATION_DEPENDENCY_TRACKING (Oracle8)

Datatype: Boolean
Default: TRUE
Range: TRUE or FALSE

The REPLICATION_DEPENDENCY_TRACKING parameter determines whether Oracle maintains information about transactional dependency which is required for parallel propagation of replicated DML. Oracle recommends using the default value of TRUE unless your replicated tables do not undergo DML.

SNAPSHOT_REFRESH_INTERVAL

Datatype: Integer
Default: 60
Range: 1 through 3600

The SNAPSHOT_REFRESH_INTERVAL parameter is obsolete. See the JOB_QUEUE_INTERVAL parameter.

SNAPSHOT_REFRESH_PROCESSES

Datatype: Integer
Default: 0
Range: 0 through 36

The SNAPSHOT_REFRESH_PROCESSES parameter is obsolete. See the JOB_QUEUE_INTERVAL parameter.

Database Links

Distributed Oracle databases are built on database links. In a nutshell, a database link is a connection from one database to another that is available to users having proper privileges any time both databases are available. The purpose of database links is to make remote data available for queries and, in some cases, updates. Because a database link is essentially a stored login to a remote database, the DBA must take care to ensure that it does not compromise the security of either the local or the remote database. This section discusses database link naming conventions, the different types of database links, different methods of creating them, restrictions, security concerns, and how to report on them.

Global Names and Database Links

If the GLOBAL_NAMES *INIT.ORA* parameter is set to its default value of FALSE, you can use any name you want for a database link. I worked at one site where one developer was partial to the name "Fred" for the links he created. Informality may be acceptable in a small organization, but not where more than three or four databases are in use.

The most intuitive approach is to use the naming convention *DB_NAME.DB_ DOMAIN* for all database links, for example, D7CA.BIGWHEEL.COM. Setting GLOBAL_NAMES to TRUE enforces this convention of database links having the same name as the database to which they connect. If you are using advanced replication, you *must* set this parameter to TRUE.

Note that you can change the global name of any database instance with an ALTER DATABASE statement:

```
ALTER DATABASE RENAME GLOBAL_NAME TO new_name
```

The global naming convention offers several advantages:

Consistency
> Administrators and users know immediately to what database a given link connects, whether they are reviewing trace files or source code or simply browsing the database.

Uniqueness
> Setting GLOBAL_NAMES to TRUE guarantees that all databases in the network community will have a unique name.

Compatibility with future releases
> Oracle has hinted in various documents that global naming will be a requirement in the future. For example, the release notes for Version 7.0.13 state: "You are encouraged to set this initialization parameter to TRUE as future releases may depend on it."

In short, there is really no reason *not* to use global naming.

 Oracle's Designer 2000 tool requires that GLOBAL_NAMES be set to FALSE if you want to use it to reverse-engineer a schema from a remote database, because it creates database links named for the schema. We have set the parameter to FALSE during the reverse-engineering procedure and set it back to TRUE when the procedure was complete.

Public, Private, and Global Database Links

Database links can be either public or private. Public links are available to all database users, while private links are available only to the creator. These levels of visibility are analogous to public and private synonyms. Because public database links provide a window into the remote database through which any user can peer, they should not be used indiscriminately.

When to use public database links

A public database link is appropriate if many users of an application must access a remote object and it is unreasonable or impossible to create individual accounts for each of them in the remote database. In this situation, the DBA can create a single account in the remote database to which the database link connects.

Remote Site	Application Site
(D7NY.BIGWHEEL.COM):	(D7CA.BIGWHEEL.COM):
	CREATE PUBLIC DATABASE
CREATE USER fromd7ca	LINK D7NY.BIGWHEEL.COM
IDENTIFIED BY waxwings	CONNECT TO fromd7ca
/	IDENTIFIED BY waxwings
GRANT CREATE SESSION TO	USING 'remotesite';
fromd7ca	
/	
GRANT remote_browse TO	
fromd7ca	
/	

If you are the DBA at the remote site (D7NY.BIGWHEEL.COM), you might also consider assigning a profile to "fromd7ca" which limits the account's connect time, concurrent sessions, and so on.

Public database links are also required for certain configurations of advanced replication. Refer to Chapter 10, *Advanced Replication Installation*, for details.

When to use private database links

From a security standpoint, private database links are preferable to public links because private links are available only to their creator. In general, you should opt for a private database link whenever possible and view the public link as a special case or last resort.

Specific scenarios that call for private links include:

- Links that are used for snapshot refreshes

- Links that are used in triggers

- Links that connect to a privileged account in the remote database

- Certain configurations of advanced replication (see Chapter 10)

In short, use private database links if you can, public database links if you must.

When to use global database links

The Oracle Names product automatically creates global database links between all databases in your networked environment. Unlike public and private database links, which Oracle stores in the data dictionary, global database links reside in the network definition file. This feature offers the obvious advantage of eliminating the need to create database links manually for all of your database instances.

By default, global database links do not use a CONNECT TO clause, which means that a user account can view data over a global database link only if the same user account exists in the remote database with the same password. These links provide the same level of security as private database links and can be used according to the same guidelines.

You can also override Oracle Names' default behavior and create global database links that do use a CONNECT TO clause by supplying this information in the Network Manager configuration tool. If you choose to create this type of global database link, you should consider the link to be public and take precautions accordingly.

Creating Database Links

The CREATE DATABASE LINK statement has a number of components that determine various properties of the database link. These include:

- The PUBLIC qualifier

- The SHARED qualifier (Oracle8)

- The connection qualifier

- The CONNECT clause

- The CURRENT_USER qualifier (Oracle8)

- The USING clause

- The AUTHENTICATED clause (Oracle8)

The syntax for the CREATE DATABASE LINK statement has many options. The creation of a database link can be as simple as

```
CREATE DATABASE LINK D7CA.BIGWHEEL.COM
/
```

or as complex as

```
CREATE SHARED PUBLIC DATABASE LINK D7CA.BIGWHEEL.COM@TCPIP
CONNECT TO cdye IDENTIFIED BY yankeeclip
AUTHENTICATED BY linkauth IDENTIFIED BY fingerprints
USING 'prodsales'
/
```

Getting It Right the First Time

Whenever you create a database link, it is well worth the effort to confirm the validity of the link immediately. Doing so can save hours of debugging and troubleshooting later on. For example:

```
SQL> CREATE DATABASE LINK D7NY.BIGWHEEL.COM
  2  CONNECT TO cdye IDENTIFIED BY yankeeclip
  3  USING 'd7ny'
  4  /

Database link created.

SQL> SELECT * FROM global_name@D7NY.BIGWHEEL.COM
  2  /

GLOBAL_NAME
----------------------------------------------------------------
D7NY.BIGWHEEL.COM

1 row selected.
```

In the sections that follow, we'll examine the components of the CREATE DATABASE LINK statement in detail.

Prerequisites for creating database links

To create a private database link, users must have the CREATE DATABASE LINK system privilege. To create a public database link, users must have the CREATE PUBLIC DATABASE LINK system privilege. In addition, the account to which the database link connects must have CREATE SESSION privileges. Note that these privileges may be granted through a role; direct grants of the system privileges are not required.

The PUBLIC qualifier

The optional PUBLIC qualifier specifies a public database link. Guidelines for when and why to use public database links are included in the earlier section, "When to use public database links."

The SHARED qualifier

The optional SHARED qualifier is a new feature of Oracle8. Shared database links can potentially reduce the number of network connections between the local and remote databases. Note that shared database links require that the local database be running multi-threaded server (MTS) and that you supply an AUTHENTI-CATED clause.

Shared database links work by reusing an existing connection from a local MTS server process to the remote database. A session can share the existing connection to the remote database only if it uses the same database link. Thus, applications that are good candidates for shared database links are those whose users utilize the same public database link and those whose users log on to a single user account, as is the case with several third-party Oracle applications.

Shared database links can actually *increase* the number of network connections. This undesirable situation can arise because repeated access to a shared link can potentially establish as many connections as you have multi-threaded server processes. Thus, if the link has fewer users than you have multi-threaded server processes, it should not be a shared link.

The connection qualifier

Oracle8 allows you to specify multiple connection paths to the same database, which is useful if you are running Oracle parallel server or multiple network protocols. For example, a site that runs both TCP/IP and DECnet could create two database links to the same database using each protocol:

```
CREATE DATABASE LINK D7CA.BIGWHEEL.COM@TCPIP
USING 'prodsales_tcpip'
/
CREATE DATABASE LINK D7CA.BIGWHEEL.COM@DECNET
USING 'prodsales_decnet'
/
```

The connection qualifier is the portion following the "@" sign in the database link name.

In order for the preceding example to function as desired, the connect strings "prodsales_tcpip" and "prodsales_decnet" would have to be configured to use the appropriate protocol; the connection qualifier itself is merely a mnemonic. In this case, the *tnsnames.ora* file contains the following entries:

```
prodsales_tcpip.bigwheel.com =
  (DESCRIPTION =
    (ADDRESS_LIST =
      (ADDRESS =
        (COMMUNITY = TCPIP)
        (PROTOCOL = TCP)
        (Host = socrates.bigwheel.com)
        (Port = 1521)
      )
    )
    (CONNECT_DATA =
      (SID = D7CA)
      (GLOBAL_NAME = d7ca.bigwheel.com)
    )
  )
prodsales_decnet.bigwheel.com =
  (DESCRIPTION =
    (ADDRESS_LIST =
      (ADDRESS =
        (PROTOCOL = DECNET)
        (NODE = socrates.bigwheel.com)
        (OBJECT = LSNR)
      )
    )
    (CONNECT_DATA =
      (SID = D7CA)
      (GLOBAL_NAME = d7ca.bigwheel.com)
    )
  )
```

The CONNECT clause

The CONNECT clause is the optional portion of the CREATE DATABASE LINK statement which supplies a username and password; for example:

```
CONNECT TO cdye IDENTIFIED BY yankeeclip
```

The connect clause creates a fixed-user database link, which means that everybody who accesses it will connect to the remote database with the same username and password. Fixed-user database links can be appropriate for public database links for which a specially designated account exists at the remote database or for private links that connect to a different user at the remote database.

If you omit the CONNECT clause, the database link will attempt to connect to the remote database using the same username and password as the user who created the link.

The CURRENT_USER qualifier

The optional CURRENT_USER qualifier causes the database link to connect to the remote database under the session's current security context. Thus, if the user is executing a procedure, package, or trigger from another schema when it accesses the database link, the link will connect to the remote database as the owner of the object being executed. If the session is not executing an object from another schema, the link will connect under the same account as the session.

This option is available only if you have configured the current user as a global user with an enterprise authentication service such as Oracle Security Server (OSS).

The USING clause

The optional USING clause supplies the connect string that the database link is to use:

```
USING 'prodsales'
```

Although this clause is optional, you must supply it unless there is already a public database link to the destination database using the desired connect string. (See the later section, "How Database Links Are Resolved," for more information.)

The AUTHENTICATED clause

The AUTHENTICATED clause is required if you are using shared database links:

```
AUTHENTICATED BY linkauth IDENTIFIED BY fingerprints
```

The account specified in the AUTHENTICATED clause must exist in the remote database with CREATE SESSION privileges. This link does not connect as this user. Rather, Oracle uses this clause as an added measure of security.

Dropping Database Links

The DROP DATABASE LINK statement has the syntax:

```
DROP [PUBLIC] DATABASE LINK dblink;
```

where dblink is the name of the link.

To drop a private database link, you must be connected as the owner of the database link. You can neither create nor drop private database links outside of your own schema. In order to drop a public database link, you must have the DROP PUBLIC DATABASE LINK system privilege, either through a direct grant or through a role.

Accessing Data over a Database Link

You can use a database link to access remote data essentially as though it were local. Oracle does handle distributed queries and updates differently from local ones, but to the end user these differences are irrelevant. (The DBA and developer, however, should consult the upcoming section "Distributed Queries and Transactions.") Oracle establishes your security context in the remote database based on the remote schema to which the link connects. This schema is

- The user specified in the link's CONNECT TO clause, if this clause is used.

- The same as the current user in the local database if the link is created with the CURRENT USER qualifier, and the local user is executing a PL/SQL object (procedure, package, or trigger).

- The same as the local connected user if neither of the preceding is true.

To reference a remote object, append an "@" sign and the name of the database link to the name of the object:

```
SQL> SELECT product_id, catalog_id, description, audit_date
  2  FROM products@D7NY.BIGWHEEL.COM
  3  /


PRODUCT_ID  CATALOG_ID DESCRIPTION                    AUDIT_DATE
----------  ---------- ------------------------------ --------------------
1000001     BIKE-0002  Boys 5 Speed Touring           28-Oct-1997 11:16:53
1000002     BIKE-0003  Girls 5 Speed Touring          28-Oct-1997 11:16:53
1000003     BIKE-0004  Mens 10 Speed Touring          28-Oct-1997 11:16:53
1000004     BIKE-0005  Mens 18 Speed Touring          28-Oct-1997 11:16:54
1000005     BIKE-0006  Mixte 10 Speed Touring         28-Oct-1997 11:16:54
1000006     BIKE-0007  Mixte 18 Speed Touring         28-Oct-1997 11:16:54
1000007     BIKE-0008  Mens 12 Speed Mountain Bike    28-Oct-1997 11:16:54
1000008     BIKE-0009  Mens 18 Speed Mountain Bike    28-Oct-1997 11:16:54
1000010     BIKE-0011  Mens 10 Speed Alloy Touring    28-Oct-1997 11:16:54
1000011     BIKE-0013  Mens 12 Speed Racing           28-Oct-1997 11:16:54
1000012     BIKE-0014  Mens 18 Speed Racing           28-Oct-1997 11:16:54
1000013     BIKE-0015  Mens 12 Speed Alloy Racing     28-Oct-1997 11:16:54
1000014     BIKE-0016  Mens 18 Speed Alloy Racing     28-Oct-1997 11:16:54
1000015     BIKE-0017  Womens 18 Speed Alloy Racing   28-Oct-1997 11:16:54

14 rows selected.
```

How Database Links Are Resolved

A database can easily have multiple database links with the same name. For example, several users may have private links to the same remote database, and there may also be a public database link to this remote site. Oracle requires a username and a connect string to establish a connection over a database link. Oracle does not necessarily obtain these two pieces of information from a single database link.

So, when a user references an object at the remote site, how does Oracle determine how to establish the remote connection?

The algorithm

When a user references a remote object, Oracle constructs the access path to the object following these steps:

1. If the reference to the database link contains only the database name portion, append the local domain name to the database name. For example, "d7ca" becomes D7CA.BIGWHEEL.COM.

2. If the user has a private database link to the remote database:

   a. If the private link contains both a CONNECT TO clause and a USING clause, use this information to establish the connection.

   b. If the private link contains a USING clause only, establish the connection using the local user's username and password at the remote database.

   c. If the private link contains a CONNECT TO clause only, look for a public database link to determine the USING clause.

   d. If the private link contains neither a CONNECT TO clause nor a USING clause, look for a public database link to determine the USING clause.

3. If there is a public database link to the remote database:

   a. If a private database link also exists but without a USING clause, obtain the USING clause from this link if possible.

   b. If no private database link exists, and the public link contains a CONNECT TO and a USING clause, use this information to establish the connection.

   c. If no private database link exists, and the public link contains a USING clause only, establish the connection using the local user's username and password at the remote database.

   d. If no private database link exists, and the public link does not contain a USING clause, look for a global database link to determine the USING clause.

4. If a global database link to the remote database exists:

   a. If neither a private nor a public database link exists, use this link to determine the USING clause for the remote destination. If this link contains a CONNECT clause, use the specified username and password; otherwise, use the local user's username and password at the remote site.

   b. If a private and/or public database link exists, but the USING clause is not specified, use this link to determine the USING clause.

Example of database link resolution

If we create a public database link specifying a USING clause only, we can then create private database links without having to specify either a CONNECT clause or a USING clause for all users who have accounts at the remote database, with the same password:

```
SQL> connect system@d7ny
Enter password:
Connected.
SQL> CREATE PUBLIC DATABASE LINK D7CA.BIGWHEEL.COM
  2  USING 'd7ca'
  3  /

Database link created.

SQL> connect cdye
Enter password:
Connected.
system@d7ny SQL> CREATE DATABASE LINK D7CA.BIGWHEEL.COM
  2  /

Database link created.

system@d7ny SQL> SELECT * FROM global_name@D7CA.BIGWHEEL.COM
  2  /

GLOBAL_NAME
-----------------------------------------------------------------
D7CA.BIGWHEEL.COM

1 row selected.
```

In this example, the statement

```
SELECT * FROM global_name@D7CA.BIGWHEEL.COM
```

uses cdye's private database link to determine the username and password to use at the remote site, and uses the public database link to determine the connect string for D7CA.BIGWHEEL.COM, that is, "d7ca".

 This example works because the cdye account exists in the local and remote databases with the same password, and the local database has the *INIT.ORA* parameter GLOBAL_NAMES set to TRUE.

Listing Information About Database Links

The data dictionary views for database link information are DBA_DB_LINKS, ALL_DB_LINKS, and USER_DB_LINKS. Table 3-2 describes the fields in these views.

Table 3-2. DBA_DB_LINKS, ALL_DB_LINKS, and USER_DB_LINKS Field Descriptions

Field Name	Description
Owner (DBA_DB_LINKS and ALL_DB_LINKS only)	The owner of the database link.
DB_LINK	The name of the database link. This is the remote database name and the domain name.
Username	The username specified in the CONNECT TO clause. NULL if the CONNECT TO clause is not supplied.
Password (USER_DB_LINKS only)	The password specified in the CONNECT TO clause. NULL if the CONNECT TO clause is not supplied.
Host	The SQL*Net connect string to the remote database. This corresponds to the USING clause. NULL if the USING clause is not supplied.
Created	Date the database link was created.

The following script lists all database links that exist in the database; you will find this script on the diskette accompanying the book.

```
-------------------------------------------------------------------------
-- Filename:     links.sql
-- Purpose:      Reports all database links in the database.
-- Author:       Chas. Dye (cdye@excitecorp.com)
-- Date:         28-May-1997
-------------------------------------------------------------------------

column owner    heading "Owner"     format a10
column db_link  heading "DB Link"   format a20
column username heading "Username"  format a12
column host     heading "Host"      format a12
column created  heading "Created"   format a20

SELECT  owner,
        db_link,
        username,
        host,
        TO_CHAR(created, 'DD-Mon-YYYY HH24:MI:SS') created
FROM    dba_db_links
ORDER BY db_link, owner
/
```

Here is a sample of the output:

```
system@d7ny SQL> @links

Owner        DB Link              Username     Host    Created
--------     ------------------   ----------   ------  --------------------
CDYE         D7CA.BIGWHEEL.COM                          04-Dec-1997 12:19:53
PUBLIC       D7CA.BIGWHEEL.COM                 d7ca     01-Oct-1997 22:24:35
REPADMIN     D7CA.BIGWHEEL.COM    REPADMIN              01-Oct-1997 22:32:05
```

```
SPROCKET      D7CA.BIGWHEEL.COM   SPROCKET      01-Oct-1997 22:42:24
SYS           D7CA.BIGWHEEL.COM   REPSYS        01-Oct-1997 22:27:21

5 rows selected.
```

Note that although the password field appears only in the USER_DB_LINKS data dictionary view, the unencrypted password is visible in the SYS.LINK$ table. Anybody with the DBA role or the SELECT ANY TABLE system privilege can see this table; for example:

```
SQL> select userid, password
  2  from sys.link$
  3  where password is not null;

USERID               PASSWORD
-------------        ------------------------------
REPSYS               ASHTABULA
SPROCKET             PEPPERPIKE
REPSYS               ORCHARDPARK
REPADMIN             HAVERFORD
OCLASS               NICHOLS

5 rows selected.
```

Similarly, the username and password supplied in the Oracle8 AUTHENTICATED clause are visible in the SYS.LINK$ fields AUTHUSR and AUTHPWD, respectively. For this reason, you should exercise extreme discretion when creating database links that specify a CONNECT TO or AUTHENTICATED clause.

Data Relocation with Database Links

Moving data from one database to another is commonplace for DBAs and developers. For example, DBAs may need to extract data from a production online transaction processing (OLTP) system into a data warehouse, or developers may need to copy a subset of data from a production database into a maintenance database to analyze a problem or to test software against production data volumes. Although the export and import utilities provide the functionality to move entire tables from one database to another, they do not allow for the horizontal and/or vertical data partitioning that is often required; the export and import utilities have only table-level granularity.

The database link is the answer when you need to copy a horizontal or vertical subset of data from one database to another. For example, suppose we have a table SALES_ITEMS that logs sales transactions, defined as follows:

```
SQL> desc sales_items
 Name                 Null?       Type
 ----------------     ---------   -----------------
 SALES_ITEM_ID        NOT NULL    NUMBER(9)
 STORE_ID             NOT NULL    NUMBER(9)
```

```
REGISTER_ID          NOT NULL    NUMBER(9)
SALES_ASSOC_ID       NOT NULL    NUMBER(9)
PRODUCT_ID           NOT NULL    NUMBER(9)
PRICE                NOT NULL    NUMBER(10, 2),
PAY_METHOD           NOT NULL    CHAR(1)
CUST_POSTCODE                    VARCHAR2(12)
AUDIT_DATE           NOT NULL    DATE
AUDIT_USER           NOT NULL    VARCHAR2(30)
GLOBAL_NAME          NOT NULL    VARCHAR2(20)
```

We wish to extract sales transactions from the normalized SALES_ITEMS table in the OLTP database into the SALES_FACTS table in our data warehouse where the marketing experts can generate their marketing segmentation reports.

```
SQL> desc sales_facts
 Name                Null?       Type
 ---------------     --------    -----------------
 JULIAN_DAY          NOT NULL    NUMBER(9)
 PRODUCT_ID          NOT NULL    NUMBER(9)
 STORE_ID            NOT NULL    NUMBER(9)
 DOLLARS_SOLD        NOT NULL    NUMBER(10, 2)
 UNITS_SOLD          NOT NULL    NUMBER(6)
```

The following example loads summarized sales data from the SALES_ITEMS table at the remote database D7CA.BIGWHEEL.COM into the SALES_FACTS table:

```
INSERT INTO sales_facts (
    julian_day,
    product_id,
    store_id,
    dollars_sold,
    units_sold )
(
SELECT  TO_CHAR( audit_date, 'J'),
        product_id,
        store_id,
        sum(dollars_sold),
        count(*)
FROM    sales_items@D7CA.BIGWHEEL.COM
GROUP BY audit_date, product_id, store_id
)
/
```

An extract of this type is simply not possible with the export/import utilities.

 You cannot use the INSERT INTO table_name ... SELECT ... to load LONG, LONG RAW, or LOB data. This restriction exists regardless of whether a database link is involved; it is a restriction of SQL. You can use the COPY command to relocate data, including LONG and LONG RAW data (under 32K) from one database to another. Although the COPY command does not use a database link, it functions in a similar way.

Restrictions on Distributed Operations over Database Links

Note the following restrictions:

- Certain operations and constructs are not supported over database links; for example, it is not possible to grant privileges on remote objects referenced through a database link, and in Oarcle8 it is not possible to DESCRIBE remote tables and views.

- Referential integrity cannot be defined or enforced over a database link.

- Database roles cannot be granted to users in a remote database.

- Queries using hash query joins cannot use multi-threaded server (MTS) connections.

Distributed Queries and Transactions

The database link is the key to location transparency in Oracle; you can perform operations on objects in multiple databases unfettered with details about where objects reside, network protocols, database names, and so on. However, if you are a DBA or a developer, you can create more efficient and robust systems by understanding the mechanisms behind distributed queries and transactions.

Table 3-3 lists the operations that Oracle supports in a distributed environment.

Table 3-3. Supported Distributed Operations

Supported DML	Supported Transaction Control
SELECT	COMMIT
SELECT FOR UPDATE	ROLLBACK
INSERT	SAVEPOINT
UPDATE	ROLLBACK TO SAVEPOINT
DELETE	
LOCK TABLE	

Behind the Scenes of a Distributed Transaction

As with local transactions, consistency is a fundamental requirement of distributed transactions. A distributed transaction must either succeed at all participating nodes or fail at all participating nodes. The classic example is the transfer of funds from one institution to another, each with its own database. The transfer must debit the payer in one database and credit the payee in the other. These updates must either succeed in both databases or fail in both databases.

Oracle ensures this transactional consistency through a mechanism called the *two-phase commit*, so named because transaction commits occur in two stages, the prepare phase and the commit phase. I'll examine the activities associated with these phases in the sections that follow.

Two-phase commit: The participants

Each participant in a distributed transaction fulfills one or more roles, each with specific responsibilities during the two-phase commit. The roles are:

Client

A client is a machine that references data in one or more remote databases. A client may or may not be a database server.

Local coordinator

A local coordinator is a database server that participates in a distributed transaction that accesses data on remote database servers. The local coordinator is responsible for the following tasks:

— Passing transaction status information among the database servers whose data it accesses

— Initiating queries on the remote database servers, possibly on behalf of other database servers (if necessary)

— Processing queries originating from remote database servers (if necessary)

— Returning results of queries to the other database servers (if necessary)

Commit point site

The commit point site effects commits or rollbacks at all participating nodes, as instructed by the global coordinator. (The commit point site and the global coordinator can be one and the same.) The site with the highest setting of the *INIT.ORA* parameter COMMIT_POINT_STRENGTH is the commit point site, with the following exceptions:

— A read-only node cannot be a commit point site.

— If two or more nodes have the same COMMIT_POINT_STRENGTH, the determination of the commit point site is not specified.

— If the global coordinator is unable to initiate the prepare phase at all participating nodes, no commit point site is designated and the global coordinator initiates a rollback at all relevant sites.

Global coordinator

The global coordinator is the database server from which the distributed transaction originates. It is responsible for the following:

— Passing SQL instructions to all directly referenced database servers

— Initiating the prepare phase of the two-phase commit on all participating nodes except for the commit point site

— Upon successful completion of the prepare phase at all participating sites, requesting the commit point site to commit the transaction

— Upon unsuccessful completion of the prepare phase at one or more participating sites, initiating a rollback of the transaction at all nodes

— Ensuring that all participants conclude the transaction with the same outcome as the commit point site—that is, the transaction either succeeds everywhere or fails everywhere

The chain of connections from the global coordinator to the local coordinator(s) and commit point site is known as the *session tree*. The global coordinator is always at the top of the session tree.

Two-phase commit: Explained

As mentioned earlier, the two phases of the two-phase commit are the *prepare phase* and the *commit phase*. During the prepare phase, the global coordinator contacts all local coordinators and instructs them to perform whatever steps are necessary to be in a position to commit their portion of the distributed transaction. These steps include the following:

- Determining whether the transaction performs any local DML

- Requesting any other dependent nodes to prepare (this stage is called "collecting"); the global coordinator must always perform the collecting step; local coordinators perform it only if they have dependents perform it

- Obtaining requisite locks

- Writing the changes required by the transaction to the redo log

After completing (or attempting to complete) these tasks, the local coordinator reports one of three possible statuses to the global coordinator:

Prepared

    The site has made all changes required by the transaction and has written the changes to the redo log. Any dependent sites have done the same.

Read-only

    The site has determined that the transaction does not modify any local data, so it need not prepare and does not participate in the commit phase of the transaction.

Abort

    The site is unable to prepare. The transaction will release any latches or locks it may have obtained before failing. When the global coordinator receives an abort status from a site, it rolls back the transaction at all other sites.

Note that the commit point site does not participate in the prepare phase. The rationale is that the commit point site is the most reliable site and therefore is the most likely to be able to commit its portion of the transaction. Since the commit point site is the most reliable, it is the most critical as well, and therefore should not be required to allocate resources for the prepare phase to a transaction that requires success on several other less reliable nodes.

If all local coordinators report back to the global coordinator with a status of *prepared*, the transaction is in a state of *in-doubt* until a commit or rollback is issued. We are now ready for the commit phase, which consists of the transaction's actual commit or rollback.

During the commit phase:

- The global coordinator instructs the commit point site to commit its portion of the transaction.

- The commit point site performs its commit. At this point the entire distributed transaction is considered to be committed because even if there is a communication failure, all other sites will automatically commit their portion(s) of the transaction when communication is reestablished.

- The commit point site informs the global coordinator that it has completed the commit. The commit point site retains information about the transaction in the data dictionary.

- The global coordinator instructs the local coordinators to commit, and commits its portion of the transaction too. All non-commit point sites write an additional entry to their redo logs indicating that the transaction is committed, and release any locks that they may have acquired for the transaction. They also inform any of their children on the session tree to perform commits.

- Local coordinators inform the global coordinator of their commits.

- The global coordinator informs the commit point site of the commit. At this point, the commit point site "forgets" about the transaction; information about it no longer exists in its data dictionary.

When Oracle commits a distributed transaction, the system change number (SCN) for the transaction is the same at all participating sites. Oracle uses the highest SCN of all the participating sites as the global SCN. The coordination of SCNs among participants in the distributed transaction simplifies recovery procedures.

When Things Go Wrong

Of course, distributed transactions can fail at any point of the two-phase commit. For example, a connection to a local coordinator could go down after the commit point site commits but before the local coordinator is instructed to commit. For the most part, Oracle is able to detect and resolve these kinds of problems, but in some cases DBA intervention is warranted.

Error messages pertaining to distributed transactions fall in the range ORA-02040 to ORA-02099. Applications that use distributed transactions should include exception handlers for all of these errors. Applications that depend on the two-phase commit protocol must have detailed strategies for dealing with the unavailability of one or more commit sites. Examples include having the application retry the operation or logging information about the failure in an error table that can be used to execute the transactions when the underlying problems are corrected.

Types of distributed transaction failures

How do you know that you have a problem in the first place? Abnormal conditions that occur during the two-phase commit generally are caused by a network or server failure that occurs between the prepare and commit phases. Since the length of time between these phases is infinitesimal, these problems are rare. The errors that you may see in the alert log are:

ORA-02050 transaction id rolled back, some remote DBs may be in-doubt
> A communication error occurred during the two-phase commit.

ORA-02053 transaction id committed, some remote DBs may be in-doubt
> The transaction was committed locally, but communication with one or more local coordinators has been lost.

ORA-02054 transaction id in-doubt
> The transaction is neither committed nor rolled back locally, and communication with the global coordinator has been lost.

In all three cases, the RECO background process will resolve the error when communications are reestablished, often before the user or DBA discovers the problem. Oracle will not close these connections until DISTRIBUTED_RECOVER_CONNECTION_HOLD_TIME seconds have elapsed.

In rare cases, an in-doubt transaction can continue to hold locks on objects if the RECO process is not able to resolve the problem. If a user attempts to perform DML on an object so locked, Oracle returns the error:

```
ORA-01591 lock held by in-doubt distributed transaction id
```

In this case, Oracle rolls back the user's attempted transaction. The DBA should now manually commit or roll back the in-doubt transaction.

A less rare and more troublesome scenario arises when distributed transactions time out waiting to acquire locks or hold locks themselves for an excessive amount of time. If a distributed transaction cannot obtain a required lock after DISTRIBUTED_LOCK_TIMEOUT seconds, Oracle returns an error:

```
ORA-02049 timeout: distributed transaction waiting for lock
```

Your only recourse is to retry the operation. Of course, you should determine what other transaction is holding the lock and verify that no other problems exist.

Forcing commits and rollbacks of distributed transactions

In cases in which in-doubt transactions hold locks, blocking access to data, the DBA(s) of the sites involved in the distributed transaction can force a commit or rollback, thereby releasing the locks. In-doubt transactions may also hold extents of a rollback segment, preventing other transactions from using it. The data dictionary views DBA_2PC_PENDING and DBA_2PC_NEIGHBORS provide information about transactions in need of recovery so that the DBA can decide whether a commit or rollback is appropriate.

Tables 3-4 and 3-5 summarize the columns in these views.

Table 3-4. DBA_2PC_PENDING Data Dictionary View

Column Name	Description
LOCAL_TRAN_ID	Local ID of the transaction. The first portion of this value is the ID of the rollback segment (as seen in DBA_ROLLBACK_SEGS) for the local transaction.
GLOBAL_TRAN_ID	Global transaction ID, unique to all sites.

STATE	One of the following:
	  Collecting
	  Prepared
	  Committed
	  Forced Commit
	  Forced Rollback

MIXED	D implies that portions of the transaction have been committed and portions rolled back (forcibly).

ADVICE	C indicates Commit
	R indicates Rollback.
	This field is populated only if the application has issued one of the statements:
	    `ALTER SESSION ADVISE COMMIT`
	or
	    `ALTER SESSION ADVISE ROLLBACK`
	before beginning the distributed transaction.

TRAN_COMMENT	Commit comment text. This field is populated only if the application has issued a COMMIT USING with a comment: `COMMIT COMMENT "comment text here."`
FAIL_TIME	Time the record was inserted into the view.

Table 3-4. DBA_2PC_PENDING Data Dictionary View (continued)

Column Name	Description
FORCE_TIME	Time the transaction was forced. NULL if the transaction has not been forced.
RETRY_TIME	Time the RECO background process last attempted to resolve the transaction.
OS_USER	Operating system user ID of the local user who created the transaction.
OS_TERMINAL	Terminal from which the local portion of the transaction originated.
HOST	Name of the machine from which the local transaction originated.
DB_USER	Oracle ID of the username originating the distributed transaction.
GLOBAL_COMMIT#	Global commit number of the transaction (if committed).

Table 3-5. DBA_2PC_NEIGHBORS Data Dictionary View

Column Name	Description
LOCAL_TRAN_ID	Local ID of the transaction.

IN_OUT	Connection type:
	  IN for incoming
	  OUT for outgoing

DATABASE	For incoming connections, the client database global name. For outgoing connections, the database link.
DBUSER_OWNER	For incoming connections, the Oracle username. For outgoing connections, the owner of the database link.
INTERFACE	Used to locate the commit point site. For incoming links, C indicates that this site or one of the descendants on an outgoing link is the commit point site. For outgoing links, C indicates that the destination database DBID is the commit point site. If we are in-doubt, INTERFACE is N and then the top-level database either is the commit point site or can locate the commit point site.
DBID	The global name of the remote database.
SESS#	Local session number for the connection. Sessions are numbered consecutively, starting with 1.
BRANCH	Transaction branch. Branch IDs for incoming connections are two-byte hexadecimal numbers; the first byte is the remote parent's session ID, and the second byte is its branch ID.

The DBA can use these views to determine how the distributed transaction has been resolved at other participating sites and act accordingly. First, query DBA_2PC_NEIGHBORS to determine whether the commit point site is a parent (INTERFACE = N). If so, query this data dictionary view in the DBID database; continue this trace until you find the database where INTERFACE is C. At this database, you can determine the state of the distributed transaction by querying the DBA_2PC_

PENDING data dictionary view. If STATE is Committed or Forced Commit, you can commit the local transaction:

```
COMMIT FORCE 'local_tran_id'
```

If the GLOBAL_COMMIT# is available in DBA_2PC_PENDING for this transaction, you should use it when you force the transaction:

```
COMMIT FORCE 'transaction_id', GLOBAL_COMMIT#
```

Otherwise, if the transaction has not been committed at the commit point site, you can roll back the local transaction:

```
ROLLBACK FORCE 'transaction_id';
```

Testing recovery of failed distributed transactions

Oracle provides a means to force distributed transactions to fail manually so that you can test your distributed transaction recovery procedures. If you issued a commit with a comment ORA-2PC-CRASH-TEST-*n*, you can test a variety of scenarios, according to the value of *n*, as shown in Table 3-6.

Table 3-6. Values of n in ORA-2PC-CRASH-TEST-n

n	Type of Failure Induced
1	Crash commit point site after collect.
2	Crash non-commit point site after collect.
3	Crash non-commit point site before prepare.
4	Crash non-commit point site after prepare.
5	Crash commit point site before commit.
6	Crash commit point site after commit.
7	Crash non-commit point site before commit.
8	Crash non-commit point site after commit.
9	Crash commit point site before forget.
11	Crash commit point site after forget.

Restrictions on Distributed Transactions

Oracle imposes the following restrictions on distributed transactions:

- All referenced LONG and LONG RAW data must be on a single server.

- DDL over database links is not supported.

- ANALYZE TABLE LIST CHAINED ROWS is not supported over a database link.

- Queries that begin after the PREPARE phase of a distributed transaction cannot access locked data until the transaction is committed or rolled back.

Distributed Backup and Recovery

If you are recovering a database that participates in distributed transactions, you may need to coordinate your recovery with the other database instances. The good news is that if you perform complete recovery (the most common type of recovery), you have nothing to worry about.

We are limiting our discussion to media recovery only, which is based on SCNs. Alternative methods, such as the import/export utilities, are not based on SCNs, and therefore you cannot coordinate them with distributed transactions in other databases.

Table 3-7 lists the possible recovery scenarios.

Table 3-7. Distributed Recovery Scenarios

Recovery Method	Impact on Databases Participating in Distributed Transactions
Restore from a cold backup	All other databases must also be restored to the same point in time.
Complete media recovery	No action required.
Incomplete media recovery	All other databases must also be restored to the same point in time.

As Table 3-7 indicates, the only recovery scenarios that impact other databases in the distributed environment are those in which the recovery is incomplete—that is, up to some time in the past. The obvious issue is that an incomplete recovery may result in data that is inconsistent globally because a distributed transaction may have been committed some time after the time to which you restore. Of course, if you can guarantee that no such transactions exist, you can recover to a time in the past without involving the other distributed databases.

If you are using the advanced replication facilities, you must always perform complete media recovery in order to guarantee the integrity of the replicated environment.

Distributed Recovery

If you cannot avoid the requirement to recover a database to a time in the past, you must roll all other databases back to the same point in time. How do you perform global transaction time-based recovery?

1. Determine the SCN to which you have recovered. This is available in the alert log; look for an entry of the form:

   ```
   RESETLOGS after incomplete recovery UNTIL CHANGE xxxxxx
   ```

2. Restore all other databases to the same SCN. (Recall that distributed transactions coordinate SCNs.)

Obviously, such a recovery can potentially force you to discard data in a healthy database just because of a failure in another. You can mitigate the impact if you export the data that you know you want to keep beforehand.

Also, if you have applications that rely heavily on distributed transactions, you can try to isolate the tables in these transactions to a single schema so that you can maximize the use of export/import to save as much of the nondistributed data as possible. Unfortunately, you cannot perform media recovery for a single schema.

Snapshots

If you perform partial recovery to a database that is the master for one or more snapshots, the snapshots may contain data from the "future." All snapshot sites should perform a complete refresh to ensure that they are consistent.

Backup Strategy Considerations

If it is conceivable that you will need to perform an incomplete backup of a database involved in distributed transactions, it is important that you have valid backups of all other participating databases from the same time. Although it is not often practical or feasible to take backups of multiple databases at exactly the same time, you should certainly have all of your systems on a similar backup schedule (e.g., weekly). Your choices for the time for recovery are limited by your backup supply.

Multiversion Interoperability

Oracle permits database links between any two RDBMS versions between Version 6 and Version 8, inclusive. However, there are restrictions, particularly when a Version 6 database is involved.

For database links going from an Oracle Version 6 database to an Oracle7 database:

- Comparisons of fixed-length strings use blank-padded semantics in the Oracle7 database, even though Oracle Version 6 itself does not.

- The link must be over a SQL*Net V2 connection if the Oracle Version is 7.3 or higher.

From an Oracle7 or Oracle8 database to an Oracle Version 6 database:

- The database link must be over a SQL*Net V2 or Net8 connection.

- The link can update only a single Version 6 database in a given statement.

- The link cannot perform distributed transactions with an Oracle Version 6 database.

4

Distributed Database Security

The manager of a distributed database environment has security considerations over and above the typical user authentication and access level concerns of the single database environment. The DBA is responsible for ensuring the privacy and integrity of the data that travels the network and for implementing an appropriately secure user authentication policy. At the same time, any single database in a distributed environment must maintain a high degree of autonomy from the databases and machines with which it interacts. Oracle provides security mechanisms at several layers, including the levels of the database, operating system, and network. This chapter discusses how to implement a secure environment with these various levels and points out some situations that you should avoid.

Privilege Management

You have a variety of choices for managing access to objects in remote databases; these choices fall into one of the following categories:

The simplistic approach
> Remote objects are accessed over a public database link, with a local public synonym for each remote object.

The mirrored account approach
> Remote objects are accessed over private database links for all user accounts, with a local public synonym for each remote object.

The local view approach
> A local view is created for remote tables. Access to remote objects is via these local objects.

The local wrapper approach
> Remote PL/SQL objects (procedures and packages) are called from local procedures; the remote procedures themselves are not available to local users.

The guidelines provided here will help you decide what is best for your applications.

The Simplistic Approach

The easiest way to provide users access to remote objects is to create a public database link to the remote database and create public synonyms for the objects there. For example, the DBA at the site D7NY.BIGWHEEL.COM could provide access to the SPROCKET.PRODUCTS table in D7CA.BIGWHEEL.COM by following these steps:

1. Create a public database link to D7CA.BIGWHEEL.COM:

   ```
   CREATE PUBLIC DATABASE LINK D7CA.BIGWHEEL.COM
   CONNECT TO d7nydba IDENTIFIED BY masquerade
   USING 'prodcal';
   ```

   We assume that the account "d7nydba" exists in D7CA.BIGWHEEL.COM, and that it has sufficient privileges to SELECT from the SPROCKET.PRODUCTS table.

2. Create a public synonym for the remote SPROCKET.PRODUCTS table:

   ```
   CREATE PUBLIC SYNONYM products
   FOR sprocket.products@D7CA.BIGWHEEL.COM;
   ```

   Actually, the public synonym is not required for users to access the remote object; they could also reference it by specifying the database link; for example:

   ```
   SELECT *
   FROM sprocket.products@D7CA.BIGWHEEL.COM;
   ```

Now any user in the local database D7NY.BIGWHEEL.COM can access the remote table SPROCKETS.PRODUCTS as though it were local and enjoy the privileges that have been granted to d7nydba.

Advantages of the simplistic approach

The primary advantage of this means of remote access is that it is extremely easy to implement, and it requires a minimal amount of coordination with the DBA at the remote site. In other words, this is the quick and dirty method, but be advised that it is *dirty*!

Disadvantages of the simplistic approach

What does it mean to say this method is dirty? Consider the following:

The simplistic approach opens the door to the remote database

Since we created a public database link to the remote database, which connects to a specific user ID, we have potentially (and probably) built a security hole. Any account in the local database can reference objects in the remote database with the privilege level of the account to which the public database link connects. Access is not restricted to the SPROCKET.PRODUCTS table for which we created the public synonym; any table, view, procedure, or package that d7nydba can access is available to all users in the local database. For example, curious users might help themselves to sensitive data as follows:

```
SELECT last_name, first_name, salary
FROM payroll@D7CA.BIGWHEEL.COM;
```

Of course, the d7nydba account in D7CA.BIGWHEEL.COM could be created with limited privileges, but it will always be able to see more than just the SPROCKET.PRODUCTS table since any objects accessible to PUBLIC are also accessible to d7nydba.

The simplistic approach provides no local control over access to remote objects

This issue is similar to that described in the previous item. Not only have we provided more access than is necessary to the remote database, but also we have no control over which local users can see the SPROCKET.PRODUCTS table; they *all* can. In addition, all users enjoy the same *level* of privileges on the table, as determined by d7nydba's privilege level in D7CA.BIG-WHEEL.COM. In other words, we cannot use database roles in the local database to define access levels. One size fits all, whether you like it or not.

The Mirrored Account Approach

The mirrored account approach entails creating user accounts in all databases in which they require access to data and private database links for these accounts from each database to all other databases they must reference. The private database links need not be created with a CONNECT or USING clause if a public database link exists to resolve link names. This is one of Oracle's recommended configurations for the advanced replication facilities with Oracle7.

Suppose we wish to create accounts for users "cdye" and "jblow" in database D7NY.BIGWHEEL.COM so that these accounts can reference remote objects in database D7CA.BIGWHEEL.COM. Here are the steps we would take:

1. Create the user accounts in D7NY.BIGWHEEL.COM and in D7CA.BIG-WHEEL.COM. If the accounts have the same passwords in both databases, we can create private database links without the CONNECT clause:

```
CREATE USER cdye IDENTIFIED BY yankeeclip
DEFAULT TABLESPACE users
TEMPORARY TABLESPACE temp;

GRANT CREATE SESSION TO cdye;

GRANT app_admin TO cdye;
```

```
CREATE USER jblow IDENTIFIED BY aoldotcom
DEFAULT TABLESPACE users
TEMPORARY TABLESPACE temp;

GRANT CREATE SESSION TO jblow;

GRANT app_user to jblow;
```

Note that in this example we have granted different roles to the different users (app_admin for cdye, and app_user for jblow); the mirrored account method allows you to tailor privileges to specific users.

2. Create a public database link from D7NY.BIGWHEEL.COM to D7CA.BIG-WHEEL.COM so that the private database links can be created without the USING clause:

```
CREATE PUBLIC DATABASE LINK D7CA.BIGWHEEL.COM
USING 'prodcal'
```

You can create this link from any account that has sufficient privileges to create public database links.

3. Create private database links from the cdye and jblow accounts.

Connected as cdye:

```
CREATE DATABASE LINK D7CA.BIGWHEEL.COM
```

Connected as jblow:

```
CREATE DATABASE LINK D7CA.BIGWHEEL.COM
```

4. Create synonyms for the remote objects in D7CA.BIGWHEEL.COM:

```
CREATE PUBLIC SYNONYM products FOR
sprocket.products@D7CA.BIGWHEEL.COM
```

The synonyms can be either public or private. From a practical standpoint, however, public synonyms make more sense since you only have to create one per object. If you do not create the synonyms, users can still reference the remote objects by specifying the database link, for example:

```
SELECT product_id, product_name
FROM products@D7CA.BIGWHEEL.COM;
```

Once you have created these accounts and links, the specified users can access remote objects, each with the access level you have granted.

Advantages of the mirrored account approach

Mirrored accounts allow you to grant access to remote objects only for those users who require it, and you can grant different privileges to different users according to their job functions and responsibilities. In addition, since the public database link we created does not include a CONNECT clause, there is no "open door" to the remote database.

Disadvantages of the mirrored account approach

Although mirrored accounts offer significant advantages over the simplistic approach, some troublesome issues persist:

- Users with remote accounts can see any objects that are available to PUBLIC, in addition to the objects to which they have been granted access either explicitly or through roles.

- Since users have accounts in the remote databases, they can log in to these databases directly, which may or may not be an issue depending on the site's security policy.

- The maintenance of user accounts, passwords, and roles in multiple databases can quickly become an administrative nightmare if there are large numbers of users or database instances. The administrators of remote database instances must sacrifice a degree of autonomy to support these users.

- There is no local control over access to remote objects. This is still an issue, as with the simplistic approach.

The Local View Approach

The local view approach entails creating a single privileged account in the remote database which has sufficient privileges on all application tables there. A local account creates a private database link that connects to the privileged account and then builds views that reference the remote objects. Since these views are local, we can use roles to define access levels.

Consider the SPROCKET.PRODUCTS table described in the previous examples. This table resides in the database instance D7CA.BIGWHEEL.COM, but users in D7NY.BIGWHEEL.COM must access it. What if some users need read-only access while other users must update it? Here is the solution:

1. Create a privileged account in D7CA.BIGWHEEL.COM that has SELECT, INSERT, UPDATE, and DELETE privileges on SPROCKET.PRODUCTS. (Assume these privileges are granted to the role product_admin.)

   ```
   CREATE USER d7nydba IDENTIFIED BY masquerade
   DEFAULT TABLESPACE USERS
   TEMPORARY TABLESPACE temp;

   GRANT CREATE SESSION TO d7nydba;

   GRANT product_admin TO d7nydba;
   ```

2. In D7NY.BIGWHEEL.COM, create a private database link to D7CA.BIG-WHEEL.COM that connects to the account created in Step 1. For the sake of clean design, this link should be created under the account that owns the

application schema, but it could be made under any account that has sufficient privileges to create views. In our case, we create the link under the SPROCKET account:

```
CREATE DATABASE LINK D7CA.BIGWHEEL.COM
CONNECT TO d7nydba IDENTIFIED BY masquerade
USING 'prodcal';
```

3. From the account that created the database link in Step 2, create a private synonym for SPROCKET.PRODUCTS@D7CA.BIGWHEEL.COM:

```
CREATE SYNONYM hq_products FOR SPROCKET.PRODUCTS@D7CA.BIGWHEEL.COM;
```

Strictly speaking, this step is optional. However, it is advisable because it eliminates the necessity to create a view that contains a database link name in the query text. This makes administrative tasks simpler, as we shall see in Chapter 6, *Oracle's Distributed System Implementation.*

4. Create a view that selects from the remote table:

```
CREATE VIEW products AS
    SELECT  product_id,
            product_type,
            catalog_id,
            description,
            rev_level,
            production_date,
            production_status
    FROM    hq_products;
```

5. Create roles and grant privileges on the view, as appropriate:

```
CREATE ROLE product_viewer;

GRANT SELECT ON products TO product_viewer;

CREATE ROLE product_admin;

GRANT SELECT, INSERT, UPDATE, DELETE ON products TO product_admin
```

6. Optionally create a public synonym for the view:

```
CREATE PUBLIC SYNONYM products FOR sprocket.products;
```

Advantages of the local view approach

The local view approach solves the problem of controlling access to remote objects with local roles. You can create as many roles as you need to provide appropriate levels of access. In addition, there is no public database link involved and therefore no open door to the remote database. In fact, in the implementation outlined here, the local account that owns the database link and the view does not even need to have CREATE SESSION privileges once the view is in place! Then nobody can use the account to exploit the private link to the remote database. (I always revoke CREATE SESSION from schema owner accounts once the schema objects are created.)

The local view approach would also work with private database links from each of the user accounts that need to reference the remote object. You could, therefore, require that local users have accounts in the remote database. This adds an additional level of security.

Disadvantages of the local view approach

Truly there are no disadvantages to this approach other than the fact that the initial setup is slightly more involved than the other techniques because you must create the local view and roles. However, this is a small price to pay for the flexibility and security that you realize.

The Local Wrapper Approach

Just as you can create local views on remote tables to control privileges, you can also write local PL/SQL procedures which execute remote procedures. By writing a local procedure or package that calls a remote procedure or package, you can use local roles to administer privileges to the remote objects. The alternative is to create database links that provide access to the remote procedures and packages and sacrifice all local control over who can execute them.

Consider the package ProductMaint, which allows users to add new products to the product table:

```
CREATE OR REPLACE PACKAGE ProductMaint IS
    PROCEDURE AddProduct   (product_type_IN     IN NUMBER,
                            catalog_id_IN       IN VARCHAR2,
                            description_IN      IN VARCHAR2,
                            rev_level_IN        IN VARCHAR2,
                            production_date_IN  IN DATE,
                            product_status_IN   IN VARCHAR);
END ProductMaint;
/
CREATE OR REPLACE PACKAGE BODY ProductMaint IS

PROCEDURE AddProduct(product_type_IN     IN NUMBER,
                     catalog_id_IN       IN VARCHAR2,
                     description_IN      IN VARCHAR2,
                     rev_level_IN        IN VARCHAR2,
                     production_date_IN  IN DATE,
                     product_status_IN   IN VARCHAR) IS
BEGIN
    INSERT INTO products (product_id,
                product_type,
                catalog_id,
                description,
```

```
                         rev_level,
                         production_date,
                         production_status,
                         audit_date,
                         audit_user,
                         global_name )
         VALUES (seq_products.nextval,
                 product_type_IN,
                 catalog_id_IN,
                 description_IN,
                 rev_level_IN,
                 production_date_IN,
                 product_status_IN,
                 SYSDATE,
                 USER,
                 DBMS_REPUTIL.GLOBAL_NAME);
     END AddProduct;

     END ProductMaint;
     /
```

If this package exists in the database D7CA.BIGWHEEL.COM, how can we give
some (but not *all*!) users in D7NY.BIGWHEEL.COM access to it? Specifically, we
wish to allow those users in D7NY.BIGWHEEL.COM with the product_admin role
the ability to execute ProductMaint.AddProduct.

The solution, of course, is to create a local procedure (or "wrapper") in
D7NY.BIGWHEEL.COM which calls the remote ProductMaint.AddProduct. Then
we can grant EXECUTE on the wrapper to the product_admin role. Here's how:

1. Create a privileged account in D7CA.BIGWHEEL.COM that has EXECUTE privileges on ProductMaint. (Assume these privileges are granted to the role
   product_admin.)

   ```
   CREATE USER d7nydba IDENTIFIED BY masquerade
   DEFAULT TABLESPACE USERS
   TEMPORARY TABLESPACE temp;

   GRANT CREATE SESSION TO d7nydba;

   GRANT product_admin TO d7nydba;
   ```

2. In D7NY.BIGWHEEL.COM, create a private database link to D7CA.BIG-
   WHEEL.COM which connects to the account created in Step 1. For the sake of
   clean design, this link should be created under the account that owns the
   application schema, but it could be made under any account that has sufficient privileges to create views. In our case, we create the link under the
   SPROCKET account:

   ```
   CREATE DATABASE LINK D7CA.BIGWHEEL.COM
   CONNECT TO d7nydba IDENTIFIED BY masquerade
   USING 'prodcal';
   ```

3. From the account that created the database link in Step 2, create a private synonym for SPROCKET.PRODUCTMAINT@D7CA.BIGWHEEL.COM:

```
CREATE SYNONYM hq_productmaint
FOR SPROCKET.PRODUCTMAINT@D7CA.BIGWHEEL.COM;
```

Strictly speaking, this step is optional. However, it is advisable because it eliminates the necessity to create a procedure that contains a database link name. This makes administrative tasks simpler, as we shall see in Chapter 6.

4. Create the "wrapper" procedure:

```
CREATE OR REPLACE PACKAGE ProductMaint IS
    PROCEDURE AddProduct(product_type_IN      IN NUMBER,
                         catalog_id_IN        IN VARCHAR2,
                         description_IN        IN VARCHAR2,
                         rev_level_IN          IN VARCHAR2,
                         production_date_IN IN DATE,
                         product_status_IN  IN VARCHAR);
END ProductMaint;
/
CREATE OR REPLACE PACKAGE BODY ProductMaint IS

PROCEDURE AddProduct (product_type_IN       IN NUMBER,
                      catalog_id_IN         IN VARCHAR2,
                      description_IN         IN VARCHAR2,
                      rev_level_IN          IN VARCHAR2,
                      production_date_IN IN DATE,
                      product_status_IN  IN VARCHAR) IS
BEGIN
    hq_ProductMaint.AddProduct(product_type_IN,
                      catalog_id_IN,
                      description_IN,
                      rev_level_IN,
                      production_date_IN,
                      product_status_IN);
END AddProduct;

END ProductMaint;
/
```

5. Grant EXECUTE privileges on the local package as appropriate:

```
GRANT EXECUTE ON ProductMaint TO product_admin;
```

Advantages of the local wrapper approach

Just as a local view of a remote object facilitates local privilege administration over remote tables, so a local wrapper facilitates local privilege administration over remote procedures and packages. In addition, the wrapper can help to ensure data consistency by performing edit checks, setting parameter values, and so on.

Disadvantages of the local wrapper approach

As with local views, the local wrapper requires a bit of extra work initially; you have to write the local procedure or package and manage the role grants.

Conclusions on Privilege Management

It is a very simple matter to offer access to objects in a remote database: just create a public database link. The challenge is to develop an access model that allows the local administrator the ability to control privilege levels on the remote objects with the same granularity that is possible with local objects. But database roles cannot manage privileges on remote objects:

```
SQL> GRANT SELECT ON sprocket.products@D7CA.BIGWHEEL.COM TO product_viewer;
GRANT SELECT ON sprocket.products@D7CA.BIGWHEEL.COM TO product_viewer
                                                        *
ERROR at line 1:
ORA-02021: DDL operations are not allowed on a remote database
```

The recommended solution is to create local views for remote tables and local wrapper functions for remote procedures and packages. You can grant privileges on these local objects to local roles.

There are, however, occasions when the local objects may not be appropriate. For example, if you are using the advanced replication facilities, the access model is quite different (as we'll see in see Chapter 10, *Advanced Replication Installation*).

Authentication Methods

One of the DBA's objectives in a distributed environment is to provide easy database access to valid users, while thwarting (or at least discouraging) unauthorized access to the database and network traffic to it (which may contain sensitive information such as passwords). There are three distinct means of authenticating users of an Oracle database, corresponding to three different types of accounts:

Database authentication

> This method corresponds to accounts made with the CREATE USER command. Users must provide a valid username/password, which the database validates with information stored in the data dictionary.

Operating system authentication

> These are Oracle accounts that correspond to operating system accounts. If a user can log in to the operating system, she is permitted to log in to the database. We often refer to these accounts as OPS$ (pronounced "ops dollar") because the corresponding database usernames are in the form OPS$*os_username* by default.

External authentication

> These are accounts that are validated by some external means, such as a fingerprint scanner or a network authentication mechanism such as Kerberos.

The sections that follow examine the considerations for each of these methods in a distributed environment and discuss implementation options.

Database Authentication

Database authenticated accounts are the type with which we are most familiar. Every Oracle database has at least two such accounts: SYS and SYSTEM. In an ideal world, you can also create an account for each user, just as the administrators of your operating system(s) do: one individual, one account in the database(s) he needs to use. This seems reasonably straightforward, but some perils do exist, for example, compromised passwords.

Most multiuser operating systems allow users to report on all of the processes running on a machine; typically, this listing displays a process ID, username, program name, and other information about CPU utilization and so on. Sometimes the listing shows the arguments that a user passed to a program. If users passed their username and password, that information may be available to one and all. The SVR4 variant of the *ps* command, found on operating systems such as Solaris, is a classic example. Here is how you can obtain passwords on a Solaris machine:

```
cdye@socrates% ps -ef | grep sql
cdye 12174 10822  0 16:03:23 pts/8  0:00 grep sql
cdye 12168 10901  0 16:01:00 pts/9  0:00 sqlplus system/twinkletoes@hr_prod
```

So, the system password for hr_prod is "twinkletoes." This problem has fueled considerable dialogue in Oracle user groups, and the consensus is that you can choose one of three remedies for it, described the following sections.

Write a wrapper command around sqlplus

In this way, the arguments are not displayed. Oracle Support has written (but does not support) a program called *hide.c* which masks arguments from the *ps* command. The program is described in Oracle Bulletin 1009091.6, which is included here:

```
                    Oracle Corporate Support
                      Problem Repository


    1. Prob# 1009091.6  HOW DO YOU HIDE USERNAME/PASSWORD IN PS?
    2. Soln# 2057042.6  USE THE HIDE.C PROGRAM


    1. Prob# 1009091.6  HOW DO YOU HIDE USERNAME/PASSWORD IN PS?


    Problem ID        : 1009091.6
    Affected Platforms : NCR Unix SVR4
    Affected Products  : SQL*Forms
    Affected Components : IAD V03.00.XX
    Affected Oracle Vsn : V07.00.13.XX


    Summary:
    HOW DO YOU HIDE USERNAME/PASSWORD IN PS?


    +=+
```

Problem Description:
====================

ps shows username/password. How can I keep this from happening?

Search words:
hide.c hide

+==+

Diagnostics and References:

 * {5038.6,Y,100}   PS SHOWS USERID AND PASSWORD

2. Soln# 2057042.6   USE THE HIDE.C PROGRAM

Solution ID   : 2057042.6
For Problem   : 1009091.6
Affected Platforms : NCR Unix SVR4
Affected Products : SQL*Forms
Affected Components : IAD V03.00.XX
Affected Oracle Vsn : V07.00.13.XX

Summary:
USE THE HIDE.C PROGRAM

+=+

Solution Description:
====================

Use the program hide.c:

```
/*--------------------------------------------------------------------------+
|     Can be used as a program prefix: hide program arguments               |
|     or as a symbolic link.  If this program is not invoked as hide, it    |
|     will hide its arguments and invoke the program name.hide              |
|     The best way to use this is to rename your critical programs to       |
|     program.hide, and create a symbolic link program to hide.            |
|     mv sqlplus sqlplus.hide; ln -s hide sqlplus                           |
|     Thus when sqlplus is invoked, its arguments will be hidden            |
|                                                                           |
| NOTES                                                                     |
|                                                                           |
| This program works by padding 3000 '/' chars in argv[0].  This fools     |
| all known ps's.  This will reduce the argument capacity of your          |
| program by 3000 chars.  A good enhancement would be to reduce the        |
| padding if needed so that no arguments are lost - would require a        |
| method of determining the max argument size on the system.  Some        |
| system's provide the E2BIG error on exec.                                |
| There is some performace penalty for using this program, but it is       |
| minimal because this program is so small - the biggest cost is the       |
| extra exec required to get this program started.                         |
| HISTORY                                                                   |
|     09/17/92  D Beusee     Fixed to compile on any system                |
+--------------------------------------------------------------------*/
/*
```

```
* $Header: /local/bin/RCS/hide.c,v 1.6 1992/09/22 22:37:17 dbeusee Exp $
*
* $Log: hide.c,v $
* Revision 1.6  1992/09/22  22:37:17  dbeusee
* Added exit(1) when cannot execvp the program.
*
* Revision 1.5  1992/09/22  11:28:44  dbeusee
* Some BSD systems have memset(), so add a #define memset MEMSET to fix
* compilation errors (like on ultrix).
*
* Revision 1.4  1992/09/22  06:34:57  dbeusee
* BSD systems need memset routine.
*
* Revision 1.3  1992/09/22  06:05:13  dbeusee
* Set JUNK_CHAR to ' ' but force last junk char to '/'. This looks prettier
* when doing 'ps'.  Also do not show full path of the program.  Also do not
* show .hide if prog is a symlink to hide.
*
* Revision 1.2  1992/09/22  05:52:26  dbeusee
* If hide could not execvp the program, give an error message.
* if hide was invoked with a full path (e.g. /usr/local/bin/hide),
* do not try to invoke PATH/hide.hide.
*
*
*/
    #include <stdio.h>
    #ifdef SYS5
    #include <string.h>
    #else
    #include <strings.h>
    #define strrchr rindex
    #define memset MEMSET /* some BSD systems have a memset() */
    char *memset();
    #endif
    #define JUNK_SIZE 3000
    #define JUNK_CHAR ' '
    char arg0buf[4096];
    char progbuf[4096];
    char errbuf[4096];
    int main(argc, argv)
    int argc;
    char *argv[];
    {
        char *name, *base;
        int firstarg;
        if (!(name = strrchr(argv[0], '/')))
            name = argv[0];
        else
            name ++; /* get past '/' */
        firstarg = (!strcmp(name, "hide")) ? 1 : 0;
        if (firstarg && (argc == 1))
        {
            fprintf(stderr, "Usage: hide program arguments\n");
            fprintf(stderr, "  ie: hide sqlplus username/password\n");
            fprintf(stderr, "if hide is not named hide, \
```

```
   it will execute name.hide (useful as a symbolic link)\n");
        exit(1);
    }
   /* Build program name.  If symbolic link mode, use argv[0] || .hide */
     strcpy(progbuf, argv[firstarg]);
     if (!(base = strrchr(argv[firstarg], '/')))
         base = argv[firstarg];
     else
         base ++; /* get past '/' */
     if (!firstarg) strcat(progbuf, ".hide");
     /* Build arg0 buffer.  First, fill it with junk */
     memset((void *)arg0buf, JUNK_CHAR, JUNK_SIZE);
     arg0buf[JUNK_SIZE-1] = '/'; /* set last char to '/' */
   /* Prepend real program name - so ps can see what prog is running */
     strncpy(arg0buf, base, strlen(base));
   /* Append real program name - so prog can see what prog is running */
     strcpy(arg0buf + JUNK_SIZE, argv[firstarg]);
     /* Assign new arg0 buffer to the argv array */
     argv[firstarg] = arg0buf;
     /* Start the new program with the shifted arguments */
     execvp(progbuf, argv + firstarg);
     sprintf(errbuf, "Could not execvp '%s'", progbuf);
     perror(errbuf);
     exit(1);
   }
   #ifndef SYS5
   char *
   memset(s, c, n)
        register char *s;
        register c, n;
   {
        register char *p = s;
        while (n-- > 0)
             *s++ = c;
        return (p);
   }
   #endif /* ifndef SYS5 */
```

DISCLAIMER:
The hide.c code is not supported by Oracle. It is provided as a courtesy,
as a workaround for SVR4 machines. BSD already hides the ps arguments.

Use operating system authenticated (OPS$) accounts

These accounts do not require a username or password:

```
cdye@socrates% sqlplus /@hr_prod
SQL*Plus: Release 8.0.4.0.0 - Production on Mon Dec 28 21:43:57 1998

(c) Copyright 1997 Oracle Corporation.  All rights reserved.

Connected to:
Oracle8 Enterprise Edition Release 8.0.4.1.0 - Production
With the Partitioning and Objects options
PL/SQL Release 8.0.4.1.0 - Production
```

```
SQL> show user
user is "OPS$CDYE"
SQL>
```

Those who attempt to obtain a password for these accounts will be disappointed, as you can see here:

```
cdye@socrates% ps -ef | grep sqlp
   cdye 12214 10822  1 18:14:05 pts/8    0:00 sqlplus /@hr_prod
   cdye 12216 10901  0 18:14:22 pts/9    0:00 grep sqlp
```

Don't invoke programs with username and password on command line

Instruct users not to enter their usernames and passwords on the command line. Let the program prompt for the password instead:

```
cdye@socrates% sqlplus cdye@hr_prod

SQL*Plus: Release 8.0.4.0.0 - Production on Mon Dec 28 21:49:14 1998

(c) Copyright 1997 Oracle Corporation.  All rights reserved.


Connected to:
Oracle8 Enterprise Edition Release 8.0.4.1.0 - Production
With the Partitioning and Objects options
PL/SQL Release 8.0.4.1.0 - Production

SQL> show user
user is "CDYE"
SQL>
```

Personally, I have not been overly successful with enforcing this approach.

Even if you use an operating system that does not display program arguments when processes are listed (such as the VMS *show system* command), passwords may still be available in network trace files.

Operating System Authentication

As mentioned earlier, you can use operating system authenticated accounts to avoid the issues of compromised database passwords. In effect, OPS$ accounts do not have passwords; their encrypted version, stored in the data dictionary view DBA_USERS, is EXTERNAL:

```
system@dc18 SQL>  SELECT username, password
  2  FROM dba_users
  3  WHERE username like 'OPS$%'
  4  /

Username          Password
---------------   ------------------
OPS$AKALIDIN      EXTERNAL
OPS$AKAPO         EXTERNAL
```

```
OPS$BONO            EXTERNAL
OPS$CDYE            EXTERNAL
OPS$CHATSINT        EXTERNAL
OPS$CHERNOVI        EXTERNAL
OPS$CKER            EXTERNAL
OPS$DEASLEY         EXTERNAL
OPS$DWEB            EXTERNAL
OPS$EDD             EXTERNAL
OPS$GKRISHNA        EXTERNAL
OPS$GWANG           EXTERNAL
OPS$IASAAD          EXTERNAL
OPS$IBALKHI         EXTERNAL
OPS$IHAB            EXTERNAL
```

 You can set the password for OPS$ accounts to whatever value you like, and they will still work.

One argument for using OPS$ accounts is that database passwords are no longer an issue: they cannot be stolen or compromised. Another reason is that these accounts are generally much more convenient for users—one less password to remember and, of course, less typing. OPS$ accounts also allow a centralized approach to account administration. Finally, auditing is simplified because trace files and audit trails containing Oracle user IDs are easy to map to operating system accounts.

If you decide to use OPS$ accounts, you are in effect telling your database that if a user can log in to the operating system successfully, then she should be able to log in to the database, too, connecting to the Oracle account corresponding to her operating system account. The Unix account cdye, for example, connects to the Oracle account OPS$CDYE:

```
SQL> CREATE USER ops$cdye
  2    IDENTIFIED EXTERNALLY;

User created.

SQL> SELECT username, password
  2    FROM dba_users
  3    WHERE username = 'OPS$CDYE';

Username       PASSWORD
-------------  -----------------------------
OPS$CDYE       EXTERNAL
```

If you keep the default encrypted password EXTERNAL for these accounts, nobody else will be able to use the OPS$ account because it is not possible to supply a password that encrypts to the string EXTERNAL. Oracle identifies users, but the operating system authenticates them.

Creating OPS$ accounts

Besides creating the database and operating system accounts themselves, there are a couple of other steps required to configure OPS$ accounts. Table 4-1 describes the relevant initialization parameters.

Table 4-1. Initialization Parameters Associated with OPS$ Logins

Parameter Name	Default Value	Description
OS_AUTHENT_PREFIX	OPS$	This is the string prepended to the name of the operating system account to form the database account.
REMOTE_OS_AUTHENT	FALSE	If TRUE, then the database will accept users who have been validated by a machine other than the one on which the database is running.

You must restart the database in order for changes to these values to take effect.

There may be additional requirements depending on your database's platform, as shown in Table 4-2.

Table 4-2. Operating-System Specific Requirements for Using OPS$ Logins

Operating System	Remarks
Unix	No additional requirements.
Microsoft NT	Operating system must exist on the NT server on which database resides; it must either share a directory from NT server to clients or use named pipes. NT clients must run 32-bit versions of Oracle client software (e.g., Forms), and the applications themselves must have been compiled with the 32-bit versions.
NetWare	For a secure OPS$ account with SQL*Net 2, the NetWare user must also be associated with an Oracle user by using the Oracle Snap-In for NetWare Administrator utility. This requires NetWare 4.1 or higher and the installation of Oracle's Novel Directory Service Authentication Adapter at the server and client.

Once you have configured your system, users can connect to the database using a connect string of the form:

```
/@sqlnet_alias
```

Note that there is no username or password.

 Not all client tools can take advantage of OPS$ logins. For example, the login screen for Designer 2000 does not accept "/" as a username.

The assumed risks of OPS$ accounts

If you set the initialization parameter REMOTE_OS_AUTHENT to TRUE, you are instructing your database to trust the authentication methods of every client on your network. As a general rule, your clients are not trustworthy. Why not? Because some operating systems permit users to masquerade as whomever they wish. Clients running Windows 3.x can set the *CONFIG.ORA* file parameter USER-NAME to identify themselves to a remote Oracle database, while Windows 95 users can set the following registry subkey:

```
My Computer\HKEY_LOCAL_MACHINE\System\CurrentControlSet\control\CurrentUser
```

Because of these security weaknesses, you should consider OPS$ accounts to be publicly available if PCs have access to your network and you have set REMOTE_OS_AUTHENT to TRUE. And even if PCs are not on your network, if people have physical access to a machine running most other operating systems, they can become whomever they want on that machine. Remember that setting REMOTE_OS_AUTHENT to TRUE means that you accept the authentication methods of all clients.

Encrypting Network Traffic

The Oracle password protocol encrypts all passwords sent over the network (Version 7.1 onward). With the advanced networking option, the password is not transmitted; rather, it is used as a key to encrypt information. Considering the wide availability of network sniffer software, encryption of passwords is essential.

External Authentication

Oracle's advanced networking option include interfaces (known as *adapters*) to a variety of third-party security services for authenticating users. You can configure these services so that users can use a single password to connect to any database on your network. The single sign-on architecture works by storing username and password information in a database or file system residing on a single server, called the *authentication server*. Oracle currently includes adapters for the following authentication services:

- Kerberos

- ICL Access Manager/SESAME

- CyberSAFE Challenger

- Bull ISM

- SecurID

- DCE Security Service (GSSAPI)

- Banyan

- Biometric (Identix)

The authentication server acts as an intermediary between client computers and database servers, as depicted in Figure 4-1.

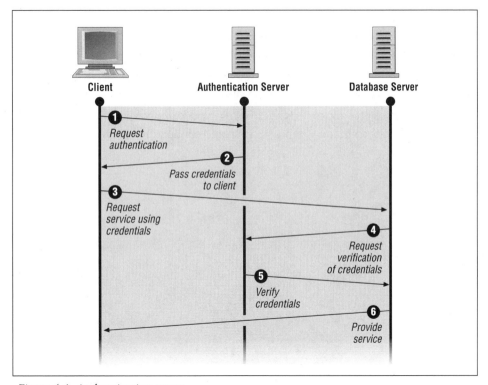

Figure 4-1. Authentication server

The sequence of events is as follows:

1. When a user on the client machine initiates a database connection, the client requests authentication credentials from the authentication server. This information is typically in the form of an encrypted key.

2. The authentication server verifies the client and sends the required credentials back.

3. The client makes a connection request to the database server, using the credentials obtained from the authentication server.

4. The database server sends the credentials to the authentication server for validation.

5. The authentication server sends verification back to the database server, which then accepts the connection request.

This architecture offers several advantages over conventional database authentication or OPS$ accounts:

- The authentication server on which passwords reside is under centralized administration, and access can (and should) be extremely limited. No interactive logins should be permitted.

- Passwords never travel over the network; instead, they are used as a key to encrypt and decrypt information during the login process.

- Users can use the same password for every database they access, with little risk that this password can be compromised.

- Besides associating passwords with users, you can associate usernames with client machines so that a given user can only connect from a given client.

5

Designing a Distributed System

Application developers and DBAs face numerous challenges and choices as they design a distributed application. Many, if not most, of these issues are not specific to the particular RDBMS vendor they have selected but are a function of business requirements and other constraints. This chapter takes a step back from Oracle specifics and examines topics common to distributed applications in general, including:

- The characteristics of a successful distributed system

- Data partitioning

- Application partitioning

- The client/server approach

- Common solutions to common problems

We introduced some of these topics in Chapter 1, *Introduction to Distributed Systems.* Chapter 6, *Oracle's Distributed System Implementation,* discusses these issues in greater detail in the context of the Oracle RDBMS.

Characteristics of a Distributed System

Before designing a distributed system, you should have a clear understanding of what a distributed system is and what requirements it must meet. In his book *An Introduction to Database Systems* (Addison-Wesley, 1995), the relational database deity C. J. (Chris) Date states his "fundamental principle of distributed database," as follows:

> To the user, a distributed system should look exactly like a nondistributed system.

Date goes on to enumerate 12 objectives that must be met in order to satisfy this principle, as follows:

1. Local autonomy

2. No reliance on a single site

3. Continuous operation

4. Location transparency

5. Fragmentation independence

6. Replication independence

7. Distributed query processing

8. Distributed transaction management

9. Hardware independence

10. Operating system independence

11. Network independence

12. RDBMS independence

Some of these requirements are quite lofty, and Chris Date himself acknowledges that these rules are not 100% achievable. Rather, they are useful primarily as guidelines to observe in the design and development of a distributed system. You can design a successful distributed database system that fails to meet every one of these objectives. Also, several of these objectives are the RDBMS vendor's responsibility, not the implementor's.

Distributed System Objectives

The following sections examine what these objectives mean, and Chapter 6 discusses Oracle's strategies for addressing them.

Local autonomy

To satisfy the local autonomy rule, a database that participates in a distributed system must be fully functional regardless of whether it is able to contact its compatriots. In addition, the data that resides with each participating database belongs to that database, in the sense that data integrity, security, and management are independent of the other sites that may be accessing or supplying the data.

No reliance on a single site

This rule is the complement to the local autonomy rule. Just as each site is self-sufficient, so there is no single master site on which others rely in the ideal distributed environment. In other words, the failure of any one site should not cripple the other sites (though it may hobble them), nor should the overall performance of the system be dependent on a single site.

Continuous operation

One of the most common reasons for developing a distributed database system is to provide redundancy and fault tolerance. By the same token, a distributed system should not require scheduled outages to perform maintenance such as adding and removing a site or upgrading software. Of course, in the ideal world we would have zero downtime, scheduled or not, but even Chris Date is willing to concede that "unplanned outages are difficult to avoid entirely."

Location transparency

Location transparency is the notion that data and data operations appear the same to users (and developers) regardless of where data resides. Users should not have to take any special measures to access data that is in multiple locations, nor should developers need to write additional code to perform a distributed transaction. Data, tables, and other objects can be viewed as logical entities, one step removed from their physical implementation. The DBA should be able to relocate data without requiring new user accounts or new code.

Fragmentation independence

The notion of fragmentation independence takes location transparency one step further. Whereas location transparency refers to the ability to locate entire tables and views transparently, fragmentation independence is the ability to partition data *within* a table (or, more accurately, within a relation) transparently. (This division of data is also known as *data partitioning*, especially in Oracle circles.) For example, an organization may keep employees' telephone extensions in one table in the corporate communications database and their department numbers in another table in the HR database. However, a user (or application) can join this data together and view it as though it were in a single table, as shown in Figure 5-1.

Data can also be partitioned horizontally. For example, individual franchises in a chain of bicycle stores track their own customers' addresses and purchases, but analysts at the headquarters site are able to view *all* register sales as though the records were in a single table, as shown in Figure 5-2.

The same restrictions apply to both updateable join views and fragmentation independence. The fact that fragmentation independence is relatively simple with relational database technology is one of the reasons why distributed databases are invariably relational databases.

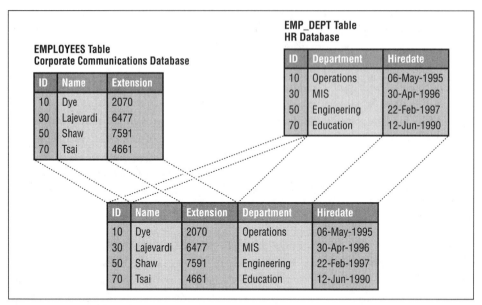

Figure 5-1. Vertical partitioning

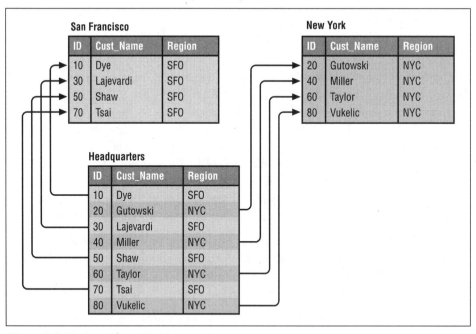

Figure 5-2. Horizontal partitioning

Replication independence

In order to meet the replication independence objective, a distributed system must provide a means of maintaining copies of the same data (i.e., tables) at multiple sites. As we shall see in Part II, reasons to replicate include performance gains and failover capability, to name a few. The challenge with providing replication independence is that when data is changed, the change must propagate to all replicas, as soon as possible. Users and applications should not be concerned with how their changes to a replicated table are propagated or whether their version of the table is up to date. Technically, replication independence requires that changes be propagated to all sites and committed as a single transaction using the two-phase commit protocol. However, enforcement of this stipulation can defeat the purpose of replicating in the first place since the additional communication required impacts performance and since processing is halted if any site is unavailable.

Distributed query processing

The performance of a query should not depend on where the data resides. The optimization of distributed queries is vital because a poor execution plan can take orders of magnitude longer than the "correct" one. For example, if a query includes a large intermediate result set, that data probably should *not* be shipped over the network to the database with a small table that is to be joined with the result set.

Distributed transaction management

A distributed system must guarantee the concurrency of distributed transactions. In other words, if a transaction is to update tables at two different sites, the transaction must either succeed both places or fail both places. This, of course, is what the two-phase commit protocol provides.

Hardware independence

The various participants in a distributed system should be able to run on whatever hardware platform suits their needs. In effect, this means that the RDBMS should run on all conceivable platforms and include the same functionality across all platforms.

Operating system independence

The RDBMS should be able to run under any operating system or at least under any of the popular operating systems. Do not allow your choice of RDBMS to tie you to a particular operating system.

Network independence

Just as it is desirable for an RDBMS to work on any hardware and any operating system, it is also desirable for it to be able to communicate with clients and other databases regardless of network protocols and architectures.

RDBMS independence

Ideally, it should be possible to create a heterogeneous distributed system. For example, we should be able to replicate data between an Oracle database and a Sybase database. In actual fact though, it can be difficult just to distribute data between two different *versions* of the same RDBMS!

Distributed System Classifications

The term *distributed database system* envelops several very different implementations and architectures. It is worthwhile to identify these various classifications before discussing design issues. The general categories are:

- Homogeneous distributed systems

- Heterogeneous distributed systems

- Federated database systems

- Redundant backup systems

These classifications are defined in the sections that follow.

Homogeneous distributed systems

The homogeneous distributed system is the classic and probably most common case. It is homogeneous because all participating databases use the same RDBMS (though not necessarily on the same platform). The second defining characteristic of a homogeneous distributed system is that data is strategically partitioned along functional and/or geographic boundaries and makes use of distributed queries and transactions. Additionally, these systems share schema under a global data dictionary. The entire database is truly the sum of its parts, yet each individual database is self-reliant, as described by Date's 12 objectives.

As an example of a homogeneous distributed system, consider the fictitious Bigwheel Bicycle company. Bigwheel's corporate headquarters is in California, and they have several retail outlets throughout the country. Bigwheel also has manufacturing sites and warehouses (see Figure 5-3). Together, these databases paint a complete picture of Bigwheel Bicycle's production, inventory, and sales. At the same time, each site can function independently from its peers (albeit in a somewhat diminished capacity in some cases).

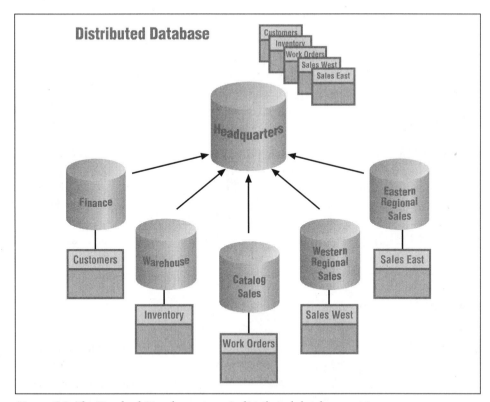

Figure 5-3. The Bigwheel Bicycle company's distributed database empire

Heterogeneous distributed systems

A heterogeneous distributed system has all the characteristics of a homogeneous system, including shared schema, except that the participating databases use two or more RDBMS engines. Generally speaking, these systems share data but are less likely to engage in distributed transactions. This restriction arises because it can be difficult to use the full functionality of an RDBMS when interfacing with an alien. Strictly speaking, different versions of RDBMS software from the same vendor can be classified as a heterogeneous distributed system and can have limitations. For example, Oracle Version 6 does not support the two-phase commit.

Federated database systems

Federated database systems differ from homogeneous and heterogeneous systems because they do not share schema. Rather, they share subsets of their data to facilitate operations at other sites, with which there is usually no functional relationship. The data that a site is willing to share is known as *exported schema*, and the remote data to which a site has access is known as *imported schema*. Participants in a federated database system are completely independent of one another and may or may not use the same RDBMS.

This independence is usually not by design. Organizations usually create federated database systems in response to needs that arise after the original systems are in production. This model is the most common type of distributed database system—perhaps because a federated database is easy to create with a minimal amount of planning.

An example of a federated database system is the fictitious Bigwheel Bicycle company's customer and sales lead databases. The customer database is the property of the customer administration group, which services the bicycle shops that have contracted to carry Bigwheel's product line. Meanwhile, the sales lead database belongs to the travelling sales force whose job is to enlist as many bicycle shops as possible to carry Bigwheel's products. The customer administrators have granted the sales force access to their database so that they can track how many of their sales leads actually become customers.

Redundant backup systems

The redundant backup system is a special case of a homogeneous system and is a popular application of replication technology. This strategy entails mirroring a primary database with an exact copy, which may be at a separate location. Using replication technology, all committed transactions in the primary database propagate to the mirror. However, unlike a homogeneous system, the mirror site is not available to users as long as the primary site is operational. If the primary site becomes unavailable, users and applications can be redirected to the mirror site where they can continue processing.

Distributed system classifications: Summary

To summarize, the factors that determine a given architecture's classification are:

* Same or different RDBMSs

* Presence or absence of shared schema and global data dictionary

* Site availability

Participants in homogeneous and heterogeneous systems share a global data dictionary, and although each member should be self-sufficient, each is a key contributor to the overall system. Federated databases, on the other hand, do not share a global data dictionary and are not complementary components of an overall system. Finally, the redundant backup system consists of a master site and its mirror. These configurations are designed to address high availability requirements.

Table 5-1 summarizes the various characteristics of distributed databases.

Table 5-1. Distributed Database Classifications

Classification	Same RDBMS	Global Data Dictionary	All Sites Available
Homogeneous	Yes	Yes	Yes
Heterogeneous	No	Yes	Yes
Federated	Maybe	No	Yes
Redundant backup	Yes	Yes	No

The Global Data Dictionary

In Table 5-1 we see that the notion of a global data dictionary is common to all but the federated model of distributed database systems. The data dictionary catalogs all objects in the distributed schema, is available at every site, and is accessed identically no matter where it is viewed. It defines the distributed database and shields users, including application developers, from the details of where data resides and how it is accessed.

Obviously, there are a number of challenges in concealing the seams of the distributed database from the users while respecting the objectives of a distributed system. Issues that must be addressed include:

- Placement of the global data dictionary

- Object naming

- The local data dictionary

- Management of interdatabase integrity constraints

- Management of user accounts and privileges

These issues are discussed in the sections that follow.

Placement of the Global Data Dictionary

The challenge here is how to make the dictionary available and identical to all sites *and* respect the 12 objectives of a successful distributed database. A centralized catalog violates the "No reliance on a single site" objective. Yet storing a complete copy of the dictionary at all sites violates the local autonomy objective since local changes must be propagated to all participating sites. Another option is to make each site responsible for its portion of the catalog only; although this meets the objectives of a distributed database, it is generally not practical since resolving the location of remote objects would launch a blind and potentially lengthy hunting expedition to the remote sites in search of the referenced object.

Clearly then, RDBMS vendors must strike some happy medium in order to support a distributed database devoid of seams and not prone to hunting expeditions or other extravagances when trying to resolve object names. The solution that Oracle and other vendors have arrived at is to store information about the location of remote objects in each local data dictionary. That is, there is no such thing as a global data dictionary in the purest sense. At first glance, this approach appears to violate the location transparency objective. Remember, though, that location transparency is in the eye of the user. As long as there is a way to shield users from the details about an object's location, which Oracle does with synonyms, location transparency is achieved. It is the DBA who has to worry about the objects' actual locations and about concealing the details of the location. We'll explore the specifics of the Oracle implementation in Chapter 6.

Object Naming

The way that Oracle and other RDBMS vendors incorporate an object's location into the data dictionary is to design object naming so that the location is a component of an object's fully qualified name. For example, table PRODUCTS is in the SPROCKET schema in the database named D7CA.BIGWHEEL.COM. Its fully qualified name is SPROCKET.PRODUCTS@D7CA.BIGWHEEL.COM. In every database in the distributed environment, this name equates to the same physical table. Unfortunately, the fully qualified name violates the location transparency objective. The solution is to create a synonym for the object so that users can reference it by the name PRODUCTS:

```
CREATE PUBLIC SYNONYM products FOR sprocket.products@D7CA.BIGWHEEL.COM;
```

Note that public synonyms do not span all databases in the distributed system. There is no guarantee that PRODUCTS in the headquarters database evaluates to the same thing as PRODUCTS in the warehouse database. Similarly, since users may be able to create private synonyms, there is not even a guarantee that PRODUCTS for user cdye refers to the same table as PRODUCTS for user jblow. All that can be guaranteed is that a fully specified name evaluates to the same thing for every user in every database. It is up to the DBA and the application developer to ensure that the proper synonyms are set up and to update these synonyms if an object (or fragment thereof) moves to another database.

Some RDBMSs (most notably IBM's R*) refer to an object's birth site rather than its location. An object's location can change, but its birth site cannot. Identifying an object by birth site reduces the data dictionary maintenance that is required when an object relocates.

From an application development perspective, object names must be selected with care so that they do not conflict with other names from other schema. Table names like USERS, CUSTOMERS, and ADDRESSES are examples of common names to avoid because they are likely to conflict with names from other application schema.

The Local Data Dictionary

In a well-designed distributed database system, the majority of data accesses will be to local data. Similarly, many, if not most, objects in the database are not accessible or known to remote sites. Therefore, it is reasonable to optimize the data dictionary for local use, while providing the extensibility needed to catalog remote objects as well. The amount of information available about remote objects varies from one RDBMS to the next, but at the very least, the physical location of remote objects must be recorded. Beyond that, it is also desirable to include statistics about the volume and distribution of the remote data so that the RDBMS can optimize queries effectively.

Management of Interdatabase Integrity Constraints

The notion of a distributed database invites the desire to enforce business rules across multiple databases. These business rules may be simple referential integrity constraints, such as "the customer ID in the ORDERS table must correspond to a customer ID in the HQ_CUSTOMERS table." Or the business rule may be a formulated one, such as "corporate shipping costs cannot exceed $10,000 per month." In a single database, these rules are simple to enforce with foreign keys and programmed logic, both of which may reside in the local data dictionary.

A distributed database, on the other hand, poses formidable challenges. To support referential integrity constraints to a parent table in a remote database, we could rely on connectivity to the remote database when updating the local child table so that we could confirm the validity of the update. Unfortunately, we would have to write our own logic to perform this validation because today's RDBMS data dictionaries do not support foreign keys defined against remote master tables, nor are they likely to in the future. Alternatively, we could maintain a copy of the master table in the local database and define foreign keys against it. The only problem is that we would have to keep that table updated as the "real" table changes. Although neither of these solutions is flawless, they are, at least, logically sound.

Enforcing formulated business rules is a much trickier task. Take the case of the $10,000 monthly shipping limit. If the corporation's cumulative shipping costs for the current month are currently $9,000, and the warehouse site needs to ship an item for $2,000, what are we to do? To reject the warehouse site's shipping order violates the database's autonomy, yet allowing the order violates the global business rule. Perhaps we should permit the shipment but send some sort of exception notification to the headquarters site. Regrettably, there is no definitive solution to this conundrum. The final solution depends on the nature of the organization—that is, the solution is specific to the application. The data dictionary cannot enforce formulated rules in a distributed system.

In short, the issues of data integrity and adherence to business rules that can be automated to a large degree in a single database are much more difficult to implement in a distributed database. You will not find a simple solution, and the solutions you choose may vary widely from one application to the next.

Management of User Accounts and Privileges

Just as data integrity is much more complex in a distributed system, so is the management of accounts and privileges. We cannot rely on the data dictionary to enforce access levels to local objects once we share data with remote sites. Yet the objective of local autonomy dictates that the local site take responsibility for the security of its data. Another conundrum? Maybe.

One solution is the concept of global users. Under this model, every user has an account in every database to which he requires access, even if the user doesn't even realize it. For example, if a user in the headquarters database requires access to the warehouse and manufacturing databases in order to view inventory, the DBAs create the requisite accounts with the requisite privileges. Since access to the data is via a synonym that masks the location of the data, the user does not even know that the other accounts exist. This situation is shown in Figure 5-4.

The attraction of this approach is that the DBA can control data access with a high degree of granularity and can administer privileges through conventional methods such as database roles. In addition, each site is solely responsible for the security of its data. The disadvantage is that the DBA could end up doing nothing but maintaining user accounts!

One alternative, as discussed in Chapter 4, *Distributed Database Security*, is to create one or more accounts that are used as global doorways into the local database. These accounts have all the privileges necessary for the operations that might be performed on the local data. Presumably, a member of a distributed database can trust the remote administrators of the remote databases to restrict access to appropriate levels.

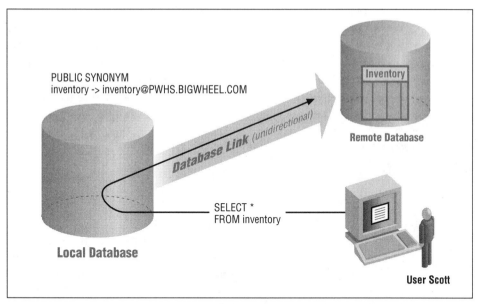

Figure 5-4. Transparent access to remote data using a private database link

We have seen that a distributed database system requires a global data dictionary that can catalog objects, constraints, and privileges just as a local data dictionary does. However, it is not reasonable to impose objectives such as location transparency on the global data dictionary itself, nor is it feasible to rely on a global data dictionary to enforce integrity constraints and user privileges on remote objects. These requirements become the responsibility of the DBAs and application developers.

Replication-Specific Issues

Building a system for replication means addressing a variety of design and configuration issues that are irrelevant in a standalone environment. As a general rule, it is not possible to "turn on" replication for an existing, standalone system, though some have tried. Items requiring attention include replication architecture, data consistency, data extraction, schema differences, primary key constraints, and confliction avoidance—to name a few. The sections that follow highlight these concerns.

Replication Architecture

There are two broad categories of replication architecture: log-based replication and transactional replication. *Log-based replication* works by examining the database's transaction logs (redo logs in the case of Oracle) and forwards committed changes to other participating databases as needed. (Quest Software's Shareplex product is an example.) *Transactional replication*, on the other hand, works by either querying the remote database (in the case of read-only snapshots) and adding triggers to replicated tables that effect the forwarding of changes to remote sites. Oracle's advanced replication facilities are an example of this technology. One of your first choices is which of these two mechanisms to use.

Log-based replication

Log-based replication has various advantages and disadvantages.

Advantages. The primary benefits of log-based replication are speed and ease of configuration. Since this technology simply forwards changes from the database transaction log to remote destinations, there is no need for a two-phase commit protocol or even interdatabase communication. That means that you can use an FTP protocol to move data, which is generally faster and simpler than, say, SQL*Net. Log-based replication can be a viable solution when you want to forward changes over the Internet.

Log-based replication is also relatively simple to configure; you do not need to generate triggers on replicated tables or design conflict resolution techniques or set up interdatabase communication.

Disadvantages. Alas, there is no free lunch. Log-based replication includes some restrictions. For example, distributed transactions become much more complex or impossible. That limits your data partitioning options. In addition, database recovery can be difficult in an environment with a high transaction rate. You must apply not only the database's transaction logs, but also the logs applied from the remote databases. Recovering multiple databases to the same point in time can be complex. Finally, adding or removing tables from the replication set can be difficult, depending on the vendor's implementation. Finally, synchronous replication is not possible.

Transactional replication

Transactional replication also has various advantages and disadvantages.

Advantages. Transactional replication technology, such as Oracle's advanced replication facilities, offers the flexibility to distribute data in a variety of ways, such as read-only snapshots, updateable snapshots, multi-master replication, and synchronous or asynchronous operation. You can mix and match your replication method to suit your needs. Because the functionality is built with the database's native programming constructs, it is readily configured and guaranteed to be supported by the RDBMS vendor. You can also partition data so that each site maintains only the data relevant to it. You also have a variety of options for resolving conflicts, as discussed in Chapter 15, *Conflict Avoidance and Resolution Techniques.*

Disadvantages. The biggest drawback to transactional replication is that large applications require a significant amount of design effort to replicate successfully. Conflict avoidance and resolution must be planned from the start; tables may need additional columns to record timestamps and site names; and database connectivity must be established with proper privileges. Another drawback is that the amount of data that must travel among sites is increased; for example, Oracle's advanced replication facilities send the new and old values of each changed column when an update occurs. Transactional replication can also be time consuming to administer. Finally, not all datatypes and objects can be replicated; Oracle does not replicate sequences or LONG or LONG RAW data (although CLOBs and BLOBs do replicate in Oracle8).

Software Compatibility

Software versions are more significant in a replicated environment because vendors often introduce new functionality and fix bugs. It is best to keep all participating databases on the exact same version of the RDBMS, despite vendor claims of interversion compatibility. This means that database upgrades must be managed more carefully; unless the vendor supports rolling upgrades, you must upgrade all databases at the same time, thus incurring downtime.

Data Consistency

Depending on the vendor's implementation, you may have to schedule data refreshes in a certain order if the source tables have referential integrity constraints defined. For example, if a snapshot site has replicas of the CUSTOMERS table and the ORDERS table, which has a foreign key to the CUSTOMERS table, you will have to refresh the CUSTOMERS table before you refresh the ORDERS table. This requirement arises because the data refresh may commit changes after each table is refreshed; if you refresh the ORDERS table first, you could insert a record that has no parent in the CUSTOMERS table.

 Oracle addresses this eventuality by allowing you to create a *snapshot group*, in which you include tables that must be refreshed as a single transaction in order to respect referential integrity constraints.

Data Extraction

Sometimes it is desirable for a site to store data in a schema that is different from the data source. For example, a data warehouse site may wish to denormalize the replicated ORDERS table so that it has a CUSTOMER_NAME field, whereas the order entry site has only CUSTOMER_ID in the table. Whenever data extractions occur against replicated tables, the designers must verify that the work required can be accomplished without interfering with the replication itself. Must the source tables be locked while the data is extracted? Can the refreshes occur while transactions are being performed, or must they be done during off-hours?

Primary Keys

Every replicated table must have either a primary key or, equivalently, a unique index. The replication mechanism uses the primary key (or unique index) to identify which rows need to be modified when changes are propagated from one site to another. Although primary keys are a sound design practice in and of themselves, you must ensure their presence on all replicated tables.

Conflict Avoidance

Any asynchronously replicated environment has the potential for update conflicts. Such a conflict arises when two sites perform DML on the same record at the same time (or at least before the changes propagate). To a large extent, you can design an application in such a way that such conflicts are rare (conflict avoidance). Beyond design considerations, most RDBMS vendors include various built-in measures for resolving conflicts when they do arise. Conflict avoidance, detection, and resolution are discussed in detail in Chapter 15.

Data Partitioning Methodologies

Partitioned data is the fundamental characteristic of a distributed database system. How that partitioning is done can make the difference between a system that can thrive and adapt and one that requires constant triage. In this section we describe a process you can use to ensure that your distributed database falls into the former category.

Many technical writings use the term *data fragmentation* instead of *data partitioning*. These terms are interchangeable. Oracle's documentation and literature prefer the latter term, possibly because data "fragmentation" in Oracle parlance has come to mean a segment that is stored in many noncontiguous extents.

The obvious approach to data partitioning is to locate data where it is used most. While this is certainly a reasonable objective, it is not always simple to realize. For example, there may be multiple sites that emerge as good candidates, owners of existing data may not be willing to relocate it, or other applications may have conflicting requirements—to name a few issues. One way to uncover these issues is to follow a step-by-step methodology that addresses potential problems and that results in a shared knowledge base of who uses data and how changes impact the distributed database.

The methodology we recommend is derived from one that Marie Buretta proposes in her book *Data Replication* (John Wiley & Sons, 1997). The process consists of the following steps:

1. Identify users, locations, and activities

2. Assess existing infrastructure

3. Identify coordinated recovery requirements

4. Map processes to data

5. Assess global requirements

6. Propose data locations

7. Validate data placement against existing constraints and capacities

8. Validate placement with service-level agreements

9. Implement

Some of these steps are actually part of the design process for every application but, in the interest of thoroughness, are restated as part of the partitioning process. What follows is an explanation of the activities associated with each of these steps.

Identify Users, Locations, and Activities

The purpose of this first step is to identify who does what where. The people to include in this step are the DBAs of all participating sites, a representative from the application development team, and a representative from each affected user community. In many cases, the distributed database being implemented must meld into an existing family of databases. And even if the implementation is completely new, it is valuable to document this information to confirm that all interested parties are in agreement and as a basis for planning the system. One cannot locate data with the sites that use it most without going through this exercise.

Table 5-2 is a sample of the information that should be collected in this step.

Table 5-2. Distributed Database Usage Matrix

Site Category	Geographic Location	Type/Number of Users	Business Processes and Transactions/ Queries per Day
Headquarters	Los Altos, CA	Sales managers/12 Sales analysts/5 Product developers/20 Support staff/4 AP staff/4 AR staff/5	Sales forecasting/10 Sales reporting/20 R & D/200 Technical support/150 Accounts payable/12 Accounts receivable/75
Manufacturing	Gilroy, CA	Plant managers/3 Procurement manager/1	Resource planning/20 Procurement/5
	King of Prussia, PA	Plant managers/2 Procurement manager/1	Resource planning/5 Procurement/1
Warehouses	Oakland, CA	Shipping admins/10	Order fulfillment/150
	Tulsa, OK	Shipping admins/5	Order fulfillment/10
	Chicago, IL	Shipping admins/3	Order fulfillment/30
	Anacostia, MD	Shipping admins/5	Order fulfillment/50
Regional sales	San Francisco, CA	Sales managers/2 Customer reps/4 Order entry clerks/15 Webmaster/1	Sales data collection/200 Customer service/10 Order entry/150 Web marketing/2000
	New York, NY	Sales manager/1 Customer reps/2 Catalog sales clerks/10	Sales data collection/300 Customer service/100 Order entry/250
	Tokyo, Japan	Sales staff/5	Sales data collection/100
	Paris, France	Sales staff/3	Sales data collection/50

This matrix provides a sound starting point for the remaining tasks at hand. It provides an overview of the locations, location types, and user types, as well as an approximation of the workload at each site. Note that we can expect similar activities and data at locations of the same type (e.g., all warehouse sites in the above example perform order fulfillment).

Assess Existing Network and Hardware Infrastructure

Now that we know what processes occur where and have an rough estimate of workload, we can verify that the organization's physical infrastructure is sufficient and appropriately deployed. To that end, we should compile an inventory of the following:

- Network topologies

- Computer equipment (servers)

- Operating system and database revision levels

- Security requirements

- System availability and support

Collecting this information will bring to light any inconsistencies, conflicts, or misallocations that may exist in the current environment. In addition, the inventory can help to justify additional equipment purchases.

The compiled data can be presented in a matrix similar to the one shown in Table 5-3.

Table 5-3. Infrastructure Summary

Location and Type	Connectivity	Servers	OS Version RDBMS	Security	Availability and Support
Los Altos Headquarters	T1—Gilroy T1—San Francisco FRa—New York FRa—Tokyo FRa—Paris 256KB—K of P 256KB—Oakland 128KB—Tulsa ISDN—Chicago ISDN—Anacostia	Sun e6000 Sun e3000	Solaris 2.6 Oracle 7.3.4	High	7x24 Full support
Gilroy Manufacturing	T1—Oakland ISDN—Tulsa 256KB—Chicago	Sun e3000	Solaris 2.6 Oracle 7.3.4	Medium	7x24 On-site support during business hours
King of Prussia Manufacturing	T1—Anacostia	Sun Ultra2	Solaris 2.6 Oracle 7.3.4	Medium	7x24 On-site support during business hours
Oakland Warehouse	T1—Gilroy 128KB—Los Altos	Sun Ultra2	Solaris 2.6 Oracle 7.3.4	Low	5x8 On-site support during business hours
Tulsa Warehouse	ISDN—Gilroy 128KB—Los Altos	Sun Ultra1	Solaris 2.6 Oracle 7.3.4	Low	5x8 Remote admin from Los Altos
Chicago Warehouse	ISDN—Los Altos 256KB—Gilroy	Sun e3000	Solaris 2.6 Oracle 7.3.4	Low	5x8 Contracted support services
Anacostia Warehouse	T1—K of P ISDN—Los Altos	Sun Ultra1	Solaris 2.6 Oracle 7.3.4	Low	5x8 Remote admin from New York
San Francisco Sales	T1—Los Altos	Sun Ultra2 Sun Ultra1	Solaris 2.6 Oracle 7.3.4	Medium	7x24 Full support

Table 5-3. Infrastructure Summary (continued)

Location and Type	Connectivity	Servers	OS Version RDBMS	Security	Availability and Support
New York Sales	FR[a]—Los Altos	Sun e3000	Solaris 2.6 Oracle 7.3.4	Medium	7x24 Full support
Tokyo Sales	FR[a]—Los Altos	Sun Ultra2	Solaris 2.6 Oracle 7.3.4	High	5x8 Remote admin from San Francisco
Paris Sales	FR[a]—Los Altos	Sun Ultra1	Solaris 2.6 Oracle 7.3.4	Medium	7x24 Full support

[a] Frame relay

Identify Coordinated Recovery Requirements

It is often the case that some sites in a distributed system are coupled more tightly than others. For example, an order entry system must have close integration with an inventory system, although it need not be closely linked with the procurement system. Tightly coupled systems must observe integrity constraints at all times and must support a coordinated recovery strategy, which means that all systems involved must be recoverable to a consistent state. Analyzing the strength of inter-site relationships ensures the survivability of the distributed database and lends insight into how data should be partitioned.

The first step in this process is to catalog all tables, relationships, and attributes that exist in the distributed database. (This catalog provides benefits in and of itself, beyond its use in data recovery.) The catalog reveals where objects are used, how critical they are, and the responsible business units. Table 5-4 outlines the information to be captured.

Table 5-4. Information for the Catalog of Tables, Relationships, and Attributes

Component	Property	Comments
Table	Name	Table name
	Description	Description of table's contents
	Primary key	Name of primary key column(s)
	Foreign keys	Columns that reference other tables
	Triggers	Description of table's triggers
	Business guardian	Organizational entity responsible for specifying requirements and business rules on the table
	Estimated size	Number of rows and bytes per row
	Estimated growth	Rate of growth (inserts) and volatility (updates)
	Confidentiality level	Indication of data sensitivity

Table 5-4. Information for the Catalog of Tables, Relationships, and Attributes (continued)

Component	Property	Comments
Relationship	Criticality level	Indication of data importance
	Users	List of who accesses the table and the type of activity they perform
	Retention requirements	How long data must remain online
	Purge conditions	When and how data is deleted
	Name	Relationship name
	Table 1 name	Name of first table in the relationship
	Table 1 cardinality	For example, one-to-many
	Table 1 optionality	Whether each row must have a correspondence in Table 2
	Table 2 name	Name of second table in the relationship
	Table 2 cardinality	For example, one-to-many
	Table 2 optionality	Whether each row must have a correspondence in Table 1
Attribute	Name	Name of the attribute
	Description	Description of what the attribute depicts
	Business name	Business entity to which the attribute corresponds
	Data type	Datatype of the attribute
	Confidentiality level	Indication of data sensitivity
	Where used	List of processes that access the attribute
	Where present	List of tables containing the attribute

The next step is to distinguish primary data sources (i.e., those with online transactions) from sites where data is copied or replicated. Start with an entity relationship diagram (ERD) so that it is easy to determine logical groupings of objects and relationships. The goal is to place every entity with a logical group. These groupings generally correspond to business activities such as order entry or procurement. These activities, in turn, generally correspond to sites. You should minimize intersite referential integrity constraints since they can be troublesome to enforce (as we discussed in the previous section). Maintaining intersite referential integrity constraints during recovery is even more challenging and generally requires that the sites involved have a coordinated backup strategy.

You will probably notice that four different types of relationships emerge among the entities in your distributed database:

Objects with strong referential links within a single data grouping
> These are objects that reside in the same database and that *must* be recovered to a state of transactional consistency. Examples include tables with a master-child relationship such as invoices and line items.

Objects with medium referential links and high volatility within a single data grouping

These are objects that *probably* reside in the same database and that *should* be recovered to a state of transactional consistency. Examples include tables with semantic referential integrity constraints such as orders and products. The high volatility refers to a high volume of updates.

Objects with medium referential links and low or medium volatility

Objects meeting these criteria are not often updated and need not be stored or recovered together. An example of this type of relationship might be a purchase order master table and a customer table. Relationships of this kind are candidates for denormalization or replication. It may also be possible to partition these objects horizontally; for example, the West Coast order entry site might also maintain customers located in that region.

 Denormalization of a distributed schema must be done with care because the task of preventing anomalies is significantly more difficult. Do not denormalize without providing processes that avoid update and delete anomalies.

Objects with weak referential links

Transaction tables whose columns are validated against lookup tables are an example of a weak referential link. For example, an address table may validate the postal code against a table of postal codes, but the postal code table itself seldom changes and can be replicated to the sites that use it for validation.

The terms *strong, weak, high, medium,* and *low* in the preceding discussion are all relative and must be assessed within the context of your environment.

The process of identifying coordinated recovery requirements should not be considered an extremely rigorous exercise; rather, it should provide an understanding of how data is used. Of course, the exercise should reveal the relationships that must be consistent at all times, but there are additional benefits as well. In particular, if you follow these recommendations you will have:

*   Identified your coordinated recovery requirements

*   Copied inventory of all lookup tables, which are candidates for snapshot replication

*   Identified candidates for partitioning

Map Processes to Data

The next phase of the process is to determine the application processes in which each data group participates and to identify the most significant processes. *Signifi-*

cant means the processes that execute frequently, that are vital to the business, that require rapid response times, or that manipulate large amounts of data.

The objective is to create a matrix depicting how processes access data. The matrix should capture the type of access each process has to the tables (i.e., SELECT, INSERT, UPDATE, and DELETE access), similar to the example in Table 5-5.

Table 5-5. Process-to-Data Mapping

Process	Customer Table	Orders Table	Product Table	Invoice Table	Sales Table
Sales data collection (high data volume)	SELECT	SELECT	SELECT	No access	SELECT INSERT UPDATE
Customer service	SELECT INSERT UPDATE	SELECT	SELECT	SELECT	SELECT
Order entry (business critical)	SELECT	SELECT INSERT UPDATE	SELECT	No access	No access
Order fulfillment (high transaction rate)	SELECT	SELECT UPDATE	SELECT	SELECT INSERT	No access
Billing (business critical)	SELECT	SELECT	SELECT	SELECT INSERT UPDATE	No access
Product development	No access	No access	SELECT INSERT UPDATE	No access	No access

Assess Global Requirements

Distributed database systems, by their very nature, service a variety of processes and applications and have a diverse user community. The preceding steps have been "application-centric"; we have not yet accounted for the requirements of other business processes and users. Even if this is a brand new system, confirming that the requirements of each business unit are understood and met means avoiding unexpected consequences later.

For data that is input for your application, you should identify the primary data source, the potential secondary sources, and the volatility of the data. This information yields insight into how you might access the data. For example, a nightly snapshot might work for data that is relatively static, whereas real-time access over a database link might be required for data that changes rapidly.

You also should establish a service-level agreement for the data that is input to your application. This entails defining the requirements for a variety of metrics, such as response time, availability, data freshness, and security. If the input data should fall outside the agreed-upon bounds, the data owners must notify you or your application, either through an automated alert or possibly through a more human form of communication. By setting these expectations prior to implementation, you can be sure that your application is able to obtain the input it needs in a timely manner, and the suppliers of the data will be prepared for the impact your application has on their infrastructure.

The process for validating your application's output data with other members of the organization is similar; you establish a service-level agreement with the data recipients in which you provide metrics about the data and arrange for automatic or manual notification of the interested parties if these metrics cannot be met.

The service-level agreements that result from this process are not the only valuable outcome. By coming to consensus, you will also verify who the organization's data caretakers are. These are the people responsible for:

- Defining and enforcing the business rules for the data

- Defining administrative procedures and administrative support

- Defining and implementing security requirements

Depending on the size and complexity of the organization, these people may all be in the same department or may be in offices in several geographic locations.

Propose and Validate Data Locations

At this point, you have sufficient information to make an educated recommendation of how data should be distributed. This information includes:

- Database usage matrix

- Infrastructure summary

- Data catalog

- Process-to-data mapping

- Service level agreements

Clearly, you are in a much better position to "put data where it is used most" than you were before going through these exercises.

Nevertheless, it *is* desirable to put the data where it is used most. Data used in active transaction processing stands to benefit the most from proper placement and to suffer the most from poor placement. Reference data (i.e., lookup tables) also needs to be deployed with care. Therefore, begin by focusing on processes with the most intensive activity (from the database usage matrix) and on the existing infrastructure to select potential data locations. If some of the databases already exist, confirm that they are deployed on hardware commensurate with their throughput requirements. Identify all viable sites, regardless of their current use.

You also should give consideration to which data distribution techniques suit your application. The options include:

Real-time access to remote data (i.e., over a database link)
This model is appropriate when the application must see the current version of the primary data source, with no latency whatsoever. For example, an order fulfillment application must have a real-time view of the organization's inventory.

Locally stored, read-only replica (i.e., a simple snapshot)
Read-only snapshots are appropriate when a certain amount of latency is acceptable, and, of course, when there is no requirement to insert or update data. For example, an order entry application can use a snapshot of the company's products that is updated every morning.

Locally stored, updateable replica (i.e., an updateable snapshot)
Updateable snapshots are an effective way to partition data horizontally. For example, the headquarters site may capture all sales data from all sales sites. All sales sites have a replica of the SALES table into which they insert records, but they neither keep nor need the sales transactions from other sales sites.

Asynchronous multi-master replication
Asynchronous multi-master replication is appropriate when a table must be shared among multiple sites, each requiring access to all records in the table, with the ability to manipulate records. For example, an ORDERS table must be accessible from the order entry site (which enters records), the shipping site (which fulfills the orders), and the billing site (which turns the orders into invoices). Generally, a certain amount of latency among peer sites is acceptable. And if it is not acceptable, many RDBMS vendors, including Oracle, support synchronous multi-master replication.

Synchronous multi-master replication
Synchronous replication ensures that transactions are committed simultaneously at all participating sites. This architecture can be used to provide a hot failover site. Since synchronous replication depends on the availability of all sites, it is not an advisable solution unless the participating hosts have very simple network connections—that is, on the same subnet with no dependency on routers. Ideally, the machines are directly connected.

Once you have determined placements and distribution methods for the application's data, you perform a "sanity check" on the emerging topology. You can estimate your network requirements by measuring the data flows generated by transaction processing and data flows generated by replication activity. Transactional data flow can be approximated as:

(bytes/transaction) × (peak transaction count/second)

The bandwidth required for replication activity is a function of the replication method, but you can make a rough estimate of the change rate for the replicated data. Finally, it never hurts to multiply your estimates by a fudge factor of 2 or three; operational behavior and load characteristics will inevitably change when the new system becomes available. At the end of this exercise, you will be able to sketch all sites in the distributed environment and the data flow required among them.

You are now in a position to validate the proposed architecture against your infrastructure's capacity as well as against other constraints such as your security requirements, service-level agreements, and availability requirements. Specific items to confirm include:

- Sufficient hardware resources for anticipated user volume and transaction rate.

- Sufficient network bandwidth.

- Support for two-phase commit protocol where required. (This is an issue primarily in heterogeneous distributed RDBMS environments.)

- Sufficient functionality and capacity of data replication technology.

- Adherence to service-level agreements reached earlier.

- Adherence to the identified security requirements.

Of course, you may need to make some adjustments to the proposed location scheme, but equipped with the information gathered during this process, you will know the consequences. In addition, the documentation this process creates is valuable not only for positioning your data but also for understanding the application as a whole.

Application Partitioning Strategies

Application partitioning refers to deploying different components of an application at various locations. For example, an order entry application may consist of:

- Data entry screens on order entry clerks' PCs

- Bar code scanners collecting shipping information at the fulfillment center

- A web server hosting management reporting

- Business rule enforcement via stored procedures in the database

The order entry application is the sum of all of these parts. The components of a partitioned, or tiered, application always fall into one of three broad categories: user interface, business logic, or data access logic.

As you design a distributed database, you must make decisions about where to locate different types of processing. Some of the choices are obvious: bar code data collection has to occur where the bar codes are. But in other cases, the decision is not so obvious. Where should we enforce the requirement that customers cannot place new orders if their accounts are more than 90 days in arrears? What factors should you consider when you make these choices?

Actually, application partitioning entails both a hardware level and a software (or logical) level. At the hardware level, we decide what equipment is best suited for various portions of the application. And at the logical level, we decide where business rules will be enforced, how the user interface will work, and what data access methods we will provide. The logical application partitioning always precedes the hardware partitioning. Table 5-6 presents these two levels in the context of the order entry application described before.

Table 5-6. Hardware and Logical Application Partitioning Considerations

Hardware Partitioning Choices	Logical Partitioning Choices
PC clients will host software for data entry.	The application's presentation layer will be written with Oracle's Developer 2000 tool set, and all textual data will be converted to uppercase before sending it to the database. All business rules will be enforced in the database with triggers and stored procedures.
Scanners from Intermec and Symbol will be used for bar code data collection.	All shipping transactions will be tracked with bar code scanners at the fulfillment center.
The web server for management reporting will run on a Sun Ultra2.	Management reporting will be provided over the intranet using a Netscape web server and CGI scripts.
The database at the order entry site will run on a Sun Enterprise 6000.	All order entry transactions will be performed in a database at the order entry site.
The database at the fulfillment site will run on a Sun Enterprise 3000.	All shipping transactions will be performed in a database at the fulfillment center.

Business rule enforcement is a pivotal issue in every application partitioning scheme. You can do it within the database, in the client portion of the application or in some intermediate tier. What are the pros and cons of these approaches?

Enforcing Business Rules in the Database Tier

One could make the argument that the database is the only sensible place to enforce business rules. By placing these requirements in the database, we can be certain that any application, current or planned, will always obey the rules that we have defined, because there is no fooling the database. For example, suppose we have a requirement that we manufacture 1000 more racing bicycles when the inventory falls below 50. We could enforce this rule by placing a trigger on the INVENTORY table which creates a record in the MANUFACTURE_QUEUE table when we hit the reorder point.

If we codify this rule in the database, we can be sure that every application will respect it, even if the developers are unaware of the rule. We can also be sure that the rule will be enforced in exactly the same way by every application; there is no room for interpretation or misinterpretation. And application code is substantially simplified. One could even make the case that performance is better because we do not need to ship the transactions related to the rule enforcement over the network. These are the compelling reasons that lead most RDBMS vendors to introduce triggers and stored procedures.

With such a convincing case for business rule enforcement in the database, why would one ever decide to do otherwise? The problem is that some applications simply are not suited to this architecture. Those that rely on message passing between application tiers or asynchronous processing cannot readily benefit from database business rule enforcement. Moreover, the fact that all rules are absolute may not be appropriate for all applications.

Enforcing Business Rules in the Presentation Tier

The dawning of powerful client development tools, coupled with the advent of powerful desktop hardware, brought about the trend to perform as much work as possible on the client. When business rules as well as a presentation layer are deployed on the client, we have a *fat client*.

Originally, the appeal of the fat client was that it could relieve the server of some of its duties, thereby improving overall performance. Although this load balancing may still be a case for the fat client, that doesn't mean we should rely on desktop machines to take up the slack for an inadequate server. But there are situations in which server-based business rule enforcement simply cannot outperform client-based logic. We have found, for example, that intensive transaction processing (i.e., hundreds of transactions per second) does better when the SQL statements come from the client as opposed to stored procedures.

The obvious disadvantage of client-based business rule enforcement is that the same logic must be coded in every interface. If you allow data entry via applications written in HTML, Power Builder, and Developer 2000, you will have to write and maintain the logic in three places.

You will also have to ensure that the logic is consistent and that there is no other access path to the database that would allow the logic to be inadvertently bypassed.

Creating a Third Tier

The emerging trend is to place a middle tier—called the *application layer*—between the client and the server. This layer may be implemented with a CORBA, DCOM, or similar object-based architecture. The advent of the Web has been a driving force behind the three-tier architecture because organizations find that they can inexpensively deploy applications that are accessible from any client that can run a browser. The client is responsible only for messaging the application tier.

 Although the application layer can include logic to enforce business rules, it is not a requirement of the three-tier approach; Oracle's Network Computing Architecture (NCA) advocates the database tier as the home for business rule logic.

Regardless of where the business rules are enforced, there are several advantages to moving application logic off both the client and the database server:

Use of "thin" clients
  As we have already stated, any machine that can run a browser can use a three-tier application. Thus, the cost of putting the application in the user's hands can be as low as the cost of a set-top box or other inexpensive device.

Implementation in a heterogeneous environment
  By storing database APIs in the application tier, clients and application modules access all databases using a single set of API calls. The database interface is the same regardless of the RDBMS. Of course, this transparency assumes that developers have designed and coded the API calls.

Scalability and load balancing
  The three-tier architecture lends itself to scalability because application components are easy to isolate and can run on equipment that is specifically sized and tuned to suit the application. Load balancing can often be realized by deploying TP monitors.

Code reuse

> Once a library of database APIs is developed, it can be used for future applications. If APIs are well documented, future development efforts should be able to pick and choose components they need and write only those pieces that are specific to the new application.

Flexibility

> If application-layer APIs are designed properly, they mask the specifics of the database interface from both the clients and other components. This transparency simplifies endeavors such as RDBMS software upgrades or even a migration to a new RDBMS engine.

Standards-based APIs

> The application-tier components should be built with languages and tools that are not specific to any particular RDBMS vendor. Most notably, using C, C++, Java, and HTML ensures that no dependencies on a proprietary language or interface sneak into the code.

Of course, there is a price exacted for all of these benefits. The principal drawback is that a multitiered environment is more complex to manage in both the development and production environments. In order to realize code reuse, for example all APIs must be thoroughly documented and must work exactly as advertised. Otherwise, duplicate functionality will creep into the API library, leading to confusion about how the APIs should be used. Version-control logistics also become more complex. New API versions must be tested and certified as being compatible with other library components. Finally, the additional tier means additional decisions about how the application can and should be partitioned. In short, the three-tier approach offers fantastic flexibility, but the additional complexity may outweigh the benefits for all but the largest systems.

How Many Tiers Are Right for You?

Now that I've explained the fundamental differences between two-tier (client/server) and three-tier architectures, how can you one decide which approach is appropriate for the application at hand? Obviously, there are no hard and fast rules, but Table 5-7 offers some guidelines.

Table 5-7. Guidelines for an Application Architecture

Situations Calling for a Two-Tier Architecture	Situations Calling for a Three-Tier Architecture
The application consists of fewer than 50 logical components. (In a typical client/server application, a logical component roughly equates to a data entry form.)	The application consists of 50 or more logical components.
The database tiers use the same RDBMS.	There is a heterogeneous database tier.

Table 5-7. Guidelines for an Application Architecture (continued)

Situations Calling for a Two-Tier Architecture	Situations Calling for a Three-Tier Architecture
The application performs fewer than 10 transactions per second.	The application has a sustained transaction rate in excess of 10 transactions per second.
The application supports 500 or fewer concurrent users.	The application supports more than 500 concurrent users.
The application is likely to be replaced or rewritten within five years.	The application's life expectancy is more than five years.

Regardless of how many tiers will house the application, you will have to perform some partitioning. In *Data Replication*, Marie Buretta proposes a step-by-step approach to decomposing an application for partitioning, summarized here:

1. Distinguish user interface components from "the rest." User interface components generally consist of data entry screens, predefined reports, and data collection equipment such as bar code scanners and cash registers.

2. That which is not a user interface component is either business logic or data access logic. Identify and separate the two.

3. Associate the business logic from Step 2 with specific business transactions, such as order entry, customer account creation, and so on.

4. Map the business transactions from Step 3 with specific database transactions. For example, taking a new order for a product would equate to something like this:

```
INSERT INTO ORDERS (order_id, customer_id, order_date)
...

INSERT INTO ORDER_ITEMS( order_id, product_id, units, uom, unit_cost )
...
```

   Note that the preceding example includes two transactions that must be completed as a unit to create an order. The mapping of business transactions to database transactions must include an account of such interdependencies.

5. Identify decision points and constraints that occur in the business transactions. An example of a decision point is the requirement to replenish stock of an item when the reorder point is reached. An example of a constraint is the refusal to accept orders from customers whose accounts are more than 90 days in arrears.

6. Identify dependencies among business transactions. For example, an order must be shipped before it can be billed. In a complex application, it may be desirable to perform operations in parallel. By identifying transactional dependencies, you will know which transactions can and cannot occur simultaneously and which transactions can be deferred.

Having determined these details about the application's transactions, you can make informed decisions about where to place its components. If you are using a client/server model, the client should host nothing more than the user interface logic; business logic belongs in the database. In the case of a three-tier architecture, business logic may be deployed in the application tier. If so, it is important that the machines that host this business logic or require a high volume of data access reside in close proximity to the RDBMS servers. In particular, these machines should not make a WAN connection to the database if it can be avoided.

Procedural Replication

Procedural replication refers to manipulating remote data indirectly by making procedure calls. For example, if you want to make a 5% price hike for all products in the remote PRODUCT_PRICES table, you might make a call like this:

```
BEGIN
    PriceMaint.PercentageIncrease( pct_in => 5);
END;
```

This procedure goes to the remote database and executes the statement:

```
UPDATE PRODUCT_PRICES
SET price = price * 1.05;
```

Since the stored procedure itself resides in the target database(s), no data travels over the network, just the name of the stored procedure and the passed parameters. Nor does the calling database need to maintain a connection to the remote database while the procedure is executed. Once the calling database delivers the call to the target locations, its work is finished.

Procedural replication is appropriate for operations that manipulate a significant amount of data on a replicated table. For example, the price increase just described changes every row in the PRODUCT_PRICES table. If you were to perform the update locally and let the row-level replication mechanism propagate all of the updated rows, the network traffic could be crippling. In general, you should not attempt to use row-level replication for any transaction that affects more than 20% of a table's records.

When using procedural replication, you must take care that procedure calls that have transactional dependencies are made in the correct order at the remote sites. For example, a call to HR_APP.HireEmployee would have to precede a call to HR_APP.PayEmployee. The replication technology that you use should ensure that the order of procedure calls is preserved.

Procedural replication is described in greater detail in Chapter 14, *Procedural Replication.*

6

Oracle's Distributed System Implementation

Oracle has gone to some lengths to ensure that their RDBMS product meets Chris Date's objectives for a distributed database system, which we described in Chapter 5, *Designing a Distributed System*. This chapter examines how Oracle networking and RDBMS products have addressed each of these objectives and discusses techniques you can utilize to achieve these goals in your own environment. I'll also look at the inherent limitations and even contradictions in realizing these goals.

Meeting the 12 Objectives with Oracle

To review, the 12 objectives for a successful distributed database system, which we discussed in Chapter 5, are:

1. Local autonomy

2. No reliance on a single site

3. Continuous operation

4. Location transparency

5. Fragmentation independence

6. Replication independence

7. Distributed query processing

8. Distributed transaction management

9. Hardware independence

10. Operating system independence

11. Network independence

12. RDBMS independence

As I said in Chapter 5, these are goals, not requirements. We cannot, for example, reasonably expect a distributed database system to provide continuous operation in perpetuity. Nevertheless, the architects of the Oracle RDBMS have answered each of these goals, as described in the following sections.

Local Autonomy

Local autonomy requires that an individual database be fully functional even if it cannot contact other systems in the distributed environment and that each site be responsible for its own data integrity, security, and management. Unfortunately, it is not possible to attain both local autonomy and location transparency, because the latter goal requires 100% availability of data at a remote location. Location transparency implies reliance on a network connection and the availability of a remote database.

Oracle introduced *snapshots* in Oracle7 as a way to make remote data accessible in the local database. A snapshot is essentially a local copy of a remote table, which (in theory) can be refreshed as often as once per second. (This frequency is only in theory because, for one thing, it may take more than one second to refresh the snapshot.) As an example, the database administrator at the sales site of the fictitious Bigwheel Bicycle company could make a snapshot of the PRODUCTS table from the headquarters site as follows:

```
CREATE SNAPSHOT products
REFRESH FAST
START WITH SYSDATE
NEXT TRUNC(sysdate+1)
AS
    SELECT  product_id, product_name
    FROM    products@PHQS.BIGWHEEL.COM;
```

This snapshot stores the contents of the headquarters PRODUCTS table in the local sales database and refreshes the contents of the table every day at midnight. The details of snapshot creation and management are described in Chapter 11, *Basic Replication.*

Snapshots are a way to view (and update with some restrictions) remote data without actually connecting to the remote site. The obvious advantage of this technique is that data is always accessible to the local site—hence local autonomy. The price for this convenience is data latency, because the data in a snapshot is only as current as the last refresh.

The second aspect of local autonomy is management independence. Oracle achieves this independence in a variety of ways. First, there is no such thing as a "child" database. Every Oracle database has its own data dictionary, its own user accounts, and its own control processes. Although a database may be logically subservient to another, Oracle does not require or include any functional dependencies. Second, Oracle guarantees interoperability among all of its supported versions on all platforms. Thus, any site in a distributed system *should* be able to follow its own upgrade path. Of course there are some limitations to this interoperability. In particular, if you are using the advanced replication facilities, Oracle generally recommends that all participating databases be on the same version of the RDBMS.

No Reliance on a Single Site

The functionality and performance of a distributed system should not depend on any single site. This is certainly a noble ambition, but there is nothing within the Oracle RDBMS that guarantees its realization. However, Oracle does provide the functionality required to design a system that meets, or nearly meets, this requirement.

The two predominant strategies for ensuring high availability are advanced replication and Oracle parallel server. These are two very different approaches, each with its inherent advantages and disadvantages. The advanced replication approach entails creating two or more separate databases that mirror specified data, as shown in Figure 6-1.

The replication can take place synchronously or asynchronously, and there is no hard limit on the number of sites that can participate. If any particular database fails or becomes unavailable, processing can be directed to a different one.

Oracle parallel server is a high-availability model in which two or more computers run Oracle instances that access the same physical database. This model protects against the loss of a computer, but the physical storage is still a single point of failure. Oracle parallel server generally requires clustering software from the operating system vendor.

To ensure that a distributed system's performance is not dictated by any single site, developers and database administrators have to examine carefully the application's distributed queries and transactions. Although Oracle can execute distributed operations without any special coding, it is often well worth the effort to tune SQL statements. In addition, the DBA should take care to configure the *INIT.ORA* parameters relevant to distributed transactions, such as COMMIT_POINT_ STRENGTH.

In short, Oracle provides the tools to design a distributed system that is free from reliance on a single site, but it is your responsibility to design it.

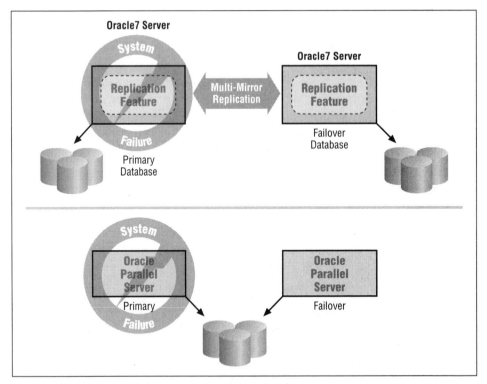

Figure 6-1. Oracle parallel server versus advanced replication

Continuous Operation

Continuous operation of a distributed system means that no maintenance tasks should require an outage of the entire system. Maintenance tasks may include upgrades to the operating system or RDBMS or the addition and deletion of participating sites.

If the Oracle distributed system is built on database links and simple replication (i.e., read-only snapshots), then there are no maintenance activities that would require an outage of the entire distributed environment. Sites can be added or removed at any time, and upgrades can be executed without impacting participating sites.

However, if you are using the advanced replication facilities, Oracle imposes certain limitations. Most significantly, if you wish to add a new master or snapshot site to a replicated environment, you must coordinate the addition so that the data at the new site includes data changes that may have occurred *while* the new site is being instantiated. Refer to the descriptions of the built-in packages DBMS_OFFLINE_SNAPSHOT and DBMS_OFFLINE_OG in Appendix A, *Built-in Packages for Distributed Systems*.

Location Transparency

Location transparency, or location independence, means that neither applications nor users need to know the actual location of the tables, views, or stored procedures they are accessing. Oracle provides support for location transparency via database links and synonyms.

Suppose that the fictitious Bigwheel Bicycle company wants to make its PRODUCTS table visible to its sales site, while the actual table resides at the headquarters site. We can configure the sales sites so that a reference to PRODUCTS maps to the table in the headquarters site by creating a database link from PSLS.BIGWHEEL.COM to PHQS.BIGWHEEL.COM and creating a synonym for the remote object:

```
CREATE DATABASE LINK PHQS.BIGWHEEL.COM
USING 'prodhq';

CREATE SYNONYM products
FOR products@PHQS.BIGWHEEL.COM;
```

 The public database link in the previous example is a private link, which means that the Oracle account that created the link is the only account that can utilize it. See Chapter 4, *Distributed Database Security*, for details about different strategies for accessing remote objects and managing privileges on remote objects specifically.

Of course, this solution is not without its limitations. For example, if the network connection between PSLS.BIGWHEEL.COM and PHQS.BIGWHEEL.COM fails, users at the sales site will become painfully aware of the fact that the PRODUCTS table resides in a remote database:

```
SQL> SELECT product_id, product_name
  2  FROM products;

ERROR at line 2:
ORA-12203: TNS:unable to connect to destination
```

Dependency on a network connection, as well as the availability of the remote database, are unavoidable side effects of providing location transparency.

Fragmentation Independence

Fragmentation refers to the partitioning of data across multiple sites. The data may be partitioned horizontally (i.e., by record) or vertically (i.e., by field). Oracle uses snapshots and/or views to support both partitioning methods.

You might want to perform horizontal partitioning if your data has a regional component. For example, if your company's sales force accesses the CUSTOMERS table, it might make sense to store only data associated with a particular region in the corresponding database.

You could implement this partitioning scheme in at least three different ways:

- Create a read-only snapshot of the headquarters-site CUSTOMERS table in each regional database. For example, in California's sales database we would create the following snapshot:

```
CREATE SNAPSHOT customers
REFRESH FAST
START WITH SYSDATE
NEXT TRUNC(sysdate+1)
AS
    SELECT  customer_id, address, state, telephone, sales_rep_id
    FROM    customers@PHQS.BIGWHEEL.COM
    WHERE   state = 'CA';
```

- If the California site requires UPDATE and INSERT privileges on the CUSTOMERS table, we could create an updateable snapshot:

```
CREATE SNAPSHOT customers
REFRESH FAST
START WITH SYSDATE
NEXT TRUNC(sysdate+1)
FOR UPDATE
AS
    SELECT  customer_id, address, state, telephone, sales_rep_id
    FROM    customers@PHQS.BIGWHEEL.COM
    WHERE   state = 'CA';
```

  The creation of the updateable snapshot assumes that the appropriate replication configuration steps have been completed. Refer to Chapter 11 for details on how to create updateable snapshots.

- We could simply create a view at the California site that references the appropriate customers in the headquarters database:

```
CREATE VIEW customers AS
    SELECT  customer_id, address, state, telephone, sales_rep_id
    FROM    customers@PHQS.BIGWHEEL.COM;
```

  Of course, this view depends on the headquarters site's availability.

Vertical partitioning makes sense when you want to view data from two or more tables at two or more sites as a single relationship or when you want to exclude columns in a table from a particular site or group of users. For example, you might want to join the CUSTOMERS table from the headquarters site (where all customer records are stored) with the ORDERS table at the catalog order site to link sales volume with regions.

We can use a view to create this relationship:

```
CREATE VIEW regional_sales_volume AS
     SELECT c.customer_id,
            c.address,
            c.state,
            c.telephone,
            c.sales_rep_id,
            o.total_amount
     FROM   customers@PHQS.BIGWHEEL.COM c,
            orders@PCOE.BIGWHEEL.COM o
     WHERE  c.customer_id = o.customer_id;
```

Note that this relationship requires the availability of the headquarters site (PHQS.BIGWHEEL.COM) and the catalog order entry site (PCOE.BIG-WHEEL.COM).

Replication Independence

Oracle introduced the *symmetric replication* feature in Version 7.1. Subsequent releases up to and including Version 8.1 have included substantial improvements to its functionality and performance. Oracle has also changed its name to the less picturesque *advanced replication* facilities. But by any name, Oracle replication offers a diverse and robust product set, including:

- Read-only and updateable snapshots

- Multi-master replication

- Built-in conflict resolution methods

- Support for BLOB and CLOB datatypes

- Synchronous or asynchronous propagation

Part II of this book is devoted to Oracle's replication products; refer to the chapters in that part for details.

Distributed Query Processing

Support for distributed query processing is a corollary of location transparency. And Oracle does allow you to issue queries against remote data, even queries that join data in multiple databases. Users and application developers need not include any special commands or incantations just because the tables being queried are in diverse locations.

However, it is worth pointing out that the *optimization* of these queries is something of a concern, at least for application developers and database administrators. The performance of a query against the same tables can vary wildly, depending on where the tables are located. Judicious use of the EXPLAIN PLAN utility and/or AUTOTRACE will help to determine whether a query is suffering because of its distributed nature. In particular, queries that join with all records in a remote table tend to perform poorly.

Distributed Transaction Management

Just as location transparency implies support for distributed query processing, it also implies support for distributed transactions. A distributed transaction is one that applies DML at multiple locations. The classic example is the credit/debit transaction: when a bank wires funds from one branch to another, it must guarantee that the account receiving the funds is credited if and only if the account sending the funds is debited. The mechanism that guarantees this integrity is the two-phase commit protocol. Oracle introduced support of the two-phase commit with Version 7.0.

As with distributed query processing, distributed transactions will work without requiring any special coding or commands, but application developers and database administrators are well advised to make accommodations for the distributed work. Specifically, the application should include logic to trap errors relating to distributed transactions; these are errors in the range ORA-02040 to ORA-02099. Similarly, database administrators should ensure that the *INIT.ORA* configuration parameters are set appropriately for all participating databases. These parameters include:

    COMMIT_POINT_STRENGTH
    COMPATIBILITY
    DISTRIBUTED_LOCK_TIMEOUT
    DISTRIBUTED_TRANSACTIONS
    GLOBAL_NAMES
    OPEN_LINKS

The DBA should also be prepared to monitor the data dictionary views DBA_2PC_NEIGHBORS and DBA_2PC_PENDING.

Hardware Independence

A distributed system should be able to run on any hardware platform. Since its earliest days, Oracle has prided itself as being the only database that runs on *anything*, even your palmtop. Although you cannot currently run an Oracle database on your pager or cell phone, it is shipping on dozens of platforms.

Operating System Independence

Oracle is certified on at least as many operating systems as hardware platforms. However, be warned that the more popular operating systems monopolize the attention of most of Oracle's development and support staff. So, if you are running on HP-UX, Sun Solaris, or Windows NT, you will not have any problems acquiring the latest versions of Oracle's RDBMS. However, those of you on operating systems that are less popular and/or nearing extinction, such as VM or VMS, will have to wait.

Network Independence

Oracle's SQL*Net and Net8 products ship with the most popular protocol adapters. Currently, these include:

TCP/IP
DECnet
SPX/IPX
LU6.2

RDBMS Independence.

Speaking of RDBMS independence may seem ironic when describing how Oracle adheres to C. J. Date's 12 requirements for an ideal distributed system. Yet Oracle can interact with other RDBMS vendors. Oracle's "Gateway" products include the following:

Transparent Gateways

Transparent Gateways provide SQL access to non-Oracle RDBMSs including DB2, SQL/400, Teradata, Rdb, RMS, Non-Stop SQL, and Bull GCOS6. These Gateway products typically run on the machine with the non-Oracle RDBMS as opposed to where the Oracle database server resides.

Procedural Gateway for APPC

This product provides remote procedure call (RPC) support via PL/SQL to execute CICS, IMS/TM, and IDMS/DC transactions accessing mainframe data sources such as Adabas, CA-IDMS, IMS, VSAM, DB2, and DatacomDB. This technology is best for accessing data sources that support OLTP applications. It's currently available on the IBM RS/6000 with porting underway to both HP-UX and Sun Solaris. Procedural Gateway for APPC does not require any Oracle software on the mainframe system.

Transparent Gateway for DRDA

Transparent Gateway for DRDA provides SQL access to DRDA-enabled databases including DB2, SQL/DS, and SQL/400. This technology is best used by sites (typically very large IBM mainframe shops) requiring IBM protocol compliance or for an application that connects to multiple DRDA-enabled databases. This product is currently available on the IBM RS/6000. Transparent Gateway for DRDA does not require Oracle software on the target system.

Open Gateway Toolkits

Open Gateway Toolkits allow you to build customized gateways to data sources that are not supported by the other Oracle gateway products. For example, you could use the Transparent Gateway Toolkit to build SQL access to a Sybase database.

Conclusions

To the extent that Chris Date's 12 objectives are attainable, Oracle has attained them. There are certain implied contradictions, such as the requirement that a distributed system supply location transparency *and* be immune from site outages. But even these challenges can be addressed with such Oracle products as the advanced replication facilities.

Oracle's Global Data Dictionary

Chapter 5 introduced the concept of a *global data dictionary*, which is a repository that uniquely identifies all objects in a distributed database system. The challenge is to implement a global data dictionary without creating a single master site in the process and without sacrificing the notion of location transparency.

Global Naming

Oracle's solution to this challenge hinges on the concept of *global naming*. In Oracle7, Oracle introduced an *INIT.ORA* parameter GLOBAL_NAMES, which, when set to TRUE, ensures that every database participating in a distributed environment has a unique name.

 You should make a habit of setting the GLOBAL_NAMES parameter to TRUE even if you are not in a distributed environment. If you ever have to switch the parameter to TRUE after it has been FALSE, you may encounter conflicts with other database names in your environment. In addition, Oracle has stated that they may require the GLOBAL_NAMES parameter to be TRUE in future versions.

You can determine the name of any given database by querying the GLOBAL_ NAME data dictionary view:

```
SQL> SELECT global_name FROM global_name;

GLOBAL_NAME
--------------------------------------------------
PHQS.BIGWHEEL.COM
```

The database's global name defaults to the concatenation of the *INIT.ORA* parameters DB_NAME and DB_DOMAIN. However, you can also change the global name to any value with an ALTER DATABASE statement:

```
ALTER DATABASE RENAME GLOBAL_NAME TO NEWNAME.BIGWHEEL.COM;
```

Why do you care about a database's global name? Because if the GLOBAL_NAMES parameter is set to TRUE, then any database link created in this database must have the same name as the global name of the database to which it connects:

The following is valid:

```
CREATE DATABASE LINK PSLS.BIGWHEEL.COM
USING 'production_sales';
```

The following is invalid:

```
CREATE DATABASE LINK prodsales
USING 'production_sales';
```

With GLOBAL_NAMES enabled, every database link with the same name connects to the same database, and every link into a given database has the same name. Thus, every object in the distributed environment is guaranteed to be uniquely identified if it is specified with a schema name and a link name; for example, SPROCKET.PRODUCTS@PHQS.BIGWHEEL.COM refers to the same object for every database in the Bigwheel Bicycle environment.

Data Dictionary Views and Location Transparency

The connection between global naming and the global data dictionary is in the Oracle data dictionary view DBA_SYNONYMS, summarized in Table 6-1.

Table 6-1. DBA_SYNONYMS Data Dictionary View

Field Name	Description
owner	The owner of the view
synonym_name	The synonym
table_owner	The owner of the object (may be a table, view, procedure, or package)
table_name	The object name
db_link	For remote objects, the name of the database link to the database in which the object resides

Obviously, if GLOBAL_NAMES is enabled, then the db_link field in this data dictionary view is not only the name of the link to the remote database but also the name of the remote database. So the same values for synonym_name, table_owner, table_name, and db_link will refer to the same object for all participants in the distributed system.

Oracle's synonyms are the key to providing location transparency because, as we have seen, a synonym can shield local users from having to know about the location of a given object. At the same time, the DBA_SYNONYMS data dictionary view contains the details about remote objects for those who need to know. Thus, synonyms solve the problem of creating a global data dictionary that uniquely identifies all objects in the distributed environment while ensuring location transparency.

7

Sample Configurations

There are probably as many distributed database configurations as there are distributed databases. This chapter provides an overview of the most common problems that distributed database systems can solve and discusses the choices and trade-offs associated with each. I hope that one or more of these sample architectures corresponds to yours.

The High-Availability System

The generally accepted definition of a *high-availability system* is one that is operational 99.9% of the time, which translates to no more than 8 hours and 45 minutes of downtime per year. Most hardware vendors have products that are designed to ensure the high availability of servers, disk drives, and other components. In the case of servers, the recommended solution is usually a clustering technology. In some cases, high-availability systems deliver the added benefit of scalability because they require redundant computers that can share the workload.

Designing high availability into a database system, however, takes more than just buying high-availability hardware. Oracle gives you three choices for creating a high-availability system:

- A hot standby database

- Oracle parallel server (OPS)

- Advanced replication

Of these three, the only one that is really a distributed database is the advanced replication solution.

The Hot Standby Database

Oracle's hot standby database solution can best be described as a database that is in a state of perpetual media recovery. The strategy is to create a backup of your database on a second machine and to ship your archived redo logs to the backup machine, where they are applied to the backup database.

In the event that your primary database fails, you can conclude the recovery process on the standby database, open it, and direct your users to it.

The steps to create a hot standby database are as follows:

1. Perform a backup (hot or cold) of your primary database. Note that your primary database must be in ARCHIVELOG mode.

2. Create a control file for the standby database by issuing the ALTER DATABASE CREATE STANDBY CONTROLFILE command from your primary database:

```
Oracle Server Manager Release 3.0.4.0.0 - Production

(c) Copyright 1997, Oracle Corporation.  All Rights Reserved.

Oracle8 Enterprise Edition Release 8.0.4.1.0 - Production
With the Partitioning and Objects options
PL/SQL Release 8.0.4.1.0 - Production

SVRMGR> connect internal
Connected.
SVRMGR> ALTER DATABASE CREATE STANDBY CONTROLFILE
  2> AS '/u/oracle/admin/PHQS/bdump/standbyPHQS.ctl'
  3> /
Statement processed.
```

3. Archive the current redo logs of the primary database:

```
SVRMGR> ALTER DATABASE ARCHIVELOG CURRENT
  2> /
Statement processed.
```

4. Transfer the files from the backup performed in Step 1, the standby control file created in Step 2, and the archived redo log from Step 3 to the backup machine.

 Your life will be much easier if you use an identical directory structure for your data, configuration, and archived redo log files on the backup machine. Oracle assumes that the structure is identical, but if you must use a different directory structure, you must set the *INIT.ORA* parameters DB_FILE_NAME_CONVERT and LOG_FILE_NAME_CONVERT in the standby database. For example:

```
FILE_NAME_CONVERT = '"/vol01/oradata/PHQS" "/vol01/
                     oradata/STANDBY/PHQS"'
```

---

5. Start the standby database on the backup machine:

```
SVRMGR> CONNECT INTERNAL
Connected.
SVRMGR> STARTUP NOMOUNT
 2> /
Statement processed.
SVRMGR> ALTER DATABASE MOUNT STANDBY DATABASE
 2> /
Statement processed.
SVRMGR> ALTER DATABASE
 2> RECOVER FROM '/u/oracle/admin/PHQS/arch'
 3> STANDBY DATABASE
 4> /
```

The standby database is now mounted and has begun media recovery, applying archived redo logs from the directory specified in the *INIT.ORA* parameter LOG_ ARCHIVE_DEST. In order to keep the standby database up to date, you must copy archived redo logs from the primary machine to the backup machine and apply them with the ALTER DATABASE RECOVER FROM command.

Advantages and disadvantages of the hot standby database

The chief advantage of the standby database (and in my opinion, its only redeeming virtue) is that it is very easy to set up and operate. Scripting the job to copy archived redo logs to the backup machine is trivial, and switching to the standby in the event of failure can be done in a matter of minutes.

However, the standby database does have some undesirable properties. First, the standby machine itself essentially goes to waste; it must be held in reserve for the event of failure, doing nothing but applying archived redo logs. Although you could use its processing power for miscellaneous jobs, they must accept the fact that they may be halted at any time. This restriction is especially frustrating because the backup machine should be of the same capacity as the machine it is mirroring—generally an expensive one!

Another downside of the standby database solution is that once the standby is activated, it completely replaces the primary database; there is no going back. Thus, once the problem on the primary machine is corrected, the only way to put it back into service is to create a hot standby database on it and activate it. This switch back to the primary machine takes at least as long as a full database backup.

 In Oracle8*i*, the hot standby database can be opened in read-only mode and can then go back to being a standby without requiring a complete rebuild.

Oracle Parallel Server

Oracle parallel server is a technology that allows one physical database to be accessed by database instances running on two or more computers. This architecture affords high availability because if one of the machines fails, processing can continue on the remaining node(s).

Oracle8 has advanced the technology so that, in some cases, users' connections are remapped to a different node transparently. And, unlike the standby database architecture, each of the nodes in an OPS configuration can be used for processing. In this sense, OPS is a high-availability architecture that also provides scalability.

Advantages and disadvantages of Oracle parallel server

The theory of OPS is fantastic: it offers high availability by virtue of multiple nodes, and it can scale since nodes can be added to the configuration. Alas, the theory of OPS differs somewhat from the reality. The most significant issue that prevents OPS from being a perfect solution is that of *pinging*. A ping occurs when a user on one node of a parallel server requests data that has been modified by a user on another node. When this happens, the data must be written from the modifying node back to the database, from which the requesting node reads it (see Figure 7-1).

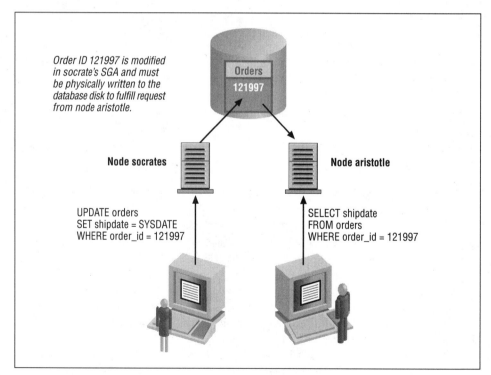

Figure 7-1. Oracle parallel server pinging

As you would imagine, pinging is extremely expensive, and an excessive amount of it can make OPS performance *worse* than the performance of a single machine! You can assume that any application that is not designed with OPS in mind will experience performance degradation with OPS.

You can design an application that minimizes pinging. The trick is to ensure that any given set of data is modified on only one node and that users on other nodes do not access data that another node modifies. For example, if the database serves multiple applications, you can designate individual nodes for specific applications. Another solution, for databases that house only one application, is to use partition tables, available with Oracle8. For example, a CUSTOMER table might be partitioned on CUSTOMER_ID, and Server A would handle activity for customers 0 through 10,000, Server B would handle customers 10,001 thorugh 20,000, and so on. Figure 7-2 shows this situation.

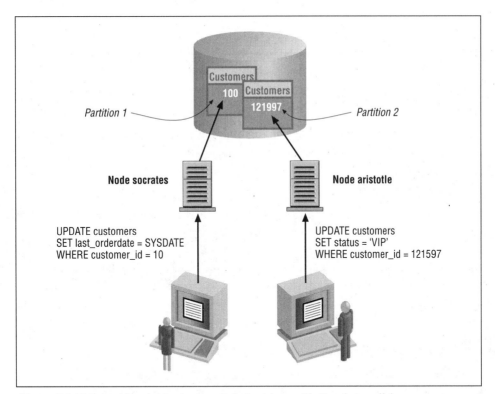

Figure 7-2. Using table partitioning to minimize pings with Oracle parallel server

In order to direct activity to the appropriate node, you would have to include a transaction monitor, or your application itself would have to have the intelligence to send transactions to the appropriate node. Of course, data partitioning is generally not this simple, and it often requires schema denormalization to be effective.

Other issues with OPS include the fact that most popular hardware vendors are still perfecting their clustering technologies. Sun, for example, has only recently shipped cluster support for more than two nodes. In addition, because of the overhead of the operating system's clustering software and the distributed lock manager, each additional node added to a cluster does not add one machine's worth of processing power, as shown in Figure 7-3.

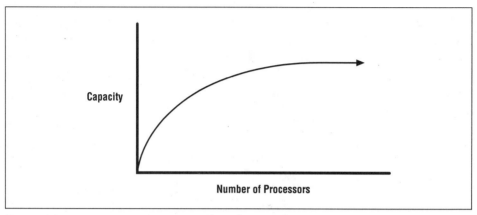

Figure 7-3. Processing power versus number of processors

In short, OPS can be an ideal solution for both high availability and scalability, but the benefits are not automatic.

Advanced Replication

One of the intended uses of advanced replication is to provide a high-availability solution. As described in Chapter 12, *Multi-Master Replication*, data changes can be propagated synchronously among the nodes participating in a replicated environment. In effect, you can have a system in which data is guaranteed to be identical at multiple locations. Such an architecture delivers not only high availability but also horizontal scalability, because application users can be directed to any node, as shown in Figure 7-4.

Advantages and disadvantages of advanced replication

Unlike the hot standby database, the advanced replication architecture allows you to utilize all machines in your environment. Unlike OPS, with advanced replication there is no issue with pinging. In addition, advanced replication provides a built-in redundancy since data is replicated at all sites. Also, there is no potential for conflicts with synchronous propagation.

Unfortunately, there is no free lunch; advanced replication in general has its costs, and synchronous propagation in particular exacts its toll. Synchronous propaga-

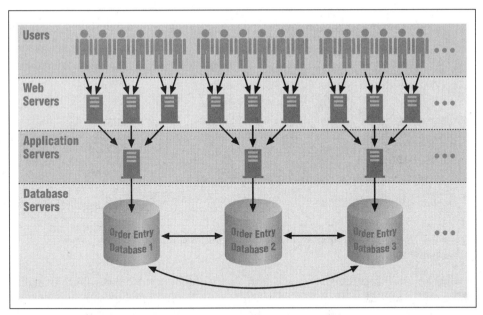

Figure 7-4. Using advanced replication to achieve horizontal scalability

tion utilizes the two-phase commit protocol to ensure that every transaction is applied at every site. The two-phase commit incurs the overhead of having to coordinate every transaction: each site must go through the prepare phase and notify the global coordinator, which then instructs all sites to commit or roll back their work. The more sites involved, the more communication necessary for each transaction. And, if any of the sites is unable to commit for any reason, such as a network problem or a database crash, all insert, update, and delete activity will cease, and the application will hang. Therefore, it is critical to provide as much redundancy as possible in terms of disk mirroring and network connectivity. Alternatively, you can use asynchronous propagation and accept the corresponding latency and potential for conflicts. Figure 7-5 shows a sample configuration.

Another issue with advanced replication is its overhead. By Oracle's account, advanced replication requires six times as much shared pool usage, and asynchronous propagation generates four times as much undo activity. As with OPS, regardless of the propagation method, the addition of a machine does not yield a corresponding increase in capacity.

Furthermore, as with OPS, it is a good idea to partition your application in such a way that the activity on any particular node accesses unique data. This is especially beneficial if you are using asynchronous propagation because partitioning will minimize the chance of conflicts. If you are using asynchronous replication with a high propagation frequency, you should include conflict resolution techniques such as Site Priority and Latest Timestamp on your replicated tables.

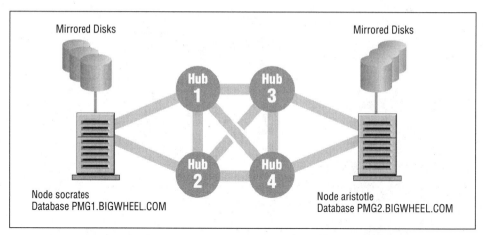

Figure 7-5. Using mirrored disks and redundant network connections in an advanced replication environment

Finally, an advanced replication solution that is intended to deliver high availability locally as well as geographic data distribution can be difficult to deliver, at least in the case of systems with high volumes of activity (i.e., tens of DML actions per second). The problem is that it is not possible to have separate propagation frequencies for replication groups propagating to the same remote site, nor is it possible to create a multi-master environment in which not all masters communicate with the remote site. If you are using asynchronous propagation, the frequency of updates is the same for all replication groups to a particular site, and every site in a multi-master environment must communicate with every other site.

It would be desirable to design a system (see Figure 7-6) in which local propagation occurs at a high frequency, while propagation to a remote site is only from a single site.

Though this example may be extreme, the concept is not entirely unreasonable. The advanced replication technology, as it exists now, would require a topology like the one shown in Figure 7-7.

You can achieve different update frequencies only by using synchronous propagation among the local sites and asynchronous propagation to the remote site.

Advanced replication can provide high availability and scalability, but it also includes overhead and may not deliver the desired flexibility in cases in which local high availability is to be coupled with geographic data distribution.

Geographic Data Distribution

As hinted in the previous section, many organizations have a requirement for global data distribution. In other words, it may be necessary to maintain the same

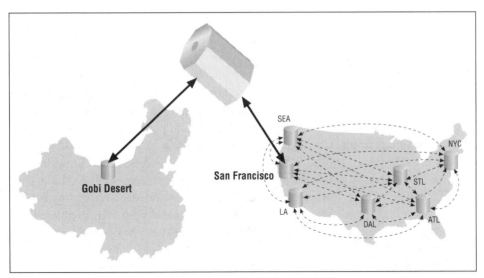

Figure 7-6. A single transcontinental link

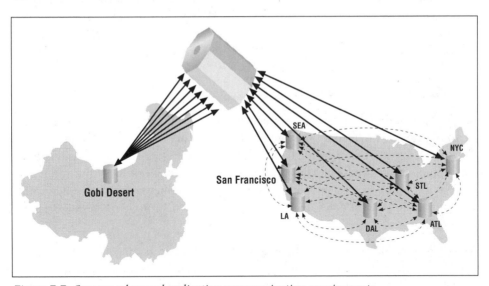

Figure 7-7. Current advanced replication communication requirements

data in separate data centers on machines that are probably not even on the same network. For example, a web site that tracks user data about news preferences may deploy databases in California, Chicago, and New York so that it can direct user traffic to a site that is nearby. Or a large corporation may replicate data about its products and prices to numerous regional headquarters.

Oracle's advanced replication is the clear choice for meeting these requirements. It can provide read/write access to data in multiple locations. In addition, if asynchronous propagation is being used, data is always fully accessible locally regardless of the availability of the remote sites. Sites also can be added or deleted as requirements change.

The most significant issues with using advanced replication for geographic data distribution are data latency and conflicts. Since synchronous propagation is not a viable option for machines that are in different locations, every site will be out of sync with its peers by at least one second (the shortest propagation frequency possible). If your application is one that allows the same tables to be updated frequently from multiple locations, this latency may be detrimental. Consider, for example, a user of a web site who changes her news preferences while she is connected to the database in Chicago. If she then leaves the site and comes back a couple of seconds later, connecting to the California database, she might not see the changes she has made. She will probably change the news preferences again, which will result in a conflict when the data from the Chicago and California sites finally do propagate.

This scenario brings us to the second caveat: conflicts. If data is propagating asynchronously, it is possible and even likely that conflicts will arise. Any replicated application must plan for and provide automatic resolution of conflicts. Please refer to Chapter 15, *Conflict Avoidance and Resolution Techniques*, for advice.

Workflow Partitioning

Workflow partitioning refers to applications that are distributed across multiple databases, each of which is associated with a particular business function. The traditional example is the distributed system that has different sites allocated to order entry, shipping, and billing. These databases may or may not be at the same geographic location and may or may not be on the same network. As a general rule, the propagation mode for these applications is asynchronous. Figure 7-8 shows partitioning among three sites.

An application that lends itself to workflow partitioning is an ideal candidate for multi-master table replication. Since the data updates that occur at each site are distinct, it is highly unlikely that conflicts will arise. And the probability of conflicts can be reduced significantly by incorporating business rules into the application. For example, in the previous example, an order cannot be billed until it has shipped. Also, Oracle provides built-in conflict resolution methods that are specifically designed for workflow partitioning, such as priority groups. Refer to Chapter 15 for details about implementing priority groups and other conflict resolution techniques.

As with other advanced replication architectures, workflow partitioning must cope with the latency inherent in asynchronous propagation.

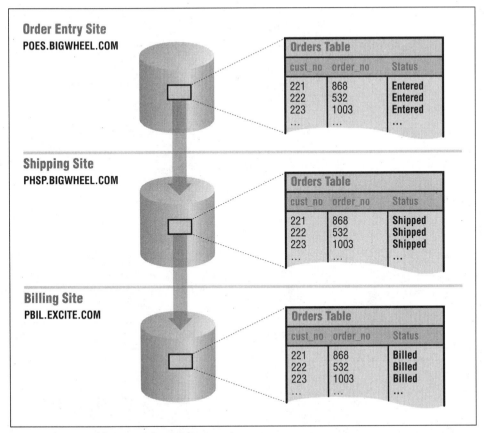

Figure 7-8. Workflow partitioning among three sites

Data Collection and Consolidation

Many organizations gather data from several locations and consolidate it into a single database. The single database is often a centralized, company-wide repository. Examples include retail chains that upload sales data from their sales outlets every night (see Figure 7-9) or a sales force armed with laptops into which they enter data about customer leads (see Figure 7-10). The distinguishing feature of these scenarios is that the databases are not expected to be in constant contact with one another; data latency can be quite high, while bandwidth can be quite low.

Both of these scenarios are perfect candidates for Oracle's updateable snapshots, a feature of advanced replication. Updateable snapshots work well in these environments because data can be horizontally partitioned and because updates to the data can be pushed to the master site on demand. The retail outlets can upload daily sales transactions after the store closes, and the traveling salespeople can send updates to headquarters when they check into their hotels and potentially receive updates that their colleagues have made.

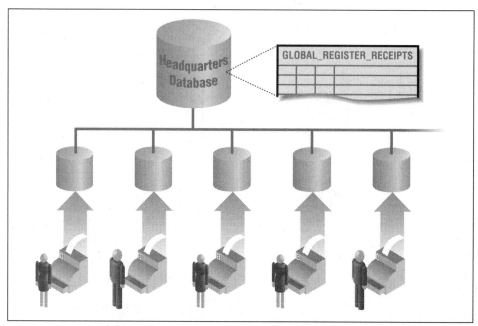

Figure 7-9. Retail stores communicate with headquarters nightly

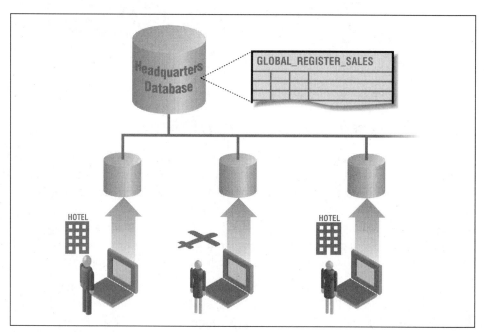

Figure 7-10. Sales personnel synchronize laptops with headquarters

As with multi-master replication, updateable snapshots may result in conflicts, and unfortunately the resolution methods are not as comprehensive as they are for multi-master replication. In effect, you must make the choice of accepting one update or the other. If possible, the application should not allow multiple snapshot sites to update the same data. Sales personnel, for example, should be allowed to update data pertaining only to customers for whom they are responsible. Furthermore, the enforcement of data integrity becomes more troublesome in an environment in which participants connect intermittently. It may not be practical to deploy all data required to validate transactions at the snapshot sites, so applications may have to include logic to perform data validation when the snapshot site connects. For example, a salesperson might book an order, only to find that the client is over his credit limit when the order is sent to headquarters.

Other issues to consider in an updateable snapshot configuration are security and the fact that the local personnel responsible for the administration of each snapshot site may lack the skills typically available at the data center that houses the master database.

Loosely Coupled Federation

If nothing else, you probably have a distributed system configuration that can best be described as a loosely coupled federation. Are you sending sales transactions from an Oracle database to a mainframe for billing? Are you extracting audit trails from your web server into a data warehouse? Are you reconciling the phone company's electronic invoices with your voice mail system? Each of these scenarios could be classified as a database federation. The data may be in disparate forms, and there are no real-time transactions taking place.

If one or more of the databases in your federation is Oracle based, you can use a variety of techniques to move data from one database to another, including:

Database links
> If both sites are Oracle based, data can be selected, inserted, or updated over a database link.

*SQL*Loader*
> This tool loads non-Oracle data from a formatted text file into an Oracle table.

*Pro*C/C++, Pro*COBOL, Pro*FORTAN, Pro*Ada*
> Oracle precompilers allow you to embed SQL statements into programs, allowing you to migrate data from a file or other external source into Oracle.

Oracle Gateway products
> These products provide SQL access from an Oracle database to a foreign data source.

The key to success with a federated database system is a written specification and robustness. Because these systems are often cobbled together over time and often viewed as informal stopgaps, their quality often suffers. It is not uncommon for such a system to come completely unraveled immediately after its chief caretaker leaves the organization.

In this chapter:
• *Schema Design and
  Integration*
• *Application Tiering*
• *Designing a
  Replicated System*

8

*Engineering
Considerations*

Any application that runs in a distributed environment must take its distributed nature into account if it is to be successful. Considerations such as data consistency, transactional integrity, conflict avoidance, and error handling are only a few of the issues to contend with. This chapter visits some of these issues and suggests best practices for addressing them.

Schema Design and Integration

As with most systems, you are fortunate if you are able to design a distributed database system from the ground up. In these cases, you have the flexibility to locate data optimally and to avoid anomalies in naming and constraint enforcement. But whether your system is prenatal or legacy, you face the challenges of data placement and schema integration for systems. Since I'm assuming in this book that all participating databases in the system are Oracle based, I won't address the additional complications associated with a heterogeneous distributed system.

The process for designing a distributed database schema is not much different from that for designing a local schema in the initial stages; entities are identified, relationships are defined, processes are mapped, and so on. The step that is unique to distributed systems is data placement, otherwise known as *data partitioning* or *data fragmenting*. Chapter 5, *Designing a Distributed System*, discussed methodologies for determining how to partition data; this chapter discusses additional considerations the application developer must take into account.

Interdatabase Referential Integrity

When you partition data among multiple databases, you may end up separating entities that have a parent-child relationship. However, Oracle does not provide declarative referential integrity constraints between databases. So, if you place your ORDERS table in one database and your ORDER_ITEMS table in another, you cannot rely on Oracle to ensure that every line item in the ORDER_ITEMS table corresponds to an order in the ORDERS table:

```
SQL> ALTER TABLE order_items ADD (
  2  CONSTRAINT fk_order_item_order_num
  3  FOREIGN KEY (order_number)
  4  REFERENCES orders@PHQS.BIGWHEEL.COM (order_number)
  5  );

REFERENCES user_profile@PHQS.EXCITE.COM (userid)
              *
ERROR at line 4:
ORA-02021: DDL operations are not allowed on a remote database
```

So, how do we establish interdatabase referential integrity? The short answer is that you shouldn't be in a position to require it! It makes no sense, for example, to separate tables with parent-child relationships into two separate databases.

Yet sometimes such separations are inevitable. Consider an organization that has its primary CUSTOMERS table in the headquarters database, but the ORDERS table for the order entry system is located in a different database at the regional sales site.

One way to handle this situation is to write a BEFORE ROW trigger on the ORDERS table that checks for the existence of a corresponding CUSTOMER_ID record in the remote CUSTOMERS table whenever a record is inserted:

```
CREATE OR REPLACE TRIGGER t_i_orders
BEFORE INSERT
ON orders
FOR EACH ROW
v_count NUMBER;
BEGIN
    SELECT count(*)
    INTO v_count
    FROM customers@PHQS.BIGWHEEL.COM c
    WHERE c.customer_id = :new.customer_id;

    IF v_count = 1
    THEN
        :new.username := USER;
        :new.rectime  := SYSDATE;
        :new.site     := DBMS_REPUTIL.GLOBAL_NAME;
    END IF;
END;
```

The downside to this solution is that it introduces a dependency on the remote database; if the remote database is unavailable, no new orders can be created. This dependency can be alleviated somewhat by including an ORDER_STATUS column in the ORDERS table which can flag orders as UNVALIDATED. Records could then be inserted into the ORDERS table even when the remote database is unavailable, and their CUSTOMER_IDs can be verified later when the remote database is available.

A simpler alternative to enforcing interdatabase referential integrity, and one which does not rely on the accessibility of the remote database, is to create a local snapshot of the master table using the WITH PRIMARY KEY clause available in Oracle8:

```
CREATE SNAPSHOT customers
TABLESPACE oe_data STORAGE (INITIAL 10M NEXT 10M PCTINCREASE 0)
REFRESH FAST
START WITH sysdate
NEXT trunc(sysdate) + 1
WITH PRIMARY KEY
AS
    SELECT customer_id, customer_name
    FROM customers@PHQS.BIGWHEEL.COM;

ALTER TABLE orders ADD (
CONSTRAINT fk_orders_customer_id
FOREIGN KEY (customer_id) REFERENCES snap$_customers(customer_id)
);
```

The WITH PRIMARY KEY clause actually creates a primary key on the SNAP$_ CUSTOMERS table, which is the table underlying the CUSTOMERS snapshot. This approach, in effect, allows a declarative referential integrity constraint on a remote object. However, snapshots by design have a certain amount of latency. The snapshot table is only as current as the most recent refresh.

Naming Conventions

Although there are no restrictions per se on object names in a distributed environment, some names are better than others. First, to the extent possible, you should try to keep names unique across all schema in the distributed environment. This is not a requirement, but it makes administration less confusing. An example of a poor choice for a table name is COUNTRY or COUNTRIES. Why? Because this name is likely to be common to more than one application and therefore several schema. When tables are replicated, either as master tables or snapshots, it may not be possible to create identical public synonyms in all databases. You can avoid name space collisions by prefixing table names with two or three characters that associate them with a given application. For example, the COUNTRIES table that the order entry system uses would become OE_COUNTRIES.

Another potential issue in a distributed database is the length of table names. Various replication-related objects have generated names that are based on a table name such as the SNAP$_CUSTOMERS of the previous example. If the generated name ends up being more than 30 characters (the maximum length of a table name in Oracle), then the name is truncated, which may result in naming conflicts. Since the longest prefix in use is seven characters (the updateable snapshot log USLOG$_), keep your table names short—never more than 23 characters.

Distributed Queries and Transactions

Oracle performs distributed queries and transactions transparently and automatically. Strictly speaking, the application need not have any knowledge of where data is actually located. However, from a practical point of view, it is in your best interest to take the location of your data into account.

Distributed queries fall into two broad categories: queries whose target tables are all located at a single remote site (also known as "remote queries") and queries whose target tables are located at multiple sites.

When an application initiates a remote query, the optimizer recognizes that the tables involved are in a single database, and it passes the entire query to the remote database, which executes it with the same efficiency as a local query. The remote database then sends that data back.

There are really no optimizations that you can make on a remote query, although if you find that your application is performing a high number of remote queries, you might consider relocating the data to the local database either in its entirety or as snapshots, thereby reducing the network traffic.

Queries that gather data from multiple sources can benefit from some optimizations as we shall see. For purposes of illustration, consider the following query:

```
SELECT    customer_name,
          TO_CHAR(order_date, 'Month') month,
          SUM(order_total) monthly_sales
FROM      customer@PHQS.BIGWHEEL.COM c,
          orders@PSLS.BIGWHEEL.COM o
WHERE     c.customer_id = o.customer_id
GROUP BY  customer_name,
          TO_CHAR(order_date, 'Month'),
          TO_CHAR(order_date, 'MM')
ORDER BY  customer_name, to_char(order_date, 'MM');


CUSTOMER_NAME          MONTH        MONTHLY_SALES
--------------         ------       -------------
Chain Reaction         June         505
Missing Link           April        345
Missing Link           May          398
Spoken Word            May          475
Spoken Word            June         305
```

To decompose this query, Oracle must first determine which columns are in which tables by querying the data dictionaries at PHQS.BIGWHEEL.COM and PSLS.BIG-WHEEL.COM. Then it retrieves the data from these two remote databases. These queries return *all* records from the remote tables.

In PHQS.BIGWHEEL.COM:

```
Statement
-----------------------------------------------------------------
SELECT "CUSTOMER_ID","CUSTOMER_NAME" FROM "CUSTOMERS" "C"
```

In PSLS.BIGWHEEL.COM:

```
Statement
-----------------------------------------------------------------
SELECT "CUSTOMER_ID","ORDER_TOTAL","ORDER_DATE" FROM "ORDERS" "O"
```

Oracle performs joins and aggregations of this data at the site at which the query originated, also known as the *driving site*. Here we see several opportunities for optimization, described in the following sections.

Control the driving site

Be mindful of how much data is being shipped to the driving site. Whenever possible, originate distributed queries from the database that holds the most target data, or use the DRIVING_SITE hint to force a specific site to be the driving site.

In our sample query, we could force the driving site to be PSLS.BIGWHEEL.COM since the ORDERS table is bigger than the CUSTOMERS table:

```
SELECT   /*+DRIVING_SITE(orders)*/
         customer_name,
         TO_CHAR(order_date, 'Month') month,
         SUM(order_total) monthly_sales
FROM     customer@PHQS.BIGWHEEL.COM c,
         orders@PSLS.BIGWHEEL.COM o
         . . .
```

This hint forces the site with the ORDERS table to perform the joins and aggregation operations the query requires. Note that the query results are still sent over the network to the site that originated the query.

Another way to force a specific site to be the driving site is to create views of remote data at the desired site. The view tricks the optimizer into thinking that the *table* is at the site. Again, referring to our example, we could force PSLS.BIG-WHEEL.COM to be the driving site by creating a view on the CUSTOMERS table there, and rewriting the query to select from that view.

At PSLS.BIGWHEEL.COM:

```
CREATE VIEW customer_view AS
SELECT customer_id, customer_name
FROM customers@PSLS.BIGWHEEL.COM;
```

At the site originating the query:

```
SELECT  customer_name,
        TO_CHAR(order_date, 'Month') month,
        SUM(order_total) monthly_sales
FROM    customer_view@PSLS.BIGWHEEL.COM c,
        orders@PSLS.BIGWHEEL.COM o
```

This query accesses the data on PHQS.BIGWHEEL.COM only indirectly. To Oracle's optimizer, it appears to be a simple remote query.

Just as important as controlling the driving site in distributed queries is controlling the use of indexes. This brings us to the next tip.

Control index usage

Regrettably, the only way that Oracle will even *consider* the use of indexes in distributed queries is if the database uses the cost-based optimizer. If your databases are configured to use the rule-based optimizer, your distributed queries are performing full table scans.

Maintenance of Database Link Connections

Whenever a user issues a remote procedure call or executes a SQL statement that references remote data and the user does not already have a connection to the remote database, Oracle automatically connects using the database link available to the user. Oracle maintains this connection either until the user logs off or until the connection is explicitly closed. In other words, connections persist even after they may no longer be necessary. This can cause undue strain on resources such as network bandwidth, machine memory, and database throughput. It can even cause unneeded expense if the connectivity is over a third-party vendor's network.

Your application can avoid all of these problems by explicitly closing database links when they are no longer necessary. To do so, all transactions that utilize the link must be completed (either committed or rolled back), and any cursors that were opened at the remote site must be closed. When these requirements are met, your application can issue this command:

```
ALTER SESSION CLOSE DATABASE LINK linkname;
```

Note that the ALTER SESSION system privilege must be granted to all users of the application. ALTER SESSION is included in the CONNECT role, but this role is not necessarily granted to all users.

Error Handling

There are a number of Oracle errors that are specific to distributed databases. An application that performs any remote or distributed operations must trap these exceptions in addition to the normal error handling of a single-database application. The following lists these Oracle errors:

ORA-00160: global transaction length num is greater than maximum num
> Cause: An external global transaction ID with a field length too large was passed in.

> Action: Report the problem to your external transaction coordinator vendor.

ORA-00161: transaction branch length num is illegal (maximum allowed num)
> Cause: An external transaction branch ID with either a length too large or 0 was passed in.

> Action: Report the problem to your external transaction coordinator vendor.

ORA-00162: external dbid length num is greater than maximum (num)
> Cause: An external database name with a field length too large was passed in.

> Action: Report the problem to your external transaction coordinator vendor.

ORA-00163: internal database name length num is greater than maximum (num)
> Cause: An internal database name with a field length too large was passed in.

> Action: Report the problem to your external transaction coordinator vendor.

The following lists messages generated during distributed transactions:

ORA-02040: remote database name does not support two-phase commit
> Cause: A distributed update of more than one database was attempted, but the named database does not support the prepare phase of the two-phase commit, as determined by its logon transaction traits. The transaction was rolled back.

> Action: Do not attempt to update the named database, unless it is the only database updated in the transaction. Distributed updates of more than one database in a single transaction can be performed only if all databases support the two-phase commit mechanism.

ORA-02041: client database did not begin a transaction
> Cause: An update occurred at a coordinated database without the coordinator beginning a distributed transaction. This may happen if a stored procedure commits and then performs updates and the stored procedure is invoked remotely. It also could happen if an external transaction monitor violates the XA protocol.

> Action: If the cause is the former, check that no commit is followed by an update.

ORA-02042: too many distributed transactions
> Cause: The distributed transaction table is full because too many distributed transactions are active.

Action: Increase the DISTRIBUTED_TRANSACTIONS parameter in the initialization parameter file, shut down and restart Oracle, or run fewer transactions. If it is certain there are not too many concurrent distributed transactions, this may be an internal error. In this case, contact customer support. Shutting down and restarting the instance could be a workaround.

ORA-02043: must end current transaction before executing command

Cause: A transaction is in progress and one of the following commands is issued: COMMIT FORCE, ROLLBACK FORCE, or ALTER SYSTEM ENABLE DISTRIBUTED RECOVERY in single process mode.

Action: Commit or roll back the current transaction and retry the command.

ORA-02044: transaction manager login denied: transaction in progress

Cause: A remote transaction manager tried to log in while a distributed transaction is in progress. A protocol error occurred in the remote transaction manager.

Action: End the current transaction.

ORA-02045: too many local sessions participating in global transactions

Cause: There are too many sessions at this site to accommodate this transaction.

Action: Use an existing database link so that another session need not be created at the remote site.

ORA-02046: distributed transaction already begun

Cause: Internal error or error in external transaction manager. A server session received a begin_tran RPC before finishing with a previous distributed transaction.

Action: Report the problem to your external transaction coordinator vendor.

Application Tiering

Application tiering refers to separating various components of an application into layers that can be managed independently. A classic example is an Internet application that must scale to support thousands or millions of users. For example, consider the case of a web site that allows users to trade stocks online via their browsers. Such an application would run on web servers, application servers, and database servers. Web servers are the "frontend" of the application, responsible for accepting requests from users and directing them to application servers. The application servers house the application's logic and interact with the database.

Scaling the web server and application server layers of a tiered application is relatively easy; just add more machines! However, it is not so easy to add databases since the data must be consistent across all databases in the environment. For example, a user who buys 100 shares of XYZ should see the trade recorded no matter what database she connects to when visiting the site. Later chapters will examine data replication, which is a means of achieving horizontal scalability of database servers.

Designing a Replicated System

There are a variety of issues that are unique to sites utilizing Oracle's advanced replication facilities. A replicated system succeeds only if the designers are aware of these idiosyncrasies and make the right implementation decisions. Again, the sooner in the process these design choices are made, the better the chances for success.

Transactional Consistency

Oracle's multi-master replication preserves the order of transactions when it replicates them to participating sites, and it also guarantees the consistency of data at all sites. So, if you have a replicated order entry system that creates an entry in the ORDERS table in one transaction and entries in the ORDER_ITEMS table as a second transaction, Oracle will apply the transactions in the same order at all remote sites.

This is a crucial property of replication; without it, transactions could fail because of violated integrity constraints, and data would not be consistent. Since Oracle respects the order of transactions, row-level transactions do not require any special handling in a replicated environment.

Oracle8 includes a feature called *parallel propagation*, which is a means to replicate multiple transactions simultaneously. Thus, it is possible, and even likely, that transactions will not be delivered to participating master sites in the same sequence in which they occurred at the originating sites. However, Oracle guarantees that parallel streams of transactions are orthogonal—that is, they are independent of one another.

Batch activity, on the other hand, is not quite as simple. Suppose, for example, that the ORDERS and ORDER_ITEMS tables were implemented as snapshots at a remote site that refreshes the snapshots once per day. We want this site to have a consistent representation of the data at all times; that means that we cannot simply refresh the ORDERS table and then the ORDER_ITEMS table, because during the time the ORDER_ITEMS table refreshes, the ORDERS table will have numerous item-less orders. And, of course, the ORDER_ITEMS table cannot be refreshed first because we would then have orphaned items.

Oracle's solution to this dilemma is the snapshot group. A *snapshot group* is a collection of two or more tables that must be refreshed as a single transaction. All tables are refreshed with a representation of the master data at a single point in time. Refer to Chapter 11, *Basic Replication*, for specifics about creating and using snapshot groups.

Schema Differences and Partitioning

In a nonreplicated distributed database, data may be fragmented vertically, and tables may be defined slightly differently at different sites. In a replicated environment, you sacrifice a certain amount of flexibility. A table that participates in peer-to-peer replication *must* have the same shape (i.e., columns) at all locations. Whenever you add or drop a column, you must quiesce the replication group and use the Oracle built-in package procedure DBMS_REPCAT.ALTER_MASTER_REP-OBJECT to change the table at all master sites.

The DBMS_REPCAT.ALTER_MASTER_REPOBJECT procedure can perform only standard DDL such as widening or adding fields. If you want to drop a column, you must create a new table without the column you are dropping, populate the new table, and add it to the replication group.

Unlike vertical partitioning, horizontal partitioning is fairly straightforward in a replicated environment. If you wish to divide a table so that a WHERE clause dictates whether records appear at specific sites, you can use updateable snapshots to bring about this partitioning. For example, a retailer may use updateable snapshots to track sales transactions at its various locations.

Horizontal partitioning can also be of tremendous use in an application that is designed to balance workload for the purpose of scalability. Consider an Internet "portal" site that allows users to personalize their view of the web page by specifying stocks in their portfolio, sports teams they track, weather reports they want, and so on. If the schema is designed so that the tables containing this personalized data can be partitioned by username, for example, then the application can direct users to specific databases in the replicated environment based on their user ID.

In order to take advantage of scalability through horizontal partitioning, the application should be able to direct users, or traffic, to a particular database based on an identifying key. Horizontal partitioning is highly desirable because it helps to avoid conflicts. It also gives you the option to use updateable snapshots or multi-master replication; updateable snapshots can take advantage of partitioning, but master tables must be replicated in their entirety. Obviously, all tables that are to be horizontally partitioned must contain the partition key.

The latter requirement generally implies denormalization of the schema. Since *every* table in the replicated schema must contain the partition key, normalizations that would be highly desirable under normal circumstances are not reasonable. For example, consider what would be involved in partitioning an order entry application. If we partition tables based on CUSTOMER_ID, then this field would have to be in not only the CUSTOMERS and ORDERS tables but also the ORDER_ITEMS table, which is highly unnatural.

If you find yourself having to denormalize your schema in absurd ways, you are probably better off either choosing a different partition key or simply using multi-master replication (and placing all data at all sites) instead. If you elect to use multi-master replication, you should still direct your application to use different databases for different subsets of data.

Row-Level Replication or Procedural Replication?

Oracle's advanced replication facility supports row-level replication and procedural replication. *Row-level replication* is transaction based; DML that is applied against a table is forwarded to other sites and applied. Every transaction creates a deferred call. *Procedural replication*, on the other hand, replicates calls to PL/SQL packaged procedures and functions.

For OLTP workloads, row-level replication makes the most sense; there is no real need or benefit to writing PL/SQL packages to perform all of an application's DML. Furthermore, row-level replication offers conflict resolution, whereas procedural replication does not.

So why would one ever want to use procedural replication? Operations that update large numbers of records do not replicate well with transaction-based replication, for a variety of reasons:

- Field values must be sent to all participating master sites. In Oracle7, both old and new column values must be sent for every column in the table, not just the changed columns. This can lead to quite a strain on the network.

- Large replicated transactions require tremendously large rollback segments. Rollback segments are required not only for the table being modified but also for the data dictionary tables that control replication.

- Conflict resolution is extremely expensive for large transactions. If a conflict arises, and you have resolution methods defined to handle it, the time required to process the conflict can easily exceed the time required to simply re-create the table.

None of these considerations is an issue with procedural replication. The only data that propagates to the participating sites is the PL/SQL call itself. Oracle executes the call at each database, requiring little more overhead than a nonreplicated procedure call uses. Since procedural replication does not utilize conflict resolution methods, no additional time or resources are required to process conflicts. Of course, the application developers have the responsibility of ensuring that the replicated procedures do not introduce conflicts and that they can handle data anomalies.

Another advantage that procedural replication has over row-level replication is that procedures can be localized. That is, they can be slightly different at different locations. This flexibility can be useful if business rules differ at various sites. For example, a price increase may trigger different customer discounts in different regions. (Again, developers and designers must ensure that any regional differences do not result in inconsistent data.) Procedural replication is described in greater detail in Chapter 14, *Procedural Replication.*

Primary Keys and Unique Indexes

Every replicated table must have either a primary key or a unique index. A primary key is preferable. The reason for this requirement should be clear; every record must be uniquely identifiable so that changes to the record can be propagated to the corresponding record in the remote databases. ROWIDs are not an option for uniquely identifying records because they contain information about the physical location of a record and are not identical across multiple databases.

As I've said, primary keys are preferable to unique indexes; in addition, a single-field key is preferable to a multivalued key. The problem with unique indexes is that the replication facility does not automatically recognize them. If you have a table with a unique index but not a primary key, you have to use the DBMS_REP-CAT.SET_COLUMNS procedure to coerce Oracle into using the index to identify records. Also, if you wish to use primary key snapshots (available in Oracle8), the master table must have a primary key. The replication software assumes that master tables have primary keys.

Primary keys should consist of a single column, preferably a numeric column. Whenever Oracle has to locate a row, which occurs quite frequently with row-level replication, the task should be as fast as possible; using a single-field primary key helps the overall performance of the replication functions. The primary advantage to using numeric fields over VARCHARs for primary keys is that indexes on numeric columns are generally much smaller than those on VARCHARs.

Foreign Keys and Referential Integrity

As stated elsewhere, Oracle's advanced replication facility preserves the order of transactions, so if a transaction creates records that respect a master-child relationship at the originating site, the relationship will be preserved at the sites to which the transaction propagates. For example, if an order entry application creates a record in the ORDERS table and multiple line items in the ORDER_ITEMS table either in a single transaction or in a series of transactions, Oracle will propagate the inserts in the same order.

Therefore, foreign key constraints are supportable and even advisable in a replicated environment. Also, unlike Oracle7, which did not allow primary keys or unique indexes on snapshot base tables, Oracle8 does support these constraints. In fact, Oracle8 can even create a primary key on snapshot base tables automatically, as described in the earlier section "Interdatabase Referential Integrity."

 Although foreign key constraints are safe to use in a replicated environment, it is not practical to use the ON DELETE CASCADE form. Foreign keys defined with cascading deletes automatically delete child records whenever a record is deleted from the parent table. If both the parent and child tables are replicated and if the constraint is defined as a cascading delete at all master sites, then deletes will be attempted twice against child tables: once because of the integrity constraint and once because of the replicated delete from the originating site.

Triggers on Replicated Tables

If your application uses triggers, make sure that the triggers do not interfere with replication functionality. For example, if you use auditing triggers that populate username and timestamp fields when a record is created or deleted, the trigger should fire at the site where the DML originated but not at the sites to which the DML is propagated. Oracle provides a built-in function called DBMS_REPUTIL.FROM_REMOTE, which you can use in your trigger body to determine whether to do anything.

```
CREATE OR REPLACE TRIGGER t_iu_orders
BEFORE INSERT OR UPDATE
ON orders
FOR EACH ROW

BEGIN
    IF (dbms_reputil.from_remote != TRUE)
    THEN
        :new.username:= USER;
        :new.rectime:= SYSDATE;
        :new.site:= DBMS_REPUTIL.GLOBAL_NAME;
    END IF;
END;
/
```

Note that this is a before-row trigger. All of Oracle's replication triggers are after-row triggers. Since it is not possible to control the firing order of triggers of the same type, it is best to guarantee that your own triggers fire before the replication triggers by making them before-row triggers. This way, your triggers will not interfere with replication functionality. Make sure that triggers that modify data fire only for the original transaction, not for propagated transactions.

Datatypes

Oracle does not replicate LONG or LONG RAW datatypes. You can still replicate a table that has LONG or LONG RAW columns, but changes to the values in such columns are not propagated. Oracle8 addresses this limitation by supporting replication of CLOB (character large object) and BLOB (binary large object) datatypes. Nevertheless, applications should perform minimal updates to these datatypes in a replicated environment because of the impact this can have on the network. In fact, Oracle8 also includes a feature called *minimum communication*, which allows you to specify the columns whose values are to be sent to remote sites when updates are propagated. If you know that the application never updates CLOB or BLOB columns, you do not need to send their values when updates propagate. See Chapter 12, *Multi-Master Replication*, for details on how to take advantage of minimum communication. If your application does allow for updates to CLOB and BLOB data, you should try to partition data vertically so that these fields are in tables that contain only the CLOB or BLOB data and a primary key:

```
SQL> desc catalog_photos
     Name                        Null?      Type
     ------------------------     --------   ----
     catalog_photo_id            NOT NULL   NUMBER(12)
     photo                       NOT NULL   BLOB
```

Oracle8 also introduced user-defined datatypes. Regrettably, user-defined datatypes do not replicate. The current recommendation is to create tables with the objects' underlying datatypes.

Time

Among the most common and easy to use methods of conflict resolution are Latest Timestamp and Earliest Timestamp. To utilize these fields, replicated tables should have a timestamp field and a before-row trigger to populate it on every insert and update. For this field to be effective, the system clocks on the machines hosting the replicated databases must be synchronized. Synchronization is particularly important for applications that perform a high rate of transactions, especially if these transactions are not partitioned to avoid conflicts.

The time zone of each database server machine may also be an issue. For example, if you have machines in New York and California and have defined Latest Timestamp conflict resolution, then the transactions originating at the New York site will prevail in most conflicts since New York is three hours ahead of California. To avoid time zone biases, you can either standardize your machines to a single time zone, such as Greenwich Mean Time (GMT), or adjust the value of the timestamp when you populate the field. The former strategy is much simpler but may cause confusion and complications if the application presents time-sensitive data to the user, such as a time and attendance system or a stock quote server. Future versions of Oracle are expected to include a timestamp component in the DATE datatype, which will simplify time zone anomalies significantly. Currently, Oracle references the computer's system clock to determine the time but does not consider the time zone.

Sequences

Oracle's advanced replication facility does not replicate sequences, which are often used to generate primary key values and other numeric keys. Because of this limitation, applications that use sequences can reference a single sequence which is located at a master site, can use their own local sequence, or can use a multicolumn primary key. Each of these strategies has its advantages and disadvantages.

Using a single sequence at a master site

If you elect to allow all databases to reference a single sequence in a remote site, you are ensured that the ordering of the numeric key in the databases represents the order in which transactions occurred. As an example, a single master sequence could be created for an order entry application that is replicated across multiple sites:

```
CREATE PUBLIC SYNONYM seq_order_num
FOR seq_order_num@PHQS.BIGWHEEL.COM
```

The ORDERS table would then have a before-row trigger to populate the ORDER_NUMBER field (as well as the other fields used for auditing and conflict avoidance).

```
CREATE OR REPLACE TRIGGER t_iu_orders
BEFORE INSERT OR UPDATE
ON orders
FOR EACH ROW

BEGIN
    IF (dbms_reputil.from_remote != TRUE)
    THEN
        :new.order_numbers := seq_order_num.next_val;
        :new.username := USER;
```

```
            :new.rectime := SYSDATE;
            :new.site := DBMS_REPUTIL.GLOBAL_NAME;
      END IF;
   END;
```

Thus, the ordering of ORDER_NUMBERs will be sequential for all orders entered at all sites.

The glaring disadvantage of this approach is the dependency on a single site. Not only must the remote database be available in order for new orders to be generated, but it must also have the capacity to support the connections and sequence requests from all users of the application. These risks are too high for most production applications.

Allocating sequence ranges to sites

An alternative is to use a local sequence in all databases in which the application runs. With a local sequence, the application can function independently from all other master sites. However, the sequences must be created so that they never collide—that is, distinct ranges of sequence numbers must be allocated to each site. You can accomplish this sequence partitioning simply by creating the sequences with different starting numbers, as follows:

Headquarters:

```
CREATE SEQUENCE seq_order_num
START WITH 1;
```

New York site:

```
CREATE SEQUENCE seq_order_num
START WITH 100000000000;
```

California site:

```
CREATE SEQUENCE seq_order_num
START WITH 200000000000;
```

It is a good idea to leave room for *plenty* of entries at each site; the preceding example allocates one hundred billion sequence numbers per site, which can support more than 300 new orders per second for 10 years. Running out of numbers is to be avoided at all costs; calculate your peak rate of record insertion and allocate enough sequence numbers to support 100 times that rate continuously for 30 years. (By then you probably won't care if it runs out of sequence numbers!)

The only disadvantages to allocated sequence ranges to sites is the loss of continuity in key values across the participating databases. Aggregate reports that sort by the key value will not be sorted by the order in which records were created. Of course, some people would find it advantageous to be able to identify where records were created just by referencing the primary key.

Using a multicolumn primary key

Finally, if neither of the previously described strategies is acceptable, the application may use two fields as the primary key for replicated tables. Typically, one of these fields would be the sequence number, as in the previous examples, and the second field would be a site identifier. For example, the ORDERS table would have its primary key defined as follows:

```
ALTER TABLE orders ADD (
CONSTRAINT pk_orders
PRIMARY KET (order_num, site_num)
);
```

The application would still use local sequences, but the sequence numbers could all start with the same value.

The advantage of this method is that its primary key values are not artificially associated with sites, and there is no danger of running out of sequence numbers at any site. In addition, new sites are simple to add. The disadvantage is that multicolumned primary keys incur additional overhead in the replication internals, and performance will be affected.

Multiple Character Sets

If your application supports multiple character sets, you must ensure that each database participating in the replicated environment is created with a compatible character set. If multiple character sets are involved, Oracle recommends the use of the UNICODE character set: AL24UTFFSS for Oracle7 databases and AL24UTFFSS or UTF8 for Oracle8 databases, because these support all mappings.

SQL*Net and Net8 perform character set conversions; there is nothing specific to replication that must be done.

II

Replication

Part II describes the details of Oracle's various distributed system products; it contains the following chapters:

- Chapter 9, *Oracle Replication Architecture*, takes a deeper look at Oracle's replication architecture; it examines the various types of replication available through Oracle, specific architectural components, installation tips, and enhancements for Oracle8 and Oracle8*i*.

- Chapter 10, *Advanced Replication Installation*, describes how to set up an advanced replication environment, including the setting of initialization parameters, the selection of redo logs and rollback segments, the size and placement of data dictionary objects, and the use of administrative accounts, privileges, and database links.

- Chapter 11, *Basic Replication*, is a detailed analysis of Oracle's basic replication (snapshot) facility.

- Chapter 12, *Multi-Master Replication*, is a detailed analysis of Oracle's multi-master replication facility.

- Chapter 13, *Updateable Snapshots*, is a detailed analysis of Oracle's updateable snapshot facility.

- Chapter 14, *Procedural Replication*, is a detailed analysis of Oracle's procedural replication facility.

- Chapter 15, *Conflict Avoidance and Resolution Techniques*, describes a variety of techniques for avoiding conflicts among the various distributed sites where data is replicated.

9

Oracle Replication Architecture

If you're going to realize the full potential of Oracle's advanced replication facilities and simultaneously avoid the pitfalls, you need to understand the architecture on which they are based. If you are new to replication or a bit unclear about how the components work together, this chapter is for you. The following chapters assume an understanding of the concepts discussed here.

What Is Oracle Replication?

Let's begin with a few simple concepts. Oracle's replication facility is a collection of tables, PL/SQL packages, and background processes that can automatically replicate data or procedure calls from one database to one or more other databases. Oracle's replication is built in to the database itself; it is not a separate application or utility like export and import. Depending on the configuration, data can be modified at all sites, or one site can be the sole writer while other sites receive read-only copies of the data. The functionality can accommodate a wide variety of business requirements. These include:

- High availability

- Scalability

- Remote data deployment

- Data extraction and consolidation

We'll examine the details of implementing these solutions in later chapters.

Note that *replicating* data is fundamentally different from *distributing* data. When data is distributed, it may be accessed transparently from multiple locations, but a given table exists in only one location, and that location is responsible for its security and integrity. Replicated data, on the other hand, resides at multiple locations, each of which shares in its maintenance. Data replication implies an increased level of complexity because it introduces issues such as data synchronization and latency. This complexity is the price to pay for continuous operations when a remote data source is unavailable.

Types of Replication

No single replication methodology can meet all of the various business requirements listed earlier. Oracle's four basic types of replication are described in Table 9-1.

Table 9-1. Types of Replication

Replication Type	Description	Example
Read-only snapshots	A master table is copied to one or more databases. Changes in the master table are reflected in the snapshot tables whenever the snapshot refreshes. The snapshot site determines the frequency of the refreshes; data is pulled.	A company may maintain its master product price list in a table at headquarters; regional sales offices or retail sites each have a snapshot of the price list in their local databases.
Updateable snapshots	Similar to read-only snapshots, except that the snapshot sites are able to modify the data and send their changes back to the master. The snapshot site determines the frequency of the refreshes and the frequency with which updates are sent back to the master.	A table of customer leads resides at headquarters. Sales staff with laptop computers visit prospective clients and enter notes about their meetings. When the sales staff dials in to the headquarters database every evening, their notes are uploaded, and they receive any updates that may have occurred since their last data refresh.
Multi-master replication	A table is copied to one or more databases, and each database has the ability to insert, update, or delete records from it. Modifications are pushed to the other database at an interval that the DBA sets for each replication group. The highest theoretical frequency is once per second.	A company achieves scalability and high availability by running its order entry system on two database instances; orders and inventory are modified on both machines.
Procedural replication	A call to a packaged procedure or function is replicated to one or more databases.	A procedure call applies a discount of 10% to all orders over US$500 by updating the ORDERS table in a replicated order entry system.

As you can see, these modes of replication are quite different, and each is suited for specific kinds of uses. A single environment can utilize all of these methods; they are not mutually exclusive.

Architecture Components

Oracle has built the replication facility on a variety of triggers, packages, background processes, jobs, and tables, all working in concert to deliver data to multiple sites as if by magic. If you are the DBA for a replicated environment, you must understand the secrets behind this magic. Read on.

The Queues

Queues are the foundation of the replication architecture. DML and DDL changes are entered into these queues, from which they are propagated to remote sites. Table 9-2 summarizes the queues.

Table 9-2. Replication Queues

Queue Name	Relevant Data Dictionary Views	Description
Deferred transaction (a.k.a. deftrans)	Primary: DEFTRAN Other: DEFTRANDEST DEFERRCOUNT DEFERROR	Local transactions that are to be replicated to remote sites are enqueued in to deftrans. A trigger on the replicated table *table_name*$RT inserts these entries. Note that in Oracle8 this trigger is internalized and is therefore not visible in the data dictionary.
Replication call (a.k.a. defcall)	Primary: DEFCALL Other: DEFCALLDEST	Remote procedure calls are enqueued into the DEFCALL view. In the case of a replicated table, there is one entry for each row that is changed.
Replication catalog (a.k.a. repcatlog)	DBA_REPCAT	DDL modifications to replicated objects as well as administrative tasks such as changing to the propagation mode are tracked in DBA_REPCAT. This view also contains information about errors that may have occurred when performing these tasks.
Job	Primary: DBA_JOBS Other: DEFSCHEDULE DBA_JOBS_RUNNING	The job queue controls scheduled jobs that run at user-defined intervals. For replication, these are recurring calls to the DBMS_REPCAT procedures that process entries in deftrans, defcall, and repcatlog and that refresh snapshots. Note that the job queue can schedule calls to any package procedure; its use is not restricted to replication-related activity.

In the case of synchronous multi-master replication, DML activity is not queued. Changes are delivered to all sites simultaneously using a two-phase commit protocol.

The next step to understanding the replication architecture is understanding the mechanisms Oracle uses to add and remove entries from these queues. As you would probably guess, it's done with triggers and packaged procedures.

The Triggers and Packages

Whether you are using snapshots, asynchronous row-level replication, or procedural replication, you are using some combination of queues, triggers, and packages. This section examines the precise mechanisms behind all of the preceding replication methods. In each case, we use an example table, called ISO_COUNTRIES, to illustrate the sequence of events that replicates an update to the table. The ISO_COUNTRIES table is defined as follows:

```
SQL> desc iso_countries
 Name            Null?       Type
 ------------    --------    --------------
 COUNTRY_ID      NOT NULL    NUMBER(6)
 ISO_CODE        NOT NULL    VARCHAR2(2)
 ISO_NAME        NOT NULL    VARCHAR2(50)
 AUDIT_DATE      NOT NULL    DATE
 AUDIT_USER      NOT NULL    VARCHAR2(30)
 GLOBAL_NAME     NOT NULL    VARCHAR2(20)
```

The primary key of the ISO_COUNTRIES table is COUNTRY_ID.

The read-only snapshot mechanism

The simplest means of replication is the read-only snapshot, which is essentially a table at the snapshot site that holds the results of a remote query. This table is refreshed at an interval that is determined when the snapshot is created and that can be modified without re-creating the snapshot.

Read-only snapshots can be created in such a way that the refreshes have to update only records that have been modified since the last refresh. This optimization is called a *fast refresh*. In order to use a fast refresh, the master table must keep track of which records have changed since the last refresh. This bookkeeping happens automatically if you create a *snapshot log* on the master table. If you do not create a snapshot log on the master table, then every snapshot will be a *complete refresh*, which means that the snapshot table is completely repopulated. Obviously this is undesirable, particularly for large snapshots.

To create a snapshot log on the ISO_COUNTRIES table, we issue the following statement:

```
CREATE SNAPSHOT LOG ON iso_countries
WITH PRIMARY KEY
TABLESPACE sprocket_data STORAGE (INITIAL 1M NEXT 1M PCTINCREASE 0)
```

 The preceding CREATE SNAPSHOT LOG statement uses the WITH PRIMARY KEY option, which is new with Oracle8. In Oracle7, changed records are tracked in the snapshot log by their ROWID. Oracle8 gives you the choice of building the snapshot log-based on primary key or ROWID.

The snapshot log on the ISO_COUNTRIES table looks like this:

```
SQL> desc SPROCKET.mlog$_iso_countries
 Name                    Null?    Type
 ----------------        -----    --------
 COUNTRY_ID                       NUMBER(6)
 SNAPTIME$$                       DATE
 DMLTYPE$$                        VARCHAR2(1)
 OLD_NEW$$                        VARCHAR2(1)
 CHANGE_VECTOR$$                  RAW(255)
```

Oracle also creates an after-row trigger on the ISO_COUNTRIES table that populates the snapshot log after every insert, update, and delete. In Oracle8, the trigger is internalized, so it is not visible in the data dictionary. In an Oracle7 database, however, we can see the text of the trigger, named TLOG$_ISO_COUNTRIES:

```
DECLARE dmltype CHAR;
BEGIN
    IF      inserting then dmltype := 'I';
    ELSIF   updating  then dmltype := 'U';
    ELSIF   deleting  then dmltype := 'D';
    END IF;

    INSERT INTO "SPROCKET"."MLOG$_ISO_COUNTRIES" (m_row$$, dmltype$$)
    VALUES (:old.rowid, dmltype);
END;
```

 The Oracle7 version of the MLOG$_ISO_COUNTRIES table identifies rows by their ROWID instead of by primary key and does not have the fields OLD_NEW$$ or CHANGE_VECTOR$$.

So far, we have only described the master site's architecture. What happens at the snapshot site when we create a snapshot?

```
CREATE SNAPSHOT iso_countries
REFRESH FAST
START WITH SYSDATE
NEXT SYSDATE+10/1440
WITH PRIMARY KEY
AS
SELECT   country_id,
         iso_code,
         iso_name,
         audit_date,
         audit_user,
         global_name
FROM     iso_countries@PHQS.BIGWHEEL.COM;
```

This CREATE SNAPSHOT statement creates a table at the snapshot site named SNAP$_ISO_COUNTRIES, which contains all columns of the master ISO_COUNTRIES table. If we use the Oracle8 WITH PRIMARY KEY syntax, the snapshot table has exactly the same columns as the master table. In Oracle7, or if we use the WITH ROWID syntax in Oracle8, the snapshot will have an extra column, M_ROW$$, which contains the ROWID corresponding to the record in the master database.

The CREATE SNAPSHOT statement also creates a view, named ISO_COUNTRIES. This view is defined as a query on the SNAP$_ISO_COUNTRIES table, which returns exactly the fields in the master table.

Finally, the CREATE SNAPSHOT statement also schedules a job in the job queue to refresh the snapshot. This job is a call to DBMS_REFRESH, and it is scheduled to recur at the frequency specified by the NEXT clause in the CREATE SNAPSHOT statement.

Table 9-3 summarizes the objects Oracle creates to support read-only snapshots.

Table 9-3. Objects Created to Support Read-Only Snapshots

Site	DDL Statement	Objects Created
Master site	CREATE SNAPSHOT LOG	Table MLOG$_*master_table_name* Trigger TLOG$_*master_table_name* (Note that the TLOG$ trigger is internalized in Oracle8 and not visible in the data dictionary.)
Snapshot site	CREATE SNAPSHOT	Table SNAP$_*master_table_name* View MLOG$_*master_table_name* (Oracle7 only) Index PK_*master_table_name* (Oracle8 only) View *master_table_name* Scheduled job to call DBMS_REFRESH

Figure 9-1 illustrates how these components work together.

At the master site, we see the TLOG$ trigger firing to populate the MLOG$ table when DML is applied to the master table. At the snapshot site, we see the SNAP$

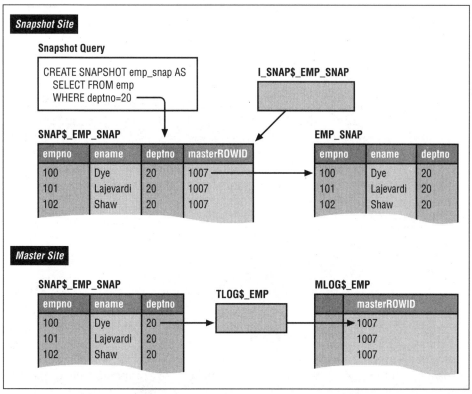

Figure 9-1. How read-only snapshots work

table, and the call to DBMS_REFRESH which reexecutes the snapshot's defining query at a specified interval.

The updateable snapshot mechanism

Updateable snapshots permit DML at the snapshot sites and propagate DML changes from the snapshot table back to the master table. The architecture of updateable snapshots is quite similar to that of read-only snapshots. The primary architectural differences are the following:

- Updateable snapshot sites maintain a table analogous to the master site's MLOG$ table, populated by a trigger analogous to the master sites TLOG$ trigger. The updateable snapshot log table is named USLOG$_*master_table_name* and the trigger is named USTRG$_*master_table_name*. As with the TLOG$ trigger, the USTRG$ trigger is internalized in Oracle8 and therefore is not visible in the data dictionary.

- Updateable snapshot sites use a trigger to post deferred RPCs that send DML changes to the master site.

Unlike read-only snapshots, updateable snapshots require that advanced replication be installed and configured.

How do these additional objects propagate updates at the snapshot site to the master site? Let us again consider our ISO_COUNTRIES table. We can create an updateable snapshot of this table as follows:

```
CREATE SNAPSHOT iso_countries
REFRESH FAST
START WITH SYSDATE
NEXT SYSDATE+10/1440
WITH PRIMARY KEY
FOR UPDATE
AS
SELECT  country_id,
        iso_code,
        iso_name,
        audit_date,
        audit_user,
        global_name
FROM    iso_countries@PHQS.BIGWHEEL.COM;
```

Again, the WITH PRIMARY KEY syntax is unique to Oracle8. When you create a snapshot with the FOR UPDATE clause and make the appropriate calls to the replication packages that create the supporting objects for the updateable snapshot, you end up with the following objects. Unless otherwise noted, these objects reside at the snapshot site:

Table SNAP$_ISO_COUNTRIES
　　Contains the results of the query that defines the snapshot, plus a field M_ ROW$$ if the snapshot site is an Oracle7 database or if the WITH ROWID syntax is used in an Oracle8 database.

Table USLOG$_ISO_COUNTRIES
　　Captures information about rows that have been changed; Oracle uses this information to update the master table.

Trigger USTRG$_ISO_COUNTRIES on table SNAP$_ISO_COUNTRIES
　　Populates the USLOG$_ISO_COUNTRIES table; visible in Oracle7 only; internalized in Oracle8.

Trigger ISO_COUNTRIES$RT on table SNAP$_ISO_COUNTRIES
　　Makes calls to ISO_COUNTRIES$TP; visible in Oracle7 only; internalized in Oracle8.

Package ISO_COUNTRIES$TP
　　Builds deferred RPCs, which call ISO_COUNTRIES$RP at the master site; visible in Oracle7 only; internalized in Oracle8.

Package ISO_COUNTRIES$RP

Performs DML on the master table.

Package ISO_COUNTRIES$RR

Defined only at the master site. This package contains routines used for conflict resolution. Oracle creates only the package at the snapshot site; at the master site Oracle creates both the package and the package body.

View ISO_COUNTRIES

View defined on the SNAP$_ISO_COUNTRIES table, which contains all columns except for the M_ROW$$ column.

Entry in job queue that calls DBMS_REFRESH

DBMS_REFRESH refreshes the snapshot and pushes DML changes back to the master.

The USLOG$_ISO_COUNTRIES table looks like the following:

Oracle7:

```
SQL>  desc uslog$_iso_countries
 Name              Null?        Type
 -----------       -----        --------------
 M_ROW$$                        VARCHAR2(255)
 SNAPTIME$$                     DATE
 DMLTYPE$$                      VARCHAR2(1)
```

Oracle8:

```
SQL>  desc uslog$_iso_countries
 Name              Null?        Type
 -----------       -----        --------------
 COUNTRY_ID                     NUMBER(6)
 SNAPTIME$$                     DATE
 DMLTYPE$$                      VARCHAR2(1)
 OLD_NEW$$                      VARCHAR2(1)
```

As is the case with the MLOG$ tables at the master site, the primary difference between the Oracle7 and Oracle8 versions of the USLOG$ table is that Oracle8 identifies rows by primary key value, whereas Oracle7 identifies them by ROWID.

The triggers USTRG$_ISO_COUNTRIES and ISO_COUNTRIES$RT are visible only in the Oracle7 data dictionary because the Oracle8 version of the trigger is internalized but logically similar. The Oracle7 triggers are defined as follows.

Trigger USTRG$_ISO_COUNTRIES:

```
declare dmltype char;

begin
    if not dbms_snapshot.I_am_a_refresh then
        if      updatingthen dmltype := 'U';
        elsif   deletingthen dmltype := 'D';
    end if;
```

```
    insert into "SPROCKET"."USLOG$_ISO_COUNTRIES"
        (m_row$$, dmltype$$, snaptime$$)
    values (:old.m_row$$,
            dmltype,
            to_date('4000-01-01:00:00:00','YYYY-MM-DD:HH24:MI:SS'));
    end if;
end;
```

The purpose of the USLOG$_ISO_COUNTRIES table is to capture information about DML that occurs at the snapshot site.

Trigger ISO_COUNTRIES$RT:

```
declare
  flag char;
begin
  if "ISO_COUNTRIES$TP".active then
    if inserting then
      flag := 'I';
    elsif updating then
      flag := 'U';
    elsif deleting then
      flag := 'D';
    end if;
    "ISO_COUNTRIES$TP".replicate(
      :old."AUDIT_DATE",:new."AUDIT_DATE",
      :old."AUDIT_USER",:new."AUDIT_USER",
      :old."COUNTRY_ID",:new."COUNTRY_ID",
      :old."GLOBAL_NAME",:new."GLOBAL_NAME",
      :old."ISO_CODE",:new."ISO_CODE",
      :old."ISO_NAME",:new."ISO_NAME",
      flag);
  end if;
end;
```

This trigger calls ISO_COUNTRIES$TP.REPLICATE, which builds a deferred RPC to propagate changes to the snapshot back to the master site.

The ISO_COUNTRIES$TP.REPLICATE procedure is defined in Example 9-1.

Example 9-1. ISO_COUNTRIES$TP Package

```
package body    "ISO_COUNTRIES$TP" as
  I_am_a_snapshot CHAR;
  is_snapshot BOOLEAN;
  function active return boolean
  is
  begin
    return (not((is_snapshot and dbms_snapshot.I_am_a_refresh) or
        not dbms_reputil.replication_is_on));
  end active;
  procedure replicate(
    "AUDIT_DATE1_o" IN DATE,        /*-- The _o and _n parameters      --*/
    "AUDIT_DATE1_n" IN DATE,        /*-- correspond to the old and new  --*/
    "AUDIT_USER2_o" IN VARCHAR2,    /*-- values of the data.            --*/
    "AUDIT_USER2_n" IN VARCHAR2,    /*-- This information is used to     --*/
```

Example 9-1. ISO_COUNTRIES$TP Package (continued)

```
      "COUNTRY_ID3_o" IN NUMBER,      /*-- check that existing row at the --*/
      "COUNTRY_ID3_n" IN NUMBER,      /*-- destination site is the same   --*/
      "GLOBAL_NAME4_o" IN VARCHAR2,   /*-- old row at the origin.          --*/
      "GLOBAL_NAME4_n" IN VARCHAR2,   /*-- If there are discrepancies,     --*/
      "ISO_CODE5_o" IN VARCHAR2,      /*-- the conflict resolution method --*/
      "ISO_CODE5_n" IN VARCHAR2,      /*-- (if defined for the table) is  --*/
      "ISO_NAME6_o" IN VARCHAR2,      /*-- invoked.                        --*/
      "ISO_NAME6_n" IN VARCHAR2,
      flag IN CHAR)
    is
    begin
      if flag = 'U' then      /*-- If updating... --*/
        dbms_defer.call('SPROCKET','ISO_COUNTRIES$RP',
            'REP_UPDATE',14,'RG_SPROCKET');
        dbms_defer.date_arg("AUDIT_DATE1_o");
        dbms_defer.date_arg("AUDIT_DATE1_n");
        dbms_defer.varchar2_arg("AUDIT_USER2_o");
        dbms_defer.varchar2_arg("AUDIT_USER2_n");
        dbms_defer.number_arg("COUNTRY_ID3_o");
        dbms_defer.number_arg("COUNTRY_ID3_n");
        dbms_defer.varchar2_arg("GLOBAL_NAME4_o");
        dbms_defer.varchar2_arg("GLOBAL_NAME4_n");
        dbms_defer.varchar2_arg("ISO_CODE5_o");
        dbms_defer.varchar2_arg("ISO_CODE5_n");
        dbms_defer.varchar2_arg("ISO_NAME6_o");
        dbms_defer.varchar2_arg("ISO_NAME6_n");
      elsif flag = 'I' then   /*-- If inserting... --*/
        dbms_defer.call('SPROCKET','ISO_COUNTRIES$RP',
            'REP_INSERT',8,'RG_SPROCKET');
        dbms_defer.date_arg("AUDIT_DATE1_n");
        dbms_defer.varchar2_arg("AUDIT_USER2_n");
        dbms_defer.number_arg("COUNTRY_ID3_n");
        dbms_defer.varchar2_arg("GLOBAL_NAME4_n");
        dbms_defer.varchar2_arg("ISO_CODE5_n");
        dbms_defer.varchar2_arg("ISO_NAME6_n");
      elsif flag = 'D' then   /*-- If deleting... */
        dbms_defer.call('SPROCKET','ISO_COUNTRIES$RP',
            'REP_DELETE',8,'RG_SPROCKET');
        dbms_defer.date_arg("AUDIT_DATE1_o");
        dbms_defer.varchar2_arg("AUDIT_USER2_o");
        dbms_defer.number_arg("COUNTRY_ID3_o");
        dbms_defer.varchar2_arg("GLOBAL_NAME4_o");
        dbms_defer.varchar2_arg("ISO_CODE5_o");
        dbms_defer.varchar2_arg("ISO_NAME6_o");
      end if;
      dbms_defer.varchar2_arg(dbms_reputil.global_name);
      dbms_defer.char_arg(I_am_a_snapshot);
    end replicate;
  begin
    select decode(master, 'N', 'Y', 'N')
      into I_am_a_snapshot
      from all_repcat where gname = 'RG_SPROCKET';
    is_snapshot := (I_am_a_snapshot = 'Y');
  end "ISO_COUNTRIES$TP";
```

Note that the calls to ISO_COUNTRIES$RP in this package are RPCs; the ISO_
COUNTRIES$RP package executes at the master site. It applies the DML from the
snapshot site to the master table. It is defined as shown in Example 9-2:

Example 9-2. ISO_COUNTRIES$RP Package

```
package body    "ISO_COUNTRIES$RP" as
  procedure rep_delete(
    "AUDIT_DATE1_o" IN DATE,
    "AUDIT_USER2_o" IN VARCHAR2,
    "COUNTRY_ID3_o" IN NUMBER,
    "GLOBAL_NAME4_o" IN VARCHAR2,
    "ISO_CODE5_o" IN VARCHAR2,
    "ISO_NAME6_o" IN VARCHAR2,
    site_name IN VARCHAR2,
    propagation_flag IN CHAR) is
  begin
    rep_delete(
      NULL,
      "AUDIT_DATE1_o",
      "AUDIT_USER2_o",
      "COUNTRY_ID3_o",
      "GLOBAL_NAME4_o",
      "ISO_CODE5_o",
      "ISO_NAME6_o",
      site_name,
      propagation_flag);
  end rep_delete;
  procedure rep_delete(
    column_changed$ IN RAW,
    "AUDIT_DATE1_o" IN DATE,
    "AUDIT_USER2_o" IN VARCHAR2,
    "COUNTRY_ID3_o" IN NUMBER,
    "GLOBAL_NAME4_o" IN VARCHAR2,
    "ISO_CODE5_o" IN VARCHAR2,
    "ISO_NAME6_o" IN VARCHAR2,
    site_name IN VARCHAR2,
    propagation_flag IN CHAR) is
    column_sent$_varchar2 VARCHAR2(6);
  begin
    column_changed$$ := column_changed$;
    if column_changed$ is not null then
      dbms_reputil.raw_to_varchar2(column_changed$,
                2,
                column_sent$_varchar2);
    end if;
    if propagation_flag = 'N' then
      dbms_reputil.replication_off;
    end if;
    dbms_reputil.rep_begin(site_name);
    dbms_reputil.global_name := site_name;
    delete from "ISO_COUNTRIES"
    where (    /*-- make sure the current row matches the origin's row --*/
        decode(substr(column_sent$_varchar2, 1, 1),
```

Example 9-2. ISO_COUNTRIES$RP Package (continued)

```
          'N', 'Y',
          decode("AUDIT_DATE1_o", "AUDIT_DATE", 'Y', 'N')) = 'Y'
  and
      decode(substr(column_sent$_varchar2, 2, 1),
          'N', 'Y',
          decode("AUDIT_USER2_o", "AUDIT_USER", 'Y', 'N')) = 'Y'
  and
      decode(substr(column_sent$_varchar2, 3, 1),
          'N', 'Y',
          decode("COUNTRY_ID3_o", "COUNTRY_ID", 'Y', 'N')) = 'Y'
  and
      decode(substr(column_sent$_varchar2, 4, 1),
      'N', 'Y',
          decode("GLOBAL_NAME4_o", "GLOBAL_NAME", 'Y', 'N')) = 'Y'
  and
      decode(substr(column_sent$_varchar2, 5, 1),
          'N', 'Y',
          decode("ISO_CODE5_o", "ISO_CODE", 'Y', 'N')) = 'Y'
  and
      decode(substr(column_sent$_varchar2, 6, 1),
          'N', 'Y',
          decode("ISO_NAME6_o", "ISO_NAME", 'Y', 'N')) = 'Y'
    );
  if sql%rowcount = 0 then
    raise no_data_found;              /*-- no records match --*/
  elsif sql%rowcount > 1 then
    raise too_many_rows;             /*-- more than one record matches --*/
  end if;
  dbms_reputil.rep_end;
exception
  when no_data_found then
    begin
    if not "ISO_COUNTRIES$RR".delete_conflict_handler(
      "AUDIT_DATE1_o",
      "AUDIT_USER2_o",
      "COUNTRY_ID3_o",
      "GLOBAL_NAME4_o",
      "ISO_CODE5_o",
      "ISO_NAME6_o",
      site_name,
      propagation_flag,
      column_changed$,
      column_sent$_varchar2) then
      dbms_reputil.rep_end;
      raise;
    end if;
    dbms_reputil.rep_end;
    exception
    when others then
      dbms_reputil.rep_end;
      raise;
    end;
```

Example 9-2. ISO_COUNTRIES$RP Package (continued)

```
  when others then
    dbms_reputil.rep_end;
    raise;
end rep_delete;
procedure rep_insert(
  "AUDIT_DATE1_n" IN DATE,
  "AUDIT_USER2_n" IN VARCHAR2,
  "COUNTRY_ID3_n" IN NUMBER,
  "GLOBAL_NAME4_n" IN VARCHAR2,
  "ISO_CODE5_n" IN VARCHAR2,
  "ISO_NAME6_n" IN VARCHAR2,
  site_name IN VARCHAR2,
  propagation_flag IN CHAR) is
begin
  if propagation_flag = 'N' then
    dbms_reputil.replication_off;
  end if;
  dbms_reputil.rep_begin(site_name);
  dbms_reputil.global_name := site_name;
  insert into "ISO_COUNTRIES" (
    "AUDIT_DATE",
    "AUDIT_USER",
    "COUNTRY_ID",
    "GLOBAL_NAME",
    "ISO_CODE",
    "ISO_NAME")
  values (
    "AUDIT_DATE1_n",
    "AUDIT_USER2_n",
    "COUNTRY_ID3_n",
    "GLOBAL_NAME4_n",
    "ISO_CODE5_n",
    "ISO_NAME6_n");
  dbms_reputil.rep_end;
exception
  when dup_val_on_index then
    begin
    if not "ISO_COUNTRIES$RR".unique_conflict_insert_handler(
      "AUDIT_DATE1_n",
      "AUDIT_USER2_n",
      "COUNTRY_ID3_n",
      "GLOBAL_NAME4_n",
      "ISO_CODE5_n",
      "ISO_NAME6_n",
      site_name,
      propagation_flag,
      SQLERRM) then
      dbms_reputil.rep_end;
      raise;
    end if;
    dbms_reputil.rep_end;
```

Example 9-2. ISO_COUNTRIES$RP Package (continued)

```
        exception
      when others then
        dbms_reputil.rep_end;
        raise;
        end;
      when others then
        dbms_reputil.rep_end;
        raise;
    end rep_insert;
    procedure rep_update(
      "AUDIT_DATE1_o" IN DATE,
      "AUDIT_DATE1_n" IN DATE,
      "AUDIT_USER2_o" IN VARCHAR2,
      "AUDIT_USER2_n" IN VARCHAR2,
      "COUNTRY_ID3_o" IN NUMBER,
      "COUNTRY_ID3_n" IN NUMBER,
      "GLOBAL_NAME4_o" IN VARCHAR2,
      "GLOBAL_NAME4_n" IN VARCHAR2,
      "ISO_CODE5_o" IN VARCHAR2,
      "ISO_CODE5_n" IN VARCHAR2,
      "ISO_NAME6_o" IN VARCHAR2,
      "ISO_NAME6_n" IN VARCHAR2,
      site_name IN VARCHAR2,
      propagation_flag IN CHAR) is
    begin
      rep_update(
        NULL,
        "AUDIT_DATE1_o",
        "AUDIT_DATE1_n",
        "AUDIT_USER2_o",
        "AUDIT_USER2_n",
        "COUNTRY_ID3_o",
        "COUNTRY_ID3_n",
        "GLOBAL_NAME4_o",
        "GLOBAL_NAME4_n",
        "ISO_CODE5_o",
        "ISO_CODE5_n",
        "ISO_NAME6_o",
        "ISO_NAME6_n",
        site_name,
        propagation_flag);
    end rep_update;
    procedure rep_update(
      column_changed$ IN RAW,
      "AUDIT_DATE1_o" IN DATE,
      "AUDIT_DATE1_n" IN DATE,
      "AUDIT_USER2_o" IN VARCHAR2,
      "AUDIT_USER2_n" IN VARCHAR2,
      "COUNTRY_ID3_o" IN NUMBER,
      "COUNTRY_ID3_n" IN NUMBER,
      "GLOBAL_NAME4_o" IN VARCHAR2,
```

Example 9-2. ISO_COUNTRIES$RP Package (continued)

```
    "GLOBAL_NAME4_n" IN VARCHAR2,
    "ISO_CODE5_o" IN VARCHAR2,
    "ISO_CODE5_n" IN VARCHAR2,
    "ISO_NAME6_o" IN VARCHAR2,
    "ISO_NAME6_n" IN VARCHAR2,
    site_name IN VARCHAR2,
    propagation_flag IN CHAR) is
    column_changed$_varchar2 VARCHAR2(6);
    column_sent$_varchar2 VARCHAR2(6);
begin
    column_changed$$ := column_changed$;
    if column_changed$ is not null then
      dbms_reputil.raw_to_varchar2(column_changed$,
                    1,
                    column_changed$_varchar2);
      dbms_reputil.raw_to_varchar2(column_changed$,
                    2,
                    column_sent$_varchar2);
    end if;
    if propagation_flag = 'N' then
      dbms_reputil.replication_off;
    end if;
    dbms_reputil.rep_begin(site_name);
    dbms_reputil.global_name := site_name;
    update "ISO_COUNTRIES" set
      "AUDIT_DATE" =
    decode(substr(column_changed$_varchar2, 1, 1),
        'N', "AUDIT_DATE",
        'Y', "AUDIT_DATE1_n",
        NULL, decode("AUDIT_DATE1_o",
              "AUDIT_DATE1_n","AUDIT_DATE",
              "AUDIT_DATE1_n")),
      "AUDIT_USER" =
    decode(substr(column_changed$_varchar2, 2, 1),
        'N', "AUDIT_USER",
        'Y', "AUDIT_USER2_n",
        NULL, decode("AUDIT_USER2_o",
              "AUDIT_USER2_n","AUDIT_USER",
              "AUDIT_USER2_n")),
      "COUNTRY_ID" =
    decode(substr(column_changed$_varchar2, 3, 1),
        'N', "COUNTRY_ID",
        'Y', "COUNTRY_ID3_n",
        NULL, decode("COUNTRY_ID3_o",
              "COUNTRY_ID3_n","COUNTRY_ID",
              "COUNTRY_ID3_n")),
      "GLOBAL_NAME" =
    decode(substr(column_changed$_varchar2, 4, 1),
        'N', "GLOBAL_NAME",
        'Y', "GLOBAL_NAME4_n",
        NULL, decode("GLOBAL_NAME4_o",
```

Example 9-2. ISO_COUNTRIES$RP Package (continued)

```
            "GLOBAL_NAME4_n","GLOBAL_NAME",
            "GLOBAL_NAME4_n")),
   "ISO_CODE" =
decode(substr(column_changed$_varchar2, 5, 1),
     'N', "ISO_CODE",
     'Y', "ISO_CODE5_n",
    NULL, decode("ISO_CODE5_o",
         "ISO_CODE5_n","ISO_CODE",
         "ISO_CODE5_n")),
   "ISO_NAME" =
decode(substr(column_changed$_varchar2, 6, 1),
     'N', "ISO_NAME",
     'Y', "ISO_NAME6_n",
    NULL, decode("ISO_NAME6_o",
         "ISO_NAME6_n","ISO_NAME",
         "ISO_NAME6_n"))
where (((decode(substr(column_changed$_varchar2, 1, 1),
         'N', 'Y',
         'Y', 'N',
         decode("AUDIT_DATE1_o", "AUDIT_DATE1_n", 'Y', 'N')) = 'Y' and

     decode(substr(column_changed$_varchar2, 2, 1),
         'N', 'Y',
         'Y', 'N',
         decode("AUDIT_USER2_o","AUDIT_USER2_n", 'Y', 'N')) = 'Y' and

     1 = 1 and
     decode(substr(column_changed$_varchar2, 4, 1),
         'N', 'Y',
         'Y', 'N',
         decode("GLOBAL_NAME4_o", "GLOBAL_NAME4_n", 'Y', 'N')) = 'Y'and

     decode(substr(column_changed$_varchar2, 5, 1),
         'N', 'Y',
         'Y', 'N',
         decode("ISO_CODE5_o", "ISO_CODE5_n", 'Y', 'N')) = 'Y' and
     decode(substr(column_changed$_varchar2, 6, 1),
         'N', 'Y',
         'Y', 'N',
         decode("ISO_NAME6_o", "ISO_NAME6_n", 'Y', 'N')) = 'Y')) or
     (decode(substr(column_sent$_varchar2, 1, 1),
         'N', 'Y',
         decode("AUDIT_DATE1_o", "AUDIT_DATE", 'Y', 'N')) = 'Y' and
     decode(substr(column_sent$_varchar2, 2, 1),
         'N', 'Y',
         decode("AUDIT_USER2_o", "AUDIT_USER", 'Y', 'N')) = 'Y' and
     1 = 1 and
     decode(substr(column_sent$_varchar2, 4, 1),
         'N', 'Y',
         decode("GLOBAL_NAME4_o", "GLOBAL_NAME", 'Y', 'N')) = 'Y' and
     decode(substr(column_sent$_varchar2, 5, 1),
```

Example 9-2. ISO_COUNTRIES$RP Package (continued)

```
            'N', 'Y',
            decode("ISO_CODE5_o", "ISO_CODE", 'Y', 'N')) = 'Y' and
        decode(substr(column_sent$_varchar2, 6, 1),
            'N', 'Y',
            decode("ISO_NAME6_o", "ISO_NAME", 'Y', 'N')) = 'Y'))
    and "COUNTRY_ID3_o" = "COUNTRY_ID";
  if sql%rowcount = 0 then
    raise no_data_found;
  elsif sql%rowcount > 1 then
    raise too_many_rows;
  end if;
  dbms_reputil.rep_end;
exception
  when no_data_found then
    begin
    if not "ISO_COUNTRIES$RR".update_conflict_handler(
      "AUDIT_DATE1_o",
      dbms_reputil2.choose_date(
          "AUDIT_DATE1_o",
          "AUDIT_DATE1_n",
          column_changed$_varchar2, 1),
      "AUDIT_USER2_o",
      dbms_reputil2.choose_varchar2(
          "AUDIT_USER2_o",
          "AUDIT_USER2_n",
          column_changed$_varchar2, 2),
      "COUNTRY_ID3_o",
      dbms_reputil2.choose_number(
          "COUNTRY_ID3_o",
          "COUNTRY_ID3_n",
          column_changed$_varchar2, 3),
      "GLOBAL_NAME4_o",
      dbms_reputil2.choose_varchar2(
          "GLOBAL_NAME4_o",
          "GLOBAL_NAME4_n",
          column_changed$_varchar2, 4),
      "ISO_CODE5_o",
      dbms_reputil2.choose_varchar2(
          "ISO_CODE5_o",
          "ISO_CODE5_n",
          column_changed$_varchar2, 5),
      "ISO_NAME6_o",
      dbms_reputil2.choose_varchar2(
          "ISO_NAME6_o",
          "ISO_NAME6_n",
          column_changed$_varchar2, 6),
      site_name,
      propagation_flag,
      column_changed$,
      column_sent$_varchar2,
      null) then
      dbms_reputil.rep_end;
```

Example 9-2. ISO_COUNTRIES$RP Package (continued)

```
      raise;
end if;
dbms_reputil.rep_end;
  exception
when others then
  dbms_reputil.rep_end;
  raise;
  end;
when dup_val_on_index then
  begin
if not "ISO_COUNTRIES$RR".unique_conflict_update_handler(
  "AUDIT_DATE1_o",
  dbms_reputil2.choose_date(
      "AUDIT_DATE1_o",
      "AUDIT_DATE1_n",
      column_changed$_varchar2, 1),
  "AUDIT_USER2_o",
  dbms_reputil2.choose_varchar2(
      "AUDIT_USER2_o",
      "AUDIT_USER2_n",
      column_changed$_varchar2, 2),
  "COUNTRY_ID3_o",
  dbms_reputil2.choose_number(
      "COUNTRY_ID3_o",
      "COUNTRY_ID3_n",
      column_changed$_varchar2, 3),
  "GLOBAL_NAME4_o",
  dbms_reputil2.choose_varchar2(
      "GLOBAL_NAME4_o",
      "GLOBAL_NAME4_n",
      column_changed$_varchar2, 4),
  "ISO_CODE5_o",
  dbms_reputil2.choose_varchar2(
      "ISO_CODE5_o",
      "ISO_CODE5_n",
      column_changed$_varchar2, 5),
  "ISO_NAME6_o",
  dbms_reputil2.choose_varchar2(
      "ISO_NAME6_o",
      "ISO_NAME6_n",
      column_changed$_varchar2, 6),
  site_name,
  propagation_flag,
  column_changed$,
  column_sent$_varchar2,
  null,
  SQLERRM) then
  dbms_reputil.rep_end;
  raise;
end if;
dbms_reputil.rep_end;
  exception
```

Example 9-2. ISO_COUNTRIES$RP Package (continued)

```
   when others then
      dbms_reputil.rep_end;
      raise;
      end;
   when others then
      dbms_reputil.rep_end;
      raise;
  end rep_update;
end "ISO_COUNTRIES$RP";
```

Note that the ISO_COUNTRIES$RP package has several references to ISO_COUN-
TRIES$RR. The $RR package contains logic to resolve conflicts.

Figure 9-2 illustrates the interaction among all of these objects.

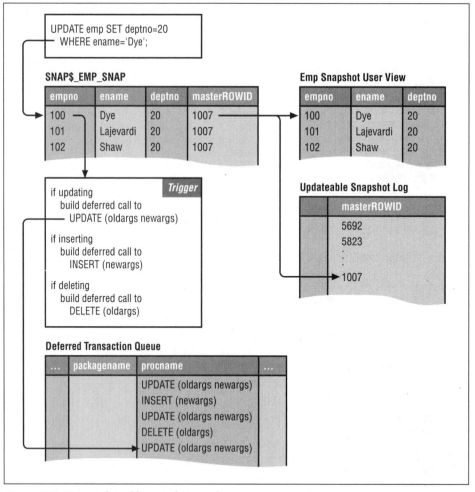

Figure 9-2. How updateable snapshots work

The multi-master replication mechanism

In some respects, the multi-master replication architecture is simpler than the updateable snapshot architecture. Because there is no distinction between master sites and snapshot sites, DML propagation is handled identically at all sites; local DML changes are queued as soon as they occur and dispatched at an interval specified in DBMS_DEFER_SYS.SCHEDULE_EXECUTION (Oracle7) or DBMS_DEFER_SYS.PUSH (Oracle8).

The mechanism behind multi-master replication consists of triggers on the replicated tables that call package procedures, which queue deferred RPCs to the remote master databases. The call to DBMS_REPCAT.GENERATE_REPLICATION_SUPPORT support generates these triggers and packages. Table 9-4 lists the objects that Oracle creates to support multi-master replication of the ISO_COUNTRIES table.

Table 9-4. Objects to Support Multi-Master Replication of Table ISO_COUNTRIES

Object Name	Object Type	Function
ISO_COUNTRIES$RT	Trigger	Trigger on ISO_COUNTRIES; makes calls to ISO_COUNTRIES$TP. Note that this trigger is internalized in Oracle8.
ISO_COUNTRIES$TP	Package	Builds deferred RPCs, which queue DML for propagation to other master sites. The deferred RPCs are to the ISO_COUNTRIES$RP package.
ISO_COUNTRIES$RP	Package	Applies DML from remote masters to the local table. Invokes ISO_COUNTRIES$RR in the event that conflicts are detected.
ISO_COUNTRIES$RR	Package	Invoked conflict resolution methods, if defined.

Figure 9-3 illustrates the interaction of these objects.

The Background Processes

The automation of data propagation in a replicated environment depends on the job queue. Oracle's job queue is analogous to a VMS batch queue or to Unix *cron* jobs; you use it to schedule activities that occur without user interaction. Just as operating system processes drive a VMS batch queue or Unix *cron* jobs, Oracle uses background processes to drive its job queue. In a Solaris environment, these processes have a name in the form ora_snp*n*_*ORACLE_SID*. For example, the PHQS instance has allocated five background processes to control its job queue:

```
socrates% ps -ef | grep snp | grep -v grep | sort
    oracle 27409   1  0   Jun 23 ?        26:10 ora_snp0_PHQS
    oracle 27411   1  0   Jun 23 ?        26:30 ora_snp1_PHQS
    oracle 27413   1  0   Jun 23 ?        26:21 ora_snp2_PHQS
```

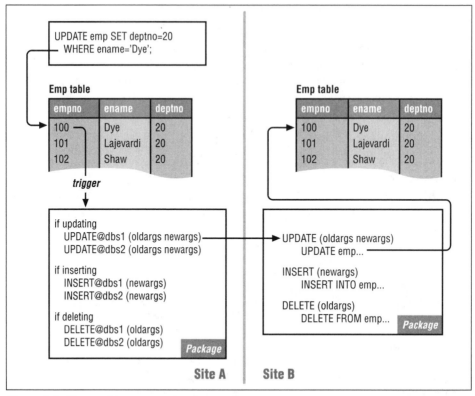

Figure 9-3. How multi-master replication works

```
oracle 27415    1  0    Jun 23 ?      27:19 ora_snp3_PHQS
oracle 27419    1  0    Jun 23 ?      26:10 ora_snp4_PHQS
```

As their name implies, these background processes also handle snapshot refreshes. In fact, the job queue itself is an extension of technology that was developed to support snapshots.

You can control how many background processes are allocated to the job queue and their behavior with two *INIT.ORA* parameters:

JOB_QUEUE_PROCESSES

Determines how many background processes to launch. Each background process can service at most one job queue entry at a time; make sure that you have enough to keep your jobs running on schedule. The maximum number allowable is 36 (snp0 through snp9 and snpA through snpZ).

JOB_QUEUE_INTERVAL

Determines how often the job queue processes "wake up" to see if there are jobs that are due to run. The range of values is 1 to 3600; the units are seconds.

Oracle Version 7.1 has a parameter, JOB_QUEUE_KEEP_CONNEC-TIONS, which can be used to keep open remote database connections that the job queue background process creates. Although this parameter also exists in Oracle Versions 7.2, 7.3, and 8.0, it is included for backward compatibility only and does not have any effect. In Version 7.2 and later, Oracle closes remote database connections after jobs execute.

If you are using the parallel propagation feature of Oracle8, then you also need to be sure to allocate the query server background processes. Although these processes generally are associated with the Parallel Query Option, Oracle also uses them to propagate DML changes in parallel. These processes are named ora_p*nnn*_ORACLE_SID. The PHQS database has eight of them:

```
socrates% ps -ef | grep ora_p0 | grep -v grep | sort
    oracle 27427    1  0    Jun 23  ?         0:00 ora_p000_PHQS
    oracle 27429    1  0    Jun 23  ?         0:00 ora_p001_PHQS
    oracle 27431    1  0    Jun 23  ?         0:00 ora_p002_PHQS
    oracle 27433    1  0    Jun 23  ?         0:00 ora_p003_PHQS
    oracle 27435    1  0    Jun 23  ?         0:00 ora_p004_PHQS
    oracle 27437    1  0    Jun 23  ?         0:00 ora_p005_PHQS
    oracle 27439    1  0    Jun 23  ?         0:00 ora_p006_PHQS
    oracle 27441    1  0    Jun 23  ?         0:00 ora_p007_PHQS
```

The following initialization parameters control the number and behavior of these background processes:

PARALLEL_MAX_SERVERS

The maximum number of background processes to create. Must be greater than or equal to PARALLEL_MIN_SERVERS. This parameter allows you to put a cap on the number of background processes Oracle spawns so that they do not consume excessive resources. However, note that you need one background process for every stream of parallel propagation. The range of values is 0 through 256.

PARALLEL_MIN_SERVERS

The minimum number of background processes to spawn.

PARALLEL_SERVER_IDLE_TIME

The amount of time a query server background process can remain idle before it is terminated.

You must set the JOB_QUEUE_PROCESSES if you want to use the job queue; the default value is 0. Similarly, if you want to utilize parallel propagation, you must set the PARALLEL_MIN_SERVERS initialization parameter.

Replication of DDL

Oracle allows you to replicate DDL as well as DML. In other words, if you want to alter a table or create a new object such as an index or synonym, you can do so at the master definition site and automatically propagate the changes to the other master sites. The procedure DBMS_REPCAT.EXECUTE_DDL provides this functionality.

The DBMS_REPCAT.EXECUTE_DDL procedure queues changes in the replication catalog queue (repcatlog), and the scheduled job DBMS_REPCAT.DO_DEFERRED_ REPCAT_ADMIN pushes the changes to the other masters. Entries in the repcatlog are visible in the DBA_REPCATLOG data dictionary view; a STATUS field contains the value ERROR when errors occur; the MESSAGE field contains the error text.

Not only does the repcatlog queue DDL to other master sites, it also queues replication administrative tasks such as quiescing the environment or adding new master sites. Chapter 12, *Multi-Master Replication*, describes these other activities in detail.

Oracle8 Enhancements

The functionality of the advanced replication facility is greatly enhanced in Oracle8—so much so that you should make every effort to upgrade to Oracle8 (if you haven't already) before creating a replicated environment. The following is a summary of the new functionality:

Parallel propagation
Oracle8 can deliver deferred transactions to remote databases in multiple streams, thereby significantly improving throughput.

Internalized triggers
The *table_name*$RT triggers are internalized in Oracle8, which improves performance and reduces administrative chores.

Reduced data propagation
Unlike Oracle7, Oracle8 sends modified column values to remote databases only when a record is updated.

Subquery snapshots
Snapshots containing subqueries can be fast-refreshed provided that they meet certain restrictions.

LOB support
Oracle8 supports the replication of LOB, CLOB, and NCLOB datatypes (which are new to Oracle8). The Oracle7 predecessors of these datatypes, LONG and LONG RAW, could not be replicated.

Fine-grained quiesce
Oracle8 can quiesce one replication group at a time. In Oracle7, quiescing one group effectively quiesces all other groups.

Primary key snapshots
Oracle8 snapshots are based on the primary key, rather than on ROWID. Thus, master tables can be reorganized without having to perform complete refreshes on all snapshot tables.

Master site snapshot registration
When you create a snapshot from an Oracle8 snapshot site to an Oracle8 master site, Oracle records the existence of the snapshot in the master site's data dictionary view DBA_REGISTERED_SNAPSHOTS.

Support for offline instantiation
The procedure for adding new master and snapshot sites requires less downtime and is more automatic.

Deferred constraint checking for updateable snapshots
Uniqueness and referential integrity constraints on updateable snapshots can be checked and enforced after a refresh is complete instead of during the refresh.

Validation procedure
Oracle8 provides the DBMS_REPCAT.VALIDATE procedure which can help to verify the correct configuration of a replicated environment.

Partitioned tables and indexes
Oracle8 supports the replication of partitioned tables and tables with partitioned indexes.

Oracle8i Enhancements

Oracle8*i* enhancements to replication focus primarily on improved performance, simpler administration, and mass deployment (e.g., hundreds of updateable snapshots from a single master table):

- The generated replication apply packages (*table_name*$RP and *table_name*$RR) are internalized instead of PL/SQL packages—that is, they are written in C and compiled directly into the database engine. This results in faster execution and generation of replication support. In addition, the packages are more secure.

- Snapshot refreshes have been optimized to support refresh groups with up to 400 snapshots per group. In addition, the refresh algorithm has been modified to significantly reduce the number of round-trips required to perform a refresh.

- Snapshot deployment templates allow the DBA to control the contents of snapshot sites. The templates are defined at the master site and deployed to snapshot sites, as opposed to snapshot sites defining their own snapshots. This ensures a uniform configuration of all snapshot sites.

- Vertical partitioning of updateable snapshots. Note that vertical partitions must include all columns that comprise the master table's primary key, and the columns that are not included must either be nullable in the master table or have default values assigned.

Alternatives to Replication

Before moving on, I want to point out that there are alternatives to advanced replication. Like advanced replication, these alternatives can create replicas of table and data at remote sites. However, unlike advanced replication, they are not automatic.

Application- and Trigger-Based Replication

If you have a relatively simple replication requirement, you might consider replicating DML yourself, either by having your application perform writes to multiple databases or by including triggers on tables that perform remote DML. This is a "quick and dirty" solution and is practical only if very few objects are being replicated.

If you choose to create your own replication functionality, you will have to be sure to address issues such as failed writes to the remote databases and degraded performance if writes to many locations are required.

Export/Import

You can use Oracle's export and import utilities to move data from one location to another. This is particularly useful if a large amount of data needs to be relocated, especially if the remote site(s) are available over a WAN or otherwise expensive network connection.

Of course, the disadvantages of the export/import utilities are that they are far from automated and are only point-in-time pictures of the database. In addition, changes you make to imported tables are not propagated back to the tables that were originally imported.

COPY/CREATE TABLE AS SELECT

You can use the SQL commands COPY or CREATE TABLE AS SELECT to make a replica of a remote table over a database link. These command are easy to use but, like the export/import utilities, do not propagate data changes back to the original tables.

In short, although there are a variety of ways to process replicated data, the advanced replication facility provides the most sophisticated and robust architecture.

10

Advanced Replication Installation

In this chapter:
- *Initialization Parameters*
- *Redo Logs and Rollback Segments*
- *Size and Placement of Data Dictionary Objects*
- *Administrative Accounts, Privileges, and Database Links*

Many of the difficulties people experience with using advanced replication stem from incorrect or incomplete installations. Unfortunately, installation errors may go undetected until you have created and instantiated replication groups. But fortunately, it is possible to validate an installation before creating objects. If you carefully follow the instructions provided here, your installations should be successful.

Initialization Parameters

Several initialization parameters have a strong bearing on the performance and reliability of advanced replication. Table 10-1 summarizes these parameters.

Table 10-1. Initialization Parameters for Advanced Replication

Parameter Name	Default Value	Value Range	Remarks
DISTRIBUTED_LOCK_TIMEOUT	60 (seconds)	60–300	The number of seconds that distributed transactions will wait for locked objects. The default may not be adequate for remote transactions to complete, particularly if you are on a slow network or a WAN.
DISTRIBUTED_TRANSACTIONS	OS dependent; approximately TRANSAC-TIONS/4	0–TRANSACTIONS	The number of distributed transactions in which the database can participate at one time. If set to 0, no distributed transactions are allowed. Make sure it is set high enough to support your site's activity.

Table 10-1. Initialization Parameters for Advanced Replication (continued)

Parameter Name	Default Value	Value Range	Remarks
GLOBAL_NAMES	FALSE	TRUE or FALSE	Enforces global naming. It *must* be set to TRUE to use advanced replication. Even if you are not using advanced replication, TRUE is the recommended setting and may be required in future Oracle releases.
JOB_QUEUE_ INTERVAL	60 (seconds)	1–3600	Sets the frequency with which job queue background processes wake up. It should be at least as frequent as your most frequent scheduled job.
JOB_QUEUE_ PROCESSES	0	0–36	This parameter dictates the number of background processes Oracle will start for the job queue. Must be at least 1. Should be at least as high as the maximum number of jobs you need to run simultaneously.
OPEN_LINKS	4	0–255	The maximum number of database links that can be open simultaneously.
PARALLEL_MAX_ SERVERS (Oracle8 only)	OS dependent; 5 on Solaris 5 on NT	0–256	Sets the maximum number of query server background processes. If you are using parallel propagation, make sure it is set high enough for your workload.
PARALLEL_MIN_ SERVERS (Oracle8 only)	0	0–PARALLEL_ MAX_SERVERS	Sets the number of query server background processes Oracle starts up. If you are using parallel propagation, you need a parallel query background process for each stream.
PARALLEL_ SERVER_IDLE_ TIME (Oracle8 only)	OS dependent; 5 on Solaris 5 on NT (minutes)	0–OS-dependent maximum	The number of minutes a query server background process is idle before Oracle terminates the process.
REPLICATION_ DEPENDENCY_ TRACKING (Oracle8 only)	TRUE	TRUE or FALSE	Enables Oracle's dependency tracking, which parallel propagation uses. Must be set to TRUE.

Table 10-1. Initialization Parameters for Advanced Replication (continued)

Parameter Name	Default Value	Value Range	Remarks
RESOURCE_LIMIT	FALSE	TRUE or FALSE	Leave this setting at FALSE; a bug causes propagation to remote sites to fail with "session limit exceeded" even if the propagator's profile has no limits set.
SHARED_POOL_SIZE	3.5MB	300K–OS-dependent limit	Advanced replication uses a significant amount of shared pool resources. Oracle Corporation has stated that the shared pool utilization for replicated DML is at least six times that of nonreplicated DML.

Of the parameters listed in Table 10-1, SHARED_POOL_SIZE is the most crucial for a successful installation. In fact, the *catrep.sql* script, which creates the data dictionary objects for replication, will fail if the shared pool is less than 11MB. As a practical matter, 32MB should be considered the absolute minimum for a replicated database.

Redo Logs and Rollback Segments

The database activity that drives the replication system generates a tremendous amount of redo and rollback activity—at least five times that of a nonreplicated environment by Oracle Corporation's own estimates. Most of this overhead is associated with internal transactions that modify data dictionary tables:

- Enqueuing and dequeueing deferred transactions update the tables SYSTEM.DEF$_AQCALL and SYSTEM.DEF$_AQERROR in Oracle8, and SYSTEM.DEF$_CALL in Oracle7.

- The scheduled jobs that propagate DML and DDL update SYS.JOB$ every time they run. These updates alone can account for many megabytes of redo logs per hour depending on the frequency with which these jobs run.

- Collecting statistics about resolved conflicts updates SYSTEM.REPCAT$_RESOLUTION_STATISTICS.

- Snapshot refreshes update the tables SYSTEM.SNAP$, SYSTEM.RGCHILD$, and (in Oracle8) SYSTEM.SNAP_REFTIME$.

Because of this additional activity, you should use more and larger redo logs and rollback segments than you would for a nonreplicated environment. A good starting point is to have five redo groups using 32MB redo logs and at least five rollback segments, with an optimal size of 64MB. This configuration is easiest to do at the time you create the database.

Size and Placement of Data Dictionary Objects

The properties of advanced replication's underpinning tables and indexes are such that they warrant their own tablespace. A default installation, however, places these objects in the SYSTEM tablespace with its default values for INITIAL and NEXT extents. The default installation quickly fragments the SYSTEM tablespace and often requires the addition of several data files to support the growth of the replication data dictionary. Fortunately, these problems are avoidable if you follow these steps when you create your database or at least before you run *catproc.sql*:

1. Create a separate tablespace for the replication data dictionary objects, and specify default storage parameters for INITIAL, NEXT, and PCTINCREASE:

```
CREATE TABLESPACE symrep_data
DATAFILE '/export/vol01/oradata/PHQS/symrep_data01.dbf' SIZE 500M
DEFAULT STORAGE (INITIAL 512K NEXT 1M PCTINCREASE 1);
```

2. Make the new tablespace the default tablespace for user SYSTEM:

```
ALTER USER system DEFAULT TABLESPACE symrep_data;
```

3. Run the *catproc.sql* script from server manager, connected as user SYS:

```
socrates% svrmgrl

Oracle Server Manager Release 3.0.4.0.0 - Production

(c) Copyright 1997, Oracle Corporation.  All Rights Reserved.

Oracle8 Enterprise Edition Release 8.0.4.1.0 - Production
With the Partitioning and Objects options
PL/SQL Release 8.0.4.1.0 - Production

SVRMGR> connect internal
Connected.
SVRMGR> @catproc
...
```

catproc.sql creates, among other things, the objects that support deferred transactions, as well as the Advanced Queueing facility in Oracle8.

4. Run the replication catalog scripts *catrep.sql* and *catrepad.sql*. You must be connected as SYS to run these scripts:

```
SVRMGR> connect internal
Connected.
SVRMGR> @catrep
...
SVRMGR> @catrepad
...
```

It is a good idea to confirm that all database objects have a status of VALID after you run the scripts *catproc.sql, catrep.sql,* and *catrepad.sql.* Query the data dictionary view DBA_OBJECTS to confirm the status, and repair any objects that are invalid either by compiling them or by increasing the shared pool and rerunning the scripts.

5. The triggers and packages that Oracle creates when you generate replication support can potentially amount to a tremendous volume of PL/SQL source in the database. If you expect to replicate more than about 20 tables, you should change the setting for the NEXT extent on the table SYS.SOURCE$ and index SYS.I_SOURCE$:

```
ALTER TABLE sys.source$ STORAGE (NEXT 1M);
ALTER INDEX sys.i_source$ STORAGE (NEXT 1M);
```

Alternatively, you can edit the catalog script which creates these objects, *sql.bsq.* This script contains the *bootstrap.sql* code that Oracle uses to build a database.

Do not modify the *sql.bsq* file unless you are certain that you understand the consequences of your modifications. Also, be aware that Oracle may not support databases that are created with a modified version of this file. We can only hope that future releases of Oracle include a variety of *sql.bsq* files so that we can create a data dictionary whose storage parameters suit specific types of databases.

Administrative Accounts, Privileges, and Database Links

Depending on whether you are running Oracle7 or Oracle8 and which security model you choose to follow, the account-creation process can be simple or tedious. In Oracle7, you have the choice of either mirrored user access or global access. In Oracle8, the management of user accounts is substantially easier; you need only to create propagator and receiver accounts. Regardless of which model you choose or which Oracle version you are using, the proper configuration of accounts, privileges, and database links is crucial. In this section we provide step-by-step procedures you can follow.

In all cases, the creation of administrative accounts and database links requires that you have already run the catalog scripts *catproc.sql, catrep.sql,* and optionally *catrepad.sql.*

Configuring Oracle7 for the Mirrored User Access Model

As its name implies, the *mirrored user access* model requires that every database have an account for every user who is allowed to perform DML against replicated tables. The onus of creating accounts for all of these users in multiple databases lies with the DBA, who must also ensure that these accounts have the same passwords in each database. In addition, these user accounts require EXECUTE privileges on the generated replication support packages for each replicated object they can manipulate. These privileges must be directly granted, not inherited through a database role. Each of these accounts also requires a private database link to each master database.

See Chapter 14, *Procedural Replication*, for a package that can create user accounts in remote databases.

Here are the steps for configuring advanced replication for mirrored user access:

1. Create public database links from every master site to every other master site. Create these links as user SYS, and do *not* use the CONNECT TO clause:

   ```
   CREATE PUBLIC DATABASE LINK PHQS.BIGWHEEL.COM
   USING 'prodhq';
   ```

   Oracle uses this database link to resolve private database links, which must be created without a USING clause (see Step 2). This public database link tells Oracle that private links named PHQS.BIGWHEEL.COM should connect to the database identified by the SQL*Net alias prodhq.

2. Create a REPSYS user in all master databases, with the same password in each database; grant this user surrogate SYS privileges:

   ```
   CREATE USER    REPSYS
   IDENTIFIED BY surrogate
   DEFAULT TABLESPACE users TEMPORARY TABLESPACE temp;

   EXECUTE dbms_repcat_auth.grant_surrogate_repcat (' REPSYS');
   ```

   The REPSYS account is the one to which private database links from user SYS in remote master databases connect. Database links that connect from SYS to SYS in the remote database compromise security because the private database links required for replication use the CONNECT TO clause, which means that usernames and unencrypted passwords are visible in the SYS.LINK$ table. The DBMS_REPCAT_AUTH.GRANT_SURROGATE_REPCAT procedure grants the account CREATE SESSION privileges, as well as the object privileges displayed by the following query:

   ```
   SQL> SELECT  owner, table_name, grantee, grantor, privilege
     2  FROM    dba_tab_privs
     3  WHERE   grantee = ' REPSYS'
     4* ORDER BY owner, table_name, grantee, grantor,  privilege;
   ```

Table Owner	Table Name	Grantee	Grantor	Granted Privilege
SYS	DBA_CONSTRAINTS	REPSYS	SYS	SELECT
SYS	DBA_CONS_COLUMNS	REPSYS	SYS	SELECT
SYS	DBA_SOURCE	REPSYS	SYS	SELECT
SYS	DBA_TABLESPACES	REPSYS	SYS	SELECT
SYS	DBA_TAB_COLUMNS	REPSYS	SYS	SELECT
SYS	DBA_TRIGGERS	REPSYS	SYS	SELECT
SYS	DBA_USERS	REPSYS	SYS	SELECT
SYS	DBA_VIEWS	REPSYS	SYS	SELECT
SYS	DBMSOBJGWRAPPER	REPSYS	SYS	EXECUTE
SYS	DBMS_DEFER	REPSYS	SYS	EXECUTE
SYS	DBMS_DEFERGEN	REPSYS	SYS	EXECUTE
SYS	DBMS_DEFER_INTERNAL_SYS	REPSYS	SYS	EXECUTE
SYS	DBMS_REPCAT	REPSYS	SYS	EXECUTE
SYS	DBMS_REPCAT_CONF	REPSYS	SYS	EXECUTE
SYS	DBMS_REPCAT_MAS	REPSYS	SYS	EXECUTE
SYS	DBMS_REPCAT_SNA	REPSYS	SYS	EXECUTE
SYS	DBMS_REPCAT_SNA_UTL	REPSYS	SYS	EXECUTE
SYS	DBMS_REPCAT_UTL	REPSYS	SYS	EXECUTE
SYS	DBMS_REPCAT_UTL2	REPSYS	SYS	EXECUTE
SYS	DBMS_REPCAT_UTL3	REPSYS	SYS	EXECUTE
SYSTEM	REPCAT$_AUDIT_ATTRIBUTE	REPSYS	SYSTEM	DELETE
SYSTEM	REPCAT$_AUDIT_ATTRIBUTE	REPSYS	SYSTEM	INSERT
SYSTEM	REPCAT$_AUDIT_ATTRIBUTE	REPSYS	SYSTEM	SELECT
SYSTEM	REPCAT$_AUDIT_COLUMN	REPSYS	SYSTEM	DELETE
SYSTEM	REPCAT$_AUDIT_COLUMN	REPSYS	SYSTEM	INSERT
SYSTEM	REPCAT$_AUDIT_COLUMN	REPSYS	SYSTEM	SELECT
SYSTEM	REPCAT$_AUDIT_COLUMN	REPSYS	SYSTEM	UPDATE
SYSTEM	REPCAT$_COLUMN_GROUP	REPSYS	SYSTEM	DELETE
SYSTEM	REPCAT$_COLUMN_GROUP	REPSYS	SYSTEM	INSERT
SYSTEM	REPCAT$_COLUMN_GROUP	REPSYS	SYSTEM	SELECT
SYSTEM	REPCAT$_CONFLICT	REPSYS	SYSTEM	DELETE
SYSTEM	REPCAT$_CONFLICT	REPSYS	SYSTEM	INSERT
SYSTEM	REPCAT$_CONFLICT	REPSYS	SYSTEM	SELECT
SYSTEM	REPCAT$_DDL	REPSYS	SYSTEM	INSERT
SYSTEM	REPCAT$_DDL	REPSYS	SYSTEM	SELECT
SYSTEM	REPCAT$_GENERATED	REPSYS	SYSTEM	SELECT
SYSTEM	REPCAT$_GROUPED_COLUMN	REPSYS	SYSTEM	DELETE
SYSTEM	REPCAT$_GROUPED_COLUMN	REPSYS	SYSTEM	INSERT
SYSTEM	REPCAT$_GROUPED_COLUMN	REPSYS	SYSTEM	SELECT
SYSTEM	REPCAT$_KEY_COLUMNS	REPSYS	SYSTEM	SELECT
SYSTEM	REPCAT$_PARAMETER_COLUMN	REPSYS	SYSTEM	DELETE
SYSTEM	REPCAT$_PARAMETER_COLUMN	REPSYS	SYSTEM	INSERT
SYSTEM	REPCAT$_PARAMETER_COLUMN	REPSYS	SYSTEM	SELECT
SYSTEM	REPCAT$_PARAMETER_COLUMN	REPSYS	SYSTEM	UPDATE
SYSTEM	REPCAT$_PRIORITY	REPSYS	SYSTEM	DELETE
SYSTEM	REPCAT$_PRIORITY	REPSYS	SYSTEM	INSERT
SYSTEM	REPCAT$_PRIORITY	REPSYS	SYSTEM	SELECT
SYSTEM	REPCAT$_PRIORITY_GROUP	REPSYS	SYSTEM	DELETE
SYSTEM	REPCAT$_PRIORITY_GROUP	REPSYS	SYSTEM	INSERT
SYSTEM	REPCAT$_PRIORITY_GROUP	REPSYS	SYSTEM	SELECT
SYSTEM	REPCAT$_REPCAT	REPSYS	SYSTEM	INSERT

SYSTEM	REPCAT$_REPCAT	REPSYS	SYSTEM	SELECT
SYSTEM	REPCAT$_REPCAT	REPSYS	SYSTEM	UPDATE
SYSTEM	REPCAT$_REPCATLOG	REPSYS	SYSTEM	DELETE
SYSTEM	REPCAT$_REPCATLOG	REPSYS	SYSTEM	INSERT
SYSTEM	REPCAT$_REPCATLOG	REPSYS	SYSTEM	SELECT
SYSTEM	REPCAT$_REPCATLOG	REPSYS	SYSTEM	UPDATE
SYSTEM	REPCAT$_REPOBJECT	REPSYS	SYSTEM	SELECT
SYSTEM	REPCAT$_REPOBJECT	REPSYS	SYSTEM	UPDATE
SYSTEM	REPCAT$_REPPROP	REPSYS	SYSTEM	DELETE
SYSTEM	REPCAT$_REPPROP	REPSYS	SYSTEM	SELECT
SYSTEM	REPCAT$_REPSCHEMA	REPSYS	SYSTEM	DELETE
SYSTEM	REPCAT$_REPSCHEMA	REPSYS	SYSTEM	INSERT
SYSTEM	REPCAT$_REPSCHEMA	REPSYS	SYSTEM	SELECT
SYSTEM	REPCAT$_REPSCHEMA	REPSYS	SYSTEM	UPDATE
SYSTEM	REPCAT$_RESOLUTION	REPSYS	SYSTEM	DELETE
SYSTEM	REPCAT$_RESOLUTION	REPSYS	SYSTEM	INSERT
SYSTEM	REPCAT$_RESOLUTION	REPSYS	SYSTEM	SELECT
SYSTEM	REPCAT$_RESOLUTION_METHOD	REPSYS	SYSTEM	DELETE
SYSTEM	REPCAT$_RESOLUTION_METHOD	REPSYS	SYSTEM	INSERT
SYSTEM	REPCAT$_RESOLUTION_METHOD	REPSYS	SYSTEM	SELECT

```
71 rows selected.
```

3. Create private database links from user SYS to user REPSYS from each master database to every other master database.

As user SYS:

```
CREATE DATABASE LINK PHQS.BIGWHEEL.COM
CONNECT TO repsys IDENTIFIED BY surrogate;
```

Note that these private database links do *not* include a USING clause.

4. Create replication administration accounts in each master database and grant this account privileges to administer any replication group and EXECUTE privileges on DBMS_DEFER. Typically, the name for this account is REPADMIN.

As user SYS:

```
CREATE USER repadmin
IDENTIFIED BY replicator
DEFAULT TABLESPACE USERS TEMPORARY TABLESPACE TEMP;

EXECUTE dbms_repcat_admin.grant_admin_any_repgroup('REPADMIN');

GRANT EXECUTE ON dbms_defer TO repadmin WITH GRANT OPTION;
```

If you intend to have multiple replication groups and you wish to administer them under separate accounts, you may do so by granting administrative privileges at the replication group level. These privileges must granted to the owner of the replicated schema, and the replication group must have the same name as the schema owner:

```
CREATE USER sprocket
IDENTIFIED BY spokes
DEFAULT TABLESPACE sprocket_data TEMPORARY TABLESPACE temp;
```

```
EXECUTE dbms_repcat.grant_admin_repgroup('SPROCKET');
```

```
GRANT EXECUTE ON dbms_defer TO sprocket WITH GRANT OPTION;
```

5. Create private database links from REPADMIN in each master database to REPADMIN in every other master database.

   As user REPADMIN:

   ```
   CREATE DATABASE LINK PHQS.BIGWHEEL.COM
   CONNECT TO repadmin IDENTIFIED BY replicator;
   ```

   Again, note that these links must be created without the USING clause.

6. Create private database links from the account owning the replicated tables to its peer account in every other master database. For example, if the Oracle user SPROCKET owns the replicated schema, we would create links as follows:

   ```
   CREATE DATABASE LINK PHQS.BIGWHEEL.COM
   CONNECT TO sprocket IDENTIFIED BY repschema;
   ```

7. Create private database links for end users of the replicated application:

   ```
   CREATE DATABASE LINK PHQS.BIGWHEEL.COM
   CONNECT TO scott IDENTIFIED BY tiger;
   ```

   Note that the end users should have identical privileges on the replicated schema in all databases. If a user changes his password in a database, then his private database links into that database must be dropped and re-created.

8. Grant EXECUTE privileges on the DBMS_DEFER package to schema owner accounts and user accounts in each database.

   As user SYS in each master database:

   ```
   GRANT EXECUTE ON dbms_defer TO repadmin;
   GRANT EXECUTE ON dbms_defer TO scott;
   ...
   ```

At this point you are ready to create replicated objects on which users can perform DML. Chapter 12, *Multi-Master Replication*, describes the procedures for creating replicated objects. Note that the execute_as_user parameter must be set to FALSE, the default, in calls to the following procedures:

```
DBMS_DEFER_SYS.EXECUTE
DBMS_DEFER_SYS.SCHEDULE_EXECUTE
DBMS_SNAPSHOT.REFRESH
DBMS_REPCAT.RESUME_MASTER_ACTIVITY
DBMS_REPCAT.SUSPEND_MASTER_ACTIVITY
```

When an end user performs DML against a table, the *table_name*$RT trigger on the table fires, queueing the DML to remote sites. Because the owner of the table owns this trigger, the table owner queues the deferred RPC. When Oracle pushes the deferred RPC to remote sites, it makes a remote connection via a database link.

Oracle first attempts to use a private link belonging to the ID that queued the transaction (i.e., the table owner). If no such private database link exists, Oracle attempts to use a private database link belonging to the *connected* user. The connected user is the user that is pushing the deferred RPC queue, typically REPADMIN.

The ID to which Oracle connects at the remote database must have EXECUTE privileges on the *table_name*$RP package at the remote site because the deferred RPC is, in fact, a call to the *table_name*$RP package. Both the table owner and the REPADMIN account have sufficient privileges to execute this package—the former because it owns the package and the latter because it has EXECUTE ANY PROCEDURE system privileges.

If you are using synchronous replication, DML is applied simultaneously to the remote sites; it is not queued. If the end user has a private database link, the user specified in the link's CONNECT TO clause must have EXECUTE privileges on the *table_name*$RP package or EXECUTE ANY PROCEDURE system privileges.

Configuring Oracle7 for the Global Access Model

If your database has tens or hundreds of user accounts, the administration of database links and passwords becomes quite daunting, even impractical. Therefore, Oracle allows you to use a single account in the master databases to replicate DML on behalf of all users. Note that this approach is simpler and closely resembles the access method used in Oracle8.

The first six steps of the procedure for configuring the global access model are the same as the mirrored access model. What you do not have to do is to create private database links for end users. To force the deferred transactions, use the REPADMIN account's private database link. The execute_as_user parameter must be set to TRUE in calls to the following procedures:

    DBMS_DEFER_SYS.EXECUTE
    DBMS_DEFER_SYS.SCHEDULE_EXECUTE
    DBMS_SNAPSHOT.REFRESH
    DBMS_REPCAT.RESUME_MASTER_ACTIVITY
    DBMS_REPCAT.SUSPEND_MASTER_ACTIVITY

Configuring Oracle8 for Advanced Replication

The configuration of Oracle8 master sites is a hybrid mix of the Oracle7 mirrored access and global access models. Oracle8 designates special *propagator* and *receiver* accounts, which process deferred RPCs. Gone are the immense database link administrative chores and the execute_as_user parameter. In general, an Oracle8 installation is much simpler than an Oracle7 installation. After you have run *catrep.sql* and *catrepad.sql*, follow these steps:

1. Create anonymous public database links in every master database to every other master database:

   ```
   CREATE PUBLIC DATABASE LINK PHQS.BIGWHEEL.COM
   using 'prodhq';
   ```

2. Create a replication administrator account in each master database. Typically, this account is named REPADMIN.

   As user SYS:

   ```
   CREATE USER repadmin
   IDENTIFIED BY replicator
   DEFAULT TABLESPACE users TEMPORARY TABLESPACE temp;
   ```

   ```
   EXECUTE dbms_repcat_admin.grant_admin_any_schema('REPADMIN');
   ```

   If you plan to have multiple replication groups and wish to administer them separately, you can grant administrative privileges to a specific schema:

   ```
   EXECUTE dbms_repcat_admin.grant_admin_schema('SPROCKET')
   ```

   This call grants the SPROCKET account privileges to perform administrative tasks on replicated objects in the SPROCKET schema. Note that the use of separate administrative accounts works only if the replication group does not span multiple schema.

3. Create private database links from the replication administrator account(s) created in Step 2 from each master database to every other master database. Note that these links must be created without specifying a USING clause:

   ```
   CREATE DATABASE LINK PHQS.BIGWHEEL.COM
   CONNECT TO repadmin IDENTIFIED BY replicator;
   ```

4. Create propagator and receiver accounts in each master database, and grant the accounts privileges to perform replicated DML:

   ```
   CREATE USER proprep IDENTIFIED BY pusher
   DEFAULT TABLESPACE users TEMPORARY TABLESPACE temp;
   ```

   ```
   EXECUTE dbms_defer_sys.register_propagator('PROPREP');
   ```

   The DBMS_DEFER_SYS.REGISTER_PROPAGATOR procedure grants the following privileges to the grantee:

   > CREATE SESSION
   > CREATE DATABASE LINK
   > CREATE PROCEDURE
   > EXECUTE ANY PROCEDURE

Usually we use the propagator account to both propagate *and* receive replicated DML, but you can also create a separate receiver account if you desire a more granular security policy:

```
CREATE USER recvrep IDENTIFIED BY receiver
DEFAULT TABLESPACE users TEMPORARY TABLESPACE temp;

GRANT CREATE SESSION TO recvrep;

GRANT EXECUTE ANY PROCEDURE TO recvrep;
```

You can designate only one propagator account per database instance, regardless of the number of replication groups.

5. Create private database links from the propagator account in each master database to the designated receiver account in every other master database.

```
CREATE DATABASE LINK PHQS.BIGWHEEL.COM
CONNECT TO proprep IDENTIFIED BY pusher;
```

You are now ready to create replication groups and objects. See Chapter 12 for details.

11

Basic Replication

The origin of Oracle's replication technology is the read-only snapshot feature, which shipped with the first Oracle7 release. Read-only snapshots, also known as *basic replication*, are essentially tables that hold the result set of a query on a remote database. We usually configure the snapshot to refresh the result set at a predetermined interval so that the data is current.

About Read-Only Snapshots

Read-only snapshots provide a means to access remote data without requiring a constant network connection. They are intended to maintain local instances of data that the remote master site maintains.

Examples of the appropriate use of read-only snapshots include the following:

- A regional sales office has a snapshot of the PRODUCT_PRICES table which the headquarters site maintains. The snapshot is refreshed once a month, when prices change.

- A retailer's data warehouse performs a snapshot of the DAILY_REGISTER_ RECEIPTS table as part of the nightly data extraction process.

- A billing system performs a snapshot of the CUSTOMER_ADDRESS table prior to each invoice run so that the bills are mailed to the correct addresses.

- A salesperson with a laptop connects to the master sales database and refreshes a snapshot of the subset of the CUSTOMER_LEAD table corresponding to her sales region.

Notice that in each case the snapshot is refreshed at an interval that ensures accurate business processing and that the master site "owns" the data—that is, only the master site can modify the data.

The basic procedure for creating read-only snapshots is as follows:

1. Identify the table(s) at the master site(s) that you want to replicate to the snapshot site and the schema that will own the snapshots. Generally, the schema that owns the snapshots should have the same name as the schema that owns the master table; although this is not a requirement, it simplifies administration.

2. Create database link(s) from the snapshot site to the master sites. These should be private database links owned by the snapshot owner. The database links must connect to an account in the master database that has sufficient privileges to issue the snapshot query.

3. Create snapshot logs in the master database for every master table. Snapshot logs are required for FAST refreshes. Snapshot logs are not required for COMPLETE refreshes.

4. Use the CREATE SNAPSHOT statement to create the snapshot(s).

5. Create one or more refresh groups at the snapshot site and assign each snapshot to a group. This step is optional but recommended.

6. Grant privileges as appropriate to other roles or accounts in the snapshot database so that they can query the snapshot.

Prerequisites and Restrictions

Read-only snapshots do not require the advanced replication facilities. You must, however, have the Procedural Option installed (i.e., the catalog script *catproc.sql* must have been run), and the scripts *dbmssnap.sql* and *prvtsnap.plb* must have been run. (Oracle runs these scripts automatically when you install the Procedural Option by running *catproc.sql*.) You also must set initialization parameters and grant appropriate system privileges to accounts that create snapshots.

Initialization Parameters

In order for snapshots to be capable of refreshing automatically, you must set the following initialization parameters:

JOB_QUEUE_PROCESSES
> This parameter should be set to at least 1. The default is 0.

JOB_QUEUE_INTERVAL
> This parameter should be set to a value that is less than or equal to your most frequent snapshot interval. The default is 60; the units are seconds.

System Privileges

The following system privileges are associated with snapshot administration:

ALTER ANY SNAPSHOT

> The grantee can change various properties of snapshots in any schema. You should reserve this privilege for DBA accounts; it is granted to the DBA role when the database is created.

CREATE ANY SNAPSHOT

> The grantee can create a snapshot in any schema. You should reserve this privilege for DBA accounts; it is granted to the roles DBA and IMP_FULL_ DATABASE when the database is created.

CREATE DATABASE LINK

> The grantee can create and drop private database links. Technically, this privilege is not required to create a snapshot because the connection to the master site could be over a public database link. However, for security's sake, snapshots should always use private database links. Of course, the account to which the database link connects must have adequate privileges on the master table(s) to execute the snapshot's defining query.

CREATE SNAPSHOT

> The grantee can create, alter, and drop snapshots under its own schema—that is, the account owns and can administer whatever snapshots it creates. This is the appropriate privilege for schema owner accounts.

CREATE VIEW

> The grantee can create views. This privilege is required because snapshots consist of an underlying table that may contain the ROWID of the master table and a view on the underlying table that contains only the fields actually queried.

DROP ANY SNAPSHOT

> The grantee can drop snapshots from any schema. You should reserve this privilege for DBA accounts; it is granted to the roles DBA and IMP_FULL_ DATABASE when the database is created.

In addition to these system privileges, the snapshot creator must also have a sufficient space quota in the tablespace(s) that will contain the snapshot base table and any indexes on this table.

Restrictions

Snapshot queries can select from SYS-owned tables or views, and they cannot contain columns of type LONG, LONG RAW, BFILE, or any user-defined datatypes. Oracle8 creates primary key snapshots by default. The master table of primary key snapshots must have a primary key defined and enabled, and the snapshot's defining query must contain all fields of the primary key.

Snapshot Creation Basics

The CREATE SNAPSHOT syntax contains several components, allowing the creator to manipulate the snapshot's physical storage, its refresh interval, and even what rollback segments to use when it refreshes if you are using Oracle8.

Let's examine the components of this statement one at a time, using the following snapshot creation statement as a sample (line numbers are included for reference):

```
 1   CREATE SNAPSHOT product_prices
 2   PCTFREE 0 PCTUSED 99
 3   TABLESPACE sprocket_data
 4       STORAGE (INITIAL 1M NEXT 1M PCTINCREASE 0)
 5   USING INDEX TABLESPACE sprocket_indx
 6       STORAGE (INITIAL 128K NEXT 128K PCTINCREASE 0)
 7   REFRESH FAST
 8       START WITH sysdate
 9       NEXT sysdate + 1
10   WITH PRIMARY KEY
11   USING LOCAL ROLLBACK SEGMENT rb_large
12   AS
13       SELECT   product_id,
14                catalog_number,
15                price,
16                effective_date
17       FROM product_prices@PHQS.BIGWHEEL.COM;
```

This statement creates a snapshot of the PRODUCT_PRICES table, mastered in database PHQS.BIGWHEEL.COM.

The Snapshot STORAGE Clause

Lines 1 through 6 specify the name of the snapshot, PRODUCT_PRICES, and specify storage parameters for the snapshot's base table and the primary key index:

```
 1   CREATE SNAPSHOT product_prices
 2   PCTFREE 0 PCTUSED 99
 3   TABLESPACE sprocket_data
 4       STORAGE (INITIAL 1M NEXT 1M PCTINCREASE 0)
 5   USING INDEX TABLESPACE sprocket_indx
 6       STORAGE (INITIAL 128K NEXT 128K PCTINCREASE 0)
```

The primary key index is an Oracle8 feature; the USING INDEX syntax does not exist in Oracle7.

You will notice that we chose extreme values for PCTFREE and PCTUSED, 0 and 99, respectively. Recall that these storage parameters govern the minimum amount of free space Oracle reserves in each block. This free space provides growing room for records that are updated. If more than PCTFREE percent of a block is empty, the block will be on the free list, which means that more records can be added to the block. Similarly, PCTUSED is the maximum amount of space that data can consume in a block.

Setting PCTFREE to 0 and PCTUSED to 99 tells Oracle to pack each block as full of data as possible; do not leave any free space for updates. We need not be concerned with updates because data in read-only snapshots is never updated, not even by the refresh procedure. (Snapshot refreshes perform updates by deleting the old record and reinserting it with its new values.) Packing the data as tightly as possible minimizes the amount of space required for a snapshot's storage, and we can expect some gains in query performance against the snapshot.

In addition to the PCTFREE and PCTUSED parameters, the tablespace in which to put the snapshot base table is specified (SNAP$_PRODUCT_PRICES in this case), as well as the size of its initial and next extents and the percent by which subsequent extents should grow. Ideally, the table will fit into a single extent.

 Measure the storage allocated to the master table so that you can set the snapshot's storage parameters appropriately. Remember that the snapshot will most likely occupy less space than the master table if you use PCTFREE 0 and PCTUSED 99.

The last portion of the STORAGE clause controls the storage of the primary key index, a feature available in Oracle8. In general, it is a wise practice to place indexes in separate tablespaces from their data. Every schema owner should utilize at least two tablespaces, one for data and one for indexes. This example uses tablespace SPROCKET_DATA and SPROCKET_INDX.

The REFRESH Clause

The REFRESH clause controls the time of the initial refresh, as well as the method and frequency of subsequent refreshes:

```
 7   REFRESH FAST
 8       START WITH sysdate
 9       NEXT sysdate + 1
10   WITH PRIMARY KEY
11   USING LOCAL ROLLBACK SEGMENT rb_large
```

If you are using Oracle8, you can also specify the snapshot type, PRIMARY KEY (the default) or ROWID. Oracle8 also allows you to specify a rollback segment to use during the snapshot refresh.

 If you plan to add the snapshot to a snapshot refresh group, then you should not specify a value for the NEXT refresh. If you do, the snapshot will refresh at the interval defined in the CREATE SNAP-SHOT statement instead of the interval defined for the refresh group.

You can specify one of three refresh methods in the REFRESH clause:

FAST

A FAST snapshot refresh queries the snapshot log on the master table to determine what records are new or have been modified since the previous refresh. Only these records are brought over to the snapshot site. FAST refreshes are possible only with simple snapshots (i.e., snapshots that query a single master table and that do not perform aggregation functions). FAST refreshes also require a snapshot log on the master table that predates the snapshot.

COMPLETE

A complete refresh reinstantiates the snapshot from scratch. Oracle must use the COMPLETE method for complex snapshots and snapshots whose master table does not have a preexisting snapshot log (or any snapshot log at all).

FORCE

You can specify REFRESH FORCE in the REFRESH clause to direct Oracle to perform a FAST refresh if possible and a COMPLETE refresh if necessary. The FORCE method avoids errors that occur when the FAST method is specified but not possible.

The Defining Query

The last element of the CREATE SNAPSHOT statement is the defining query:

```
12  AS
13      SELECT  product_id,
14              catalog_number,
15              price,
16              effective_date
17      FROM product_prices@PHQS.BIGWHEEL.COM;
```

The result set of the query is stored in the snapshot base table. Any query that does not select fields of type LONG, LONG RAW, or user-defined datatypes and that does not contain an ORDER BY clause is valid as a snapshot's defining query. However, not all queries can be refreshed with the FAST REFRESH method.

Referencing Remote Tables

Oracle's documentation recommends that the defining query reference table names in the form *owner.table_name*. This way, you can be sure of what the master table is and not mistakenly point to the wrong table because a synonym changed.

We discourage this practice because it comes at the expense of flexibility. Of course, you do need to be mindful of what tables are visible over the database link that you use to create and to refresh snapshots, but these are details over which the DBA has control, particularly in a production environment.

Simple Versus Complex Snapshots

Simple snapshots are the only type that can use the FAST REFRESH method. A snapshot is considered *simple* if the defining query meets the following criteria:

*   It does not contain any DISTINCT or aggregation functions.

*   It does not contain a GROUP BY or CONNECT BY clause.

*   It does not perform set operations (UNION, UNION ALL, INTERSECT, etc.).

*   It does not perform joins other than those used for subquery subsetting.

Essentially, a simple snapshot is one that selects from a single table and that may or may not use a WHERE clause.

Oracle8 extends the universe of simple snapshots with a feature known as subquery subsetting, described in the later section entitled "Subquery Subsetting."

Not surprisingly, any snapshot that is not a simple snapshot is a *complex* snapshot. Complex snapshots can only use COMPLETE refreshes, which are not always practical. For tables of more than about 100,000 rows, COMPLETE refreshes can be quite unwieldy.

You can often avoid this situation by creating simple snapshots of individual tables at the master site and performing the offending query against the local snapshots. For example, avoid creating a complex snapshot such as the following:

```
CREATE SNAPSHOT sales_by_region
REFRESH COMPLETE
START WITH sysdate
```

```
NEXT sysdate + 1
AS
SELECT   r.region_name,
         r.sales_rep,
         p.product_id,
         count(*) num_sold,
         sum(sales_price)
FROM     product_sales@PHQS.BIGWHEEL.COM p,
         regions@PHQS.BIGWHEEL.COM r
WHERE    p.region_id = r.region_id
```

which must reinstantiate the snapshot completely with every refresh. Instead, simply create two simple snapshots, one on the PRODUCT_SALES table and the other on the REGIONS table. Both snapshots can use a FAST refresh, and you can issue the desired query locally.

Snapshot Logs

A snapshot log is a table that resides at the master site and that keeps track of changes to a master table. The name of the snapshot log table is MLOG$_*master_ table_name.* Snapshot logs make FAST refreshes possible because the refresh process can consult the snapshot log to determine which rows have changed since the previous refresh; it then applies only these changes instead of replacing every record in the snapshot. In other words, snapshot logs enable the use of FAST refreshes. For tables with more than 100,000 records, a FAST refresh is the only viable means of maintaining a snapshot.

 In order for Oracle to utilize the FAST refresh mechanism, the snapshot log must be created at the master site before the snapshot itself.

Restrictions on Snapshot Logs

Please note that in Oracle8, which uses primary keys to identify records in the master table, the master table must have a primary key defined and enabled in order to create a snapshot log.

Creation Tips

Records in a snapshot log are never updated, so you should create them with storage parameters that pack records as tightly as possible so you will realize the best performance and most efficient use of space.

Snapshot Logs for ROWID Snapshots

If your master table is in an Oracle8 database and the snapshot either is in an Oracle7 database or was created using the WITH ROWID option, then you must also create the snapshot log using the WITH ROWID option. Try to use primary key snapshots whenever possible because of the flexibility they impart to routine tasks such as reorganizing the master table or the snapshot base table. Note that snapshots logs can contain both ROWIDs and primary keys in order to support both Oracle7 and Oracle8 snapshots.

Subquery Subsetting

Subquery subsetting is one of the most significant feature additions to replication in Oracle8. This is a method that allows you to create snapshot sites containing only the data that is locally relevant without having to have a distinguishing key in every table for which you create a snapshot. For example, an order fulfillment center might process orders only from customers in California, yet it needs data from tables CUSTOMERS, ORDERS, and ORDER_ITEMS.

The challenge is to create snapshots of the ORDERS and ORDER_ITEMS tables that contain data for the California customers only. However, the ORDERS table has a customer_id field and no state field, while the ORDER_ITEMS table doesn't even have a customer_id field. In other words, the schema is normalized. Clearly adding and maintaining a state field in the ORDERS and ORDER_ITEMS table would be awkward at best.

Rather than denormalize the schema by putting the state field in all of the tables for which you created a snapshot, we can use a subquery subset snapshot, which takes advantage of foreign keys defined on the tables to determine which records of the ORDERS and ORDER_ITEMS tables the snapshot site needs to see. We can create the snapshots as follows:

1. Create a snapshot on the CUSTOMERS table containing only the records where state = CA:

```
CREATE SNAPSHOT customers
REFRESH FAST
START WITH sysdate
NEXT sysdate + 1
AS
SELECT  customer_id,
        sales_rep_id,
        first_name,
        last_name,
        addr_line_1,
        addr_line_2,
```

```
               city,
               state,
               zip
FROM       customers@PHQS.BIGWHEEL.COM
WHERE      state = 'CA';
```

2. Create a subquery subset snapshot on ORDERS containing only the orders associated with customers from California:

```
CREATE SNAPSHOT orders
REFRESH FAST
START WITH sysdate
NEXT sysdate + 1
AS
SELECT  order_id,
        customer_id,
        purchase_order_id,
        order_date,
        order_taker,
        status
FROM    orders@PHQS.BIGWHEEL.COM o
WHERE   EXISTS (SELECT  customer_id
               FROM    customers@PHQS.BIGWHEEL.COM c
               WHERE   c.customer_id = o.customer_id
               AND     c.state = 'CA');
```

3. Create a subquery subset snapshot on the ORDER_ITEMS table containing only the records associated with the orders for California customers:

```
CREATE SNAPSHOT order_items
REFRESH FAST
START WITH sysdate
NEXT sysdate + 1
AS
SELECT  order_line_id,
        order_id,
        item_number,
        product_id,
        quantity,
        unit_of_measure,
        unit_price,
        extended_price,
        status
FROM    order_items@PHQS.BIGWHEEL.COM i
WHERE   EXISTS (SELECT  order_id
               FROM    orders@PHQS.BIGWHEEL.COM o
               WHERE   i.order_id = o.order_id
               AND EXISTS (SELECT  customer_id
                          FROM    customers@PHQS.BIGWHEEL.COM c
                          WHERE   c.customer_id = o.customer_id
                          AND     c.state = 'CA'));
```

Thus, we have created three separate snapshots that obtain the subset of data the snapshot site requires without having to denormalize the schema or modify the application code in any way. In other words, we can create a snapshot for records associated with the filter column state even though the master tables ORDERS and ORDER_ITEMS do not contain the filter column. Notice that these snapshots can all use the FAST refresh (assuming that the master tables have snapshot logs defined).

Updates to the filter column, though permitted, should be avoided.

Restrictions on Subquery Subsets

Of course, not all operations or relationships can benefit from subquery snapshots. Specifically, subquery subsetting works only if the following restrictions are met:

- The defining query does not include explicit joins, aggregation operations, set operations, GROUP BY, HAVING, or CONNECT BY.
- Each master table referenced in the defining query must have a primary key.
- All master tables must reside in the same database instance.
- All subqueries must be positive and formulated with the EXISTS clause—that is, explicit joins and NOT EXISTS are not permitted.
- The subqueries must use equijoins on columns that have a many-to-one relationship.
- All master tables referenced in the defining query must have a snapshot log, even if you are using a COMPLETE refresh.
- Snapshot logs must contain primary key values.
- Snapshot logs must contain all filter columns.

Subquery Subset Snapshot Base Tables

You will notice that the base table of subquery subset snapshots contains fields in addition to those of the master table. For example, the ORDER_ITEMS snapshot base table, SNAP$_ORDER_ITEMS, contains a customer_id field. Snapshot base tables must contain the primary key values of each table referenced in the subquery. Oracle automatically adds these fields if and only if they are not part of the SELECT list in the snapshot's defining query. In addition, Oracle automatically creates indexes on these hidden columns when the snapshot is created.

A Special Case

In the previous example, ORDERS and ORDER_ITEMS records were filtered to those associated with customers in California. Suppose we wish to further restrict the query to California customers whose sales representative is John Smith. Assume a many-to-many relationship between the CUSTOMERS table and the SALES_REPS table. In other words, a sales representative can handle many customers, and a given customer may have more than one representative. The CUSTOMER_REP_INTERSECT table resolves the many-to-many relationship between CUSTOMERS and SALES_REPS.

Oracle's subquery subsetting allows us to snapshot data associated with customers meeting two restrictions: they are from California, and their sales rep is John Smith. The snapshot on the ORDER_ITEMS table would be defined as follows:

```
CREATE SNAPSHOT order_items
REFRESH FAST
START WITH sysdate
NEXT sysdate + 1
AS
SELECT  order_line_id,
        order_id,
        item_number,
        product_id,
        quantity,
        unit_of_measure,
        unit_price,
        extended_price,
        status
FROM    order_items@PHQS.BIGWHEEL.COM i
WHERE   EXISTS (SELECT  order_id
               FROM     orders@PHQS.BIGWHEEL.COM o
               WHERE    i.order_id = o.order_id
               AND EXISTS  (SELECT  customer_id
                           FROM     customers@PHQS.BIGWHEEL.COM c
                           WHERE    c.customer_id = o.customer_id
                           AND      c.state = 'CA'
               AND EXISTS  (SELECT  sales_rep_id
                           FROM     customer_rep_intersect i
                           WHERE    i.customer_id = c.customer_id
               AND EXISTS  (SELECT  sales_rep_id
                           FROM     sales_reps r
                           WHERE    r.sales_rep_id = i.sales_rep_id
                           AND      r.rep_name =  'John Smith'))))
```

While subquery subset snapshots of this complexity are possible, there does come a point where the performance of the subquery snapshot lags behind that of snapshots containing all records from a master table. You will have to experiment to determine which approach works better for you.

Refresh Groups

As in the previous example, often you need snapshots on a group of related tables, which may have interdependencies. If you refresh snapshots individually, the resulting data is not guaranteed to have a point-in-time consistency; in fact, it probably will not. For example, if we were to refresh the ORDER_ITEMS snapshot followed by the ORDERS table, we could end up with entries in ORDERS that have no corresponding entries in ORDER_ITEMS if users create orders while the ORDER_ITEMS table refreshes. Obviously, this is not an acceptable state of affairs.

Oracle uses the concept of a *refresh group* to encapsulate snapshots that must have point-in-time consistency. You are guaranteed that all snapshots in a single refresh group will be refreshed with data from the master tables as of a single point in time. In addition, refresh groups provide ease of management because Oracle includes a variety of built-in procedures in the package DBMS_REFRESH for their maintenance. The following procedures manipulate refresh groups at the snapshot site:

DBMS_REFRESH.ADD
> Adds a snapshot to an existing group.

DBMS_REFRESH.CHANGE
> Modifies properties of a refresh group, such as refresh interval, next refresh time, and so on.

DBMS_REFRESH.DESTROY
> Drops a refresh group.

DBMS_REFRESH.MAKE
> Creates a refresh group.

DBMS_REFRESH.SUBTRACT
> Removes a snapshot from an existing refresh group.

The following sections provide brief examples of using these procedures; refer to Appendix A, *Built-in Packages for Distributed Systems*, for the complete API reference to these procedures.

Refresh groups are applicable to updateable snapshots as well as to read-only snapshots.

Creating and Destroying Refresh Groups

Use the built-in package procedure DBMS_REFRESH.MAKE to create a refresh group and DBMS_REFRESH.DESTROY to drop it; execute both of these procedures from the snapshot site. The following examples illustrate their use.

Creating a snapshot refresh group of read-only snapshots

This example shows the simplest invocation of DBMS_REFRESH.MAKE; defaults are used for all parameters possible. This call creates a refresh group on four related tables and schedules them to be refreshed every day at midnight:

```
DECLARE
vSnapshotList dbms_utility.uncl_array;
BEGIN
    vSnapshotList(1) := 'CUSTOMERS';
    vSnapshotList(2) := 'ORDERS';
    vSnapshotList(3) := 'ORDER_ITEMS';
    vSnapshotList(4) := 'CUSTOMER_REP_INTERSECT';

    DBMS_REFRESH.MAKE(      name => 'SG_CUST_ORDERS',
                            tab => vSnapShotList,
                            next_date => TRUNC(sysdate) + 1,
                            interval => 'SYSDATE + 1');
END;
```

Creating a snapshot refresh group of read-only snapshots with specialized parameters

```
DECLARE
vSnapshotList dbms_utility.uncl_array
BEGIN
    vSnapshotList(1) = 'CUSTOMERS'
    vSnapshotList(2) = 'ORDERS'
    vSnapshotList(3) = 'ORDER_ITEMS'
    vSnapshotList(4) = 'CUSTOMER_REP_INTERSECT'

    DBMS_REFRESH.MAKE(      name => 'SG_CUST_ORDERS',
                            tab => vSnapShotList,
                            next_date => TRUNC(sysdate) + 1,
                            interval => 'SYSDATE + 1',
                            implicit_destroy => TRUE,
                            lax => TRUE,
                            rollback_segment 'RB1');
END;
```

This example creates the same refresh group as in the first example but with the following additional properties:

implicit_destroy => TRUE

This setting causes the refresh group SG_CUST_ORDERS to be destroyed if all of the snapshots in the group are dropped. The default behavior is to preserve the refresh group, even if it has no members.

lax => TRUE

> If any of the snapshots being added to SG_CUST_ORDERS exist in another refresh group, this setting instructs Oracle to remove them from the other group before adding them to the new group. A snapshot cannot be a member of more than one refresh group.

rollback_segment => 'RB1'

> This setting causes Oracle to use rollback segment RB1 whenever it refreshes refresh group SG_CUST_ORDERS. You should consider specifying rollback segments if your snapshot refreshes result in long transactions requiring a large rollback segment.

Creating a snapshot refresh group that uses parallel propagation (Oracle8 only)

This example sets parallelism to 4, so that Oracle uses four processes to perform the refresh:

```
DECLARE
vSnapshotList dbms_utility.uncl_array
BEGIN
    vSnapshotList(1) = 'CUSTOMERS'
    vSnapshotList(2) = 'ORDERS'
    vSnapshotList(3) = 'ORDER_ITEMS'
    vSnapshotList(4) = 'CUSTOMER_REP_INTERSECT'

    DBMS_REFRESH.MAKE(      name => 'SG_CUST_ORDERS',
                            tab => vSnapShotList,
                            next_date => TRUNC(sysdate) + 1,
                            interval => 'SYSDATE + 1',
                            parallelism => 4,);
END;
```

 In order to take advantage of parallel propagation, you must have parallel query slave background processes running. The number of processes is controlled by the initialization parameters PARALLEL_MIN_SERVERS and PARALLEL_MAX_SERVERS.

Dropping a refresh group

This example destroys the snapshot group SG_CUST_ORDERS. It does not drop the member snapshots themselves; however, they will not be refreshed again unless you either add them to another snapshot group or refresh them manually with DBMS_SNAPSHOT.REFRESH:

```
BEGIN
    DBMS_REFRESH.DESTROY(name => 'SG_CUST_ORDERS' );
END;
```

Management and Optimization

Snapshots require a certain amount of DBA attention in order to keep them running optimally. In addition, Oracle provides packaged procedures to render the DBA's responsibilities less taxing. This section discusses your options for squeezing optimal performance out of snapshots and offers some common solutions to common problems.

Tuning Snapshots

The earlier section "Snapshot Creation Basics" recommended that you select PCT-FREE and PCTUSED settings that will pack the data in your read-only snapshot base tables as tightly as possible, thus preserving disk space and reducing the expense of scanning the table. You can also take the following steps to enhance the performance of queries against the snapshot base tables and the snapshot refresh itself:

Index the snapshot base table

> You can place indexes on the columns of the snapshot base table to enhance the performance of your application's queries. Note, however, that you cannot use unique indexes if you are using Oracle7; if you are using Oracle8, unique constraints must be deferrable. This restriction exists because uniqueness is not guaranteed during the period of the actual snapshot refresh.

Cluster read-only snapshot base tables

> If you snapshot several tables that share common keys, consider using a cluster index for the key as was done in the CUSTOMERS, ORDERS, ORDER_ITEMS example.

Tune the defining query

> When you create subquery subset snapshots, be sure that the defining query is optimized. You can create the appropriate indexes on the master tables and/or use EXPLAIN PLAN, TKPROF, or another utility to tune the statements themselves.

Analyze the snapshot log

> If you are using the cost-based optimizer, be sure to ANALYZE the snapshot log tables at the master site. Oracle recommends analyzing the snapshot log when it is empty or nearly so.

Administrative Tasks

The DBMS_REFRESH and DBMS_SNAPSHOT built-in packages include a variety of routines the DBA can use to manage snapshots and snapshot logs. In addition to the procedures mentioned for maintaining snapshot logs and refresh groups, the following procedures are available:

DBMS_REFRESH.REFRESH

Refreshes a snapshot refresh group.

DBMS_REFRESH.USER_EXPORT

Produces the SQL statement required to create a given refresh group (Oracle8 only).

DBMS_REFRESH.USER_EXPORT_CHILD

Produces the SQL statement required to create a given snapshot within a refresh group (Oracle8 only).

DBMS_SNAPSHOT.REFRESH

Refreshes a specific snapshot.

DBMS_SNAPSHOT.REFRESH_ALL

Refreshes all snapshots that are due to be refreshed.

DBMS_SNAPSHOT.I_AM_A_REFRESH

Queries a state variable for a session to determine whether it is acting on behalf of a snapshot refresh.

DBMS_SNAPSHOT.SET_I_AM_A_REFRESH

Sets a session state variable to indicate that the session is acting on behalf of a snapshot refresh.

DBMS_SNAPSHOT.BEGIN_TABLE_REORGANIZATION

Called prior to reorganizing a master table in order to preserve snapshot log information (Oracle8 only).

DBMS_SNAPSHOT.END_TABLE_REORGANIZATION

Called at the conclusion of a master table reorganization to resume normal logging of DML (Oracle8 only).

DBMS_SNAPSHOT.REGISTER_SNAPSHOT

Creates an entry for a snapshot in the data dictionary view DBA_REGISTERED_SNAPSHOTS at the master site.

DBMS_SNAPSHOT.UNREGISTER_SNAPSHOT

Removes the entry for a snapshot in the data dictionary view DBA_REGISTERED_SNAPSHOTS at the master site.

The full specification of these procedures is provided in Appendix A.

Reorganizing a Master Table in Oracle8

Occasionally, a DBA must reorganize a table—that is, coalesce its extents and reduce row chaining. These two new modules in Oracle8 allow you to reorganize a master table without invalidating its snapshot log. Therefore, you do not have to perform complete refreshes of the table's snapshots after it is reorganized. To take advantage of this new feature, you must be using primary key snapshots. The procedure is to call DBMS_SNAPSHOT.BEGIN_REORGANIZATION before reorganizing the table and DBMS_SNAPSHOT.END_REORGANIZATION when you are finished.

The following sections illustrate how to use these procedures as part of a table reorganization.

Steps for reorganizing a master table using truncation

1. Call DBMS_SNAPSHOT.BEGIN_TABLE_REORGANIZATION:

```
EXECUTE DBMS_SNAPSHOT.BEGIN_TABLE_REORGANIZATION (
    tabowner => 'SPROCKET',
    tabname  => 'COUNTRIES');
```

2. Back up the table by exporting it or spooling it to a flat file.

3. Truncate the master table, preserving the snapshot log:

```
TRUNCATE TABLE countries PRESERVE SNAPSHOT LOG;
```

4. Restore the table from the export file or flat file.

5. Call DBMS_SNAPSHOT.END_TABLE_REORGANIZATION:

```
EXECUTE DBMS_SNAPSHOT.END_TABLE_REORGANIZATION (
    tabowner => 'SPROCKET',
    tabname  => 'COUNTRIES');
```

Steps for reorganizing a master table by renaming

1. Call DBMS_SNAPSHOT.BEGIN_TABLE_REORGANIZATION:

```
EXECUTE DBMS_SNAPSHOT.BEGIN_TABLE_REORGANIZATION (
    tabowner => 'SPROCKET',
    tabname  => 'COUNTRIES');
```

2. Rename the table:

```
RENAME TABLE countries TO countries_pre_reorg;
```

3. Create a new version of the table:

```
CREATE TABLE countries AS SELECT * FROM countries_pre_reorg;
```

4. Call DBMS_SNAPSHOT.END_TABLE_REORGANIZATION:

```
EXECUTE DBMS_SNAPSHOT.END_TABLE_REORGANIZATION (
    tabowner => 'SPROCKET',
    tabname  => 'COUNTRIES');
```

5. Re-create any triggers that were defined on the table.

In both of these examples, snapshots will be able to use the snapshot log for FAST refreshes after the table reorganization is complete.

Offline Instantiation of Snapshots

In cases in which you wish to instantiate a snapshot site with a large amount of data in an advanced replication environment, offline instantiation may be more convenient than using the DBMS_REPCAT methods. Offline instantiation refers to the population of snapshots with the import and export utilities as opposed to using the DBMS_SNAPSHOT.REFRESH procedure. This technique is less time consuming and less taxing on your network, and it minimizes the time your environment must be quiesced. The DBMS_OFFLINE_SNAPSHOT package provides the bulk of the functionality of offline instantiation. You must also call DBMS_REPCAT.CREATE_SNAPSHOT_REPGROUP to create a new replicated snapshot group.

The procedure for performing offline instantiation of snapshots in an advanced replication environment is as follows:

1. Create a snapshot log for each master table if one does not already exist.

2. Create a snapshot of each master table in the master database and in the same schema as the master table. Of course, the name of the snapshot will have to be different from the name of the master table. The CREATE SNAPSHOT statement must also include a loopback database link qualifier:

```
CREATE SNAPSHOT snp_countries
AS SELECT * FROM countries@D7CA.BIGWHEEL.COM
```

3. Perform user exports of all schemas that own master tables. You should be logged on to the schema owner account for these exports. The only tables that you need to export are the snapshot base tables (i.e., those whose names begin with SNAP$_).

4. Copy the export dump file(s) to the new snapshot site(s).

5. Use DBMS_REPCAT.CREATE_SNAPSHOT_REPGROUP at the snapshot sites to create a new snapshot replication object group. The name of this object group should be the same as the name of the replication group of which the master tables are members:

```
EXECUTE DBMS_REPCAT.CREATE_SNAPSHOT_REPGROUP(
    gname                => 'SPROCKET',
    master               => 'D7CA.BIGWHEEL.COM',
    comment              => 'Group created on '||sysdate|| ' by '||user,
    propagation_mode     => 'ASYNCHRONOUS');
```

6. Call DBMS_OFFLINE_SNAPSHOT.BEGIN_LOAD to begin loading the data from the export file(s). You must call the procedure for every snapshot you plan to import:

```
EXECUTE DBMS_OFFLINE_SNAPSHOT.BEGIN_LOAD(
    gname                => 'SPROCKET',
    sname                => 'SPROCKET',
    master_site          => 'D7CA.BIGWHEEL.COM'
```

```
    snapshot_oname  => 'SNP_COUNTRIES'
    storage_c       => 'TABLESPACE sprocket_data STORAGE (INITIAL 64K)'
    comment         => 'Load of COUNTRIES snapshot begun at '||sysdate);
```

7. Import the snapshot base table(s) from the export file(s) created in Step 4.

8. Call DBMS_OFFLINE_SNAPSHOT.END_LOAD for each snapshot when the load is complete:

```
EXECUTE DBMS_OFFLINE_SNAPSHOT.END_LOAD(
    gname           => 'SPROCKET'
    sname           => 'SPROCKET'
    snapshot_oname  => 'SNP_COUNTRIES');
```

Troubleshooting

The following sections describe solutions to some common problems that arise when using snapshots.

Snapshots are not refreshing

When snapshots fail to refresh, it is generally because of either a connectivity problem (i.e., the snapshot site cannot connect to the master site) or a privilege problem. When a snapshot first fails to refresh, Oracle retries the operation one minute later. If the refresh continues to fail, Oracle reattempts two minutes later, then four minutes later, and so on. If the retry interval exceeds the snapshot refresh interval, then Oracle retries at the refresh interval. If the refresh fails 16 times, then Oracle marks the snapshot as BROKEN in the DBA_REFRESH and DBA_REFRESH_CHILDREN data dictionary views.

This behavior is the same as for jobs in the job queue precisely because snapshot refresh jobs are jobs in the job queue.

When you notice that a snapshot is not refreshing, you can almost always determine the problem by looking for a trace file in the directory specified by the initialization parameter BACKGROUND_DUMP_DEST. The trace file will have information about whatever errors the snapshot background process has encountered. For example, if the database link from the snapshot site to the master site attempts to connect with an invalid username or password, the trace file contains entries like this:

```
*** SESSION ID:(10.9446) 1998.06.21.21.19.47.000
ORA-12012: error on auto execute of job 29
ORA-01017: invalid username/password; logon denied
ORA-06512: at "SYS.DBMS_SNAPSHOT", line 380
ORA-06512: at "SYS.DBMS_IREFRESH", line 450
```

```
ORA-06512: at "SYS.DBMS_REFRESH", line 182
ORA-06512: at line 1
Sun Jun 21 21:19:47 1998
```

Usually, the problem is reasonably easy to diagnose by looking in the trace file.

Snapshots refreshing continuously

At the other end of the spectrum is a situation in which snapshots refresh constantly. This can occur if the interval specified for the refresh is less than the time it takes to actually refresh the snapshot. In other words, the snapshot is overdue for a refresh after it completes each refresh. The solution to this problem is to modify the snapshot's refresh interval accordingly, either with the package procedure DBMS_REFRESH.CHANGE (if the snapshot is a member of a refresh group) or with the ALTER SNAPSHOT command (for snapshots that are not members of refresh groups).

Snapshot logs are growing uncontrollably

One of the most commonly reported problems with snapshot logs is a log that continues growing seemingly without bounds. This can occur if the master site thinks that there are unrefreshed snapshot sites that still need to reference the log. Oracle does not remove entries from the snapshot log until all snapshots have "seen" it. So, if a site becomes unavailable for an extended period of time, or if a snapshot is dropped, the snapshot log can continue to queue records for the non-existent snapshot.

Oracle provides several package procedures that allow you to rid the snapshot log of irrelevant records or to purge the log entirely:

DBMS_SNAPSHOT.GET_LOG_AGE
> Finds the age of the oldest record in the snapshot log (Oracle8 only).

DBMS_SNAPSHOT.PURGE_LOG
> Deletes some or all records from a snapshot log.

DBMS_SNAPSHOT.PURGE_SNAPSHOT_FROM_LOG
> Removes log entries associated with a particular snapshot from the snapshot log.

Refer to Appendix A for the complete API reference for these procedures.

Scripts

Several scripts provided in Appendix B, *Scripts and Utilities*, are particularly useful for providing information about snapshots in your environment. See *snaps.sql*, *reqsnaps.sql*, and *mastersnapinfo.sql*. These scripts are also included on the accompanying diskette.

12

Multi-Master Replication

Multi-master replication, also known as *advanced replication* or *symmetric replication*, allows you to maintain multiple sets of identical data at various sites; Oracle can automatically synchronize all DDL and DML changes. Obviously, this functionality comes at the expense of additional planning and administrative tasks and introduces a new level of sophistication to the environment. This chapter describes how to create and maintain a replicated environment and how to assess its health.

Concepts and Terminology

As you embark down the road of replication, you will encounter several phrases repeatedly; these include:

- Deferred transaction

- Replication group

- Quiescence

- Master definition site

- Master site

- Replication support

- Conflict

- Propagation latency

- Instantiation

The following sections briefly describe what these phrases mean.

Deferred Transaction

A *deferred transaction* is a transaction that is queued for delivery to one or more remote databases. If you use multi-master replication with asynchronous propagation, Oracle creates deferred transactions for all local DML activity against the replicated tables.

Replication Group

A *replication group* is a collection of one or more replicated objects (typically tables) that are administrated together. Very generally speaking, the objects in a given replication group are logically related; for example, they are often the set of objects that a given application uses. Prior to Oracle Version 7.3, the concept of a replication group did not exist; instead, objects had to be replicated on a schema-by-schema basis. Beginning with Version 7.3, Oracle organized replicated objects into replication groups. A given replication group can contain objects from multiple schema, and a given schema can have objects in more than one replication group. However, any given object can be in only one replication group.

The most significant property of replication groups is that all objects in a given group are quiesced together. That is, DML activity is enabled and disabled for all group members simultaneously.

Quiescence

Quiescence is the act of suspending DML activity for all tables in a given replication group. This is required in order to perform certain administrative tasks on objects in a replication group, such as altering a table. The Oracle built-in package procedure call that quiesces a replication group is DBMS_REPCAT.SUSPEND_MASTER_ACTIVITY.

Prior to Oracle8, quiescing a single replication group actually caused all groups to be quiesced, even though the DBMS_REPCAT.SUSPEND_MASTER_ACTIVITY call requires that you specify a single group. Oracle refers to the ability to quiesce a single replication group as a *fine-grained quiesce.*

Master Definition Site

The *master definition site* of a replication group is the database instance from which the group is administered. This site is usually, but not necessarily, the site at which the replication group was originally created. (You can use the built-in package procedure DMBS_REPCAT.RELOCATE_MASTERDEF to change a replication group's master definition site.) Activities such as quiescence and DDL on replicated objects must be performed at the master definition site. There is exactly one master definition site for each replication group.

It is worth noting that the behavior of DML is the same at the master definition site as at any other site. In other words, DML performed at the master definition site does not have any precedence over DML performed at other master sites.

Master Site

A *master site* is a site that is participating in one or more replication groups but is not the master definition site.

Replication Support

Replication support refers to the packages and triggers that Oracle creates in order to propagate changes to replicated objects, to detect and resolve conflicts, and so on. See Chapter 9, *Oracle Replication Architecture*, for a description of these objects.

Conflict

When Oracle propagates an update to destination tables, it expects the current data for the row at the destination to match the data at the originating site prior to the update. If the data is not the same, an update *conflict* results. Similarly, if an insert fails because of a primary key violation (i.e., a unique constraint violation) the result is a uniqueness conflict or violation. And, if the target row of a delete does not exist at the destination site, a delete conflict results. Chapter 15, *Conflict Avoidance and Resolution Techniques*, discusses advanced techniques for detecting and resolving conflicts automatically.

Propagation Latency

Unless you are propagating changes among master sites synchronously, there is a delay between the time a DML change is applied at the originating database and the time the transaction reaches the destination databases. This lag is known as *propagation latency*.

Instantiation

Instantiation is the act of creating and populating a table so that it has identical structure and data as its replica in other master databases.

Getting Started

Before setting up tables for replication, you must complete the preliminary tasks described in Chapter 10, *Advanced Replication Installation*. These tasks include the following:

- Determining and setting initialization parameters appropriately
- Sizing rollback segments and redo logs
- Running *catproc.sql* and *catrep.sql* (and optionally *catrepad.sql*)
- Creating administrative accounts with appropriate privileges
- Creating necessary database links

If you have accomplished these tasks, you are ready to create replication groups, configure tables, and other objects for replication and add master databases.

The Quick-and-Dirty Setup

Many people want to configure objects for replication as quickly and simply as possible so that they can get a sense of the administration and performance considerations and to learn about how replication works firsthand. To speed these people on their way, the steps required to set up a bare-bones replicated environment are included here. The main distinction between this minimal configuration and one that is appropriate for production is that it does not include any conflict resolution logic.

 Although these steps will indeed create a replicated environment, it is not suitable for a production installation because it does not take conflicts into account, rendering it anything but robust.

This procedure assumes that you have set the proper initialization parameters, run the required catalog scripts, and created necessary database links and administrative accounts. Now, with no further ado, the minimal procedure for replicating an object is to follow these steps:

1. Create the object in all master databases; if it is a table, you can populate it with identical data at all locations before configuring it for replication, or you can let Oracle's replication packages populate the table.

2. Create one or more replication groups using the package procedure DBMS_REPCAT.CREATE_MASTER_REPGROUP.

3. Add objects to the replication groups using the package procedure DBMS_REPCAT.CREATE_MASTER_REPOBJECT.

4. Generate replication support for each object using the package procedure DBMS_REPCAT.GENERATE_REPLICATION_SUPPORT.

5. Add one or more master sites to the replication group using the package procedure DBMS_REPCAT.ADD_MASTER_DATABASE.

6. Schedule the propagation of DML changes and replicated procedure calls to each master site using DBMS_DEFER_SYS.SCHEDULE_PUSH (for Oracle8 databases) or DBMS_DEFER_SYS.SCHEDULE_EXECUTION (for Oracle7 databases).

 Although Oracle8 includes the DBMS_DEFER_SYS.SCHEDULE_EXE-CUTION package procedure, it is intended for backward compatibility only. Always use DBMS_DEFER_SYS.SCHEDULE_PUSH.

---

7. (Oracle8 only) Schedule the purging of the deftran queue using the DBMS_DEFER_SYS.SCHEDULE_PURGE.

A Quick-and-Dirty Example

Here are the steps to go through to replicate a single table named SPROCKET.REGIONS at sites PHQS.BIGWHEEL.COM and PSLS.BIGWHEEL.COM. Suppose this table looks like this:

```
SQL> describe regions
 Name                Null?      Type
 --------------      --------   ---------
 REGION_ID           NOT NULL   NUMBER(6)
 COUNTRY_ID          NOT NULL   NUMBER(6)
 REGION_NAME         NOT NULL   VARCHAR2(15)
 AUDIT_DATE          NOT NULL   DATE
 AUDIT_USER          NOT NULL   VARCHAR2(30)
 GLOBAL_NAME         NOT NULL   VARCHAR2(20)
```

For the purposes of this example, assume that PHQS.BIGWHEEL.COM is the master definition site and that the REGIONS table has already been created and populated at both sites. Perform all of the following steps connected to the master definition site under the replication administrator account, typically REPADMIN.

1. Create a replication group, in this case named RG_SALES:

```
EXECUTE dbms_repcat.create_master_repgroup( -
gname          => 'RG_SALES', -
group_comment  => 'Created by ' ||user|| ' on ' || sysdate, -
master_comment => 'Created by ' ||user|| ' on ' || sysdate)
```

2. Add REGIONS to the RG_SALES replication group:

```
EXECUTE dbms_repcat.create_master_repobject(-
sname               => 'SPROCKET',-
oname               => 'REGIONS',-
type                => 'TABLE',-
use_existing_object => TRUE,-
comment             => 'Added by '||lower(user)||' on '||sysdate,-
copy_rows           => FALSE,-
gname               => 'RG_SALES');
```

3. Generate replication support for the REGIONS table:

```
EXECUTE dbms_repcat.generate_replication_support( -
sname       => 'SPROCKET',-
oname       => 'REGIONS',-
type        => 'TABLE',-
distributed => TRUE);
```

4. Add the master site PSLS.BIGWHEEL.COM to the replication group:

```
EXECUTEdbms_repcat.add_master_database( -
gname                => 'RG_THROW', -
master               => 'PHQS.BIGWHEEL.COM', -
use_existing_objects => TRUE, -
copy_rows            => FALSE, -
comment              => 'PSLS.BIGWHEEL.COM added on '||sysdate, -
propagation_mode     => 'ASYNCHRONOUS');
```

 Actually, you can add master databases to a replication group as soon as you create the group. However, it is faster to generate replication support for all replicated objects *before* adding masters. Whenever possible, generate replication support for objects first.

---

5. Schedule propagation between the databases PHQS.BIGWHEEL.COM and PSLS.BIGWHEEL.COM. In this case, the propagation interval is once per minute (there are 1440 minutes in a day).

In PHQS.BIGWHEEL.COM (master definition site):

Oracle8 syntax:

```
EXECUTE dbms_defer_sys.schedule_push( -
destination => 'PSLS.BIGWHEEL.COM', -
interval    => 'SYSDATE+1/1440', -
next_date   => SYSDATE+1/1440);
```

Oracle7 syntax:

```
EXECUTE dbms_defer_sys.schedule_execution( -
destination => 'PSLS.BIGWHEEL.COM', -
interval    => 'SYSDATE+1/1440', -
next_date   => SYSDATE+1/1440);
```

In PSLS.BIGWHEEL.COM (master site):

Oracle8 syntax:

```
EXECUTE dbms_defer_sys.schedule_push( -
destination => 'PHQS.BIGWHEEL.COM', -
interval    => 'SYSDATE+1/1440', -
next_date   => SYSDATE+1/1440);
```

Oracle7 syntax:

```
EXECUTE dbms_defer_sys.schedule_execution( -
destination => 'PHQS.BIGWHEEL.COM', -
interval    => 'SYSDATE+1/1440', -
next_date   => SYSDATE+1/1440);
```

6. For Oracle8 databases, you must also schedule a periodic purge of the deftran queue. Here the purge is scheduled to run every 10 minutes in both databases (Oracle8 only).

In PHQS.BIGWHEEL.COM (master definition site):

```
EXECUTE dbms_defer_sys.schedule_purge( -
interval    => 'SYSDATE+10/1440', -
next_date   => SYSDATE+10/1440);
```

In PSLS.BIGWHEEL.COM (master site):

```
EXECUTE dbms_defer_sys.schedule_purge( -
interval    => 'SYSDATE+10/1440', -
next_date   => SYSDATE+10/1440);
```

7. Enable replication. From the master definition site, PHQS.BIGWHEEL.COM, call DBMS_REPCAT.RESUME_MASTER_ACTIVITY:

```
EXECUTE dbms_repcat.resume_master_activity(gname => 'RG_SALES');
```

At this point, you should be able to perform inserts, updates, and deletes on the REGIONS table from either site and see the transaction applied at the other site within approximately 1 minute.

Now, if you want to create a robust replicated environment that will stand up to real-world production usage, read on.

Replication Groups

As described earlier, a replication group is a collection of one or more objects, generally tables, that are logically related and that can or should be administered together. As a very general guideline, you can place all replicated objects associated with a given application into a single group. A common practice is to create all of an application's objects under a single schema (i.e., Oracle user account); in such cases, it often makes sense to use a one-to-one correspondence between schema and replication groups. In fact, prior to Oracle 7.3, that was not only the assumption but also the requirement.

API Calls

Oracle furnishes the following built-in package procedures to create and drop replication groups:

DBMS_REPCAT.CREATE_MASTER_REPGROUP

Creates a replication group. The group is initially quiesced and contains no objects.

DBMS_REPCAT.DROP_MASTER_REPGROUP

Drops a replication group.

DBMS_REPCAT.COMMENT_ON_REPGROUP

Creates or replaces a comment on a replication group, visible in the DBA_REPGROUP data dictionary view.

Refer to Appendix A, *Built-in Packages for Distributed Systems*, for the complete API reference to these procedures.

The data dictionary view DBA_REPGROUP contains information about all replication groups at the current site.

 The call to DBMS_REPCAT.CREATE_MASTER_REPGROUP automatically creates an entry in the job queue to process tasks in the repcatlog queue. This scheduled job calls DBMS_REPCAT.DO_DEFERRED_REPCAT_ADMIN every 10 minutes.

Naming Conventions

Oracle replication has many different entities associated with it: replication groups, column groups, site priorities, and so on. We find that administration is simplified immensely if such objects are named according to a uniform convention. With this end in mind, we recommend naming replication groups in the form RG_*name*. If you are creating a replication group that will include all replicated objects for a single schema, then *name* should be the name of the schema. You can use the following script to report on all replication groups:

```
-------------------------------------------------------------------------
-- Filename:     repgroup.sql
-- Purpose:      Lists status of all replication groups.
-- Author:       Chas. Dye (cdye@excitecorp.com)
-- Date:         28-Jun-1996
-------------------------------------------------------------------------

column MASTER              heading "Mast|Site"      format a4
column MASTERDEF           heading "Mast|Def|Site"  format a4
```

```
column STATUS           heading "Status"      format a9
column GNAME            heading "Group"       format a12
column SCHEMA_COMMENT   heading "Comment"     format a45

SELECT  g.gname,
        decode(g.master, 'N', 'No', 'Y', 'Yes') master,
        decode(s.masterdef, 'Y', 'Yes', 'N', 'No') masterdef,
        g.status,
        g.schema_comment
FROM    dba_repgroup g,
        dba_repsites s
WHERE   g.gname = s.gname
AND     s.my_dblink = 'Y'
/
```

Which Tables Belong in the Same Replication Group?

In the majority of cases, the easiest strategy is to associate a single replication group with a single schema. However, this advice comes with the caveats listed here:

- Do not allow transactions to cross replication group boundaries.

  If you have transactions that manipulate multiple tables, make sure that all affected tables are in the same replication group. This approach ensures that DML is either enabled for all tables in the transaction or disabled for all tables in the transaction. In other words, either all or none of the tables in the transaction will be quiesced at any given time.

- Do not allow referential integrity constraints to cross replication group boundaries.

  Common sense and experience have shown that a table with foreign keys should be in the same replication group as the table that parents the keys. Although DML is not necessarily prevented when one or the other table is quiesced, applications often modify such tables together, albeit not always in a single transaction. For example, an order entry application may insert a record into the ORDERS table in one transaction and the ORDER_ITEMS table in the next. Of course this is not a hard-and-fast rule, but unless you have a good reason to separate tables that are bound by integrity constraints, keep them in the same replication group.

- Identify and isolate "problem" tables into separate replication groups.

  Does your application include a few tables that are substantially larger or hotter than the others? It is often worthwhile to put such tables in their own replication groups so that you can perform maintenance on them without having to quiesce the rest of the schema.

Oracle introduced the concept of a replication group in Oracle 7.3. Prior to Oracle 7.3, you had to replicate objects on a schema-by-schema basis; in other words, objects belonging to a given schema had to be managed together.

How to Drop a Replication Group

You can drop a replication group with a call to DBMS_REPCAT.DROP_MASTER_ REPGROUP, which can also drop the underlying objects in the replication group if you wish. The procedure is defined as follows:

```
PROCEDURE drop_master_repgroup(
    gname          IN VARCHAR2,
    drop_contents  IN BOOLEAN := FALSE,
    all_sites      IN BOOLEAN := FALSE);
```

You are not required to quiesce the replication group before dropping it, but the call will fail if there are transactions associated with the group in the deftran queue.

Table 12-1 describes the behavior of the drop_contents and all_sites parameters.

Table 12-1. Effect of drop_contents and all_sites in DROP_MASTER_REPGROUP

Calling Site	drop_contents	all_sites	Effect
Master definition site	TRUE	TRUE	Replication group gname and its underlying objects are dropped from all sites.
Master definition site	FALSE	TRUE	Replication group gname is dropped from all master sites.
Master definition site	TRUE	FALSE	Replication group gname and underlying contents are dropped from the master definition site only.
Master definition site	FALSE	FALSE	Replication group gname is dropped from the master definition site only. Underlying objects remain at all sites.
Master site	TRUE	FALSE	Replication group gname and all underlying objects are dropped at the calling site.
Master site	FALSE	FALSE	Replication group gname is dropped; underlying objects are unaffected.

The all_sites parameter must be set to FALSE if the calling site is not the master definition site.

When Oracle drops the replication group, that means that all replication support packages and triggers associated with the replication group are dropped, and the replication group is removed from all relevant data dictionary views.

Master Site Maintenance and Propagation

The site at which you create a replication group is automatically the master definition site for that replication group. Of course, for replication to have any meaning, you will need to add at least one master site. The DBMS_REPCAT package includes procedures for adding and removing master sites. You also need to control how DML changes propagate between sites; the DBMS_DEFER_SYS package contains the procedures for configuring the properties of propagation.

API Calls

The following procedures manipulate master sites:

DBMS_REPCAT.ADD_MASTER_DATABASE

Adds a master database to the specified replication group. The call can create the objects if they do not already exist at the master site, populate replicated tables if they do not contain any data, or utilize the tables and data that are already at the new master site.

DBMS_REPCAT.RELOCATE_MASTERDEF

Changes the location of a replication group's master definition site. This procedure is useful if the existing master definition site becomes unavailable or otherwise irrelevant.

DBMS_REPCAT.REMOVE_MASTER_DATABASES

Removes a master site from a replication group.

Refer to Appendix A for the complete API reference to these procedures.

Adding a Master Site

If you are creating a brand new replication group, your primary tasks are to instantiate the data at all master sites, generate replication support for all objects, and add all sites to the environment. There are a number of ways to accomplish these tasks, and some are more effective than others. Experience has taught that, given a choice, you should add master sites *after* you have added objects to the replication group at the master definition site and that you should pre-create and instantiate replicated tables at all master sites.

You will notice that the DBMS_REPCAT.ADD_MASTER_DATABASE procedure includes parameters for creating and instantiating objects at the new master:

```
PROCEDURE add_master_database(
                    gname               IN VARCHAR2,
                    master              IN VARCHAR2,
                    use_existing_objects IN BOOLEAN := TRUE,
                    copy_rows           IN BOOLEAN := TRUE,
                    comment             IN VARCHAR2 := '',
                    propagation_mode    IN VARCHAR2 := 'ASYNCHRONOUS');
```

I strongly advise you to *not* rely on this procedure to create or instantiate objects. Although this procedure may work adequately for small and simple tables, you effectively relinquish control of the instantiation process and may end up waiting a very long time before learning of problems.

Instead, follow these steps at each intended master site:

1. Create the tables and procedures that are in the replication group.

2. Populate tables with identical data, using utilities such as import/export or SQL*Loader.

3. Create primary keys and other indexes on all replicated tables.

4. Create any user-defined triggers on replicated tables. User-defined triggers are particularly useful for populating columns that are used for conflict resolution.

5. Add the site by calling DBMS_REPCAT.ADD_MASTER_DATABASE at the master definition site, with the parameters:

```
use_existing_objects => TRUE
copy_rows => FALSE
```

It is quite easy to follow this methodology if you maintain appropriate scripts to create your schema objects. For example, maintaining the REGIONS table used in the earlier quick-and-dirty example are the scripts *cr_regions.sql* (which creates the table and synonyms), *pk_regions.sql* (which creates the constraints and indexes on the table), and *trg_regions.sql* (which creates the user-defined triggers). The contents of these scripts follow.

Admittedly, creating these scripts can be a chore, but it is well worth the effort if you are attempting to maintain replicated schema at multiple master sites.

Creating the REGIONS table

```
-------------------------------------------------------------------------
-- Filename:    cr_regions.sql
-- Purpose:     Creates the REGIONS table and its public synonym.
-- Author:      Chas. Dye (cdye@excitecorp.com)
-- Date:        12-Jan-1998
-------------------------------------------------------------------------
```

```
set echo on
set termout on
spool regions.log

DROP PUBLIC SYNONYM regions
/
DROP TABLE regions CASCADE CONSTRAINTS
/
CREATE TABLE regions (
region_id    NUMBER(6)     NOT NULL,
country_id   NUMBER(6)     NOT NULL,
region_name  VARCHAR2(15)  NOT NULL,
audit_date   DATE          NOT NULL,
audit_user   VARCHAR2(30)  NOT NULL,
global_name  VARCHAR2(20)  NOT NULL
)
TABLESPACE sprocket_data STORAGE (INITIAL 16K NEXT 16K PCTINCREASE 0)
/

CREATE PUBLIC SYNONYM regions FOR regions
/

spool off
```

Creating constraints and indexes on REGIONS table

```
--------------------------------------------------------------------------
-- Filename:    pk_regions.sql
-- Purpose:     Creates the constraints and indexes on table REGIONS.
-- Author:      Chas. Dye (cdye@excitecorp.com)
-- Date:        12-Jan-1998
--------------------------------------------------------------------------
set echo on
set termout on
spool pk_regions.log

ALTER TABLE regions ADD (
CONSTRAINT pk_regions
PRIMARY KEY (region_id)
USING INDEX TABLESPACE sprocket_indx
STORAGE (INITIAL 16K NEXT 16K PCTINCREASE 0)
)
/

ALTER TABLE regions ADD (
CONSTRAINT fk_regions_country_id
FOREIGN KEY (country_id)
REFERENCES countries (country_id)
)
/

CREATE INDEX i_region_country_id ON regions(country_id)
TABLESPACE sprocket_indx STORAGE (INITIAL 16K NEXT 16K PCTINCREASE 0)
/

spool off
```

Creating user-defined triggers on the REGIONS table

```
-------------------------------------------------------------------------
-- Filename:      trg_regions.sql
-- Purpose:       Creates trigger(s) on table REGIONS.
-- Author:        Chas. Dye (cdye@excitecorp.com)
-- Date:          12-Jan-1998
-------------------------------------------------------------------------
set echo on
set termout on
spool trg_regions.log

CREATE OR REPLACE TRIGGER t_br_iu_regions
BEFORE INSERT OR UPDATE
ON regions
FOR EACH ROW

BEGIN
    IF (dbms_reputil.from_remote != TRUE)
    THEN
        :new.audit_date  := SYSDATE;
        :new.audit_user  := USER;
        :new.global_name := DBMS_REPUTIL.GLOBAL_NAME;
    END IF;
END;
/

spool off
```

Dropping a Master Site

If you need to drop a master site from a replication group, you can do so by calling the built-in package procedure DBMS_REPCAT.REMOVE_MASTER_DATABASES. You may use this procedure even if the master sites referenced in the call are not accessible; however, the remaining master sites do need to be accessible. In addition, you must call REMOVE_MASTER_DATABASES from the replication group's master definition site.

REMOVE_MASTER_DATABASES is overloaded—that is, the list of master sites may be passed either as a comma-separated string of database names or as a PL/SQL table of database names:

```
PROCEDURE remove_master_databases(
    gname       IN VARCHAR2,
    master_list IN VARCHAR2);

PROCEDURE remove_master_databases(
    gname        IN VARCHAR2,
    master_table IN dbms_utility.dblink_array);
```

The following examples illustrate how to call the procedure in either of its incarnations. In both cases, we drop the master sites PSLS.BIGWHEEL.COM and PMFG.BIGWHEEL.COM from the replication group RG_SALES:

- Calling REMOVE_MASTER_DATABASE with the master_list parameter:

```
EXECUTE dbms_repcat.remove_master_database( -
    gname             => 'RG_SALES', -
    master_list       => 'PSLS.BIGWHEEL.COM,PMFG.BIGWHEEL.COM');
```

- Calling REMOVE_MASTER_DATABASES with the master_table parameter:

```
DECLARE
    vMasterTable dbms_utility.dblink_array;
BEGIN
    vMasterTable(1) := 'PSLS.BIGWHEEL.COM';
    vMasterTable(2) := 'PMFG.BIGWHEEL.COM';

    dbms_repcat.remove_master_database(
        gname             => 'RG_SALES',
        master_table      => vMasterTable);
END;
```

After removing the master database, you should call DBMS_REP-CAT.DROP_MASTER_REPGROUP at each of the master sites you removed. This procedure removes all replication support objects and associated data dictionary entries. Although you do not need to quiesce the replication group to remove one or more master database(s), you are strongly encouraged to do so. Otherwise, you will have to clear the RPC queue manually and resolve any inconsistencies.

Relocating a Master Definition Site

If your master definition site becomes unusable or if you simply want to replace it with another site, you can use the DBMS_REPCAT.RELOCATE_MASTERDEF procedure to effect the change. The specification of this procedure is as follows:

```
PROCEDURE relocate_masterdef(
    gname                   IN VARCHAR2,
    old_masterdef           IN VARCHAR2,
    new_masterdef           IN VARCHAR2,
    notify_masters          IN BOOLEAN := TRUE,
    include_old_masterdef   IN BOOLEAN := TRUE);
```

We recommend following these guidelines when relocating a master definition site:

- If your relocation is planned (i.e., all sites are up and reachable), set the notify_masters and include_old_masterdef parameters to TRUE.

- It the current master definition site is not available, set the notify_masters parameter to TRUE and include_old_masterdef to FALSE.

- If the master definition site as well as some master sites are unavailable, invoke the RELOCATE_MASTERDEF procedure from each functioning master site with the parameters notify_masters and include_old_masterdef set to FALSE.

 Advanced replication will continue to function even without a master definition site. The master definition site is only required for administrative tasks such as performing DDL or quiescing a replication group.

Controlling Propagation

We can measure the success of a replicated environment by determining how quickly and efficiently DML changes and RPCs are delivered to their destinations. In order to deliver changes to remote sites as quickly as possible, most people succumb to the temptation to propagate changes as frequently as Oracle will allow, which is once per second. In some cases, such an aggressive schedule is warranted, but in most it is not.

Consider the analogy of grocery shopping. Perhaps you maintain a list (or queue) of items that you need to pick up during your next shopping expedition. Do you run to the grocery store every time an item is added to the list, or do you wait until the list is sufficiently long to merit a shopping expedition? Most likely, you wait until the trip is worthwhile.

So it is with propagating DML among master sites. The problem with the one-second propagation strategy is that it generally takes longer than one second to perform a push! Therefore, you may actually end up falling behind if you opt for such a frequent schedule. On the other hand, if you opt for infrequent propagation, the likelihood of conflicts increases. The optimal situation is to schedule pushes in such a way that they deliver a fairly constant number of transactions with each push and the average latency of transactions does not exceed the push interval.

 Scheduled jobs cause updates to data dictionary tables such as SYS.JOB$ every time they run. Therefore, the more frequent a job is pushed, the greater the volume of redo log activity. Beware that frequent pushes will result in a significant volume of redo, which you will have to accommodate if your database is in ARCHIVELOG mode.

API Calls

The following built-in package procedures maintain propagation properties:

DBMS_REPCAT.ALTER_MASTER_PROPAGATION
> Switches the propagation mode between SYNCHRONOUS and ASYNCHRO-NOUS.

DBMS_DEFER_SYS.SCHEDULE_EXECUTION (Oracle7)
> Schedules automatic push of the deftran queue to the specified master database. In Oracle8 this procedure is replaced with SCHEDULE_PUSH, though Oracle8 includes this procedure for backward compatibility.

DBMS_DEFER_SYS.UNSCHEDULE_EXECUTION
> Removes the scheduled DBMS_DEFER_SYS.EXECUTE job from the job queue. Oracle8 includes this procedure for backward compatibility only.

DBMS_DEFER_SYS.SCHEDULE_PURGE (Oracle8 only)
> Oracle8 does not rely on the two-phase commit protocol to deliver transactions to remote master databases. The scheduled purge operation confirms the delivery of transactions to remote databases and removes delivered transactions from the deftran queue.

DBMS_DEFER_SYS.UNSCHEDULE_PURGE (Oracle8 only)
> Removes the scheduled DBMS_DEFER_SYS.PURGE job from the job queue for the specified master database.

DBMS_DEFER_SYS.SCHEDULE_PUSH (Oracle8 only)
> Schedules an automatic push of the deftran queue to the specified master database.

DBMS_DEFER_SYS.UNSCHEDULE_PUSH (Oracle8 only)
> Removes the scheduled DBMS_DEFER_SYS.PUSH job from the job queue.

Refer to Appendix A for the complete API reference to these procedures.

As you can see, Oracle8 has introduced significant changes in the way that replicated actions propagate. One fundamental difference between propagation in Oracle7 and Oracle8 is that Oracle7 relies on a two-phase commit to deliver transactions to the destination site, while Oracle8 does not. Oracle8 delivers entries in the deftran queue to other master sites but does not wait for the receiving site to confirm receipt (the reason for the two-phase commit). Instead, Oracle8 visits the destination sites later to confirm the delivery of defran entries—hence the need for SCHEDULE_PURGE and its complement UNSCHEDULE_PURGE. These procedures schedule a delivery confirmation at all destination sites.

Another fundamental difference between Oracle7 and Oracle8 is support for parallel propagation. *Parallel propagation* means that Oracle will invoke multiple connections to databases receiving DML changes and apply multiple transactions in deftran simultaneously. Of course, Oracle ensures that these transactions are independent of each other, so transactional consistency is preserved. In order to support parallel propagation in Oracle8, the Oracle7 procedure SCHEDULE_ EXECUTION is replaced with SCHEDULE_PUSH in Oracle8. And UNSCHEDULE_ EXECUTION gives way to UNSCHEDULE_PUSH.

The specification for the procedures SCHEDULE_EXECUTION and SCHEDULE_ PUSH is as follows:

```
PROCEDURE schedule_execution(
    dblink              IN VARCHAR2,
    interval            IN VARCHAR2,
    next_date           IN DATE,
    reset               IN BOOLEAN default FALSE,
    stop_on_error       IN BOOLEAN := NULL,
    transaction_count   IN BINARY_INTEGER := NULL,
    execution_seconds   IN BINARY_INTEGER := NULL,
    execute_as_user     IN BOOLEAN,
    delay_seconds       IN NATURAL := NULL,
    batch_size          IN NATURAL := NULL);

PROCEDURE schedule_push(
    destination         IN VARCHAR2,
    interval            IN VARCHAR2,
    next_date           IN DATE,
    reset               IN BOOLEAN := FALSE,
    parallelism         IN BINARY_INTEGER := NULL,
    heap_size           IN BINARY_INTEGER := NULL,
    stop_on_error       IN BOOLEAN := NULL,
    write_trace         IN BOOLEAN := NULL,
    startup_seconds     IN BINARY_INTEGER := NULL,
    execution_seconds   IN BINARY_INTEGER := NULL,
    delay_seconds       IN BINARY_INTEGER := NULL,
    transaction_count   IN BINARY_INTEGER := NULL);
```

About the Parameters

Some of the parameters in SCHEDULE_EXECUTION and SCHEDULE_PUSH are not intuitive. Here we discuss the nonobvious parameters:

stop_on_error

Setting the Boolean parameter stop_on_error to FALSE (the default) causes Oracle to continue propagating and executing deferred RPCs at dblink (Oracle7) or destination (Oracle8) even if one or more of the calls encounters an error. Setting this parameter to TRUE causes execution of deferred RPCs to stop if an error occurs at the destination site.

transaction_count and execution_seconds

These two parameters are usually used in tandem. They cause propagation of RPCs to destination to cease after execution_seconds seconds or transaction_ count transactions, whichever comes first. These parameters provide a method of throttling the time and resources that are consumed during any one call to DBMS_DEFER_SYS.EXECUTE (Oracle7) or DBMS_DEFER_SYS.PUSH (Oracle8). Since these settings may cause the propagation to stop before all deferred RPCs are sent, it is your responsibility to monitor the DEFTRANDEST data dictionary view and/or schedule automatic propagation at intervals. The default for both of these parameters is 0, which means that no such limits are set.

execute_as_user (obsolete in Oracle8)

This parameter determines the privilege domain under which the procedure call executes at the destination. Setting execute_as_user to FALSE (the default) causes the call to execute under the privilege domain of the user who queued the call originally, as seen in the ORIGIN_USER column of the DEFTRAN data dictionary view. Setting it to TRUE executes the call under the privilege domain of the session that calls DBMS_DEFER_SYS.EXECUTE (Oracle7) or DBMS_DEFER_SYS.PUSH (Oracle8). The *user* in execute_as_user refers to the user calling DBMS_DEFER_SYS.EXECUTE (Oracle7) or DBMS_DEFER_SYS.PUSH (Oracle8), not to the user who queued the call.

delay_seconds

This parameter causes DBMS_DEFER_SYS.EXECUTE (Oracle7) or DBMS_DEFER_SYS.PUSH (Oracle8) to sleep for delay_seconds seconds before returning when it finishes propagating the queued transactions to destination. The primary purpose of this parameter is to delay the next call to DBMS_DEFER_SYS.EXECUTE (Oracle7) or DBMS_DEFER_SYS.PUSH (Oracle8), the idea being that more transactions will have a chance to accumulate and be pushed by the same call to DBMS_DEFER_SYS.EXECUTE (Oracle7) or DBMS_DEFER_SYS.PUSH (Oracle8). It is more efficient to propagate five deferred RPCs with one call to DBMS_DEFER_SYS.EXECUTE (Oracle7) or DBMS_DEFER_SYS.PUSH (Oracle8) than with five calls. This parameter is relevant only if you have scheduled automatic propagation. You can simulate synchronous propagation by setting delay_seconds to a very high value.

batch_size

batch_size is the number of deferred calls to execute between commits. The default is 0, which means that a commit should occur for each deferred transaction that is propagated.

If you are queuing a relatively low volume of deferred RPCs, these additional parameters controlling the volume and timing of deliveries are not extremely relevant. They are really provided for fine-tuning the behavior and performance of automatically scheduled RPCs, such as those associated with the advanced replication facilities.

Parallel Propagation

In Oracle7, the database pushes the deftran queue to each master site serially, so transactions are applied in the same order at the destination database as they were at the originating database. This methodology is adequate for applications that do not generate a tremendous volume of DML activity, but for high throughput applications such as OLTP or many web-based applications, the serial push can have a hard time keeping up with the transaction flow.

Even if you set parallelism to 1, you will notice improved throughput over serial propagation of DML pushes because serial propagation uses a two-phase commit protocol, while parallel propagation does not.

The engineers at Oracle recognized that transactions do not necessarily need to be applied in the same chronological order at both the origin and the destination. For example, transactions against tables that have no relationship with one another can be applied simultaneously. The actual algorithm that Oracle uses to determine transaction dependencies is based on the SCN (system change number) in the blocks that the transaction modifies. So, updates to the same table may be candidates for parallel propagation. There are a number of factors that can influence the performance gain you realize by using parallel propagation, such as how densely your data is packed; the more records a table stores in a single block, the less likely that transactions against the table can be parallelized because of the increased likelihood that multiple transactions touch the same block. (You can control data density with the storage parameters PCTFREE and PCTUSED.)

Another behavior of parallel propagation is that transactions originating from the same database session are not parallelized. So, applications that run with one (or very few) database connections are not likely to notice a tremendous boost. Applications that have numerous connections performing DML and those with a mix of independent transactions will notice a significant benefit.

It is actually possible to enable parallel propagation of a single session's transactios by issuing this command:

```
ALTER SESSION SET EVENTS '26567 TRACE NAME CONNECT
FOREVER, LEVEL'
```

Managing parallel propagation

To enable parallel propagation, you must set the parallelism parameter in the call to DBMS_DEFER_SYS.SCHEDULE_PUSH. For example:

```
execute dbms_defer_sys.schedule_push( -
destination       => 'PMFG.BIGWHEEL.COM', -
interval          => 'SYSDATE+5/86400', -
next_date         => SYSDATE+5/86400, -
transaction_count => 10000, -
parallelism       => 8);
```

This call enables parallel propagation for all replication groups' deftran pushes to the database PMFG.BIGWHEEL.COM.

Parallel propagation relies on the parallel query background processes to do its bidding. To ensure that the propagations have the resources they need, do the following:

- Note the settings of the initialization parameters PARALLEL_MIN_SERVERS and PARALLEL_MAX_SERVERS. The default value for PARALLEL_MIN_SERVERS is 0. You should set this value at least as high as the highest degree of parallelism you have specified in your calls to DBMS_DEFER_SYS.SCHEDULE_PUSH, preferably higher. The PARALLEL_MAX_SERVERS value should be set high enough to support simultaneous parallel pushes to all master databases.

- Be aware that the server background processes that service parallel propagation are the same background processes that support parallel queries. Therefore, if your application utilized the parallel query option (i.e., DEGREE is greater than 1 for any tables in DBA_TABLES) make sure that your PARALLEL_MAX_SERVERS can support the replication propagation and the parallel query activity. I recommend against using the parallel query option on replicated tables if you are also using parallel propagation.

 When using parallel propagation, Oracle must be able to use the same number of parallel query background processes as the value of parallelism in the call to DBMS_DEFER_SYS.PUSH. This behavior differs from parallel queries, which can function even if the query cannot allocate the number of parallel query background processes required to support the requested degree of parallelism.

If a parallel push fails because it could not acquire enough parallel query background processes, the push will fail; Oracle does not reattempt the push using serial propagation.

Checking parallel pushes

When a parallel push executes successfully, you will see multiple connections to the destination database:

```
SELECT  sid,
        serial#,
        username,
        osuser,
        process,
        substr(program,
                decode  (instr(program,':'),0,1,
                        (instr(program,':')+1)),32)  program
FROM v$session
WHERE username = 'PROPREP'
ORDER BY username


   SID      S# Username  OS User    PROCESS  PROGRAM
   -----  ------ --------- --------- --------- ------------------------
      18   17700 PROPREP   oracle        4014  oracle@walrus (P004)
      20   41600 PROPREP   oracle        4012  oracle@walrus (P003)
      22   62490 PROPREP   oracle        4016  oracle@walrus (P005)
      38    7124 PROPREP   oracle        4010  oracle@walrus (P002)
      63   58713 PROPREP   oracle        4020  oracle@walrus (P007)
      72   42205 PROPREP   oracle        4006  oracle@walrus (P000)
      64   50893 PROPREP   oracle        4018  oracle@walrus (P006)
      58   41460 PROPREP   oracle        4008  oracle@walrus (P001)
 8 rows selected.
```

These sessions exist in the destination database only during the actual deftran push. If things are working smoothly, they should not stay connected for very long—typically less than a minute. If the connections remain for longer, it often indicates that Oracle has detected and is resolving a conflict.

Parallel push errors

Under certain circumstances, it is possible for parallel propagation to "seize up" by encountering an error from which it cannot recover. These errors are usually related to resource issues rather then propagation conflicts. The symptoms are usually alarmingly obvious; transactions are queueing up at the origin site(s), and there is no propagation activity at the destination sites. You also may see errors like this in trace files or at the SQL*Plus prompt if you attempt to push the queue manually:

```
ORA-12012: error on auto execute of job 501
ORA-23388: replication parallel push watermark error
ORA-06512: at "SYS.DBMS_DEFER_SYS", line 1448
ORA-06512: at line 1
```

The root of the problem is a record in the table SYSTEM.DEF$_DESTINATION at the originating site. This table contains one record for every database that is receiving pushes. The value of the last_seq column is normally either NULL or 0. If it holds another value, then the last parallel push failed; the last_error_number and last_error_message fields should contain details.

For example, suppose that propagation from our headquarters site (PHQS.BIG-WHEEL.COM) to our manufacturing site (PMFG.BIGWHEEL.COM) has ceased. We can query SYSTEM.DEF$_DESTINATION at the headquarters site to get an idea of the problem:

```
SELECT  dblink,
        last_delivered,
        last_enq_tid,
        last_seq,
        disabled,
        job,
        last_txn_count,
        last_error_number,
        last_error_message
FROM    system.def$_destination
/
```

DB Link	Last Delivered	Last Enq TID	Last Seq	Disabled	Job	Last Txn Count	Last Error Number	Last Error Message
PSLS.BIGWHEEL.COM	525424		0		271	262		
PMFG.BIGWHEEL.COM	525424		1		382	1301	-2395	Exceeded call limit on io usage

Here we see that the propagation to PMFG.BIGWHEEL.COM failed because the propagator process in the remote database exceeded a resource limit. We can remedy the situation by following these steps:

1. Query the table SYSTEM.DEF$_ORIGIN at the destination site (PMFG.BIG-WHEEL.COM in this case) to determine what transactions have already been delivered from PHQS.BIGWHEEL.COM:

```
SELECT  enq_tid, origin_dblink
FROM    system.def$_origin
WHERE   enq_tid = 'PHQS.BIGWHEEL.COM'
/
```

ENQ_TID	ORIGIN_DBLINK
3.6.436763	PHQS.BIGWHEEL.COM
6.2.4574	PHQS.BIGWHEEL.COM
5.8.53272	PHQS.BIGWHEEL.COM

2. Delete these transactions from the deftran queue at the origin site (PHQS.BIG-WHEEL.COM):

```
EXECUTE dbms_defer_sys.delete_tran('3.6.436763', 'PHQS.BIGWHEEL.COM');
PL/SQL procedure successfully completed.

EXECUTE dbms_defer_sys.delete_tran('6.2.4574', 'PHQS.BIGWHEEL.COM');
PL/SQL procedure successfully completed.

EXECUTE dbms_defer_sys.delete_tran('5.8.53272', 'PHQS.BIGWHEEL.COM');
PL/SQL procedure successfully completed.

COMMIT;
```

3. Update the table SYSTEM.DEF$_DESTINATION at the origin site (PHQS.BIG-WHEEL.COM):

```
UPDATE SYSTEM.DEF$_DESTINATION
SET last_seq = 0
WHERE dblink = 'PMFG.BIGHWEEL.COM
/
1 row updated.
```

4. At this point, you should be able to resume propagation from PHQS.BIG-WHEEL.COM to PMFG.BIGWHEEL.COM. It is best to attempt a manual serial push first, followed by a manual parallel push. If these pushes are successful, you can safely reschedule automatic propagation.

 Do not use this procedure unless you are sure that propagation has ceased. Symptoms include propagators logged in to the destination accounts that are not doing anything and a lack of network traffic between the originating database server and the destination database server.

Synchronous versus asynchronous propagation

Synchronous propagation uses a two-phase commit protocol to guarantee that transactions are committed locally if and only if they are also applied at the destination database(s). Therefore, if a remote database cannot be reached or if a transaction cannot be committed for *any* reason, then all DML activity will hang. Because synchronous replication has such stringent requirements and because a failure has such dramatic consequences, most sites do not use it. Instead of adding a level of redundancy, synchronous replication effectively adds an additional dependency.

We recommend the use of asynchronous propagation unless your business case clearly calls for the synchronous approach. That being said, if you wish to switch

Bug Update

Oracle has identified two bugs (numbers 737918 and 734902) that can cause dscn to be greater than cscn in the table SYSTEM.DEF$_AQCALL. When this corruption occurs, parallel propagation hangs.

With Oracle's blessing, using a BEFORE UPDATE trigger on the table avoids the corruption as follows:

```
CREATE OR REPLACE TRIGGER t_bu_def$_aqcall
BEFORE UPDATE
ON def$_aqcall
FOR EACH ROW

BEGIN
    IF (:new.dscn > :new.cscn)
    THEN
        :new.dscn := :new.cscn;
    END IF;
END;
/
```

These bugs are slated to be fixed in version 8.0.4.4. We recommend contacting Oracle Worldwide Support for a status update if you intend to use parallel propagation.

between propagation modes, you can do so using the package procedure DBMS_REPCAT.ALTER_MASTER_PROPAGATION:

```
PROCEDURE alter_master_propagation(
        gname               IN VARCHAR2,
        master              IN VARCHAR2,
        dblink_table        IN dbms_utility.dblink_array,
        propagation_mode    IN VARCHAR2 := 'ASYNCHRONOUS',
        comment             IN VARCHAR2 := '');

PROCEDURE alter_master_propagation(
        gname               IN VARCHAR2,
        master              IN VARCHAR2,
        dblink_list         IN VARCHAR2,
        propagation_mode    IN VARCHAR2 := 'ASYNCHRONOUS',
        comment             IN VARCHAR2 := '');
```

The replication group gname must be quiesced in order to use the ALTER_MASTER_PROPAGATION procedure. In addition, you must regenerate replication support for all objects in the group before resuming normal activity.

Scheduling multiple push intervals for the same database

One of the limitations of advanced replication is that you cannot schedule different propagation intervals for different replication groups. The propagation interval between master sites is the same for all replication groups at those sites. It might be convenient, for example, to push changes to inventory more frequently than changes in prices.

Of course, there is a workaround, which is, in effect, to give the same destination database multiple names and schedule different propagation intervals to the different names. How do you give a database two names? By using connection qualifiers. For example, you could create two names for the PMFG site by creating database links as follows:

```
CREATE PUBLIC DATABASE LINK PMFG.BIGWHEEL.COM
USING 'prodmanufacturing';
```

and

```
CREATE PUBLIC DATABASE LINK PMFG.BIGWHEEL.COM@TCP
USING 'prodmanufacturing';
```

Then you can use different propagation intervals to these two "different" sites and add our replication groups to one site or the other based on how frequently the group's data is updated.

Beware that this solution is not without cost. Maintenance tasks become more complicated. For example, if you want to take the manufacturing site out of service, you must issue two calls to DBMS_DEFER_SYS.UNSCHEDULE_EXECU-TION—one for each name. You must also create additional database links using each name for accounts such as REPADMIN and the replication propagator account. Finally, you should avoid configurations that lead to transactions that involve multiple replication groups.

The Replication Catalog

The *replication catalog* is the subset of the data dictionary that contains information about replicated objects at all master sites and, to a certain extent, snapshot sites. Operations that modify the data in the replication catalog, such as adding or removing master objects, must be propagated from the master definition site to other master sites. In general, changes to the replication catalog require that the affected replication group be quiesced. Just as Oracle maintains a deferred transaction queue (deftran) for queued transactions, it also maintains a queue for replication catalog changes, known as the repcatlog.

The 10 DBMS_REPCAT calls which create entries in the repcatlog queue are:

DBMS_REPCAT.ADD_MASTER_DATABASE
DBMS_REPCAT.ALTER_MASTER_PROPAGATION
DBMS_REPCAT.ALTER_MASTER_REPOBJECT
DBMS_REPCAT.CREATE_MASTER_REPOBJECT
DBMS_REPCAT.DROP_MASTER_REPGROUP
DBMS_REPCAT.DROP_MASTER_REPOBJECT
DBMS_REPCAT.EXECUTE_DDL
DBMS_REPCAT.GENERATE_REPLICATION_SUPPORT
DBMS_REPCAT.RESUME_MASTER_ACTIVITY
DBMS_REPCAT.SUSPEND_MASTER_ACTIVITY

Replication Catalog Data Dictionary Views

The data dictionary views that make up the replication catalog are the following:

DBA_REPCAT

Name, status, and comment for every replication group. (Same as DBA_REP-GROUP.)

DBA_REPCATLOG

Lists all items in the repcatlog queue.

DBA_REPDDL

Lists all DDL calls in the repcatlog queue.

DBA_REPGENERATED

Lists all replication support objects.

DBA_REPGROUP

Name, status, and comment for every replication group. (Same as DBA_REP-CAT.)

DBA_REPKEY_COLUMNS

Lists key columns for all replicated tables. These columns are either primary key columns or columns that have been identified with DBMS_REPCAT.SET_COLUMNS.

DBA_REPOBJECT

Lists all replicated objects.

DBA_REPPROP

Lists propagation mode for all replicated objects to all sites.

DBA_REPSITES

Lists sites that are members of each replication group.

Appendix B, *Scripts and Utilities*, includes scripts to generate useful reports from these data dictionary views.

Pushing repcatlog Entries

You may have noticed that whenever you create a replication group, Oracle automatically makes an entry in the job queue that looks something like this:

```
system@live SQL> SELECT job, what
  2  FROM dba_jobs
  3  WHERE what like '%do_deferred_repcat_admin%'
  4  /

Job What
---- ----------------------------------------------------------------------
 241 dbms_repcat.do_deferred_repcat_admin('"RG_SPROCKET"', FALSE);
```

DBMS_REPCAT.DO_DEFERRED_REPCAT_ADMIN is the procedure that processes
repcatlog entries in the local database. If the procedure is called with all_sites set
to TRUE, the procedure will also perform the administrative tasks at remote masters. By default, Oracle schedules this job at every master database to run once
every 10 minutes, with all_sites set to FALSE. The most common chores for entries
in the repcatlog queue are suspending or resuming master activity, adding and
dropping replicated objects, and generating replication support.

The default frequency of 10 minutes is adequate for most situations, but if you
wish to expedite the repcatlog queue executes, you can call DBMS_REPCAT.DO_
DEFERRED_REPCAT_ADMIN manually when logged in to the replication administrator (REPADMIN) account.

Monitoring Progress

Once you create entries in the repcatlog queue with calls to procedures such as
DBMS_REPCAT.ADD_MASTER_DATABASE, you can query the data dictionary
view DBA_REPCATLOG at all master sites to determine the status of your operations. Table 12-2 describes the meanings of all possible status values.

Table 12-2. Explanation of Status Column in DBA_REPCATLOG

Status	Meaning
READY	The site is ready to execute the request. The next call to DBMS_REPCAT.DO_DEFERRED_REPCAT_ADMIN will execute the pending request.
DO_CALLBACK	Oracle is updating the status of a request from a remote database.
AWAIT_CALLBACK	Oracle is awaiting feedback from a remote database about the completion of a task, such as generating replication support.
ERROR	The request has failed. Information about the failure is available in the DBA_REPCATLOG fields ERRNUM and MESSAGE.

Similarly, the REQUEST field tells what the current repcatlog request is. Table 12-3
describes the requests that can be queued.

Table 12-3. Explanation of REQUEST Column in DBA_REPCATLOG

Request	Meaning
CREATE_MASTER_REPOBJECT	Add new replicated object.
DROP_MASTER_REPSCHEMA	Drop replication group.
ADD_MASTER_DATABASE	Add master database to replication group.
ALTER_MASTER_REPOBJECT	Perform DDL on an existing replicated object.
DROP_MASTER_REPOBJECT	Drop a master replicated object.
SUSPEND_MASTER_ACTIVITY	Quiesce a replication group.
RESUME_MASTER_ACTIVITY	Resume normal activity for a replication group.
EXECUTE_DDL	Perform DDL.
GENERATE_REPLICATION_SUPPORT	Begin generation of replication support for a replicated object.
GENERATE_SUPPORT_PHASE_1	Generate replication support; phase 1.
GENERATE_SUPPORT_PHASE_2	Generate replication support; phase 2
ALTER_MASTER_PROPAGATION	Alter propagation mode (between SYNCHRONOUS and ASYNCHRONOUS).
END_PHASE_2	End of replication support generation.

 It is usually best not to submit numerous (as in scores) of requests to the repcatlog all at once, because an error in any one request can delay subsequent requests.

The following script reports the relevant details about requests in the repcatlog queue:

```
-------------------------------------------------------------------------
-- Filename:    repcatlog.sql
-- Purpose:     Lists all tasks pending in dba_repcatlog queue.
-- Author:      Chas. Dye (cdye@excitecorp.com)
-- Date:        28-Jun-1996
-------------------------------------------------------------------------
column SOURCE            heading "Source"     format a6
column MASTER            heading "Master"     format a6
column SNAME             heading "Group"      format a10
column STATUS            heading "Status"     format a14
column REQUEST           heading "Request"    format a28
column TIMESTAMP         heading "Time"       format a8

SELECT  substr(source, 1, instr(source, '.', 1) -1 ) source,
        substr(master, 1, instr(master, '.', 1) -1 ) master
        sname,
        status,
        request, to_char(timestamp, 'HH24:MI:SS') timestamp
FROM    dba_repcatlog
ORDER BY master
/
```

Correcting Errors

Errors that occur during repcatlog executions log diagnostics in the ERRNUM and MESSAGE fields of DBA_REPCATLOG. You can either correct the cause of the error (such as a privilege shortage) or remove the request from the repcatlog queue.

The following script reports on errors and generates the text of the required call to DBMS_REPCAT.PURGE_MASTER_LOG to delete the repcatlog queue entry:

```
------------------------------------------------------------------------
-- Filename:    repcaterr.sql
-- Purpose:     Lists entries in dba_repcatlog with error status.
-- Author:      Chas. Dye (cdye@excitecorp.com)
-- Date:        28-Jun-1996
------------------------------------------------------------------------
column ID              heading "Id"        format 9999
column SOURCE          heading "Source"    format a20
column SNAME           heading "Schema"    format a8
column REQUEST         heading "Request"   format a22
column ONAME           heading "Object"    format a20
column ERRNUM          heading "Error"     format 99999
column MESSAGE         heading "Message"   format a74

SELECT  id, status, sname, request, oname, errnum
FROM    dba_repcatlog
WHERE   status = 'ERROR'
ORDER BY id
/

SELECT  id, message
FROM    dba_repcatlog
WHERE   status = 'ERROR'
ORDER BY id
/

set head off
SELECT 'Run these commands to purge...'
FROM dual
/
set head on

SELECT
      'EXECUTE dbms_repcat.purge_master_log('||
         id ||', '
   ||chr(39)||rtrim(source)||chr(39)||', '
   ||chr(39)||gname||chr(39)||');'         command
FROM    dba_repcatlog
WHERE   status = 'ERROR'
/
```

Sample output:

```
SQL> @repcaterr

    Id Status      Schema Request                Object        Error
 ----- --------- -------- ---------------------- ------------- ------
   664 ERROR      SPROCKET DROP_MASTER_REPOBJECT  PRODUCTS      -1013

1 row selected.

    Id Message
 ----- ------------------------------------------------------------------
   664 ORA-01013: user requested cancel of current operation

1 row selected.

Run these commands to purge...

1 row selected.

COMMAND
 --------------------------------------------------------------------------
EXECUTE dbms_repcat.purge_master_log(664, 'LIVE.WORLD', 'RG_LIVESTK');

1 row selected.
```

The DBMS_REPCAT package does not include a procedure to retry failed repcat-log requests, so you must always delete the failed entry and retry the request after the underlying problem is corrected.

> You must issue a COMMIT after calling DBMS_REPCAT.PURGE_MASTER_LOG.

Table Replication

Certainly the most versatile and intriguing component of Oracle's advanced replication facility is multi-master table replication. Any replicated table can be updated anywhere, and the changes will appear in all participating master sites. However, as with any sophisticated technology, you must configure multi-master replication with great care in order to avoid perils and pitfalls.

This section describes the API calls used to create and to maintain replicated tables, points out techniques to make the administration job easier, and describes some practices that will help you to avoid trouble.

API Calls

The fundamental DBMS_REPCAT procedures for administering replicated tables are as follows:

DBMS_REPCAT.ADD_UNIQUE_RESOLUTION
> Adds a uniqueness conflict resolution handler to the table.

DBMS_REPCAT.ADD_UPDATE_RESOLUTION
> Adds an update conflict resolution handler to the table.

DBMS_REPCAT.DEFINE_COLUMN_GROUP
> Creates an empty column group.

DBMS_REPCAT.DROP_COLUMN_GROUP
> Drops a column group.

DBMS_REPCAT.DROP_UNIQUE_RESOLUTION
> Drops a uniqueness conflict handler.

DBMS_REPCAT.DROP_UPDATE_RESOLUTION
> Drops an update conflict handler.

DBMS_REPCAT.MAKE_COLUMN_GROUP
> Creates a column group and assigns columns to the group.

DBMS_REPCAT.SEND_AND_COMPARE_OLD_VALUES
> Specifies which columns should send their previous values to remote sites for comparison during updates and deletes.

DBMS_REPCAT.SET_COLUMNS
> Specifies the column(s) to use to uniquely identify records in the table.

You may notice that many of these procedures are associated with configuring conflict resolution methods, which is a testament to the fact that conflict detection and resolution is a crucial component of a multi-master replicated environment. Chapter 15 is devoted to conflict resolution techniques.

Column Groups

I recommend that you specifically define column groups for every replicated table, as opposed to allowing columns to be assigned to the "shadow" column group that Oracle creates by default. This way, it is easier to administer conflict resolution for the table.

For tables whose conflict resolution methods are not dictated by specific business rules or other requirements, I suggest including a timestamp and site_name field so that you can easily assign both a time-based and site-priority-based resolution method to the table, as follows.

Consider the table REGIONS:

```
system@d8ca SQL> desc regions
 Name            Null?     Type
 ------------    --------  -----------
 REGION_ID       NOT NULL  NUMBER(6)
 COUNTRY_ID      NOT NULL  NUMBER(6)
 REGION_NAME     NOT NULL  VARCHAR2(15)
 AUDIT_DATE      NOT NULL  DATE
 AUDIT_USER      NOT NULL  VARCHAR2(30)
 GLOBAL_NAME     NOT NULL  VARCHAR2(20)
```

The following procedure calls create a column group CG_REGIONS and assign time-based and site-priority-based conflict resolution methods:

```
-- Create the column group; include all columns.
EXECUTE dbms_repcat.make_column_group( -
sname                   => 'SPROCKET',-
oname                   => 'REGIONS',-
column_group            => 'CG_REGIONS',-
list_of_column_names    => '*');

-- Add a site-priority-based resolution method.  (This assumes the site
-- priority group SP_SPROCKET_SITE has already been created.)
EXECUTE dbms_repcat.add_update_resolution( -
sname                   => 'SPROCKET', -
oname                   => 'REGIONS', -
column_group            => 'CG_REGIONS', -
sequence_no             => 20, -
method                  => 'SITE PRIORITY', -
parameter_column_name   => 'GLOBAL_NAME', -
priority_group          => 'SP_SPROCKET_SITE', -
comment                 => 'Added by '||user||' on '||sysdate);

-- Add a timestamp-based resolution method.
EXECUTE dbms_repcat.add_update_resolution( -
sname                   => 'SPROCKET', -
oname                   => 'REGIONS', -
column_group            => 'CG_REGIONS', -
sequence_no             => 10, -
method                  => 'LATEST TIMESTAMP', -
parameter_column_name   => 'AUDIT_DATE', -
comment                 => 'Added by '||user||' on '||sysdate);
```

The overhead of processing unresolved conflicts, while reduced in Oracle8, is still expensive, especially in an environment with a high transaction volume. It is imperative that every replicated table have at least one, and preferably two, conflict resolution methods defined. You will find that conflicts will arise no matter how carefully you design the application.

Chapter 15 contains information about more advanced usages of column groups. For tables that don't require advanced techniques, you can use the method just described.

Minimum Communication and SEND_AND_COMPARE_OLD_VALUES

When Oracle replicates an update or delete operation, it ensures that the row it updates or deletes in the remote database(s) is the same as the record that it updated or deleted in the local database. The default behavior is to compare the current data in every field of the remote database with the prechange data in the local database.

Needless to say, this comparison can lead to a great deal of network traffic and substantial processing overhead, particularly for large VARCHAR fields.

Enter Oracle8 and the *minimum communication* option. This feature allows you to specify that updates compare the values of changed column groups only. The min_communication parameter in the DBMS_REPCAT.GENERATE_REPLICATION_ SUPPORT procedure dictates whether the minimum communication feature is activated. The parameter is set to TRUE by default.

The DBMS_REPCAT.SEND_AND_COMPARE_OLD_VALUES procedure, also new to Oracle8, allows you to take minimum communication to an extreme by letting you define what columns to compare on updates and deletes. If you want to, you can restrict the comparison of old and new values to the primary key columns only. Although drastic, this minimization can be appropriate for certain OLTP applications and/or for databases that are connected by an expensive and/or inefficient interface, such as a satellite relay or the Internet. As a practical matter, the most minimization that you should consider would include primary key columns and all columns used in conflict resolution methods.

 Indiscriminate use of SEND_AND_COMPARE_OLD_VALUES can effectively disable all conflict resolution techniques, resulting in divergent data.

The specification for DBMS_REPCAT.SEND_AND_COMPARE_OLD_VALUES is as follows:

```
PROCEDURE send_and_compare_old_values(
    sname       IN VARCHAR2,
    oname       IN VARCHAR2,
    column_list IN VARCHAR2,
    operation   IN VARCHAR2 := 'UPDATE',
    send        IN BOOLEAN := TRUE);
```

```
PROCEDURE send_and_compare_old_values(
    sname        IN VARCHAR2,
    oname        IN VARCHAR2,
    column_table IN dbms_repcat.varchar2s,
    operation    IN VARCHAR2 := 'UPDATE',
    send         IN BOOLEAN := TRUE);
```

Table 12-4 describes the usage of these parameters in the SEND_AND_COMPARE_OLD_VALUES procedure.

Table 12-4. Parameter Usage for SEND_AND_COMPARE_OLD_VALUES

Parameter Name	Comments
sname	The owner of the replicated table.
oname	The name of the replicated table
column_list	A comma-separated string of columns to operate on. An asterisk (*) indicates all nonkey columns. Use either column_list or column_table.
column_table	A PL/SQL table of columns to operate on. Use either column_list or column_table.
operation	One of UPDATE, DELETE, or *, with * meaning both UPDATE and DELETE.
send	If send is TRUE, the specified columns are sent. If FALSE, the specified columns are not sent. Unspecified columns are not affected.

Changes specified in calls to SEND_AND_COMPARE_OLD_VALUES take effect the next time you generate replication support for the table.

Returning to the REGIONS table, you could make the following call to restrict the old values that Oracle sends to remote databases to REGION_ID (the primary key), AUDIT_DATE, and GLOBAL_NAME:

```
EXECUTE dbms_repcat.send_and_compare_old_values( -
sname        => 'SPROCKET', -
oname        => 'REGIONS', -
column_list => 'COUNTRY_ID,REGION_NAME,AUDIT_USER', -
operation    => '*', -
send         => FALSE);

EXECUTE dbms_repcat.generate_replication_support( -
sname               => 'SPROCKET', -
oname               => 'REGIONS', -
type                => 'TABLE', -
distributed         => TRUE, -
min_communication   => TRUE);
```

Triggers on Replicated Tables

Triggers on replicated tables must take into account that DML activity may be the result of Oracle's replicating a remote transaction. For example, if you have an INSERT trigger that populates a timestamp field, you would probably want the trigger to fire when the INSERT occurs at the original site, but not at all of the other replicated master sites. You may also wish to use triggers to populate fields that Oracle uses for conflict resolution, such as the AUDIT_DATE and GLOBAL_ NAME fields. The examples in the following sections demonstrate how to write triggers on replicated tables.

A trigger to populate fields at the originating site only

Because of the condition—IF (dbms_reputil.from_remote != TRUE)—this trigger updates the AUDIT_DATE and GLOBAL_NAME fields only if the DML is local, as opposed to a deferred transaction from a remote database:

```
CREATE OR REPLACE TRIGGER t_br_iu_regions
BEFORE INSERT OR UPDATE
ON regions
FOR EACH ROW

BEGIN
    IF (dbms_reputil.from_remote != TRUE)
    THEN
        :new.audit_date      := SYSDATE;
        :new.global_name     := DBMS_REPUTIL.GLOBAL_NAME;
    END IF;
END;
/
```

A trigger to populate a field from a sequence on inserts and fields used for conflict resolution

This trigger illustrates how to populate primary key fields from sequences for replicated tables:

```
CREATE OR REPLACE TRIGGER t_br_iu_regions
BEFORE INSERT OR UPDATE
ON regions
FOR EACH ROW

BEGIN
    IF (dbms_reputil.from_remote != TRUE)
    THEN
        IF INSERTING
        THEN
            SELECT  seq_regions.nextval
            INTO    :new.region_id
            FROM dual;
        END IF;
        :new.rectime    := SYSDATE;
        :new.site       := DBMS_REPUTIL.GLOBAL_NAME;
    END IF;
END;
/
```

All of the triggers that Oracle creates to support the replication of a table are after-row triggers. It is best for applications to use before-row triggers so that they are guaranteed to fire before the replication triggers.

Replicating triggers themselves

You can use the DBMS_REPCAT.CREATE_MASTER_REPOBJECT procedure if you wish, or you can simply build the triggers individually in each database. I have found the latter method to be more efficient.

Using Offline Instantiation

Suppose you want to create replicated tables at a new master site. One way to do so is to quiesce the replication group, export the tables, import them at the new site, generate replication support for them at the new site, and finally resume normal activity for the replication group. Although this methodology ensures that the new tables will be in sync with the original ones, the duration of the quiescence may be unacceptably long. Offline instantiation is a technique you can use to deploy replicated tables at new sites without having to quiesce the table's replication group at the master site during the entire data loading process. Table 12-5 describes how to use DBMS_OFFLINE_OG.

Table 12-5. Instantiating a Table at a New Site with DBMS_OFFLINE_OG

Step	Where Performed	Activity
1	Master definition site	DBMS_REPCAT.ADD_MASTER_DATABASE
2	Master definition site	DBMS_REPCAT.SUSPEND_MASTER_ACTIVITY
3	Master definition site	DBMS_OFFLINE_OG.BEGIN_INSTANTIATION
4	Any existing master site	Export replicated schema
5	Master definition site	DBMS_OFFLINE_OG.RESUME_SUBSET_OF_MASTERS
6	New site	DBMS_OFFLINE_OG.BEGIN_LOAD
7	New site	Import data from Step 4
8	New Site	DBMS_OFFLINE_OG.END_LOAD
9	Master definition site	DBMS_OFFLINE_OG.END_INSTANTIATION

The following scenario shows how you would instantiate a new site. Here, the site PFIN.BIGWHEEL.COM is added to the replication group RG_SPROCKET using DBMS_OFFLINE_OG. Assume that the master definition site is PHQS.BIGWHEEL.COM.

1. From master definition site PHQS.BIGWHEEL.COM, add the new master site, quiesce the replication group, and call DBMS_OFFLINE_OG.BEGIN_INSTANTIATION:

```
EXECUTE DBMS_REPCAT.ADD_MASTER_DATABASE( -
        gname   => 'RG_SPROCKET', -
        master  => 'PFIN.BIGWHEEL.COM');

EXECUTE DBMS_REPCAT.SUSPEND_MASTER_ACTIVITY(gname => 'RG_SPROCKET');

EXECUTE DBMS_OFFLINE_OG.BEGIN_INSTANTIATION( -
        gname     => 'RG_SPROCKET', -
        new_site  => 'PFIN.BIGWHEEL.COM');
```

2. Perform export of schema SPROCKET from any existing master site.

3. Call RESUME_SUBSET_OF_MASTERS at the master definition site.

4. Call BEGIN_LOAD from the new master site PFIN.BIGWHEEL.COM:

```
EXECUTE DBMS_OFFLINE_OG.BEGIN_LOAD( -
        gname     => 'RG_SPROCKET', -
        new_site  => 'PFIN.BIGWHEEL.COM');
```

5. Import the RG_SPROCKET schema into PFIN.BIGWHEEL.COM using the export file created in Step 2.

6. Call END_LOAD from the new master site, PFIN.BIGWHEEL.COM:

```
EXECUTE DBMS_OFFLINE_OG.END_LOAD( -
        gname     => 'RG_SPROCKET', -
        new_site  => 'PFIN.BIGWHEEL.COM');
```

7. Call END_INSTANTIATION from the master definition site:

```
EXECUTE DBMS_OFFLINE_OG.END_INSTANTIATION( -
        gname => 'RG_SPROCKET', -
        new_site => 'PFIN.BIGWHEEL.COM');
```

Offline instantiation caveats

Offline instantiation has one noticeable drawback, which is that Oracle queues *all* transactions destined for new_site. Therefore, if you use this technique to add a table to a master site that is already participating in the replication of other tables, transactions against those other tables will not be delivered until the call to DBMS_ OFFLINE_OG.END_INSTANTIATION. In other words, the DBMS_OFFLINE.BEGIN_ INSTANTIATION call disables all pushes to new_site.

This behavior is generally not an issue if you are adding a brand new master site, but if you're trying to roll out a new table to an existing site, you should be prepared to queue transactions to that new site for as long as it takes to perform your export and import.

As of this writing, DBMS_OFFLINE_OG does not support connection qualifiers (bugs 659595 and 729672); see the earlier sidebar, "Bug Update."

An alternative to DBMS_OFFLINE_OG

If you need to add a replicated table to an existing master database with a minimal amount of transaction queueing to the master, you might consider this procedure. The basic idea is to create a temporary replication group that uses a connection qualifier to identify the master. For purposes of illustration, assume that we wish to add the table SPROCKET.PRODUCTS to the existing master site PFIN.BIGWHEEL.COM.

1. Create a new database link to PFIN.BIGWHEEL.COM using connection qualifiers:

   ```
   CREATE PUBLIC DATABASE LINK PFIN.BIGWHEEL.COM@TCP
   USING 'prodfinance'
   ```

   Note that in addition to the public database link, you also need to create private links for your REPADMIN and PROGAGATOR accounts.

2. Create a temporary replication group RG_SPROCKET_TEMP:

   ```
   EXECUTE DBMS_REPCAT.CREATE_MASTER_REPGROUP(-
       gname => 'RG_SPROCKET_TEMP', -
       qualifier => '@TCP');
   ```

3. Add the PFIN.BIGWHEEL.COM database to the temporary group:

   ```
   EXECUTE DBMS_REPCAT.ADD_MASTER_DATABASE( -
       gname => 'RG_SPROCKET_TEMP', -
       master => 'PFIN.BIGWHEEL.COM@TCP'
   ```

4. Add table SPROCKET.PRODUCTS to the replication group RG_SPROCKET_TEMP and generate replication support:

   ```
   EXECUTE DBMS_REPCAT.CREATE_MASTER_REPOBJECT( -
       sname => 'SPROCKET', -
       oname => 'PRODUCTS', -
       type  => 'TABLE', -
       copy_rows => FALSE, -
       gname => 'RG_SPROCKET_TEMP');

   EXECUTE DBMS_REPCAT.GENERATE_REPLICATION_SUPPORT( -
       sname => 'SPROCKET', -
       oname => 'PRODUCTS', -
       type  => 'TABLE');
   ```

   You should also add conflict resolution to the table at this time.

5. Export table SPROCKET.PRODUCTS.

6. Resume master activity for the replication group RG_SPROCKET_TEMP:

```
EXECUTE DBMS_REPCAT.RESUME_MASTER_ACTIVITY( -
gname => 'RG_SPROCKET_TEMP');
```

7. Import SPROCKET.PRODUCTS at the new master site without firing any of the replication triggers (disable all triggers on the table first).

8. When the import is finished, push the queued transactions to PFIN.BIG-WHEEL.COM@TCP:

```
VARIABLE rc NUMBER
BEGIN
    rc := EXECUTE DBMS_DEFER_SYS.PUSH(
        destination := 'PFIN.BIGWHEEL.COM@TCP');
END;
/
```

9. Quiesce the temporary group RG_SPROCKET_TEMP:

```
EXECUTE DBMS_REPCAT.SUSPEND_MASTER_ACTIVITY(-
    gname => 'RG_SPROCKET_TEMP');
```

At this point, the PRODUCTS table should be in sync at all sites.

10. Remove SPROCKET.PRODUCTS from the temporary replication group:

```
EXECUTE DBMS_REPCAT.DROP_MASTER_REPOBJECT( -
    sname => 'SPROCKET'
    oname => 'PRODUCTS', -
    type => 'TABLE',       -
    drop_objects => FALSE);
```

11. Quiesce the replication group RG_SPROCKET and add the table SPROCKET.PRODUCTS to it:

```
EXECUTE DBMS_REPCAT.SUSPEND_MASTER_ACTIVITY( -
    gname => 'RG_SPROCKET');

EXECUTE DBMS_REPCAT.CREATE_MASTER_REPOBJECT( -
    sname => 'SPROCKET',  -
    oname => 'PRODUCTS',  -
    type => 'TABLE',      -
    gname => 'RG_SPROCKET');

EXECUTE DBMS_REPCAT.GENERATE_REPLICATION_SUPPORT( -
    sname       => 'SPROCKET',  -
    oname       => 'PRODUCTS',  -
    type        => 'TABLE',     -
    distributed => TRUE);
```

12. Resume master activity, with the SPROCKET.PRODUCTS table in replication group RG_SPROCKET, instantiated at the site PFIN.BIGWHEEL.COM:

```
EXECUTE DBMS_REPCAT.RESUME_MASTER_ACTIVITY('RG_SPROCKET');
```

Adding and Removing Tables

Use the built-in package procedures DBMS_REPCAT.CREATE_MASTER_REPOB-
JECT and DBMS_REPCAT.REMOVE_MASTER_REPOBJECT to add and remove
tables (and any other replicated objects) from a replication group. The specifications for these packages are as follows:

```
PROCEDURE create_master_repobject(
sname                IN VARCHAR2,
oname                IN VARCHAR2,
type                 IN VARCHAR2,
use_existing_object  IN BOOLEAN := TRUE,
ddl_text             IN VARCHAR2 := NULL,
comment              IN VARCHAR2 := '',
retry                IN BOOLEAN := FALSE,
copy_rows            IN BOOLEAN := TRUE,
gname                IN VARCHAR2 := '');

PROCEDURE drop_master_repobject(
sname          IN VARCHAR2,
oname          IN VARCHAR2,
type           IN VARCHAR2,
drop_objects   IN BOOLEAN := FALSE);
```

Note that CREATE_MASTER_REPOBJECT requires the quiescence of the replication group to which the table belongs, while DROP_MASTER_REPOBJECT does
not. Both procedures must be called from the master definition site.

Adding replicated tables.

The following examples illustrate various strategies for adding a table to a replication group.

This call adds table SPROCKET.PRODUCTS to the replication group SPROCKET:

```
EXECUTE DBMS_REPCAT.CREATE_MASTER_REPOBJECT( -
sname   => 'SPROCKET',  -
oname   => 'PRODUCTS',  -
type    => 'TABLE',  -
gname   => 'RG_SPROCKET');
```

Since we have not specified the ddl_text parameter in this example, the table must
already exist.

In the next example, CREATE_MASTER_REPOBJECT is used to create an object at
the master definition site and simultaneously add it to the replication group:

```
EXECUTE DBMS_REPCAT.CREATE_MASTER_REPOBJECT( -
sname   => 'SPROCKET',  -
oname   => 'STATES',  -
type    => 'TABLE' -
ddl_text => 'CREATE TABLE  sprocket.states (state_id VARCHAR2(2),
    state_name VARCHAR2(20))',
gname   => 'RG_SPROCKET');
```

Notice that the CREATE TABLE statement in this example specifies the owner of the table. Typically, the replication administrator account uses DBMS_REPCAT, not the schema owner account. Therefore, when the REPADMIN account is calling the procedure, you must be sure to specify the schema in which to create objects. One of the privileges granted through DBMS_REPCAT_ADMIN.GRANT_ADMIN_ANY_ REPGROUP is CREATE ANY TABLE.

In all likelihood, you will not create objects with the CREATE_MASTER_REPOB-JECT procedure very often because doing so is rather clumsy for all but the most simple objects. But, it's there if you want it.

By setting the retry and use_existing_object parameters to TRUE in the following example, Oracle creates the table PRODUCTS at all master sites where it does not already exist and, by setting copy_rows to TRUE, copies the data from the master definition site to the master sites:

```
EXECUTE DBMS_REPCAT.CREATE_MASTER_REPOBJECT( -
sname               => 'SPROCKET',  -
oname               => 'PRODUCTS',  -
type                => 'TABLE',  -
use_existing_object => TRUE, -
retry               => TRUE, -
copy_rows           => TRUE, -
gname               => 'SPROCKET');
```

If tables exist at master sites, but do not have the same shape as at the master definition site, Oracle returns an error.

 I strongly recommend pre-creating and populating tables at master sites as opposed to relying on the CREATE_MASTER_REPOBJECT procedure to do it for you, especially if the objects have interdependencies. At our sites, we always run a catalog script to create all schema objects, including triggers, primary and foreign key definitions, check constraints, and so on. We then let Oracle generate the replication support objects. This methodology gives us complete control over how the schema is created, and all environments are easily reproduced.

Removing replicated tables

The DBMS_REPCAT.DROP_MASTER_REPOBJECT procedure removes a table (or other replicated object) from a replication group and optionally drops the table itself if the DROP_OBJECTS parameter is set to TRUE. Executing this package is very straightforward, as the following example shows.

In this example, we remove the table SPROCKET.PRODUCTS from its replication group while leaving the table and its data intact:

```
EXECUTE DBMS_REPCAT.DROP_MASTER_REPOBJECT( -
sname        => 'SPROCKET',
oname        => 'PRODUCTS',
type         => 'TABLE',
drop_objects => FALSE);
```

Notice that this procedure does not have a gname parameter for specifying the replication group; since an object can be a member of exactly one replication group, identifying the table name and owner is sufficient.

Dropping replicated tables: caveats

Before dropping a replicated table, you should make every effort to delete all deferred transactions that affect the table. Oracle makes no effort to check for or to delete these transactions. Although deferred transactions against nonexistent replicated tables will not break or corrupt the replicated environment, they will incur the overhead of being logged as errors.

To clear the deferred transactions associated with a table, you need to delete them from the originating site. To find these transactions, you can query the DEFTRAN and DEFCALL data dictionary views, as illustrated in the following example.

The query in this example generates the calls to DBMS_DEFER_SYS.DELETE_ TRAN required to delete all transactions against the PRODUCTS table that originated at this site:

```
SELECT
'EXECUTE DBMS_DEFER_SYS.DELETE_TRAN('||chr(39)||
deferred_tran_id||chr(39)||', NULL);'||chr(10)||'COMMIT;' delete_command
FROM deftran t
WHERE EXISTS (
        SELECT deferred_tran_id
        FROM   defcall c
        WHERE  c.deferred_tran_id = t.deferred_tran_id
        AND    c.packagename = 'PRODUCTS$RP')
/
DELETE_COMMAND
--------------------------------------------------------------------
EXECUTE DBMS_DEFER_SYS.DELETE_TRAN('16.67.151601', NULL);
COMMIT;

EXECUTE DBMS_DEFER_SYS.DELETE_TRAN('19.0.145356', NULL);
COMMIT;

EXECUTE DBMS_DEFER_SYS.DELETE_TRAN('19.75.145358', NULL);
COMMIT;
```

```
EXECUTE DBMS_DEFER_SYS.DELETE_TRAN('21.14.146003', NULL);
COMMIT;

EXECUTE DBMS_DEFER_SYS.DELETE_TRAN('21.35.146000', NULL);
COMMIT;
```

Partially dropped tables (Oracle8 only)

Another caveat to consider when dropping replicated tables is that the call to
DBMS_REPCAT.DROP_MASTER_REPOBJECT may fail to drop all of the replication support triggers and packages associated with the target table. This partial
drop situation is a distinct possibility if the table is an active one. The symptoms of
an incomplete execution of DBMS_REPCAT.DROP_MASTER_REPOBJECT include
returning a lock timeout error and the continued queuing of transactions against
the table even though it no longer appears in the DBA_REPOBJECT data dictionary view. This scenario is particularly vexing since replication support triggers are
internalized and therefore invisible in Oracle8. To recover from this, you must call
the undocumented package procedures:

> DBMS_REPCAT_CACHE.PURGE_OBJECT_GROUP
> DBMS_REPCAT_UTL.DESTROY_INTERNAL_TRIGGER
> DBMS_REPCAT_UTL.REMOVE_REPOBJECT

The specifications for these procedures are as follows:

```
PROCEDURE destroy_internal_trigger(
canon_sname    IN VARCHAR2,      /*--- the owner of the table ---*/
canon_oname    IN VARCHAR2,      /*--- the table name ---*/
type_id        IN NUMBER);       /*--- use 2 ---*/

PROCEDURE remove_repobject(
canon_sname    IN VARCHAR2,      /*--- the owner of the table ---*/
canon_oname    IN VARCHAR2,      /*--- the table name ---*/
type_id        IN NUMBER);       /*--- use 2 ---*/

PROCEDURE purge_object_group(
cannon_gname   IN VARCHAR2       /*--- the replication group name ---*/
);
```

To use these procedures, follow these steps:

1. In each master database, log in to the SYS account and execute the procedures DBMS_REPCAT_UTL.DESTROY_INTERNAL_TRIGGER and DBMS_REP-
   CAT_UTL.REMOVE_REPOBJECT. For example:

```
EXECUTE dbms_repcat_utl.destroy_internal_trigger( -
    canon_sname => 'SPROCKET', -
    canon_oname => 'PRODUCTS', -
    type_id     => 2);
```

```
EXECUTE dbms_repcat_utl.remove_object( -
    canon_sname => 'SPROCKET', -
    canon_oname => 'PRODUCTS', -
    type_id     => 2);

COMMIT;
```

Note that these calls may result in lock timeout errors. Continue attempting them until they complete successfully.

2. In each master database, log in to the SYS account and execute DBMS_REPCAT_CACHE.PURGE_OBJECT_GROUP. For example:

```
EXECUTE dbms_repcat_cache.purge_object_group( -
    canon_gname => 'RG_SPROCKET'

COMMIT;
```

You should contact Oracle Support before attempting these procedures. Since the procedures are undocumented, they may change in future releases of the database. The procedure shown here works for Oracle 8.0.4.

Replicating DDL

The advanced replication facilities include support for replicating DDL commands to all master databases in a replication group. The DBMS_REPCAT procedures that provide this support are DBMS_REPCAT.ALTER_MASTER_REPOBJECT and DBMS_REPCAT.EXECUTE_DDL; their specifications follow:

```
PROCEDURE alter_master_repobject(
    sname    IN VARCHAR2,
    oname    IN VARCHAR2,
    type     IN VARCHAR2,
    ddl_text IN VARCHAR2,
    comment  IN VARCHAR2 := '',
    retry    IN BOOLEAN  := FALSE);

PROCEDURE execute_DDL(
    gname       IN VARCHAR2,
    master_list IN VARCHAR2 := NULL,
    ddl_text    IN VARCHAR2);

PROCEDURE execute_DDL(
    gname        IN VARCHAR2,
    master_table IN dbms_utility.dblink_array,
    ddl_text     IN VARCHAR2);
```

Notice that ALTER_MASTER_REPOBJECT does not allow you to specify master sites, whereas EXECUTE_DDL does. ALTER_MASTER_
REPOBJECT operates only on existing replicated objects and therefore executes at all master sites, whereas EXECUTE_DDL allows you
to perform DDL operations independent of replicated objects. For
example, you can use EXECUTE_DDL to create users at a remote site.

Restrictions

Note the following restrictions on DDL replication:

- Both DBMS_REPCAT.ALTER_MASTER_REPOBJECT and DBMS_REPCAT.EXE-
  CUTE_DDL must be called from the master definition site.

- DBMS_REPCAT.ALTER_MASTER_REPOBJECT requires the replication group to
  be quiesced.

- You must call regenerate replication support for tables that you alter with a
  call to DBMS_REPCAT.ALTER_MASTER_REPOBJECT.

Examples

The following examples demonstrate how to use the DDL replication procedures.

Creating an index

This example uses the DBMS_REPCAT.EXECUTE_DDL procedure to create an
index on the SPROCKET.STATES table at sites PFIN.BIGWHEEL.COM and
PMFG.BIGWHEEL.COM. Note that, as with CREATE_MASTER_REPOBJECT, we
must specify the schema in which to create the index.

```
DECLARE vMasters VARCHAR2(30);
BEGIN
    vMasters := 'PFIN.BIGWHEEL.COM,PMFG.BIGWHEEL.COM';
    DBMS_REPCAT.EXECUTE_DDL(
        gname       => 'SPROCKET',
        master_list => vMasters,
        ddl_text    => 'CREATE INDEX sprocket.i_state_id
            ON sprocket.tstates(state_id)',
        sname       =>'SPROCKET');
END;
```

Compiling a replicated package body

In this example, we use the DBMS_REPCAT.ALTER_MASTER_REPOBJECT procedure to set the retry parameter to TRUE so that ALTER_MASTER_REPOBJECT
applies the DDL only at sites at which the package body's status is INVALID.

```
DBMS_REPCAT.ALTER_MASTER_REPOBJECT( -
        sname        => 'SPROCKET', -
        oname        => 'PRODUCTMAINT', -
        type         => 'PACKAGE BODY', -
        ddl_text     => 'ALTER PACKAGE SPROCKET.PRODUCTMAINT COMPILE BODY', -
        comment      => 'Recompiled on '||sysdate|| ' by '||user, -
        retry        => TRUE );
```

Notice that the schema is specified for the object being altered. As with DBMS_REPCAT.EXECUTE_DDL, the ALTER_MASTER_REPOBJECT procedure operates on objects in the caller's schema by default, and the caller is generally the replication administrator account, not the schema account.

Altering a column in a replicated table

This example uses the DBMS_REPCAT.ALTER_MASTER_REPOBJECT procedure to alter the width of the state_id column in table SPROCKET.STATES at *all* sites:

```
DBMS_REPCAT.ALTER_MASTER_REPOBJECT( -
    sname    => 'SPROCKET', -
    oname    => 'STATES', -
    type     => 'TABLE', -
    ddl_text => 'ALTER TABLE SPROCKET.STATES MODIFY (STATE_ID NUMBER(10))' , -
    comment => 'state_id widened on '||sysdate|| ' by '||user);
```

You may find it convenient to create a special replication group, RG_DBA, to which you can use DBMS_REPCAT.EXCECUTE_DDL to "broadcast" administrative tasks such as creating users or coalescing tablespaces to all master databases.

Manually Executing Entries in the repcatlog

The procedures DBMS_REPCAT.ALTER_MASTER_REPOBJECT and DBMS_REPCAT.EXECUTE_DDL both put entries in the local repcatlog. These entries cause the commands to be executed at remote sites. By default, Oracle executes entries in the repcatlog every 10 minutes. However, if you wish, you can execute repcatlog entries manually by calling DBMS_REPCAT.DO_DEFERRED_REPCAT_ADMIN. For example, the following call executes repcatlog entries associated with the replication group RG_SPROCKET:

```
EXECUTE DBMS_REPCAT.DO_DEFERRED_REPCAT_ADMIN( gname => 'RG_SPROCKET');
```

Deleting Errors from the repcatlog

Use the procedure DBMS_REPCAT.PURGE_MASTER_LOG to delete errors from the repcatlog. The DBA_REPCATLOG data dictionary view retains entries for DDL propagations that have failed, and these entries are not removed when you resolve the problem that caused the failure. You may notice entries such as these:

```
SELECT source, status, request, to_char(timestamp, 'HH24:MI:SS') timestamp
FROM    dba_repcatlog
ORDER BY id
/
```

```
Source                  Status   Request                    Time
----------------        ------   ----------------------     -----------
D7CA.BIGWHEEL.COM       ERROR    CREATE_MASTER_REPOBJECT    23:13:07
D7CA.BIGWHEEL.COM       ERROR    CREATE_MASTER_REPOBJECT    23:13:07
D7CA.BIGWHEEL.COM       ERROR    CREATE_MASTER_REPOBJECT    23:25:20
D7CA.BIGWHEEL.COM       ERROR    CREATE_MASTER_REPOBJECT    23:25:20
D7CA.BIGWHEEL.COM       ERROR    CREATE_MASTER_REPOBJECT    23:26:53
D7CA.BIGWHEEL.COM       ERROR    CREATE_MASTER_REPOBJECT    23:26:53
D7CA.BIGWHEEL.COM       ERROR    DROP_MASTER_REPOBJECT      14:03:27
D7CA.BIGWHEEL.COM       ERROR    DROP_MASTER_REPOBJECT      14:03:27
```

```
8 rows selected.
```

The PURGE_MASTER_LOG procedure removes these entries from DBA_REPCAT-LOG. You can specify records to delete by ID, originating master, replication group, and schema. If any of the parameters is NULL, it is treated as a wildcard. Specifications differ for Oracle7 and Oracle8 as follows.

Oracle7 specification:

```
PROCEDURE DBMS_REPCAT.PURGE_MASTER_LOG(
    id      IN NATURAL,
    source IN VARCHAR2,
    gname  IN VARCHAR2 := '',
    sname  IN VARCHAR2 := '');
```

Oracle8 specification:

```
PROCEDURE DBMS_REPCAT.PURGE_MASTER_LOG(
    id      IN NATURAL,
    source IN VARCHAR2,
    gname  IN VARCHAR2);
```

The following call removes all entries associated with replication group SPROCKET from the DBA_REPCATLOG data dictionary view:

```
DBMS_REPCAT.PURGE_MASTER_LOG (gname => 'SPROCKET' );
```

To clear all entries from the DBA_REPCATLOG data dictionary view, set all parameters to NULL.

Your Replicated Environment

Once you have a replicated system up and running, you need to monitor it to ensure that you detect problems early. The most important things to monitor are:

- The number of transactions queued at each originating site

- The number of unresolved errors at each destination site

- The number of entries in each snapshot log

If any of these three counts becomes too high, it can be very time-consuming to recover. By the same token, all are usually easy to correct if you catch them early.

Monitoring Queued Transactions

The following SQL query returns the number of deferred transactions that are currently queued:

```
SELECT   count(*)
FROM     deftrandest d, deftran t
WHERE    d.deferred_tran_id    = t.deferred_tran_id
AND      d.delivery_order      = t.delivery_order;
```

This query has been incorporated into a Unix shell script, *checklatency*, shown here, which sends email to the DBA when the number of deferred transactions exceeds 150:

```
#! /bin/ksh
#-----------------------------------------------------------------------
# Filename: checklatency
# Purpose:  Notifies the dba when more than 150 replicated transactions
#             are queued.
# Author:   Chas. Dye (cdye@excitecorp.com)
# Date:     21-Oct-1998
# Remarks:  Requires OPS$ account for whichever OS user crons this script.
#-----------------------------------------------------------------------
HOST=`/bin/uname -n`
MAIL=/bin/mailx
DISTLIST="beepdba@yoursite.com"
export HOST MAIL DISTLIST
#
ORACLE_HOME=/u/oracle/product/8.0.4.2 ; export ORACLE_HOME
ORACLE_SID=PHQS ; export ORACLE_SID
PATH=$ORACLE_HOME/bin:/bin:{PATH} ; export PATH
LD_LIBRARY_PATH=$ORACLE_HOME/lib:${LD_LIBRARY_PATH}; export LD_LIBRARY_PATH
#
cd ${HOME}/bin
#
sqlplus -s / << EOF
set echo off
```

```
set head off
set feedback on
spool /u/oracle/admin/PHQS/logbook/latent.log
SELECT   count(*)
FROM     deftrandest d, deftran t
WHERE    d.deferred_tran_id      = t.deferred_tran_id
AND      d.delivery_order        = t.delivery_order
HAVING   count(*) > 150;
spool off
EOF
#
grep 1 latent.log > latent.err
if [ -s latent.err ]
then
        $MAIL -s"${ORACLE_SID}@${HOST} latency alert" $DISTLIST < latent.log
fi
#
rm -f latent.err
rm -f latent.log
```

You may also be interested in the age and count of transactions to specific destinations. This script, *latent.sql,* provides precisely that information. This is possibly
the single most valuable script for checking the health of a replicated environment:

```
---------------------------------------------------------------------------
-- Filename:     latent.sql
-- Purpose:      Lists outstanding transactions by destination.
-- Author:       Chas. Dye (cdye@excitecorp.com)
-- Date:         09-Jul-1996
---------------------------------------------------------------------------

col dblink     heading "Destination"                          format a16
col earliest   heading "Least Recently|Queued Transaction"    format a20
col latest     heading "Most Recently|Queued Transaction"     format a20
col out        heading "Total|Txns|Queued"                    format 999,999
col timenow    heading "Current|Time"                         format a8
col latency    heading "Maximum|Latency|dd:hh:mi:ss"          format a12

clear breaks
clear computes

set head off
set feedback off
select 'Propagation Latency Instance: '||name||'.  Time: ' ||
       to_char(sysdate, 'DD-Mon-YY HH24:mi:ss')
from v$database
/
set head on
set feedback on

compute sum of out on report
break on report skip 1
```

```
SELECT  d.dblink,
        min(t.start_time) earliest,
        max(t.start_time) latest,
        count(*) out,
        ltrim(to_char(trunc(sysdate-( min(start_time)) ), '09')) || ':' ||
        ltrim(to_char(trunc(24*((sysdate-min(start_time)) -
                trunc(sysdate-min(start_time)))), '09'))||':' ||
        ltrim(to_char(mod(trunc(1440*((sysdate-min(start_time)) -
                trunc(sysdate-min(start_time)))), 60), '09')) ||':' ||
        ltrim(to_char(mod(trunc(86400*((sysdate-min(start_time)) -
                trunc(sysdate-min(start_time)))), 60), '09')) latency
FROM    deftrandest d, deftran t
WHERE   d.deferred_tran_id    = t.deferred_tran_id
AND     d.delivery_order      = t.delivery_order
GROUP BY d.dblink
/
```

Sample output follows:

```
Propagation Latency Instance: PMFG.  Time: 22-Nov-98 10:06:09

                                                      Total    Maximum
                        Least Recently     Most Recently   Txns    Latency
Destination         Queued Transaction  Queued Transaction  Qud dd:hh:mi:ss
---------------     ------------------- ------------------- ---- -----------
PMFG.EXCITE.COM  22-Nov-1998 10:06:05 22-Nov-1998 10:06:09   20 00:00:00:04
PSLS.EXCITE.COM  22-Nov-1998 10:04:52 22-Nov-1998 10:06:22   72 00:00:01:33
                                                            ----
sum                                                           92

1 row selected.
```

Monitoring Deferred Transaction Errors

If you allow errors to accumulate at destination sites, it can be very difficult to clear them. In an ideal world, your conflict resolution techniques will detect and resolve errors. However, experience has shown that it is best to expect the unexpected. The utilities in this section will help you to keep tabs on deferred transaction errors so that you can respond in a timely fashion.

The first script, *deferror.sql* (*deferror8.sql* for Oracle8) lists unresolved errors and generates the calls to DBMS_DEFER_SYS.DELETE_ERROR to delete the errors and DBMS_DEFER_SYS.EXECUTE_ERROR to retry the transaction.

Due to differences in the Oracle7 and Oracle8 data dictionaries, the scripts *deferror.sql* (for Oracle7) and *deferror8.sql* (for Oracle8) are slightly different. We show only the Oracle8 version of the script here, though both scripts are on the diskette accompanying this book.

```
-------------------------------------------------------------------------
-- Filename:      deferror8.sql
-- Purpose:       Reports on deferred transactions with errors and generates
--                call to dbms_defer_sys.execute_error to clear them.
-- Author:        Chas. Dye (cdye@excitecorp.com)
-- Date:          28-Jun-1996
--
-- Modification History
-- --------------------
-- 13-Aug-1998 : Chas. : Updated for Oracle8; added commands to delete error.
-- 09-Oct-1998 : Chas. : Added ORDER BY start_time
-------------------------------------------------------------------------

column ORIGIN_TRAN_DB    heading "Origin|Tran|DB"        format a15
column DEFERRED_TRAN_ID  heading "Deferred|Tran|ID"      format a15
column DESTINATION       heading "Destination"           format a15
column ERROR_TIME        heading "Error Time"            format a22
column ERROR_NUMBER      heading "Error#"                format 999999
column FIX               heading "Run This to Clear"     format a80
column DITCH             heading "Run This to Delete"    format a80


SELECT   deferred_tran_id,
         origin_tran_db,
         destination,
         to_char(start_time, 'DD-Mon-YYYY hh24:mi:ss') error_time,
         error_number
FROM     deferror
ORDER BY start_time
/

SELECT   'EXECUTE dbms_defer_sys.execute_error(' || chr(39) ||
         deferred_tran_id || chr(39) || ', '|| chr(39) ||
         destination || chr(39) || ' )'  fix
FROM     deferror
ORDER BY start_time
/

SELECT   'EXECUTE dbms_defer_sys.delete_error(' || chr(39) ||
         deferred_tran_id || chr(39) || ', '|| chr(39) ||
         destination || chr(39) || ' )'  ditch
FROM     deferror
ORDER BY start_time
/
```

Sample output follows:

```
Deferred    Origin
Tran        Tran
ID          DB              Destination     Error Time             Error#
----------  --------------- --------------- ---------------------- -------
6.19.63683  LIVE.WORLD      PLV2.EXCITE.COM 06-Nov-1998 15:33:50   1403

1 row selected.
```

```
Run This to Clear
------------------------------------------------------------------------
EXECUTE dbms_defer_sys.execute_error('6.19.63683', 'PLV2.EXCITE.COM' )

1 row selected.


Run This to Delete
------------------------------------------------------------------------
EXECUTE dbms_defer_sys.delete_error('6.19.63683', 'PLV2.EXCITE.COM' )

1 row selected.
```

Before you delete or reexecute a transaction that has resulted in an error, you will probably want to know what operation the transaction was attempting against what table. However, that information is not available in the DEFERROR data dictionary view. The script *errorinfo.sql* culls the relevant information from DEFERROR and DEFCALL.

```
------------------------------------------------------------------------
-- Filename:      errorinfo.sql
-- Purpose:       Reports on all errors.
-- Author:        Chas. Dye (cdye@excitecorp.com)
-- Date:          28-Jun-1996
--
-- Modification History
-- -------------------
-- 03-Jun-1998 : Chas. : Removed deferred_tran_db field (not in Oracle8)
-- 09-Oct-1998 : Chas. : Added ORDER BY e.start_time
------------------------------------------------------------------------

col callno              heading "Call|No"            format 9999
col deferred_tran_id    heading "Deferred|Tran|ID"   format a12
col schemaname          heading "Schema|Name"        format a8
col packagename         heading "Package|Name"       format a25
col procname            heading "Procedure|Name"     format a10
col argcount            heading "Arg|Count"          format 999
col origin_tran_db      heading "Origin"             format a17

SELECT  c.callno,
        c.deferred_tran_id,
        c.packagename,
        c.procname,
        c.argcount,
        e.origin_tran_db
FROM    defcall c, deferror e
WHERE   c.deferred_tran_id = e.deferred_tran_id
AND     c.callno = e.callno
ORDER BY e.start_time
/
```

Sample output follows:

```
          Deferred
     Call Tran          Package                  Procedure  Arg
       No ID            Name                     Name       Count Origin
     ----- ------------ -------------------- ---------- ----- ----------------
         0 4.38.5528    COMM$RP                  REP_INSERT     14 PTHA.EXCITE.COM
         0 7.97.5526    COMMPROPSWELCOME$RP      REP_UPDATE     33 PTHA.EXCITE.COM
        12 6.68.7736    CONTACT$RP               REP_DELETE     22 PTHA.EXCITE.COM
```

Finally, if you want to find out exactly what parameters have been used in a given call, you can use the script *defcallinfo.sql* to find out:

```
-------------------------------------------------------------------------
-- Filename:    defcallinfo.sql
-- Purpose:     Lists information about deferred calls.
-- Author:      Chas. Dye (cdye@excitecorp.com)
-- Date:        10-Jul-1998
-------------------------------------------------------------------------

set serveroutput on size 100000
set verify off
undef callno
undef argcnt
undef tran_db
undef tran_id

DECLARE
        vTypes  dbms_defer_query.type_ary;
        vVals   dbms_defer_query.val_ary;
        indx    NUMBER;
BEGIN
        dbms_defer_query.get_call_args(
                callno          => '&&callno',
                startarg        => 1,
                argcnt          => &&argcnt,
                argsize         => 128,
                tran_db         => '&&tran_db',
                tran_id         => '&&tran_id',
                date_fmt        => 'DD-Mon-YYYY HH24:MI:SS',
                types           => vTypes,
                vals            => vVals );

        FOR indx IN 1..&&argcnt LOOP
            dbms_output.put_line('Arg '|| indx || ' Value '|| vVals(indx));
        END LOOP;
END;
/
```

Sample output follows:

```
SQL> @defcallinfo
Enter value for callno: 0
Enter value for argcnt: 14
```

```
Enter value for tran_db: PTHA.EXCITE.COM
Enter value for tran_id: 4.38.5528
Arg 1 Value 42397
Arg 2 Value 16-Oct-1998 13:00:06
Arg 3 Value 79EA878A35EB4002
Arg 4 Value Cadillac Voodoo Choir
Arg 5 Value 0
Arg 6 Value 16-Oct-1998 13:00:06
Arg 7 Value PTHA.EXCITE.COM
Arg 8 Value NULL
Arg 9 Value NULL
Arg 10 Value NULL
Arg 11 Value NULL
Arg 12 Value 0
Arg 13 Value PTHA.EXCITE.COM
Arg 14 Value N
```

The arguments here refer to the old and new column values that Oracle sends to the destination site when it propagates the transaction.

Automatic Notification Mechanism

I have developed a tool to send email to appropriate people and pagers when it detects errors in the DEFERROR view. The tool uses a PL/SQL package that checks the view at destination databases and the DBMS_PIPE utility to send the email request. Please refer to Appendix B for the installation instructions; the tool is provided on the diskette.

Monitoring Snapshot Logs

If you have created snapshot logs on master tables, you should check the size of the snapshot logs periodically to ensure that they are not growing too large. If you notice that a snapshot log has many entries (i.e., thousands), it may be because either not all snapshots that are mastered to the master table are firing or because their refresh interval is too long.

The script *mlogs.sql* generates the SQL statements to select the record count for all snapshot logs in the database:

```
----------------------------------------------------------------------
-- Filename:    mlogs.sql
-- Purpose:     Generates SELECT statements to find the count of entries in
--              all snapshot logs.
-- Author:      Chas. Dye (cdye@excitecorp.com)
-- Date:        27-May-1998
----------------------------------------------------------------------
```

```
SELECT
        'SELECT count(*) FROM '||lower(owner)||'.'||lower(table_name)||';'
FROM    dba_tables
WHERE   table_name like 'MLOG$_%'
AND     owner not like 'SYS%'
ORDER BY owner, table_name
/
```

Monitoring: Summary

I have found the scripts described in the preceding section to be invaluable in helping to maintain a replicated environment. If you are responsible for more than two or three replicated applications, I strongly encourage you to automate as much of the monitoring as possible. As mentioned, most problems are easy to resolve if you spot them early but become exponentially more difficult to correct if they are allowed to persist unchecked.

Advanced Replication Limitations

Finally, note that there are some restrictions on what you can and cannot do in a replicated environment:

- There is no support for cascading deletes. As an alternative, you may consider writing a trigger on the master table to delete child records.

- Sequences do not replicate. If you use sequences to populate key fields, be sure to designate a range of sequence values in each master database that is large enough to avoid key collisions for the life of the application.

- There is no support for local customization of replicated tables. In other words, replicated tables must have an identical shape in each master database.

- The datatypes LONG, LONG RAW, and HHCODE do not replicate. You may replicate tables containing columns of these datatypes, but DML to these columns will not propagate to other master sites. I recommend using the CLOB and LOB datatypes available in Oracle8.

13

Updateable Snapshots

Updateable snapshots offer a means of deploying updateable copies of data at multiple sites. Unlike multi-master replication, which maintains copies of all records in a table at multiple sites, updateable snapshots may be partitioned horizontally. Another key difference between updateable snapshots and multi-master table replication is that updateable snapshot sites need not be in constant communication with the master site. Common usages of updateable snapshots include sales lead data on a salesperson's laptop computer or grocery register receipt data. In both cases, the master data would reside at a headquarters site, and the updateable snapshot might push data back to the headquarters site at the end of the business day.

About Updateable Snapshots

As described in Chapter 11, *Basic Replication*, updateable snapshots function by placing triggers on the master and snapshot tables. The trigger on the master table (TLOG$_*table_name*) populates the snapshot log table (MLOG$_*table_name*) at the master site. Similarly, the trigger on the snapshot base table (USTRG$_*master_ table_name*) populates the snapshot log table (USLOG$_*table_name*) at the snapshot site.

Like their read-only counterparts, updateable snapshots must be refreshed in order to reflect changes that have occurred to the master table. In addition, updateable snapshots must propagate changes from the snapshot site back to the master table. This propagation can happen either at the same time as the snapshot refresh or at a different scheduled interval. My recommendation is to propagate changes from the snapshot site to the master site during the same "conversation" as the snapshot refresh. This recommendation is particularly relevant if the snapshot site is not in constant contact with the master site.

Restrictions

As with read-only snapshots, Oracle imposes certain restrictions on updateable snapshots:

- Updateable snapshots must be simple snapshots. That is, they must be snapshots against a single table without DISTINCT, GROUP BY, or CONNECT BY operators or any subqueries.

- Columns of type LONG and LONG RAW cannot be used.

- Updateable snapshots must include all columns of the master table. Therefore, vertical partitioning is not possible.

- In Oracle7, updateable snapshots must have the same name as the master table.

Creating Updateable Snapshots

Updateable snapshots require components at both the master site and the snapshot site. To illustrate the procedure, I'll trace the steps required to create an updateable snapshot on the table SPROCKET.DAILY_SALES defined as follows:

```
SQL> desc daily_sales
 Name                Null?    Type
 ---------------- -------- ----
 SALES_ID            NOT NULL NUMBER(9)
 DISTRIBUTOR_ID      NOT NULL NUMBER(6)
 PRODUCT_ID          NOT NULL NUMBER(9)
 UNITS               NOT NULL NUMBER(9,2)
 REGION              NOT NULL VARCHAR2(3)
 AUDIT_DATE          NOT NULL DATE
 AUDIT_USER          NOT NULL VARCHAR2(30)
 GLOBAL_NAME         NOT NULL VARCHAR2(20)
```

Each retail outlet of the fictitious Bigwheel Bicycle company updates a local snapshot of this table with each customer purchase. The outlet stores send their data back to the headquarters database each evening. For the purposes of our example, suppose that the headquarters database is named PHQS.BIGWHEEL.COM and that the retail store's database is named PSFO.BIGWHEEL.COM.

Preliminary Steps

Before creating updateable snapshots, the master and snapshot databases must be configured for replication as described in Chapter 12, *Multi-Master Replication*. In addition to running the *catproc.sql* and *catrep.sql* scripts at both sites, you must ensure the following:

- Replication administrator accounts exist with proper privileges at the master and all snapshot sites. (Typically, the replication administrator account is REPADMIN.)

- Database links must be in place. The links from the snapshot site to the master site must connect to an account that either is the owner of the master table or has replication administrator privileges. In addition, the account at the master site must have EXECUTE privileges on the package SYS.DBMSOBJGWRAPPER.

- The table to be replicated exists at the master site and has a primary key defined.

- The account that creates the updateable snapshot must have the privileges CREATE SNAPSHOT, CREATE TABLE, CREATE TRIGGER, and CREATE VIEW.

- If the snapshot is to be created in a different schema (i.e., owned by a different Oracle account from the one issuing the CREATE SNAPSHOT statement), then the account must have the CREATE ANY SNAPSHOT privilege.

Preparing the Master Table

An important difference between read-only snapshots and updateable snapshots is that the master table for the latter must be defined as a replicated object. The master table also must have a snapshot log. Follow these steps:

1. Make the table a replicated object; run the following from the replication administrator account:

```
EXECUTE dbms_repcat.create_master_repgroup( -
gname=>'RG_SPROCKET', -
group_comment=>'Created by '||user||' on '||sysdate);

EXECUTE dbms_repcat.create_master_repobject( -
sname                 => 'SPROCKET', -
oname                 => 'DAILY_SALES', -
type                  => 'TABLE', -
use_existing_object   => TRUE, -
comment               => 'Added by '||lower(user)||' on '||sysdate, -
copy_rows             => FALSE, -
gname                 => 'RG_SPROCKET');

EXECUTE dbms_repcat.generate_replication_support( -
sname       => 'SPROCKET', -
oname       => 'DAILY_SALES', -
type        => 'TABLE', -
distributed => TRUE);

EXECUTE dbms_repcat.resume_master_activity('RG_SPROCKET');
```

2. Create a snapshot log on the master table; run the following from the account that owns the master table:

```
CREATE SNAPSHOT LOG ON daily_sales
PCTFREE 5 PCTUSED 90
TABLESPACE sprocket_data STORAGE (INITIAL 1M NEXT 1M PCTINCREASE 0)
WITH PRIMARY KEY        Oracle8 only
/
```

Prior to Oracle8, Oracle recorded a row's ROWID in the snapshot log to identify it as having been changed. Since ROWIDs can change if a table is moved, or exported and imported, this meant that tables with snapshot logs could not be rebuilt without rebuilding the snapshot log and therefore requiring a complete refresh of all snapshots. Oracle8, on the other hand, allows you to identify changed records in the snapshot log by their primary key, affording you the flexibility of rebuilding a master table without being forced to perform a complete refresh of all of its snapshots.

Preparing the Snapshot Site

At the snapshot site, we must first create the actual snapshot, either with the CREATE SNAPSHOT statement or by supplying the DDL in the call to DBMS_REPCAT.CREATE_SNAPSHOT_REPOBJECT.

Also, note that in the CREATE SNAPSHOT statement, we do not specify a NEXT time for the refreshes. We omit this component because we will put the updateable snapshot into a refresh group which controls the refresh schedule. By default, Oracle creates a refresh group with the same name as the snapshot itself when you issue a CREATE SNAPSHOT statement.

Finally, notice that the defining query of the CREATE SNAPSHOT statement uses "SELECT *" instead of specifying field names. Updateable snapshots must contain every field in the table, and the SELECT * syntax is the only method Oracle supports.

Follow these steps:

1. Create the snapshot using the FOR UPDATE clause in the CREATE SNAPSHOT statement. Create the snapshot when logged in to the schema owner account, preferably with the same account name as the owner of the master table.

   Oracle8 syntax:

   ```
   CREATE SNAPSHOT daily_sales
   TABLESPACE sprocket_data
       STORAGE (INITIAL 1M NEXT 1M PCTINCREASE 0)
   USING INDEX TABLESPACE sprocket_indx
       STORAGE (INITIAL 128K NEXT 128K PCTINCREASE 0)
   REFRESH FAST
   START WITH sysdate
   WITH PRIMARY KEY
   FOR UPDATE
   AS
       SELECT  *
   ```

```
    FROM      product_prices@PHQS.BIGWHEEL.COM
    WHERE     region = 'SFO';
```

Oracle7 syntax:

```
CREATE SNAPSHOT daily_sales
TABLESPACE sprocket_data
    STORAGE (INITIAL 1M NEXT 1M PCTINCREASE 0)
REFRESH FAST
START WITH sysdate
FOR UPDATE
AS
    SELECT  *
    FROM      product_prices@PHQS.BIGWHEEL.COM;
```

2. Create a snapshot replication group. Run these commands under the replication administrator account:

```
EXECUTE dbms_repcat.create_snapshot_repgroup( -
    gname            => 'RG_SPROCKET', -
    master           => 'PHQS.BIGWHEEL.COM', -
    comment          => 'Created on '||sysdate||' by '||user, -
    propagation_mode=> 'ASYNCHRONOUS');
```

The name of the snapshot replication group must be the same as the name of the master replication group to which the master table belongs.

3. Add the snapshot to the snapshot group from the replication administrator account:

```
EXECUTE dbms_repcat.create_snapshot_repobject( -
    sname            => 'SPROCKET', -
    oname            => 'DAILY_SALES', -
    type             => 'SNAPSHOT', -
    comment          => 'Created on '||sysdate||' by '||user, -
    gen_objs_owner => 'REPADMIN');
```

4. Create a snapshot refresh group, and add the snapshot to the group (optional, but recommended):

```
EXECUTE dbms_refresh.make( -
    name                => 'RG_SPROCKET', -
    list                =>'SPROCKET.DAILY_SALES', -
    next_date           => SYSDATE, -
    interval            => 'TRUNC(SYSDATE+1)+23/24', -
    push_deferred_rpc   => TRUE, -
    purge_option        => 1, -          Oracle8 only
    parallelism         => 4, -          Oracle8 only
    lax                 => TRUE);

EXECUTE dbms_refresh.add( -
    name    => 'RG_SPROCKET', -
    list    => 'SPROCKET.DAILY_SALES', -
    lax     => TRUE );
```

At this point, we have created an updateable snapshot on SPROCKET.DAILY_SALES, which refreshes once a day at 11:00 P.M.

User-Defined Triggers on Updateable Snapshots

You may have noticed the fields audit_date, audit_user, and global_name in the table SPROCKET.DAILY_SALES. These fields are intended to track the time that records are inserted or deleted, who performed the operation, and in which database. You can use triggers to populate these fields, but you must make sure that they fire for local DML only; they must not fire because of the DML associated with a snapshot refresh. Use the Oracle built-in package function DBMS_SNAP-SHOT.I_AM_A_REFRESH to determine whether the trigger should fire. The following code creates the audit trigger on the SPROCKET.DAILY_SALES updateable snapshot:

```
CREATE OR REPLACE TRIGGER t_iu_snap$_daily_sales
BEFORE INSERT OR UPDATE
ON snap$_daily_sales
FOR EACH ROW

BEGIN
    IF (dbms_snapshot.i_am_a_refresh != TRUE)
    THEN
        :new.audit_date      := SYSDATE;
        :new.audit_user      := USER;
        :new.global_name     := DBMS_REPUTIL.GLOBAL_NAME;
    END IF;
END;
/
```

Notice that the trigger is defined on the snapshot base table SNAP$_DAILY_SALES.

Communication Flow

Your replicated environment is probably not as simple as a master site and a snapshot site. Oracle allows you to mix and match endless permutations of masters and snapshots. A site can even be a snapshot site for one set of tables and a master site for another. Somehow, all of the data gets to its destination.

The most complex configuration for updateable snapshots is one in which two or more multi-master sites have their own snapshot sites, as shown in Figure 13-1.

Suppose that a user at the snapshot site PSLS.BIGWHEEL.COM makes an update to the SALES_LEADS table. How does that change propagate to the updateable snapshot of the same name at site PSFO.BIGWHEEL.COM? The process is as follows:

1. The user updates the snapshot SALES_LEADS.

2. The trigger USTRG$_SALES_LEADS creates an entry in the snapshot log USLOG$_SALES_LEADS. (In Oracle8, this trigger is internalized and therefore not visible in the data dictionary.)

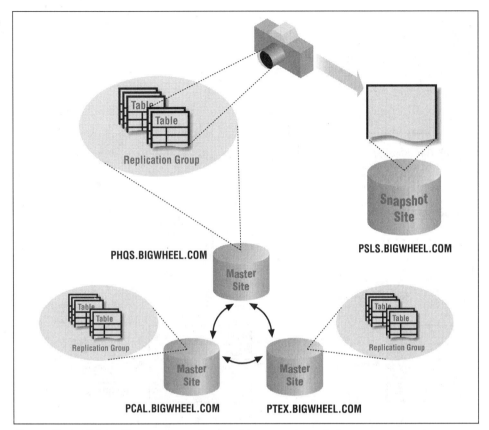

Figure 13-1. Updateable snapshots where multi-masters have their own snapshot sites

3. The snapshot refresh updates master table in PHQS.BIGWHEEL.COM.

4. The replication trigger SALES_LEADS$RT in PHQS.BIGWHEEL.COM queues the update for propagation to its companion master, PCAL.BIGWHEEL.COM. (In Oracle8, this trigger is internalized and therefore not visible in the data dictionary.)

5. When the update is applied at PCAL.BIGWHEEL.COM, the trigger TLOG$_SALES_LEADS creates an entry in the snapshot log MLOG$_SALES_LEADS. (In Oracle8, this trigger is internalized and therefore not visible in the data dictionary.)

6. The refresh from PSFO.BIGWHEEL.COM to PCAL.BIGWHEEL.COM reads the snapshot log and applies the change.

Figure 13-2 depicts this chain of events.

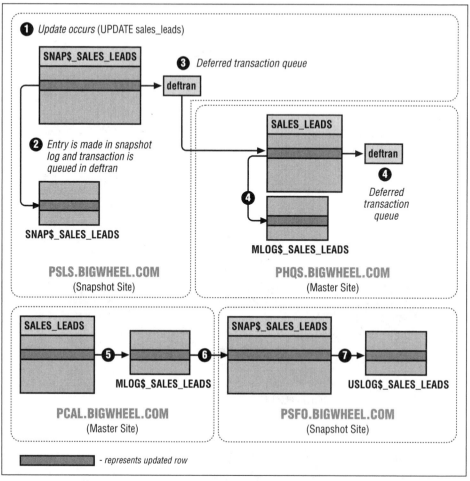

Figure 13-2. Propagating a snapshot to another site

Controlling Propagation and Refreshes

As with multi-master table replication, updateable snapshots can propagate their changes back to the master table either synchronously or asynchronously. Unlike multi-master table replication, you can control asynchronous propagation so that DML is sent back to the master table either at the time of snapshot refreshes or at some other scheduled interval. You should evaluate your data flow requirements to determine what best suits your needs. This section presents recommendations for some common scenarios.

Although updateable snapshots can propagate changes back to the master table synchronously, snapshot refreshes (propagation of changes from the master table to the snapshot) are always asynchronous; the snapshot site always polls the master site for refreshes.

Real-Time (Synchronous) Propagation

You can specify synchronous propagation either by specifying propagation_mode => 'SYNCHRONOUS' in the call to DBMS_REPCAT.CREATE_SNAPSHOT_REP-GROUP or by using DBMS_REPCAT.ALTER_SNAPSHOT_PROPAGATION to change the propagation mode if the snapshot replication group already exists.

If you elect to use synchronous propagation, Oracle follows these steps to forward updateable snapshot DML back to the master site:

1. Oracle locks the record in the snapshot base table and performs the update.

2. Oracle fires the USTRG$_*snapshot_name* trigger which invokes the *table_ name*$RP package at the master site.

3. The *table_name*$RP package at the master site locks and updates the record in the master table.

4. If an unresolvable conflict arises at the master site, the *table_name*$RP package raises an exception.

5. Oracle commits the transaction (or rolls back in the event of an error) using the two-phase commit protocol. All locks are then released.

You should not use synchronous propagation unless you are certain that the network connection between the two databases will not go down, or you can tolerate interruptions in service if the connection is unavailable.

Once-a-Day Propagation

Applications that accumulate data through the course of the day and feed it to the master database are candidates for a once-per-day propagation scenario. Typically, the only time when the snapshot and master database are in contact is during this data upload period. Therefore, the snapshot site should not only upload the local changes but also refresh snapshots with new data from the master. We can force Oracle to push queued DML from the updateable snapshot in the course of performing refreshes by setting the parameter push_deferred_rpc to TRUE in the call to DBMS_REFRESH.MAKE:

```
EXECUTE dbms_refresh.make( -
     name                 => 'RG_SPROCKET', -
     list                 => 'SPROCKET.DAILY_SALES', -
     next_date            => TRUNC(SYSDATE+1) + 1/24, -
     interval             => 'TRUNC(SYSDATE+1)+23/24', -
     push_deferred_rpc    => TRUE, -
     lax                  => TRUE);
```

This call adds the snapshot to the RG_SPROCKET snapshot refresh group and schedules it for its initial refresh tomorrow at 1:00 A.M.:

```
     next_date            => TRUNC(SYSDATE+1) + 1/24, -
```

The call also schedules a job queue entry which performs all future refreshes for 11:00 P.M. nightly (by a call to DBMS_REFRESH.REFRESH):

```
     interval             => 'TRUNC(SYSDATE+1)+23/24', -
```

Propagation on Demand

Another scenario calling for an updateable snapshot involves the traveling salesperson who enters sales leads and customer information into a laptop computer and who dials in to the headquarters site at unpredictable times. This person needs to upload the information from the laptop to the headquarters site and refresh snapshots on demand. It does not really make sense to schedule a job on the laptop machine because there is no guarantee that the master database will be reachable when the job runs.

Instead, we create the snapshot refresh group without specifying a refresh interval. We do, however, specify next_date to be SYSDATE because we want to populate the snapshots when the refresh group is originally created:

```
EXECUTE dbms_refresh.make( -
     name                 => 'RG_SPROCKET', -
     list                 => 'SPROCKET.DAILY_SALES', -
     next_date            => SYSDATE, -
     push_deferred_rpc    => TRUE, -
     lax                  => TRUE);
```

To perform the data upload and snapshot refresh on demand, the salesperson simply calls DBMS_REFRESH.REFRESH:

```
EXECUTE dbms_refresh.refresh('RG_SPROCKET')
```

Of course, you may wish to create a script that allows the salesperson to perform the refresh by clicking on an icon rather than having to use SQL*Plus!

> ## DBMS_REFRESH.REFRESH Versus DBMS_SNAPSHOT.REFRESH
>
> You may have noticed that Oracle provides two different REFRESH procedures, one in DBMS_REFRESH and the other in DBMS_SNAPSHOT. Why? The DBMS_REFRESH version of REFRESH operates on all snapshots in a single refresh group, and this methodology is the direction in which the replication technology is moving. The DBMS_SNAPSHOT version of REFRESH allows you do refresh snapshots that are not members of a refresh group or a set of snapshots that are members of different refresh groups. The DBMS_SNAPSHOT version also allows you to specify various parameters, such as rollback_segs, whereas snapshot refresh groups have these settings defined in the call to DBMS_REFRESH.MAKE.
>
> Snapshot refresh groups are generally much easier to maintain than multiple ungrouped snapshots. Our recommendation is to group all snapshots so you will be able to use DBMS_REFRESH.REFRESH.

Maintenance

In addition to the administrative tasks associated with read-only snapshots, updateable snapshots require the database administrator to perform a number of maintenance tasks.

Altering the Master Table

If the structure of the updateable snapshot's master table changes, the updateable snapshot must reflect the modification. Since updateable snapshots are registered as replicated objects, a change to a master table will generate appropriate DDL calls for all snapshot sites. However, unlike DDL changes in a multi-master replicated environment that Oracle propagates when you call DBMS_REPCAT.GENERATE_REPLICATION_SUPPORT, the snapshot site must request the DDL changes from the master. The built-in package procedure DBMS_REPCAT.REFRESH_SNAPSHOT_REPGROUP makes this request.

Suppose you wish to make the distributor_id column nullable in the table SPROCKET.DAILY_SALES. You would follow these steps:

1. Alter the table at the master site, connected to the replication administrator account at the master site:

   ```
   EXECUTE dbms_repcat.suspend_master_activity('RG_SPROCKET');
   ```

```
EXECUTE dbms_repcat.alter_master_repobject( -
    sname        => 'SPROCKET', -
    oname        => 'DAILY_SALES', -
    type         => 'TABLE', -
    ddl_text     => 'ALTER TABLE SPROCKET.DAILY_SALES
                    MODIFY (DISTRIBUTOR_ID NULL)');

EXECUTE dbms_repcat.generate_replication_support( -
    sname        => 'SPROCKET', -
    oname        => 'DAILY_SALES', -
    type         => 'TABLE');

EXECUTE dbms_repcat.resume_master_activity('RG_SPROCKET');
```

2. At the snapshot site, request the changes. Connect to the replication administrator account at the snapshot site:

```
EXECUTE dbms_repcat.refresh_snapshot_repgroup( -
    gname                => 'RG_SPROCKET'
    refresh_snapshots    => TRUE);
```

Refer to Appendix A, *Built-in Packages for Distributed Systems*, for a complete
description of the parameters in the DBMS_REPCAT.REFRESH_SNAPSHOT_REP-
GROUP procedure.

    If you change the *shape* of a master table by adding columns or
changing the size of columns, you are required to drop and re-create
the snapshot.

Dropping a Replicated Snapshot Object

You may wish to drop a snapshot, either because it is no longer required at the
snapshot site or because the master table no longer exists. Here we describe how
to approach both scenarios.

Master table still exists

Use DBMS_REPCAT.DROP_SNAPSHOT_REPOBJECT to drop a specific snapshot
from a snapshot refresh group or DBMS_REPCAT.DROP_SNAPSHOT_REPGROUP
to drop the entire group. The first example drops an updateable snapshot from a
snapshot refresh group:

```
EXECUTE dbms_repcat.drop_snapshot_repobject( -
    sname            => 'RG_SPROCKET', -
    oname            => 'DAILY_SALES', -
    type             => 'SNAPSHOT'
    drop_objects     => TRUE);
```

The next example drops the snapshot replication group:

```
EXCUTE dbms_repcat.drop_snapshot_repgroup( -
    gname          => 'RG_SPROCKET', -
    drop_contents  => TRUE)'
```

Refer to Appendix A for a complete description of the parameters to these procedures.

Remastering a snapshot

If a snapshot's master table is part of a multi-master replicated environment, you can "remaster" your snapshot to any of the other master sites if the original master becomes unavailable or otherwise irrelevant. The built-in package procedure to use is DBMS_REPCAT.SWITCH_SNAPSHOT_MASTER:

```
EXECUTE dbms_repcat.switch_snapshot_master(
    gname  => 'RG_SPROCKET' -
    master => 'PHKG.BIGWHEEL.COM);
```

Note the following when using this procedure:

- You must call this procedure from the snapshot site.

- At the time of the switch, Oracle will perform a complete refresh of the snapshots in the refresh group using master tables at the new master table.

- You are encouraged to build snapshot logs on the master tables at the new site if they do not already exist.

- If the original master site is not available when SWITCH_SNAPSHOT_MASTER is called, the original master site does not receive notification that it is no longer the master. Therefore, you should purge or drop the master log, if one exists; if you are using Oracle8, you should call DBMS_REPCAT.UNREGISTER_ SNAPSHOT_REPGROUP at the original master site.

14

Procedural Replication

In this chapter:
- *When to Use Procedural Replication*
- *How Procedural Replication Works*
- *Creating a Replicated Package Procedure*
- *Restrictions on Procedural Replication*
- *An Example*

The row-level, or multi-master, component of Oracle's advanced replication facilities were never intended to support transactions that modify numerous records. Instead, using procedural replication you can write PL/SQL procedures around such operations and replicate calls to the procedures instead of to the row-level transactions.

When to Use Procedural Replication

There is no hard limit on how many records a single transaction can modify in a table that is undergoing row-level replication, but as a general rule, modifying more than about 100 records in a single transaction is not advisable, at least not on a regular basis. Bear in mind that even though you may use a single transaction to modify multiple records, Oracle queues an RPC for each modified record. Before you know it, the deferred transaction queue may have thousands of entries.

Typical operations that are ideal candidates for procedural replication include the following:

Batch updates
> For example, a transaction that adjusts the price of all items in a catalog

Data purging
> For example, deleting all records that are older than a certain date

Data archiving
> For example, moving sales records from the previous quarter into an archive table

Specialty operations
> For example, creating or dropping a user in multiple databases (see the example in this chapter)

This list is by no means exhaustive. Row-level replication is best suited for transactions that modify a single record. Consider procedural replication for everything else.

How Procedural Replication Works

Procedural replication executes your procedure call in the local database and queues a call to the procedure in all other master databases in the replication group, using whatever parameters you pass. This mechanism requires a "wrapper" procedure that calls the procedure that locally does the queueing. It also requires that the procedure be registered as a replicated object in all databases in the replication group.

As an example, suppose that we have a package procedure USER_ADMIN. CREATE_USER and a replicated wrapper package DEFER_USER_ADMIN. A call to the wrapper package results in the following chain of events:

1. Call to DEFER_USER_ADMIN.CREATE_USER('SCOTT', 'TIGER').

2. DEFER_USER_ADMIN calls USER_ADMIN.CREATE_USER('SCOTT', 'TIGER').

3. Procedure USER_ADMIN.CREATE_USER executes locally.

4. DEFER_USER_ADMIN builds a remote call to USER_ADMIN.CREATE_USER in other master databases in the same replication group. The remote call is placed in the deferred transaction queue.

5. Procedure USER_ADMIN.CREATE_USER executes at remote databases.

Figure 14-1 depicts these events.

Creating a Replicated Package Procedure

Creating a replicated package procedure is easy. Simply register an existing package as a replicated object with DBMS_REPCAT.CREATE_MASTER_REPOBJECT and then generate replication support for it. I recommend that you pre-create your packages in all master databases before registering them for replication.

If your replicated procedure modifies a table that is undergoing row-level replication, you should disable replication within the procedure by calling DBMS_REPUTIL.REPLICATION_OFF before any SQL statements that perform DML on the table. Be sure to call DBMS_REPUTIL.REPLICATION_ON after these SQL statements.

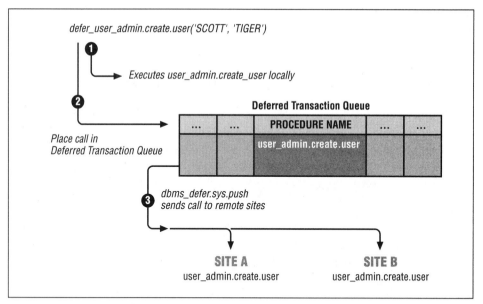

Figure 14-1. How procedural replication works

To enable replicated calls to the package USERADMIN, we would make these DBMS_REPCAT calls:

```
EXECUTE dbms_repcat.create_master_repobject( -
sname              => 'SYSTEM', -
oname              => 'USER_ADMIN', -
type               => 'PACKAGE', -
use_existing_object => TRUE, -
retry              => FALSE, -
gname              => 'RG_SPROCKET');

EXECUTE dbms_repcat.create_master_repobject( -
sname              => 'SYSTEM', -
oname              => 'USER_ADMIN', -
type               => 'PACKAGE BODY', -
use_existing_object => TRUE, -
retry              => FALSE, -
gname              => 'RG_SPROCKET');

EXECUTE dbms_repcat.generate_replication_support( -
name               => 'SYSTEM', -
oname              => 'USER_ADMIN', -
type               => 'PACKAGE', -
package_prefix     => 'DEFER_');

EXECUTE dbms_repcat.generate_replication_support( -
sname              => 'SYSTEM', -
oname              => 'USER_ADMIN', -
type               => 'PACKAGE BODY', -
package_prefix     => 'DEFER_');
```

Note that we must call the CREATE_MASTER_REPOBJECT and GENERATE_REPLICATION_SUPPORT packages for the package as well as the package body.

The net result of these calls is the creation of a wrapper package called DEFER_USER_ADMIN. This package is the one to invoke if you want calls to USER_ADMIN to be replicated; it builds the RPCs required to replicate the call. You can also use the wrapper to execute USER_ADMIN at remote sites only or at the local site only, because it adds the parameters CALL_LOCAL and CALL_REMOTE to each procedure within the original package.

The specification for the generated package DEFER_USER_ADMIN is as follows:

```
package DEFER_USER_ADMIN as
   I_am_a_snapshot CHAR;
   procedure CHANGEPASS(
      IN_USERNAME IN varchar2,
      IN_PASSWORD IN varchar2,
      call_local IN char := 'N',
      call_remote IN char := 'Y');
   procedure CREATEUSER(
      IN_USERNAME IN varchar2,
      IN_PASSWORD IN varchar2,
      call_local IN char := 'N',
      call_remote IN char := 'Y');
   procedure DROPUSER(
      IN_USERNAME IN varchar2,
      call_local IN char := 'N',
      call_remote IN char := 'Y');
   procedure GRANTROLE(
      IN_USERNAME IN varchar2,
      IN_ROLE IN varchar2,
      IN_DEFAULTYN IN varchar2,
      call_local IN char := 'N',
      call_remote IN char := 'Y');
   procedure REVOKEROLE(
      IN_USERNAME IN varchar2,
      IN_ROLE IN varchar2,
      call_local IN char := 'N',
      call_remote IN char := 'Y');
end DEFER_USER_ADMIN;
```

 In Oracle8 the wrapper package is owned by the replication propagator account (typically PROPREP). If you unregister the propagator account, all wrapper procedures will be dropped.

Each of the procedures in DEFER_USER_ADMIN builds a deferred call to the corresponding call in USER_ADMIN if the call_remote parameter is set to 'Y'. For

example, the procedure DEFER_USER_ADMIN.CREATE_USER builds a deferred
call to USER_ADMIN.CREATE_USER:

```
procedure "CREATE_USER"(
  "IN_USERNAME" IN VARCHAR2,
  "IN_PASSWORD" IN VARCHAR2,
  call_local IN char := 'N',
  call_remote IN char := 'Y') is
begin
  select decode(master, 'N', 'Y', 'N')
    into I_am_a_snapshot
    from all_repcat where gname = 'RG_SPROCKET';
  if call_local = 'Y' then
    "SYSTEM"."USER_ADMIN"."CREATE_USER"(
  "IN_USERNAME",
  "IN_PASSWORD");
  end if;
  if call_remote = 'Y' then
    dbms_defer.call('SYSTEM', 'USER_ADMIN', 'CREATE_USER', 2, 'RG_LIVE');
    dbms_defer.varchar2_arg("IN_USERNAME");
    dbms_defer.varchar2_arg("IN_PASSWORD");
  end if;
end "CREATE_USER";
```

Restrictions on Procedural Replication

Oracle imposes various restrictions on replicated procedures, as follows:

- All replicated procedures must be *package* procedures.

- Replication of functions is not supported.

- All procedure parameters must be IN parameters; OUT and IN OUT parameters are not supported.

- Parameters of type BOOLEAN are not supported.

- Oracle supplies no conflict resolution techniques for procedural replication.

- Replicated procedures should not manipulate remote data.

- All replication groups must be in NORMAL mode when making a replicated
  procedure call (i.e., no replication groups can be quiesced).

An Example

Since data dictionary tables cannot be replicated, the DBA must perform various
administrative tasks in multiple sites. One particular task that I have found to be a
needless nuisance is user administration, so I have created the package USERAD-
MIN to replicate calls to create and drop users and to grant and revoke roles. The
scripts to create the package are:

cr_seq_audit_admin.sql

Creates the sequence SEQ_AUDIT_ADMIN which is used to populate the ID field in the table AUDIT_ADMIN.

cr_audit_admin.sql

Creates the table AUDIT_ADMIN, which logs usage of the USERADMIN package.

pl_useradmin.sql

Calls the scripts *cr_seq_audit_admin.sql* and *cr_audit_admin.sql* and creates the package USERADMIN. This script should be run by user SYSTEM.

These scripts are included here, as well as on the accompanying diskette.

cr_seq_audit_admin.sql

```
---------------------------------------------------------------------------
-- Filename:     cr_seq_audit_admin.sql
-- Purpose:      Creates SEQ_AUDIT_ADMIN used by USER_ADMIN procedure
-- Author:       Chas. Dye (cdye@excitecorp.com)
-- Date:         5-Mar-1998
---------------------------------------------------------------------------

set echo on
set termout on
spool seq_audit_admin.log

DROP PUBLIC SYNONYM seq_audit_admin
/
DROP SEQUENCE seq_audit_admin
/
CREATE SEQUENCE seq_audit_admin
START WITH 1
/
CREATE PUBLIC SYNONYM seq_audit_admin FOR seq_audit_admin
/

spool off
```

cr_audit_admin.sql

```
---------------------------------------------------------------------------
-- Filename:     cr_audit_admin.sql
-- Purpose:      Creates table to be used by USER_ADMIN procedure.
-- Author:       Chas. Dye (cdye@excitecorp.com)
-- Date:         5-Mar-1998
---------------------------------------------------------------------------

set echo on
set termout on
spool audit_admin.log

DROP PUBLIC SYNONYM audit_admin
```

```
/
DROP TABLE audit_admin CASCADE CONSTRAINTS
/
CREATE TABLE audit_admin (
audit_id     NUMBER(10)NOT NULL,
procname     VARCHAR2(12),
info         VARCHAR2(40),
errornum     NUMBER(6),
audit_user   VARCHAR2(30),
audit_date   DATE
)
/

CREATE PUBLIC SYNONYM audit_admin FOR audit_admin
/

ALTER TABLE audit_admin ADD (
CONSTRAINT pk_audit_admin
PRIMARY KEY (audit_id)
)
/

CREATE OR REPLACE TRIGGER t_brr_iu_audit_admin
BEFORE INSERT OR UPDATE
ON audit_admin
FOR EACH ROW

BEGIN
    :new.audit_user := USER;
    :new.audit_date := SYSDATE;
END;
/

spool off
```

pl_useradmin.sql

```
-------------------------------------------------------------------------
-- Filename:    pl_useradmin.sql
-- Purpose:     Utility to perform user administration on multiple databases.
-- Author:      Chas. Dye (cdye@excitecorp.com)
-- Date:        5-Mar-1998
-------------------------------------------------------------------------

set echo on
set termout on

@@cr_seq_audit_admin
@@cr_audit_admin

spool useradmin.log

DROP PUBLIC SYNONYM UserAdmin
/
```

rep_useradmin.sql

```
CREATE OR REPLACE PACKAGE UserAdmin IS
    PROCEDURE CreateUser(IN_Username VARCHAR2,
                IN_Password VARCHAR2 );
    PROCEDURE DropUser(IN_Username VARCHAR2 );
    PROCEDURE ChangePass(IN_Username VARCHAR2,
                IN_Password VARCHAR2 );
    PROCEDURE GrantRole(IN_Username VARCHAR2,
                IN_Role VARCHAR2,
                IN_DefaultYN VARCHAR2 DEFAULT 'N' );
    PROCEDURE RevokeRole(IN_Username VARCHAR2,
                IN_Role VARCHAR2 );
END UserAdmin;
/

CREATE OR REPLACE PACKAGE BODY  UserAdmin IS


----------------------------------------------------------------------------
-- Note:    This package should be owned by SYSTEM because it must be owned
--          by an id that has CREATE SESSION privileges (schema IDs should
--          NOT).
--          Also, SYS must make the following explicit grants to SYSTEM:
--              GRANT ALTER USER TO system
--              GRANT CREATE USER TO system
--              GRANT CREATE SESSION TO system WITH ADMIN OPTION
--              GRANT DROP USER TO system
--              GRANT GRANT ANY ROLE TO system
--              GRANT SELECT ON DBA_ROLE_PRIVS TO system
--              GRANT SELECT ON DBA_SEGMENTS TO system
--          Optional Grants:
--              GRANT SELECT ON dba_role_privs TO access_admin
--              GRANT SELECT ON dba_roles      TO access_admin
----------------------------------------------------------------------------

PROCEDURE AuditUserAdmin   (IN_Proc  VARCHAR2,
                            IN_Info  VARCHAR2    DEFAULT NULL,
                            IN_Error NUMBER      DEFAULT NULL ) IS
BEGIN
    INSERT INTO audit_admin
            (audit_id,
            procname,
            info,
            errornum,
            audit_user,
            audit_date
        )
    VALUES (seq_audit_admin.nextval,
            IN_Proc,
            IN_info,
            IN_Error,
            user,
            sysdate
        );
```

```
        COMMIT;
END AuditUserAdmin;


--------------------------------------------------------------------------
-- PROCEDURE CreateUser creates a user and grants CREATE SESSION to him/her
--------------------------------------------------------------------------
PROCEDURE CreateUser( IN_Username VARCHAR2, IN_Password VARCHAR2 ) IS
hCursor     NUMBER;
vProcName   audit_admin.procname%TYPE    := 'CreateUser';
vInfo       audit_admin.info%TYPE        := NULL;
BadPassword EXCEPTION;
UserExists  EXCEPTION;
NameTooLong EXCEPTION;

BEGIN
    IF UPPER(IN_Username) = UPPER(IN_Password)
    THEN
        RAISE BadPassword;
    END IF;

    IF length(IN_Username) > 8
    THEN
        RAISE NameTooLong;
    END IF;

    hCursor := dbms_sql.open_cursor;
    dbms_sql.parse(hCursor,
            'CREATE USER '      || IN_Username ||
            ' IDENTIFIED BY '   || IN_Password ||
            ' DEFAULT TABLESPACE users TEMPORARY TABLESPACE temp',
            dbms_sql.v7);
    dbms_sql.close_cursor( hCursor);

    hCursor := dbms_sql.open_cursor;
    dbms_sql.parse(    hCursor,
            'GRANT CREATE SESSION TO ' || IN_Username,
            dbms_sql.v7);
    dbms_sql.close_cursor( hCursor);

    vInfo := 'Created ' || IN_Username || ' Password ' || IN_Password;
    AuditUserAdmin( vProcName, vInfo );

EXCEPTION
    WHEN NameTooLong THEN
        vInfo := '!Bad Username: ' || IN_Username;
        AuditUserAdmin( vProcName, vInfo );
        dbms_output.put_line( 'Username must be 8 chars or less.');
        RAISE_APPLICATION_ERROR(-20010, 'CreateUser:Username too long');
    WHEN BadPassword THEN
        vInfo := '!Bad Password for ' || IN_Username;
        AuditUserAdmin( vProcName, vInfo );
        dbms_output.put_line( 'Username and Password must differ.');
        RAISE_APPLICATION_ERROR(-20020, 'CreateUser:Username=Password');
```

```
        WHEN OTHERS THEN
            vInfo := '!Create User ' || IN_Username;
            AuditUserAdmin( vProcName, vInfo , sqlcode);
            dbms_output.put_line('error ' || sqlerrm);
            RAISE_APPLICATION_ERROR(-20030, 'CreateUser:Error ' || sqlerrm);
END CreateUser;


-------------------------------------------------------------------------
-- PROCEDURE DropUser drops a user.
-------------------------------------------------------------------------
PROCEDURE DropUser( IN_Username VARCHAR2 ) IS
hCursor         NUMBER;
vProcName       audit_admin.procname%TYPE    := 'DropUser';
vInfo           audit_admin.info%TYPE        := NULL;
vSegCount       NUMBER;
UserHasObjects  EXCEPTION;
UserIsDBA       EXCEPTION;
BEGIN
    IF upper( IN_Username ) IN ('SYS', 'SYSTEM')
    THEN
        RAISE UserIsDBA;
    END IF;

    SELECT  count(*)
    INTO    vSegCount
    FROM    dba_segments
    WHERE   owner = UPPER( IN_Username );

    IF vSegCount > 0
    THEN
        RAISE UserHasObjects;
    END IF;

    hCursor := dbms_sql.open_cursor;
    dbms_sql.parse( hCursor,
            'DROP USER ' || IN_Username || ' CASCADE',
            dbms_sql.v7);
    dbms_sql.close_cursor( hCursor );

    vInfo := 'Dropped ' || IN_Username;
    AuditUserAdmin( vProcName, vInfo );

EXCEPTION
    WHEN UserIsDBA THEN
        vInfo := '!DROP ' || IN_Username;
        AuditUserAdmin( vProcName, vInfo );
        dbms_output.put_line('Cannot drop SYS or SYSTEM accounts.');
        RAISE_APPLICATION_ERROR(-2110, 'DropUser: User is DBA');
    WHEN UserHasObjects THEN
        vInfo := '!DROP ' || IN_Username;
        AuditUserAdmin( vProcName, vInfo );
        RAISE_APPLICATION_ERROR(-20120, 'DropUser: User owns objects');
    WHEN OTHERS THEN
        vInfo := '!DROP ' || IN_Username;
```

```
            AuditUserAdmin( vProcName, vInfo, sqlcode );
            dbms_output.put_line('error ' || sqlerrm);
            RAISE_APPLICATION_ERROR(-20130, 'DropUser: Error ' || sqlerrm);
END DropUser;


-------------------------------------------------------------------------
-- PROCEDURE ChangePass changes a user's password.
-------------------------------------------------------------------------
PROCEDURE ChangePass(IN_Username VARCHAR2, IN_Password VARCHAR2 ) IS
hCursor         NUMBER;
vProcName       audit_admin.procname%TYPE    := 'ChangePass';
vInfo           audit_admin.info%TYPE        := NULL;
BadPassword     EXCEPTION;
PassTooLong     EXCEPTION;
UserIsDBA       EXCEPTION;
BEGIN
    IF upper( IN_Username ) IN ('SYS', 'SYSTEM')
    THEN
        RAISE UserIsDBA;
    END IF;

    IF UPPER(IN_Username) = UPPER(IN_Password)
    THEN
        RAISE BadPassword;
    END IF;

    IF length(IN_Password) > 30
    THEN
        RAISE PassTooLong;
    END IF;

    hCursor := dbms_sql.open_cursor;
    dbms_sql.parse(hCursor,
            'ALTER USER '          || IN_Username    ||
            ' IDENTIFIED BY '      || IN_Password,
            dbms_sql.v7);
    dbms_sql.close_cursor( hCursor);

    vInfo := 'Changed ' || IN_Username || ' Password ' || IN_Password;
    AuditUserAdmin( vProcName, vInfo );

EXCEPTION
    WHEN UserIsDBA THEN
        vInfo := '!DROP ' || IN_Username;
        AuditUserAdmin( vProcName, vInfo );
        dbms_output.put_line('Cannot change SYS or SYSTEM passwords.');
        RAISE_APPLICATION_ERROR(-20210, 'ChangePass:Cannot change DBA');
    WHEN PassTooLong THEN
        vInfo := '!Bad Username: ' || IN_Username;
        AuditUserAdmin( vProcName, vInfo );
        dbms_output.put_line( 'Password must be 30 chars or less.');
        RAISE_APPLICATION_ERROR(-20220, 'ChangePass:password>30 chars');
    WHEN BadPassword THEN
        vInfo := '!Bad Password for ' || IN_Username;
```

```
            AuditUserAdmin( vProcName, vInfo );
            dbms_output.put_line( 'Username and Password must differ.');
            RAISE_APPLICATION_ERROR(-20230, 'ChangePass:username=password');
        WHEN OTHERS THEN
            vInfo := '!Create User ' || IN_Username;
            AuditUserAdmin( vProcName, vInfo , sqlcode);
            RAISE_APPLICATION_ERROR(-20240, 'ChangePass:Error ' || sqlerrm);
END ChangePass;


-------------------------------------------------------------------------
-- PROCEDURE GrantRole grants roles.
-------------------------------------------------------------------------
PROCEDURE GrantRole(IN_Username VARCHAR2,
            IN_Role VARCHAR2,
        IN_DefaultYN VARCHAR2 DEFAULT 'N') IS
CURSOR cDefRole IS
    SELECT  granted_role
    FROM    dba_role_privs
    WHERE   grantee = UPPER(IN_Username)
    AND     default_role = 'YES';

hCursor          NUMBER;
vProcName        audit_admin.procname%TYPE   := 'GrantRole';
vInfo            audit_admin.info%TYPE        := NULL;
vRoleStr         VARCHAR2(2000)               := NULL;
vDefRoleCount    NUMBER        := 0;
vHasDefRoles     BOOLEAN       := FALSE;
vRoleCheck       NUMBER        := 0;
UserIsDBA        EXCEPTION;
NoPrivRoles      EXCEPTION;
RoleAlready      EXCEPTION;
BEGIN
    vInfo := 'Grant ' || IN_Role || ' to ' || IN_Username;

    IF UPPER(IN_Username) IN ('SYS', 'SYSTEM')
    THEN
        RAISE UserIsDBA;
    END IF;

    IF UPPER(IN_Role) IN (  'DBA', 'CONNECT', 'RESOURCE')
    THEN
        RAISE NoPrivRoles;
    END IF;

    SELECT  count(*)
    INTO    vRoleCheck
    FROM    dba_role_privs
    WHERE   grantee        = UPPER(IN_Username)
    AND     granted_role   = UPPER(IN_Role);

    IF vRoleCheck > 0
    THEN
        RAISE RoleAlready;
    END IF;
```

```
    FOR rDefRole IN cDefRole LOOP
        vRoleStr          := vRoleStr || rDefRole.granted_role || ',';
        vDefRoleCount     := vDefRoleCount + 1;
    END LOOP;

    IF ( vDefRoleCount > 0 ) OR ( IN_DefaultYN = 'Y' )
    THEN
        vHasDefRoles := TRUE;
        IF ( vDefRoleCount > 0 ) AND ( IN_DefaultYN = 'N' )
        THEN
            vRoleStr := substr(vRoleStr, 1, length(vRoleStr) - 1 );
        ELSIF ( vDefRoleCount > 0 ) AND ( IN_DefaultYN = 'Y' )
            THEN
                vRoleStr := vRoleStr || ' ' || IN_Role;
        ELSIF ( vDefRoleCount = 0 ) AND ( IN_DefaultYN = 'Y' )
            THEN
                vRoleStr := IN_Role;
        END IF;
    END IF;
----------------------------
-- First grant the new role --
----------------------------
    hCursor := dbms_sql.open_cursor;
    dbms_sql.parse  (hCursor,
            'GRANT ' || IN_Role || ' TO '|| IN_Username,
            dbms_sql.v7);
    dbms_sql.close_cursor( hCursor);


--------------------------------------
-- Now set user to no default roles --
--------------------------------------
    hCursor := dbms_sql.open_cursor;
    dbms_sql.parse  (hCursor,
            'ALTER USER ' || IN_Username || ' DEFAULT ROLE NONE',
            dbms_sql.v7);
    dbms_sql.close_cursor( hCursor);


--------------------------------
-- Now grant any default roles --
--------------------------------
    IF vHasDefRoles = TRUE
    THEN
        hCursor := dbms_sql.open_cursor;
        dbms_sql.parse(hCursor,
            'ALTER USER ' ||IN_Username||' DEFAULT ROLE '||vRoleStr,
            dbms_sql.v7);
        dbms_sql.close_cursor( hCursor);

    END IF;

    AuditUserAdmin( vProcName, vInfo );

EXCEPTION
    WHEN UserIsDBA THEN
```

```
                vInfo := '!' || vInfo;
                AuditUserAdmin( vProcName, vInfo );
                dbms_output.put_line('Cannot grant to SYS or SYSTEM accounts.');
                RAISE_APPLICATION_ERROR(-2410, 'GrantRole: Cannot grant SYS');
        WHEN RoleAlready THEN
                vInfo := '!' || vInfo;
                AuditUserAdmin( vProcName, vInfo );
                dbms_output.put_line(IN_Username ||' already has ' || IN_Role);
                RAISE_APPLICATION_ERROR(-20420, 'GrantRole:Role already grntd');
        WHEN NoPrivRoles THEN
                vInfo := '!' || vInfo;
                AuditUserAdmin( vProcName, vInfo );
                dbms_output.put_line('Not authorized to grant ' || IN_Role);
                RAISE_APPLICATION_ERROR(-20430, 'GrantRole: Cannot grant DBA');
        WHEN OTHERS THEN
            _ vInfo := '!' || vInfo;
                AuditUserAdmin( vProcName, vInfo, sqlcode );
                dbms_output.put_line('error ' || sqlerrm);
                RAISE_APPLICATION_ERROR(-20440, 'GrantRole: Error ' || sqlerrm);

END GrantRole;


-------------------------------------------------------------------------------
-- PROCEDURE RevokeRole   revokes roles.
-------------------------------------------------------------------------------
PROCEDURE RevokeRole( IN_Username VARCHAR2, IN_Role VARCHAR2 ) IS
hCursor      NUMBER;
vProcName    audit_admin.procname%TYPE    := 'RevokeRole';
vInfo        audit_admin.info%TYPE        := NULL;
UserIsDBA    EXCEPTION;

BEGIN
    IF UPPER(IN_Username) IN ('SYS', 'SYSTEM')
    THEN
        RAISE UserIsDBA;
    END IF;

    hCursor := dbms_sql.open_cursor;
    dbms_sql.parse(hCursor,
            'REVOKE ' || IN_Role || ' FROM ' || IN_Username,
            dbms_sql.v7);
    dbms_sql.close_cursor( hCursor);

    vInfo := 'Revoke ' || IN_Role || ' from ' || IN_Username;
    AuditUserAdmin( vProcName, vInfo );

EXCEPTION
    WHEN UserIsDBA THEN
        vInfo := '!Revoke ' || IN_Role || ' FROM ' || IN_Username;
        AuditUserAdmin( vProcName, vInfo );
        dbms_output.put_line('Cannot revoke from SYS or SYSTEM.');
        RAISE_APPLICATION_ERROR(-20510, 'RevokeRole:Cannot revoke SYS');
    WHEN OTHERS THEN
        vInfo := '!Revoke ' || IN_Role || ' FROM ' || IN_Username;
```

```
            AuditUserAdmin( vProcName, vInfo, sqlcode );
            dbms_output.put_line('error ' || sqlerrm);
            RAISE_APPLICATION_ERROR(-20520, 'RevokeRole:Error ' || sqlerrm);

END RevokeRole;

END UserAdmin;
/

CREATE PUBLIC SYNONYM UserAdmin FOR UserAdmin
/
CREATE ROLE access_admin
/
GRANT EXECUTE ON useradmin TO access_admin
/

spool off
```

15

Conflict Avoidance and Resolution Techniques

Data integrity and consistency are perhaps the most significant challenges for the administrator of an advanced replication environment. Since users can perform DML on a given table in multiple Oracle instances, the administrator's responsibility expands from guaranteeing data integrity locally to ensuring data convergence globally. For example, if two users at two sites update an employee's salary to two different values, how do we determine which value to accept and how do we ensure that the correct value is propagated to all sites that have the replicated table? It can be done, and Oracle provides a variety of built-in conflict resolution handlers, but to use these techniques successfully, developers and administrators must understand and anticipate all likely scenarios that would result in conflicts. They also must understand how Oracle replicates DML and consider the limitations of the conflict handlers.

Data Integrity Versus Data Convergence

Data integrity refers to data that is consistent with the constraints that are defined for it. These constraints may be referential integrity constraints. For example, the value of the Po_Num field for records in table LINE_ITEMS might be restricted to values of Po_Num that exist in the PURCHASE_ORDERS table. Data also may be restricted to ranges that are independent of other tables; a gender field may be restricted to the values M and F. Other examples of integrity constraints include NOT NULL fields and UNIQUE constraints.

If you design a schema using the constraint-checking functionality that is built into the database (primary keys, foreign keys, check constraints, etc.), you are guaranteed that the data within that schema will always adhere to the rules you have defined. If your schema exists in only one database instance, your concerns about data integrity should be few, and your concerns about data convergence should be none.

However, if you are responsible for a replicated environment, you must ensure that data is consistent within and *among* database instances. *Data convergence* refers to the scenario in which all replicated tables contain identical data that is consistent with the constraints defined in each database. Oracle does not provide a means to enforce referential integrity among databases, nor should it; the model of advanced replication is that local transactions succeed regardless of problems that may occur at other sites. Therefore, DML that results in a conflict at the destination site must be resolved at the destination site. Since the objective is for data to converge, the conflict resolution could ultimately result in overwriting the change at the originating site. For example, an optimistic user of an order entry system may process an order and update its status to SHIPPED in her database, which is replicated to the order fulfillment database. The user at the order fulfillment site sees that the item is out of stock and updates the status to BACKORDERED. Ultimately, the order should have a status of BACKORDERED in both databases.

Applications That Avoid Conflicts

Ideally, applications never have conflicts, certainly never any unresolved conflicts. Although it is highly unlikely that any significant application can avoid conflicts entirely, such conflicts can certainly be kept to a minimum by observing some common sense and by taking advantage of the techniques that are available with the advanced replication facilities. The time you spend during the design phase to make your application "replication ready" will save considerable frustration later.

Normalize

Yes, once again, somebody is telling you to normalize your schema. In addition to the benefits of normalization that are extolled elsewhere, a normalized schema is far easier to replicate. Why? Consider a schema that is in first normal form (1NF)—that is, its tables contain redundant data. For example, a CUSTOMER table might have a column company_name. If this table contains 1000 records for customers who work for Acme Tire and Rubber, then 1000 records will have to be updated when Acme Tire and Rubber changes its name to Acme Tire and Rubber and Lawn Furniture. Since every update is a potential conflict, updates should be kept to a minimum. In addition, if a field such as company_name appears in numerous tables, you will have to devote significant effort to devising methods to ensure that an update to the field in one table affects the appropriate updates in the other tables not only locally, but also globally.

A more practical concern with a denormalized schema is that such schemas are typically characterized by tables with many (i.e., tens of) columns. Since replicated DML must compare the old and new values of every column of every changed row, performance will suffer.

An unfortunate myth among database designers is that normalization reduces performance. The thinking is that since a denormalization can lead to a performance gain, any steps in the opposite direction must lead to performance losses. This conclusion is far from accurate; do not denormalize for performance without the metrics to justify it.

Designate a Governing Column for Column Groups

Replicated applications invariably use built-in resolution techniques based on column groups. To make column groups work most efficiently, you should design tables in such a way that one column is the "governing" column for each group. For example, in a table with two column groups, the timestamp field might govern a Latest Timestamp resolution method that is associated with one group, while a global_name field governs the second group whose resolution method is Site Priority. It is quite conceivable that a table could have two column groups which both use Latest Timestamp as a resolution method, which would mean having two timestamp fields in the table (with different names, of course).

The main point to remember is that you must have a governing field for each column group that uses any of the following resolution methods:

- Earliest/Latest Timestamp
- Priority Group
- Site Priority

Standardize on a Time Zone

If you plan to use timestamps to resolve conflicts, it is vital that the timestamps from the various sites participating in replication are based on the same time zone; timestamps in the Oracle RDBMS do not include a time zone component. Therefore, you are strongly encouraged to put your database servers on Greenwich Mean Time (GMT) or some other mutually acceptable time zone, preferably one that does not observe daylight savings time. This is the only way to guarantee that timestamps are performed correctly.

Of course, there is some inconvenience if your application contains data that is time critical, such as a time and attendance system. However, it is far simpler to have the application perform time arithmetic for display and reporting purposes than to rewrite the timestamp conflict resolution routines to calculate the time differences among your sites.

Identify Workflow

The workflow of a replicated application should be well defined and well understood. The more often a row is updated during its lifetime, the more challenging it is for multiple sites to converge on the "correct" values for that row, especially if multiple sites are able to perform updates simultaneously.

To the greatest extent possible, the application should associate certain types of activities with certain sites. For example, updates associated with credit card information should occur at the billing location, and updates associated with shipments should happen at the shipping location. Such restrictions are known as workflow partitioning or dynamic ownership.

Workflow partitioning is possible only if it is designed into the application from the beginning; imposing it later is generally not an option. This approach avoids conflicts by associating data with a certain site when it is in a certain state (i.e., when a specific WHERE clause is true). In the preceding example, the billing location owns rows WHERE location = 'BILLING'. The application does not allow sites to update rows unless they own them.

Ownership of the row can change but only if the site that currently owns the row changes it or "pushes" it to the next site. The classic example is the manufacturing application in which orders with a status of ORDERED can be modified only at the order entry site, which updates records to SHIP. Then ownership transfers to the order fulfillment site, which updates the status to BILL, thereby transferring ownership to the accounts receivable site.

You must designate a column to hold status values that determine row ownership. Any conflicts that arise in such an application can be resolved with the Priority Group method, as we shall see later.

Consider Token Passing

If the dynamic data ownership model does not match your application's business rules, you can achieve similar results by using the technique known as token passing. As with the workflow partitioning method, token passing associates row ownership with a single site at any one time. But unlike workflow partitioning, token passing allows *any* site to take ownership of the row.

You must add two columns to any table that is to use token passing: epoch and global_name. The epoch field holds a number that is increased whenever ownership of the row changes, and the global_name field holds the global name of the database that owns the row for that value of epoch. The current owner of the row is the site associated with the highest value of the epoch field. To obtain ownership of a row, your application must:

1. Find the highest value in the epoch column and the associated global_name for that row.

2. Lock the row.

3. Update the global_name of the row to the local global name and perform the same update at the previous owner site. Turn replication off when updating the previous owner site by calling the DBMS_REPUTIL.REPLICATION_OFF procedure.

4. Turn replication off at the local site and update the row with data from the previous owner site.

5. Turn replication back on (DBMS_REPUTIL.REPLICATION_ON), increment the epoch field at the local site, and perform the rest of the intended update.

In order for token passing to work, you must include a Maximum Value resolution handler so that updates with the highest epoch value always take precedence.

Perform Strategic Administration

Other techniques for avoiding conflicts include the judicious timing of RPC pushes and the consistent use of secondary resolution methods to handle unusual or unforeseen situations. Every replicated table should have at least two conflict handlers. Although it is generally not advisable to push transactions more than once every five minutes or so, the longer you wait, the more likely it is that conflicts will arise when you finally perform the push, since users at the destination sites have been performing their own updates for a longer time.

You also should implement automated notification mechanisms so that you receive a page or email to alert you to conflicts that have managed to escape resolution, as well as any other exceptions.

Types of Conflicts Detected

Oracle detects conflicts based on PL/SQL exceptions, as summarized in Table 15-1, only at the destination site. Note that conflict detection does not imply conflict resolution.

Table 15-1. Detectable PL/SQL Exceptions

Type of DML	Potential Conflicts
INSERT	DUP_VAL_ON_INDEX
UPDATE	SQL%ROWCOUNT = 0 (NO_DATA_FOUND) SQL%ROWCOUNT > 1 (TOO_MANY_ROWS) DUP_VAL_ON_INDEX
DELETE	SQL%ROWCOUNT = 0 (NO_DATA_FOUND) SQL%ROWCOUNT > 1 (TOO_MANY_ROWS)

The situations for which Oracle does not resolve conflicts include:

- Deletes that raise NO_DATA_FOUND errors (even though they are detected)

- Deletes that raise TOO_MANY_ROWS errors

- Use of NULL values in columns used for conflict resolution

- DML that violates referential integrity constraints

- Conflicts arising from procedural replication

Why not? A brief analysis of Oracle's implementation reveals why these restrictions must exist.

Limitations of Delete Conflict Resolution

Because of the difficulties of processing delete conflicts, Oracle's recommendation is to design replicated applications to *flag* records as deleted. Include a STATUS column in the table and update it to D, for example, instead of actually deleting the row. This way, you can avoid all potential delete conflicts and avoid the task of writing your own delete conflict handling procedure. You can perform the actual delete at scheduled intervals using procedural replication. If this is not an option for your application, then consider the following alternatives.

If a row deleted at one site maps to more than one row at the destination site (i.e., the delete raises TOO_MANY_ROWS at the destination site), there is no general algorithm that can determine which of the rows should *really* be deleted at the destination site. Although Oracle detects the condition, it is not possible to pass it to an exception handler without modifying the code generated from the DBMS_REPCAT.GENERATE_REPLICATION_SUPPORT procedure. Remember, though, that all replicated tables *must* have primary keys. Therefore, if such a conflict ever did arise, it would indicate that the primary key on the table has been dropped or disabled, which is certainly an avoidable scenario.

The scenario of a delete that cannot find the matching row at the destination site, however, is quite plausible and should be anticipated. The DBMS_REPCAT.ADD_DELETE_RESOLUTION procedure associates a user-defined conflict handler package with deletes that raise NO_DATA_FOUND. Again, there is no general algorithm to determine what to do if the row to be deleted does not exist at the destination site. This could happen if the row were deleted or updated at the destination site. Should it be deleted from the originating site? Perhaps, but that is a decision for *you* to make during the design phase. But no matter what, any application that allows deletes from replicated tables must include a conflict handler package that resolves deletes that raise a NO_DATA_FOUND exception because Oracle will attempt to invoke it.

Defining a delete conflict handler

You should define a conflict handler for every table for which your application allows deletes. Remember, this conflict handler will be invoked only if the delete raises the NO_DATA_FOUND exception—that is, the row to be deleted does not exist at the destination site. A reasonable course of action under these circumstances is to insert the row into a log table, which the DBA can review.

Suppose you are replicating the table DEPT, as defined in the following table:

Column Name	Type
deptno	NUMBER(2)
dname	VARCHAR2(13)
loc	VARCHAR2(14)

You would write a function that inserts the record into table DEPT_DEL_ERR, as defined in the next table:

Column Name	Type
deptno	NUMBER(2)
dname	VARCHAR2(13)
loc	VARCHAR2(14)
timestamp	DATE
username	VARCHAR2(30)

The function is defined as follows:

```
CREATE OR REPLACE FUNCTION resolve_dept_delete(
        io_deptno               IN OUT dept.deptno%TYPE,
        io_dname                IN OUT dept.dname%TYPE,
        io_loc                  IN OUT dept.loc%TYPE,
        io_ignore_discard_flag  IN OUT BOOLEAN)
RETURN BOOLEAN IS
vRowCount NUMBER := 0;

BEGIN
```

```
---------------------------------------------------------------------
-- See if the row exists based on the primary key (deptno).
-- This finds rows that have been updated at this site.
---------------------------------------------------------------------
    SELECT  count(*)
    INTO    vRowCount
    FROM    dept
    WHERE   deptno = io_deptno;


---------------------------------------------------------------------
-- If the record exists, delete it, and return success; otherwise, put
-- the info from the passed parameters row in the DEPT_DEL_ERR table.
---------------------------------------------------------------------
    IF vRowCount = 1 THEN
        DELETE  FROM dept
        WHERE   deptno = io_deptno;
    ELSE
        INSERT INTO dept_del_err(  deptno,
                                   dname,
                                   loc,
                                   timestamp,
                                   username )

        VALUES (io_deptno,
                io_dname,
                io_loc,
                sysdate,
                user );
    END IF;

    COMMIT;

    RETURN (TRUE);
END resolve_dept_delete;
/
```

Note that the parameters to this function call are the columns of the DEPT table and that they are all IN OUT parameters; delete handlers must accept all columns as parameters, and they all must be in IN OUT mode. You will also notice that this function always returns TRUE. There is no way that deletes on this table will fail to replicate, but the DBA still has to monitor the DEPT_DEL_ERR table for errors. Obviously, your application's requirements may dictate different behavior.

To designate RESOLVE_DEPT_DELETE as the handler for the DEPT table, you must quiesce the replication group:

```
EXECUTE dbms_repcat.suspend_master_activity('MOSS')
```

The required procedure calls to make RESOLVE_DEPT_DELETE the delete conflict handler for the DEPT table are as follows:

```
-- Make RESOLVE_DEPT_DELETE a replicated object.
EXECUTE dbms_repcat.create_master_repobject(       -
    sname              => 'CDYE',                   -
    oname              => 'RESOLVE_DEPT_DELETE',-
```

```
    type                 => 'FUNCTION',           -
    use_existing_object  => FALSE,                 -
    gname                => 'CDYE')

-- Designate RESOLVE_DEPT_DELETE as the DELETE handler for DEPT.
EXECUTE dbms_repcat.add_delete_resolution(           -
    sname                 => 'CDYE',                 -
    oname                 => 'DEPT',                 -
    sequence_no           => 1,                      -
    parameter_column_name => 'DEPTNO, DNAME, LOC',   -
    function_name         => 'RESOLVE_DEPT_DELETE',  -
    comment               => 'Added on '|| sysdate )

-- Generate replication support for the function.
EXECUTE dbms_repcat.generate_replication_package( -
    sname   => 'CDYE', -
    oname   => 'RESOLVE_DEPT_DELETE')
```

Because of the complications of avoiding and resolving delete conflicts, the best policy is not to perform deletes at all. Instead, include a STATUS field in your replicated tables that designates a row as deleted. This way, your application only inserts and updates records. Conflict avoidance and resolution for inserts and updates are significantly easier to implement.

Limitations of NULL Values in Conflict Resolution

When you designate one of the built-in conflict resolution methods with your table, such as Site Priority, Oracle *depends* on the values in the relevant columns and assumes that these columns are NOT NULL. If, for example, the global_name field used for Site Priority is NULL when the conflict handler executes, the conflict will go unresolved and Oracle will make an entry in the DEFERROR data dictionary view. The reason for this restriction should be rather obvious: NULL values cannot be used in comparisons!

The moral is that you should design your replicated tables so that columns used in conflict resolution always have the NOT NULL attribute.

Referential Integrity Violations and Conflict Resolution

As discussed earlier, there is a distinction between data integrity and data convergence, and the means of ensuring both are also distinct. Data integrity is enforced by mechanisms that are built into the RDBMS, such as referential integrity constraints. Unlike data integrity, which Oracle guarantees if you use these mechanisms, there is no mechanism to guarantee data convergence.

Integrity constraints are neither designed for nor intended to enforce data integrity between databases. And it is possible that a replicated transaction may violate an integrity constraint at the destination database, even though it was permitted locally.

The best policy is to maintain identical integrity constraints among all sites participating in replication and to replicate tables whose primary keys are foreign keys of any replicated table. For example, if you have a COUNTRY table whose primary key (e.g., country_code) is a foreign key to the country_code in your replicated ADDRESS table, then you should also replicate the COUNTRY table. Do not be fooled by claims such as "The COUNTRY table never changes; we don't need to worry about replicating it." Such assumptions invariably lead to conflicts, which are quite easy to avoid.

Conflicts Arising from Procedural Replication

Oracle does not provide any means of resolving conflicts that arise from procedural replication. All resolution methods are for row-level replication. Therefore, any replicated procedures you write must include logic to detect and resolve conflicts.

To avoid conflicts in your replicated procedures, Oracle Corporation recommends these guidelines:

- Disable row-level replication in the procedure by calling the DBMS_REPUTIL.REPLICATION_OFF procedure. Be sure to re-enable replication by calling DBMS_REPUTIL.REPLICATION_ON before the procedure exits.

- Do not call more than one replicated procedure at a time.

- Replicated procedures must be within a package that does not contain any functions.

- Do not reference remote objects in a replicated procedure.

- Avoid references to values determined locally, such as SYSDATE.

- If you are using token passing, do not change the ownership of rows.

How Oracle Detects and Resolves Conflicts

The package procedure *table_name*$RP is the package that detects conflicts as it applies DML at the destination site. Generating replication support for a table creates this package. As an example, generating replication support for the table DEPT produces the package DEPT$RP (shown in Example 15-1), which contains a procedure for each of the three types of DML: REP_DELETE, REP_INSERT, and REP_UPDATE. Each of these procedures passes exceptions on to the appropriate conflict resolution handler.

The boldfaced areas show how exceptions are passed to conflict handlers. As you can see, relatively few exceptions have a chance to be resolved: NO_DATA_FOUND for deletes (line 25) and updates (line 135) and DUP_VAL_ON_INDEX for inserts (line 68) and updates (line 155). Any other exceptions, such as VALUE_ERROR, result in entries in the DEFERROR data dictionary view.

Example 15-1. Detecting Conflicts with DEPT$RP

```
 1 package body     "DEPT$RP" as
 2   procedure rep_delete(
 3     "DEPTNO1_o" IN NUMBER,
 4     "DNAME2_o" IN VARCHAR2,
 5     "LOC3_o" IN VARCHAR2,
 6     site_name IN VARCHAR2,
 7     propagation_flag IN CHAR) is
 8   begin
 9     if propagation_flag = 'N' then
10       dbms_reputil.replication_off;
11     end if;
12     dbms_reputil.rep_begin;
13     dbms_reputil.global_name := site_name;
14     delete from "DEPT"
15     where ("DEPTNO1_o" = "DEPTNO"
16     and  (("DNAME2_o" = "DNAME") or ("DNAME2_o" is NULL and "DNAME" is NULL))
17     and  (("LOC3_o" = "LOC") or ("LOC3_o" is NULL and "LOC" is NULL)));
18     if sql%rowcount = 0 then
19       raise no_data_found;
20     elsif sql%rowcount > 1 then
21       raise too_many_rows;
22     end if;
23     dbms_reputil.rep_end;
24   exception
25     when no_data_found then
26       begin
27         if not "DEPT$RR".delete_conflict_handler(
28         "DEPTNO1_o",
29         "DNAME2_o",
30         "LOC3_o",
31         site_name,
32         propagation_flag) then
33         dbms_reputil.rep_end;
34         raise;
35         end if;
36         dbms_reputil.rep_end;
37       exception
38         when others then
39         dbms_reputil.rep_end;
40         raise;
41       end;
42     when others then
43       dbms_reputil.rep_end;
44       raise;
```

Example 15-1. Detecting Conflicts with DEPT$RP (continued)

```
45   end rep_delete;
46   procedure rep_insert(
47     "DEPTNO1_n" IN NUMBER,
48     "DNAME2_n" IN VARCHAR2,
49     "LOC3_n" IN VARCHAR2,
50     site_name IN VARCHAR2,
51     propagation_flag IN CHAR) is
52   begin
53     if propagation_flag = 'N' then
54       dbms_reputil.replication_off;
55     end if;
56     dbms_reputil.rep_begin;
57     dbms_reputil.global_name := site_name;
58     insert into "DEPT" (
59       "DEPTNO",
60       "DNAME",
61       "LOC")
62     values (
63       "DEPTNO1_n",
64       "DNAME2_n",
65       "LOC3_n");
66     dbms_reputil.rep_end;
67   exception
68     when dup_val_on_index then
69       begin
70         if not "DEPT$RR".unique_conflict_insert_handler(
71       "DEPTNO1_n",
72       "DNAME2_n",
73       "LOC3_n",
74       site_name,
75       propagation_flag,
76       SQLERRM) then
77       dbms_reputil.rep_end;
78       raise;
79         end if;
80         dbms_reputil.rep_end;
81       exception
82         when others then
83       dbms_reputil.rep_end;
84       raise;
85       end;
86     when others then
87       dbms_reputil.rep_end;
88       raise;
89   end rep_insert;
90   procedure rep_update(
91     "DEPTNO1_o" IN NUMBER,
92     "DEPTNO1_n" IN NUMBER,
93     "DNAME2_o" IN VARCHAR2,
94     "DNAME2_n" IN VARCHAR2,
95     "LOC3_o" IN VARCHAR2,
```

Example 15-1. Detecting Conflicts with DEPT$RP (continued)

```
 96     "LOC3_n" IN VARCHAR2,
 97     site_name IN VARCHAR2,
 98     propagation_flag IN CHAR) is
 99   begin
100     if propagation_flag = 'N' then
101       dbms_reputil.replication_off;
102     end if;
103     dbms_reputil.rep_begin;
104     dbms_reputil.global_name := site_name;
105     update "DEPT" set
106       "DEPTNO" = "DEPTNO1_n",
107       "DNAME" =
108         decode("DNAME2_o",
109           "DNAME2_n", "DNAME",
110           null, nvl("DNAME2_n", "DNAME"),
111           "DNAME2_n"),
112       "LOC" =
113         decode("LOC3_o",
114           "LOC3_n", "LOC",
115           null, nvl("LOC3_n", "LOC"),
116           "LOC3_n")
117     where (((1 = 1 and
118         ("DNAME2_o" = "DNAME2_n" or
119         ("DNAME2_o" is null and "DNAME2_n" is null)) and
120         ("LOC3_o" = "LOC3_n" or
121         ("LOC3_o" is null and "LOC3_n" is null)))) or
122        (1 = 1 and
123         ("DNAME2_o" = "DNAME" or
124         ("DNAME2_o" is null and "DNAME" is null)) and
125         ("LOC3_o" = "LOC" or
126         ("LOC3_o" is null and "LOC" is null))))
127       and "DEPTNO1_o" = "DEPTNO";
128     if sql%rowcount = 0 then
129       raise no_data_found;
130     elsif sql%rowcount > 1 then
131       raise too_many_rows;
132     end if;
133     dbms_reputil.rep_end;
134   exception
135     when no_data_found then
136       begin
137         if not "DEPT$RR".update_conflict_handler(
138       "DEPTNO1_o",
139       "DEPTNO1_n",
140       "DNAME2_o",
141       "DNAME2_n",
142       "LOC3_o",
143       "LOC3_n",
144       site_name,
145       propagation_flag) then
146       dbms_reputil.rep_end;
```

Example 15-1. Detecting Conflicts with DEPT$RP (continued)

```
147        raise;
148          end if;
149          dbms_reputil.rep_end;
150        exception
151          when others then
152        dbms_reputil.rep_end;
153        raise;
154        end;
155     when dup_val_on_index then
156        begin
157          if not "DEPT$RR".unique_conflict_update_handler(
158        "DEPTNO1_o",
159        "DEPTNO1_n",
160        "DNAME2_o",
161        "DNAME2_n",
162        "LOC3_o",
163        "LOC3_n",
164        site_name,
165        propagation_flag,
166        SQLERRM) then
167        dbms_reputil.rep_end;
168        raise;
169          end if;
170          dbms_reputil.rep_end;
171        exception
172          when others then
173        dbms_reputil.rep_end;
174        raise;
175        end;
176     when others then
177        dbms_reputil.rep_end;
178        raise;
179   end rep_update;
180 end "DEPT$RP";
```

Column Groups and Priority Groups

Column groups and priority groups provide interfaces to a variety of built-in conflict resolution techniques and the easiest way to configure your application to resolve conflicts automatically. Let's look at them one at a time.

Column Groups

A column group is a set of one or more columns associated with a single conflict resolution method. A column cannot belong to more than one column group, and columns that are not explicitly assigned to a column group are members of a shadow column group, which Oracle creates by default and which uses the default conflict resolution methods.

For example, suppose that you want to define a column group for the EMPLOY-EES table described in the following table:

Column Name	Type
EMPLOYEE_ID	NUMBER(10)
LAST_NAME	VARCHAR2(30)
FIRST_NAME	VARCHAR2(20)
SOCIAL_SECURITY_NO	VARCHAR2(11)
MARITAL_STATUS	VARCHAR2(1)
HOME_PHONE	VARCHAR2(12)
PERS_GLOBAL_NAME	VARCHAR2(30)
PERS_TIMESTAMP	DATE
MANAGER	NUMBER(3)
DEPT	NUMBER(3)
SAL_GRADE	NUMBER(3)
SENIORITY	VARCHAR2(10)
PAYROLL_GLOBAL_NAME	VARCHAR2(30)
PAYROLL_TIMESTAMP	DATE

Use the procedure DBMS_REPCAT.MAKE_COLUMN_GROUP to define a column group for fields that the personnel site maintains (i.e., LAST_NAME, FIRST_NAME, SOCIAL_SECURITY_NO, MARITAL_STATUS, HOME_PHONE). The application records information about changes to these fields in PERS_GLOBAL_NAME and PERS_TIMESTAMP.

```
EXECUTE dbms_repcat.make_column_group(                  -
    gname                 => 'HR',                      -
    oname                 => 'EMPLOYEES',               -
    column_group          => 'CG_EMP_PERSONNEL',        -
    list_of_column_names  => -
        'LAST_NAME, FIRST_NAME, SOCIAL_SECURITY_NUM, MARITAL_STATUS, -
        HOME_PHONE, PERS_GLOBAL_NAME, PERS_TIMESTAMP' )
```

To add update conflict resolution to this column group based on the Latest Timestamp technique and a backup resolution method based on the Overwrite technique, make these calls:

```
EXECUTE dbms_repcat.add_update_resolution(             -
    sname                  => 'HR',                     -
    oname                  => 'EMPLOYEES',              -
    column_group           => 'CG_EMP_PERSONNEL',       -
    sequence_no            => 1,                        -
    method                 => 'LATEST TIMESTAMP',       -
    parameter_column_name  => 'PERS_TIMESTAMP',         -
    comment                => 'Method 1 added on ' || sysdate);
```

```
EXECUTE dbms_repcat.add_update_resolution(            -
        sname                  => 'HR',              -
        oname                  => 'EMPLOYEES',       -
        column_group           => 'CG_EMP_PERSONNEL', -
        sequence_no            => 2,                 -
        method                 => 'OVERWRITE',       -
        parameter_column_name  => '*',               -
        comment                => 'Method 2 added on ' || sysdate);
```

As with any other modifications to replicated objects, you must add column groups from the master definition site when the environment is quiesced. You must also regenerate replication support for any table for which you modify a column group:

```
EXECUTE dbms_repcat.generate_replication_support(  -
        sname   => 'HR',                            -
        oname   => 'EMPLOYEES',                     -
        type    => 'TABLE' )
```

Column groups provide a means to assign different resolution techniques to different types of data; numeric techniques for numeric data, timestamp techniques for date fields, and so on. It also allows you to group related fields, such as the components of an address.

Dividing the fields of a table into column groups raises the possibility that the "resolved" data for a single row may contain values from different sites. In the EMPLOYEES table example, we could define a second column group containing the fields MANAGER, DEPT, SALGRADE, SENIORITY, PERS_GLOBAL_NAME, and PERS_TIMESTAMP. One site could update MARITAL_STATUS, and another could update SAL_GRADE, and the resulting row would be the combination of the two updates. Since data can be merged this way, it is vital to keep related columns in the same column group; you would not want to put FIRST_NAME in one column group and LAST_NAME in another.

How the column group resolution mechanism works

Oracle detects conflicts by scanning every field in every column group, comparing the old value from the origination site with the current value at the destination site. If Oracle detects a difference (because, for example, a change at the destination site had not yet been propagated), it invokes the conflict resolution technique(s) for the corresponding column group. If the column group has more than one resolution technique (as it should), they are called in descending priority order until the conflict is resolved. The shadow column group that contains columns that have not been explicitly assigned to any group is scanned last.

If all conflicts are resolved, the resolved data is committed. Otherwise, the transaction is written to the DEFERROR data dictionary view.

APIs for column groups

The following lists the APIs that manipulate column groups:

DBMS_REPCAT.DEFINE_COLUMN_GROUP
    Creates a column group with no member columns.

DBMS_REPCAT.DROP_COLUMN_GROUP
    Drops a column group.

DBMS_REPCAT.ADD_GROUPED_COLUMN
    Adds a column to an existing column group.

DBMS_REPCAT.DROP_GROUPED_COLUMN
    Removes a column from a column group.

DBMS_REPCAT.MAKE_COLUMN_GROUP
    Creates a column group and adds columns to it.

Appendix A, *Built-in Packages for Distributed Systems*, contains a complete reference to these APIs.

Priority Groups

Priority groups rank a finite list of possible values for a column so that, in the event of a conflict, Oracle updates the destination table if and only if the new value from the originating site has a higher priority. This method is designed to work with applications that use workflow partitioning. Unlike column groups, which are defined at the table level, priority groups can be used by multiple tables. A site priority is a priority group in which the range of values for a column is the list of global names of databases participating in the replication.

If you choose to implement priority groups, you must select a priority column, and you must rank all potential values of that column. Consider the SENIORITY column of the EMPLOYEES table. Suppose that its range of possible values is PROBATION, REGULAR, and TENURED. Assuming that this organization never demotes an employee's seniority, you could define a priority group to enforce the workflow of orders from PROBATION to REGULAR to TENURED:

```
-- Create a column group which includes the SENIORITY column.
EXECUTE dbms_repcat.make_column_group(           -
        sname                => 'HR',            -
        oname                => 'EMPLOYEES',     -
        column_group         => 'CG_HR',         -
        list_of_column_names => -
    'MANAGER, DEPT, SALGRADE, SENIORITY, PERS_GLOBAL_NAME, PERS_TIMESTAMP')

-- Define a priority group using the SENIORITY column.
EXECUTE dbms_repcat.define_priority_group(       -
        gname          => 'HR',                  -
        pgroup         => 'SENIORITY',            -
```

```
        datatype        => 'VARCHAR2',              -
        fixed_length    => NULL,                     -
        comment         => 'SENIORITY created on ' || sysdate)

-- Associate priorities with the various possible values.  The higher the
-- priority, the higher the precedence.
EXECUTE dbms_repcat.add_priority_varchar2(          -
        gname           => 'HR',                    -
        pgroup          => 'SENIORITY',             -
        value           => 'PROBATION',             -
        priority        => 1 )

EXECUTE dbms_repcat.add_priority_varchar2(          -
        gname           => 'HR',                    -
        pgroup          => 'SENIORITY',             -
        value           => 'REGULAR',               -
        priority        => 2 )

EXECUTE dbms_repcat.add_priority_varchar2(          -
        gname           => 'HR',                    -
        pgroup          => 'SENIORITY',             -
        value           => 'TENURED',               -
        priority        => 3 )

EXECUTE dbms_repcat.generate_replication_support( -
        sname           => 'HR',                    -
        oname           => 'EMPLOYEES',             -
        type            => 'TABLE' )
```

As usual, you must perform these steps from the master definition site while the environment is quiesced. A priority group is a very powerful resolution method because it guarantees data convergence if the priority of the column is always increasing, which is why it is perfect for applications that can use workflow partitioning.

Site Priority

A site priority is essentially a priority group in which the priority column holds the global name of the database that updates the data. The following procedure calls set up site priorities for three locations participating in a replicated environment: ALBANY.COM, BUFFALO.COM, and CLEVELAND.COM:

```
-- Define the site priority.
EXECUTE dbms_repcat.define_site_priority(          -
        gname   => 'HR',                            -
        name    => 'HR_SITES',                      -
        comment => 'Site Priority define on ' || sysdate)

-- Add the sites.
-- ALBANY.COM has highest priority, CLEVELAND.COM has lowest.
EXECUTE dbms_repcat.add_priority_site(              -
        gname           => 'HR',                    -
        name            => 'HR_SITES',              -
```

```
            site            => 'ALBANY.COM',          -
            priority        => 3)

EXECUTE dbms_repcat.add_priority_site(                -
            gname           => 'HR',                  -
            name            => 'HR_SITES',            -
            site            => 'BUFFALO.COM',         -
            priority        => 2)

EXECUTE dbms_repcat.add_priority_site(                -
            gname           => 'HR',                  -
            name            => 'HR_SITES',            -
            site            => 'CLEVELAND.COM',       -
            priority        => 1)
```

You would typically use site priority as a backup resolution method to act as a final tiebreaker that is invoked when other methods fail to resolve the conflict. If each of your sites is associated with an event or status in the workflow model, then you should use priority groups instead of site priority to effect data convergence. As Table 15-2 illustrates, site priority does not guarantee data convergence with more than two master sites.

Table 15-2. How Site Priority Can Fail with More Than Two Sites

Time	ALBANY.COM Priority = 3	BUFFALO.COM Priority = 2	CLEVELAND.COM Priority = 1
12:00	signal = GREEN	signal = GREEN	signal = GREEN
12:05	signal = GREEN	signal = GREEN	*site down*
12:10	signal = YELLOW	signal = GREEN	*site down*
12:15	signal = YELLOW	signal = YELLOW	*site down*
12:20	signal = YELLOW	signal = RED	signal = GREEN
12:25	signal = YELLOW	signal = RED	signal = RED
12:30	signal = YELLOW	signal = RED	signal = YELLOW
12:35	signal = RED	signal = RED	signal = YELLOW

Consider the time line:

- 12:00: All sites are in agreement.

- 12:05: CLEVELAND.COM goes down; all sites are still in agreement.

- 12:10: ALBANY.COM updates signal to YELLOW; CLEVELAND.COM is still down.

- 12:15: BUFFALO.COM receives and applies update from ALBANY.COM; CLEVELAND.COM is still down.

- 12:20: BUFFALO.COM updates signal to RED; CLEVELAND.COM comes back online.

- 12:25: CLEVELAND.COM receives the update from BUFFALO.COM. Site Priority conflict resolution gives precedence to BUFFALO.COM's update, so CLEVELAND.COM sets signal to RED.

- 12:30: CLEVELAND.COM receives an update from ALBANY.COM (from 12:10). The site priority conflict gives precedence to ALBANY.COM's update, so CLEVELAND.COM sets signal to YELLOW.

- 12:35 ALBANY.COM receives update from BUFFALO.COM and applies it without any conflict.

So, after all transactions have been replicated, there are no unresolved conflicts, but the data does not agree! Of course, if ALBANY.COM or BUFFALO.COM updates this particular row at some later date, the data could converge once again. Unfortunately for CLEVELAND.COM, no such update is imminent; you certainly cannot depend on additional updates to attain data convergence. Similar risks of data divergence exist for the Earliest Timestamp resolution method and for priority groups that do not follow a workflow model. This example would have resulted in data convergence if we had used priority groups, assuming that the column values always progress from GREEN to YELLOW to RED.

APIs for priority groups and site priority

The DBMS_REPCAT APIs for priority groups and site priority are summarized here. Possible values for *datatype* are CHAR, VARCHAR2, NUMBER, DATE, and RAW.

DBMS_REPCAT.DEFINE_PRIORITY_GROUP
> Creates a priority group.

DBMS_REPCAT.DROP_PRIORITY_GROUP
> Drops a priority group.

DBMS_REPCAT.ADD_PRIORITY_datatype
> Adds a new value of type *datatype* to an existing priority group.

DBMS_REPCAT.ALTER_PRIORITY_datatype
> Changes the priority of an existing column value.

DBMS_REPCAT.DROP_PRIORITY
> Drops a member of a priority group with a specified priority.

DBMS_REPCAT.DROP_PRIORITY_datatype
> Drops a member of a priority group for a specific column.

DBMS_REPCAT.DROP_SITE_PRIORITY
> Drops an existing site priority group.

DBMS_REPCAT.ALTER_SITE_PRIORITY_SITE
> Changes the site associated with a specific priority value.

DMBS_REPCAT.ALTER_SITE_PRIORITY
> Changes the priority of a specific site.

DMBS_REPCAT.DROP_SITE_PRIORITY_SITE
> Drops a site from the site priority group.

Appendix A contains a complete reference to these APIs.

The Built-in Methods

Oracle supplies 11 built-in conflict resolution methods (see Table 15-3), which you can designate for column groups and priority groups. You will notice that data convergence for replicated environments of three or more sites is very challenging to obtain.

Table 15-3. Built-in Conflict Resolution Methods

Method	DML Supported	> 1 Master?	Convergence Requirements
Minimum Value	UPDATE	Yes	Always decreasing or < 3 masters
Maximum Value	UPDATE	Yes	Always increasing or < 3 masters
Earliest Timestamp	UPDATE	Yes	< 3 masters
Latest Timestamp	UPDATE	Yes	Always increasing or < 3 masters
Overwrite Update	UPDATE	No	< 2 masters
Discard Update	UPDATE	No	< 2 masters
Average	UPDATE	No	< 2 masters
Additive	UPDATE	Yes	Always converges
Append Site Name	INSERT	Yes	Never guaranteed to converge
Append Sequence	INSERT	Yes	Never guaranteed to converge
Ignore Insert/Discard Insert	INSERT	Yes	Never guaranteed to converge

For the most part, these techniques are self-explanatory, but certain peculiarities of their usage warrant further explanation.

Minimum Value/Maximum Value

The Minimum Value and Maximum Value methods are appropriate for sites with any number of masters and can be used with any replicatable datatype. Data is always guaranteed to converge with two masters and with three masters if values are always decreasing (for Minimum Value) or always increasing (for Maximum Value). If the data from the originating site and destination site are the same, these resolution techniques will fail. Therefore, you should always provide a backup method, such as site priority to handle this situation.

Earliest Timestamp/Latest Timestamp

The Earliest Timestamp and Latest Timestamp techniques are basically the same as the Minimum and Maximum Value techniques, except that they only apply to DATE columns. However, they do introduce the issue of differing time zones. As I mentioned earlier, Oracle strongly recommends putting systems in multiple time zones on Greenwich Mean Time (GMT) if you plan to use timestamp-based conflict resolution, since Oracle's DATE datatype does not have a time zone component. The Latest Timestamp method is guaranteed to converge for any number of master sites, although Earliest Timestamp is not. Earliest Timestamp does not necessarily converge because such values are not necessarily always decreasing, whereas Latest Timestamps must always be increasing.

As with the Minimum and Maximum Value techniques, you are strongly encouraged to supply a backup resolution method to break ties that occur when the timestamps are equal. Note that the Earliest and Latest Timestamp methods may not be appropriate for data that can be updated at multiple sites, since the "correct" value may not necessarily be associated with the earliest (or latest) timestamp.

Overwrite Update/Discard Update

The Overwrite Update and Discard Update methods of conflict resolution are primarily intended for environments with a single master site and several snapshot sites. These methods either overwrite or discard data at either the origination or the destination and do not guarantee convergence in a multi-master environment. Specifically, the Overwrite Update method simply replaces the data at the destination with the new originating site's data, and the Discard Update method does nothing at all with the update. If you choose to use the Overwrite Update or Discard Update conflict resolution techniques in a multi-master environment, you should do so in conjunction with a notification facility to alert the DBA.

Average/Additive

The Additive and Average methods work with numeric data only. The Additive method adds the delta at the originating site to the destination site, while the Average method averages the new value from the originating site with the current value at the destination site. The Additive method always converges, and the Average method converges with two or fewer master sites.

Append Site Name/Append Sequence

The Append Site Name and Append Sequence techniques are intended to resolve inserts that result in unique constraint violations. Although appending a global name or sequence number to the violated key may circumvent the conflict, it does not guarantee data convergence. These methods may be appropriate for situations in which data availability is more important than data accuracy. These techniques should also be used in conjunction with a notification facility.

Ignore Insert/Discard Insert

The Ignore Insert and Discard Insert techniques are also used to resolve unique constraint violations on inserts. The Ignore Insert method does nothing with the update, and the Discard Insert method deletes the row from the originating site. Again, these methods do not guarantee data convergence and should be used only in conjunction with a notification facility.

Writing Your Own Conflict Resolution Handler

If the conflict resolution techniques that Oracle supplies do not meet your requirements, you are free to write your own routine. An example of such a routine is the one with the delete conflict handler shown earlier in this chapter. When you sit down to write your conflict resolution function, it is probably easiest to begin with the code that Oracle generates for the corresponding built-in resolution technique, which you can extract from the DBA_SOURCE data dictionary view. You should also consider building a notification method.

Oracle's requirements for user-defined conflict resolution techniques are as follows:

* Use PL/SQL.

* Return Boolean TRUE if successful, FALSE otherwise.

* Update handlers require Old, New, and Current column values for columns specified in the parameter_column_name parameter of DBMS_REPCAT.ADD_ UPDATE_RESOLUTION.

* Delete handlers require Old column values for the entire row.

* Uniqueness handlers require New values for columns specified in the parameter_column_name parameter of DBMS_REPCAT.ADD_UPDATE_RESO- LUTION.

* Do not perform DDL (i.e., through dynamic SQL).

* Do not perform transaction control (e.g., ROLLBACK).

* Do not perform session control (e.g., ALTER SESSION...).

* Do not perform system control (e.g. ALTER SYSTEM...).

When you are ready to add your conflict resolution function to the table, follow these steps:

1. Quiesce the replication group.

2. Call DBMS_REPCAT.CREATE_MASTER_REPOBJECT to make your function a replicated object.

3. Call DBMS_REPCAT.ADD_*conflicttype*_RESOLUTION (where *type* may be UPDATE, DELETE, or UNIQUE) to associate your function with the table.

4. Call DBMS_REPCAT.GENERATE_REPLICATION_PACKAGE to generate replication support for your function.

5. Call DBMS_REPCAT.RESUME_MASTER_ACTIVITY to resume replication.

III

Appendixes

This part of the book contains the following appendixes:

- Appendix A, *Built-in Packages for Distributed Systems*, is the API reference; it contains summaries of all specifications, parameters, exceptions, and restrictions for the procedures and functions available through the Oracle built-in packages used with distributed systems.

- Appendix B, *Scripts and Utilities*, contains the code for a variety of scripts mentioned in this book.

A

Built-in Packages for Distributed Systems

This appendix summarizes the Application Programming Interface (API) calls to the procedures and functions in the various Oracle built-in packages that support distributed systems. It covers the packages listed in Table A-1.

For each package, I'll describe briefly how to find the package and how to call each of its programs. I'll also show exceptions and other nonprogram elements. For each procedure and function provided in the package, I'll show, in a quick-reference format, the specifications, parameters, exceptions, and any restrictions.

 In addition to the distributed system packages described here, Oracle provides many other built-in packages (e.g., DBMS_SQL and DBMS_UTILITY). For a full discussion of all of the packages, see *Oracle Built-in Packages* by Steven Feuerstein, Charles Dye, and John Beresniewicz (O'Reilly & Associates, 1998).

Table A-1. Built-in Packages for Distributed Systems

Package	Description
DBMS_DEFER	Builds deferred calls.
DBMS_DEFER_QUERY	Provides access to parameters passed to deferred calls, primarily for diagnostic purposes.
DBMS_DEFER_SYS	Performs administrative tasks such as scheduling, executing, and deleting queued transactions.
DBMS_OFFLINE_OG	Instantiates sites—that is, lets you export data from an existing master site and import it into the new master site.

Table A-1. Built-in Packages for Distributed Systems (continued)

Package	Description
DBMS_OFFLINE_SNAPSHOT	Allows you to instantiate snapshots without having to run the CREATE SNAPSHOT command over the network. This package is particularly useful if you need to instantiate extremely large snapshots.
DBMS_RECTIFIER_DIFF	Compares the replicated tables at two master sites and allows you to synchronize them if they are different.
DBMS_REFRESH	Administers snapshot groups at a snapshot site.
DBMS_REPCAT	Performs a number of replication, administration, snapshot, and conflict resolution operations.
DBMS_REPCAT_ADMIN	Creates administrator accounts for replication.
DBMS_REPCAT_AUTH	Grants and revokes "surrogate SYS" privileges for an administrator account.
DBMS_REPUTIL	Enables and disables replication at the session level.
DBMS_SNAPSHOT	Lets you maintain snapshots and snapshot logs.

DBMS_DEFER: Building Deferred Calls

The DBMS_DEFER package queues deferred transactions. These transactions are typically remote procedure calls (RPCs), but you can also defer procedure calls locally. The advanced replication facilities use this package transparently and extensively, but you can also access it directly for other purposes.

How the Package Is Used

You queue procedure calls by calling the TRANSACTION or CALL procedure. A call to TRANSACTION is followed by one or more deferred RPCs, which are followed by a COMMIT.

DBMS_DEFER can execute procedures at remote sites under a highly privileged account, such as the replication administrator account. Therefore, EXECUTE privileges on DBMS_DEFER should not be widely granted. As a general rule, you should restrict it to DBA accounts. If you want to provide end users with the ability to create their own deferred calls, you should create a cover package and grant EXECUTE on it to end users or end user roles.

Installation and Access

The DBMS_DEFER package is created when the Oracle database is installed. The *dbmsdefr.sql* script (found in the built-in packages source directory), contains the source code for this package's specification. This script is called by *catrep.sql*, which must be run to install the advanced replication packages. The script creates the public synonym DBMS_DEFER. EXECUTE privileges on DBMS_DEFER are not granted.

DBMS_DEFER Procedures

Procedure Name	Description
CALL	Defines a remote procedure call.
COMMIT_WORK	Commits deferred RPC transaction.
*datatype*_ARG	Adds parameter of specified datatype to a deferred call; *datatype* may be CHAR, DATE, NUMBER, RAW, ROWID, or VARCHAR2.
TRANSACTION	Marks a transaction as deferred.

DBMS_DEFER Exceptions

Exception Name	Number	Description
bad_param_type	−23325	Parameter type does not match actual type.
commfailure	−23302	Remote update failed due to communication failure.
dbms_defererror	−23305	Generic internal errors.
deferred_rpc_quiesce	−23326	Database is quiescing.
executiondisabled	−23354	Deferred RPC execution is disabled.
malformedcall	−23304	Argument count mismatches, etc.
mixeddest	−23301	Destinations for transaction not specified consistently.
parameterlength	−23323	Parameter length exceeds limits (2000 for CHAR/VARCHAR, 255 for RAW).
updateconflict	−23303	Remote update failed due to conflict.

DBMS_DEFER Nonprogram Elements

In the following list, the node_list_t element is a PL/SQL table whose first entry is always placed in row 1. It is filled sequentially, with each subsequent entry placed in row node_list_t.last + 1.

Element Type and Name	Description
CONSTANT arg_csetid_none (Oracle8 only)	Internal character set ID. Value = 0. Includes types DATE, NUMBER, ROWID, RAW, and BLOB.
CONSTANT arg_form_any (Oracle8 only)	Internal character set ID. Value = 4.
CONSTANT arg_form_implicit (Oracle8 only)	Internal character set ID. Value = 1. Includes types CHAR, VARCHAR2, and CLOB.
CONSTANT arg_form_nchar (Oracle8 only)	Internal character set ID. Value = 2. Includes types NCHAR, NVARCHAR2, and NCLOB.
CONSTANT arg_form_none (Oracle8 only)	Internal character set ID. Value = 0. Includes types DATE, NUMBER, ROWID, RAW, and BLOB.
CONSTANT arg_type_blob (Oracle8 only)	Used in arg_type column of def$_args table. Value = 113.
CONSTANT arg_type_clob (Oracle8 only)	Used in arg_type column of def$_args table. Value = 112.

Element Type and Name	Description
CONSTANT arg_type_bfil (Oracle8 only)	Used in arg_type column of def$_args table. Value = 114.
CONSTANT arg_type_cfil (Oracle8 only)	Used in arg_type column of def$_args table. Value = 115.
CONSTANT arg_type_num	Used in arg_type column of def$_args table. Value = 2.
CONSTANT arg_type_char	Used in arg_type column of def$_args table. Value = 96.
CONSTANT arg_type_varchar2	Used in arg_type column of def$_args table. Value = 1.
CONSTANT arg_type_date	Used in arg_type column of def$_args table. Value = 12.
CONSTANT arg_type_rowid	Used in arg_type column of def$_args table. Value = 11.
CONSTANT arg_type_raw	Used in arg_type column of def$_args table. Value = 23.
CONSTANT repcat_status_normal	Signals normal successful completion. Value = 0.0.
TYPE node_list_t	Table of VARCHAR2(128).

DBMS_DEFER.CALL

The CALL procedure queues an RPC to the destination specified in the DEFDE-FAULTDEST data dictionary view. It calls TRANSACTION automatically if it is the first call of a transaction. If you do not specify a value for the nodes parameter, the destination of the RPC will be the locations in the data dictionary view DEFDE-FAULTDEST.

```
PROCEDURE DBMS_DEFER.CALL
   (schema_name IN VARCHAR2,
    package_name IN VARCHAR2,
    proc_name IN VARCHAR2,
    arg_count IN NATURAL,
    {group_name IN VARCHAR2 := ''|
    nodes IN node_list_t});
```

Parameters

Parameter Name	Description
schema_name	Name of the schema queuing the call.
package_name	Name of the package containing the procedure that is being queued.
proc_name	Name of the procedure being queued.
arg_count	Number of parameters being passed to the procedure. You must have one call to DBMS_DEFER.*datatype*_ARG for each parameter.

Parameter Name	Description
group_name	Optional. Reserved for internal use.
nodes	Optional. List of destination nodes (global_names) where the procedure is to be executed. If nodes are not specified, destinations are determined by the list passed to TRANSACTION.

Exceptions

Exception Name	Number	Description
malformedcall	−23304	Number of arguments in the call does not match value of arg_count.
ORA-23319	−23319	The parameter is NULL, misspelled, or not allowed.
ORA-23352	−23352	The nodes list contains a duplicate.

Restrictions

The procedures used in deferred RPCs must be part of a package; it is not possible to queue standalone procedures.

DBMS_DEFER.COMMIT_WORK

The COMMIT_WORK procedure issues a COMMIT command to commit the transaction constructed by the preceding TRANSACTION and CALL procedures.

```
PROCEDURE DBMS_DEFER.COMMIT_WORK
    (commit_work_comment IN VARCHAR2);
```

commit_work_comment is a description of the transaction. The comment may be up to 50 characters.

Exceptions

Exception Name	Number	Description
malformedcall	−23304	Number of arguments in the CALL procedure does not match value arg_count, there are missing calls to the *datatype*_ARG procedure, or the TRANSACTION procedure was not called for this transaction.

Restrictions

If the destination nodes are not specified in DBMS_REPCAT, they are determined by one of the following, in order of procedure:

* List of nodes in parameter passed to CALL
* List of nodes in parameter passed to TRANSACTION
* Entries in DEFTRANDEST

DBMS_DEFER.*datatype*_ARG

This *datatype*_ARG procedure specifies an argument for a procedure being built for a remote procedure call. The argument is of the datatype specified in *datatype*.

```
PROCEDURE DBMS_DEFER.datatype_ARG (arg IN datatype)
```

Parameters

Specifications differ for different datatypes, depending on whether you are using Oracle7 or Oracle8. *datatype* can be any type in the following table.

Oracle7 and Oracle8	Oracle8 Only
NUMBER	NVARCHAR2
DATE	ANY_VARCHAR2
VARCHAR2	NCHAR
CHAR	ANY_VARCHAR
ROWID	BLOB
RAW	CLOB
	ANY_CLOB
	NCLOB

The arg parameter is the value to pass to the parameter of the same datatype in the procedure previously queued via CALL; it may not exceed the following:

- 2000 for CHAR and VARCHAR2

- 255 for RAW

The various alternatives are listed here.

These specifications apply to both Oracle7 and Oracle8:

```
PROCEDURE NUMBER_ARG (arg IN NUMBER);
PROCEDURE DATE_ARG (arg IN DATE);
PROCEDURE VARCHAR2_ARG (arg IN VARCHAR2);
PROCEDURE CHAR_ARG (arg IN CHAR);
PROCEDURE ROWID_ARG (arg IN ROWID);
PROCEDURE RAW_ARG (arg IN RAW);
```

These specifications apply only to Oracle8:

```
PROCEDURE NVARCHAR2_ARG (arg IN NVARCHAR2);
PROCEDURE ANY_VARCHAR2_ARG (arg  IN VARCHAR2 CHARACTER SET ANY_CS);
PROCEDURE NCHAR_ARG (arg IN NCHAR);
PROCEDURE ANY_CHAR_ARG (arg IN CHAR CHARACTER SET ANY_CS);
PROCEDURE BLOB_ARG (arg IN BLOB);
PROCEDURE CLOB_ARG (arg IN CLOB);
PROCEDURE ANY_CLOB_ARG (arg IN CLOB CHARACTER SET ANY_CS);
PROCEDURE NCLOB_ARG (arg IN NCLOB);
```

Exceptions

Exception Name	Number	Description
paramlen_num	−23323	Parameter is too long.

Restrictions

- This procedure is used only in conjunction with CALL.

- ROWID parameters can only be used for RPCs queued for the local node.

DBMS_DEFER.TRANSACTION

The TRANSACTION procedure allows you to specify destination sites for the ensuing call(s) to the CALL procedure. It marks a transaction as "deferred"—that is, the transaction contains RPCs. This call is optional because CALL also calls it. There are two main reasons why you might wish to identify destinations this way:

- You might wish to override the destinations in the DBA_REPSITES data dictionary view.

- You might be making several calls to CALL and not wish to specify the destinations in the nodes parameter individually each time.

The TRANSACTION procedure is overloaded in such a way that the nodes parameter is optional. You can specify either:

```
PROCEDURE DBMS_DEFER.TRANSACTION;
```

or:

```
PROCEDURE DBMS_DEFER.TRANSACTION
    (nodes IN node_list_t);
```

If specified, nodes is a PL/SQL table containing the list of nodes that should receive the RPC. If you do not specify the nodes parameter, the ensuing call(s) to CALL will queue the calls to destinations in DEFDEFAULTDEST. If you do specify the nodes parameter, you must populate it with the global name of target destinations.

Exceptions

Exception Name	Number	Description
malformedcall	−23304	Transaction is not properly formed, or transaction terminated.
ORA-23319	−23319	Parameter value is not appropriate.
ORA-23352	−23352	node_list_t contains duplicates.

Restrictions

You can call the TRANSACTION procedure only in conjunction with CALL.

DBMS_DEFER_QUERY: Performing Diagnostics and Maintenance

Occasionally, you may want to see details about deferred RPCs in the queue, such as what procedure and parameters are used. The DBMS_DEFER_QUERY package contains procedures to display this data.

How the Package Is Used

Typically, this package is used to assist in debugging errors and conflicts that have occurred during the execution of an RPC.

Installation and Access

The DBMS_REPCAT_QUERY package is created when the Oracle database is installed. The *dbmsdefr.sql* script (found in the built-in packages source directory) contains the source code for this package's specification. This script is called by *catrep.sql*, which must be run to install the advanced replication packages. The wrapped SQL script *prvtrctf.sql* creates the public synonym DBMS_REPCAT_QUERY. No EXECUTE privileges are granted on DBMS_REPCAT_QUERY; only the owner (SYS) and those with the EXECUTE ANY PROCEDURE system privilege may execute the package.

There are no exceptions defined for this package.

DBMS_DEFER_QUERY Procedures

Procedure Name	Description
GET_ARG_TYPE	Returns the type of a parameter in a deferred call
GET_CALL_ARGS	Returns information about parameters in text form
GET_*datatype*_ARG	Returns the value of a parameter whose type is *datatype*; values can be CHAR, DATE, NUMBER, RAW, ROWID, or VARCHAR2

DBMS_DEFER_QUERY Nonprogram Elements

Type and Name	Description
TYPE type_ary	Table of NUMBER
TYPE val_ary	Table of VARCHAR2(2000)

The PL/SQL tables type_ary and val_ary are both used in parameters to the procedure GET_CALL_ARGS; type_ary is an output array for RPC parameter datatypes, and val_ary is an output array of the parameter values. The following table shows the mapping of numbers to datatypes in type_ary:

Datatype	Numeric Value in type_ary
BFILE (Oracle8 only)	114
BLOB (Oracle8 only)	113
CFIL (Oracle8 only)	115
CHAR	96
CLOB (Oracle8 only)	112
DATE	12
NUMBER	2
RAW	23
ROWID	11
VARCHAR2	1

DBMS_DEFER_QUERY.GET_ARG_TYPE

You can use this function in conjunction with GET_*datatype*_ARG or GET_CALL_ARGS to determine information about the deferred RPCs in the queue. GET_ARG_TYPE returns a number corresponding to the argument's datatype.

```
FUNCTION DBMS_DEFER_QUEUE.GET_ARG_TYPE
    (callno IN NUMBER,
     deferred_tran_db IN VARCHAR2,
     arg_no IN  NUMBER,
     deferred_tran_id IN VARCHAR2)
  RETURN NUMBER;
```

The following table shows the mapping of datatypes to return values:

Argument Datatype	GET_ARG_TYPE Return Code
BFILE (Oracle8 only)	114
BLOB (Oracle8 only)	113
CFIL (Oracle8 only)	115
CHAR	96
CLOB (Oracle8 only)	112
DATE	12
NUMBER	2
RAW	23
ROWID	11
VARCHAR2	1

Notice that the datatypes here are limited to the Oracle-supplied datatypes; you cannot, for example, defer a call to a procedure that accepts a PL/SQL table as a parameter.

There are no restrictions on calling GET_ARG_TYPE.

Parameters

Parameter Name	Description
callno	The CALLNO of the RPC, as stored in the DEFCALL data dictionary view
deferred_tran_db	Global name of the database deferring the call (also stored in DEFCALL)
arg_no	The position of the argument in the RPC
deferred_tran_id	The deferred_tran_id for the call (also stored in DEFCALL)

Exceptions

Exception Name	Number	Description
NO_DATA_FOUND	–00100	Specified argument does not exist for specified RPC.

DBMS_DEFER_QUERY.GET_CALL_ARGS

The GET_CALL_ARGS procedure allows you to obtain the datatypes and values for all arguments passed to a procedure in a single call. This is the easiest way to obtain information about the datatypes and values of all passed parameters.

```
PROCEDURE DBMS_DEFER_QUERY.GET_CALL_ARGS
    (callno IN NUMBER,
     startarg IN NUMBER := 1,
     argcnt IN NUMBER,
     argsize IN NUMBER,
     tran_db IN VARCHAR2,
     tran_id IN VARCHAR2,
     date_fmt IN VARCHAR2,
     types OUT TYPE_ARY,
     vals OUT VAL_ARY);
```

There are no restrictions on calling the GET_CALL_ARGS procedure.

Parameters

Parameter Name	Description
callno	The CALLNO of the RPC as stored in the DEFCALL data dictionary view
startarg	First argument to fetch
argcnt	Number of arguments to fetch
argsize	Largest size of a returned argument
tran_db	Global name of database deferring the call (also stored in DEF-CALL)
tran_id	The deferred_tran_id parameter for the call (also stored in DEF-CALL)
date_fmt	Date format mask

Parameter Name	Description
types	Output array for argument types
vals	Output array for argument values

Exceptions

Exception Name	Number	Description
NO_DATA_FOUND	–00100	Specified argument does not exist for specified RPC.

DBMS_DEFER_QUERY.GET_*datatype*_ARG

The GET_*datatype*_ARG function returns a value of a certain type (specified by *datatype*). The type of the returned value corresponds to the value of the argument specified by arg_no in the deferred RPC corresponding to callno.

There is one variant of the GET_*datatype*_ARG function for each of the Oracle-supplied datatypes.

```
FUNCTION DBMS_DEFER_QUERY.GET_datatype_ARG
   (callno IN NUMBER,
    deferred_tran_db IN VARCHAR2
    arg_no IN NUMBER,
    deferred_tran_id IN VARCHAR2 DEFAULT NULL)
   RETURN arg;
```

datatype can be any type in the following table.

Oracle7 and Oracle8	Oracle8 Only
CHAR	NCHAR
DATE	NVARCHAR2
NUMBER	BLOB
RAW	CLOB
ROWID	NCLOB
VARCHAR2	

Therefore, any of the following are valid:

```
FUNCTION DBMS_DEFER_QUERY.GET_CHAR_ARG...
FUNCTION DBMS_DEFER_QUERY.GET_DATE_ARG...
FUNCTION DBMS_DEFER_QUERY.GET_NUMBER_ARG...
FUNCTION DBMS_DEFER_QUERY.GET_RAW_ARG...
FUNCTION DBMS_DEFER_QUERY.GET_ROWID_ARG...
FUNCTION DBMS_DEFER_QUERY.GET_VARCHAR2_ARG...
FUNCTION DBMS_DEFER_QUERY.GET_NCHAR_ARG...
FUNCTION DBMS_DEFER_QUERY.GET_NVARCHAR2_ARG...
FUNCTION DBMS_DEFER_QUERY.GET_BLOB_ARG...
FUNCTION DBMS_DEFER_QUERY.GET_CLOB_ARG...
FUNCTION DBMS_DEFER_QUERY.GET_NCLOB_ARG...
```

Parameters have the same meanings described for the GET_ARG_TYPE procedure.

Exceptions

Exception Name	Number	Description
NO_DATA_FOUND	–00100	Specified argument does not exist for specified RPC.
WRONG_TYPE	–26564	Specified argument is not of type *datatype*.

DBMS_DEFER_SYS: Managing Deferred Transactions

The DBMS_DEFER_SYS package provides a number of programs for administrative tasks associated with deferred transactions.

How the Package Is Used

This package is used primarily to administer an advanced replication environment. DBAs can use the procedures to execute deferred transactions, to control what nodes are available for them, and to schedule their execution.

Installation and Access

The DBMS_DEFER_SYS package is created when the Oracle database is installed. The *dbmsdefr.sql* script (found in the built-in packages source directory), contains the source code for this package's specification. This script is called by *catrep.sql*, which must be run to install the advanced replication packages. The wrapped SQL script *prvtrctf.sql* creates the public synonym DBMS_DEFER_SYS. No EXECUTE privileges are granted on DBMS_DEFER_SYS; only the owner (SYS) and those with the EXECUTE ANY PROCEDURE system privilege may execute the package.

DBMS_DEFER_SYS Procedures

Procedure Name	Description
ADD_DEFAULT_DEST	Adds a destination to the DEFDEFAULTDEST data dictionary view
COPY	Creates a copy of an RPC with a different destination
DELETE_DEFAULT_DEST	Deletes a destination from the DEFDEFAULTDEST data dictionary view
DELETE_ERROR	Deletes an error from the DEFERROR data dictionary view
DELETE_TRAN	Deletes a transaction from the DEFTRANDEST data dictionary view
DISABLED	Returns a Boolean indicating whether deferred transactions from the current site to the destination site are disabled

Procedure Name	Description
EXCLUDE_PUSH	Acquires a lock to disable deferred pushes
EXECUTE	Executes an RPC immediately
EXECUTE_ERROR	Reexecutes an RPC that failed previously
PURGE	Purges transactions that have been propagated from the deferred transaction queue
PUSH	Pushes a queued transaction to a destination node
REGISTER_PROPAGATOR	Makes the designated user the propagator for the local database
SCHEDULE_EXECUTION	Schedules automatic RPC pushes between a master or snapshot site and another master site
SCHEDULE_PURGE	Schedules the automatic purge of transactions that have been propagated from the queue
SCHEDULE_PUSH	Schedules automatic pushes to destination node
SET_DISABLED	Disables deferred transactions between the current site and a destination site
UNREGISTER_PROPAGATOR	Complement to REGISTER_PROPAGATOR; revokes privileges granted to make user the local database's propagator
UNSCHEDULE_EXECUTION	Stops automatic RPC pushes between a master or snapshot site and another master site
UNSCHEDULE_PURGE	Complement to SCHEDULE_PURGE; unschedules the automatic purge of transactions that have been propagated to the queue
UNSCHEDULE_PUSH	Complement to SCHEDULE_PUSH; unschedules automatic pushes to destination node

DBMS_DEFER_SYS Exceptions

Exception Name	Number	Description
crt_err_err	−23324	Parameter type does not match actual type.

DBMS_DEFER_SYS Nonprogram Elements

The following constants defined in the DBMS_DEFER_SYS are used internally in the package:

Type and Name	Description
CONSTANT parm_buffer_size	Size of long buffer used for packing parameters (= 4096)
CONSTANT default_alert_name	VARCHAR2(30) := ORA$DEFER_ALERT

DBMS_DEFER_SYS.ADD_DEFAULT_DEST

The ADD_DEFAULT_DEST procedure adds records in the DEFDEFAULTDEST data dictionary view. Adding a record to this view effectively specifies a default destination for deferred RPCs.

```
PROCEDURE DBMS_DEFER_SYS.ADD_DEFAULT_DEST
    (dblink IN VARCHAR2);
```

dblink is the global name of the destination site being added.

There are no restrictions on calling ADD_DEFAULT.DEST. Changes you make to DEFDEFAULTDEST affect future calls only, not calls that may already be queued.

Exceptions

Exception Name	Number	Description
ORA-23352	−23352	Specified destination is already in the DEFDEFAULT-DEST data dictionary view.

DBMS_DEFER_SYS.COPY (Oracle7 only)

The COPY procedure copies a specified deferred transaction. Oracle queues the copied transaction to the new destinations that you specify.

```
PROCEDURE DBMS_DEFER_SYS.COPY
    (deferred_tran_id IN VARCHAR2,
     deferred_tran_db IN VARCHAR2,
     destination_list IN dbms_defer.node_list_t,
     destination_count IN BINARY_INTEGER);
```

There are no restrictions on calling COPY.

Parameters

Parameter Name	Description
deferred_tran_id	ID from the DEFTRAN data dictionary view to be copied
deferred_tran_db	Global name of the originating database
destination_list	PL/SQL table listing global names of databases to which the transaction is to be sent
destination_count	Number of entries in destination_list

Exceptions

Exception Name	Number	Description
NO_DATA_FOUND	−01403	Specified deferred_tran_id does not exist.

DBMS_DEFER.SYS.DELETE_DEFAULT_DEST

The DELETE_DEFAULT_DEST procedure deletes records in the DEFDEFAULT-DEST data dictionary view. Deleting a record effectively removes a default destination for deferred RPCs.

```
PROCEDURE DBMS_DEFER_SYS.DELETE_DEFAULT_DEST
    (dblink IN VARCHAR2);
```

dblink is the global name of the destination site being deleted.

There are no restrictions on calling DELETE_DEFAULT_DEST, and the procedure raises no exceptions.

DBMS_DEFER_SYS.DELETE_ERROR

The DELETE_ERROR procedure allows you to delete transactions from the DEF-ERROR data dictionary view. The procedure also deletes the related entries from DEFCALL, DEFTRAN, and DEFTRANDEST. Use DELETE_ERROR if you have manually resolved a transaction that initially failed.

```
PROCEDURE DBMS_DEFER_SYS.DELETE_ERROR
    (deferred_tran_id IN VARCHAR2,
     deferred_tran_db IN VARCHAR2,
     destination      IN VARCHAR2);
```

There are no restrictions on calling DELETE_ERROR.

Parameters

Parameter Name	Description
deferred_tran_id	ID from the DEFTRAN data dictionary view of the transaction to be deleted from DEFERROR. If NULL, all entries for the specified deferred_tran_db and destination are deleted.
deferred_tran_db	Global name of the originating database. If NULL, all entries for the specified deferred_tran_id and destination are deleted.
destination	Global name of the destination database. If NULL, all entries for the specified deferred_tran_id and deferred_tran_db are deleted.

Exceptions

Exception Name	Number	Description
NO_DATA_FOUND	−01403	Specified deferred_tran_id does not exist, specified deferred_tran_db does not exist, or specified destination does not exist.

DBMS_DEFER_SYS.DELETE_TRAN

The DELETE_TRAN procedure deletes deferred transactions. You might want to do this if you have applied the call manually or if you remove a node from your environment. The procedure deletes the call from the DEFTRANDEST data dictionary view and also from DEFCALLDEST (if it is an RPC). If the original call has been applied to all other destinations, then the procedure also removes the entries from DEFCALL and DEFTRAN.

```
PROCEDURE DBMS_DEFER_SYS.DELETE_TRAN
    (deferred_tran_id IN VARCHAR2,
     deferred_tran_db IN VARCHAR2,
     destination      IN VARCHAR2);
```

There are no restrictions on calling DELETE_TRAN.

Parameters

Parameter Name	Description
deferred_tran_id	ID from the DEFTRAN data dictionary view of the transaction to be deleted from DEFERROR. If NULL, all entries for the specified deferred_tran_db and destination are deleted.
deferred_tran_db	Global name of the originating database. If NULL, all entries for the specified deferred_tran_id and destination are deleted.
destination	Global name of the destination database. If NULL, all entries for the specified deferred_tran_id and deferred_tran_db are deleted.

Exceptions

Exception Name	Number	Description
NO_DATA_FOUND	–01403	Specified deferred_tran_id does not exist, specified deferred_tran_db does not exist, or specified destination does not exist.

DBMS_DEFER_SYS.DISABLED

The DISABLED function returns the Boolean value TRUE if the deferred RPCs to the specified destination have been disabled (with SET_DISABLED) and returns FALSE otherwise.

```
FUNCTION DBMS_DEFER_SYS.DISABLED
    (destination IN VARCHAR2) RETURN BOOLEAN;
```

destination is the global name of the destination database.

There are no restrictions on calling the DISABLED function.

Exceptions

Exception Name	Number	Description
NO_DATA_FOUND	−01403	Specified destination is not in the DEFSCHEDULE data dictionary view.

DBMS_DEFER_SYS.EXCLUDE_PUSH (Oracle8 Only)

Oracle8 uses a slightly different mechanism to propagate transactions to remote databases. Instead of deleting transactions from the local queue as soon as they are delivered to a remote site, Oracle purges the queue as a separate process. This strategy enhances performance because there is no need for a two-phase commit when transactions are propagated. In addition, Oracle8 includes support for parallel propagation, which means that multiple transactions can be delivered to the destinations simultaneously if they are not dependent on each other.

```
FUNCTION DBMS_DEFER_SYS.EXCLUDE_PUSH
    (timeout IN INTEGER) RETURN INTEGER;
```

timeout is the time to wait to acquire a lock that disables pushes. Specify DBMS_LOCK.MAXWAIT to wait indefinitely.

The EXCLUDE_PUSH function may return the values shown in the following table:

Value	Meaning
0	Normal successful completion
1	Timed out waiting for lock
2	Unsuccessful due to deadlock
4	Lock is already owned

DBMS_DEFER_SYS.EXECUTE

The DBMS_DEFER.CALL procedure, discussed earlier, neither executes nor pushes transactions to the destination databases; it simply queues them. In order to propagate the deferred call to the destinations and to execute it there, you must use the DBMS_DEFER_SYS package's EXECUTE procedure. EXECUTE forces immediate execution of a deferred transaction from the current master or snapshot site.

```
PROCEDURE DBMS_DEFER_SYS.EXECUTE
    (destination IN VARCHAR2,
     stop_on_error IN BOOLEAN := FALSE,
     transaction_count IN BINARY_INTEGER := 0,
     execution_seconds IN BINARY_INTEGER := 0,
     execute_as_user IN BOOLEAN := FALSE,
     delay_seconds IN NATURAL := 0,
     batch_size IN NATURAL := 0);
```

There are no restrictions on calling EXECUTE.

Parameters

Parameter Name	Description
destination	Global name of the destination database.
stop_on_error	If TRUE, execution of queued transactions stops if an error is encountered. If FALSE (the default), execution continues unless destination is unavailable.
transaction_count	If > 0, maximum number of transactions to execute.
execution_seconds	If > 0, maximum number of seconds to spend executing transactions.
execute_as_user	If TRUE, the execution of deferred transactions is authenticated at the remote system using the authentication context of the session user. If FALSE (the default), the execution is authenticated at the remote system using the authentication contexts of the users that originally queued the deferred transactions (indicated in the origin_user column of the DEFTRAN data dictionary view). This parameter is obsolete in Oracle8, which executes transactions under the context of the propagator.
delay_seconds	If > 0, routine sleeps for this many seconds before resuming when there are no more transactions to push to destination.
batch_size	The number of deferred transactions executed before committing. If batch_size = 0, a commit occurs after each deferred transaction. If batch_size > 0, a commit occurs when the total number of deferred calls executed exceeds batch_size and a complete transaction has been executed.

Exceptions

If execution stops because of an exception, the EXECUTE procedure raises the last exception encountered.

DBMS_DEFER_SYS.EXECUTE_ERROR

The EXECUTE_ERROR procedure executes transactions in the DEFERROR data dictionary view after the cause of the error has been resolved. As with the DELETE_ERROR and DELETE_TRAN procedures, you may pass NULLs to indicate wildcards.

```
PROCEDURE DBMS_DEFER_SYS.EXECUTE_ERROR
   (deferred_tran_id IN VARCHAR2,
    deferred_tran_db IN VARCHAR2,
    destination      IN VARCHAR2);
```

Parameters

Parameter Name	Description
deferred_tran_id	ID of transaction in the DEFERROR data dictionary view
deferred_tran_db	Global name of database that originated or copied the transaction originally
destination	Global name of destination database

Exceptions

Exception Name	Number	Description
ORA-24275	−24275	destination is NULL, or deferred_tran_id and deferred_tran_db are neither both NULL nor both NOT NULL.

If execution stops because of an exception, the EXECUTE_ERROR procedure raises the last exception encountered.

Restrictions

- The destination parameter may not be NULL.

- The deferred_tran_id and deferred_tran_db parameters must either both be NULL or both be NOT NULL. If they are NULL, all transactions in DEFERROR destined for destination are applied.

DBMS_DEFER_SYS.PURGE (Oracle8 Only)

The PURGE procedure purges transactions that have been propagated from the deferred transaction queue.

```
FUNCTION DBMS_DEFER_SYS.PURGE(
    purge_method IN BINARY_INTEGER := purge_method_quick,
    rollback_segment IN VARCHAR2 := NULL,
    startup_seconds IN BINARY_INTEGER := 0,
    execution_seconds IN BINARY_INTEGER := seconds_infinity,
    delay_seconds IN BINARY_INTEGER := 0,
    transaction_count IN BINARY_INTEGER := transactions_infinity,
    write_trace IN BOOLEAN := FALSE )
RETURN BINARY_INTEGER;
```

Parameters

Parameter Name	Description
purge_method	1 = purge_method_quick (not necessarily complete, but faster). 2 = purge_method_precise (complete purge).
rollback_segment	Which rollback segment should be used.
startup_seconds	Maximum number of seconds to wait for the completion of a previous push to the same destination.
execution_seconds	If > 0, maximum number of seconds to spend executing transactions.
delay_seconds	If > 0, routine sleeps for this many seconds before resuming when there are no more transactions to push to destination.
transaction_count	Maximum number of transactions to push per execution.
write_trace	If TRUE, record result in a trace file.

The return values for PURGE are listed in the following table:

Value	Meaning
0	Normal completion after delay_seconds expired
1	Terminated by lock timeout while starting
2	Terminated by exceeding execution_seconds
3	Terminated by exceeding transaction_count
4	Terminated at delivery_order_limit
5	Terminated after errors

Exceptions

Exception Name	Number	Description
argoutofrange	–23427	A parameter value is out of range.
executiondisabled	–23354	Execution is disabled at destination.
dbms_defererror	–23305	An internal error occurred.

DBMS_DEFER_SYS.PUSH

The PUSH function pushes a queued transaction to a destination node.

```
FUNCTION DBMS_DEFER_SYS.PUSH(
    destination IN VARCHAR2,
    parallelism IN BINARY_INTEGER := 0,
    heap_size IN BINARY_INTEGER := 0,
    stop_on_error IN BOOLEAN := FALSE,
    write_trace IN BOOLEAN := FALSE,
    startup_seconds IN BINARY_INTEGER := 0,
    execution_seconds IN BINARY_INTEGER := seconds_infinity,
    delay_seconds IN BINARY_INTEGER := 0,
    transaction_count IN BINARY_INTEGER := transactions_infinity,
    delivery_order_limit IN NUMBER := delivery_order_infinity )
    RETURN BINARY_INTEGER;
```

Parameters

Parameter Name	Description
destination	Global name of the destination database.
parallelism	Degree of parallelism: 　0 = serial (no parallelism) 　1 = parallel propagation with one slave 　n = parallel propagation with n slaves
heap_size	If > 0, maximum number of transactions to examine simultaneously for parallel scheduling computation. If 0, compute this number based on parallelism parameter.
stop_on_error	If TRUE, then stop on the first error, even if not fatal.

Parameter Name	Description
write_trace	If TRUE, record result in a trace file.
startup_seconds	Maximum number of seconds to wait for the completion of a previous push to the same destination.
execution_seconds	Maximum number of seconds to spend on the push before shutting down; defaults to seconds_infinity (i.e., unlimited).
delay_seconds	Shut down push cleanly if queue is empty for this many seconds.
transaction_count	Maximum number of transactions to push per execution.
delivery_order_limit	Shut down cleanly before pushing a transaction with delivery_order > delivery_order_limit.

Return values for PUSH are listed in the following table:

Value	Meaning
0	Normal completion after delay_seconds expired
1	Terminated by lock timeout while starting
2	Terminated by exceeding execution_seconds
3	Terminated by exceeding transaction_count
4	Terminated at delivery_order_limit
5	Terminated after errors

Exceptions

Exception Name	Number	Description
commfailure	−23302	Communication failure.
crt_err_err	−23324	Error creating DEFERROR entry.
deferred_rpc_quiesce	−23326	The system is being quiesced.
executiondisabled	−23354	Execution is disabled at destination.
incompleteparallelpush	−23388	Internal error.
missingpropagator	−23357	A propagator does not exist.

DBMS_DEFER_SYS.REGISTER_PROPAGATOR (Oracle8 Only)

The REGISTER_PROPAGATOR procedure makes a designated user the propagator for the local database.

```
PROCEDURE DBMS_DEFER_SYS.REGISTER_PROPAGATOR
    (username IN VARCHAR2);
```

username is the name of the account to which privileges are to be granted.

Exceptions

Exception Name	Number	Description
alreadypropagator	–23393	User username is already the propagator for this database.
duplicatepropagator	–23394	Database already has a propagator account.
missinguser	–23362	User username does not exist.

DBMS_DEFER_SYS.SCHEDULE_EXECUTION

If you are using the advanced replication facilities or if your application queues deferred RPCs on a continual basis, then you should schedule the calls to the EXECUTE procedure at prescribed intervals for each destination. The SCHEDULE_EXECUTION procedure does just that by placing calls to the EXECUTE procedure in the job queue.

```
PROCEDURE DBMS_DEFER_SYS.SCHEDULE_EXECUTION
    (dblink IN VARCHAR2,
     interval IN VARCHAR2,
     next_date IN DATE,
     reset IN BOOLEAN default FALSE,
     stop_on_error IN BOOLEAN := NULL,
     transaction_count IN BINARY_INTEGER := NULL,
     execution_seconds IN BINARY_INTEGER := NULL,
     execute_as_user IN BOOLEAN := NULL,
     delay_seconds IN NATURAL := NULL,
     batch_size IN NATURAL := NULL);
```

The SCHEDULE_EXECUTION procedure does not raise any exceptions nor are there any restrictions on calling this procedure.

Parameters

Parameter Name	Description
dblink	Global name of the destination database.
interval	Frequency with which to execute the RPC.
next_date	First time to execute transactions queued for dblink.
reset	If TRUE, then last_txn_count, last_error, and last_msg are nulled in DEFSCHEDULE data dictionary view for this dblink.
stop_on_error	If not NULL, value is used by the call to EXECUTE.
transaction_count	If not NULL, value is used by the call to EXECUTE.
execution_seconds	If not NULL, value is used by the call to EXECUTE.
execute_as_user	If not NULL, value is used by the call to DBMS_DEFER_SYS.EXECUTE (obsolete in Oracle8).
delay_seconds	If not NULL, value is used by the call to EXECUTE.
batch_size	If not NULL, value is used by the call to EXECUTE.

If an entry for dblink already exists in the DEFSCHEDULE data dictionary view with non-NULL values for next_date and interval, you do not need to specify these values in the call to SCHEDULE_EXECUTION. If you do specify interval and/or next_date, then any previous values in DEFSCHEDULE will be overwritten. If there is no entry for dblink in DEFSCHEDULE, then you must supply a value for interval and/or next_date.

DBMS_DEFER_SYS.SCHEDULE_PURGE (Oracle8 Only)

The SCHEDULE_PURGE procedure schedules the automatic purge of transactions that have been propagated from the queue.

```
PROCEDURE DBMS_DEFER_SYS.SCHEDULE_PURGE(
    interval IN VARCHAR2,
    next_date IN DATE,
    reset IN BOOLEAN := FALSE,
    purge_method IN BINARY_INTEGER := NULL,
    rollback_segment IN VARCHAR2 := NULL,
    startup_seconds IN BINARY_INTEGER := NULL,
    execution_seconds IN BINARY_INTEGER := NULL,
    delay_seconds IN BINARY_INTEGER := NULL,
    transaction_count IN BINARY_INTEGER := NULL,
    write_trace IN BOOLEAN := NULL );
```

Parameters

Parameter Name	Description
interval	Frequency with which to execute the call.
next_date	First time to execute the purge.
reset	If TRUE, last_txn_count, last_error, and last_msg are nulled in DEFSCHEDULE data dictionary view.
purge_method	1 = purge_method_quick (not necessarily complete, but faster). 2 = purge_method_precise (complete purge).
rollback_segment	Which rollback segment should be used.
startup_seconds	Maximum number of seconds to wait for the completion of a previous push to the same destination.
execution_seconds	Maximum number of seconds to spend on the push before shutting down; defaults to seconds_infinity (i.e., unlimited).
delay_seconds	If > 0, routine sleeps for this many seconds before resuming when there are no more transactions to push to destination.
transaction_count	Maximum number of transactions to push per execution.
write_trace	If TRUE, record the result in a trace file.

DBMS_DEFER_SYS.SCHEDULE_PUSH (Oracle8 Only)

The SCHEDULE_PUSH procedure schedules automatic pushes to the destination node.

```
PROCEDURE DBMS_DEFER_SYS.SCHEDULE_PUSH(
    destination IN VARCHAR2,
    interval IN VARCHAR2,
    next_date IN DATE,
    reset IN BOOLEAN := FALSE,
    parallelism IN BINARY_INTEGER := NULL,
    heap_size IN BINARY_INTEGER := NULL,
    stop_on_error IN BOOLEAN := NULL,
    write_trace IN BOOLEAN := NULL,
    startup_seconds IN BINARY_INTEGER := NULL,
    execution_seconds IN BINARY_INTEGER := NULL,
    delay_seconds IN BINARY_INTEGER := NULL,
    transaction_count IN BINARY_INTEGER := NULL );
```

Parameters

Parameter Name	Description
destination	Global name of the destination database.
interval	Frequency with which to execute the call.
next_date	First time to push transactions queued for destination.
reset	If TRUE, last_txn_count, last_error, and last_msg are nulled in DEFSCHEDULE data dictionary view for this destination.

parallelism	Degree of parallelism:
	    0 = serial (no parallelism)
	    1 = parallel propagation with one slave
	    n = parallel propagation with n slaves

heap_size	If > 0, maximum number of transactions to examine simultaneously for parallel scheduling computation. If 0, compute this number based on parallelism parameter.
stop_on_error	If TRUE, stop on the first error, even if not fatal.
write_trace	If TRUE, record the result in a trace file.
startup_seconds	Maximum number of seconds to wait for the completion of a previous push to the same destination.
execution_seconds	Maximum number of seconds to spend on the push before shutting down; defaults to seconds_infinity (i.e., unlimited).
delay_seconds	If > 0, routine sleeps for this many seconds before resuming when there are no more transactions to push to destination.
transaction_count	Maximum number of transactions to push per execution.

DBMS_DEFER_SYS.SET_DISABLED

The SET_DISABLED procedure disables or enables propagation to the specified destination. If you are managing a replicated environment, you might want to disable propagation to a given site while you perform maintenance. If you disable propagation while RPCs are being delivered to the destination database, the delivery will be allowed to complete.

```
PROCEDURE DBMS_DEFER_SYS.SET_DISABLED
    (destination IN VARCHAR2,
     disabled IN BOOLEAN := TRUE);
```

Parameters

Parameter Name	Description
destination	Global name of the destination database
disabled	Flag indicating whether calls are to be disabled (TRUE) or enabled (FALSE)

If disabled is set to TRUE, propagation to the destination is disabled, although any transactions in progress are allowed to complete. If disabled is set to FALSE, propagation to the destination is enabled, although this does not call EXECUTE.

Exceptions

Exception Name	Number	Description
NO_DATA_FOUND	–01403	Specified destination is not in the DEFSCHEDULE data dictionary view.

Restrictions

You must execute a COMMIT after a call to the SET_DISABLED procedure for the changes to take effect.

DBMS_DEFER_SYS.UNREGISTER_PROPAGATOR (Oracle8 Only)

The UNREGISTER_PROPAGATOR procedure revokes the privileges granted to make a particular user the local database propagator.

```
PROCEDURE DBMS_DEFER_SYS.UNREGISTER_PROPAGATOR
    (username IN VARCHAR2,
     timeout  IN INTEGER  DEFAULT dbms_lock.maxwait);
```

I recommend using the same username as the propagator at all database sites. Also, make sure that the account is the same as the replication administrator (REPADMIN) account.

Parameters

Parameter Name	Description
username	Name of the account for which privileges are to be revoked
timeout	Number of seconds to wait if the propagator account is in use when the call to UNREGISTER_PROPAGATOR is made

Exceptions

Exception Name	Number	Description
missingpropagator	−23357	User username is not a propagator.
propagator_inuse	−23418	The propagator account is in use, and timeout seconds have elapsed.

DBMS_DEFER_SYS.UNSCHEDULE_EXECUTION

When you need to stop the propagation of deferred calls to a given destination, you can do so with the UNSCHEDULE_EXECUTION procedure.

```
PROCEDURE DBMS_DEFER_SYS.UNSCHEDULE_EXECUTION
    (dblink IN VARCHAR2);
```

dblink is the global name of the destination database.

Calling this procedure is analogous to calling DBMS_JOB.REMOVE to remove the job that SCHEDULE_EXECUTION scheduled. The job is removed from the queue, and automatic propagation to the database specified by dblink ceases. Whenever you remove a master definition site, call UNCHEDULE_EXECUTION for the site.

There are no restrictions on calling UNSCHEDULE_EXECUTION.

Exceptions

Exception Name	Number	Description
NO_DATA_FOUND	−01403	Specified destination is not in the DEFSCHEDULE data dictionary view.

DBMS_DEFER_SYS.UNSCHEDULE_PURGE (Oracle8 Only)

The UNSCHEDULE_PURGE procedure is the complement to the SCHEDULE_ PURGE procedure. This procedure unschedules the automatic purge of transactions that have been propagated to the queue.

```
PROCEDURE DBMS_DEFER_SYS.UNSCHEDULE_PURGE;
```

DBMS_DEFER_SYS.UNSCHEDULE_PUSH (Oracle8 Only)

The UNSCHEDULE_PUSH procedure is the complement to the SCHEDULE_PUSH procedure. This procedure unschedules automatic pushes to the destination node.

```
PROCEDURE DBMS_DEFER_SYS.UNSCHEDULE_PUSH(dblink IN VARCHAR2);
```

dblink is the global name of the database to which pushes are to be unscheduled.

Exceptions

Exception Name	Number	Description
NO_DATA_FOUND	–00100	No pushes to dblink exist.

DBMS_OFFLINE_OG: Performing Site Instantiation

When you add a new site to your replicated environment, you must not only create the replicated objects but also populate snapshots and replicated tables with a copy of the current data. Although you can set the copy_rows parameter to TRUE in your call to the DBMS_REPCAT package's CREATE_MASTER_REPOBJECT or ADD_MASTER_DATABASE procedure, this option is not practical for schemas that are large or complex.

The DBMS_OFFLINE_OG package provides a more feasible method of site instantiation. The general idea is that you export data from an existing master site and import it into the new master site. While the import is taking place, the existing master site's queue data updates to the new site, but the updates are not actually sent until the load is complete. This package lets you perform much of the instantiation without quiescing the entire replication group.

How the Package Is Used

The following table summarizes the steps you follow when using DBMS_OFFLINE_OG.

Step	Where Performed	Activity
1	Master definition site	DBMS_REPCAT.ADD_MASTER_DATABASE
2	Master definition site	DBMS_REPCAT.SUSPEND_MASTER_ACTIVITY
3	Master definition site	DBMS_OFFLINE_OG.BEGIN_INSTANTIATION
4	Any master site	Export replicated schema
5	Master definition site	DBMS_OFFLINE_OG.RESUME_SUBSET_OF_MASTERS
6	New site	DBMS_OFFLINE_OG.BEGIN_LOAD
7	New site	Import data from Step 4
8	New site	DBMS_OFFLINE_OG.END_LOAD
9	Master definition site	DBMS_OFFLINE_OG.END_INSTANTIATION

Installation and Access

The DBMS_OFFLINE_OG package is created when the Oracle database is installed. The *dbmsofln.sql* script (found in the built-in packages source directory) contains the source code for this package's specification. This script is called by *catrep.sql*, which must be run to install the advanced replication packages. The wrapped SQL script *prvtofln.plb* creates the public synonym DBMS_OFFLINE_OG. No EXECUTE privileges are granted on DBMS_OFFLINE_OG; only the owner (SYS) and those with the EXECUTE ANY PROCEDURE system privilege may execute the package.

DBMS_OFFLINE_OG Procedures

Procedure Name	Description
BEGIN_INSTANTIATION	Call from master definition site to flag beginning of offline instantiation
BEGIN_LOAD	Call from new master site prior to importing data
END_INSTANTIATION	Call from master definition site to flag end of offline instantiation
END_LOAD	Call from new master site after importing data
RESUME_SUBSET_OF_MASTERS	Call from master definition site to resume replication activity for existing sites while new site is instantiated

DBMS_OFFLINE_OG Exceptions

Name	Number	Description
badargument	−23430	gname, sname, master_site, or snapshot_oname is NULL or ' '.
sitealreadyexists	−23432	new_site already exists.
unknownsite	−23434	new_site is not known at the master definition site (i.e., not in the DBA_REPSITES data dictionary view).
wrongsite	−23433	BEGIN_LOAD is executed at a site other than new_site.
wrongstate	−23431	The site is not in the appropriate state (normal or quiesced) for the attempted activity.

DBMS_OFFLINE_OG Nonprogram Elements

Type and Name	Description
TYPE SetOfSiteType	Table of VARCHAR2(256)

SetOfSiteType is a PL/SQL table that is used internally.

DBMS_OFFLINE_OG.BEGIN_INSTANTIATION

The BEGIN_INSTANTIATION procedure is called from the master definition site to flag the beginning of offline instantiation.

```
PROCEDURE DBMS_OFFLINE_OG.BEGIN_INSTANTIATION
   (gname IN VARCHAR2,
    new_site IN VARCHAR2);
```

Parameters

Parameter Name	Description
gname	The replication group to which the site is being added
new_site	The global name of the new site

Exceptions

Exception Name	Number	Description
badargument	−23430	Group gname is NULL or ' '.
missingrepgroup	−23373	Group gname does not exist.
nonmasterdef	−23312	Routine is not being called from the master definition site.
sitealreadyexists	−23432	new_site already exists.
wrongstate	−23431	Group gname is not in NORMAL state at the master definition site.

Restrictions

- This procedure must be run from the master definition site.

- Group gname must be quiesced.

DBMS_OFFLINE_OG.BEGIN_LOAD

Call the BEGIN_LOAD procedure from the new master site before you begin importing data. The effect is to disable triggers so that data cannot be modified during the import and to disable the propagation of changes to other master sites.

```
PROCEDURE DBMS_OFFLINE_OG.BEGIN_LOAD
    (gname IN VARCHAR2,
     new_site IN VARCHAR2);
```

Parameters are identical to those given for the BEGIN_INSTANTIATION procedure.

Exceptions

Exception Name	Number	Description
badargument	−23430	Group gname is NULL or ' '.
missingrepgroup	−23373	Group gname does not exist.
wrongsite	−23433	BEGIN_LOAD or END_LOAD is executed at a site other than new_site.
wrongstate	−23431	Group gname is not in NORMAL state at the master definition site.

Restrictions

This procedure must be run from the new site prior to importing the replicated schema. The effect is to add the new site to the set of masters in a normal state—that is, all propagation is enabled among all sites.

DBMS_OFFLINE_OG.END_INSTANTIATION

You call the END_INSTANTIATION procedure from the master definition site to flag the end of offline instantiation.

```
PROCEDURE DBMS_OFFLINE_OG.END_INSTANTIATION
    (gname IN VARCHAR2,
     new_site IN VARCHAR2);
```

Parameters are identical to those described for the BEGIN_INSTANTIATION procedure.

Exceptions

Exception Name	Number	Description
badargument	−23430	Group gname is NULL or ' '.
missingrepgroup	−23373	Group gname does not exist.
nonmasterdef	−23312	Routine is not being called from the master definition site.
sitealreadyexists	−23432	new_site already exists.
wrongstate	−23431	Group gname is not in NORMAL state at the master definition site.

Restrictions

- This procedure must be run from the master definition site.

- Group gname must be in the NORMAL state at the master definition site.

DBMS_OFFLINE_OG.END_LOAD

Call the END_LOAD procedure from the new master site when you are finished importing data. The effect is to enable propagation to all other sites participating in the replication.

```
PROCEDURE DBMS_OFFLINE_OG.END_LOAD
    (gname IN VARCHAR2,
     new_site IN VARCHAR2);
```

Parameters are identical to those given for the BEGIN_INSTANTIATION procedure.

Exceptions

Exception Name	Number	Description
badargument	−23430	Group gname is NULL or ' '.
missingrepgroup	−23373	Group gname does not exist.
wrongsite	−23433	BEGIN_LOAD or END_LOAD is executed at a site other than new_site.
wrongstate	−23431	Group gname is not in NORMAL state at the master definition site.

Restrictions

This procedure must be run from the new site after the data is imported.

DBMS_OFFLINE_OG.RESUME_SUBSET_OF_MASTERS

Call this procedure from the master definition site to allow propagation of replication activity among all master sites except the site indicated by the new_site parameter. Upon successful completion, the status of gname is NORMAL in all master sites except for new_site, where the group is still quiesced.

```
PROCEDURE DBMS_OFFLINE_OG.RESUME_SUBSET_OF_MASTERS
    (gname IN VARCHAR2,
    new_site IN VARCHAR2);
```

Parameters are identical to those given for the BEGIN_INSTANTIATION procedure.

Exceptions

Exception Name	Number	Description
badargument	−23430	Group gname is NULL or ' '.
missingrepgroup	−23373	Group gname does not exist.
nonmasterdef	−23312	Routine is not being called from master definition site.
sitealreadyexists	−23432	new_site already exists.
wrongstate	−23431	Group gname is not in NORMAL state at the master definition site.

Restrictions

* This procedure must be run from the master definition site.
* Group gname must be in the quiesced state at the master definition site.

DBMS_OFFLINE_SNAPSHOT: Performing Offline Snapshot Instantiation

The DBMS_OFFLINE_SNAPSHOT package allows you to instantiate snapshots without having to run the CREATE SNAPSHOT command or the DBMS_ REPCAT.SNAPSHOT_REPOBJECT procedure over the network. Doing offline instantiation in this way is particularly useful in cases in which you wish to instantiate a snapshot site with a large amount of data in an advanced replication environment. Offline instantiation refers to the population of snapshots with the import and export utilities, as opposed to using the DBMS_SNAPSHOT.REFRESH procedure. This technique is less time consuming and less taxing on your network, and it minimizes the time your environment must be quiesced.

How the Package Is Used

The following table summarizes the steps you follow when using DBMS_ OFFLINE_SNAPSHOT:

Step	Where Performed	Activity
1	Master site	Create snapshot log on table(s) to be snapshotted (optional, but recommended).
2	Master site	Create a snapshot locally on the table(s) to be snapshotted.
3	Master site	Export SNAP$_*table_name* table(s) created in Step 2 as the schema owner.
4	New snapshot site	DBMS_REPCAT.CREATE_SNAPSHOT_REPGROUP.
5	New snapshot site	DBMS_OFFLINE_SNAPSHOT.BEGIN_LOAD.
6	New snapshot site	Import SNAP$_*table_name* tables from export file created in Step 3.
7	New snapshot site	DBMS_OFFLINE_SNAPSHOT.END_LOAD.
8	Master site	Drop snapshot(s) created in Step 2.

Installation and Access

The DBMS_OFFLINE_SNAPSHOT package is created when the Oracle database is installed. The *dbmsofln.sql* script (found in the built-in packages source directory) contains the source code for this package's specification. This script is called by *catrep.sql*, which must be run to install the advanced replication packages. The wrapped SQL script *prvtofln.plb* creates the public synonym DBMS_OFFLINE_ SNAPSHOT. No EXECUTE privileges are granted on DBMS_OFFLINE_SNAPSHOT; only the owner (SYS) and those with the EXECUTE ANY PROCEDURE system privilege may execute the package.

DBMS_OFFLINE_SNAPSHOT *Procedures*

Name	Description
BEGIN_LOAD	Call before beginning to load data from an export file
END_LOAD	Call after the load is complete

DBMS_OFFLINE_SNAPSHOT *Exceptions*

Name	Number	Description
badargument	−23430	The gname, sname, master_site, or snapshot_oname parameter is NULL or ' '.
missingremotesnap	−23361	The snapshot_oname parameter does not exist at the remote master site (master_site parameter).
snaptabmismatch	−23363	The base table name of the snapshot at the master site and snapshot site do not match.

DBMS_OFFLINE_SNAPSHOT.BEGIN_LOAD

Call the BEGIN_LOAD procedure from the new snapshot site prior to importing the SNAP$*table_name* tables that were exported from the master site. This call creates empty snapshots and supporting objects. The specifications for the Oracle7 and Oracle8 versions differ as follows.

Oracle7 specification:

```
PROCEDURE DBMS_OFFLINE_SNAPSHOT.BEGIN_LOAD
    (gname IN VARCHAR2,
     sname IN VARCHAR2,
     master_site IN VARCHAR2,
     snapshot_oname IN VARCHAR2,
     storage_c IN VARCHAR2 := '',
     comment IN VARCHAR2 := '');
```

Oracle8 specification:

```
PROCEDURE DBMS_OFFLINE_SNAPSHOT.BEGIN_LOAD
    (gname IN VARCHAR2,
     sname IN VARCHAR2,
     master_site IN VARCHAR2,
     snapshot_oname IN VARCHAR2,
     storage_c IN VARCHAR2 := '',
     comment IN VARCHAR2 := '',
     min_communication IN BOOLEAN := TRUE );
```

The BEGIN_LOAD procedure does not raise any exceptions.

Parameters

Parameter Name	Description
gname	The replication group to which the new snapshot belongs.
sname	The schema that owns the new snapshot.
master_site	The global name of the snapshot master site.
snapshot_oname	The name of the temporary snapshot created at the master site.
storage_c	Optional storage clause for the new snapshot.
comment	Optional comment for the snapshot; stored with entry in DBA_SNAPSHOTS if supplied.
min_communication (Oracle8 only)	The min_communication parameter controls how the update trigger on updateable snapshot queues changes back to the master site. If this parameter is set to TRUE (the default), then old column values are sent only if the update changes their value. New column values are sent only if the column is part of the primary key or if the column is in a column group that has been modified.

Restrictions

This procedure must be run from the new snapshot site prior to importing the replicated schema.

DBMS_OFFLINE_SNAPSHOT.END_LOAD

Call the END_LOAD procedure after the data import (initiated by the BEGIN_LOAD procedure) is complete. Upon successful completion, the new snapshot is instantiated and operational. The specification is the same for Oracle7 and Oracle8:

```
PROCEDURE DBMS_OFFLINE_SNAPSHOT.END_LOAD
    (gname IN VARCHAR2,
     sname IN VARCHAR2,
     snapshot_oname IN VARCHAR2);
```

Parameters have the same meanings as for the BEGIN_LOAD procedure. The END_LOAD procedure does not raise any exceptions.

Restrictions

This procedure must be run from the new snapshot site after importing the replicated schema.

DBMS_RECTIFIER_DIFF: Comparing Replicated Tables

If you are not sure whether the data at two sites are identical, you can use the DBMS_RECTIFIER_DIFF package to find out.

How the Package Is Used

The DBMS_RECTIFIER_DIFF's DIFFERENCES procedure compares two instantiations of a table. The table at one of two sites is considered the reference, or "truth" table, and the other is the "comparison" table. The procedure stores discrepancies between the truth table and comparison table in a "missing rows" table, which the user must create. If differences exist, the DBA can use the RECTIFY procedure to synchronize the comparison table with the truth table. The truth table is not modified.

Installation and Access

The DBMS_RECTIFIER_DIFF package is created when the Oracle database is installed. The *dbmsrepc.sql* script (found in the built-in packages source directory) contains the source code for this package's specification. This script is called by *catrep.sql*, which must be run to install the advanced replication packages. The wrapped SQL script *prvtrctf.sql* creates the public synonym DBMS_RECTIFIER_ DIFF. No EXECUTE privileges are granted on DBMS_RECTIFIER_DIFF; only the owner (SYS) and those with the EXECUTE ANY PROCEDURE system privilege may execute the package.

DBMS_RECTIFIER_DIFF Procedures

Procedure Name	Description
DIFFERENCES	Determines differences between the truth table and the comparison table
RECTIFY	Synchronizes the comparison table with the truth table

DBMS_RECTIFIER_DIFF Exceptions

Exception Name	Number	Description
badmrname	−23377	Truth table and missing rows table are the same.
badname	−23368	sname, oname, missing_rows_sname, or missing_rows_oname is NULL or ' ' .
badnumber	−23366	max_missing is less than 1 or NULL.

Exception Name	Number	Description
cannotbenull	−23369	max_missing is NULL.
dbms_repcat.commfailure	−23302	Remote site is not accessible.
dbms_repcat.missingobject	−23308	One or more of the tables oname1, oname2, missing_rows_oname1, or missing_rows_oname2 do not exist.
dbms_repcat.norepoption	−02094	Replication option is not linked to kernel.
missingprimarykey	−23367	column_list does not contain the table's primary keys. If multiple columns constitute the primary key, then all columns must be specified in column_list.
nosuchsite	−23365	reference_site, comparison_site, or missing_rows_site does not name a site.
notshapeequivalent	−23370	Columns specified in column_list are not the same for sname1.oname1 at site reference_site and sname2.oname2 at site comparison_site.
unknowncolumn	−23371	Columns specified in column_list do not exist in sname1.oname1 and/or sname2.oname2.
unsupportedtype	−23372	column_list contains columns of type LONG, LONG RAW, or MLSLABEL.

DBMS_RECTIFIER_DIFF.DIFFERENCES

The DIFFERENCES procedure compares the data in a table at a master site with the same table at a reference site. The reference site need not be the master definition site.

The procedure stores discrepancies between the reference table and comparison table in a "missing rows" table, which the user must create. It populates the table specified by the missing_rows_oname1 parameter with rows that exist in the reference table but not the comparison table and rows that exist in the comparison table but not the reference table. The table identified by the missing_rows_oname2 parameter has one record for every record in missing_rows_oname1, which identifies which site has the record.

```
PROCEDURE DBMS_RECTIFIER_DIFF.DIFFERENCES
    (sname1 IN VARCHAR2,
     oname1 IN VARCHAR2,
     reference_site IN VARCHAR2 := '',
     sname2 IN VARCHAR2,
     oname2 IN VARCHAR2,
     comparison_site IN VARCHAR2 := '',
     where_clause IN VARCHAR2 := '',
     {column_list IN VARCHAR2 := '' |
     array_columns IN dbms_utility.name_array,},
     missing_rows_sname IN VARCHAR2,
```

```
missing_rows_oname1 IN VARCHAR2,
missing_rows_oname2 IN VARCHAR2,
missing_rows_site IN VARCHAR2 := '',
max_missing IN INTEGER,
commit_rows IN INTEGER := 500);
```

This procedure can take a long time to run and only identifies differences, which then need to be processed with DBMS_RECTIFIER_DIFF.RECTIFY. If the volume of data is significant, it will probably be easier for you to simply reinstantiate the comparison table by importing an export of the reference table.

Parameters

Parameter Name	Description
sname1	Name of the schema that owns oname1.
oname1	Table at the reference site (truth table).
reference_site	The global name of site withthe truth table. If NULL or ' ' (default), the truth table is assumed to be local.
sname2	Name of the schema that owns oname2.
oname2	The comparison table.
comparison_site	The global name of the site with comparison table. If NULL or ' ', table is assumed to be local.
where_clause	Optional predicate that can be used to limit set of rows compared (e.g.,WHERE STATE = 'CA').
column_list	Comma-separated list of one or more columns whose values are to be compared. If NULL or ' ' (default), then all columns are used. There should not be any whitespace after the commas.
array_columns	PL/SQL table of column names; either column_list or array_columns can be passed, not both.
missing_rows_sname	Name of schema that owns missing_rows_oname1.
missing_rows_oname1	Name of table containing records that do not exist in both the truth table and the comparison table.
missing_rows_oname2	Table that holds information telling which table owns each record in missing_rows_oname1.
missing_rows_site	The global name of site where tables missing_rows_oname1 and missing_rows_oname2 exist; if NULL or ' ' (default), tables are assumed to be local.
max_missing	The maximum number of rows to insert into missing_rows_oname1 before exiting; it can be any value > 1.
commit_rows	Commit rows inserted into missing_rows_oname1 after this many records.

Exceptions

Exception Name	Number	Description
badmrname	−23377	oname1 is the same as missing_rows_oname1.
badname	−23368	sname, oname, missing_rows_sname, or missing_rows_oname is NULL or ' '.
badnumber	−23366	max_missing is less than 1 or NULL.
dbms_repcat.commfailure	−23302	Remote site is not accessible.
dbms_repcat.missingobject	−23308	One or more of the tables oname1, oname2, missing_rows_oname1, or missing_rows_oname2 does not exist.
nosuchsite	−23365	reference_site, comparison_site, or missing_rows_site does not name a site.

Restrictions

* You must create tables named in the form missing_rows_sname.missing_rows_oname1 and missing_rows_sname.missing_rows_oname2 before running this procedure.

* The columns in table missing_rows_oname1 must match the columns passed to column_list or array_columns exactly.

* The replication group to which the tables belong must be quiesced.

DBMS_RECTIFIER_DIFF.RECTIFY

The DIFFERENCES procedure paves the way for its companion procedure, REC-TIFY, which synchronizes the reference table (oname1). Before running the REC-TIFY procedure, always make sure that the updates to the comparison table (oname2) will not violate any integrity, check, or NOT NULL constraints. Note that this procedure does not modify the reference table.

The DIFFERENCES and RECTIFY procedures can take a long time to run. If the volume of data is significant, it will probably be easier for you to simply reinstantiate the comparison table by importing an export of the reference table.

```
PROCEDURE DBMS_RECTIFIER_DIFF.RECTIFY
   (sname1 IN VARCHAR2,
   oname1 IN VARCHAR2,
   reference_site IN VARCHAR2 := '',
   sname2 IN VARCHAR2,
   oname2 IN VARCHAR2,
   comparison_site IN VARCHAR2 := '',
   {column_list := '' |
   array_columns IN dbms_utility.name_array},
   missing_rows_sname IN VARCHAR2,
   missing_rows_oname1 IN VARCHAR2,
```

```
missing_rows_oname2 IN VARCHAR2,
missing_rows_site IN VARCHAR2 := '',
commit_rows IN INTEGER := 500);
```

Parameters

Parameter Name	Description
sname1	Name of the schema that owns oname1.
oname1	Table at the reference_site (truth table).
reference_site	The global name of the site with truth table; if NULL or ' ' (default), the truth table is assumed to be local.
sname2	Name of the schema that owns oname2.
oname2	The comparison table.
comparison_site	The global name of the site with comparison table. If NULL or ' ', table is assumed to be local.
column_list	A comma-separated list of one or more columns whose values are to be compared; if NULL or ' ' (default), then all columns are used. There should not be any whitespace after the commas.
array_columns	PL/SQL table of column names; either column_list or array_columns can be passed, not both.
missing_rows_sname	Name of the schema that owns missing_rows_oname1.
missing_rows_oname1	The name of the table containing records that do not exist in both the truth table and the comparison table.
missing_rows_oname2	The table that holds information telling which table owns each record in missing_rows_oname1.
missing_rows_site	The global name of the site where tables missing_rows_oname1 and missing_rows_oname2 exist; if NULL or ' ' (default), tables are assumed to be local.
commit_rows	Commit rows inserted into missing_row_oname1 after this many records.

Exceptions

Exception Name	Number	Description
badname	−23368	sname, oname, missing_rows_sname, or missing_rows_oname is NULL or ' '.
badnumber	−23366	max_missing is less than 1 or NULL.
dbms_repcat.commfailure	−23302	Remote site is not accessible.
dbms_repcat.missingobject	−23308	The table oname1, oname2, missing_rows_oname1, or missing_rows_oname2 does not exist.
dbms_repcat.norepoption	−2094	Replication option is not linked to kernel.
nosuchsite	−23365	reference_site, comparison_site, or missing_rows_site does not name a site.

Restrictions

- The DIFFERENCES procedure must have been run prior to running RECTIFY.

- The replication group to which the tables belong should still be quiesced.

- If duplicate rows exist in the reference table but not the comparison table, they will be inserted into the comparison table.

- If duplicate rows exist in the comparison table but not the reference table, they will be deleted from the comparison table.

DBMS_REFRESH: Managing Snapshot Groups

The DBMS_REFRESH package contains procedures for administering snapshot groups.

How the Package Is Used

A snapshot group is a collection of one or more snapshots that Oracle refreshes in an atomic transaction, guaranteeing that relationships among the master tables are preserved in the snapshot tables.

Installation and Access

The DBMS_REFRESH package is created when the Oracle database is installed. The *dbmssnap.sql* script (found in the built-in packages source directory) contains the source code for this package's specification. This script is called by *catproc.sql*, which is normally run immediately after database creation. The script creates the public synonym DBMS_REFRESH for the package and grants the EXECUTE privilege on the package to public. All Oracle users can reference and make use of this package.

DBMS_REFRESH Procedures

Procedure Name	Description
ADD	Adds one or more snapshots to an existing refresh group
CHANGE	Changes parameters associated with a refresh group
DESTROY	Removes a refresh group
MAKE	Creates a refresh group
REFRESH	Forces a refresh of a refresh group
SUBTRACT	Removes one or more snapshots from a refresh group

DBMS_REFRESH does not define any exceptions.

DBMS_REFRESH Nonprogram Elements

Element Name/Type	Description
aaspriv/BINARY INTEGER	Privilege number for ALTER ANY SNAPSHOT system privilege (107)

DBMS_REFRESH.ADD

Call the ADD procedure to add one or more snapshots to all existing snapshot groups or move a snapshot from one group to another.

```
PROCEDURE DBMS_REFRESH.ADD
    (name IN VARCHAR2,
    {list IN VARCHAR2,| tab IN dbms_utility.uncl_array,}
     lax IN BOOLEAN DEFAULT FALSE );
```

A snapshot group cannot have more than 100 members.

In both Oracle7 and Oracle8, the ADD procedure is overloaded; you can supply the list of snapshots either as a comma-separated string with the list parameter, or as a PL/SQL table with the tab parameter. You must select either the list or tab parameter, but not both.

Parameters

Parameter Name	Description
name	Name of the refresh group to create.
list	A comma-delimited string of snapshots to include in the new refresh group. Use either list or tab to specify the snapshot(s) you want to add.
tab	A PL/SQL table of snapshots to include in the new refresh group. Use either list or tab to specify the snapshot(s) you want to add.
lax	If set to TRUE and the snapshots already exist in a refresh group other than name, the snapshots are first removed from the other group.

Exceptions

Exception Name/Type	Description
aaspriv/BINARY INTEGER	Privilege number for ALTER ANY SNAPSHOT system privilege

Restrictions

- This procedure must be run from the snapshot site.
- A snapshot cannot belong to more than one refresh group.
- If you want to move a snapshot from one refresh group to another, the lax parameter must be set to TRUE, which is not the default.

DBMS_REFRESH.CHANGE

The CHANGE procedure allows you to modify settings associated with a snapshot group. You can change most of the parameters that are available in ADD.

The specifications for CHANGE differ for Oracle7 and Oracle8 as follows. Note that the difference between the Oracle7 and Oracle8 CHANGE specifications is the inclusion of support for parallel propagation and purging in the Oracle8 version.

Oracle7 specification:

```
PROCEDURE DBMS_REFRESH.CHANGE
    (name IN VARCHAR2,
     next_date IN DATE DEFAULT NULL,
     interval IN VARCHAR2 DEFAULT NULL,
     implicit_destroy IN BOOLEAN DEFAULT NULL,
     rollback_seg IN VARCHAR2 DEFAULT NULL,
     push_deferred_rpc IN BOOLEAN DEFAULT NULL,
     refresh_after_errors IN BOOLEAN DEFAULT NULL);
```

Oracle8 specification:

```
PROCEDURE DBMS_REFRESH.CHANGE
    (name IN VARCHAR2,
     next_date IN DATE := NULL,
     interval IN VARCHAR2 := NULL,
     implicit_destroy IN BOOLEAN := NULL,
     rollback_seg IN VARCHAR2 := NULL,
     push_deferred_rpc IN BOOLEAN := NULL,
     refresh_after_errors IN BOOLEAN := NULL,
     purge_option IN BINARY_INTEGER := NULL,
     parallelism IN BINARY_INTEGER := NULL,
     heap_size IN BINARY_INTEGER := NULL);
```

Refer to the ADD section for an explanation of these parameters.

Exceptions

Exception Name	Number	Description
ORA-23404	−23404	Refresh group name does not exist.

Restrictions

This procedure must be run from the snapshot site.

DBMS_REFRESH.DESTROY

Call the DESTROY procedure to destroy a snapshot group. For both Oracle7 and Oracle8, you call DESTROY as follows:

```
PROCEDURE DBMS_REFRESH.DESTROY (name IN VARCHAR2);
```

name is the name of the snapshot group to be destroyed.

Exceptions

Exception Name	Number	Description
ORA-23404	–23404	Refresh group name does not exist.

Restrictions

This procedure must be run from the snapshot site.

DBMS_REFRESH.MAKE

Call the MAKE procedure to create a snapshot group. The specifications for the Oracle7 and Oracle8 versions differ as follows.

Oracle7 specification:

```
PROCEDURE DBMS_REFRESH.MAKE
   (name IN VARCHAR2,
   {list IN VARCHAR2, | tab IN dbms_utility.uncl_array,}
   next_date IN DATE,
   interval IN VARCHAR2,
   implicit_destroy IN BOOLEAN DEFAULT FALSE,
   lax IN BOOLEAN DEFAULT FALSE,
   job IN BINARY_INTEGER DEFAULT 0,
   rollback_seg IN VARCHAR2 DEFAULT NULL,
   push_deferred_rpc IN BOOLEAN DEFAULT TRUE,
   refresh_after_errors IN BOOLEAN DEFAULT FALSE );
```

Oracle8 specification:

```
PROCEDURE DBMS_REFRESH.MAKE
   (name IN VARCHAR2,
   {list IN VARCHAR2, | tab IN dmbs_utility.uncl_array,}
   next_date IN DATE,
   interval IN VARCHAR2,
   implicit_destroy IN BOOLEAN := FALSE,
   lax IN BOOLEAN := FALSE,
   job IN BINARY_INTEGER := 0,
   rollback_seg IN VARCHAR2 := NULL,
   push_deferred_rpc IN BOOLEAN := TRUE,
   refresh_after_errors IN BOOLEAN := FALSE,
   purge_option  IN BINARY_INTEGER := 1,
   parallelism IN BINARY_INTEGER := 0,
   heap_size IN BINARY_INTEGER := 0);
```

The MAKE procedure does not raise any exceptions.

Parameters

Parameter Name	Description
name	Name of the refresh group to create.
list	A comma-delimited string of snapshots to include in the new refresh group. Use either list or tab to specify the snapshot(s) you want to add.

Parameter Name	Description
tab	A PL/SQL table of snapshots to include in the new refresh group. Use either list or tab to specify the snapshot(s) you want to add.
next_date	The time of the next refresh.
interval	A DATE expression indicating the snapshot group's refresh interval.
implicit_destroy	If set to TRUE, the snapshot group is destroyed if all snapshots are removed from it.
lax	If set to TRUE and the snapshot(s) already exist in a refresh group other than name, the snapshot(s) are first removed from the other group.
job	Used by import utility. Always use default value of 0.
rollback_seg	Specifies the rollback segment to use during snapshot refreshes. If set to NULL, the default rollback segment is used.
push_deferred_rpc	For updateable snapshots only. Setting this parameter to TRUE indicates that local updates will be pushed back to the master site (otherwise, local updates will not be visible during the refresh).
refresh_after_errors	For updateable snapshots only. Setting this parameter to TRUE indicates that refreshes should occur even if errors exist in the DEFERROR data dictionary view.

purge_option (Oracle8 only)	If push_deferred_rpc is TRUE, this designates the purge method; default is 1.
	    0 = no purge
	    1 = lazy purge (optimized for time)
	    2 = aggressive purge (complete)

parallelism (Oracle8 only)	If push_deferred_rpc is TRUE, this determines the maximum degree of parallelism; default is 1.
	    0 = serial
	    1 = parallel with 1 slave
	    n = parallel with n slaves ($n > 1$)

heap_size (Oracle8 only)	Used only if parallelism > 0. Sets the maximum number of transactions to be examined simultaneously for determining parallel scheduling. Oracle determines this value internally; you are advised not to use it.

Restrictions

This procedure must be run from the snapshot site.

DBMS_REFRESH.REFRESH

Call REFRESH to refresh a snapshot group. A call to REFRESH causes all members of snapshot group name to be refreshed with the settings that you have designated in MAKE and/or CHANGE.

```
PROCEDURE DBMS_REFRESH.REFRESH (name IN VARCHAR2);
```

name identifies the snapshot group.

Exceptions

Exception Name	Number	Description
ORA-23404	–23404	Refresh group name does not exist.

Restrictions

This procedure must be run from the snapshot site.

DBMS_REFRESH.SUBTRACT

Call the SUBTRACT procedure to subtract a snapshot group.

```
PROCEDURE DBMS_REFRESH.SUBTRACT
    (name IN VARCHAR2,
    {list IN VARCHAR2,| tab IN dbms_utility.uncl_array,}
     lax IN BOOLEAN DEFAULT FALSE );
```

The parameters for the SUBTRACT procedure have the same meaning as in the ADD procedure; refer to the parameter table in that section. Note that you must select the list or tab parameter, but not both.

Exceptions

Exception Name	Number	Description
ORA-23404	–23404	Refresh group name does not exist.

Restrictions

This procedure must be run from the snapshot site.

DBMS_REPCAT: Performing Replication Administration

The DBMS_REPCAT package is the foundation of the replication API. It allows you to perform a wide variety of operations in several categories: advanced replication administration, snapshots, and conflict resolution.

How the Package Is Used

DBMS_REPCAT contains the procedures required to maintain the following aspects of a replicated environment:

- Site priority information
- Column group configuration
- Priority group configuration

- Conflict resolution techniques
- Snapshot propagation
- Object replication support
- Statistics
- Master site configuration

Installation and Access

The DBMS_REPCAT package is created when the Oracle database is installed. The *dbmsrepc.sql* script (found in the built-in packages source directory) contains the source code for this package's specification. This script is called by *catrep.sql*, which must be run to install the advanced replication packages. The script creates the public synonym DBMS_REPCAT. The package procedure DBMS_REPCAT_AUTH.GRANT_SURROGATE_REPCAT grants EXECUTE privileges on the package to the specified grantee. In addition, the package owner (SYS) and users with the EXECUTE ANY PROCEDURE system privilege may execute it.

DBMS_REPCAT Procedures

Procedure Name	Description
ADD_*conflicttype*_RESOLUTION	Adds a custom conflict resolution handler for update, delete, or uniqueness conflicts.
ADD_GROUPED_COLUMN	Adds table column(s) to an existing column group.
ADD_MASTER_DATABASE	Adds a master database to a replication group.
ADD_PRIORITY_*datatype*	Adds a member to an existing priority group.
ADD_SITE_PRIORITY_SITE	Adds a site to an existing site priority group.
ALTER_MASTER_PROPAGATION	Alters the propagation method for a replication group at a given site. Options are SYNCHRONOUS or ASYNCHRONOUS.
ALTER_MASTER_REPOBJECT	Performs DDL on a replicated object.
ALTER_PRIORITY	Changes priority level for a member of a priority group.
ALTER_PRIORITY_*datatype*	Alters the value of a member of a priority group.
ALTER_SITE_PRIORITY	Alters priority level of a site.
ALTER_SITE_PRIORITY_SITE	Designates a site to a given priority level.
ALTER_SNAPSHOT_PROPAGATION	Alters the propagation method for a replication group at a snapshot site.
CANCEL_STATISTICS	Cancels collection of statistics about conflict resolution for a table.

Procedure Name	Description
COMMENT_ON_*conflicttype_*RESOLUTION	Creates a comment on a conflict resolution method, visible in DBA_REPRESOLUTION data dictionary view.
COMMENT_ON_COLUMN_GROUP	Creates or updates a comment on a column group, visible in DBA_REPCOLUMN_GROUP data dictionary view.
COMMENT_ON_PRIORITY_GROUP	Creates or updates comment on a priority group, visible in DBA_REPPRIORITY_GROUP.
COMMENT_ON_REPGROUP	Creates or updates a comment on a replication group, visible in DBA_REPGROUP data dictionary view.
COMMENT_ON_REPOBJECT	Creates or updates a comment on a replicated object, visible in DBA_REPOBJECT data dictionary view.
COMMENT_ON_REPSITES	Creates or updates a comment on a replication site, visible in DBA_REPSITES data dictionary view.
COMMENT_ON_SITE_PRIORITY	Creates or updates a comment on a site priority, visible in DBA_REPRIORITY_GROUP data dictionary view.
CREATE_MASTER_REPGROUP	Creates a master replication group.
CREATE_MASTER_REPOBJECT	Adds an object to a replication group.
CREATE_SNAPSHOT_REPGROUP	Creates a snapshot replication group.
CREATE_SNAPSHOT_REPOBJECT	Adds an object to a snapshot replication group.
DEFINE_COLUMN_GROUP	Creates an empty column group for a replication group.
DEFINE_PRIORITY_GROUP	Creates a priority group for a replication group.
DEFINE_SITE_PRIORITY	Creates a site priority group for a replication group.
DO_DEFERRED_REPCAT_ADMIN	Performs outstanding administrative tasks at local master site.
DROP_*conflicttype*_RESOLUTION	Drops an update, delete, or uniqueness conflict resolution handling technique from a replication group.
DROP_COLUMN_GROUP	Drops a column group from a replication group.
DROP_GROUPED_COLUMN	Drops a column from a column group.
DROP_MASTER_REPGROUP	Drops a replication group.
DROP_MASTER_REPOBJECT	Drops an object from a replication group.
DROP_PRIORITY	Drops a member of a priority group, selected by priority level.
DROP_PRIORITY_*datatype*	Drops a member of a priority group, selected by value.

Procedure Name	Description
DROP_PRIORITY_GROUP	Drops a priority group from a replication group.
DROP_SITE_PRIORITY	Drops a site priority group from a replication group.
DROP_SITE_PRIORITY_SITE	Drops a site from a site priority group, selected by site name.
DROP_SNAPSHOT_REPGROUP	Drops a snapshot replication group.
DROP_SNAPSHOT_REPOBJECT	Drops an object from a snapshot replication group.
EXECUTE_DDL	Specifies DDL to execute at master sites.
GENERATE_REPLICATION_PACKAGE	Generates packages required to replicate a given table.
GENERATE_REPLICATION_SUPPORT	Generates triggers, packages, and procedures required to replicate a given table.
GENERATE_REPLICATION_TRIGGER	Generates triggers and packages required to replicate a given table.
MAKE_COLUMN_GROUP	Creates a column group and adds one or more columns.
PURGE_MASTER_LOG	Deletes entries from the local repcatlog (DBA_REPCATLOG).
PURGE_STATISTICS	Deletes entries from the DBA_REPRESOLU-TION_STATISTICS data dictionary view.
REFRESH_SNAPSHOT_REPGROUP	Refreshes a snapshot replication group.
REGISTER_STATISTICS	Starts collection of statistics for the resolution of update, delete, and uniqueness conflicts for a given table.
RELOCATE_MASTERDEF	Changes the master definition site for a replication group.
REMOVE_MASTER_DATABASES	Drops one or more master databases from a replication group.
REPCAT_IMPORT_CHECK	Confirms a replicated object's validity after an import.
RESUME_MASTER_ACTIVITY	Enables propagation of a replication group that had been quiesced.
SEND_AND_COMPARE_OLD_VALUES	Avoids sending unchanged values when propagation updates to participating master sites.
SET_COLUMNS	Designates alternative column(s) to use instead of a primary to uniquely identify rows of a replicated table.
SUSPEND_MASTER_ACTIVITY	Quiesces a replication group.
SWITCH_SNAPSHOT_MASTER	Remasters a snapshot site to another master site.

Procedure Name	Description
VALIDATE	Diagnoses the status of your replicated environment.
WAIT_MASTER_LOG	Determines whether asynchronous DML has been applied at a master site.

DBMS_REPCAT Exceptions

Exception Name	Number	Description
badsnapname	−23328	Invalid snapshot name (used internally).
commfailure	−23317	Unable to communicate with remote site.
corrupt	−23320	Corruption occurred (used internally during generation of replication support objects).
dbnotcompatible	−23375	Operation not available for current version of RDBMS.
ddlfailure	−23318	DDL failed during object creation or maintenance activity.
duplicatecolumn	−23333	Attempt to add duplicate column to column group.
duplicategroup	−23330	Attempt to add duplicate column group to a replicated table.
duplicateobject	−23309	Replicated object already exists.
duplicateprioritygroup	−23335	Attempt to create duplicate priority group.
duplicaterepgroup	−23374	Attempt to create duplicate snapshot replication group.
duplicateresolution	−23339	Attempt to create duplicate resolution method.
duplicateschema	−23307	Attempt to create duplicate replication group.
duplicatevalue	−23338	Attempt to create duplicate value in a priority group.
fullqueue	−23353	Attempt to drop replication group or schema for which RPC entries are queued.
invalidmethod	−23340	Attempt to use nonexistent conflict resolution method.
invalidparameter	−23342	Invalid number of columns in call to ADD_UNIQUE_RESOLUTION.
invalidpropmode	−23380	Invalid propagation mode (used internally).
invalidqualifier	−23378	Invalid qualifier (used internally).
masternotremoved	−23356	Master site not removed (used internally).
missingcolumn	−23334	Reference to nonexistent column.
missingconstraint	−23344	Missing constraint (used internally).
missingfunction	−23341	User function does not exist.
missinggroup	−23331	Column group does not exist.

Exception Name	Number	Description
missingobject	-23308	Object does not exist as a table.
missingprioritygroup	-23336	Priority group does not exist.
missingremoteobject	-23381	Master object has not had replication support generated.
missingrepgroup	-23373	Replication group does not exist.
missingresolution	-23343	Referenced conflict resolution method does not exist.
missingschema	-23306	Schema does not exist.
missingvalue	-23337	Missing value (used internally).
misssnapobject	-23355	Snapshot object does not exist.
nonmaster	-23313	Site is not a master site.
nonmasterdef	-23312	Site is not a master definition site.
nonsnapshot	-23314	Site is not a snapshot site.
norepoption	-23364	Replication option not installed.
notnormal	-23311	Replication group is not in normal propagation mode.
notquiesced	-23310	Replication group is not quiesced.
onlyonesnap	-23360	Only one snapshot (used internally).
paramtype	-23325	Invalid parameter type (used internally).
qualifiertoolong	-23379	Qualifier parameter too long (used internally).
reconfigerror	-23316	Attempt to drop master definition site with REMOVE_MASTER_DATABASES.
referenced	-23332	Attempt to drop column group used for conflict resolution.
repnotcompatible	-23376	Replication versions not compatible (used internally).
statnotreg	-23345	Conflict resolution statistics not registered (used internally).
typefailure	-23319	Attempt to replicate nonsupported datatype.
version	-23315	Replication versions not compatible (used internally).

DBMS_REPCAT Nonprogram Elements

In addition to programs and exceptions, the DBMS_REPCAT package defines the VARCHAR2S constant. This is a PL/SQL table of VARCHAR2(60) indexed by BINARY INTEGER. This type can be used to supply a list of column names to the following procedures:

ADD_GROUPED_COLUMN	ADD_UPDATE_RESOLUTION
MAKE_COLUMN_GROUP	ADD_DELETE_RESOLUTION
DROP_COLUMN_GROUP	ADD_UNIQUE_RESOLUTION

DBMS_REPCAT.ADD_conflicttype_RESOLUTION

The ADD_*conflicttype*_RESOLUTION procedure adds a built-in or user-defined conflict resolution type to a table. The value of *conflicttype* can be UPDATE, UNIQUE, or DELETE.

The built-in conflict resolution types for update conflicts are the following:

- Minimum Value

- Maximum Value

- Latest Timestamp

- Earliest Timestamp

- Additive

- Average

- Priority Group

- Site Priority

- Overwrite

- Discard

The built-in conflict resolution methods for uniqueness conflicts are as follows:

- Append Site Name

- Append Sequence Number

- Discard

Oracle does not provide any conflict resolution techniques for delete conflicts.

Here are the specifications:

```
PROCEDURE DBMS_REPCAT.ADD_UPDATE_RESOLUTION
    (sname IN VARCHAR2,
     oname IN VARCHAR2,
     column_group IN VARCHAR2,
     sequence_no IN NUMBER,
     method IN VARCHAR2,
     {parameter_column_name  IN dbms_repcat.varchar2s, |
     parameter_column_name IN VARCHAR2,}
     priority_group IN VARCHAR2 := NULL,
     function_name IN VARCHAR2 := NULL,
     comment IN VARCHAR2 := NULL);

PROCEDURE DBMS_REPCAT.ADD_UNIQUE_RESOLUTION
    (sname IN VARCHAR2,
     oname IN VARCHAR2,
     constraint_name IN VARCHAR2,
     sequence_no IN NUMBER,
     method IN VARCHAR2,
```

```
    {parameter_column_name IN dbms_repcat.varchar2s, |
    parameter_column_name IN VARCHAR2,}
    comment IN VARCHAR2 := NULL);

PROCEDURE DBMS_REPCAT.ADD_DELETE_RESOLUTION
    (sname IN VARCHAR2,
    oname IN VARCHAR2,
    sequence_no IN NUMBER,
    {parameter_column_name IN dbms_repcat.varchar2s, |
    parameter_column_name IN VARCHAR2,}
    function_name IN VARCHAR2 := NULL,
    comment IN VARCHAR2 := NULL);
```

Always define more than one conflict resolution method for a given column or priority group. No single resolution method is completely foolproof.

Parameters

Parameter Name	Description
sname	Name of the schema containing the replicated schema. Defaults to current user.
oname	Name of the replicated table.
column_group	ADD_UPDATE_RESOLUTION only. Column group for which the conflict resolution method is being defined.
constraint_name	ADD_UNIQUE_RESOLUTION only. Name of the constraint name or unique index for which the conflict resolution method is being added.
sequence_no	Number indicating when this conflict resolution method should be applied relative to other methods defined for the same column group or priority group.

method	The conflict resolution method. Valid values are:
	    Priority Group
	    Site Priority
	    User Function
	or one of the built-in types listed earlier.

parameter_column_name	Comma-separated list of columns to be used to resolve the conflict (if VARCHAR2) or a PL/SQL table of column names. If column_group is passed, the column(s) passed to parameter_column_name must be in the group. An asterisk (*) indicates that all columns in the table or column group should be passed to the conflict resolution function, in alphabetical order.
priority_group	ADD_UPDATE_RESOLUTION only. If using a priority group or site priority group, the name of the group.
function_name	If designating a user-defined conflict resolution method, the name of the user function.
comment	Comment on the conflict resolution method, visible in the DBA_REPRESOLUTION data dictionary view.

Exceptions

Exception Name	Number	Description
duplicatesequence	–00001	Resolution method already exists with sequence number sequence_no for this column or priority group.
invalidmethod	–23340	Resolution method does not exist.
invalidparameter	–23342	Column(s) specified in parameter_column_name invalid.
missingcolumn	–23334	Specified column(s) do not exist in table oname.
missingconstraint	–23344	Constraint constraint_name specified in ADD_ UNIQUE_RESOLUTION does not exist.
missingfunction	–23341	User-defined function function_name does not exist.
missinggroup	–23331	column_group does not exist.
missingobject	–23308	Table oname does not exist in the replication group.
missingpriority-group	–23336	priority_group does not exist.
nonmasterdef	–23312	Calling site is not the master definition site.
typefailure	–23319	Datatype of one of the columns specified in parameter_column_name is not appropriate for the resolution method.

Restrictions

• You must call this procedure from the master definition site.

• After this call, you must generate replication support for the table passed to oname.

DBMS_REPCAT.ADD_GROUPED_COLUMN

The ADD_GROUPED_COLUMN procedure adds a member column to a column group. You can call this procedure after you have created a new, empty column group with DEFINE_COLUMN_GROUP or if your schema or conflict resolution requirements change.

```
PROCEDURE DBMS_REPCAT.ADD_GROUPED_COLUMN
    (sname IN VARCHAR2,
     oname IN VARCHAR2,
     column_group IN VARCHAR2,
     {list_of_column_names IN VARCHAR2 |
     list_of_column_names IN dbms_repcat.varchar2s});
```

Note that you must specify only one of the list_of_column_names parameters.

Parameters

Parameter Name	Description
sname	Name of the schema that owns the replicated table.
oname	Name of the table with the column_group.
column_group	Name of the column_group to which column(s) will be added.
list_of_column_names	A comma-delimited list of column names, or a PL/SQL table of column names. Use an asterick (*) to add all columns in the table to the column group.

Exceptions

Exception Name	Number	Description
duplicatecolumn	−23333	Column(s) specified already exist in column_group.
missingcolumn	−23334	Column(s) specified do not exist in table oname.
missinggroup	−23331	Column group column_group does not exist.
missingobject	−23308	Table oname does not exist.
missingschema	−23306	Schema sname does not exist.
nonmasterdef	−23312	Invoking site is not master definition site.

Restrictions

- You must call this procedure from the quiesced master definition site.

- You must regenerate replication support for the table after defining the column group with the GENERATE_REPLICATION_SUPPORT procedure.

DBMS_REPCAT.ADD_MASTER_DATABASE

The ADD_MASTER_DATABASE procedure adds a master site to an existing replication group and initializes all objects at the new site. The specifications differ for Oracle7 and Oracle8 as follows.

Oracle7 specification:

```
PROCEDURE DBMS_REPCAT.ADD_MASTER_DATABASE
    (gname     IN VARCHAR2 := '',
    master     IN VARCHAR2,
    use_existing_objects IN BOOLEAN := TRUE,
    copy_rows IN BOOLEAN := TRUE,
    comment    IN VARCHAR2 := '',
    propagation_mode IN VARCHAR2 := 'ASYNCHRONOUS',
    sname IN VARCHAR2 := '');
```

Oracle8 specification:

```
PROCEDURE DBMS_REPCAT.ADD_MASTER_DATABASE
    (gname     IN VARCHAR2 := '',
```

```
master    IN VARCHAR2,
use_existing_objects IN BOOLEAN := TRUE,
copy_rows IN BOOLEAN := TRUE,
comment   IN VARCHAR2 := '',
propagation_mode IN VARCHAR2 := 'ASYNCHRONOUS');
```

It is generally easier to instantiate all objects at the new master site first. That way, the call to ADD_MASTER_DATABASE does not have to perform DDL to create the schema or send all of the data across a network link. If you instantiate the objects first, the call to ADD_MASTER_DATABASE only has to generate replication support for the objects and update other master sites with the new master's existence.

Parameters

Parameter Name	Description
gname	Name of the replication group to which master site is being added.
master	Global name of the new master site.
use_existing_objects	Reuse existing objects at the new site.
copy_rows	Copy rows from the invoking site to the new master site.
comment	Comment on new master site, visible in DBA_REPSITES data dictionary view.
propagation_mode	Propagation mode (SYNCHRONOUS or ASYNCHRONOUS).
sname (Oracle7 only)	Schema name (provided for pre-Oracle 7.3 compatibility).

Exceptions

Exception Name	Number	Description
commfailure	−23317	Site master is not reachable.
duplicateschema	−23307	Replication group gname already exists at site master.
invalidpropmode	−23380	Propagation_mode is not SYNCHRONOUS or ASYNCHRONOUS.
missingrepgroup	−23373	Replication group gname does not exist at the calling site.
nonmasterdef	−23312	Calling site is not the master definition site.
notquiesced	−23310	Replication group gname is not quiesced.
repnotcompatible	−23376	Replication group gname does not exist at master, and master is a pre-7.3 release.

Restrictions

- This procedure must be run from the master definition site.
- The replication group must be quiesced.

DBMS_REPCAT.ADD_PRIORITY_*datatype*

 Each of the procedures containing the *datatype* suffix actually has five different versions in Oracle7, one for each of the datatypes CHAR, VARCHAR2, NUMBER, RAW, and DATE. Oracle8 adds support for two more datatypes: NCHAR and NVARCHAR2. The usage of each of these packages is identical.

The ADD_PRIORITY_*datatype* procedure adds a member (of the specified datatype) to an existing priority group. The addition of the new priority and value takes effect immediately. Values with higher numeric priorities take precedence— that is, the value with priority 1 has the lowest priority. The specifications differ for Oracle7 and Oracle8 as follows.

Oracle7 specification:

```
PROCEDURE DBMS_REPCAT.ADD_PRIORITY_datatype
    (gname IN VARCHAR2 := '',
    pgroup IN VARCHAR2,
    value IN {CHAR|VARCHAR2|NUMBER|DATE|RAW,
    priority IN NUMBER,
    sname IN VARCHAR2 := '');
```

Oracle8 specification:

```
PROCEDURE DBMS_REPCAT.ADD_PRIORITY_datatype
    (gname IN VARCHAR2 := '',
    pgroup IN VARCHAR2,
    value IN {CHAR|NCHAR|VARCHAR2|NUMBER|DATE|RAW,
    priority IN NUMBER)
```

In these specifications, *datatype* can be any of the following, and value can be any of these types:

Oracle7 and Oracle8	Oracle8 Only
CHAR	NCHAR
VARCHAR2	NVARCHAR2
NUMBER	
DATE	
RAW	

Parameters

Parameter Name	Description
gname	Name of the replication group to which priority group pgroup belongs
pgroup	Priority group to which new value and priority are being added

Parameter Name	Description
value	Literal value that is being assigned added to pgroup
priority	Priority designated to value; it is a good idea to number priorities in multiples of 10 or more so that you can easily add new priority values later as requirements change.
sname (Oracle7 only)	Schema name (provided for pre-Oracle 7.3 compatibility)

Exceptions

Exception Name	Number	Description
duplicatepriority	−23335	Another value is already designated with the specified priority.
duplicatevalue	−23338	Value is already in the priority group pgroup.
missingprioritygroup	−23336	Priority group pgroup does not exist.
missingrepgroup	−23373	Replication group gname does not exist.
nonmasterdef	−23312	Calling site is not the master definition site.
typefailure	−23319	Datatype of value is not the same as the datatype for priority group pgroup.

Restrictions

- The new value must be unique within the priority group.

- The new priority must be unique within the priority group.

- ADD_PRIORITY_*datatype* must be called from the master definition site.

DBMS_REPCAT.ADD_SITE_PRIORITY_SITE

The ADD_SITE_PRIORITY_SITE procedure adds a new site to an existing site priority group. The addition of the new site takes effect immediately. Specifications for Oracle7 and Oracle8 differ as follows.

Oracle7 specification:

```
PROCEDURE DBMS_REPCAT.ADD_SITE_PRIORITY_SITE
    (gname IN VARCHAR2 := '',
    name IN VARCHAR2,
    site IN VARCHAR2,
    priority IN NUMBER,
    sname IN VARCHAR2 := '');
```

Oracle8 specification:

```
PROCEDURE DBMS_REPCAT.ADD_SITE_PRIORITY_SITE
    (gname IN VARCHAR2 := '',
    name IN VARCHAR2,
    site IN VARCHAR2,
    priority IN NUMBER);
```

Parameters

Parameter Name	Description
gname	Name of the replication group to which site priority group name belongs
name	Name of the site priority group
site	Global name of the new site
priority	Priority designated to site; it is a good idea to number priorities in multiples of 10 or more so that you can easily add new priority values later as requirements change.
sname (Oracle7 only)	Schema name (provided for pre-Oracle 7.3 compatibility)

Exceptions

Exception Name	Number	Description
duplicatepriority	−23335	Another site is already designated with the priority specified by the priority parameter.
duplicatesite	−23338	Site is already in the site priority group name.
missingpriority	−1403	Site does not exist.
missingrepgroup	−23373	Replication group gname does not exist.
nonmasterdef	−23312	Calling site is not the master definition site.

Restrictions

* You must call the ADD_SITE_PRIORITY_SITE procedure from the master definition site.

* The new priority must be unique within the site priority group.

DBMS_REPCAT.ALTER_MASTER_PROPAGATION

The ALTER_MASTER_PROPAGATION procedure changes the propagation mode between specified master sites (from synchronous to asynchronous, or vice versa).

```
PROCEDURE DBMS_REPCAT.ALTER_MASTER_PROPAGATION
    (gname IN VARCHAR2,
    master IN VARCHAR2,
    {dblink_table IN dbms_utility.dblink_array | dblink_list IN VARCHAR2},
    propagation_modee IN VARCHAR2 := 'ASYNCHRONOUS',
    comment IN VARCHAR2 := '');
```

ALTER_MASTER_PROPAGATION does not automatically generate replication support triggers. After altering the propagation method, you must call GENERATE_REPLICATION_TRIGGER for replicated table in the replication group.

Parameters

Parameter Name	Description
gname	Name of the replication group whose propagation mode is being altered
master	Global name of the master site having its propagation mode altered
dblink_list	List of database links for which the master's propagation mode is being altered
propagation_mode	New propagation mode (SYNCHRONOUS or ASYNCHRONOUS)
comment	Comment visible in DBA_REPPROP data dictionary view

Exceptions

Exception Name	Number	Description
nonmaster	−23312	One of the sites in dblink_list is not a master site.
nonmasterdef	−23312	Calling site is not the master definition site.
notquiesced	−23310	Replication group gname is not quiesced.
typefailure	−23319	The propagation_mode is not SYNCHRONOUS or ASYNCHRONOUS.

Restrictions

- You must run this procedure from the master definition site.

- The replication group must be quiesced.

DBMS_REPCAT.ALTER_MASTER_REPOBJECT

Just as you can propagate DDL to create objects with the EXECUTE_DDL procedure, you can also propagate DDL to alter objects with ALTER_MASTER_REPOB-
JECT. Unlike EXECUTE_DDL, ALTER_MASTER_REPOBJECT does not allow you to
specify a list of master sites; the call affects all masters. In other words, Oracle
does not support site-specific customizations of replicated objects.

You can perform DDL on any of these objects:

Function	Synonym
Index	Table
Package	Trigger
Package body	View
Procedure	

Here is the specification:

```
PROCEDURE DBMS_REPCAT.ALTER_MASTER_REPOBJECT
    (sname IN VARCHAR2,
     oname IN VARCHAR2,
     type IN VARCHAR2,
     ddl_text IN VARCHAR2,
     comment IN VARCHAR2 := '',
     retry IN BOOLEAN := FALSE);
```

Parameters

Parameter Name	Description
sname	Name of the schema to which object oname belongs.
oname	Name of the object to alter.
type	The oname object type. Supported types: FUNCTION, INDEX, PACKAGE, PACKAGE BODY, SYNONYM, TABLE, TRIGGER, and VIEW.
ddl_text	Text of DDL statement to apply.
comment	Comment visible in DBA_REPOBJECT data dictionary view.
retry	If set to TRUE, procedure alters only objects whose status is not VALID at master sites.

Exceptions

Exception Name	Number	Description
commfailure	–23317	Unable to communicate with one or more master sites.
ddlfailure	–23318	DDL at master definition site failed.
missingobject	–23308	Object oname does not exist.
nonmasterdef	–23312	Calling site is not the master definition site.
notquiesced	–23310	Replication group gname is not quiesced.
typefailure	–23319	DDL on objects of the specified type is not supported.

Restrictions

- This procedure must be run from the master definition site.

- The replication group must be quiesced.

- You must call GENERATE_REPLICATION_SUPPORT for the altered object before resuming replication.

DBMS_REPCAT.ALTER_PRIORITY

The ALTER_PRIORITY procedure lets you change the priority associated with a specific value in a priority group. The change takes place immediately. The specifications differ for Oracle7 and Oracle8 as follows.

Oracle7 specification:

```
PROCEDURE DBMS_REPCAT.ALTER_PRIORITY
    (gname IN VARCHAR2 := '',
     pgroup IN VARCHAR2,
     old_priority IN NUMBER,
     new_priority IN NUMBER,
     sname IN VARCHAR2 := '');
```

Oracle8 specification:

```
PROCEDURE DBMS_REPCAT.ALTER_PRIORITY
    (gname IN VARCHAR2 := '',
     pgroup IN VARCHAR2,
     old_priority IN NUMBER,          ·
     new_priority IN NUMBER)
```

Parameters

Parameter Name	Description
gname	Name of the replication group to which priority group pgroup belongs
pgroup	Name of the priority group whose priority is being altered
old_priority	pgroup's previous priority value
new_priority	pgroup's new priority value
sname (Oracle7 only)	Schema name (provided for pre-Oracle 7.3 compatibility)

Exceptions

Exception Name	Number	Description
duplicatepriority	−23335	Priority new_priority already exists in priority group pgroup.
missingprioritygroup	−23336	Priority group pgroup does not exist.
missingvalue	−23337	Value was not registered with a call to ADD_PRIORITY_*datatype*.
nonmasterdef	−23312	Calling site is not the master definition site.

Restrictions

- You must call the ALTER_PRIORITY procedure from the master definition site.
- The new priority must be unique within the priority group.

DBMS_REPCAT.ALTER_PRIORITY_*datatype*

The ALTER_PRIORITY_*datatype* procedures let you alter the data value associated with a specific priority for a priority group. For example, in the priority group PG_MFG_STAT, the value associated with priority 1 could be changed from CONCEPT to PLANNED. The change takes effect immediately. The specifications differ for Oracle7 and Oracle8 as follows.

Oracle7 specification:

```
PROCEDURE DBMS_REPCAT.ALTER_PRIORITY_datatype
    (gname      IN VARCHAR2 := '',
     pgroup     IN VARCHAR2,
     old_value  IN {CHAR|VARCHAR2|NUMBER|DATE|RAW},
     new_value  IN {CHAR|VARCHAR2|NUMBER|DATE|RAW},
     sname      IN VARCHAR2 := '');
```

Oracle8 specification:

```
PROCEDURE DBMS_REPCAT.ALTER_PRIORITY_datatype
    (gname      IN VARCHAR2 := '',
     pgroup     IN VARCHAR2,
     old_value  IN {CHAR|NCHAR|VARCHAR2|NUMBER|DATE|RAW},
     new_value  IN {CHAR|NCHAR|VARCHAR2|NUMBER|DATE|RAW});
```

datatype, value, and old_value can be any of the types in the following table.

Oracle7 and Oracle8	Oracle8 Only
CHAR	NCHAR
VARCHAR2	NVARCHAR2
NUMBER	
DATE	
RAW	

Parameters

Parameter Name	Description
gname	Name of the replication group to which priority group pgroup belongs
pgroup	Name of the priority group whose priority is being altered
old_value	Current value of the priority group member
new_value	New value of the priority group member
sname (Oracle7 only)	Schema name (provided for pre-Oracle 7.3 compatibility)

Exceptions

Exception Name	Number	Description
duplicatevalue	–23338	Value new_value is already designated a priority in priority group pgroup.
missingprioritygroup	–23336	Priority group pgroup does not exist.
missingvalue	–23337	Value was not registered with a call to ADD_PRIORITY_*datatype*.
nonmasterdef	–23312	Calling site is not the master definition site.

Restrictions

- You must call the ALTER_PRIORITY_*datatype* procedure from the master definition site.

- The new priority must be unique within the priority group.

DBMS_REPCAT.ALTER_SITE_PRIORITY

Just as you can change the priority of a value in a priority group, you can change the priority of a site in a site priority group. Use the ALTER_SITE_PRIORITY procedure to do this. The specifications for Oracle7 and Oracle8 differ as follows.

Oracle7 specification:

```
PROCEDURE DBMS_REPCAT.ALTER_SITE_PRIORITY
    (gname IN VARCHAR2 := '',
    name IN VARCHAR2,
    old_priority IN NUMBER,
    new_priority IN NUMBER,
    sname IN VARCHAR2 := '');
```

Oracle8 specification:

```
PROCEDURE DBMS_REPCAT.ALTER_SITE_PRIORITY
    (gname IN VARCHAR2 := '',
    name IN VARCHAR2,
    old_priority IN NUMBER,
    new_priority IN NUMBER);
    site IN VARCHAR2);
```

Parameters

Parameter Name	Description
gname	Name of the replication group to which the site priority group name belongs
name	Name of the site priority group
old_priority	Site's current priority
new_priority	Site's new priority
sname (Oracle7 only)	Schema name (provided for pre-Oracle 7.3 compatibility)
site	Global name of the site

Exceptions

Exception Name	Number	Description
duplicatepriority	−00001	Priority new_priority already exists for the site priority group name.
missingpriority	−01403	Priority old_priority is not associated with any sites.
missingrepgroup	−23373	Replication group gname does not exist.
missingvalue	−23337	Value old_value does not already exist.

Exception Name	Number	Description
nonmasterdef	–23312	Calling site is not the master definition site.
paramtype	–23325	Parameter new_value is incorrect datatype.

Restrictions

- You must run this procedure from the master definition site.

- The new priority must be unique within the site priority group.

DBMS_REPCAT.ALTER_SITE_PRIORITY_SITE

The ALTER_SITE_PRIORITY_SITE procedure is analogous to the ADD_PRIORITY_ *datatype* procedure; use it to change the site name for an existing named site in a site priority group. The specifications for Oracle7 and Oracle8 differ as follows.

Oracle7 specification:

```
PROCEDURE DBMS_REPCAT.ALTER_SITE_PRIORITY_SITE
    (gname IN VARCHAR2 := '',
    name IN VARCHAR2,
    old_site IN VARCHAR2,
    new_site IN VARCHAR2,
    sname IN VARCHAR2 := '');
```

Oracle8 specification:

```
PROCEDURE DBMS_REPCAT.ALTER_SITE_PRIORITY_SITE
    (gname IN VARCHAR2 := '',
    name IN VARCHAR2,
    old_site IN VARCHAR2,
    new_site IN VARCHAR2);
```

Parameters

Parameter Name	Description
gname	Name of the replication group to which the site priority group name belongs
name	Name of the site priority group
old_site	Global name of the site currently associated with the priority level
new_site	Global name of the site that is to replace old_site at old_site's priority level
sname (Oracle7 only)	Schema name (provided for pre-Oracle 7.3 compatibility)

Exceptions

Exception Name	Number	Description
duplicatesite	–00001	new_site is already in the site priority group.
missingpriority	–01403	Site priority group name does not exist.

Exception Name	Number	Description
missingrepgroup	−23373	Replication group gname does not exist.
missingvalue	−23337	old_site is not in the site priority group.
nonmasterdef	−23312	Calling site is not the master definition site.

Restrictions

* You must call this procedure from the master definition site.

* The new site must be unique in the site priority group.

DBMS_REPCAT.ALTER_SNAPSHOT_PROPAGATION

Call the ALTER_SNAPSHOT_PROPAGATION procedure to change the propagation mode of a particular snapshot. Specifications for Oracle7 and Oracle8 differ.

Oracle7 specification:

```
PROCEDURE DBMS_REPCAT.ALTER_SNAPSHOT_PROPAGATION
    (gname IN VARCHAR2,
     propagation_mode IN VARCHAR2,
     comment IN VARCHAR2 := '',
     execute_as_user IN BOOLEAN  := FALSE);
```

Oracle8 specification:

```
PROCEDURE DBMS_REPCAT.ALTER_SNAPSHOT_PROPAGATION
    (gname IN VARCHAR2,
     propagation_mode IN VARCHAR2,
     comment IN VARCHAR2 := '' );
```

Parameters

Parameter Name	Description
gname	Name of the replication group to be altered.
propagation_mode	The new propagation mode to use (SYNCHRONOUS or ASYNCHRONOUS).
comment	Comment visible in DBA_REPPROP data dictionary view.
execute_as_user (Oracle7 only)	FALSE (default) indicates that remote system will authenticate calls using authentication context user who originally queued the RPC; TRUE indicates that remote system will use authentication context of the session user.

Exceptions

Exception Name	Number	Description
dbnotcompatible	−23375	Database version is not 7.3 or later.
missingrepgroup	−23373	Replication group gname does not exist.
typefailure	−23319	Invalid propagation_mode.

Restrictions

This procedure must be called from a snapshot site.

DBMS_REPCAT.CANCEL_STATISTICS

The CANCEL_STATISTICS procedure disables the gathering of conflict resolution statistics.

```
PROCEDURE DBMS_REPCAT.CANCEL_STATISTICS
    (sname IN VARCHAR2,
     oname IN VARCHAR2);
```

There are no restrictions on calling CANCEL_STATISTICS.

Parameters

Parameter Name	Description
sname	Name of the schema to which the replicated table belongs
oname	Name of the replicated table

Exceptions

Exception Name	Number	Description
missingobject	−23308	Table oname does not exist.
missingschema	−23306	Schema sname does not exist.
statnotreg	−23345	Statistics have not been registered for object oname.

DBMS_REPCAT.COMMENT_ON_*conflicttype*_RESOLUTION

You can use the COMMENT_ON_*conflicttype*_RESOLUTION procedure to add or replace a comment for a given conflict resolution type. You can see this comment in the DBA_REPRESOLUTION data dictionary view. Following are the specifications for the three values of *conflicttype* (UPDATE, UNIQUE, DELETE):

```
PROCEDURE DBMS_REPCAT.COMMENT_ON_UPDATE_RESOLUTION
    (sname IN VARCHAR2,
     oname IN VARCHAR2,
     column_group IN VARCHAR2,
     sequence_no IN NUMBER,
     comment IN VARCHAR2);

PROCEDURE DBMS_REPCAT.COMMENT_ON_UNIQUE_RESOLUTION
    (sname IN VARCHAR2,
     oname in VARCHAR2,
     constraint_name IN VARCHAR2,
     sequence_no IN NUMBER,
     comment IN VARCHAR2) ;
```

```
PROCEDURE DBMS_REPCAT.COMMENT_ON_DELETE_RESOLUTION
    (sname IN VARCHAR2,
     oname IN VARCHAR2,
     sequence_no IN NUMBER,
     comment IN VARCHAR2) ;
```

Parameters

Parameter Name	Description
sname	Name of the schema to which object oname belongs
oname	Name of the object
column_group	Name of column group for which conflict resolution method is defined
constraint_name	Name of unique constraint the method resolves (COMMENT_ON_UNIQUE_RESOLUTION only)
sequence_no	Sequence number associated with the resolution method
comment	Comment

Exceptions

Exception Name	Number	Description
missingobject	−23308	Object oname does not exist.
missingresolution	−23343	No resolution method exists for column_group and sequence_no.
nonmasterdef	−23312	Calling site is not the master definition site.

Restrictions

- You must call this procedure from the master definition site.

- After this call, you must generate replication support for the table passed to oname.

- Comments do not take effect until there is a call to GENERATE_REPLICA-TION_SUPPORT.

DBMS_REPCAT.COMMENT_ON_COLUMN_GROUP

The COMMENT_ON_COLUMN_GROUP procedure adds or changes the comment associated with a column group. This comment is visible in the DBA_REPCOL-UMN_GROUP data dictionary view.

```
PROCEDURE DBMS_REPCAT.COMMENT_ON_COLUMN_GROUP
    (sname IN VARCHAR2,
     oname IN VARCHAR2,
     column_group IN VARCHAR2,
     comment IN VARCHAR2);
```

Parameters

Parameter Name	Description
sname	Name of the schema to which the replicated table belongs
oname	Name of the replicated table containing the column group
column_group	Name of the column group
comment	Comment

Exceptions

Exception Name	Number	Description
missinggroup	–23331	column_group does not exist.
nonmasterdef	–23312	Calling site is not the master definition site.

Restrictions

The COMMENT_ON_COLUMN_GROUP procedure must be called from the master definition site.

DBMS_REPCAT.COMMENT_ON_PRIORITY_GROUP

The COMMENT_ON_PRIORITY_GROUP procedure allows you to add or replace the comment for a priority group (as seen in the DBA_REPPRIORITY_GROUP data dictionary view). The specifications for Oracle7 and Oracle8 differ as follows.

Oracle7 specification:

```
PROCEDURE DBMS_REPCAT.COMMENT_ON_PRIORITY_GROUP
    (gname IN VARCHAR2 := '',
    pgroup IN VARCHAR2,
    comment IN VARCHAR2,
    sname IN VARCHAR2 := '');
```

Oracle8 specification:

```
PROCEDURE DBMS_REPCAT.COMMENT_ON_PRIORITY_GROUP
    (gname IN VARCHAR2 := '',
    pgroup IN VARCHAR2,
    comment IN VARCHAR2);
```

Parameters

Parameter Name	Description
gname	Name of the replication group containing the priority group
pgroup	Name of the priority group
comment	Comment
sname (Oracle7 only)	Schema name (provided for pre-Oracle 7.3 compatibility)

Exceptions

Exception Name	Number	Description
missingprioritygroup	–23336	Priority group pgroup does not exist.
missingrepgroup	–23373	Replication group gname does not exist.
nonmasterdef	–23312	Calling site is not the master definition site.

Restrictions

You must call COMMENT_ON_PRIORITY_GROUP from the master definition site.

DBMS_REPCAT.COMMENT_ON_REPGROUP

This procedure adds a new schema comment field to the DBA_REPCAT data dictionary view or changes an existing one. The specifications differ for Oracle7 and Oracle8 as follows.

Oracle7 specification:

```
PROCEDURE DMBS_REPCAT.COMMENT_ON_REPGROUP
    (gname IN VARCHAR2 := '',
     comment IN VARCHAR2,
     sname IN VARCHAR2 := '');
```

Oracle8 specification:

```
PROCEDURE DMBS_REPCAT.COMMENT_ON_REPGROUP
    (gname IN VARCHAR2,
     comment IN VARCHAR2);
```

Parameters

Parameter Name	Description
gname	Replication group to which comment is added
comment	Comment
sname (Oracle7 only)	Schema name (provided for pre-Oracle 7.3 compatibility)

Exceptions

Exception Name	Number	Description
commfailure	–23317	Unable to communicate with one or more master sites.
missinggroup	–23331	Replication group gname does not exist.
nonmasterdef	–23312	Calling site is not master definition site.

Restrictions

The COMMENT_ON_REPGROUP procedure must be called from the master definition site.

DBMS_REPCAT.COMMENT_ON_REPOBJECT

As you have seen, you can associate comments with a replicated object when you create or alter it by passing a VARCHAR2 string to the comment parameter. You can see these comments in the object_comment field of DBA_REPOBJECTS. Also, you can create comments without creating or altering the object with DBMS_REP-CAT's COMMENT_ON_REPOBJECT procedure.

```
PROCEDURE DBMS_REPCAT.COMMENT_ON_REPOBJECT
    (sname IN VARCHAR2,
     oname IN VARCHAR2,
     type IN VARCHAR2,
     comment IN VARCHAR2);
```

Parameters

Parameter Name	Description
sname	Name of schema to which object belongs
oname	Name of the object
type	Object type
comment	Comment

Exceptions

Exception Name	Number	Description
commfailure	−23317	Unable to communicate with one or more master sites.
missingobject	−23308	Object oname does not exist.
nonmasterdef	−23312	Calling site is not master definition site.
typefailure	−23319	Object type is not supported.

Restrictions

The COMMENT_ON_REPOBJECT procedure must be called from the master definition site.

DBMS_REPCAT.COMMENT_ON_REPSITES

The COMMENT_ON_REPSITES procedure allows you to add or change a comment associated with a master site, which is visible in the DBA_REPSITES data dictionary view.

```
PROCEDURE DBMS_REPCAT.COMMENT_ON_REPSITES
    (gname IN VARCHAR2,
     master IN VARCHAR,
     comment IN VARCHAR2);
```

Parameters

Parameter Name	Description
gname	Name of the replication group to which master belongs
master	Global name of master site
comment	Comment

Exceptions

Exception Name	Number	Description
commfailure	−23317	Unable to communicate with one or more master sites.
nonmaster	−23313	The master is not a master site.
nonmasterdef	−23312	Calling site is not master definition site.

Restrictions

You must call the COMMENT_ON_REPSITES procedure from the master definition site.

DBMS_REPCAT.COMMENT_ON_SITE_PRIORITY

The COMMENT_ON_SITE_PRIORITY procedure adds or replaces the comment field in the DBA_REPPRIORITY_GROUP data dictionary view for the specified site priority group. Specifications differ for Oracle7 and Oracle8 as follows.

Oracle7 specification:

```
PROCEDURE DBMS_REPCAT.COMMENT_ON_SITE_PRIORITY
    (gname IN VARCHAR2 := '',
     name IN VARCHAR2,
     comment IN VARCHAR2,
     sname IN VARCHAR2 := '');
```

Oracle8 specification:

```
PROCEDURE DBMS_REPCAT.COMMENT_ON_SITE_PRIORITY
    (gname IN VARCHAR2 := '',
     name IN VARCHAR2,
     comment IN VARCHAR2)
```

Parameters

Parameter Name	Description
gname	Name of the replication group containing the priority group
name	Name of the site priority group
comment	Comment
sname (Oracle7 only)	Schema name (provided for pre-Oracle 7.3 compatibility)

Exceptions

Exception Name	Number	Description
missingpriority	−1403	Site priority group name does not exist.
missingrepgroup	−23373	Replication group gname does not exist.
nonmasterdef	−23312	Calling site is not master definition site.

Restrictions

You must call COMMENT_ON_SITE_PRIORITY from the master definition site.

DBMS_REPCAT.CREATE_MASTER_REPGROUP

The CREATE_MASTER_REPGROUP procedure creates a new, empty, quiesced replication group at the master definition site. The calling site is the master definition site for the new group.

```
PROCEDURE DBMS_REPCAT.CREATE_MASTER_REPGROUP
    (gname IN VARCHAR2,
     group_comment  IN VARCHAR2 := '',
     master_comment IN VARCHAR2 := '',
     qualifier      IN VARCHAR2 := '');
```

Parameters

Parameter Name	Description
gname	Name of the new replication group
group_comment	Comment for new replication group, visible in DBA_REPGROUP data dictionary view
master_comment	Comment for the calling site, visible in DBA_REPSITES data dictionary view
qualifier	For internal use

Exceptions

Exception Name	Number	Description
ddlfailure	−23318	Unable to create REP$WHAT_AM_I package or package body.
duplicaterepgroup	−23374	Replication group gname already exists.
duplicateschema	−23307	Schema gname is already a replication group.
missingrepgroup	−23373	The gname was not specified correctly.
norepoption	−23364	Replication option not installed.
dbnotcompatible	−23375	The gname is not a schema name, and RDBMS is a pre-7.3 release.

Restrictions

You must be connected to the replication administrator account (typically REPAD-MIN) to call CREATE_MASTER_REPGROUP.

DBMS_REPCAT.CREATE_MASTER_REPOBJECT

The CREATE_MASTER_REPOBJECT procedure adds a new replicated object to an existing replication group.

```
PROCEDURE DBMS_REPCAT.CREATE_MASTER_REPOBJECT(
    sname IN VARCHAR2,
    oname IN VARCHAR2,
    type IN VARCHAR2,
    use_existing_object IN BOOLEAN := TRUE,
    ddl_text IN VARCHAR2 := NULL,
    comment IN VARCHAR2 := '',
    retry IN BOOLEAN := FALSE,
    copy_rows IN BOOLEAN := TRUE,
    gname IN VARCHAR2 := '');
```

It is generally easier to instantiate objects that you intend to replicate at all partici-pating master sites before calling CREATE_MASTER_REPOBJECT. This avoids the additional time and complexity of having the procedure create and populate the replicated objects itself.

Parameters

Parameter Name	Description
sname	Name of the schema to which oname belongs.
oname	Name of the object to be added.
type	Object type. Valid types: TABLE, INDEX, SYNONYM, TRIGGER, VIEW, PROCEDURE, FUNCTION, PACKAGE, and PACKAGE BODY.
use_existing_object	Set to TRUE to reuse existing objects with the same name and structure at master sites.
ddl_text	Text of DDL statement to create object oname (use this parameter if and only if object does not already exist).
comment	Comment on replicated object, visible in DBA_REPOBJECT data dictionary view.
retry	Flag indicating that this call is a reattempt of an earlier call. An attempt is made to create object only at master sites where it does not exist with a status of VALID.
copy_rows	Populate tables and other master sites with data from master defi-nition site.
gname	Name of the replication group to which oname should be added.

Exceptions

Exception Name	Number	Description
commfailure	–23317	Not all master sites are reachable.
ddlfailure	–23309	Object oname already exists in replication group gname, and retry is not set to TRUE.
duplicateobject	–23374	Replication group gname already exists.
missingobject	–23308	Object oname does not exist.
nonmasterdef	–23373	Calling site is not the master definition site for replication group gname.
notquiesced	–23310	Replication group gname is not quiesced.
typefailure	–23319	The type is not supported.

Restrictions

- This procedure must be called from the master definition site.

- The replication group must already exist and be quiesced.

DBMS_REPCAT.CREATE_SNAPSHOT_REPGROUP

This procedure creates a new, empty snapshot replication group. If you will be creating the snapshot group at multiple sites, it is advisable to create a script to perform this call because there is no analogy to ADD_MASTER_DATABASE for snapshot groups.

PROCEDURE DBMS_REPCAT.CREATE_SNAPSHOT_REPGROUP

```
(gname IN VARCHAR2,
master IN VARCHAR2,
comment IN VARCHAR2 := '',
propagation_mode IN VARCHAR2 := 'ASYNCHRONOUS');
```

Parameters

Parameter Name	Description
gname	Name of the new snapshot group
master	Global name of master site
comment	Comment for the snapshot group, visible in DBA_REPSITES data dictionary view
propagation_mode	Snapshot propagation mode (SYNCHRONOUS or ASYNCHRONOUS)

Exceptions

Exception Name	Number	Description
commfailure	−23317	Unable to communicate with master.
dbnotcompatible	−23375	Attempt to use SYNCHRONOUS propagation in pre-7.3 database.
duplicaterepgroup	−23374	Replication group gname already exists.
nonmaster	−23312	The master parameter is not a master site.
norepoption	−23364	Replication option not installed.
typefailure	−23319	propagation_mode not specified correctly.

Restrictions

* You must be connected to the replication administrator account (typically REPADMIN) to call the CREATE_SNAPSHOT_REPGROUP procedure.

* The snapshot group name must match the name of the master replication group.

* You must invoke this procedure from the snapshot site.

DBMS_REPCAT.CREATE_SNAPSHOT_REPOBJECT

The CREATE_SNAPSHOT_REPOBJECT procedure adds an object to a specified snapshot replication group at a snapshot site. For new snapshot objects, this procedure generates row-level replication triggers for snapshots if the master table uses row-level replication. The specifications differ for Oracle7 and Oracle8 as follows. (Note the addition of the min_communication parameter in Oracle8.)

Oracle7 specification:

```
PROCEDURE DBMS_REPCAT. CREATE_SNAPSHOT_REPOBJECT
    (sname IN VARCHAR2,
     oname IN VARCHAR2,
     type IN VARCHAR2,
     ddl_text IN VARCHAR2 := '',
     comment IN VARCHAR2 := '',
     gname IN VARCHAR2 := '',
     gen_objs_owner IN VARCHAR2 := '');
```

Oracle8 specification:

```
PROCEDURE DBMS_REPCAT.CREATE_SNAPSHOT_REPOBJECT
    (sname IN VARCHAR2,
     oname IN VARCHAR2,
     type IN VARCHAR2,
     ddl_text IN VARCHAR2 := '',
     comment IN VARCHAR2 := '',
     gname IN VARCHAR2 := '',
     gen_objs_owner IN VARCHAR2 := '',
     min_communication IN BOOLEAN := TRUE);
```

Parameters

Parameter Name	Description
sname	Name of schema to which oname belongs.
oname	Name of object to be added.
type	Object type. Supported types are PACKAGE, PACKAGE BODY, PROCEDURE, SNAPSHOT, SYNONYM, and VIEW.
ddl_text	DDL used to create object (for type SNAPSHOT only).
comment	Comment on object, visible in DBA_REPOBJECT data dictionary view.
gname	Name of snapshot group to which object is being added. Defaults to sname if not specified.
gen_objs_owner	Name of the schema in which to create the generated trigger and trigger package or procedure wrapper for the object. Defaults to sname.
drop_objects	If set to TRUE, object is dropped too. If FALSE (the default), object is removed only from the snapshot group.
min_communication (Oracle8 only)	Must be FALSE if any master site is running Oracle7. TRUE, the default setting, uses the minimum communication algorithm.

Exceptions

Exception Name	Number	Description
commfailure	−23317	Unable to communicate with master site.
ddlfailure	−23318	Unable to perform DDL.
duplicateobject	−23309	Object oname already exists.
missingobject	−23308	Object oname does not exist in master's replication group gname.
missingremoteobject	−23381	Master site has not generated replication support for oname.
missingschema	−23306	Schema sname does not exist.
misssnapobject	−23355	Object oname does not exist at master.
nonmaster	−23312	Master site associated with snapshot group is no longer a master site.
nonsnapshot	−23314	Calling site is not a snapshot site.
typefailure	−23319	Invalid value for type.

Restrictions

- You must be connected to the replication administrator account (typically REPADMIN).

- If you are creating an snapshot with ddl_text, be sure to specify the schema in which it should be created (if other than the replication administrator).

DBMS_REPCAT.DEFINE_COLUMN_GROUP

The DEFINE_COLUMN_GROUP procedure creates a column group with no member columns. The new column group does not take effect until you call GENERATE_REPLICATION_SUPPORT for the table.

```
PROCEDURE DBMS_REPCAT.DEFINE_COLUMN_GROUP
    (sname IN VARCHAR2,
     oname IN VARCHAR2,
     column_group IN VARCHAR2,
     comment IN VARCHAR@ := NULL);
```

Parameters

Parameter Name	Description
sname	Name of the schema to which the replicated table belongs
oname	Name of the replicated table containing the column group
column_group	Name of the column group
comment	Comment

Exceptions

Exception Name	Number	Description
duplicategroup	−23330	Column_group already exists.
missingobject	−23308	Object oname does not exist.
nonmasterdef	−23312	Calling site is not master definition site.

Restrictions

You must call this procedure from the quiesced master definition site.

DBMS_REPCAT.DEFINE_PRIORITY_GROUP

The DEFINE_PRIORITY_GROUP procedure creates a new priority group. The new group does not take effect until you call GENERATE_REPLICATION_SUPPORT for the table. The specifications differ for Oracle7 and Oracle8 as follows.

Oracle7 specification:

```
PROCEDURE DBMS_REPCAT.DEFINE_PRIORITY_GROUP
    (gname IN VARCHAR2 := '',
     pgroup IN VARCHAR2,
     datatype IN VARCHAR2,
     fixed_length IN INTEGER := NULL,
     comment IN VARCHAR2 := NULL,
     sname IN VARCHAR2 := '');
```

Oracle8 specification:

```
PROCEDURE DBMS_REPCAT.DEFINE_PRIORITY_GROUP
   (gname IN VARCHAR2 := '',
    pgroup IN VARCHAR2,
    datatype IN VARCHAR2,
    fixed_length IN INTEGER := NULL,
    comment IN VARCHAR2 := NULL);
```

Parameters

Parameter Name	Description
gname	Name of the replication group containing the priority group.
pgroup	Name of the priority group.
datatype	Datatype for the value used in the priority group. Supported datatypes: CHAR NCHAR (Oracle8 only) VARCHAR2 NUMBER DATE RAW
fixed_length	Fixed length for values. Used only for datatype CHAR.
comment	Comment.
sname (Oracle7 only)	Schema name (provided for pre-Oracle 7.3 compatibility).

Exceptions

Exception Name	Number	Description
duplicateprioritygroup	−23335	Priority group pgroup already exists.
missingschema	−23306	Schema does not exist.
nonmasterdef	−23312	Calling site is not the master definition site.
typefailure	−23319	Datatype not supported.

Restrictions

You must call the DEFINE_PRIORITY_GROUP procedure from the master definition site.

DBMS_REPCAT.DEFINE_SITE_PRIORITY

The DEFINE_SITE_PRIORITY procedure creates a site priority group. You can add sites to this group later. The new site priority does not take effect until you call GENERATE_REPLICATION_SUPPORT for the table. Specifications differ for Oracle7 and Oracle8 as follows.

Oracle7 specification:

```
PROCEDURE DBMS_REPCAT.DEFINE_SITE_PRIORITY
    (gname IN VARCHAR2 := '',
    name IN VARCHAR2,
    comment IN VARCHAR2 := NULL,
    sname IN VARCHAR2 := '');
```

Oracle8 specification:

```
PROCEDURE DBMS_REPCAT.DEFINE_SITE_PRIORITY
    (gname IN VARCHAR2 := '',
    name IN VARCHAR2,
    comment IN VARCHAR2 := NULL)
```

Parameters

Parameter Name	Description
gname	Name of the replication group containing the site priority group
name	Name of the site priority group
comment	Comment, visible in DBA_REPPRIORITY_GROUP data dictionary view
sname (Oracle7 only)	Schema name (provided for pre-Oracle 7.3 compatibility)

Exceptions

Exception Name	Number	Description
duplicateprioritygroup	−23335	Site priority group name already exists.
missingrepgroup	−23373	Replication group gname does not exist.
nonmasterdef	−23312	Calling site is not the master definition site.

Restrictions

You must call DEFINE_SITE_PRIORITY from the master definition site.

DBMS_REPCAT.DO_DEFERRED_REPCAT_ADMIN

Whenever you create or alter replicated objects—for example, with the GENER-ATE_REPLICATION_SUPPORT or ALTER_MASTER_REPOBJECT procedure—Oracle queues the changes in the repcatlog queue; the entries in this queue correspond to entries in the DBA_REPCATLOG data dictionary view. All DDL changes must originate at the master definition site, but the repcatlog queue exists at every master site.

The DO_DEFERRED_REPCAT_ADMIN procedure performs administrative tasks queued in DBA_REPCAT for the specific replication group at the master site from which the call is made. If the all_sites parameter is set to TRUE, the tasks are applied at all masters. The specifications differ for Oracle7 and Oracle8 as follows.

Oracle7 specification:

```
PROCEDURE DBMS_REPCAT.DO_DEFERRED_REPCAT_ADMIN
    (gname IN VARCHAR2 := '',
     all_sites IN BOOLEAN := FALSE,
     sname IN VARCHAR2 := '');
```

Oracle8 specification:

```
PROCEDURE DBMS_REPCAT.DO_DEFERRED_REPCAT_ADMIN
    (gname IN VARCHAR2,
     all_sites IN BOOLEAN := FALSE);
```

Parameters

Parameter Name	Description
gname	Name of the replication group for which to push the repcatlog queue
all_sites	If TRUE, execute queued procedures at every master site
sname (Oracle7 only)	Schema name (provided for pre-Oracle 7.3 compatibility)

Exceptions

Exception Name	Number	Description
commfailure	–23317	Unable to communicate with master site.
nonmaster	–23312	Master site associated with snapshot group is no longer a master site.

Restrictions

The DO_DEFERRED_REPCAT_ADMIN procedure performs only the procedures that have been queued by the invoking user. Note that the job queue is used to perform the queued procedures automatically.

DBMS_REPCAT.DROP_*conflicttype*_RESOLUTION

The DROP_*conflicttype*_RESOLUTION procedure removes a conflict resolution type from a replicated table. The value of *conflicttype* can be UPDATE, UNIQUE, or DELETE.

```
PROCEDURE DBMS_REPCAT.DROP_UPDATE_RESOLUTION
    (sname IN VARCHAR2,
     oname IN VARCHAR2,
     column_group IN VARCHAR2,
     sequence_no IN NUMBER) ;
```

```
PROCEDURE DBMS_REPCAT.DROP_UNIQUE_RESOLUTION
    (sname IN VARCHAR2,
     oname IN VARCHAR2,
     constraint_name IN VARCHAR2,
     sequence_no IN NUMBER) ;

PROCEDURE DBMS_REPCAT.DROP_DELETE_RESOLUTION
    (sname IN VARCHAR2,
     oname IN VARCHAR2,
     sequence_no IN NUMBER) ;
```

Parameters

Parameter Name	Description
sname	Name of the schema containing the replicated schema. Defaults to current user.
oname	Name of the replicated table.
column_group	Column group for which the conflict resolution method is defined.
constraint_name	For procedure DROP_UNIQUE_RESOLUTION only. Name of the constraint name or unique index for which the conflict resolution method is defined.
sequence_no	Number indicating when this conflict resolution method is applied relative to other conflict resolution methods defined for the same column group or priority group.

Exceptions

Exception Name	Number	Description
missingobject	−23308	Table oname does not exist in the replication group.
missingschema	−23306	Schema sname does not exist.
nonmasterdef	−23312	Calling site is not the master definition site.

Restrictions

- You must call this procedure from the master definition site.

- After this call, you must generate replication support for the table passed to oname.

DBMS_REPCAT.DROP_COLUMN_GROUP

The DROP_COLUMN_GROUP procedure drops a column group that you've previously created. The change does not take effect until you call GENERATE_REPLICATION_SUPPORT for the table for which the column group is defined.

```
PROCEDURE DBMS_REPCAT.DROP_COLUMN_GROUP
    (sname IN VARCHAR2,
     oname IN VARCHAR2,
     column_group IN VARCHAR2);
```

Parameters

Parameter Name	Description
sname	Name of the schema to which the replicated table belongs
oname	Name of the replicated table containing the column group
column_group	Name of the column group

Exceptions

Exception Name	Number	Description
missinggroup	–23331	The column_group does not exist.
missingobject	–23308	The object oname does not exist.
missingschema	–23306	The schema sname does not exist.
nonmasterdef	–23312	Calling site is not master definition site.
referenced	–23332	The column_group is used by existing conflict resolution methods.

Restrictions

You must call this procedure from the quiesced master definition site.

DBMS_REPCAT.DROP_GROUPED_COLUMN

The DROP_GROUPED_COLUMN procedure allows you to drop one or more columns from a column group. Dropping a column from a column group is quite similar to adding one. Make sure, however, that none of your conflict resolution methods reference the column(s) that you are dropping. Changes do not take effect until GENERATE_REPLICATION_SUPPORT is called.

As with the other procedures with a list_of_column_names parameter, you can pass an asterisk (*) to the parameter to indicate all fields in table oname.

```
PROCEDURE DBMS_REPCAT.DROP_GROUPED_COLUMN
    (sname IN VARCHAR2,
     oname IN VARCHAR2,
     column_group IN VARCHAR2,
     {list_of_column_names IN VARCHAR2 |
     list_of_column_names IN dbms_repcat.varchar2s});
```

Note that you must specify only one of the list_of_column_names parameters.

Parameters

Parameter Name	Description
sname	Name of the schema that owns the replicated table
oname	Name of the table with the column_group

Parameter Name	Description
column_group	Name of the column_group from which column(s) will be dropped
list_of_column_names	A comma-delimited list of column names or a PL/SQL table of column names

Exceptions

Exception Name	Number	Description
missinggroup	−23331	Column group column_group does not exist.
missingobject	−23308	Table oname does not exist.
missingschema	−23306	Schema sname does not exist.
nonmasterdef	−23312	Invoking site is not the master definition site.

Restrictions

You must not call this procedure from the quiesced master definition site.

DBMS_REPCAT.DROP_MASTER_REPGROUP

The DROP_MASTER_REPGROUP procedure drops one or more replication groups (and optionally all of its contents) at the master definition site. Changes do not take effect until GENERATE_REPLICATION_SUPPORT is called.

Before calling DROP_MASTER_REPGROUP, call REMOVE_MASTER_DATABASES from the master definition site to remove all masters for which you plan to drop the group and that do not contain any other replication groups. In addition, you can avoid the fullqueue error by quiescing the replication group before attempting to drop the replication group.

```
PROCEDURE DBMS_REPCAT.DROP_MASTER_REPGROUP
    (gname IN VARCHAR2,
     drop_contents IN BOOLEAN := FALSE,
     all_sites IN BOOLEAN := FALSE);
```

Parameters

Parameter Name	Description
all_sites	If TRUE and call is the master definition site, then drop the replication group from all sites in the environment.
drop_contents	If TRUE, drop the objects in the replication group as well as the group itself.
gname	Name of the new replication group.

Exceptions

Exception Name	Number	Description
commfailure	−23317	Unable to communicate with all masters, and all_sites is TRUE.
fullqueue	−23353	Outstanding transactions queued for replication group gname.
missingrepgroup	−23373	gname is not specified correctly.
nonmaster	−23313	Calling site is not a master site.
nonmasterdef	−23312	Calling site is not a master definition site, and all_sites is TRUE.

Restrictions

- You must be connected to the replication administrator account (typically REPADMIN) to call DROP_MASTER_REPGROUP.

- DROP_MASTER_REPGROUP does not drop all snapshots if the gname parameter is the master of any snapshot groups. Dropping a master site does not necessarily remove it from the DBA_REPSITES at other masters.

DBMS_REPCAT.DROP_MASTER_REPOBJECT

The DROP_MASTER_REPOBJECT procedure drops a replicated object in an existing replication group at the master site and optionally drops the object from all sites. Do not drop tables to which snapshots are mastered.

```
PROCEDURE DBMS_REPOBJECT.DROP_MASTER_REPOBJECT
   (sname IN VARCHAR2,
    oname IN VARCHAR2,
    type IN VARCHAR2,
    drop_objects IN BOOLEAN := FALSE);
```

Parameters

Parameter Name	Description
sname	Name of the schema to which oname belongs.
oname	Name of the object to be added.
type	Object type. Valid types: TABLE, INDEX, SYNONYM, TRIGGER, VIEW, PROCEDURE, FUNCTION, PACKAGE, and PACKAGE BODY.
drop_objects	If TRUE, drop the object at all master sites; default is FALSE.

Exceptions

Exception Name	Number	Description
commfailure	−23317	Not all master sites are reachable.
missingobject	−23308	Object oname does not exist.

Exception Name	Number	Description
nonmasterdef	−23373	Calling site is not the master definition site for replication group gname.
typefailure	−23319	The type is not supported.

Restrictions

- This procedure must be called from the master definition site.

- The replication group must already exist and be quiesced.

DBMS_REPCAT.DROP_PRIORITY

The DROP_PRIORITY procedure removes a value from a priority group. The change takes effect immediately. The specifications differ for Oracle7 and Oracle8 as follows.

Oracle7 specification:

```
PROCEDURE DBMS_REPCAT.DROP_PRIORITY
    (gname IN VARCHAR2 := '',
     pgroup IN VARCHAR2,
     priority_num IN NUMBER,
     sname IN VARCHAR2 := '');
```

Oracle8 specification:

```
PROCEDURE DBMS_REPCAT.DROP_PRIORITY
    (gname IN VARCHAR2 := '',
     pgroup IN VARCHAR2,
     priority_num IN NUMBER);
```

Parameters

Parameter Name	Description
gname	Name of the replication group to which priority group pgroup belongs
pgroup	Name of the priority group whose priority is being altered
priority_num	Priority for the value to be dropped
sname (Oracle7 only)	Schema name (provided for pre-Oracle 7.3 compatibility)

Exceptions

Exception Name	Number	Description
missingprioritygroup	−23336	Priority group pgroup does not exist.
missingrepgroup	−23373	Replication group gname does not exist.
nonmasterdef	−23312	Calling site is not the master definition site.

Restrictions

You must call the DROP_PRIORITY procedure from the master definition site.

DBMS_REPCAT.DROP_PRIORITY_*datatype*

The DROP_PRIORITY_*datatype* procedure removes a value from a priority group. In this version of the procedure, you can specify the value by data value. The removal of a priority and value takes effect immediately.

The specifications differ for Oracle7 and Oracle 8 as follows.

Oracle7 specification:

```
PROCEDURE DBMS_REPCAT.DROP_PRIORITY_datatype
    (gname  IN VARCHAR2 := '',
     pgroup IN VARCHAR2,
     value  IN {CHAR|VARCHAR2|NUMBER|DATE|RAW},
     sname  IN VARCHAR2 := '');
```

Oracle8 specification:

```
PROCEDURE DBMS_REPCAT.DROP_PRIORITY_datatype
    (name   IN VARCHAR2 := '',
     pgroup IN VARCHAR2,
     value  IN {CHAR|NCHAR|VARCHAR2|NUMBER|DATE|RAW},
     sname  IN VARCHAR2 := '');
```

datatype and value can be any of the types in the following table.

Oracle7 and Oracle8	Oracle8 Only
CHAR	NCHAR
VARCHAR2	NVARCHAR2
NUMBER	
DATE	
RAW	

Parameters

Parameter Name	Description
gname	Name of the replication group to which priority group pgroup belongs
pgroup	Priority group to which new value and priority are being added
value	Literal value that is being assigned to pgroup
sname (Oracle7 only)	Schema name (provided for pre-Oracle 7.3 compatibility)

Exceptions

Exception Name	Number	Description
missingprioritygroup	–23336	Priority group pgroup does not exist.
missingrepgroup	–23373	Replication group gname does not exist.
nonmasterdef	–23312	Calling site is not the master definition site.
paramtype	–23325	Datatype of value is not the same as the datatype for priority group pgroup.

Restrictions

You must call DROP_PRIORITY_*datatype* from the master definition site.

DBMS_REPCAT.DROP_PRIORITY_GROUP

The DROP_PRIORITY_GROUP procedure lets you drop a priority group that you have defined. The change does not go into effect until the next call to GENERATE_REPLICATION_SUPPORT. Do not drop a priority group that you have designated as an UPDATE conflict resolution method for a column group. You must first use DROP_UPDATE_RESOLUTION for the column group. Records in the data dictionary view DBA_REPRESOLUTION indicate if and where the priority group is used. Attempting to drop a priority group that is in use raises the referenced exception.

The specifications differ for Oracle7 and Oracle8 as follows.

Oracle7 specification:

```
PROCEDURE DBMS_REPCAT.DROP_PRIORITY_GROUP
    (gname IN VARCHAR2 := '',
     pgroup IN VARCHAR2,
     sname IN VARCHAR2 := '');
```

Oracle8 specification:

```
PROCEDURE DBMS_REPCAT.DROP_PRIORITY_GROUP
    (gname IN VARCHAR2 := '',
     pgroup IN VARCHAR2);
```

Parameters

Parameter Name	Description
gname	Name of the replication group containing the priority group
pgroup	Name of the priority group to drop
sname (Oracle7 only)	Schema name (provided for pre-Oracle 7.3 compatibility)

Exceptions

Exception Name	Number	Description
missingrepgroup	−23373	Replication group gname does not exist.
nonmasterdef	−23312	Calling site is not the master definition site.
referenced	−23332	Priority group pgroup is used by existing conflict resolution methods.

Restrictions

You must call DROP_PRIORITY_GROUP from the master definition site.

DBMS_REPCAT.DROP_SITE_PRIORITY

The DROP_SITE_PRIORITY procedure drops an existing site priority group that is no longer in use. The change does not go into effect until the next call to GENERATE_REPLICATION_SUPPORT. As with the DROP_PRIORITY_GROUP procedure, do not attempt to drop a site priority group that is acting as an UPDATE conflict resolution handler for a column group. First, use DROP_UPDATE_RESO-LUTION to drop the conflict handler for the column group.

Specifications differ for Oracle7 and Oracle8 as follows.

Oracle7 specification:

```
PROCEDURE DBMS_REPCAT.DROP_SITE_PRIORITY
    (gname IN VARCHAR2 := '',
    name IN VARCHAR2,
    sname IN VARCHAR2 := '');
```

Oracle8 specification:

```
PROCEDURE DBMS_REPCAT.DROP_SITE_PRIORITY
    (gname IN VARCHAR2 := '',
    name IN VARCHAR2)
```

Parameters

Parameter Name	Description
gname	Name of the replication group containing the site priority group
name	Name of the site priority group
sname (Oracle7 only)	Schema name (provided for pre-Oracle 7.3 compatibility)

Exceptions

Exception Name	Number	Description
missingrepgroup	−23373	Replication group gname does not exist.
nonmasterdef	−23312	Calling site is not the master definition site.

Exception Name	Number	Description
referenced	−23332	Site priority group is used by existing conflict resolution method.

Restrictions

You must call DROP_SITE_PRIORITY from the master definition site.

DBMS_REPCAT.DROP_SITE_PRIORITY_SITE

The DROP_SITE_PRIORITY_SITE procedure removes a site from a site priority. The change takes effect immediately. Specifications for Oracle7 and Oracle8 differ as follows.

Oracle7 specification:

```
PROCEDURE DBMS_REPCAT.DROP_SITE_PRIORITY_SITE
   (gname IN VARCHAR2 := '',
    name IN VARCHAR2,
    site IN VARCHAR2,
    sname IN VARCHAR2 := '');
```

Oracle8 specification:

```
PROCEDURE DBMS_REPCAT.DROP_SITE_PRIORITY_SITE
   (gname IN VARCHAR2 := '',
    name IN VARCHAR2,
    site IN VARCHAR2);
```

Parameters

Parameter Name	Description
gname	Name of the replication group to which site priority group name belongs
name	Name of the site priority group
site	Global name of the new site
sname (Oracle7 only)	Schema name (provided for pre-Oracle 7.3 compatibility)

Exceptions

Exception Name	Number	Description
missingpriority	−1403	Site priority does not exist.
missingrepgroup	−23373	Replication group gname does not exist.
nonmasterdef	−23312	Calling site is not the master definition site.

Restrictions

You must call DROP_SITE_PRIORITY_SITE from the master definition site.

DBMS_REPCAT.DROP_SNAPSHOT_REPGROUP

The DBMS_REPCAT package's DROP_SNAPSHOT_REPGROUP procedure is the counterpart to the CREATE_SNAPSHOT_REPGROUP procedure. This procedure drops an existing snapshot replication group and, optionally, all of its contents.

```
PROCEDURE DBMS_REPCAT>DROP_SNAPSHOT_REPGROUP
    (gname IN VARCHAR2,
     drop_contents IN BOOLEAN := FALSE);
```

Parameters

Parameter Name	Description
gname	Name of the snapshot group.
drop_contents	If TRUE, objects in gname are dropped. If FALSE (the default) they are simply no longer replicated.

Exceptions

Exception Name	Number	Description
missingrepgroup	−23373	Replication group gname does not exist.
nonmaster	−23313	Calling site is not a snapshot site.

Restrictions

If drop_contents is set to FALSE, the triggers created to support snapshot modifications remain.

DBMS_REPCAT.DROP_SNAPSHOT_REPOBJECT

The DROP_SNAPSHOT_REPOBJECT procedure drops an object from a snapshot replication group at the snapshot site and, optionally, drops the object and its dependents as well.

```
PROCEDURE DBMS_REPCAT.DROP_SNAPSHOT_REPOBJECT
    (sname IN VARCHAR2,
     oname IN VARCHAR2,
     type IN VARCHAR2,
     drop_objects IN BOOLEAN := FALSE);.
```

For parameter descriptions, see the CREATE_SNAPSHOT_REPOBJECT procedure.

Exceptions

Exception Name	Number	Description
missingobject	−23308	Object oname does not exist in master's replication group gname.

Exception Name	Number	Description
nonsnapshot	–23314	Calling site is not a snapshot site.
typefailure	–23319	Invalid value for type.

Restrictions

If the type parameter is SNAPSHOT and you do not set the drop_objects parameter to TRUE, replication triggers and associated packages remain in the schema, and deferred transactions (if any) remain in the deftran queue.

DBMS_REPCAT.EXECUTE_DDL

CREATE_MASTER_REPOBJECT and DROP_MASTER_REPOBJECT do not support every type of object. For example, you cannot use these procedures to drop and create constraints. Enter the EXECUTE_DDL procedure. EXECUTE_DDL allows you to perform DDL at one or more master sites. The replication group may or may not be quiesced. You can monitor the progress of the DDL call by monitoring the REPCATLOG data dictionary view (DBA_REPCATLOG).

```
PROCEDURE DBMS_DEFER_SYS.EXECUTE_DDL
    (gname       IN VARCHAR2 := '',
    {master_list IN VARCHAR2 := NULL, |
    master_table IN dbms_utility.dblink_array,}
    ddl_text     IN VARCHAR2,
    sname        IN VARCHAR2 := '');
```

Parameters

Parameter Name	Description
gname	Name of the replicated object group.
master_list	Comma-separated string of master site global names at which DDL is to be performed. If NULL (the default), DDL is applied at all master sites in the replication group. Use either parameter master_list or master_table.
master_table	PL/SQL table of master site global names at which DDL is to be performed. Use either parameter master_list or master_table.
ddl_text	DDL statement to apply.
sname (Oracle7 only)	Schema name (provided for pre-Oracle 7.3 compatibility).

Exceptions

Exception Name	Number	Description
commfailure	–23317	Unable to communicate with the master site.
ddlfailure	–23318	Unable to perform DDL.

Exception Name	Number	Description
nonmaster	−23312	At least one site in master_list or master_table is not a master site.
nonmasterdef	−23312	Calling site is not a master definition site.

Restrictions

- This procedure must be called from the master definition site.
- The replication group must already exist.

DBMS_REPCAT.GENERATE_REPLICATION_PACKAGE

In some situations, you may wish to generate only replication support packages. GENERATE_REPLICATION_PACKAGE generates the *table_name*$RP package for the specified object at all master sites. The package is required for all tables participating in low-level replication.

```
PROCEDURE DBMS_REPCAT.GENERATE_REPLICATION__PACKAGE
    (sname IN VARCHAR2,
     oname IN VARCHAR2);
```

Parameters

Parameter Name	Description
sname	Name of the schema to which table oname belongs
oname	Name of table for which package is being generated

Exceptions

Exception Name	Number	Description
commfailure	−23317	Unable to communicate with all masters.
dbnotcompatible	−23375	One or more masters is a pre-7.3 release.
missingobject	−23308	Table oname does not exist in schema sname.
nonmasterdef	−23312	Calling site is not a master definition site.
notquiesced	−23310	Replication group to which object belongs is not quiesced.

Restrictions

- You must call this procedure from the master definition site.
- The replication group must be quiesced.
- The Oracle version must be 7.3 or later.

DBMS_REPCAT.GENERATE_REPLICATION_SUPPORT

The GENERATE_REPLICATION_SUPPORT procedure generates support for replicated tables, packages, and package bodies required to support replication of the
specified object, which can be a table, procedure, package, or package body. The
typical use of GENERATE_REPLICATION_SUPPORT is to regenerate the replication support triggers and procedures after changing a replication group's mode of
propagation.

If the object is a table, GENERATE_REPLICATION_SUPPORT creates the *table_
name*$RT triggers on the table, as well as the *table_name*$RP and *table_name*$RR
packages at all master sites.

If the object is a procedure, package or package body, GENERATE_REPLICA-
TION_SUPPORT generates the requisite procedure wrappers for it. The name of
the wrapper procedure is in the format *package_prefixoname* for packages and
package bodies, and *procedure_prefixoname* for procedures. If the parameters
package_prefix or procedure_prefix are not supplied, the default prefix DEFER_ is
used.

The specifications differ for Oracle7 and Oracle8 as follows.

Oracle7 specification:

```
PROCEDURE DBMS_REPCAT.GENERATE_REPLICATION_SUPPORT
    (sname              IN VARCHAR2,
     oname              IN VARCHAR2,    .
     type               IN VARCHAR2,
     package_prefix     IN VARCHAR2 := NULL,
     procedure_prefix   IN VARCHAR2 := NULL,
     distributed        IN BOOLEAN  := TRUE,
     gen_objs_owner     IN VARCHAR2 := NULL,
     gen_rep2_trigger   IN BOOLEAN  := FALSE);
```

Oracle8 specification:

```
PROCEDURE DBMS_REPCAT.GENERATE_REPLICATION_SUPPORT
    (sname              IN VARCHAR2,
     oname              IN VARCHAR2,
     type               IN VARCHAR2,
     package_prefix     IN VARCHAR2 := NULL,
     procedure_prefix   IN VARCHAR2 := NULL,
     distributed        IN BOOLEAN  := TRUE,
     gen_objs_owner     IN VARCHAR2 := NULL,
     min_communication  IN BOOLEAN  := TRUE);
```

Although it can take time for each call to GENERATE_REPLICATION_SUPPORT to
generate all required packages at all master sites, you can call it numerous times
(for all objects you are replicating) without waiting for each call to finish its work.

Parameters

Parameter Name	Description
sname	Name of the schema to which table oname belongs.
oname	Name of table for which package is being generated.
type	Object type. Supported types: TABLE, PROCEDURE, PACKAGE, and PACKAGE BODY.
package_prefix	Prefix used to name generated wrapper package for packages and package bodies.
procedure_prefix	Prefix used to name generated wrapper package for procedures.
distributed	If TRUE (the default), generate replication support for the object at each master; if FALSE, copy the replication support objects generated at the master definition site.
gen_objs_owner	Specifies schema in which to generate replication support objects; if NULL (the default), objects are generated under schema sname.
gen_rep2_trigger (Oracle7 only)	Provided for backward compatibility; if any masters are pre-7.3 releases, this must be set to TRUE. The default is FALSE.
min_communication (Oracle8 only)	If TRUE (the default), Oracle propagates changes with the minimum communication parameter, which avoids sending the old and new column values of unmodified fields.

Exceptions

Exception Name	Number	Description
commfailure	−23317	Unable to communicate with all masters.
dbnotcompatible	−23375	One or more masters is a pre-7.3 release.
missingobject	−23308	Table oname does not exist in schema sname.
missingschema	−23306	Schema sname does not exist.
nonmasterdef	−23312	Calling site is not a master definition site.
notquiesced	−23310	Replication group to which object belongs is not quiesced.
typefailure	−23319	Specified type is not a supported type.

Restrictions

- You must call this procedure from the master definition site for each object in the replication group.

- The replication group must be quiesced.

- If the object is not owned by the replication administrator account, the owner must have explicit EXECUTE privileges on the DBMS_DEFER package.

- If the *INIT.ORA* parameter COMPATIBLE is 7.3 or higher, the distributed parameter must be set to TRUE.

- If the *INIT.ORA* parameter COMPATIBLE is less than 7.3 in any snapshot sites, the gen_rep2_trigger parameter must be set to TRUE, and the COMPATIBLE parameter at the master definition site must be set to 7.3.0.0 or greater.

DBMS_REPCAT.GENERATE_REPLICATION_TRIGGER

The GENERATE_REPLICATION_TRIGGER procedure allows you to generate replication support triggers. The procedure generates the *table_name*$TP trigger and associated packages for the specified object. The specifications differ for Oracle7 and Oracle8 as follows. The first form of the procedure shown here generates the objects at all masters. Either form can be used to generate support at specific master sites.

Oracle7 specification:

```
PROCEDURE DBMS_REPCAT.GENERATE_REPLICATION_TRIGGER
    (sname IN VARCHAR2,
     oname IN VARCHAR2,
     gen_objs_owner IN VARCHAR2 := NULL,
     gen_rep2_trigger IN BOOLEAN := FALSE);

PROCEDURE DBMS_REPCAT.GENERATE_REPLICATION_TRIGGER
    (gname IN VARCHAR2,
     {master_list IN VARCHAR2 := NULL |
     master_table IN dbms_utility.dblink_array},
     gen_objs_owner IN VARCHAR2 := NULL);
```

Oracle8 specification:

```
PROCEDURE DBMS_REPCAT.GENERATE_REPLICATION_TRIGGER
    (sname IN VARCHAR2,
     oname IN VARCHAR2,
     gen_objs_owner IN VARCHAR2 := NULL,
     min_communication IN BOOLEAN  := TRUE);

PROCEDURE DBMS_REPCAT.GENERATE_REPLICATION_TRIGGER
    (gname IN VARCHAR2,
     gen_objs_owner IN VARCHAR2 := NULL,
     min_communication IN BOOLEAN := NULL);
```

Parameters

Parameter Name	Description
sname	Name of the schema to which table oname belongs.
oname	Name of object for which support objects are being generated.
gen_rep2_trigger (Oracle7 only)	Provided for backward compatibility; if any master sites are pre-7.3 releases, this parameter must be set to TRUE (default is FALSE).
gname	The replication group to which oname belongs.

Parameter Name	Description
master_list	Comma-delimited string of global names for masters in which support objects are to be generated.
master_table	PL/SQL table of global names for masters in which support objects are to be generated.
gen_objs_owner	Specifies schema in which to generate replication support objects; if NULL (the default), objects are generated under schema in which they currently reside.
min_communication (Oracle8 only)	If TRUE (the default), the generated trigger sends the new value of a column only if the value has changed. Old field values are sent only if the field is part of the primary key or part of a column group for which member columns have changed.

Exceptions

Exception Name	Number	Description
commfailure	−23317	Unable to communicate with all masters.
dbnotcompatible	−23375	One or more masters is a pre-7.3 release and gen_rep2_trigger is not set to TRUE.
missingobject	−23308	Table oname does not exist in schema sname.
missingschema	−23306	Schema sname does not exist.
nonmasterdef	−23312	Calling site is not a master definition site.
notquiesced	−23310	Replication group to which object belongs is not quiesced.

Restrictions

- You must call this procedure from the master definition site.

- The replication group must be quiesced.

- The GENERATE_REPLICATION_SUPPORT or GENERATE_REPLICATION_PACKAGE must previously have been called for the object specified in the oname parameter.

DBMS_REPCAT.MAKE_COLUMN_GROUP

The MAKE_COLUMN_GROUP procedure creates a new column group and designates columns to it. It provides the functional equivalent of calling DEFINE_COLUMN_GROUP followed by ADD_GROUPED_COLUMN.

```
PROCEDURE DBMS_REPCAT.MAKE_COLUMN_GROUP
    (sname IN VARCHAR2,
     oname IN VARCHAR2,
     column_group IN VARCHAR2,
     {list_of_column_names IN VARCHAR2 |
     list_of_column_names IN dbms_repcat.varchar2s} );
```

Note that you must specify only one of the list_of_column_names parameters.

Parameters

Parameter Name	Description
sname	Name of the schema to which the replicated table belongs.
oname	Name of the replicated table containing the column group.
column_group	Name of the column group.
list_of_column_names	A comma-delimited list of column names or a PL/SQL table of column names. Use an asterisk (*) to add all columns in the table.

Exceptions

Exception Name	Number	Description
duplicatecolumn	−23333	Column(s) already a member of a different column group.
duplicategroup	−23330	column_group already exists.
missingcolumn	−23334	Column(s) specified do not exist in table oname.
missingobject	−23308	Object oname does not exist.
nonmasterdef	−23312	Calling site is not master definition site.

Restrictions

- You must call this procedure from the quiesced master definition site.

- You must regenerate replication support for the table after defining the column group with the GENERATE_REPLICATION_SUPPORT procedure.

DBMS_REPCAT.PURGE_MASTER_LOG

The PURGE_MASTER_LOG procedure removes records from the DBA_REPCAT-LOG data dictionary view. Records may be removed by ID, originating master, replication group, or schema. If any of the parameters is NULL, it is treated as a wildcard. Specifications differ for Oracle7 and Oracle8 as follows.

Oracle7 specification:

```
PROCEDURE DBMS_REPCAT.PURGE_MASTER_LOG
    (id IN NATURAL,
     source IN VARCHAR2,
     gname IN VARCHAR2 := '',
     sname IN VARCHAR2 := '');
```

Oracle8 specification:

```
PROCEDURE DBMS_REPCAT.PURGE_MASTER_LOG
    (id IN NATURAL,
     source IN VARCHAR2,
     gname IN VARCHAR2);
```

To clear all entries from the DBA_REPCATLOG data dictionary view, set all parameters to NULL.

Parameters

Parameter Name	Description
id	Identification of the request (i.e., the ID field in DBA_REPCATLOG data dictionary view)
source	Global name of originating master
gname	Name of the replication group for which request was made
sname (Oracle7 only)	Schema name (provided for pre-Oracle 7.3 compatibility)

ExceptionsRestrictions

Exception Name	Number	Description
nonmaster	−23312	The gname is NULL, and calling site is not a master site.

The calling site must be a master site.

DBMS_REPCAT.PURGE_STATISTICS

If you are collecting conflict resolution statistics, you can purge this information periodically using the PURGE_STATISTICS procedure. This procedure removes records from the DBA_REPRESOLUTION.STATISTICS data dictionary view. Records may be specified by data range.

```
PROCEDURE DBMS_REPCAT.PURGE_STATISTICS
    (sname IN VARCHAR2,
     oname IN VARCHAR2,
     start_date IN DATE,
     end_date IN DATE);
```

To clear all entries in DBA_REPRESOLUTION_STATISTICS, set the start_date and end_date parameters to NULL.

There are no restrictions on calling PURGE_STATISTICS.

Parameters

Parameter Name	Description
sname	Name of the schema that owns oname.
oname	Table whose conflict resolution statistics are to be deleted.
start_date	Beginning of date range for which statistics are to be deleted. If NULL, all entries less than end_date are deleted.
end_date	End of date range for which statistics are to be deleted. If NULL, all entries greater than end_date are deleted.

Exceptions

Exception Name	Number	Description
missingobject	–23308	Object oname does not exist.
missingschema	–23306	Schema sname does not exist.

DBMS_REPCAT.REFRESH_SNAPSHOT_REPGROUP

The REFRESH_SNAPSHOT_REPGROUP procedure refreshes the snapshot replication group manually. Specifications differ for Oracle7 and Oracle8 as follows.

Oracle7 specification:

```
PROCEDURE DBMS_REPCAT.REFRESH_SNAPSHOT_REPGROUP
    (gname IN VARCHAR2,
     drop_missing_contents IN BOOLEAN := FALSE,
     refresh_snapshots IN BOOLEAN := FALSE,
     refresh_other_objects IN BOOLEAN := FALSE,
     execute_as_user IN BOOLEAN:= FALSE);
```

Oracle8 specification:

```
PROCEDURE DBMS_REPCAT.REFRESH_SNAPSHOT_REPGROUP
    (gname IN VARCHAR2,
     drop_missing_contents IN BOOLEAN := FALSE,
     refresh_other_objects IN BOOLEAN := FALSE )
```

The procedure can optionally drop objects that are no longer in the group and/or refresh the snapshots and other objects.

The REFRESH_SNAPSHOT_REPGROUP procedure replaces the REFRESH_SNAP-SHOT_REPSCHEMA procedure. Although REFRESH_SNAPSHOT_REPSCHEMA still exists (as of Oracle 7.3.3), do not use it; it does not exist in Oracle 8.0.3.

Parameters

Parameter Name	Description
gname	Name of the replication group.
drop_missing_contents	If TRUE, drop schema objects that are no longer in the snapshot group. If FALSE (the default), objects are simply no longer replicated.
refresh_snapshots	If TRUE, force a refresh of snapshots in gname. Default is FALSE.
refresh_other_objects	If TRUE, refresh nonsnapshot objects in gname, such as views and procedures. Nonsnapshot objects are refreshed by dropping and re-creating them. Default is FALSE.
execute_as_user (Oracle7 only)	FALSE (default) indicates that the remote system will authenticate calls using the authentication context user who originally queued the RPC; TRUE indicates that remote system will use authentication context of the session user.

Exceptions

Exception Name	Number	Description
commfailure	−23317	Unable to communicate with the master site.
nonmaster	−23313	Master is no longer a master database.
nonsnapshot	−23314	Calling site is not a snapshot site.

Restrictions

REFRESH_SNAPSHOT_REPGROUP must be called from a snapshot site.

DBMS_REPCAT.REGISTER_STATISTICS

The REGISTER_STATISTICS procedure enables the collection of data about the successful resolution of update, uniqueness, and delete conflicts. This information is visible in the DBA_REPRESOLUTION_STATISTICS data dictionary view.

```
PROCEDURE DBMS_REPCAT.REGISTER_STATISTICS
    (sname IN VARCHAR2,
     oname IN VARCHAR2);
```

These are no restrictions on calling REGISTER_STATISTICS.

Parameters

Parameter Name	Description
sname	Name of the schema to which the replicated table belongs
oname	Name of the replicated table

Exceptions

Exception Name	Number	Description
missingobject	−23308	Table oname does not exist.
missingschema	−23306	Schema sname does not exist.

DBMS_REPCAT.RELOCATE_MASTERDEF

If your master definition site becomes unusable or if you simply want another site to serve that role, you can configure a different master site as the master definition site with the RELOCATE_MASTERDEF procedure. Follow these guidelines:

- If your relocation is planned (i.e., all sites are up and reachable), set the notify_masters and include_old_masterdef parameters to TRUE.

- If the current master definition site is not available, set the notify_masters parameter to TRUE, and set include_old_masterdef to FALSE.

- If the master definition site as well as some master sites are unavailable, invoke the RELOCATE_MASTERDEF procedure from each functioning master site with both the notify_masters and the include_old_masterdef parameters set to FALSE.

Neither the current master definition site nor the new master definition site need be reachable to run this procedure successfully from any given master site.

The specifications differ for Oracle7 and Oracle8 as follows.

Oracle7 specification:

```
PROCEDURE DBMS_REPCAT.RELOCATE_MASTERDEF
    (gname IN VARCHAR2 := '',
     old_masterdef IN VARCHAR2,
     new_masterdef IN VARCHAR2,
     notify_masters IN BOOLEAN := TRUE,
     include_old_masterdef IN BOOLEAN := TRUE,
     sname IN VARCHAR2 := '')
```

Oracle8 specification:

```
PROCEDURE DBMS_REPCAT.RELOCATE_MASTERDEF
    (gname IN VARCHAR2,
     old_masterdef IN VARCHAR2,
     new_masterdef IN VARCHAR2,
     notify_masters IN BOOLEAN := TRUE,
     include_old_masterdef IN BOOLEAN := TRUE);
```

Parameters

Parameter Name	Description
gname	Name of the replication group.
old_masterdef	Global name of the current master definition site.
new_masterdef	Global name of the new master definition site.
notify_masters	If TRUE (the default), synchronously multicast information about the change to all masters; if FALSE, do not inform masters.
include_old_masterdef	If TRUE (the default), notify current master definition site of the change.
sname (Oracle7 only)	Schema name (provided for pre-Oracle 7.3 compatibility).

Exceptions

Exception Name	Number	Description
commfailure	−23317	Unable to communicate with master site(s) and notify_masters is TRUE.
nonmaster	−23313	The new_masterdef is not a master site.
nonmasterdef	−23312	The old_masterdef is not the master definition site.

Restrictions

You must call RELOCATE_MASTERDEF from a master or master definition site.

DBMS_REPCAT.REMOVE_MASTER_DATABASES

The REMOVE_MASTER_DATABASES procedure complements the ADD_MASTER_ DATABASE procedure by removing one or more master databases from a replication group. The master sites being removed do not need to be accessible, but all other masters do. After removing master sites with REMOVE_MASTER_DATA- BASES, you should call DROP_MASTER_REPGROUP at each of the master sites you removed. Although you do not need to quiesce the replication group to remove one or more master database(s), you are strongly encouraged to do so. Otherwise, you will manually have to clear the RPC queue and resolve any inconsistencies.

Specification differ for Oracle7 and Oracle8 as follows.

Oracle7 specification:

```
PROCEDURE DBMS_REPCAT.REMOVE_MASTER_DATABASES
    (gname IN VARCHAR2 := '',
     master_list IN VARCHAR2,
     sname IN VARCHAR2 := '');
```

Oracle8 specification:

```
PROCEDURE DBMS_REPCAT.REMOVE_MASTER_DATABASES
    (gname IN VARCHAR2 := '',
     master_list IN VARCHAR2);,
```

Parameters

Parameter Name	Description
gname	Name of the replication group from which the master site(s) will be removed.
master_list	A comma-delimited list of global_names of master sites to be removed; use either master_list or master_table.
sname (Oracle7 only)	Schema name (provided for pre-Oracle 7.3 compatibility).

Exceptions

Exception Name	Number	Description
commfailure	−23317	One or more remaining master sites is not reachable.
nonmaster	−23313	One or more of the specified masters is not a master database.
nonmasterdef	−23312	Calling site is not the master definition site.
reconfigerror	−23316	One of the specified masters is the master definition site.

Restrictions

The REMOVE_MASTER_DATABASES procedure must be run from the master definition site.

DBMS_REPCAT.REPCAT_IMPORT_CHECK

From time to time, you may need to rebuild a master site from an export dump file as either a recovery or maintenance procedure. Because object ID numbers (as seen in SYS.OBJ$.OBJ# and DBA_OBJECTS.OBJECT_ID) change during these rebuilds, Oracle supplies a procedure (REPCAT_IMPORT_CHECK) that you must run immediately after an import of any master site to synchronize the new ID numbers with the data stored in the table SYSTEM.REPCAT$_REPOBJECT. Objects with a status of VALID in REPCAT$_REPOBJECT are not affected.

The specifications differ for Oracle7 and Oracle8 as follows.

Oracle7 specification:

```
PROCEDURE DBMS_REPCAT.REPCAT_IMPORT_CHECK
    (gname IN VARCHAR2 := '',
     master IN BOOLEAN,
     sname IN VARCHAR2 := '');
```

Oracle8 specification:

```
PROCEDURE DBMS_REPCAT.REPCAT_IMPORT_CHECK
    (gname IN VARCHAR2 := '',
     master IN BOOLEAN);
```

There are no restrictions on calling REPCAT_IMPORT_CHECK.

Call REPCAT_IMPORT_CHECK with sname and master set to NULL (or with no parameters) to validate all replication groups at the site.

Parameters

Parameter Name	Description
gname	Name of the replication group being revalidated
master	Set to TRUE if site is a master, FALSE if it is a snapshot site
sname (Oracle7 only)	Schema name (provided for pre-Oracle 7.3 compatibility)

Exceptions

Exception Name	Number	Description
missingobject	−23308	Object with a status of VALID in REPCAT$_REPOBJECT does not exist.
missingschema	−23306	Schema sname does not exist.
nonmaster	−23312	Master is set to TRUE, but the calling site is not a master or not the expected database.

Exception Name	Number	Description
nonsnapshot	−23314	Master is set to FALSE but the calling site is not a snapshot site.

DBMS_REPCAT.RESUME_MASTER_ACTIVITY

The RESUME_MASTER_ACTIVITY procedure starts up an environment that has been or is in the process of being quiesced. The specifications differ for Oracle7 and Oracle8 as follows.

Oracle7 specification:

```
PROCEDURE DBMS_REPCAT.RESUME_MASTER_ACTIVITY
    (gname IN VARCHAR2 := '',
     override IN BOOLEAN := FALSE,
     sname IN VARCHAR2 := '');
```

Oracle8 specification:

```
PROCEDURE DBMS_REPCAT.RESUME_MASTER_ACTIVITY
    (gname IN VARCHAR2,
     override IN BOOLEAN := FALSE);
```

Parameters

Parameter Name	Description
gname	Name of the replication group for which replication activity is to be resumed.
override	If FALSE (the default), activity is resumed only after all deferred REPCAT activity is completed; if set to TRUE, activity is resumed as soon as possible.
sname (Oracle7 only)	Schema name (provided for pre-Oracle 7.3 compatibility).

Exceptions

Exception Name	Number	Description
commfailure	−23317	Unable to communicate with one or more master sites.
nonmasterdef	−23312	Calling site is not the master definition site.
notquiesced	−23310	Replication group gname is not quiesced.

Restrictions

- You must run this procedure from the master definition site.

- The replication group must be quiesced or quiescing.

DBMS_REPCAT.SEND_AND_COMPARE_OLD_VALUES (Oracle8 Only)

The default behavior of advanced replication is to send the old and new values of every column to participating master sites whenever you update a row in a replicated table. At the destination sites, Oracle uses this information to ensure that the version of the row that you updated matches the version of the row currently at the destination. However, if you know that certain columns in a table will never change, you can avoid sending the data in these columns when you propagate updates to participating master sites. Using the SEND_AND_COMPARE_OLD_VALUES procedure (available only in Oracle8) in this way, you'll reduce propagation overhead.

```
PROCEDURE DBMS_REPCAT.SEND_AND_COMPARE_OLD_VALUES
    (sname IN VARCHAR2
     oname IN VARCHAR2,
     {column_list IN VARCHAR2 | column_table IN dbms_repcat.varchar2s},
     operation IN VARCHAR2 := 'UPDATE',
     send IN BOOLEAN := TRUE);
```

The configuration changes you specify with this procedure do not take effect unless the min_communication parameter is TRUE for the table in question. That is, you must have executed GENERATE_REPLICATION_SUPPORT for the table with min_communication = TRUE.

If you change the propagation mode in Oracle8, you must also regenerate the SEND_AND_COMPARE_OLD_VALUES procedure.

Parameters

Parameter Name	Description
sname	Name of the replication group whose propagation mode is being altered.
oname	Table being altered.
column_list	Comma-separated list of columns whose propagation mode is being altered; an asterisk (*) indicates all nonkey columns.
column_table	PL/SQL table of containing columns whose propagation is being altered.
operation	Operation for which this change applies; this may be UPDATE, DELETE, or an asterisk (*) (indicating both updates and deletes).
send	If TRUE (the default), then the old values for the columns are sent; if FALSE, then old values are not sent.

Exceptions

Exception Name	Number	Description
missingcolumn	−23334	Column(s) specified do not exist in table oname.
missingobject	−23308	Object oname does not exist.
nonmasterdef	−23312	Calling site is not the master definition site.
notquiesced	−23310	Replication group gname is not quiesced.
typefailure	−23319	The oname is not a table.

Restrictions

- You must call this procedure from the master definition site.

- The replication group sname must be quiesced.

DBMS_REPCAT.SET_COLUMNS

When you replicate a table, Oracle must be able to uniquely identify each record in the table so that it can propagate changes to the correct row or rows. By default, the advanced replication facilities use the primary key to identify rows. However, if your table does not have a primary key or if you wish to use a different criterion to uniquely identify records, you can use SET_COLUMNS to designate a pseudo primary key. Columns designated with this procedure may contain NULL values.

```
PROCEDURE DBMS_REPCAT.SET_COLUMNS
   (sname IN VARCHAR2,
    oname IN VARCHAR2,
    column_list IN VARCHAR2 | column_table IN dbms_utility.name_array);
```

Parameters

Parameter Name	Description
sname	Name of the schema that owns the replicated table.
oname	Name of the table with the column_group.
column_list	A comma-delimited list of column names to use as the pseudo primary key. Use either column_list or column_table.
column_table	A PL/SQL table of column names. Use either column_list or column_table.

Exceptions

Exception Name	Number	Description
missingcolumn	–23334	Column(s) specified do not exist in table oname.
missingobject	–23308	Table oname does not exist.
nonmasterdef	–23312	Invoking site is not the master definition site.

Restrictions

- SET_COLUMNS must be run from the master definition site.

- The changes do not take effect until the next call to GENERATE_REPLICATION_SUPPORT.

DBMS_REPCAT.SUSPEND_MASTER_ACTIVITY

You may have noticed that many of the DBMS_REPCAT procedures require you to quiesce the environment before using them. *Quiescence,* as it is called, accomplishes two things:

*   It applies all outstanding DML for the replication group at all master sites.

*   It prevents any additional DML on any of the replicated objects at all master sites.

In other words, quiescence ensures that all sites are up to date and forces the replicated environment to stand still.

Do not attempt to quiesce an environment that has unresolved errors or any other serious problems. If you cannot complete outstanding transactions, you will not be able to quiesce the environment.

The SUSPEND_MASTER_ACTIVITY procedure quiesces an environment. It propagates all deferred transactions and RPCs and then disables all replication activity. Although this procedure allows you to specify a replication group in Version 7.x databases, all replication groups whose master definition site is the invoking site are quiesced. Group-level quiescence is available with Oracle8. This call can take some time to complete if you have many master sites or many outstanding transactions. You can monitor the progress by querying the status field in the DBA_REPCATLOG data dictionary view.

The specifications differ for Oracle7 and Oracle8 as follows.

Oracle7 specification:

```
PROCEDURE DBMS_REPCAT.SUSPEND_MASTER_ACTIVITY
    (gname IN VARCHAR2 := '',
     execute_as_user IN BOOLEAN := FALSE,
     sname IN VARCHAR2 := '');
```

Oracle8 specification:

```
PROCEDURE DBMS_REPCAT.SUSPEND_MASTER_ACTIVITY
    (gname IN VARCHAR2,
     override IN BOOLEAN := FALSE);
```

Parameters

Parameter Name	Description
gname	Name of the replication group for which replication activity is to be suspended.

Parameter Name	Description
execute_as_user	FALSE (the default) indicates that the remote system will authenticate calls using the authentication context user who originally queued the RPC; TRUE indicates that the remote system will use authentication context of the session user.
sname (Oracle7 only)	Schema name (provided for pre-Oracle 7.3 compatibility).

Exceptions

Exception Name	Number	Description
commfailure	–23317	Unable to communicate with one or more master sites.
nonmasterdef	–23312	Calling site is not the master definition site.
notnormal	–23311	Replication group gname is not in NORMAL state.

Restrictions

- You must run this procedure from the master definition site.

- Prior to Oracle8, this procedure quiesces all replication groups at the master definition site, not just the group specified by the gname parameter.

DBMS_REPCAT.SWITCH_SNAPSHOT_MASTER

The SWITCH_SNAPSHOT_MASTER procedure lets you switch a snapshot replication group to a different master site. This procedure changes the master site for the specified snapshot group. The new master site must contain a replica of the replication group gname. The next time the snapshot group refreshes, Oracle performs a full refresh. Put snapshot logs on the master tables at the new master site so that you can use fast refreshes.

The specifications differ for Oracle7 and Oracle8 as follows.

Oracle7 specification:

```
PROCEDURE DBMS_REPCAT.SWITCH_SNAPSHOT_MASTER
    (gname IN VARCHAR2 := '',
    master IN VARCHAR2,
    execute_as_user IN BOOLEAN := FALSE,
    sname IN VARCHAR2 := '');
```

Oracle8 specification:

```
PROCEDURE DBMS_REPCAT.SWITCH_SNAPSHOT_MASTER
    (gname IN VARCHAR2 := '',
    master IN VARCHAR2)
```

Parameters

Parameter Name	Description
gname	Name of the snapshot group.
master	Name of the new master site.
execute_as_user (Oracle7 only)	FALSE (the default) indicates that the remote system will authenticate calls using the authentication context user who originally queued the RPC; TRUE indicates that the remote system will use authentication context of the session user.
sname (Oracle7 only)	Schema name (provided for pre-Oracle 7.3 compatibility).

Exceptions

Exception Name	Number	Description
commfailure	−23317	Unable to communicate with the master site.
nonmaster	−23312	The master parameter is not a master site.
nonsnapshot	−23314	Calling site is not a snapshot site.

Restrictions

- The new master site must contain a replica of the replication group gname.

- Snapshots whose query is greater than 32K cannot be remastered.

DBMS_REPCAT.VALIDATE

The VALIDATE function diagnoses the status of your replicated environment and returns any errors in either a PL/SQL array of records (error_table) or a pair of arrays with error text (error_msg_table) and error numbers (error_num_table).

```
FUNCTION validate(gname            IN   VARCHAR2,
                  check_genflags   IN   BOOLEAN := FALSE,
                  check_valid_objs IN   BOOLEAN := FALSE,
                  check_links_sched IN  BOOLEAN := FALSE,
                  check_links      IN   BOOLEAN := FALSE,
                  error_table          OUT dbms_repcat.validate_err_table)

FUNCTION validate(gname            IN   VARCHAR2,
                  check_genflags   IN   BOOLEAN := FALSE,
                  check_valid_objs IN   BOOLEAN := FALSE,
                  check_links_sched IN  BOOLEAN := FALSE,
                  check_links      IN   BOOLEAN := FALSE,
                  error_msg_table      OUT dbms_utility.uncl_array,
                  error_num_table      OUT dbms_utility.number_array)
                  RETURN BINARY_INTEGER;
```

The return value of these functions is the number of errors detected.

There are no restrictions on calling this function.

Parameters

Parameter Name	Description
gname	Name of the replication group.
check_genflags	Boolean flag indicating whether to check that all replicated objects have replication support generated.
check_valid_objs	Boolean flag which checks whether or not all replicated objects are valid. This check is performed at all master sites.
check_links_sched	Boolean flag to check if pushes are scheduled to all master databases.
check_links	Boolean flag which checks if the user invoking the procedure has valid database links to all master databases.
error_table	PL/SQL table of errors found.
error_msg_table	Error message text of any errors found.
error_num_table	Oracle error number for any errors found.

Exceptions

Exception Name	Number	Description
missingdblink	−23396	The database link does not exist for the replication propagator account, or pushes are not scheduled.
dblinkmismatch	−23397	The database link name at the local site does not match the global name of the database to which it connects.
dblinkuidmismatch	−23398	The replication propagator accounts are not the same at all sites.
objectnotgenerated	−23399	Replication support has not been generated for the object at all master sites.
opnotsupported	−23408	Not all sites are Oracle8.

DBMS_REPCAT.WAIT_MASTER_LOG

You can use the WAIT_MASTER_LOG procedure to ascertain whether the changes in the repcatlog queue have reached the master sites. However, you might find it more convenient to query the DBA_REPCATLOG data dictionary view directly. This procedure has an OUT parameter, true_count, which the procedure populates with the number of outstanding (incomplete) tasks. The specifications differ for Oracle7 and Oracle8 as follows.

Oracle7 specification:

```
PROCEDURE DBMS_REPCAT.WAIT_MASTER_LOG
    (gname IN VARCHAR2 := '',
    record_count IN NATURAL,
    timeout IN NATURAL,
    true_count OUT NATURAL,
    sname IN VARCHAR2 := '');
```

Oracle8 specification:

```
PROCEDURE DBMS_REPCAT.WAIT_MASTER_LOG
    (gname IN VARCHAR2,
     record_count IN NATURAL,
     timeout IN NATURAL,
     true_count OUT NATURAL);
```

There are no restrictions on calling WAIT_MASTER_LOG.

Parameters

Parameter Name	Description
gname	Name of the replication group
record_count	Number of records to allow to be entered in the DBA_REPCAT-LOG data dictionary view before returning
timeout	Number of seconds to wait before returning
true_count	Output variable containing the actual number of incomplete activities queued in the DBA_REPCATLOG data dictionary view
sname (Oracle7 only)	Schema name (provided for pre-Oracle 7.3 compatibility)

Exceptions

Exception Name	Number	Description
nonmaster	−23312	Calling site is not a master site.

DBMS_REPCAT_ADMIN: Setting Up Administrative Accounts

The first step in creating an advanced replication environment is to create administrative and end user accounts. The DBMS_REPCAT_AUTH and DBMS_REPCAT_ADMIN packages contain programs that grant and revoke the privileges required in such an environment.

How the Package Is Used

The replication administration account or a DBA account uses the procedures in DBMS_REPCAT_ADMIN to grant or revoke the specified privileges.

Installation and Access

The DBMS_REPCAT_ADMIN package is created when the Oracle database is installed. The *dbmsrepc.sql* script (found in the built-in packages source directory) contains the source code for this package's specification. This script is called by *catrep.sql*, which must be run to install the advanced replication packages. The wrapped SQL script *prvtrepc.sql* creates the public synonym DBMS_REPCAT_ ADMIN. No EXECUTE privileges are granted on DBMS_REPCAT_ADMIN; only the owner (SYS) and those with the EXECUTE ANY PROCEDURE system privilege may execute the package.

DBMS_REPCAT_ADMIN Procedures

 Oracle8 documents only the REPGROUP procedures listed here, although the REPSCHEMA procedures also exist. The functionality is identical.

Procedure Name	Description
GRANT_ADMIN_ANY_REPGROUP (Oracle8)	Grants privileges required to administer any replication group at the current site
GRANT_ADMIN_ANY_REPSCHEMA	Grants privileges required to administer any replication schema at the current site
GRANT_ADMIN_REPGROUP (Oracle8)	Grants privileges required to administer the replication group for which the user is the schema owner
GRANT_ADMIN_REPSCHEMA	Grants privileges required to administer the replication schema for which the user is the schema owner
REVOKE_ADMIN_ANY_REPGROUP (Oracle8)	Revokes privileges required to administer all replication groups
REVOKE_ADMIN_ANY_REPSCHEMA	Revokes privileges required to administer all replication schemas
REVOKE_ADMIN_REPGROUP (Oracle8)	Revokes privileges required to administer the replication group for which the user is the schema owner
REVOKE_ADMIN_REPSCHEMA	Revokes privileges required to administer the replication schema for which the user is the schema owner

DBMS_REPCAT_ADMIN Exceptions

The DBMS_REPCAT_ADMIN package may raise exception ORA-01917 if the specified user does not exist.

DBMS_REPCAT_ADMIN.GRANT_ADMIN_ANY_REPGROUP

The GRANT_ADMIN_ANY_REPGROUP procedure grants the privileges required to administer any replication group at the current site.

```
PROCEDURE DBMS_REPCAT_ADMIN.GRANT_ADMIN_ANY_REPGROUP
    (userid IN VARCHAR2);
```

userid is the Oracle user ID for whom you are granting privileges.

There are no restrictions on calling GRANT_ADMIN_ANY_REPGROUP.

This procedure replaces GRANT_ADMIN_ANY_REPSCHEMA. The specific privileges granted are:

ALTER ANY CLUSTER	ALTER ANY INDEX
ALTER ANY PROCEDURE	ALTER ANY SEQUENCE
ALTER ANY SNAPSHOT	ALTER ANY TABLE
ALTER ANY TRIGGER	ALTER SESSION
CREATE ANY CLUSTER	CREATE ANY INDEX
CREATE ANY PROCEDURE	CREATE ANY SEQUENCE
CREATE ANY SNAPSHOT	CREATE ANY SYNONYM
CREATE ANY TABLE	CREATE ANY TRIGGER
CREATE ANY VIEW	CREATE DATABASE LINK
CREATE SESSION	DELETE ANY TABLE
DROP ANY CLUSTER	DROP ANY INDEX
DROP ANY PROCEDURE	DROP ANY SEQUENCE
DROP ANY SNAPSHOT	DROP ANY SYNONYM
DROP ANY TABLE	DROP ANY TRIGGER
DROP ANY VIEW	EXECUTE ANY PROCEDURE
INSERT ANY TABLE	SELECT ANY TABLE
UNLIMITED TABLESPACE	

Because the privileges granted to userid are relatively powerful, recipients of these grants should be kept to an absolute minimum.

Be sure to set up a replication administrator account at every master site of a multi-master replication environment. In addition, administration will be easiest if you use the same account name in all locations.

Exceptions

GRANT_ADMIN_ANY_REPGROUP may raise exception ORA-01917 if the specified user does not exist.

DBMS_REPCAT_ADMIN.GRANT_ADMIN_REPGROUP

The GRANT_ADMIN_REPGROUP procedure grants the privileges required to administer a replication group for which the user is the schema owner.

```
PROCEDURE DBMS_REPCAT_ADMIN.GRANT_ADMIN_REPGROUP
    (userid IN VARCHAR2);
```

userid is the Oracle user ID for whom you are granting privileges.

This procedure replaces GRANT_ADMIN_REPSCHEMA. The specific privileges granted are:

ALTER SESSION	CREATE CLUSTER
CREATE DATABASE LINK	CREATE PROCEDURE
CREATE SEQUENCE	CREATE SESSION
CREATE SNAPSHOT	CREATE SYNONYM
CREATE TABLE	CREATE TRIGGER
CREATE VIEW	EXECUTE ON SYS.DBMS_DEFER
EXECUTE ON SYS.DBMS_DEFER_SYS	EXECUTE ON SYS.DBMS_REPCAT
EXECUTE ON SYS.DBMSOBJGWRAPPER	UNLIMITED TABLESPACE

GRANT_ADMIN_REPGROUP is not useful if your replication group contains objects belonging to multiple schemas. Such a replication group has to be administered by a user who has been granted privileges via GRANT_ADMIN_ANY_REPGROUP.

There are no restrictions on calling GRANT_ADMIN_REPGROUP.

Exceptions

GRANT_ADMIN.REPGROUP may raise exception ORA-01917 if the specified user does not exist.

DBMS_REPCAT_ADMIN.REVOKE_ADMIN_ANY_REPGROUP

The REVOKE_ADMIN_ANY_REPGROUP procedure revokes the privileges required to administer any replication group at the current site (see GRANT_ADMIN_ANY_ REPGROUP for a list of these privileges). Note that REVOKE_ADMIN_ANY_REP-GROUP revokes privileges regardless of whether or not they were obtained via GRANT_ADMIN_ANY_REPGROUP. This procedure replaces REVOKE_ADMIN_ ANY_SCHEMA, which is now obsolete.

```
PROCEDURE DBMS_REPCAT_ADMIN.REVOKE_ADMIN_ANY_REPGROUP
    (userid IN VARCHAR2);
```

userid is the Oracle user ID for whom you are revoking privileges.

There are no restrictions on calling REVOKE_ADMIN_ANY_REPGROUP.

Exceptions

REVOKE_ADMIN_REPGROUP may raise exception ORA-01917 if the specified user does not exist.

DBMS_REPCAT_ADMIN.REVOKE_ADMIN_REPGROUP

REVOKE_ADMIN_REPGROUP revokes from userid all privileges required to administer a replication group with the same name as userid (see GRANT_ADMIN_REPGROUP for a list of these privileges). Note that REVOKE_ADMIN_REP-GROUP revokes privileges regardless of whether they were obtained via GRANT_ADMIN_REPGROUP. This procedure replaces REVOKE_ADMIN_REPSCHEMA, which is now obsolete.

```
PROCEDURE DBMS_REPCAT_ADMIN.REVOKE_ADMIN_REPGROUP
   (userid IN VARCHAR2);
```

userid is the Oracle user ID for whom you are revoking privileges.

There are no restrictions on calling REVOKE_ADMIN_REPGROUP.

Exceptions

REVOKE_ADMIN_REPGROUP may raise exception ORA-01917 if the specified user does not exist.

DBMS_REPCAT_AUTH: Setting Up More Administrative Accounts

DBMS_REPCAT_AUTH grants and revokes privileges to a user ID that is designated at each master site to perform replication activities on behalf of other remote masters. In effect, the existence of such a user ID eliminates the need for SYS-owned database links between master sites.

How the Package Is Used

The replication administration account and/or a DBA account uses the two procedures in DBMS_REPCAT_AUTH to grant or revoke the specified privileges.

Installation and Access

The DBMS_REPCAT_AUTH package is created when the Oracle database is installed. The *dbmsrepc.sql* script (found in the built-in packages source directory) contains the source code for this package's specification. This script is called by *catrep.sql*, which must be run to install the advanced replication packages. The wrapped SQL script *prvtrepc.sql* creates the public synonym DBMS_REPCAT_AUTH. No EXECUTE privileges are granted on DBMS_REPCAT_AUTH; only the owner (SYS) and those with the EXECUTE ANY PROCEDURE system privilege may execute the package.

DBMS_REPCAT_AUTH Procedures.

Procedure Name	Description
GRANT_SURROGATE_REPCAT	Grants required privileges to a specified user
REVOKE_SURROGATE_REPCAT	Revokes required privileges from a specified user

DBMS_REPCAT_AUTH Exceptions

The DBMS_REPCAT_AUTH package may raise exception ORA-01917 if the specified user does not exist.

DBMS_REPCAT_AUTH.GRANT_SURROGATE_REPCAT

GRANT_SURROGATE_REPCAT grants userid all privileges required to perform required replication activities on behalf of the SYS user at remote masters. Because the privileges granted to userid are relatively powerful, recipients of these grants should be limited to a single account that is used solely for this purpose (i.e., this account is never used interactively). It is most convenient to use the same account name for the surrogate SYS user in all master databases.

```
PROCEDURE DBMS_REPCAT_AUTH.GRANT_SURROGATE_REPCAT
     (userid IN VARCHAR2);
```

userid is the Oracle user ID for whom you are granting privileges.

There are no restrictions on calling GRANT_SURROGATE_REPCAT.

Exceptions

The GRANT_SURROGATE_REPCAT procedure may raise the exception ORA-01917 if the specified user does not exist.

DBMS_REPCAT_AUTH.REVOKE_SURROGATE_REPCAT

REVOKE_SURROGATE_REPCAT revokes from userid all privileges required to perform required replication activities on behalf of the SYS user at remote masters. Note that these privileges will be revoked regardless of whether they were obtained via GRANT_SURROGATE_REPCAT. In addition, any private synonyms with the same name as those created by REVOKE_SURROGATE_REPCAT will also be dropped.

```
PROCEDURE DBMS_REPCAT_AUTH.REVOKE_SURROGATE_REPCAT
     (userid IN VARCHAR2);
```

userid is the Oracle user ID for whom you are revoking privileges.

There are no restrictions on calling REVOKE_SURROGATE_REPCAT.

Exceptions

The REVOKE_SURROGATE_REPCAT procedure may raise exception ORA-01917 if the specified user does not exist.

DBMS_REPUTIL: Enabling and Disabling Replication

Situations will arise in which you need to perform DML on a replicated table *without* propagating the changes to other master sites. For example, if you have resolved a conflict and wish to update a row manually, you would not want to propagate your change. Or you might have a trigger on a replicated table that you want to fire only for updates that originate locally. The DBMS_REPUTIL package allows you to control whether updates propagate for the current session. It does this by setting the global variable replication_is_on, which the replication triggers and packages reference.

How the Package Is Used

The procedures REPLICATION_ON and REPLICATION_OFF are useful for controlling the replication of DML. A typical example is DML that is performed to get a local table synchronized with other masters.

Installation and Access

The DBMS_REPUTIL package is created when the Oracle database is installed. The *dbmsgen.sql* script (found in the built-in packages source directory) contains the source code for this package's specification. This script is called by *catrep.sql*, which must be run to install the advanced replication packages. The script creates the public synonym DBMS_REPUTIL for the package and grants EXECUTE privileges on the package to public. All Oracle users can reference and make use of this package.

DBMS_REPUTIL Procedures

Procedure Name	Description
REPLICATION_OFF	Turns replication off for the current session
REPLICATION_ON	Turns replication on for the current session

DBMS_REPUTIL Nonprogram Elements

Element Name/Type	Description
replication_is_on/BOOLEAN	Flag indicating whether DML should be queued for replication
from_remote/BOOLEAN	Flag indicating whether DML was initiated at another master site
global_name/VARCHAR2(128)	Global name of the current database

DBMS_REPUTIL.REPLICATION_OFF

The REPLICATION_OFF procedure works by setting the package variable replication_is_on to FALSE. The replication triggers and procedures can subsequently query this variable. This procedure is as simple as it can be: no parameters, no exceptions, and no restrictions.

```
PROCEDURE DBMS_REPUTIL.REPLICATION_OFF;
```

DBMS_REPUTIL.REPLICATION_ON

The REPLICATION_ON procedure reverses the effect of the REPLICATION_OFF procedure. It sets the package variable replication_is_on to TRUE.

```
PROCEDURE DBMS_REPUTIL.REPLICATION_ON;
```

There are no exceptions or restrictions for this procedure.

DBMS_SNAPSHOT: Managing Snapshots

The DBMS_SNAPSHOT package contains programs that allow you to maintain snapshots and snapshot logs and to set and query package state variables associated with the advanced replication facilities.

How the Package Is Used

The procedures I_AM_A_REFRESH and SET_I_AM_A_REFRESH are used to check and set the package variable REP$WHAT_AM_I.I_AM_A_SNAPSHOT, which numerous replication triggers and procedures reference. The procedures PURGE_LOG and REFRESH are typically run by the DBA and/or scheduled in the job queue.

Installation and Access

The DBMS_SNAPSHOT package is created when the Oracle database is installed. The *dbmssnap.sql* script (found in the built-in packages source directory) contains the source code for this package's specification. This script is called by *catproc.sql*, which is normally run immediately after database creation. The script creates the public synonym DBMS_SNAPSHOT for the package and grants the EXECUTE privilege on the package to public. All Oracle users can reference and make use of this package.

DBMS_SNAPSHOT Procedures

Name	Description
BEGIN_TABLE_REORGA-NIZATION (Oracle8 only)	Called prior to reorganizing a master table (e.g., through export/import); saves data required to refresh snapshots
END_TABLE_REORGANI-ZATION (Oracle8 only)	Called after reorganizing a master table (e.g., through export/import); validates data required to refresh snapshots
I_AM_A_REFRESH	Returns value of REP$WHAT_AM_I.I_AM_A_SNAPSHOT
PURGE_LOG	Purges snapshot log
REFRESH	Refreshes a snapshot
REFRESH_ALL	Refreshes all snapshots due to be executed.
REGISTER_SNAPSHOT (Oracle8 only)	Records information about snapshots at the master site in the DBA_REGISTERED_SNAPSHOTS data dictionary view
SET_I_AM_A_REFRESH	Sets REP$WHAT_AM_I.I_AM_A_SNAPSHOT to specified value
UNREGISTER_SNAPSHOT (Oracle8 only)	Removes information about snapshots at the master site from the DBA_REGISTERED_SNAPSHOTS data dictionary view

All of the programs in DBMS_SNAPSHOT are available regardless of whether you are using snapshot groups or the advanced replication facilities.

DBMS_SNAPSHOT does not define any exceptions.

DBMS_SNAPSHOT.BEGIN_TABLE_REORGANIZATION (Oracle8 Only)

If you are reorganizing a table, call the BEGIN_TABLE_REORGANIZATION procedure before reorganizing the table and the END_TABLE_REORGANIZATION procedure when you are finished.

```
PROCEDURE DBMS_SNAPSHOT.BEGIN_TABLE_REORGANIZATION
    (tabowner IN VARCHAR2,
     tabname  IN VARCHAR2);
```

There are no exceptions or restrictions for this procedure.Parameters

Parameter Name	Description
tabowner	Owner of the master table
tabname	Name of the master table being reorganized

DBMS_SNAPSHOT.END_TABLE_REORGANIZATION (Oracle8 Only)

Call the END_TABLE_REORGANIZATION procedure when you are finished reorganizing a table.

```
PROCEDURE DBMS_SNAPSHOT.END_TABLE_REORGANIZATION
    (tabowner   IN VARCHAR2
     tablename IN VARCHAR2);
```

Parameters are the same as those for BEGIN_TABLE_REORGANIZATION. This procedure does not raise any exceptions, and there are no restrictions on calling it.

DBMS_SNAPSHOT.I_AM_A_REFRESH

The I_AM_A_REFRESH function queries the REP$I_AM_A_REFRESH package variable. If this variable is TRUE, then the session is refreshing a snapshot or applying propagated DML to a replicated table. This DML is performed on behalf of a replicated transaction that was initiated at another master—that is, the DML performed by this session will not be replicated because it is the local application of remote DML. I_AM_A_REFRESH is used by numerous replication triggers and procedures to determine whether DML should be replicated.

```
FUNCTION DBMS_SNAPSHOT.I_AM_A_REFRESH RETURN BOOLEAN;
```

All row-level replication triggers are after-row triggers. Although a table can have multiple triggers of the same type, you cannot control the order in which they are fired. Therefore, it is safest to use before-row triggers to perform auditing on replicated tables; in this way, you are guaranteed that before-row triggers fire before after-row triggers.

The function does not raise any exceptions, and there are no restrictions on calling it.

DBMS_SNAPSHOT.PURGE_LOG

Call the PURGE_LOG procedure to delete snapshot log records.

```
PROCEDURE DBMS_SNAPSHOT.PURGE_LOG
    (master VARCHAR2,
     num BINARY_INTEGER DEFAULT 1,
     flag VARCHAR2 DEFAULT 'NOP' );
```

To delete all records from a snapshot log, set the num parameter to a high value (greater than the number of snapshots mastered to the master table, specified in the master parameter).

The PURGE_LOG procedure does not raise any exceptions, and there are no restrictions on calling it.

Parameters

Parameter Name	Description
master	Name of the master table.
num	Delete records required to refresh the oldest number of unrefreshed snapshot; default is 1.
flag	Set to DELETE to guarantee that records are deleted for at least one snapshot regardless of the setting of num.

DBMS_SNAPSHOT.REFRESH

Call the REFRESH procedure to force a snapshot refresh. The specifications for the Oracle7 and Oracle8 versions of the REFRESH procedure differ. Note that the Version 8.0 implementation adds parameters that support parallelism and drops the execute_as_user parameter. Both versions are overloaded, allowing you to specify the list of snapshots as a comma-delimited string in the list parameter or as a PL/SQL table in the tab parameter. The other parameters are identical for the two versions.

Oracle7 specification:

```
PROCEDURE DBMS_SNAPSHOT.REFRESH
    (list IN VARCHAR2,
     method IN VARCHAR2 DEFAULT NULL,
     rollback_seg IN VARCHAR2 DEFAULT NULL,
     push_deferred_rpc IN BOOLEAN DEFAULT TRUE,
     refresh_after_errors IN BOOLEAN DEFAULT FALSE,
     execute_as_user IN BOOLEAN DEFAULT FALSE );

PROCEDURE DBMS_SNAPSHOT.REFRESH
    (tab IN OUT dbms_utility.uncl_array,
     method  IN VARCHAR2 DEFAULT NULL,
     rollback_seg IN VARCHAR2 DEFAULT NULL,
     push_deferred_rpc IN BOOLEAN DEFAULT TRUE,
     refresh_after_errors IN BOOLEAN DEFAULT FALSE,
     execute_as_user IN BOOLEAN DEFAULT FALSE );
```

Oracle8 specification:

```
PROCEDURE DBMS_SNAPSHOT.REFRESH
    (list IN VARCHAR2,
     method  IN VARCHAR2 := NULL,
     rollback_seg IN VARCHAR2 := NULL,
     push_deferred_rpc IN BOOLEAN := TRUE,
     refresh_after_errors IN BOOLEAN := FALSE,
     purge_option IN BINARY_INTEGER := 1,
     parallelism IN BINARY_INTEGER := 0,
     heap_size IN BINARY_INTEGER := 0);

PROCEDURE DBMS_SNAPSHOT.REFRESH
    (tab IN OUT dbms_utility.uncl_array,
     method IN VARCHAR2 := NULL,
```

```
rollback_seg IN VARCHAR2 := NULL,
push_deferred_rpc IN BOOLEAN := TRUE,
refresh_after_errors IN BOOLEAN := FALSE,
purge_option IN BINARY_INTEGER := 1,
parallelism IN BINARY_INTEGER := 0,
heap_size IN BINARY_INTEGER := 0);
```

The REFRESH procedure does not raise any exceptions.

Parameters

Parameter Name	Description
list	Comma-separated list of snapshots to be refreshed. Use list or tab.
tab	PL/SQL table of snapshots to be refreshed. Use list or tab.
method	Refresh method: "?" uses the default refresh method. If you specified a refresh method when you created the snapshot, that is the default method. Otherwise, Oracle uses a fast refresh if possible and a complete refresh if not. "F" or "f" uses fast refresh if possible and returns ORA-12004 if not. "C" or "c" uses a complete refresh. This parameter should include a single character for each snapshot specified in list or tab, in the same order as the snapshot names appear. If list or tab contains more snapshots than the method list, the additional snapshots are refreshed with their default method.
rollback_seg	Optional; specifies the rollback segment to use for the refresh.
push_deferred_rpc	Optional; for updateable snapshots only. If TRUE (the default), then local updates are sent back to the master site before the snapshot is refreshed (otherwise, local updates will be temporarily overwritten).
refresh_after_errors	Optional; for updateable snapshots only. If TRUE, proceed with the refresh even if outstanding errors (conflicts) are logged in the DEFERROR data dictionary view at the master site. Default is FALSE.
execute_as_user (Oracle7 only)	If FALSE (the default), then the call to the remote system is performed under the privilege domain of the user that created the snapshot. If TRUE, the call is performed as the user calling the refresh procedure.

purge_option
(Oracle8 only)
	If push_deferred_rpc is TRUE, this designates the purge method; default is 1.
	    0 = no purge
	    1 = lazy purge (optimized for time)
	    2 = aggressive purge (complete)

parallelism
(Oracle8 only)
	If push_deferred_rpc is TRUE, this determines the maximum degree of parallelism; default is 1.
	    0 = serial
	    1 = parallel with one slave
	    n = parallel with n slaves ($n > 1$)

Parameter Name	Description
heap_size (Oracle8 only)	Used only if parallelism > 0. Sets the maximum number of transactions to be examined simultaneously for determining parallel scheduling. Oracle determines this value internally; you are advised not to use it.

The purge_option parameter controls how Oracle purges the snapshot site's deferred transaction queue; Oracle8 does not purge the queue automatically when the transactions propagate, so you must use DBMS_DEFER_SYS.SCHEDULE_PURGE to schedule a job to purge the queue, lest it become large and unmanageable. The purge_option parameter in REFRESH provides an opportunity to purge the queue of transactions associated with the updateable snapshots you are refreshing.

Restrictions

You can call REFRESH only from a snapshot site.

DBMS_SNAPSHOT.REFRESH_ALL

The DBMS_SNAPSHOT.REFRESH_ALL refreshes all snapshots that are due to be executed.

```
PROCEDURE DBMS_REFRESH.REFRESH_ALL
```

This procedure has no parameters, exceptions, or restrictions.

DBMS_SNAPSHOT.REGISTER_SNAPSHOT (Oracle8 Only)

Generally, the registration and unregistration of snapshots is automatic if both the master and snapshot databases are Oracle8. However, in case the snapshot site is running Oracle7 or if the automatic registration fails, you can use the Oracle8 procedure, REGISTER_SNAPSHOT, to register the snapshot manually.

One of the most significant improvements in Oracle8 is the automatic registration of snapshots at the master site. In Oracle7, there was no easy way to determine the location—or even the existence—of snapshots with master table(s) in your instance. But when you create a snapshot in Oracle8, Oracle puts a record in the DBA_REGISTERED_SNAPSHOTS data dictionary view. Similarly, when you drop a snapshot, Oracle deletes the record from DBA_REGISTERED_SNAPSHOTS.

The REGISTER and UNREGISTER procedures let you manually maintain the DBS_REGISTERED_SNAPSHOTS data dictionary view, shown here:

Column Name	Description
OWNER	Snapshot owner.
NAME	Snapshot name.
SNAPSHOT_SITE	Global name of database where snapshot resides.

Column Name	Description
CAN_USE_LOG	If YES, then snapshot refreshes can use snapshot log.
UPDATABLE	If YES, then snapshot is an updateable snapshot.
REFRESH_METHOD	Refresh method; either ROWID or PRIMARY KEY.
SNAPSHOT_ID	Unique ID of snapshot used for fast refreshes.
VERSION	Version of the snapshot. Possible values are REG_ UNKNOWN, REG_V7_GROUP, REG_V8_GROUP, and REG_ REPAPI_GROUP.
QUERY_TXT	Text of the snapshot's query.

The registration of snapshots is not mandatory; it records data in DBA_ REGISTERED_SNAPSHOTS that is for informational use only. You should not rely on the contents of this data dictionary view. The REGISTER_SNAPSHOT procedure is overloaded; snapshot_id is a DATE type if the snapshot site is an Oracle7 database and BINARY_INTEGER if it is an Oracle8 database.

```
PROCEDURE DBMS_SNAPSHOT.REGISTER_SNAPSHOT
    (snapowner    IN VARCHAR2,
     snapname     IN VARCHAR2,
     snapsite     IN VARCHAR2,
     snapshot_id  IN DATE | BINARY_INTEGER,
     flag         IN BINARY_INTEGER,
     qry_txt      IN VARCHAR2,
     rep_type     IN BINARY_INTEGER := dbms_snapshot.reg_unknown);
```

REGISTER_SNAPSHOT does not raise any exceptions, and there are no restrictions on calling it.

Parameters

Parameter Name	Description
snapowner	Owner of the snapshot.
snapname	Name of the snapshot.
snapsite	Global name of snapshot site database instance.
snapshot_id	ID of the snapshot. Use DATE datatype for Oracle7 snapshot sites, BINARY_INTEGER for Oracle8 snapshot sites. The snapshot_id and flag parameters are mutually exclusive.
flag	PL/SQL variable dictating whether future moves and creates are registered in the qry_text parameter; this flag does not appear to be used.
qry_txt	Up to 32,000 characters of the text of the snapshot query.
rep_type	Binary integer indicating the version of the snapshot. Possible values are: REG_UNKNOWN = 0 (the default) REG_V7_GROUP = 1 REG_V8_GROUP = 2 REG_REPAPI_GROUP = 3

DBMS_SNAPSHOT.SET_I_AM_A_REFRESH

The SET_I_AM_A_REFRESH procedure sets the REP$WHAT_AM_I.I_AM_A_SNAP-SHOT package variable to a specified value. If this variable is TRUE, then the session making the call is performing local DML on behalf of a replicated transaction that was initiated at another master. That is, the DML performed by this session will not be replicated because it is the local application of remote DML. Use this package carefully, because disabling replication triggers effectively disables any conflict resolution mechanisms you may have defined.

```
PROCEDURE DBMS_SNAPSHOT.SET_I_AM_A_REFRESH   (value IN BOOLEAN);
```

value is the value (Y or N) being set.

This procedure does not raise any exceptions.

DBMS_SNAPSHOT.UNREGISTER_SNAPSHOT (Oracle8 Only)

The UNREGISTER_SNAPSHOT procedure is the flip side of the REGISTER_SNAP-SHOT procedure. You use UNREGISTER_SNAPSHOT when you need to manually unregister a snapshot. This procedure unregisters snapshots at the master site, regardless of whether they were registered manually or automatically.

```
PROCEDURE DBMS_SNAPSHOT.UNREGISTER_SNAPSHOT
    (snapowner IN VARCHAR,
     snapname IN VARCHAR2,
     snapsite IN VARCHAR2)
```

See the description of parameters under the REGISTER_SNAPSHOT procedure.

UNREGISTER_SNAPSHOT does not raise any exceptions and there are no restrictions on calling it. Unregistering a snapshot has no effect on the snapshot itself.

B

Scripts and Utilities

This appendix contains a collection of scripts and utilities that I find useful when administering distributed systems. Many of the scripts are described, or at least mentioned, in this book. Each contains a brief description of its function. Although I have tested these scripts and utilities and use them on a regular basis, platforms and configurations differ, so be sure to test them in your own environment. These scripts and utilities are also available on the accompanying diskette and at the O'Reilly web site; see the Preface for details.

busycirc.sql

```
-------------------------------------------------------------------------
-- Filename:    busycirc.sql
-- Purpose:     Provides stats indicating whether or not a given circuit
--              is overly taxed in a Multi-Threaded Server environment.
-- Author:      Chas. Dye (cdye@excitecorp.com)
-- Date:        6-Aug-1998
-------------------------------------------------------------------------
column server    heading "Server"                       format a8
column circuit   heading "Name"                         format a8
column status    heading "Status"                       format a8
column message0  heading "Bytes|in|First|Msg|Buf"       format 9,999
column message1  heading "Bytes|in|Second|Msg|Buf"      format 9,999
column messages  heading "Messages|Processed"           format 999,999
column queue     heading "Queue"                        format a10
column bytes     heading "Bytes"                        format 9,999,999
column breaks    heading "Brks"                         format 999

SELECT  server,
        circuit,
        status,
        queue,
        message0,
```

```
                message1,
                messages,
                bytes,
                breaks
     FROM     v$circuit
     ORDER BY server
     /
```

busydisp.sql

```
     --------------------------------------------------------------------------
     -- Filename:    busydisp.sql
     -- Purpose:     Provides stats indicating whether the dispatcher processes
     --              are overly taxed.
     -- Author:      Chas. Dye (cdye@excitecorp.com)
     -- Date:        6-Aug-1998
     --------------------------------------------------------------------------
     column network  heading "Protocol"                          format a40
     column rate      heading "Total Busy Rate|>50%=>Add Dispatchers" format 99.99

     SELECT   network,
              100*(sum(busy)/(sum(busy)+sum(idle))) rate
     FROM     v$dispatcher
     GROUP BY network
     /
     column protocol heading "Protocol"                          format a40
     column Wait     heading "Average Wait|(hundredths of seconds)"  format a30

     SELECT   network Protocol,
              decode( sum(totalq), 0, 'No Responses',
              to_char(sum(wait)/sum(totalq), 'FM9999.90')) Wait
     FROM     v$queue q, v$dispatcher d
     WHERE    q.type = 'DISPATCHER'
     AND      q.paddr = d.paddr
     GROUP BY network
     /
```

busyq.sql

```
     --------------------------------------------------------------------------
     -- Filename:    busyq.sql
     -- Purpose:     Provides stats indicating whether a given queue is overly
     --              taxed in a Multi-Threaded Server environment.
     --              If the COMMON queue is overly taxed, consider adding more
     --              servers.
     -- Author:      Chas. Dye (cdye@excitecorp.com)
     -- Date:        6-Aug-1998
     --------------------------------------------------------------------------
     column type     heading "Queue|Type"             format a10
     column circuit  heading "Name"                   format a8
     column queued   heading "Items|Queued"           format 999,999
     column wait     heading "Total|Time|Waited"      format 999,999,999
     column totalq   heading "Total|Items|Processed"  format 999,999,999,999
     column avgwait  heading "Average|Wait"           format 9,999.90
```

```
set head off
set feedback off

SELECT  sysdate
FROM    dual
/
set head on
set feedback on

SELECT  paddr,
        type,
        queued,
        wait,
        totalq,
        decode(totalq, 0, 0, wait)/decode(totalq, 0, 1, totalq) avgwait
FROM    v$queue
/
```

checklatency

```
#! /bin/ksh
#-------------------------------------------------------------------------
# Filename: checklatency
# Purpose:  Notifies dba when more than 150 replicated transactions are
#           queued.
# Author:   Chas. Dye (cdye@excitecorp.com)
# Date:     21-Oct-1998
# Remarks:  Requires OPS$ account for whichever OS user crons this script.
#-------------------------------------------------------------------------
HOST=`/bin/uname -n`
MAIL=/bin/mailx
DISTLIST="beepdba@yoursite.com"
export HOST MAIL DISTLIST
#
ORACLE_HOME=/u/oracle/product/8.0.4.2 ; export ORACLE_HOME
ORACLE_SID=PHQS ; export ORACLE_SID
PATH=$ORACLE_HOME/bin:/bin:{PATH} ; export PATH
LD_LIBRARY_PATH=$ORACLE_HOME/lib:${LD_LIBRARY_PATH} ; export LD_LIBRARY_PATH
#
cd ${HOME}/bin
#
sqlplus -s / << EOF
set echo off
set head off
set feedback on
spool /u/oracle/admin/PHQS/logbook/latent.log
SELECT  count(*)
FROM    deftrandest d, deftran t
WHERE   d.deferred_tran_id    = t.deferred_tran_id
AND     d.delivery_order      = t.delivery_order
HAVING  count(*) > 150;
spool off
EOF
#
```

```
grep 1 latent.log > latent.err
if [ -s latent.err ]
then
        $MAIL -s"${ORACLE_SID}@${HOST} latency alert" $DISTLIST < latent.log
fi
#
rm -f latent.err
rm -f latent.log
```

colgroups.sql

```
---------------------------------------------------------------------------
-- Filename:      colgroups.sql
-- Purpose:       Lists all defined column groups.
-- Author:        Chas. Dye (cdye@excitecorp.com)
-- Date:          27-May-1998
---------------------------------------------------------------------------
column sname                    heading "Schema|Name"     format a8
column oname                    heading "Table|Name"      format a30
column group_name               heading "Column|Group"    format a30
column group_comment            heading "Comment"         format a19

SELECT  sname,
        oname,
        group_name
FROM    dba_repcolumn_group
ORDER BY sname, oname, group_name
/
```

confstats.sql

```
---------------------------------------------------------------------------
-- Filename:      confstats.sql
-- Purpose:       Lists conflicts for which statistics are being gathered.
-- Author:        Chas. Dye (cdye@excitecorp.com)
-- Date:          11-Jun-1998
--
-- Modification History
-- -------------------
-- 11-Jun-1998 : Chas. : Creation
---------------------------------------------------------------------------
col primary_key_value    form a10
col oname                form a25
col conflict_type        form a10
col method_name          form a20

SELECT  oname,
        created,
        status_update_date
FROM    dba_represol_stats_control
/
```

cr_regions.sql

```
-------------------------------------------------------------------------
-- Filename:    cr_regions.sql
-- Purpose:     Creates the REGIONS table and its public synonym.
-- Author:      Chas. Dye (cdye@excitecorp.com)
-- Date:        12-Jan-1998
-------------------------------------------------------------------------
set echo on
set termout on
spool regions.log

DROP PUBLIC SYNONYM regions
/
DROP TABLE regions CASCADE CONSTRAINTS
/
CREATE TABLE regions (
region_id    NUMBER(6)       NOT NULL,
country_id   NUMBER(6)       NOT NULL,
region_name  VARCHAR2(15)    NOT NULL,
audit_date   DATE            NOT NULL,
audit_user   VARCHAR2(30)    NOT NULL,
global_name  VARCHAR2(20)    NOT NULL
)
TABLESPACE sprocket_data STORAGE (INITIAL 16K NEXT 16K PCTINCREASE 0)
/

CREATE PUBLIC SYNONYM regions FOR regions
/

spool off
```

defcall.sql

```
-------------------------------------------------------------------------
-- Filename:    defcall.sql
-- Purpose:     Reports on all queued calls in defcall.
-- Author:      Chas. Dye (cdye@excitecorp.com)
-- Date:        28-Jun-1996
--
-- Modification History
-- --------------------
-- 03-Jun-1998 : Chas. : Removed deferred_tran_db field (not in Oracle8)
-------------------------------------------------------------------------
col callno              heading "Call|No"            format 9999
col deferred_tran_id    heading "Deferred|Tran|ID"   format a12
col schemaname          heading "Schema|Name"        format a8
col packagename         heading "Package|Name"       format a25
col procname            heading "Procedure|Name"     format a10
col argcount            heading "Arg|Count"          format 999
col dblink              heading "Destination"        format a17

SELECT  c.callno,
        c.deferred_tran_id,
```

```
            c.packagename,
            c.procname,
            c.argcount,
            d.dblink
FROM        defcall c, defcalldest d
WHERE       c.callno = d.callno
AND         c.deferred_tran_id = d.deferred_tran_id
/
```

defcalldest.sql

```
--------------------------------------------------------------------------
-- Filename:    defcalldest.sql
-- Purpose:     Lists all calls in defcalldest.
-- Author:      Chas. Dye (cdye@excitecorp.com)
-- Date:        28-Jun-1996
--------------------------------------------------------------------------
col callno              heading "Call No"           format 9999999999999
col deferred_tran_db    heading "Deferred|Tran|DB"  format a19
col deferred_tran_id    heading "Deferred|Tran|ID"  format a15
col dblink              heading "DB Link"           format a20
col start_time          heading "Start|Time"        format a20

SELECT  c.callno,
        c.deferred_tran_id,
        c.dblink,
        t.start_time
FROM    defcalldest c, deftran t
WHERE   c.deferred_tran_id = t.deferred_tran_id
/
```

defcallinfo.sql

```
--------------------------------------------------------------------------
-- Filename:    defcallinfo.sql
-- Purpose:     Lists information about deferred calls.
-- Author:      Chas. Dye (cdye@excitecorp.com)
-- Date:        10-Jul-1998
--------------------------------------------------------------------------
set serveroutput on size 100000
set verify off
undef callno
undef argcnt
undef tran_db
undef tran_id

DECLARE
        vTypes  dbms_defer_query.type_ary;
        vVals   dbms_defer_query.val_ary;
        indx    NUMBER;
BEGIN
        dbms_defer_query.get_call_args(
                callno          => '&&callno',
```

```
                    startarg          => 1,
                    argcnt            => &&argcnt,
                    argsize           => 128,
                    tran_db           => '&&tran_db',
                    tran_id           => '&&tran_id',
                    date_fmt          => 'DD-Mon-YYYY HH24:MI:SS',
                    types             => vTypes,
                    vals              => vVals );

            FOR indx IN 1..&&argcnt LOOP
                dbms_output.put_line('Arg '|| indx || ' Value '|| vVals(indx));
            END LOOP;
    END;
    /
```

defdest.sql

```
--------------------------------------------------------------------------
-- Filename:     defdest.sql
-- Purpose:      Lists data from system.def$_destination.
-- Author:       Chas. Dye (cdye@excitecorp.com)
-- Date:         27-May-1998
--------------------------------------------------------------------------
column dblink              heading "DB Link"               format a15
column last_delivered      heading "Last|Delivered"        format 9999999999
column last_enq_tid        heading "Last|Enq|TID"          format a5
column last_seq            heading "Last|Seq"              format 999
column disabled            heading "D|i|s|a|b|l|e|d"        format a1
column job                 heading "Job"                   format 9999
column last_txn_count      heading "Last|Txn|Count"        format 9999
column last_error_number   heading "Last|Error|Number"     format 999999
column last_error_Message  heading "Last|Error|Message"    format a19

SELECT  dblink,
        last_delivered,
        last_enq_tid,
        last_seq,
        disabled,
        job,
        last_txn_count,
        last_error_number,
        last_error_message
FROM    system.def$_destination
/
```

deferror.sql

```
--------------------------------------------------------------------------
-- Filename:     deferror.sql
-- Purpose:      Reports on deferred transaction with errors and generates
--               call to dbms_defer_sys.execute_error to clear them.
-- Author:       Chas. Dye (cdye@excitecorp.com)
-- Date:         28-Jun-1996
--------------------------------------------------------------------------
```

```
column ORIGIN_TRAN_DB        heading "Origin|Tran|DB"      format a15
column DEFERRED_TRAN_ID      heading "Deferred|Tran|ID"    format a15
column DESTINATION           heading "Destination"         format a15
column ERROR_TIME            heading "Error Time"          format a22
column ERROR_NUMBER          heading "Error#"              format 999999
column FIX                   heading "Run This to Clear"   format a80

SELECT  deferred_tran_id,
        origin_tran_db,
        destination,
        to_char(start_time, 'DD-Mon-YYYY hh24:mi:ss') error_time,
        error_number
FROM    deferror
/

SELECT  'EXECUTE dbms_defer_sys.execute_error(' || chr(39) ||
        deferred_tran_id || chr(39) || ', '|| chr(39) ||
        origin_tran_db || chr(39) || ', - '|| chr(10) ||chr(39) ||
        destination || chr(39) || ' )'  fix
FROM    deferror
/
```

deferror8.sql

```
-------------------------------------------------------------------------
-- Filename:      deferror8.sql
-- Purpose:       Reports on deferred transaction with errors and generates
--                call to dbms_defer_sys.execute_error to clear them.
-- Author:        Chas. Dye (cdye@excitecorp.com)
-- Date:          28-Jun-1996
--
-- Modification History
-- --------------------
-- 13-Aug-1998 : Chas. : Updated for Oracle8; added commands to delete error.
-- 09-Oct-1998 : Chas. : Added ORDER BY start_time
-------------------------------------------------------------------------
column ORIGIN_TRAN_DB        heading "Origin|Tran|DB"      format a15
column DEFERRED_TRAN_ID      heading "Deferred|Tran|ID"    format a15
column DESTINATION           heading "Destination"         format a15
column ERROR_TIME            heading "Error Time"          format a22
column ERROR_NUMBER          heading "Error#"              format 999999
column FIX                   heading "Run This to Clear"   format a80
column DITCH                 heading "Run This to Delete"  format a80

SELECT  deferred_tran_id,
        origin_tran_db,
        destination,
        to_char(start_time, 'DD-Mon-YYYY hh24:mi:ss') error_time,
        error_number
FROM    deferror
ORDER BY start_time
/

SELECT  'EXECUTE dbms_defer_sys.execute_error(' || chr(39) ||
        deferred_tran_id || chr(39) || ', '|| chr(39) ||
```

```
        destination || chr(39) || ' )'  fix
FROM    deferror
ORDER BY start_time
/

SELECT  'EXECUTE dbms_defer_sys.delete_error(' || chr(39) ||
        deferred_tran_id || chr(39) || ', '|| chr(39) ||
        destination || chr(39) || ' )'  ditch
FROM    deferror
ORDER BY start_time
/
```

deforigin.sql

```
--------------------------------------------------------------------------
-- Filename:    deforigin.sql
-- Purpose:     Lists data from system.def$_origin.
-- Author:      Chas. Dye (cdye@excitecorp.com)
-- Date:        27-May-1998
--------------------------------------------------------------------------
column origin_db        heading "Origin|DB"         format a15
column origin_dblink    heading "Origin|DB Link"    format a15
column inusr            heading "INUSR"             format 99999
column cscn             heading "CSCN"              format 999999999
column eng_tid          heading "Enqueue|Txn ID"    format a15
column reco_seq_no      heading "Reco|Seq|No"       format 99999

SELECT  origin_db,
        origin_dblink,
        inusr,
        cscn,
        enq_tid,
        reco_seq_no
FROM    system.def$_origin
/
```

defschedule.sql

```
--------------------------------------------------------------------------
-- Filename:    defschedule.sql
-- Purpose:     Returns information about scheduled transactions.
-- Author:      Chas.Dye (cdye@excitecorp.com)
-- Date:        31-Jul-1996
--------------------------------------------------------------------------
column dblink           heading "DB Link"           format a20
column JOB              heading "Job"               format 999
column LAST_DATE        heading "Last Date"         format a20
column NEXT_DATE        heading "Next Date"         format a20
column BROKEN           heading "B|r|o|k|e|n"       format a3
column INTERVAL         heading "Interval"          format a22
column FAILURES         heading "F|a|i|l"           format 999
column WHAT             heading "What"              format a75
column last_txn_count   heading "Last|Txn|Count"    format 999
```

```
SELECT  dblink,
        job,
        to_char(next_date, 'DD-Mon-YYYY HH24:mi:ss') next_date,
        to_char(last_date, 'DD-Mon-YYYY HH24:mi:ss') last_date,
        disabled,
        last_txn_count
FROM    defschedule
/
```

deftran.sql

```
----------------------------------------------------------------------------
-- Filename:    deftran.sql
-- Purpose:     Reports on all deferred transactions in deftran.
-- Author:      Chas. Dye (cdye@excitecorp.com)
-- Date:        11-Jun-1998
--
-- Modification History
-- --------------------
-- 11-Jun-1998 : Chas. : Creation
----------------------------------------------------------------------------
col deferred_tran_id heading "Deferred|Tran|ID" format a15

SELECT  deferred_tran_id,
        delivery_order,
        destination_list,
        start_time
FROM    deftran
ORDER BY start_time
/
```

deftrandest.sql

```
----------------------------------------------------------------------------
-- Filename:    deftrandest.sql
-- Purpose:     Lists all databases in deftrandest.
-- Author:      Chas. Dye (cdye@excitecorp.com)
-- Date:        28-Jun-1996
----------------------------------------------------------------------------

col callno              heading "Call No"           format 9999999999999
col deferred_tran_db    heading "Deferred|Tran|DB"  format a20
col deferred_tran_id    heading "Deferred|Tran|ID"  format a20
col dblink              heading "DB Link"           format a20
col start_time          heading "Start Time"        format a20

SELECT  d.deferred_tran_id,
        d.delivery_order,
        d.dblink,
        t.start_time
FROM    deftrandest d, deftran t
WHERE   d.deferred_tran_id = t.deferred_tran_id
AND     d.delivery_order = t.delivery_order
/
```

disprate.sql

```
-------------------------------------------------------------------------
-- Filename:    disprate.sql
-- Purpose:     Queries v$dispatcher_rate.
-- Author:      Chas. Dye (cdye@excitecorp.com)
-- Date:        24-Nov-1998
-------------------------------------------------------------------------

col name format a8

col CUR_MSG_RATE   format 999999
col MAX_MSG_RATE   format 999999
col AVG_MSG_RATE   format 999999

SELECT name,
       CUR_MSG_RATE,
       MAX_MSG_RATE,
       AVG_MSG_RATE
FROM   v$dispatcher_rate
/

col CUR_SVR_BYTE_PER_BUF   format 999999 heading "CUR|SVR|BYTE|PER|BUF"
col CUR_CLT_BYTE_PER_BUF   format 999999 heading "CUR|CLT|BYTE|PER|BUF"
col MAX_SVR_BYTE_PER_BUF   format 999999 heading "MAX|SVR|BYTE|PER|BUF"
col MAX_CLT_BYTE_PER_BUF   format 999999 heading "MAX|CLT|BYTE|PER|BUF"
col AVG_SVR_BYTE_PER_BUF   format 999999 heading "AVG|SVR|BYTE|PER|BUF"
col AVG_CLT_BYTE_PER_BUF   format 999999 heading "AVG|CLT|BYTE|PER|BUF"

SELECT  name,
        CUR_SVR_BYTE_PER_BUF,
        CUR_CLT_BYTE_PER_BUF,
        MAX_SVR_BYTE_PER_BUF,
        MAX_CLT_BYTE_PER_BUF,
        AVG_SVR_BYTE_PER_BUF,
        MAX_CLT_BYTE_PER_BUF
FROM    v$dispatcher_rate
/
```

errorinfo.sql

```
-------------------------------------------------------------------------
-- Filename:    errorinfo.sql
-- Purpose:     Reports on all errors.
-- Author:      Chas. Dye (cdye@excitecorp.com)
-- Date:        28-Jun-1996
--
-- Modification History
-- --------------------
-- 03-Jun-1998 : Chas. : Removed deferred_tran_db field (not in Oracle8)
-- 09-Oct-1998 : Chas. : Added ORDER BY e.start_time
-------------------------------------------------------------------------
```

```
col callno                heading "Call|No"              format 9999
col deferred_tran_id      heading "Deferred|Tran|ID"     format a12
col schemaname            heading "Schema|Name"          format a8
col packagename           heading "Package|Name"         format a25
col procname              heading "Procedure|Name"       format a10
col argcount              heading "Arg|Count"            format 999
col origin_tran_db        heading "Origin"               format a17

SELECT  c.callno,
        c.deferred_tran_id,
        c.packagename,
        c.procname,
        c.argcount,
        e.origin_tran_db
FROM    defcall c, deferror e
WHERE   c.deferred_tran_id = e.deferred_tran_id
AND     c.callno = e.callno
ORDER BY e.start_time
/
```

fixdefer.sql

```
----------------------------------------------------------------------
-- Filename:    fixdefer.sql
-- Purpose:     Reports on deferred transaction with errors and generates
--              call to dbms_defer_sys.execute_error to clear them.
-- Author:      Chas. Dye (cdye@excitecorp.com)
-- Date:        28-Jun-1996
----------------------------------------------------------------------
column DEFERRED_TRAN_DB    heading "Deferred|Tran|DB"     format a15
column DEFERRED_TRAN_ID    heading "Deffered|Tran|ID"     format a15
column DESTINATION         heading "Destination"          format a15
column ERROR_TIME          heading "Error Time"           format a22
column ERROR_NUMBER        heading "Error#"               format 999999
column FIX                 heading "Run This to Clear"    format a80


SELECT  deferred_tran_id,
        deferred_tran_db,
        destination,
        to_char(error_time, 'DD-Mon-YYYY hh24:mi:ss') error_time,
        error_number
FROM    deferror
/

SELECT  'EXECUTE dbms_defer_sys.execute_error(' || chr(39) ||
        deferred_tran_id || chr(39) || ', '|| chr(39) ||
        deferred_tran_db || chr(39) || ', - '|| chr(10) ||chr(39) ||
        destination || chr(39) || ' )'  fix
FROM    deferror
/
```

gendelerrtran.sql

```
-------------------------------------------------------------------------
-- Filename:       gendelerrtran.sql
-- Purpose:        Generates calls to dbms_defer_sys to delete transactions
--                 that have resulted in errors for a particular table.
-- Author:         Chas. Dye (cdye@excitecorp.com)
-- Date:           27-May-1998
-------------------------------------------------------------------------
SELECT   'EXECUTE dbms_defer_sys.delete_error(' || chr(39) ||
         deferred_tran_id || chr(39) || ', '|| chr(39) ||
         destination || chr(39) || ' );', 'COMMIT;'
FROM     deferror e
WHERE EXISTS (
         SELECT   deferred_tran_id
         FROM     defcall c
         WHERE    c.deferred_tran_id = e.deferred_tran_id
         AND      c.packagename like upper('%&target_table%'))
/
```

gendeltran.sql

```
-------------------------------------------------------------------------
-- Filename:       gendeltran.sql
-- Purpose:        Generates calls to dbms_defer_sys to delete transactions
--                 for a particular table.
-- Author:         Chas. Dye (cdye@excitecorp.com)
-- Date:           27-May-1998
-------------------------------------------------------------------------
select
'exec dbms_defer_sys.delete_tran('||chr(39)||deferred_tran_id||chr(39)||','||
chr(39)||'PLV2.EXCITE.COM'||chr(39)||');'||chr(10)||'commit;'
from deftran t
where exists
(select DEFERRED_TRAN_ID from defcall c
where c.DEFERRED_TRAN_ID = t.DEFERRED_TRAN_ID
and c.packagename like upper('&target_table$%'))
/
```

gengensup.sql

```
-------------------------------------------------------------------------
-- Filename:       gengensup.sql
-- Purpose:        Generates calls to generate_replication_support.
-- Author:         Chas. Dye (cdye@excitecorp.com)
-- Date:           27-May-1998
-------------------------------------------------------------------------
undef schema_name

SELECT
         'EXECUTE dbms_repcat.generate_replication_support( -'||chr(10)||
         'sname=>'||chr(39)||upper('&&schema_name')||chr(39)||', -'||chr(10)||
```

```
                'oname=>'||chr(39)||oname||chr(39)||', -'||chr(10)||
                'type=>'||chr(39)||type||chr(39)||', -'||chr(10)||
                'distributed=>TRUE);'
    FROM    dba_repobject
    WHERE   oname NOT LIKE '%$R%'
    AND     sname = upper('&&schema_name')
    ORDER BY sname, type, oname
    /

    undef schema_name
```

groupedcols.sql

```
    ------------------------------------------------------------------------
    -- Filename:    groupedcols.sql
    -- Purpose:     Lists all grouped columns.
    -- Author:      Chas. Dye (cdye@excitecorp.com)
    -- Date:        27-May-1998
    ------------------------------------------------------------------------
    column sname            heading "Schema|Name"    format a8
    column oname            heading "Table|Name"     format a25
    column group_name       heading "Column|Group"   format a25
    column column_name      heading "Column|Name"    format a19

    clear breaks
    break on sname on oname skip 1

    SELECT  sname,
            substr(oname, 1, 25)            oname,
            substr(group_name, 1, 25)       group_name,
            substr(column_name, 1, 19)      column_name
    FROM    dba_repgrouped_column
    ORDER BY sname, oname, group_name, column_name
    /

    clear breaks
```

invalids.sql

```
    ------------------------------------------------------------------------
    -- Filename:    invalids.sql
    -- Purpose:     Lists all invalid objects and provides SQL to (attempt to)
    --              repair them.
    -- Author:      Chas. Dye (cdye@excitecorp.com)
    -- Date:        28-Jun-1996
    ------------------------------------------------------------------------
    column object_name   format a25      heading "Object Name"
    column status        format a7       heading "Status"
    column owner         format a12      heading "Owner"
    column object_type   format a12      heading "Object Type"
    column created       format a20      heading "Date Created"
    column fix           format a70      heading "Run these statements to repair"
```

```
SELECT   object_name, status, object_type, owner, created
FROM     dba_objects
WHERE    status != 'VALID'
/

SELECT
         'ALTER ' ||
         DECODE( object_type, 'PACKAGE BODY', 'PACKAGE', object_type) || ' ' ||
         lower(owner)||'.'|| lower(object_name) ||
         DECODE( object_type, 'PACKAGE BODY', ' COMPILE BODY;', ' COMPILE;') fix
FROM     dba_objects
WHERE object_type IN (            'FUNCTION',
                                  'PACKAGE',
                                  'PACKAGE BODY',
                                  'PROCEDURE',
                                  'TYPE',
                                  'TRIGGER',
                                  'VIEW'
                        )
AND      status = 'INVALID'
/
```

jobs.sql

```
rem -------------------------------------------------------------------
rem Filename:    jobs.sql
rem Purpose:     Returns information about jobs in the job queue.
rem Author:      cdye@excitecorp.com
rem Date:        31-Jul-1996
rem -------------------------------------------------------------------
column JOB              heading "Job"           format 9999
column LAST_DATE        heading "Last Date"     format a20
column NEXT_DATE        heading "Next Date"     format a20
column BROKEN           heading "B|r|o|k|e|n"   format a3
column INTERVAL         heading "Interval"      format a24
column FAILURES         heading "F|a|i|l"       format 99
column WHAT             heading "What"          format a74

SELECT   job,
         to_char(last_date, 'DD-Mon-YYYY HH24:mi:ss') last_date,
         to_char(next_date, 'DD-Mon-YYYY HH24:mi:ss') next_date,
         decode(broken, 'Y', 'Yes', 'No') broken,
         interval,
         failures
FROM     dba_jobs
/

SELECT   job,
         what
FROM     dba_jobs
/
```

keycols.sql

```
--------------------------------------------------------------------------
-- Filename:     keycols.sql
-- Purpose:      Lists columns identified by DBMS_REPCAT.SET_COLUMNS.
-- Author:       Chas. Dye (cdye@excitecorp.com)
-- Date:         27-May-1998
--------------------------------------------------------------------------
col sname          heading "Schema"          format a12
col oname          heading "Table Name"      format a30
col col            heading "Column Name"     format a30

clear breaks

break on sname on oname skip 1

SELECT  sname, oname, col
FROM    dba_repkey_columns
ORDER BY sname, oname
/

clear breaks
```

lastsnap.sql

```
--------------------------------------------------------------------------
-- Filename:     lastsnap.sql
-- Purpose:      Lists registered snapshots (run from master site).
-- Author:       Chas. Dye (cdye@excitecorp.com)
-- Date:         29-Aug-1998
--------------------------------------------------------------------------
column owner                  heading "Owner"            format a8
column name                   heading "Name"             format a22
column snapshot_site          heading "Snapshot|Site"    format a15
column refresh_method         heading "Refresh|Method"   format a11
column version                heading "Version"          format a10
column current_snapshots      heading "Last|Refresh"     format a20

SELECT  r.owner,
        r.name,
        r.snapshot_site,
        r.refresh_method,
        nvl(  to_char(l.current_snapshots, 'DD-Mon-YYYY HH24:MI:SS'),
              '   -- Unknown --') current_snapshots
FROM    dba_registered_snapshots r,
        dba_snapshot_logs l
WHERE   l.log_owner(+) = r.owner
AND     l.master(+) = r.name
/
```

latent.sql

```
----------------------------------------------------------------------------
-- Filename:     latent.sql
-- Purpose:      Lists outstanding transactions by destination.
-- Author:       Chas. Dye (cdye@excitecorp.com)
-- Date:         09-Jul-1996
----------------------------------------------------------------------------
col dblink        heading "Destination"                         format a16
col earliest      heading "Least Recently|Queued Transaction"   format a20
col latest        heading "Most Recently|Queued Transaction"    format a20
col out           heading "Total|Txns|Queued"                   format 999,999
col timenow       heading "Current|Time"                        format a8
col latency       heading "Maximum|Latency|dd:hh:mi:ss"         format a12

clear breaks
clear computes

set head off
set feedback off
select 'Propagation Latency Instance: '||name||'.  Time: ' ||
       to_char(sysdate, 'DD-Mon-YY HH24:mi:ss')
from v$database
/
set head on
set feedback on

compute sum of out on report
break on report skip 1

SELECT  d.dblink,
        min(t.start_time) earliest,
        max(t.start_time) latest,
        count(*) out,
        ltrim(to_char(trunc( sysdate - ( min(start_time)) ), '09')) || ':' ||
        ltrim(to_char(trunc(24*((sysdate-min(start_time)) -
               trunc(sysdate-min(start_time)))), '09'))||':' ||
        ltrim(to_char(mod(trunc(1440*((sysdate-min(start_time)) -
               trunc(sysdate-min(start_time)))), 60), '09')) ||':' ||
        ltrim(to_char(mod(trunc(86400*((sysdate-min(start_time)) -
               trunc(sysdate-min(start_time)))), 60), '09')) latency
FROM    deftrandest d, deftran t
WHERE   d.deferred_tran_id     = t.deferred_tran_id
AND     d.delivery_order       = t.delivery_order
GROUP BY d.dblink
/

clear breaks
clear computes
```

links.sql

```
-------------------------------------------------------------------------
-- Filename:    links.sql
-- Purpose:     Reports all database links in the database.
-- Author       Chas. Dye (cdye@excitecorp.com)
-- Date:        28-May-1997
-------------------------------------------------------------------------
column owner           heading "Owner"       format a10
column db_link         heading "DB Link"     format a20
column username        heading "Username"    format a12
column host            heading "Host"        format a12
column created         heading "Created"     format a20

clear breaks
break on db_link skip 1

SELECT  db_link,
        owner,
        nvl(username, '--------') username,
        host,
        TO_CHAR(created, 'DD-Mon-YYYY HH24:MI:SS') created
FROM    dba_db_links
ORDER BY db_link, host, owner
/

clear breaks
```

mastersnapinfo.sql

```
-------------------------------------------------------------------------
-- Filename:    mastersnapinfo.sql
-- Purpose:     Lists info about all registered snapshots.
--              Requires Oracle8.
-- Author:      Chas. Dye (cdye@excitecorp.com)
-- Date:        28-Jun-1997
-------------------------------------------------------------------------
column owner                 format a10
column name                  format a20
column snapshot_site         format a15
column current_snapshot      format a22

SELECT  r.owner,
        r.name,
        r.snapshot_site,
        l.current_snapshots
FROM    dba_registered_snapshots r,
        dba_snapshot_logs l
WHERE   r.snapshot_id = l.snapshot_id(+)
/
```

mlogs.sql

```
--------------------------------------------------------------------------
-- Filename:    mlogs.sql
-- Purpose:     Generates SELECT statements to find count of entries in all
--              snapshot logs.
-- Author:      Chas. Dye (cdye@excitecorp.com)
-- Date:        27-May-1998
--------------------------------------------------------------------------
SELECT
        'SELECT count(*) FROM '||lower(owner)||'.'||lower(table_name)||';'
FROM    dba_tables
WHERE   table_name like 'MLOG$_%'
AND     owner not like 'SYS%'
ORDER BY owner, table_name
/
```

needsgen.sql

```
--------------------------------------------------------------------------
-- Filename:    needsgen.sql
-- Purpose:     Lists all replicated objects.
-- Author:      Chas. Dye (cdye@excitecorp.com)
-- Date:        28-Jun-1996
--------------------------------------------------------------------------
column  SNAME    heading "Schema"      format a8
column  ONAME    heading "Object"      format a30
column  TYPE     heading "Type"        format a15
column  STATUS   heading "Status"      format a9
column  ID       heading "ID"          format 9999
column  GNAME    heading "Group"       format a8


SELECT  id, gname, sname, oname, type, status
FROM    dba_repobject
WHERE   generation_status = 'NEEDSGEN'
ORDER BY gname, sname, type, oname
/
```

nonrepobjects.sql

```
--------------------------------------------------------------------------
-- Filename:    nonrepobjects.sql
-- Purpose:     Lists objects in a schema that are NOT replicated.
--              Oracle8 only.
-- Author:      Chas. Dye (cdye@excitecorp.com)
-- Date:        29-Aug-1998
--------------------------------------------------------------------------
undef table_owner
set verify off

column owner                      heading "Owner"         format a10
column name                       heading "Name"          format a30
```

```
column table_name                    heading "Table Name"            format a30
column tablespace_name               heading "Tablespace"            format a20

SELECT   t.owner,
         t.table_name,
         t.tablespace_name
FROM     dba_tables t
WHERE    owner = upper('&&table_owner')
AND      table_name NOT LIKE 'MLOG$_%'
AND      table_name NOT LIKE 'SNAP$_%'
AND      table_name NOT LIKE 'ULOG$_%'
AND      table_name NOT IN (
                 SELECT   oname
                 FROM     dba_repobject
                 WHERE    sname = upper('&&table_owner'))
AND      table_name NOT IN (
                 SELECT   name
                 FROM     dba_registered_snapshots )
ORDER BY table_name
/

undef table_owner
```

pk_regions.sql

```
-------------------------------------------------------------------------
-- Filename:     pk_regions.sql
-- Purpose:      Creates the constraints and indexes on table REGIONS.
-- Author:       Chas. Dye (cdye@excitecorp.com)
-- Date:         12-Jan-1998
-------------------------------------------------------------------------
set echo on
set termout on
spool pk_regions.log

ALTER TABLE regions ADD (
CONSTRAINT pk_regions
PRIMARY KEY (region_id)
USING INDEX TABLESPACE sprocket_indx
STORAGE (INITIAL 16K NEXT 16K PCTINCREASE 0)
)
/

ALTER TABLE regions ADD (
CONSTRAINT fk_regions_country_id
FOREIGN KEY (country_id)
REFERENCES countries (country_id)
)
/

CREATE INDEX i_region_country_id ON regions(country_id)
TABLESPACE sprocket_indx STORAGE (INITIAL 16K NEXT 16K PCTINCREASE 0)
/

spool off
```

prioritygroups.sql

```
------------------------------------------------------------------------
-- Filename:      prioritygroups.sql
-- Purpose:       Lists all defined priority groups.
-- Author:        Chas. Dye (cdye@excitecorp.com)
-- Date:          27-May-1998
------------------------------------------------------------------------
column sname               heading "Rep|Group"           format a15
column priority_group      heading "Priority|Group"      format a15
column data_type           heading "Data|Type"           format a9
column priority_comment    heading "Comment"             format a35

SELECT  sname,
        priority_group,
        data_type,
        substr(priority_comment, 1, 35) priority_comment
FROM    dba_reppriority_group
ORDER BY sname, priority_group
/
```

prioritysites.sql

```
------------------------------------------------------------------------
-- Filename:      prioritysites.sql
-- Purpose:       Lists all defined priority sites.
-- Author:        Chas. Dye (cdye@excitecorp.com)
-- Date:          27-May-1998
------------------------------------------------------------------------
column sname               heading "Rep|Group"               format a15
column priority_group      heading "Site|Priority|Name"      format a15
column priority            heading "Priority"                format 9999
column varchar2_value      heading "Site|Name"               format a20
column priority_comment    heading "Comment"                 format a35

SELECT  sname,
        priority_group,
        varchar2_value,
        priority
FROM    dba_reppriority
ORDER BY sname, priority_group
/
```

propmode.sql

```
------------------------------------------------------------------------
-- Filename:      propmode.sql
-- Purpose:       Lists all replication sites and propagation modes.
-- Author:        Chas. Dye (cdye@excitecorp.com)
-- Date:          28-Jun-1996
------------------------------------------------------------------------
column SNAME               heading "Group"           format a8
column DBLINK              heading "DB-Link"          format a20
```

```
    column HOW                    heading "Prop|Mode"              format 999,999,999

    clear breaks
    break on dblink skip 1

    SELECT  distinct(l1.dblink) dblink, l2.sname, l2.how
    FROM    dba_repprop l1, dba_repprop l2
    WHERE   l1.dblink = l2.dblink
    AND     l2.how != 'NONE'
    /

    clear breaks
```

refgroups.sql

```
    ------------------------------------------------------------------------
    -- Filename:     refgroups.sql
    -- Purpose:      Lists all refresh groups in the database.
    -- Author:       Chas. Dye (cdye@excitecorp.com)
    -- Date:         17-Jan-1997
    ------------------------------------------------------------------------
    column rname                  heading "Refresh|Group"          format a15
    column owner                  heading "Snapshot|Owner"         format a10
    column name                   heading "Table Name"             format a25
    column next_date              heading "Next Refresh"           format a20
    column parallelism            heading "P|a|r|a|l|l|e|l"         format 99999

    clear breaks
    break on rname skip 1

    SELECT  rname,
            owner,
            name,
            next_date,
            parallelism
    FROM    dba_refresh_children
    ORDER BY rname, owner, name
    /

    clear breaks
```

regsnaps.sql

```
    ------------------------------------------------------------------------
    -- Filename:     regsnaps.sql
    -- Purpose:      Lists registered snapshots (run from master site).
    -- Author:       Chas. Dye (cdye@excitecorp.com)
    -- Date:         24-Jun-1998
    ------------------------------------------------------------------------
    column owner                  heading "Owner"                  format a8
    column name                   heading "Name"                   format a20
    column snapshot_site          heading "Snapshot|Site"          format a15
    column can_use_log            heading "Can|Use|Log"            format a3
    column updatable              heading "Upd"                    format a3
```

```
column refresh_method     heading "Refresh|Method"     format a11
column version            heading "Version"            format a10

SELECT  owner,
        name,
        snapshot_site,
        can_use_log,
        updatable,
        refresh_method,
        substr(version, 1, 8) version
FROM    dba_registered_snapshots
/
```

repcaterr.sql

```
-------------------------------------------------------------------------
-- Filename:     repcaterr.sql
-- Purpose:      Lists entries in dba_repcatlog with error status.
-- Author:       Chas. Dye (cdye@excitecorp.com)
-- Date:         28-Jun-1996
-------------------------------------------------------------------------
column ID              heading "Id"         format 9999
column SOURCE          heading "Source"     format a20
column SNAME           heading "Schema"     format a8
column REQUEST         heading "Request"    format a22
column ONAME           heading "Object"     format a20
column ERRNUM          heading "Error"      format 99999
column MESSAGE         heading "Message"    format a74

SELECT  id, status, sname, request, oname, errnum
FROM    dba_repcatlog
WHERE   status = 'ERROR'
ORDER BY id
/

SELECT  id, message
FROM    dba_repcatlog
WHERE   status = 'ERROR'
ORDER BY id
/

set head off
SELECT 'Run these commands to purge...'
FROM dual
/
set head on

SELECT
        'EXECUTE dbms_repcat.purge_master_log('||
        id ||', '
        ||chr(39)||rtrim(source)||chr(39)||', '
        ||chr(39)||gname||chr(39)||');'      command
FROM    dba_repcatlog
WHERE   status = 'ERROR'
/
```

repcatlog.sql

```
-------------------------------------------------------------------------
-- Filename:    repcatlog.sql
-- Purpose:     Lists all tasks pending in dba_repcatlog queue.
-- Author:      Chas. Dye (cdye@excitecorp.com)
-- Date:        28-Jun-1996
-------------------------------------------------------------------------
column SOURCE              heading "Source"          format a6
column MASTER              heading "Master"          format a6
column SNAME               heading "Group"           format a10
column STATUS              heading "Status"          format a14
column REQUEST             heading "Request"         format a28
column TIMESTAMP           heading "Time"            format a8


SELECT   substr(source, 1, instr(source, '.', 1) -1 ) source,
         substr(master, 1, instr(master, '.', 1) -1 ) master,
         sname,
         status,
         request, to_char(timestamp, 'HH24:MI:SS') timestamp
FROM     dba_repcatlog
ORDER BY master
/
```

repconflict.sql

```
-------------------------------------------------------------------------
-- Filename:    repconflict.sql
-- Purpose:     Lists all defined conflict resolution methods.
-- Author:      Chas. Dye (cdye@excitecorp.com)
-- Date:        27-May-1998
-------------------------------------------------------------------------
column sname               heading "Schema|Name"        format a10
column oname               heading "Table|Name"         format a25
column conflict_type       heading "Conf|Type"          format a10
column reference_name      heading "Reference|Name"     format a30

SELECT   sname, oname, conflict_type, reference_name
FROM     dba_repconflict
ORDER BY sname, oname
/
```

repgroup.sql

```
-------------------------------------------------------------------------
-- Filename:    repgroup.sql
-- Purpose:     Lists status of all replication groups.
-- Author:      Chas. Dye (cdye@excitecorp.com)
-- Date:        28-Jun-1996
-------------------------------------------------------------------------
column MASTER              heading "Mast|Site"          format a4
column MASTERDEF           heading "Mast|Def|Site"      format a4
```

```
column STATUS              heading "Status"              format a9
column GNAME               heading "Group"               format a12
column SCHEMA_COMMENT      heading "Comment"             format a45

SELECT  g.gname,
        decode(g.master, 'N', 'No', 'Y', 'Yes') master,
        decode(s.masterdef, 'Y', 'Yes', 'N', 'No') masterdef,
        g.status,
        g.schema_comment
FROM    dba_repgroup g,
        dba_repsites s
WHERE   g.gname = s.gname
AND     s.my_dblink = 'Y'
/
```

repobjects.sql

```
---------------------------------------------------------------------------
-- Filename:     repobjects.sql
-- Purpose:      Lists all replicated objects.
-- Author:       Chas. Dye (cdye@excitecorp.com)
-- Date:         28-Jun-1996
---------------------------------------------------------------------------
column  SNAME              heading "Schema"              format a8
column  ONAME              heading "Object"              format a30
column  TYPE               heading "Type"                format a15
column  STATUS             heading "Status"              format a7
column  ID                 heading "ID"                  format 9999
column  GNAME              heading "Group"               format a10

SELECT  id, gname, sname, oname, type, status
FROM    dba_repobject
ORDER BY gname, sname, type, oname
/
```

repres.sql

```
---------------------------------------------------------------------------
-- Filename:     repres.sql
-- Purpose:      Lists all conflict resolution techniques.
-- Author:       Chas. Dye (cdye@excitecorp.com)
-- Date:         27-May-1998
---------------------------------------------------------------------------
column sname               heading "Schema|Name"     format a8
column oname               heading "Table|Name"      format a25
column conflict_type       heading "Conflict|Type"   format a10
column method_name         heading "Method"          format a18
column sequence_no         heading "Seq"             format 99

clear breaks
break on sname on oname skip 1

SELECT  sname,
        substr(oname, 1, 25)                oname,
```

```
            conflict_type,
            method_name,
            sequence_no
FROM    dba_represolution
ORDER BY sname, oname
/

clear breaks
```

repsites.sql

```
--------------------------------------------------------------------------
-- Filename:    repsites.sql
-- Purpose:     Lists all replication sites.
-- Author:      Chas. Dye (cdye@excitecorp.com)
-- Date:        28-Jun-1996
--------------------------------------------------------------------------
column GNAME              heading "Group"              format a15
column DBLINK             heading "DB-Link"            format a20
column MASTERDEF          heading "Master|Def|Site?"   format a6
column MASTER             heading "Master|Site?"       format a6
column PROP_UPDATES       heading "Update|Requests"    format 999,999,999
column MY_DBLINK          heading "Is|This|Database?"  format a9

SELECT  gname,
        dblink,
        decode(masterdef, 'Y', 'Yes', 'No') masterdef,
        decode(master, 'Y', 'Yes', 'No') master,
        prop_updates,
        decode(my_dblink, 'Y', 'Yes', 'No') my_dblink
FROM    dba_repsites
ORDER BY gname ASC, masterdef DESC
/
```

resconfs.sql

```
--------------------------------------------------------------------------
-- Filename:    resconfs.sql
-- Purpose:     Reports on all resolved conflicts.
-- Author:      Chas. Dye (cdye@excitecorp.com)
-- Date:        11-Jun-1998
--
-- Modification History
-- -------------------
-- 11-Jun-1998 : Chas. : Creation
--------------------------------------------------------------------------
col primary_key_value   form a10      heading "Primary|Key"
col oname               form a25      heading "Object Name"
col conflict_type       form a8       heading "Conflict|Type"
col method_name         form a18      heading "Resolution|Method"
col resolved_date       form a15      heading "Resolution|Date"
```

```
SELECT  oname,
        primary_key_value,
        conflict_type,
        method_name,
        to_char(resolved_date, 'DD-Mon HH24:MI:SS') resolved_date
FROM    dba_represolution_statistics
/
```

snaps.sql

```
-------------------------------------------------------------------------
-- Filename:    snaps.sql
-- Purpose:     Lists all snapshots in the database.
-- Author       Chas. Dye (cdye@excitecorp.com)
-- Date:        17-Jan-1997
-------------------------------------------------------------------------
column owner       format a9
column name        format a15
column table_name  format a27
column link        format a5      heading "Link"
column last_refresh format a20

SELECT  d.owner,
        d.name,
        d.table_name,
        substr(d.master_link, 1, 5) link,
        s.snaptime last_refresh
/*--
        to_char(last_refresh, 'DD-Mon-YYYY hh24:mi:ss') last_refresh
--*/
FROM    dba_snapshots d,
        sys.snap_reftime$ s
WHERE   d.owner = s.sowner
AND     d.name = s.vname
ORDER BY d.owner, d.name
/
```

snaps7.sql

```
-------------------------------------------------------------------------
-- Filename:    snaps7.sql
-- Purpose:     Lists all snapshots in the database.
-- Author       Chas. Dye (cdye@excitecorp.com)
-- Date:        17-Jan-1997
-------------------------------------------------------------------------
column owner       format a9
column name        format a15
column table_name  format a27
column link        format a5      heading "Link"
column last_refresh format a20

SELECT  owner,
        name,
        table_name,
```

```
            substr(master_link, 1, 5) link,
            to_char(last_refresh, 'DD-Mon-YYYY hh24:mi:ss') last_refresh
   FROM     dba_snapshots
   ORDER BY owner, name
   /
```

trg_regions.sql

```
-------------------------------------------------------------------------
-- Filename:    trg_regions.sql
-- Purpose:     Creates trigger(s) on table REGIONS.
-- Author:      Chas. Dye (cdye@excitecorp.com)
-- Date:        12-Jan-1998
-------------------------------------------------------------------------
set echo on
set termout on
spool trg_regions.log

CREATE OR REPLACE TRIGGER t_br_iu_regions
BEFORE INSERT OR UPDATE
ON regions
FOR EACH ROW

BEGIN
    IF (dbms_reputil.from_remote != TRUE)
    THEN
        :new.audit_date  := SYSDATE;
        :new.audit_user  := USER;
        :new.global_name := DBMS_REPUTIL.GLOBAL_NAME;
    END IF;
END;
/

spool off
```

UserAdmin

The UserAdmin package allows you to create and drop users and grant and revoke privileges. Using procedural replication, this package provides a means to maintain user accounts in multiple databases without having to actually log into each database to perform the administrative tasks. The package is quite lengthy and is already included in Chapter 14, *Procedural Replication* (see scripts *cr_seq_audit_admin.sql*, *cr_audit_admin.sql*, and *pl_useradmin.sql*, so I have not duplicated the code here. However, you will find it on the accompanying diskette and at the O'Reilly web site.

Index

D

About the Author

Charles Dye is the Database Architect for Excite, Inc., where he manages some of the world's busiest databases, which supply content to one of the world's hottest web sites. Prior to joining Excite, Charles was the Senior DBA at the Dialog Corporation, where, among other things, he designed a distributed database environment serving hundreds of thousands of customers.

In addition to authoring *Oracle Distributed Systems*, Charles also coauthored *Oracle Built-in Packages* with Steven Feuerstein and John Beresniewicz (O'Reilly & Associates, 1998). He is also a frequent speaker at Oracle Open World and IOUG-A conferences.

Colophon

Butterflies are featured on the cover of *Oracle Distributed Systems*. These are three of the thousands of species of butterfly. Butterflies, along with moths and skippers, make up the order Lepidoptera. The word "Lepidoptera" is derived from the Greek words *lepic*, meaning "scale," and *pteron*, meaning "wing." And, in fact, butterfly and moth wings are covered entirely in tiny, overlapping scales. The coloration of these fragile scales is what creates the spectacular, shimmering colors of the butterfly. The wing membrane itself is transparent and without color. Butterfly scales and hairs are covered in a thin layer of wax, making these insects water-repellent.

Most butterflies fly by fluttering their wings at a relatively slow rate, sometimes as slowly as 10 beats per second, approximately four miles per hour. Unlike many other insects, who beat their wings so fast that they become just a blur in flight, the butterfly's wings are clearly visible during its fluttering flight.

Butterflies are as well known for their four-stage metamorphosis as they are for their colorful wings and graceful fluttering. An adult female butterfly lays a large number of eggs, usually on or near food plants. The larva, better known as the caterpillar, develops within the egg and eats its way out. It then continues to eat almost constantly for a period ranging from one month to two years, depending on the butterfly species, periodically molting its skin during the process. The caterpillar then produces a pupa, or chrysalis, a mummylike structure. When the adult butterfly is fully formed, it breaks out of the pupa, its body and wings harden, and it takes off in search of food.

Melanie Wang was the production editor, and Norma Emory was the copy editor for *Oracle Distributed Systems*. Sheryl Avruch was the production manager, and

Jane Ellin and Ellie Maden provided quality control reviews. Betty Hugh and Sebastian Banker provided production support. Chris Reilley created the illustrations using Adobe Photoshop 5 and Macromedia FreeHand 8. Mike Sierra provided FrameMaker technical support. Ruth Rautenberg wrote the index.

Edie Freedman designed the cover of this book, using a 19th-century engraving from the Dover Pictorial Archive. The cover layout was produced by Kathleen Wilson with QuarkXPress 3.32 using the ITC Garamond font. Kathleen Wilson designed the diskette label.

The inside layout was designed by Nancy Priest and Alicia Cech and implemented in FrameMaker 5.5 by Mike Sierra. The text and heading fonts are ITC Garamond Light and Garamond Book. This colophon was written by Clairemarie Fisher O'Leary.

Whenever possible, our books use a durable and flexible lay-flat binding, either RepKover™ or Otabind™. If the page count exceeds the mamximum bulk possible for this type of binding, perfect binding is used.

 # More Titles from O'Reilly

Oracle

Oracle PL/SQL Programming, 2nd Edition

By Steven Feuerstein with Bill Pribyl
2nd Edition September 1997
1028 pages, Includes diskette
ISBN 1-56592-335-9

The first edition of *Oracle PL/SQL Programming* quickly became an indispensable reference for PL/SQL developers. This new edition covers Oracle8 and includes chapters on Oracle8 object types, object views, collections, and external procedures. It also covers new data types and functions, and contains new chapters on tuning, tracing, and debugging PL/SQL programs. The companion diskette contains an online Windows-based tool offering access to more than 100 files of source code and documentation prepared by the authors.

Advanced Oracle PL/SQL *Programming with Packages*

By Steven Feuerstein,
1st Edition Oct.1996, 690 pages,
plus diskette, ISBN 1-56592-238-7

This book explains the best way to construct packages, a powerful part of Oracle's PL/SQL procedural language that can dramatically improve your programming productivity and code quality, while preparing you for object-oriented development in Oracle technology. It comes with PL/Vision software, a library of PL/SQL packages developed by the author, and takes you behind the scenes as it examines how and why the PL/Vision packages were implemented the way they were.

Oracle8 Design Tips

By Dave Ensor & Ian Stevenson
1st Edition September 1997
130 pages, ISBN 1-56592-361-8

The newest version of the Oracle DBMS, Oracle8, offers some dramatically different features from previous versions, including better scalability, reliability, and security; an object-relational model; additional datatypes; and more. To get peak performance out of an Oracle8 system, databases and code need to be designed with these new features in mind. This small book tells Oracle designers and developers just what they need to know to use the Oracle8 features to best advantage.

Oracle Security

By Marlene Theriault & William Heney
1st Edition October 1998
446 pages, ISBN 1-56592-450-9

This book covers the field of Oracle security from simple to complex. It describes basic RDBMS security features (e.g., passwords, profiles, roles, privileges, synonyms) and includes many practical strategies for securing an Oracle system, developing auditing and backup plans, and using the Oracle Enterprise Manager and Oracle Security Server. Also touches on advanced security features, such as encryption, Trusted Oracle, and Internet and Web protection.

Oracle Design

By Dave Ensor & Ian Stevenson
1st Edition March 1997
546 pages, 1-56592-268-9

This book looks thoroughly at the field of Oracle relational database design, an often neglected area of Oracle, but one that has an enormous impact on the ultimate power and performance of a system. Focuses on both database and code design, including such special design areas as data models, enormalization, the use of keys and indexes, temporal data, special architectures (client/server, distributed database, parallel processing), and data warehouses.

Oracle Scripts

By Brian Lomasky & David C. Kreines
1st Edition May 1998
200 pages, Includes CD-ROM
ISBN 1-56592-438-X

A powerful toolset for Oracle DBAs and developers, these scripts will simplify everyday tasks—monitoring databases, protecting against data loss, improving security and performance, and helping to diagnose problems and repair databases in emergencies. The accompanying CD-ROM contains complete source code and additional monitoring and tuning software.

Oracle

Oracle Built-In Packages

By Steven Feuerstein
1st Edition March 1998
600 pages, Includes diskette
ISBN 1-56592-375-8

Oracle's built-in packages dramatically extend the power of the PL/SQL language, but few developers know how to use them effectively. This book is a complete reference to all of the built-ins, including those new to Oracle8. The enclosed diskette includes an online tool that provides easy access to the many files of source code and documentation developed by the authors.

Oracle PL/SQL Built-ins Pocket Reference

By Steven Feuerstein,
John Beresniewicz & Chip Dawes
1st Edition October 1998
78 pages, ISBN 1-56592-456-8

This companion to Steven Feuerstein's bestselling Oracle PL/SQL Programming and Oracle Built-in Packages provides quick-reference information on how to call Oracle's built-in functions and packages, including those new to Oracle8. It shows how to call all types of functions (numeric, character, date, conversion, large object [LOB], and miscellaneous) and packages (e.g., DBMS_SQL, DBMS_OUTPUT).

Oracle Performance Tuning, 2nd Edition

By Mark Gurry & Peter Corrigan
2nd Edition November 1996
964 pages, Includes diskette
ISBN 1-56592-237-9

Performance tuning is crucial in any modern relational database management system. The first edition of this book became a classic for developers and DBAs. This edition offers 400 pages of new material on new Oracle features, including parallel server, parallel query, Oracle Performance Pack, disk striping and mirroring, RAID, MPPs, SMPs, distributed databases, backup and recovery, and much more. Includes diskette.

O'REILLY®

TO ORDER: **800-998-9938** • **order@oreilly.com** • **http://www.oreilly.com/**
OUR PRODUCTS ARE AVAILABLE AT A BOOKSTORE OR SOFTWARE STORE NEAR YOU.
FOR INFORMATION: **800-998-9938** • **707-829-0515** • **info@oreilly.com**

How to stay in touch with O'Reilly

1. Visit Our Award-Winning Web Site

http://www.oreilly.com/

★ "Top 100 Sites on the Web" —*PC Magazine*
★ "Top 5% Web sites" —*Point Communications*
★ "3-Star site" —*The McKinley Group*

Our web site contains a library of comprehensive product information (including book excerpts and tables of contents), downloadable software, background articles, interviews with technology leaders, links to relevant sites, book cover art, and more. File us in your Bookmarks or Hotlist!

2. Join Our Email Mailing Lists

New Product Releases

To receive automatic email with brief descriptions of all new O'Reilly products as they are released, send email to:
listproc@online.oreilly.com
Put the following information in the first line of your message (*not* in the Subject field):
subscribe oreilly-news

O'Reilly Events

If you'd also like us to send information about trade show events, special promotions, and other O'Reilly events, send email to:
listproc@online.oreilly.com
Put the following information in the first line of your message (*not* in the Subject field):
subscribe oreilly-events

3. Get Examples from Our Books via FTP

There are two ways to access an archive of example files from our books:

Regular FTP

*   ftp to:
    ftp.oreilly.com
    (login: anonymous
    password: your email address)
*   Point your web browser to:
    ftp://ftp.oreilly.com/

FTPMAIL

*   Send an email message to:
    ftpmail@online.oreilly.com
    (Write "help" in the message body)

4. Contact Us via Email

order@oreilly.com
To place a book or software order online. Good for North American and international customers.

subscriptions@oreilly.com
To place an order for any of our newsletters or periodicals.

books@oreilly.com
General questions about any of our books.

software@oreilly.com
For general questions and product information about our software. Check out O'Reilly Software Online at **http://software.oreilly.com/** for software and technical support information. Registered O'Reilly software users send your questions to: **website-support@oreilly.com**

cs@oreilly.com
For answers to problems regarding your order or our products.

booktech@oreilly.com
For book content technical questions or corrections.

proposals@oreilly.com
To submit new book or software proposals to our editors and product managers.

international@oreilly.com
For information about our international distributors or translation queries. For a list of our distributors outside of North America check out:
http://www.oreilly.com/www/order/country.html

O'Reilly & Associates, Inc.
101 Morris Street, Sebastopol, CA 95472 USA
TEL   707-829-0515 or 800-998-9938
       (6am to 5pm PST)
FAX   707-829-0104

International Distributors

UK, EUROPE, MIDDLE EAST AND AFRICA (EXCEPT FRANCE, GERMANY, AUSTRIA, SWITZERLAND, LUXEMBOURG, LIECHTENSTEIN, AND EASTERN EUROPE)

INQUIRIES
O'Reilly UK Limited
4 Castle Street
Farnham
Surrey, GU9 7HS
United Kingdom
Telephone: 44-1252-711776
Fax: 44-1252-734211
Email: josette@oreilly.com

ORDERS
Wiley Distribution Services Ltd.
1 Oldlands Way
Bognor Regis
West Sussex PO22 9SA
United Kingdom
Telephone: 44-1243-779777
Fax: 44-1243-820250
Email: cs-books@wiley.co.uk

FRANCE

ORDERS
GEODIF
61, Bd Saint-Germain
75240 Paris Cedex 05, France
Tel: 33-1-44-41-46-16 (French books)
Tel: 33-1-44-41-11-87 (English books)
Fax: 33-1-44-41-11-44
Email: distribution@eyrolles.com

INQUIRIES
Éditions O'Reilly
18 rue Séguier
75006 Paris, France
Tel: 33-1-40-51-52-30
Fax: 33-1-40-51-52-31
Email: france@editions-oreilly.fr

GERMANY, SWITZERLAND, AUSTRIA, EASTERN EUROPE, LUXEMBOURG, AND LIECHTENSTEIN

INQUIRIES & ORDERS
O'Reilly Verlag
Balthasarstr. 81
D-50670 Köln
Germany
Telephone: 49-221-973160-91
Fax: 49-221-973160-8
Email: anfragen@oreilly.de (inquiries)
Email: order@oreilly.de (orders)

CANADA (FRENCH LANGUAGE BOOKS)

Les Éditions Flammarion ltée
375, Avenue Laurier Ouest
Montréal (Québec) H2V 2K3
Tel: 00-1-514-277-8807
Fax: 00-1-514-278-2085
Email: info@flammarion.qc.ca

HONG KONG

City Discount Subscription Service, Ltd.
Unit D, 3rd Floor, Yan's Tower
27 Wong Chuk Hang Road
Aberdeen, Hong Kong
Tel: 852-2580-3539
Fax: 852-2580-6463
Email: citydis@ppn.com.hk

KOREA

Hanbit Media, Inc.
Sonyoung Bldg. 202
Yeksam-dong 736-36
Kangnam-ku
Seoul, Korea
Tel: 822-554-9610
Fax: 822-556-0363
Email: hant93@chollian.dacom.co.kr

PHILIPPINES

Mutual Books, Inc.
429-D Shaw Boulevard
Mandaluyong City, Metro
Manila, Philippines
Tel: 632-725-7538
Fax: 632-721-3056
Email: mbikikog@mnl.sequel.net

TAIWAN

O'Reilly Taiwan
No. 3, Lane 131
Hang-Chow South Road
Section 1, Taipei, Taiwan
Tel: 886-2-23968990
Fax: 886-2-23968916
Email: benh@oreilly.com

CHINA

O'Reilly Beijing
Room 2410
160, FuXingMenNeiDaJie
XiCheng District
Beijing, China PR 100031
Tel: 86-10-86631006
Fax: 86-10-86631007
Email: frederic@oreilly.com

INDIA

Computer Bookshop (India) Pvt. Ltd.
190 Dr. D.N. Road, Fort
Bombay 400 001 India
Tel: 91-22-207-0989
Fax: 91-22-262-3551
Email: cbsbom@giasbm01.vsnl.net.in

JAPAN

O'Reilly Japan, Inc.
Kiyoshige Building 2F
12-Bancho, Sanei-cho
Shinjuku-ku
Tokyo 160-0008 Japan
Tel: 81-3-3356-5227
Fax: 81-3-3356-5261
Email: japan@oreilly.com

ALL OTHER ASIAN COUNTRIES

O'Reilly & Associates, Inc.
101 Morris Street
Sebastopol, CA 95472 USA
Tel: 707-829-0515
Fax: 707-829-0104
Email: order@oreilly.com

AUSTRALIA

WoodsLane Pty., Ltd.
7/5 Vuko Place
Warriewood NSW 2102
Australia
Tel: 61-2-9970-5111
Fax: 61-2-9970-5002
Email: info@woodslane.com.au

NEW ZEALAND

Woodslane New Zealand, Ltd.
21 Cooks Street (P.O. Box 575)
Waganui, New Zealand
Tel: 64-6-347-6543
Fax: 64-6-345-4840
Email: info@woodslane.com.au

LATIN AMERICA

McGraw-Hill Interamericana
Editores, S.A. de C.V.
Cedro No. 512
Col. Atlampa
06450, Mexico, D.F.
Tel: 52-5-547-6777
Fax: 52-5-547-3336
Email: mcgraw-hill@infosel.net.mx

O'REILLY®